GROUP WORK

PROCESSES AND APPLICATIONS

Bradley T. Erford
Loyola University Maryland

Boston   Columbus   Indianapolis   New York   San Francisco   Upper Saddle River
Amsterdam   Cape Town   Dubai   London   Madrid   Milan   Munich   Paris   Montreal   Toronto
Delhi   Mexico City   Sao Paulo   Sydney   Hong Kong   Seoul   Singapore   Taipei   Tokyo

Vice President and Editor in Chief: Jeffery W. Johnston
Acquisitions Editor: Meredith D. Fossel
Editorial Assistant: Nancy Holstein
Vice President, Director of Marketing: Quinn Perkson
Sr. Marketing Manager: Chris Barry
Marketing Manager: Amanda Stedke
Senior Managing Editor: Pamela D. Bennett
Sr. Production Editor: Mary Irvin
Project Manager: Susan Hannahs

Art Director: Jayne Conte
Cover Designer: Karen Salzbach
Cover Art: SuperStock
Full-Service Project Manager: Suganya Karuppasamy
Composition: GGS Higher Education Resources, A division of PreMedia Global, Inc.
Text Printer/Bindery: Hamilton Inc.
Cover Printer: Lehigh/Phoenix Color, Inc.
Text Font: Garamond

Credits and acknowledgments borrowed from other sources and reproduced, with permission, in this textbook appear on appropriate page within text.

Every effort has been made to provide accurate and current Internet information in this book. However, the Internet and information posted on it are constantly changing, so it is inevitable that some of the Internet addresses listed in this textbook will change.

Library of Congress Cataloging-in-Publication Data

Group work : processes and applications / [edited by] Bradley T. Erford.
    p. cm.
Includes bibliographical references and index.
ISBN-13: 978-0-13-171410-6
ISBN-10: 0-13-171410-4
1. Group counseling. 2. Group psychotherapy. 3. Social group work. I. Erford, Bradley T.
BF636.7.G76G79 2011
158'.35--dc22

2009038217

10 9 8 7 6 5 4 3 2 1

www.pearsonhighered.com

ISBN 10:   0-13-171410-4
ISBN 13: 978-0-13-171410-6

This effort is dedicated to The One: the Giver of energy, passion, and understanding; Who makes life worth living and endeavors worth pursuing and accomplishing; the Teacher of love and forgiveness.

PREFACE

The preparation of professional counselors has become increasingly more specialized over the past several decades, stemming primarily from systemic changes in the nature of what professional counselors do. These changes were brought about by several professional and societal changes, including the managed-care movement, school reform, and calls for greater cost efficiency and therapeutic effectiveness. Today, counselors need to know how to lead task, psychoeducational, counseling, and psychotherapy groups, rather than focusing only on traditional counseling and psychotherapy. In addition, while underlying theoretical orientations are important, few group leaders anchor themselves in a single approach to group work; the vast majority of group leaders operate from a systemic, integrative perspective. Thus, in-depth study of a dozen or more theoretical approaches is less important today than it was to past generations of group counselors and psychotherapists. There is also often a lack of focus in group work texts on what works and what doesn't work in groups, and how to help group leaders assess and evaluate the effectiveness of group interventions. It is also critical that leaders address the multicultural, ethical, and legal implications and applications within group work and address leader and group member roles from a prodevelopmental perspective (i.e., one that does not pathologize members as problematic and helps leaders address these members using positive approaches and interventions).

The overriding theme of *Group Work: Processes and Applications* is a focus on the specialized group work that counselors perform from a systemic perspective in a multicultural context. A number of group counseling and psychotherapy texts focus exclusively on counseling or conducting psychotherapy with small groups of clients, but counselors also run psychoeducational groups and task groups to address the developmental needs of clients and organizations. Most group counseling texts do not address psychoeducational and task groups. In addition, today counselors leading counseling and psychotherapy groups have a marked tendency to use a theoretically integrative counseling approach, rather than a specific theoretical orientation, such as person-centered, rational-emotive behavior; Adlerian; or Gestalt therapy. Other group psychotherapy texts make these theoretical approaches the core of the leader learning experience. This text briefly covers these traditional theoretical approaches, focusing more on the techniques and applications of the approaches, but the core of the text involves the systemic approach to group work: that is, preparing group leaders to facilitate the systemic group process, from planning the group through the four stages of group work: forming and orienting, transition, working, and termination. Mastering the facilitation of these defined stages of group work allows leaders to work effectively with clients in all types of group contexts and topics, and from a theoretically integrative perspective.

The content of *Group Work: Processes and Applications* is precisely aligned with the 2009 Council for the Accreditation of Counseling and Related Educational Programs (CACREP) standards because CACREP defines the standard of quality in the counselor preparation field. Thus, this text helps CACREP-accredited programs meet the CACREP Standards, and helps non-CACREP programs provide counselors-in-training with the most current, highest level professional training standards.

The text is divided into four sections: Section 1, Foundations of Group Work; Section 2, Systemic Group Work: Planning and Process; Section 3, Group Work in Action: Models and Theoretical Approaches; and Section 4, Special Issues in Group Work. Students will appreciate that numerous specific group work techniques are integrated and exemplified throughout the book; these techniques include drawing out, giving feedback, I-statements, pairing, paradox, reframing, self-disclosure, active listening, blocking, clarifying, confrontation, empathy, evaluating skills, initiating skills, instructing skills, linking, modeling, questioning, summarizing, using enthusiasm, holding the focus, shifting focus, cutting off, journal writing, rounds, dyads, sentence completion, scaling, values contract, journaling, reunions, scrapbooks, comfort zone, and personal growth charts. Numerous other techniques, covered in Chapters 13–18, are linked with specific theoretical orientations.

Section 1, "Foundations of Group Work" (Chapters 1–5), begins by acquainting students with the four Association for Specialists in Group Work (ASGW) functional group models and allows students to explore the historical forces that shaped group work in schools today, the therapeutic factors that underlie effective group approaches, and the advantages and disadvantages of group work in the schools. These topics are covered in Chapter 1, "The Value of Group Work: Functional Group Models and Historical Perspectives," written by Julia A. Southern, Bradley T. Erford, Ann Vernon, and Darcie Davis-Gage. This initial chapter leads the reader to appreciate the value of group work approaches. To understand group work models, leaders need to consider model characteristics, subtypes, stages, and the classic role and function of the leader. To accomplish this objective, Chapter 1 presents an overview of the four main types of functional group models categorized by the Association for Specialists in Group Work (ASGW): task groups, psychoeducational groups, counseling groups, and psychotherapy groups.

In Chapter 2, "Ethical and Legal Foundations of Group Work," by Lynn E. Linde, Bradley T. Erford, Danica G. Hays, and F. Robert Wilson, readers encounter the essential ethical and legal issues in group work, including confidentiality, informed consent, relationships among group members, termination issues, group participation, diversity issues, the Health Information Portability and Accountability Act (HIPAA), and the Family Educational Rights and Privacy Act (FERPA).

In Chapter 3, "Multicultural Issues in Group Work," by Cheryl Holcomb–McCoy and Cheryl Moore-Thomas, students will build a foundation of multicultural group work attitudes, knowledge, and skills. Chapter 3 addresses group work with diverse clients using oppression and marginalization as the frameworks from which group leaders can conceptualize group members' problems, behaviors, and actions. Because research indicates that people from oppressed backgrounds (e.g., ethnic minorities, disabled persons, the materially poor, gay and lesbian persons) are more likely to avoid counseling experiences, drop out prematurely from counseling, and report lower outcomes, it is important that group leaders become more responsive to member experiences of discrimination, prejudice, and inequities. Leaders can and should act to prevent or address these issues in the group. Also, because oppressed and marginalized members are accustomed to being silenced, being made to feel inferior, and having no voice, leaders must be skilled in working with members who are quiet, suspicious, pessimistic, cynical, and even angry. The authors also address how issues of oppression and marginalization may influence each stage of the systemic group process and provide a discussion of dilemmas that may arise when implementing groups with culturally diverse members.

While so many texts portray group member roles from a negative or destructive perspective, this text looks at the prodevelopmental needs of group members, with a focus on helping members to appropriately self-disclose and give and receive feedback to enhance the therapeutic value of the group experience. Thus, Chapter 4, "Distinguishing Group Member Roles," by George R. Leddick provides a discussion of what members should both do and not do. Chapter 4 begins by describing essential tasks for group members (i.e., self-disclosure and feedback) and later identifies ways member behavior might prove challenging for leaders. This approach does not pathologize the group member. It helps the leader to understand effective leader techniques and strategies to move the group forward, while emphasizing that members also have responsibilities to the group and that those members who fill specific roles can be handled in prodevelopmental ways that help promote the group process.

Leader skills are emphasized early in the text to help Leaders understand and master the role of the leader as a facilitator of group process. Techniques are provided that help group leaders move groups in a positive direction. Chapter 5, "Leading Groups," by Amy Milsom, addresses the common concern that leading a group can feel overwhelming for many leaders-in-training. Dr. Milsom acknowledges that, for students who may be just starting to feel comfortable conducting counseling sessions with one client, thinking about how to effectively attend to and facilitate interaction among many members might seem nearly impossible. Basic knowledge of important group leadership styles, characteristics, and skills for effective group leadership are provided in Chapter 5 to help ease the transition to effective group work.

Leaders almost always use a systemic process orientation when planning and running groups (i.e., planning, forming and orienting, transition, working, termination) rather than a strictly theoretical orientation (e.g., rational-emotive behavior therapy [REBT], Gestalt). Section 2, "Systemic Group Work: Planning and Process" (Chapters 6–10), addresses this systemic approach to group work and gives leaders real-life examples of leader and member responses within the context of the group process under discussion. In Chapter 6, "Planning for Group Work," by F. Robert Wilson, planning is proposed as an essential component of successful school-based group work. Key elements of planning, drawn from group work best practices and group work training standards, are identified and discussed within this chapter; these key elements include screening, selecting, and preparing members; selecting methods for deriving meaning and transferring learning; determining needed resources; measuring outcomes; and using closed or open groups.

Chapter 7, "Forming and Orienting Groups," by Nathaniel N. Ivers and Debbie W. Newsome, provides an overview of the forming and orienting stage of group work, including descriptions of primary tasks that are accomplished during the forming and orienting stage, discussion of responsibilities of the group leader during this stage, and a case example that illustrates what might occur during an initial group session.

The theory behind the developmental and systemic tasks of the transition stage in groups is explored in Chapter 8, "The Transition Stage in Group Work," by D. Paige Bentley Greason. Topics include the internal and external determinants of transition dynamics, how these dynamics manifest in the group, and what leaders can do to effectively work with the sometimes intense emotions and behaviors of this transition stage.

For as long as groups have been studied, researchers have noted the part in the life of the group where members actively and freely work on group and personal goals, honestly share aspects of self, courageously give feedback, and feel a sense of "we-ness" that enable members to truly believe in the process of group like never before. Chapter 9, "The Working Stage," by Kevin A. Fall, H. George McMahon, and Danica G. Hays, provides an overview of the working stage of group work, with an emphasis on member and leader functions within this important part of the group process. Components of this stage related to group foundations and design are also discussed to illustrate indicators for optimal working stage process.

Chapter 10, "Termination," by Danica G. Hays, Tammi F. Milliken, and Catherine Y. Chang, provides an overview of the termination stage, including a general description of termination characteristics, goals, and benefits and challenges. Following these general descriptions, three types of termination were discussed: premature termination, termination of group sessions, and termination of the group.

Section 3 of the text is entitled "Group Work in Action: Models and Theoretical Approaches" (Chapters 11–18). This section includes entire chapters on using task groups, psychoeducational groups, and theoretically based models for counseling and psychotherapy groups. Each of these chapters describes in depth how to effectively facilitate task, psychoeducational, and counseling and psychotherapy groups, and provides numerous real-life examples that help expose students to and ground them in the true-to-life context of group work. Task and psychoeducational groups require different skills and approaches than do counseling and psychotherapy groups. Including all four approaches to group work recognizes the role that mental health practitioners can play as a systemic change agent.

Chapter 11, "Leading Task Groups," by Janice L. DeLucia-Waack and Amy Nitza, starts with the observation that, if you look hard enough, task groups are everywhere. Clubs, classrooms, and most meetings can all be defined as task groups because task groups involve groups of people who come together to accomplish a common goal. Chapter 11 provides strategies for using group dynamics, group process, and leadership skills to create successful task groups. Guidelines for leading effective task groups are included; these guidelines focus on task groups of students (e.g., clubs, community service projects, student government) and also task groups of staff (e.g., department or team meetings, curriculum committees, intervention teams). Case examples are included to illustrate successful strategies and leadership styles.

Chapter 12, "Leading Psychoeducational Groups," by Sam Steen, Julia Bryan, and Norma L. Day-Vines, acknowledges that psychoeducational groups provide unique learning experiences that support traditional learning. Chapter 12 provides information about psychoeducational groups, with a focus on both small-group and large-group formats and strategies for enhancing the delivery of classroom or large-group guidance. A group model developed by Dr. Steen, Achieving Success Everyday (ASE), and strategies for incorporating culturally relevant bibliotherapy into group work, as pioneered by Dr. Day-Vines, are provided.

Nearly all mental health professionals use a focused, integrated approach aimed at achieving group goals when running counseling or psychotherapy groups. However, a working knowledge of various theoretical approaches to group work is essential, whether one uses a single theoretical approach or an integrative approach. Chapters 13–18 review the major theoretical approaches to group work, with a special focus on the primary techniques used by practitioners. In addition, transcripts of sessions are provided to give the reader an idea of how the approach and techniques would occur in diverse group formats. Here is a list of these chapters:

- Chapter 13, "Person-Centered and Existential Approaches to Counseling and Psychotherapy Groups," by Laura R. Simpson and Joel F. Diambra

- Chapter 14, "The Rational-Emotive Behavior Therapy Approaches to Group Counseling and Psychotherapy: Theory, Techniques, and Applications," by Ann Vernon
- Chapter 15, "Reality Therapy and Behavioral Approaches to Counseling and Psychotherapy Groups," by Ann Vernon
- Chapter 16, "Adlerian and Transactional Analysis Approaches to Counseling and Psychotherapy Groups," by Laura R. Simpson, Ann Vernon, and Bradley T. Erford
- Chapter 17, "Gestalt and Psychodrama Approaches to Counseling and Psychotherapy Groups," by Darcie Davis-Gage
- Chapter 18: "Family, Couples, T-Group, and Self-Help Approaches to Counseling and Psychotherapy Groups," by Ann Vernon and Darcie Davis-Gage

The final section (Section 4) is entitled "Special Issues in Group Work." Chapter 19, "Special Issues in Group Work with Children and Adolescents," by Susan H. Eaves and Carl J. Sheperis, highlights the special developmental issues of school-age children. The chapter also introduces the reader to major group counseling, child-centered themes, allowing a head start on how to address these issues with members of psychoeducational and counseling groups. The chapter includes the basic principles of group work with children of alcoholics, children of divorce, sexual abuse victims, adolescents struggling with addictions, and social skills training. Chapter 20, "Group Work with Adult Populations," by Susan H. Eaves and Carl J. Sheperis, addresses aspects of group work with adults, including the basic principles of group work with elderly clients, survivors and perpetrators of sexual abuse, and substance abuse.

Outcomes research in group work and accountability practices and procedures are presented to help leaders understand what works in group work and to help them document the outcomes of the member experience to determine the effectiveness of group interventions. Chapter 21, "Accountability in Group Work," by Bradley T. Erford, addresses the following facets of accountability: needs assessment, program evaluation, process evaluation, and outcome studies. Each facet contributes to a cycle of quality improvement for group work practice. In addition, Chapter 22, "Outcome Research in Group Work," by Bradley T. Erford, reminds the reader that group work leaders have an ethical responsibility to "use techniques/procedures/modalities that are grounded in theory and/or have an empirical or scientific foundation" (Herlihy & Corey, 2006, p. 39). Research has concluded that group work can affect members in powerful ways, and Chapter 22 reviews research on the effectiveness of group work with children and adolescents in schools.

Group Work: Processes and Applications provides a wealth of information on the foundations, systemic perspectives, and current critical topics and issues in group work practice. *Group Work: Processes and Applications* was specifically designed to enhance the knowledge, skills, and attitudes of group work leaders who conduct task groups, psychoeducational groups, and counseling and psychotherapy groups. Enjoy!

SUPPLEMENTAL INSTRUCTIONAL FEATURES

Supplemental pedagogical tools helpful to counselor educators choosing to use this book as a course textbook are provided. The companion Instructor's Manual contains at least 25 multiple-choice questions, 10 essay questions, and 10 suggested in-class or out-of-class activities per chapter. Numerous case studies and activities included in the text can also stimulate lively classroom discussions.

ACKNOWLEDGMENTS

I thank Megan Earl, Lacey Wallace, and Emily Miller, graduate assistants extraordinaire, for their tireless assistance in the preparation of the original manuscript. All of the contributing authors are to be commended for lending their expertise in the various topical areas. As always, Meredith Fossel, my editor at Pearson, has been wonderfully responsive and supportive, as was her production staff, including Nancy Holstein. Finally, special thanks go to the outside reviewers whose comments helped to provide substantive improvement to the original manuscript: James M. Benshoff, University of North Carolina at Greensboro; Robert C. Berg, University of North Texas; Sheli Bernstein-Goff, West Liberty State College; William J. Casle, Duquesne University; Devika Dibya Choudhuri, Eastern Michigan University; Deborah A. Gerrity, University of Buffalo; Cynthia Kalodner, Towson University; Simone Lambert, Virginia Tech; Susan Dana Leone, Virginia Commonwealth University; Sandy Magnuson, University of Northern Colorado; Nicholas Mazza, Florida State University; J. Jeffries McWhirter, Arizona State University; Michael Moyer, University of Texas-San Antonio; and Tarrell Portman, The University of Iowa.

BRIEF CONTENTS

SECTION 4   Special Issues in Group Work

CONTENTS

Chapter 3   Multicultural Issues in Group Work   39

Cheryl Holcomb-McCoy and Cheryl Moore-Thomas

Chapter 4   Distinguishing Group Member Roles   52

George R. Leddick

SECTION 2   Systemic Group Work: Planning and Process

SECTION 3   Group Work in Action: Models and Theoretical Approaches

Chapter 13 Person-Centered and Existential Approaches to Counseling and Psychotherapy Groups 202

Laura R. Simpson and Joel F. Diambra

Chapter 14 The Rational-Emotive Behavior Therapy Approaches to Group Counseling and Psychotherapy: Theory, Techniques, and Applications 213

Ann Vernon

Chapter 17   Gestalt and Psychodrama Approaches to Counseling and Psychotherapy Groups   249

Darcie Davis-Gage

Chapter 18   Family, Couples, T-Group, and Self-Help Approaches to Counseling and Psychotherapy Groups   258

Ann Vernon and Darcie Davis-Gage

SECTION 4   Special Issues in Group Work

Chapter 19   Special Issues in Group Work with Children and Adolescents   263
Susan H. Eaves and Carl J. Sheperis

ABOUT THE EDITOR

Bradley T. Erford Ph.D., NCC, LCPC, LPC, LP, is a professor in the School Counseling Program of the Educational Specialties Department in the School of Education at Loyola University Maryland. He is the recipient of the American Counseling Association (ACA) Research Award, ACA Hitchcock Distinguished Professional Service Award, ACA Professional Development Award, and ACA Carl D. Perkins Government Relations Award. He was also inducted as an ACA Fellow. In addition, he has received the Association for Assessment in Counseling and Education (AACE)/Measurement and Evaluation in Counseling and Development (MECD) AACE/MECD Research Award, the AACE Exemplary Practices Award, the AACE President's Special Merit Award, the Association for Counselor Education and Supervision's (ACES) Robert O. Stripling Award for Excellence in Standards, Maryland Association for Counseling and Development (MACD) Maryland Counselor of the Year, MACD Counselor Advocacy Award, MACD Professional Development Award, MACD Professional Service Award, MACD Outstanding Programming Award, and MACD Counselor Visibility Award. He has coauthored, edited, and coedited a number of texts, including: *The American Counseling Association Encyclopedia of Counseling* (ACA, 2009), *Transforming the School Counseling Profession* (2010; 1st, 2nd, and 3rd editions; Pearson/Merrill), *Professional School Counseling: A Handbook of Principles, Programs and Practices* (2009, 1st and 2nd editions, Pro-ed), *35 Techniques Every Counselor Should Know* (2010, Pearson/Merrill), *Group Work in the Schools* (2010, Pearson/Merrill), *Orientation to the Counseling Profession* (2009, Pearson/Merrill), *Developing Multicultural Competence: A System's Approach* (2009, Pearson/Merrill), *Assessment for Counselors* (2007, Cengage), *Research and Evaluation in Counseling* (2008, Cengage), and *The Counselor's Guide to Clinical, Personality and Behavioral Assessment* (2005, Cengage). His research specialization falls primarily in development and technical analysis of psychoeducational tests and has resulted in the publication of numerous refereed journal articles, book chapters, and published tests. He is an ACA Governing Council Representative, Past President of AACE, Past Chair and Parliamentarian of the American Counseling Association-Southern (U.S.) Region; Past President of the Maryland Association for Counseling and Development (MACD); Past Chair of ACA's Task Force on High Stakes Testing; Past Chair of ACA's Standards for Test Users Task Force; Past Chair of ACA's Interprofessional Committee; Past Chair of the American Counseling Association's (ACA) Public Awareness and Support Committee; Chair of the Convention and past Chair of the Screening Assessment Instruments Committees for AACE; past president of Maryland Association for Counselor Education and Supervision (MACES); past president of Maryland Association for Measurement and Evaluation (MAME); and past president of the Maryland Association for Mental Health Counselors (MAMHC). Dr. Erford has been a faculty member at Loyola since 1993 and is a Licensed Clinical Professional Counselor, Licensed Professional Counselor, Nationally Certified Counselor, Licensed Psychologist, and Licensed School Psychologist. Prior to arriving at Loyola, Dr. Erford was a school psychologist/counselor in the Chesterfield County (VA) Public Schools. He maintains a private practice specializing in assessment and treatment of children and adolescents. He holds a Ph.D. in counselor education from The University of Virginia, M.A. in school psychology from Bucknell University, and B.S. in Biology/Psychology from Grove City College (PA). He teaches courses in Testing and Measurement, Lifespan Development, Research and Evaluation in Counseling, and Stress Management (not that he needs it).

ABOUT THE AUTHORS

Julia Bryan received her Ph.D. in counselor education from the University of Maryland. She is currently an assistant professor of education and director of the school counseling program at The University of Maryland. Her research interests focus on school family community partnerships in school counseling, the affect of school counselor contact on student outcomes, group work with children and adolescents, and experiences of Caribbean immigrant students.

Catherine Y. Chang, Ph.D., is an associate professor and program coordinator of the Counselor Education and Practice Doctoral Program in the Department of Counseling and Psychological Services at Georgia State University. She received her doctorate in counselor education from the University of North Carolina at Greensboro. Her areas of research interest include multicultural counseling and supervision, Asian and Korean concerns, and multicultural issues in assessment.

Darcie Davis-Gage, Ph.D., LPC, received her Masters and Specialist Degrees from Pittsburg State University and her Ph.D. from the University of Iowa. She currently is an assistant professor at the University of Northern Iowa. She has presented and published in the areas of group counseling, supervision, and ethics.

Norma L. Day-Vines, Ph.D., is an associate professor in the counselor education program at Virginia Polytechnic Institute and State University. She writes extensively about culturally responsive strategies for working more effectively with ethnic minority students in general and African American students in particular.

Janice L. DeLucia-Waack, Ph.D., is an associate professor in the Department of Counseling, School, and Educational Psychology at the University at Buffalo, SUNY. She is the former editor of the *Journal for Specialists in Group Work,* and is a fellow in the Association for Specialists in Group Work (ASGW) and American Psychological Association Division 49: Group Psychology and Group Psychotherapy. She is author or co-author of six books, past secretary of APA Division 49, and past president of ASGW. She is also a group co-facilitator in the DVD available from ACA: *Leading Groups for Adolescents.*

Joel F. Diambra, Ed.D., LPC-MHSP, NCC, is an associate professor and Ph.D. program coordinator in counselor education at the University of Tennessee. He teaches courses on theories, supervision, practicum, internship, group counseling, and advanced group counseling. He has published and presented in the areas of school counseling, human services, student development, and service learning. He also serves as co-editor of the *Tennessee Counseling Association Journal.*

Susan H. Eaves, Ph.D., NCC, LPC, received her doctorate in counselor education from Mississippi State University. She has worked with children, adolescents, and adults, with emphasized experience conducting group therapy and commitment screenings. Dr. Eaves's research interests include marital infidelity, sexually risky behaviors, assessment, and Borderline Personality Disorder.

Kevin A. Fall, Ph.D., is chair and associate professor of the Department of Counseling, Loyola University, New Orleans. Dr. Fall is the author of several books, including *Group*

Counseling: Concepts and Procedures (with Berg and Landreth) and *Theoretical Models of Counseling and Psychotherapy* (with Holden and Marquis). He has published articles and presented at conferences on the topics of group work, ethics, and Adlerian theory. He also maintains a private practice focusing on adolescents and their families.

D. Paige Bentley Greason, MA.Ed., LPC, NCC, is a doctoral candidate in the Department of Counseling and Counselor Education at UNC-Greensboro and professional counselor in private practice in Winston-Salem, NC. She has extensive experience leading therapy and psychoeducational groups in both her private practice and previous work as a counselor at a local mental health agency. She earned her bachelor's and master's degrees at Wake Forest University.

Danica G. Hays, Ph.D., LPC, NCC, is an assistant professor in the Department of Educational Leadership and Counseling at Old Dominion University. She has conducted individual and group counseling in community mental health, university, and hospital settings. Her research interests include qualitative methodology, assessment and diagnosis, domestic violence intervention, and multicultural and social justice issues in counselor preparation and community mental health.

Cheryl Holcomb-McCoy received her Ph.D. in counseling and educational development from the University of North Carolina at Greensboro (UNCG). She is an associate professor in the Department of Counseling and Personnel Services at the University of Maryland, College Park, and is the former director of the School Counseling Program at Brooklyn College of the City University of New York. Her areas of research specialization include multicultural school counseling, school counselor multicultural self-efficacy, and urban school counselor preparation. She has written over 40 book chapters and refereed articles on issues pertaining to diversity in school counselor education. Dr. Holcomb-McCoy is a former elementary school counselor and kindergarten teacher.

Nathaniel N. Ivers is a doctoral student in the Counseling and Educational Development program at UNC-Greensboro. He received his M.A. in counseling from Wake Forest University. He has practiced counseling primarily with the Latino/Latina Spanish-speaking population.

George R. Leddick, Ph.D., earned his doctorate at Purdue University and was influenced by group work pioneers Allan Dye, Allen Segrist, John Sherwood, and Rex Stockton. For the past 25 years he has conducted both beginning and advanced group work practica in graduate schools in Indiana, South Carolina, New York, and Texas. He also taught organizational development consulting courses and maintained a private consulting practice. He served on the editorial board of the *Journal for Specialists in Group Work,* was elected a Fellow of the Association for Specialists in Group Work (ASGW), and was also elected the organization's president. He currently represents ASGW on the Governing Council of the American Counseling Association (ACA).

Lynn E. Linde, Ed.D., is Coordinator of Clinical Experiences in the School Counseling Program at Loyola University Maryland. She received her doctorate in counseling from George Washington University. She is a former branch chief for Pupil Services at the Maryland State Department of Education and representative to the ACA Governing Council. She is the 2009–2010 ACA President, an ACA Fellow, past chair of ACA-Southern Region, and past president of the Maryland Association for Counseling and Development.

H. George McMahon, Ph.D., is an assistant professor in the Counseling and Psychological Services Department at Georgia State University in Atlanta. He is a former middle and elementary school counselor who received his Ph.D. in Counseling Psychology from The University of Georgia and his M.Ed. in School Counseling from The University of Virginia. He has led groups in schools, psychiatric hospitals, residential treatment centers, and substance abuse programs. He has co-authored journal articles and book chapters, and has presented at state, regional, and national conferences on various topics related to group work. His professional interests include school counselor preparation, group work in school settings, and the role of counselors of privilege in multiculturalism.

Tammi F. Milliken, Ph.D., NCC, is an assistant professor of human services in the Department of Educational Leadership and Counseling at Old Dominion University. She received her doctorate in counselor education with an emphasis in family-school collaboration from the College of William and Mary, and her M.S. in education from Old Dominion University. Her work experience includes serving as Director of Project EMPOWER, a school-based prevention program, as an elementary school counselor in Norfolk Public Schools in Virginia, and as a family counselor for New Horizons at the College of William and Mary. She is an endorsed Harvard Mind/Body Stress Management Education Initiative facilitator and trainer. Dr. Milliken's research interests include critical issues in human services, developmental theory and application, adult development and learning, ethics, and multicultural competence in human services.

Amy Milsom Ph.D., NCC, LPC, is an assistant professor at the University of North Carolina at Greensboro. She earned her doctorate from Penn State University and is a former middle and high school counselor. Her primary research interests are in the areas of students with disabilities, school counselor preparation and professionalism, and group work.

Cheryl Moore-Thomas, Ph.D., NCC, is an associate professor of education in the school counseling program at Loyola University Maryland, where she teaches courses in group and multicultural counseling. She has published and presented in the areas of multicultural counseling competence, racial identity development, spiritual identity development in African American children and adolescents, and accountability in school counseling programs. Dr. Moore-Thomas also consults with public school systems on issues of diversity and academic achievement.

Debbie W. Newsome, Ph.D., LPC, NCC, is an associate professor of counselor education at Wake Forest University, where she teaches courses in career counseling, appraisal procedures, and statistics, and supervises master's students in their field experiences. She also serves as an adjunct clinician at a nonprofit mental health organization, where she counsels children, adolescents, and families.

Amy Nitza, Ph.D., is an assistant professor of counseling and counselor education in the School of Education at Indiana University-Purdue University, Fort Wayne. She is the producer of a group training DVD *Leading Groups for Adolescents,* co-author of a group workbook, editor of the newsletter of the ASGW, and the author of several journal articles on group topics. Her research interests include the use of psychoeducational groups for prevention, and therapeutic factors in groups for children and adolescents.

Carl J. Sheperis, Ph.D., NCC, LPC, is the Director of Academic Programs in Counselor Education and Human Services for Walden University. His research interests include Reactive Attachment Disorder, parent-child relationships, and peer confiict.

Laura R. Simpson, Ph.D. is an assistant professor of counselor education at Delta State University. Dr. Simpson is a Licensed Professional Counselor, National Certified Counselor, and Approved Clinical Supervisor whose teaching responsibilities include Social and Cultural Foundations, Group Counseling, Psychodiagnostics, General Internship, Spirituality in Counseling, and Substance Abuse Counseling. Recently appointed to serve on the Mississippi Licensed Professional Counselors Board of Examiners, she also serves on the executive board for the Mississippi Counseling Association and Mississippi Licensed Professional Counselor Association. Her writings and presentations include counselor wellness and secondary trauma, spirituality, group work, and supervision.

Julia A. Southern, M.Ed., received her master's in school counseling from Loyola College in Maryland. She is a professional school counselor in the Howard County Public School System of Maryland and an experienced public relations and events professional.

Sam Steen, Ph.D., is an assistant professor of school counseling at the George Washington University, Washington, DC, where he teaches courses in theories, techniques, and group counseling. His research interests include group counseling practice and evaluation with children and adolescents in school settings. Specifically, his publications include topics such as cross-cultural group counseling, using literacy to promote achievement in group counseling as well as integrating academic and personal/social development through group work. Prior to working in academia, he was employed as a professional school counselor for approximately 10 years in northern Virginia.

Ann Vernon, Ph.D., NCC, LMHC, is professor emeritus, former coordinator of counseling at the University of Northern Iowa, and a therapist in private practice where she works extensively with children, adolescents, and their parents. Dr. Vernon is the former director of the Midwest Center for rational-emotive behavior therapy (REBT) and Vice President of the Albert Ellis Board of Trustees. She is the author of numerous chapters, articles, and books including *Thinking, Feeling, Behaving* and *What Works When with Children and Adolescents.*

F. Robert Wilson, Ph.D., has been a member of the University of Cincinnati counseling faculty for nearly 30 years, where he coordinates the master's program in mental health counseling. In addition to teaching courses in clinical mental health counseling, group work, and the foundations of counseling, he supervises beginning and advanced master's counseling interns. His research and clinical interests include service to indigent and homeless people with mental illnesses; assessment, problem identification, and diagnosis; and individual and group treatment modalities, with an emphasis on ecological psychotherapy and evidence-based clinical practices. Dr. Wilson received his doctorate from Michigan State University and completed postdoctoral training in Gestalt Therapy at the Cincinnati Gestalt Institute. He is licensed to practice counseling in both the state of Ohio and the commonwealth of Kentucky, and is a Nationally Certified Counselor and an Approved Clinical Supervisor. He is a Fellow of the Association for Specialists in Group Work and was recently recognized as the Susan J. Sears "Counselor of the Year" by the Ohio Counseling Association. An active professional leader, he has served as president of the Association for Assessment in Counseling and Education, vice chair of Council for the Accreditation of Counseling and Related Educational Programs (CACREP), member of the Governing Council of the American Counseling Association, and member of the governing board of the Ohio Mental Health Counseling Association.

CHAPTER 1

The Value of Group Work
Functional Group Models and Historical Perspectives

Julia A. Southern, Bradley T. Erford, Ann Vernon, and Darcie Davis-Gage

PREVIEW

This initial chapter provides a tour through the essential historical and foundational issues of group work, leading the reader to appreciate the value of these approaches. To understand group work models, leaders need to consider model characteristics, subtypes, stages, and classic roles and functions of the leader. This chapter presents an overview of the four main types of group formats categorized by the Association for Specialists in Group Work (ASGW): task groups, psychoeducational groups, counseling groups, and psychotherapy groups.

DEFINING GROUP WORK

Throughout time, humans have naturally gathered together in groups for the purpose of ensuring their survival and development. Most individuals spend a considerable amount of time in groups for social, professional, religious, and other purposes. But what exactly defines a group? Do specific parameters exist? Researchers in the field have proposed varying descriptions to categorize a group's unique characteristics. Charles Cooley defined the primary group concept as a face-to-face encounter between individuals, involving intimate cooperation. Gladding (2008) expanded on these concepts by defining a group as two or more individuals who meet interdependently, with the awareness that each belongs for the purpose of achieving mutually set goals.

Gladding's (2008) depiction of groups as functional organisms led to his description and use of the term *group work*, characterized as the application of knowledge and skill in group facilitation to assist members in reaching their mutual goals. These goals include work or education-related tasks, personal development, problem solving, and the remediation of disorders. These goals can be accomplished through different procedures, processes, and approaches, broadly categorized as functional group models.

FUNCTIONAL GROUP MODELS

The Association for Specialists in Group Work (ASGW) (2007) categorized various functional types of group work experiences as task groups, psychoeducational groups, counseling groups, and psychotherapy groups. Each of these group models will be discussed below in relation to characteristics, subtypes, stages, and the role and function of the leader, and each of these group work types will be discussed in even greater depth in Chapters 11–18.

But how does a group leader know which type of group model to use? Leaders determine which type of group model to implement depending on the structure and goals of the group. For example, task groups ordinarily are formed with the goal of accomplishing some task or solving some problem. Once the problem is addressed, the group terminates. Examples of task groups include student assistance teams in schools or a task force formed by a professional association to address a specific problem or produce a written document or product.

Psychoeducational groups ordinarily are formed with the primary goal of conveying knowledge and skills to members through psychoeducational techniques, either in small groups or through large-group classroom guidance. Examples of psychoeducational groups include a teacher/student training on implementing a peer mediation program or a small social skills group meant to help students with social or interactional difficulties to develop the knowledge, skills, and attitudes to increase successes in peer and adult relationships.

Group counseling may also address member knowledge and skill deficiencies but through application of a process-oriented, theoretically based counseling approach (e.g., humanistic, rational-emotive behavior therapy, reality therapy, integrative approach). Goals for counseling group members ordinarily are written to address cognitive, affective, and behavioral changes agreed to by the leader and members. Counseling groups are usually time-limited (e.g., 6 to 25 sessions in clinics; 6 to12 sessions in schools) and may address issues such as dealing with "changing families" or grief and loss, which are meant to help

small groups of students adjust to the developmental changes required of life changes and loss.

Psychotherapy groups involve in-depth, long-term commitments (i.e., 12 to 50 or more sessions) and, usually, advanced levels of training and expertise on the part of the leader. Examples of psychotherapy group topics include coping with long-term, traumatic occurrences of physical abuse or sexual abuse; groups for members with complicated bereavement; or groups for individuals with personality disorders, with the goals of personality restructuring and reintegration. School counselors rarely have the luxury of dedicating the time required to successfully complete these types of psychotherapy groups and therefore can be an excellent source of referrals for students in need of group psychotherapy for private or community service providers. The characteristics, types, roles, and function of the leader and the stages of each of these group models (i.e., task, psychoeducational, counseling, and psychotherapy) will be reviewed in the following pages.

Task Groups

Task groups occur in a variety of settings, from schools and mental health agencies to large businesses and corporations. Task groups are designed around accomplishing a specific goal. Task groups use principles of group dynamics and incorporate methods such as collaboration, problem solving, and team-building exercises to reach goals. The focus is not on changing people but on completing the task at hand in an efficient and effective manner. For example, if a community wanted to address the complex problems of adolescents at-risk of academic failure and delinquency from a systemic, multidisciplinary perspective, the city council may appoint members of a task group to identify and then establish authentic partnerships with community and governmental organizations.

Hulse-Killacky, Killacky, and Donigian (2001) identified elements of successful task groups, including having well-defined goals and purposes, addressing and processing conflicts between members, blending content and process, and encouraging members to give and receive feedback as well as reflect on their work as a group. Leaders of task groups should have a clear purpose, take time to build rapport, encourage members to be reflective and active, and pay attention to the here and now.

CHARACTERISTICS OF TASK GROUPS Task groups can vary greatly in size, but they often function more effectively if there are fewer than 12 people to avoid problems with subgrouping. With younger school-age children, task groups of 6 to 8 students often work best. Task groups also vary in duration and the number of sessions, and they usually depend on accomplishing the identified goal. Once the goal is accomplished, the group generally disbands unless another task is identified. Task group members also tend to have contact with each other outside the group, which is one of the unique characteristics of task groups not often encountered in counseling or psychotherapy groups.

TYPES OF TASK GROUPS There are as many different types of task groups as there are tasks. Examples of task groups in schools include determining procedures and policies about the treatment of clients, planning a conference, resolving a conflict among employees, choosing officers for a club or professional organization, planning a fundraising event or social function, or developing a crisis plan for a university counseling center. ASGW standards identified committees, task forces, and learning groups as types of task groups. Upon completion of a task or at a logical point within group meetings, members can evaluate how well they worked together, reflecting on roles each member played and what, if anything, interfered with their functioning well as a group. Age-appropriate formats can be devised using typical process observer criteria such as:

a. What role did you play in the group? Were you a leader or a follower?
b. How successful was the group in completing the task?

c. If you did not complete the task, what prevented you from completing it?
d. If you worked as a group again, how could you work more effectively?

Questions such as these can be adapted and expanded upon depending on the age of the group members. At times it is also effective to assign one or two members to be process observers and give feedback to the rest of the group members.

ROLE AND FUNCTION OF THE LEADER IN TASK GROUPS The leaders of task groups tend to take on the role of process consultant (Kottler, 2001). A task group leader's main goal is to help the group complete a task or reach a goal. This is best facilitated when a leader is able to strike a balance between content and process, while still accomplishing the task at hand in a timely manner. Leaders of task groups need to be able to facilitate communication and keep the group focused on the goals of the group. When a member is the leader of the task group, that member may struggle with the content and/or process facilitation and may need more assistance from the leader.

STAGES OF TASK GROUPS Hulse-Killacky, Kraus, and Schumacher (1999) described a conceptual framework that a group leader can use when conducting task groups. Within this framework, the authors identified three stages: a warming-up period, followed by a working stage, and ending with termination of the group. Although these phases may be present in other types of groups such as psychoeducational or counseling groups, they seem to be particularly applicable to task or work groups. Using these stages allows trust and cohesion to form, which will in turn facilitate a more productive task group.

During the first stage, Hulse-Killacky et al. (1999) stressed that members should introduce themselves to one another and identify the task and purpose of the group. The second stage includes working on accomplishing the identified task while also developing an understanding of how members will work together. During this phase, it is important for the leader to work within the here-and-now context while emphasizing direct communication and feedback between members. To achieve a balance between content and process, it may also be helpful for the leader to pay attention to how members are interacting and not overemphasize completion of the task. The final stage involves bringing the group to completion, which is best accomplished by having members reflect on the progress as well as the process of the group. Hulse-Killacky et al. (1999) emphasized that leaders should maintain a balance of content and process throughout all stages because without this balance, groups risk becoming stagnant and unproductive.

Within a school setting and when using task groups with students, the stages may show some variation. For example, the teacher or professional school counselor will most likely structure some rapport building during the warming-up stage, may identify the task, and give specific instructions for the working stage.

SOME FINAL COMMENTS ON TASK GROUPS   Task groups are designed around accomplishment of a certain task. They are an effective way of accomplishing that task because the group members bring various perspectives and multiple sources of energy and expertise together to accomplish their goals. By employing various group principles, leaders can help task groups be more productive and complete their goals in a timely manner. Personal change and growth usually do not occur in task groups, but if task groups are properly facilitated, members may leave the group with a better understanding of group dynamics as well as possibly gaining insight into their individual interpersonal skills. In the school setting, task groups are an exceptionally good way to educate young people about group roles and group dynamics that will facilitate their group participation in the present as well as the future. Task groups are covered in much greater detail in Chapter 11.

Psychoeducational Groups

Psychoeducational groups were originally developed for use in schools, but they are also increasingly used in mental health agencies, hospitals, social service agencies, and universities (Aasheim & Niemann, 2006). These groups are more structured than counseling or psychotherapy groups, emphasizing skill development through various nonthreatening skill-building exercises, but at the same time encouraging discussion, sharing, and feedback among members (Corey, Corey, Callahan, & Russell, 2004). The goal of psychoeducational group work is to prevent psychological disturbance by increasing self-awareness, knowledge, and skills about specific developmentally relevant issues. The fact that a psychoeducational group can be preventive, growth-oriented, or remedial makes it a very versatile type of group model. The psychoeducational group model is commonly used in PreK–12 comprehensive developmental school-counseling programs, whether in small groups to address study or social skills or in large-group classroom guidance to address educational planning or career developmental goals.

CHARACTERISTICS OF PSYCHOEDUCATIONAL GROUPS   Psychoeducational groups are appropriate for all age groups and can be adapted to the specific needs of group members. In the school setting, they may be called guidance groups and are "more structured, issue specific, and leader directed" (Aasheim & Niemann, 2006, p. 269). Psychoeducational groups serve several purposes, including giving information, encouraging members to share common experiences, teaching participants problem-solving skills, and helping them create their own support systems outside the group setting. The focus is both educational and therapeutic in that information about the specific topic is shared and self-development is emphasized (Ivey, Pedersen, & Ivey, 2001).

TYPES OF PSYCHOEDUCATIONAL GROUPS Aasheim and Niemann (2006) identified three types of psychoeducational groups: (a) education groups that focus on presenting new information and concepts, (b) skills-training groups that are generally experiential and emphasize skill acquisition, and (c) self-understanding groups that are similar to counseling groups but focus less on self-disclosure and more on building self-confidence by giving feedback about members' behavior and how it affects others. This latter type of group is more appropriate for adolescents and adults than for children, although it could be beneficial with elementary-age children, depending on their maturity and the group composition.

Psychoeducational groups are typically centered around a particular topic and have been widely used to address broad-ranging issues such as stress management, assertion, interpersonal skills, substance abuse, eating disorders, anger, loss, self-esteem, domestic violence, responsible sexual behavior, healthy choices, and diversity awareness, among many others. Other topics applicable in a school setting include improving study skills, getting along with friends, career decision making, or dealing with family changes. Regardless of the type of group, growth is acquired through knowledge. This knowledge may be presented through discussions, presentations, videos, computer-assisted programs, or activities and exercises. Depending on the age level of members, games, simulations, role playing, and worksheets designed to convey information and stimulate discussion may also be used.

ROLE AND FUNCTION OF THE LEADER IN PSYCHOEDUCATIONAL GROUPS Because this type of group is based on presenting knowledge and helping members change perceptions, the leader needs to have expertise in the content area as well as group facilitation skills. It is also imperative that the group leader create a safe environment so that members feel comfortable sharing feelings and engaging in self-disclosure. Because this type of group is more structured than psychotherapy or counseling groups, the leader must engage in careful planning that includes having a well-designed curriculum to allow sufficient time for group members to process and discuss the information presented.

The leader also needs to be adept at juggling content as well as process, and at the same time be sensitive to the times when group members are ready to address various issues and engage in certain activities. Planning is essential in psychoeducational groups, including planning for session length, frequency, number of sessions, content, and follow-up sessions. Although these factors may vary due to member age and setting, typically adult groups last 60 to 90 minutes and meet once per week, groups in a high school setting last 45 to 60 minutes and meet once a week, and 30 to 45 minutes ordinarily is sufficient with elementary students. The number of sessions varies widely depending on the topic and depth of coverage, but the average is 6 to 12 sessions. The optimal number of members in a psychoeducational group also varies widely, but with children and adolescents, 6 to 10 members is the ideal composition in order to facilitate discussion and feedback; adult groups usually have 6 to 12 members. Classroom guidance lessons are frequently conducted with 20 to 30 students, but such large groups allow for less discussion, feedback, and individualized attention.

It is also beneficial for the leader of a psychoeducational group to help members clarify what they want from the group and translate these vague goals into specific, measurable objectives. Asking members to write down their goals or write a description of what they hope to get from the group experience can help. Having members complete contracts that identify specific, realistic, and attainable goals is also a useful strategy.

STAGES OF A PSYCHOEDUCATIONAL GROUP The beginning and closing stages are often shorter in psychoeducational groups than in counseling or psychotherapy groups, but the leader nevertheless has to plan for these stages. The middle stage includes delivery of content, which may be through a short lecture or a variety of experientially based activities that introduce the topic and engage members in learning more about it. In this stage, the leader's job is to shift between giving information and facilitating discussion, which helps members learn the information and apply it to their own lives. All too often inexperienced leaders focus too much on providing information and lose sight of the group process, or leaders allow too much sharing and don't have enough information. A good balance of information and interaction is essential.

SOME FINAL COMMENTS ON PSYCHOEDU-CATIONAL GROUPS The Association for Specialists in Group Work (ASGW) *Best Practice Guidelines* (2007) state that psychoeducational groups stress growth through knowledge. Through this approach, students of all ages can benefit from the learning and support that this type of group offers, and they can apply what they learned to their real-life situations. Psychoeducational groups have extensive applicability in schools because of the variety of topics that can be introduced to help students acquire knowledge and skills that enhance their development. Group leaders can structure age-appropriate activities that stimulate discussion and application of concepts, thus increasing children's and adolescents' ability to deal with present and future concerns. Leaders of psychoeducational groups walk a fine line between presenting information and facilitating the group process that encourages sharing and self-disclosure, which are essential to an effective group. Psychoeducational group approaches are covered in much greater detail in Chapter 12.

Counseling Groups

Counseling groups are designed to help members work on interpersonal problems and promote behavioral changes related to these problems. Counseling groups are typically problem-oriented, helping members explore their problems and seek resolution, but counseling groups can also be preventive, growth-oriented, or remedial.

Kottler (2001) described counseling groups as relatively short in length, focusing on adjustment issues for individuals who function relatively normally. People usually come to group counseling because they are experiencing some sort of problem, such as dealing with family issues, difficult relationships, or stress-related problems.

CHARACTERISTICS OF COUNSELING GROUPS Various goals of members can be addressed in counseling groups. For example, counseling groups help members explore issues affecting their development, experience acceptance and support from their peers while exploring various problems, and increase coping skills. As a result of attending counseling groups, members may also improve their abilities to build and maintain healthy relationships. Counseling groups can help members develop more positive attitudes about interpersonal functioning. The fact that the member can practice these skills in a group forum may increase the member's interpersonal effectiveness. Once these behavior changes occur in the group setting, members should be able to transfer the skills into their everyday living.

To maintain the personal focus, counseling groups for children (grades PreK–5) ordinarily range in size from four to six individuals. Leaders might consider having three to four students in a group if they are working with students with attention difficulties or severe behavioral problems. In adolescent counseling groups, numbers ordinarily range from six to eight students. In adult counseling groups, six to ten members is usual. Typically, the number of sessions can range from 6 to 12, depending on the issues being addressed and the age of the members, although some adult groups may meet for up to 20 sessions. Group sessions ideally run for 30 to 60 minutes for students in school, again depending on the age of the members and the amount of time available in the school's class schedule. Groups for adolescents and adults in clinical settings usually meet for 60 to 90 minutes.

TYPES OF COUNSELING GROUPS Various types of counseling groups may be offered in a multitude of settings, and participation can have multiple benefits for members of any age. Counseling groups for children may focus on adjusting to parental divorce or dealing with other types of loss. The goal would be to help children develop coping skills, share feelings about their situations, and gain support from others who are experiencing similar circumstances. Counseling groups may also prevent more serious problems from occurring.

Counseling groups are also helpful for adolescents. Groups appropriate for adolescents include sexual orientation issues, teenage pregnancy and parenting, and relationship skills, among numerous other potential topics. By attending group sessions, members are given a chance to process their problems, receive constructive feedback, and work on interpersonal relationship skills.

Counseling groups are frequently helpful for adults. Some examples of counseling groups for adults include groups for cancer patients, adult survivors of childhood abuse, or couples with relationship difficulties (Chen & Rybak, 2004). By attending group sessions, members are given a chance to process their problems, receive constructive feedback, and work on interpersonal relationship skills.

ROLE AND FUNCTION OF THE LEADER IN COUNSELING GROUPS Group leaders tend to be less directive in a counseling group than in a psychoeducational group. When working with children and adolescents, leaders must also be aware of students' developmental levels and choose age-appropriate topics and activities. When forming counseling groups, leaders should also try to make them as heterogeneous as possible in regard to diversity (e.g., race, ethnicity, socioeconomic level, sexual orientation, and so on) so that members can experience a wide variety of interactions that mirror the pluralistic society.

Leaders have various functions when facilitating counseling groups. First, they build an atmosphere that is conducive to members openly sharing their problems without fear of rejection or ridicule. Leaders also facilitate communication and protect members if necessary. Group leaders also need to help members apply the insight they gain in the group to their lives outside the group.

STAGES OF COUNSELING GROUPS The development of a counseling group depends on effective leadership and knowledge about how groups transition through various stages. In the beginning of the counseling group experience, members spend time getting acquainted and sharing information about themselves. This phase can last from one to three sessions. Some groups may cycle through a transition period during this beginning phase, when the group members may challenge the leader or may share only superficial information about themselves and their issues.

Next, members will enter the working stage, where participants begin to work on the issues that brought them to group. Leaders need to be skilled in helping to link members as they share similar problems to help build cohesion and universality. The ending phase usually lasts one to two sessions and the focus is on processing feelings related to the termination of the group. These stages of group process are expanded upon in Chapters 6–10.

SOME FINAL COMMENTS ON COUNSELING GROUPS Counseling groups can prevent problems and help improve members' interpersonal skills. Counseling groups are most helpful for people who are having difficulties adjusting to a variety of life circumstances and could benefit from a growth-producing experience. Counseling groups are often provided for children and adolescents as part of a comprehensive school-counseling program. Counseling groups outside the school system may be more difficult to access if potential members do not have adequate health insurance coverage or the means to pay for the services because counseling groups are usually offered by trained professionals and may be rather expensive. Regardless of the cost, group counseling may be more beneficial than individual counseling for certain types of problems (see Chapter 22). Counseling groups are covered in much greater detail in Chapters 13–18.

Psychotherapy Groups

Psychotherapy groups can be used with children and adolescents with most types of mental illness (Carrier & Haley, 2006), and they are designed to treat those who may be experiencing severe or chronic problems in their lives. Ordinarily, members in psychotherapy groups display more dysfunctional behavior and typically carry a psychiatric (i.e., Diagnostic and Statistical Manual of Mental Disorders [DSM]) diagnosis.

Psychotherapy groups are typically offered by agencies and in residential treatment settings, but they are increasingly being offered in alternative schools or full-service schools that may offer school-based mental health services. Psychotherapy groups are rarely conducted in comprehensive developmental school-counseling programs because of the time-intensive commitment involved and because psychotherapy groups sometimes require advanced training and knowledge. Still, professional school counselors should understand what is involved in psychotherapy groups, at least so that appropriate referrals can be made to practitioners outside the school setting.

Members of psychotherapy groups are usually identified through a screening process; although some individuals who participate in psychotherapy groups may have problems similar to members in counseling groups, psychotherapy groups are more appropriate for individuals whose symptoms are more severe or pervasive. The goal of a psychotherapy group, compared to the goals of other types of groups, is to change people on a deeper level (Carrier & Haley, 2006) by engaging in a process of personality reconstruction. This makes changing personality traits, cognitive distortions, and behavioral patterns that interfere with a member's functioning a major focus.

CHARACTERISTICS OF PSYCHOTHERAPY GROUPS
Psychotherapy groups tend to have fewer members than psychoeducational or task groups, but they may be similar in size to counseling groups. Psychotherapy groups typically range from four to six members, but they can range from as few as two to three members up to perhaps eight or nine members. Co-leadership may be helpful for psychotherapy groups with more than eight members.

Typically, psychotherapy groups last from 45 to 90 minutes, one or more times a week, depending on the setting. Spitz and Spitz (1999) found that psychotherapy groups vary in duration from a brief number of sessions (e.g., 8 to 15) to longer-term treatment (e.g., years). When conducting school-based group psychotherapy, the leaders must be conscious of the academic schedule; thus, groups may be offered twice a week but for shorter periods of time. Nonresidential treatment facilities tend to offer groups for longer periods of time, while residential treatment facilities may offer more group sessions per week but for shorter lengths of time, depending on how long clients are in the residential treatment center. Spitz and Spitz (1999) proposed that sessions lasting longer than 90 minutes ordinarily are "beyond the adaptive capacity of most seriously impaired psychiatric inpatients" (p. 17).

Spitz and Spitz (1999) emphasized that the goals of the individual members and the group should drive the decision regarding length of treatment. Brief psychotherapy groups are appropriate when member goals focus on a reduction of mild symptoms or on an increase in social skills. Shorter groups also tend to be more effective if the members have similar psychological problems or disorders. Longer-term groups tend to focus on building insight and self-awareness, examining the past, and working on the relationship with one's family.

TYPES OF PSYCHOTHERAPY GROUPS   Psychotherapy groups are usually reserved for people who have a clinical diagnosis or have serious problems of adjustment (Spitz & Spitz, 1999). Some psychotherapy groups are heterogeneous. For example, many inpatient hospitalization units offer group psychotherapy for patients with many different problems and diagnoses, as long as all patients can benefit from the interpersonal interaction as well as constructive feedback from the leaders and other members. Other groups are homogeneous with regard to the type of diagnosis or problem. Examples of homogeneous groups are people diagnosed with Posttraumatic Stress Disorder (PTSD), childhood sexual abuse survivors, people experiencing addictions, chronically depressed or anxious individuals, or those suffering from eating disorders. Sometimes these homogeneous groups are single-sex groups.

Psychotherapy groups for children and adolescents offered in the school setting are usually offered by practitioners from local mental health agencies. These types of groups are usually provided to children and adolescents with problems such as depression, substance abuse, and disruptive behavioral disorders. For these types of groups to be successful in the schools, group leaders should establish therapeutic and educational goals as part of their groups. For example, educational goals can include improving school attendance, increasing individual grade point average, or reducing detentions. Psychotherapy groups in the schools are usually most successful if the leader carefully considers and respects the context, culture, and rules of the school.

ROLE AND FUNCTION OF THE LEADER IN PSYCHOTHERAPY GROUPS Spitz and Spitz (1999) stressed that psychotherapy groups should be led by a professionally trained group facilitator who is familiar with and has experience serving individuals with severe and pervasive problems. In addition, psychotherapy group leaders must be active facilitators who screen members and carefully select appropriate interventions based on the composition and goals of the group. Because members of psychotherapy groups tend to have more serious problems, it is especially important that leaders have training in abnormal psychology, psychopathology, and diagnosis (Association for Specialists in Group Work [ASGW], 2000).

Leaders of psychotherapy groups usually operate from a theoretical framework as well (see Chapters 13–18). To work with members of psychotherapy groups, leaders must also have knowledge of Yalom's therapeutic factors (Yalom & Leszcz, 2005), which are reviewed later in this chapter. Leaders should be able to use these therapeutic factors to promote and facilitate change among group members.

STAGES OF PSYCHOTHERAPY GROUPS Although the stages of psychotherapy groups can depend on the length of the group and the theoretical orientation of the group leader, some general commonalities exist. As mentioned above, the planning phase is critical to the success of a psychotherapy group because of the importance of screening and selection of members. Spitz and Spitz (1999) emphasized that psychotherapy groups begin with a warm-up stage where members introduce themselves and learn about others. This is followed by a period of vying for power and control in the group (i.e., transition), after which time, group rules and norms are often formed. Once those issues are resolved, the group moves into a working stage where members address issues with intimacy, dependency, and independence. The group then concludes with a termination phase, in which the group members are able to reflect on their accomplishments while also dealing with issues of grief and loss. These stages are expanded upon in Chapters 6–10.

SOME FINAL COMMENTS ON PSYCHOTHERAPY GROUPS Psychotherapy groups can be beneficial for a variety of people with many different problems, but they are particularly beneficial for those with serious problems who may need the support of a group. Psychotherapy groups can be very cost-effective; treatment offers a level of support to individuals and also provides an opportunity for members to experience caring relationships. Psychotherapy groups are typically reserved for people with the most severe problems, and this approach allows members to reconstruct parts of their personalities in a safe environment where they can receive constructive feedback and the space to practice new skills in living. Psychotherapy groups are covered in much greater detail in Chapters 13–18.

AN INTRODUCTION TO THE STAGES OF GROUP WORK PROCESS

During the introduction of functional group models provided above, you might have found it hard not to notice that different researchers and authors conceptualized the stages of different functional group models differently. Some suggested a three-stage, four-stage, five-stage (or even more) model. The identification of stages in group work is often helpful when teaching counselors-in-training about group process and development, as well as when helping leaders evaluate the progress that group members are making from session to session. For the purpose of this book, we have chosen to identify the stages of group work as: (1) the forming and orienting stage, (2) the transition stage, (3) the working stage, and (4) the termination stage. The precursor to these four stages is known as the planning phase. These phases and stages will be expanded upon substantially in Chapters 6–Chapters 10, but for now, a very brief explanation of each is necessary for general knowledge and identification purposes.

The planning phase occurs well before the first group meeting. Planning involves identifying potential group members and screening the members to determine their appropriateness for the group (e.g., willingness to participate, consistency of personal goals with group goals). The planning phase also allows the leader to discuss confidentiality, limits of confidentiality, informed consent, and myriad other details related to setting up and running a group in schools. Planning also infers that the leader has researched and selected essential content to be conveyed (in the case of psychoeducational or counseling groups); decided on any experiential activities that will be implemented; and, in general, is ready to lead the group and infuse relevant content. Once the potential members have been screened and the members are selected, the group sessions are ready to commence.

Forming and orienting, the initial stage of group process, is an interesting and sometimes anxiety-producing time for members and the leader. During the first couple of sessions, the leader seeks to collaboratively determine goals, orient the members to the goals of the group, collaboratively set ground rules with members, and structure the sessions to help members communicate and give feedback to each other. The leader's style of interaction is very important during this stage because it sets the tone for member interactions. At this point, many task and psychoeducational groups have been structured and led so that they are ready to begin the working stage because the leader is usually using an active and directive approach, the group's goals

are well-defined, and the group is time-limited. However, leaders of counseling and psychotherapy groups ordinarily are less directive and attempt to harness the experiences and power of group process, transferring responsibility for group and member successes to the members themselves. This transfer of responsibility is accomplished through the stage known as transition, which is frequently anxiety-producing for both members and leaders. As members take responsibility for the group, become familiar with each other, and become serious about making progress toward meeting their goals, the group is poised to enter the working stage. Navigating the transition stage takes a great deal of skill on the part of the group leader.

Ordinarily, most of the group meeting time is spent in the working stage, accomplishing the goals the members committed to achieving during the planning phase and when the group experience commenced. During this stage, leaders must skillfully facilitate group process while empowering members to take control, and pursue and accomplish individual and group goals. As goals are accomplished and the time approaches for the group experience to end, the termination stage arrives. While evaluation of group content and process is conducted throughout the duration of the group experience, assessment of group and individual goals becomes particularly important in this final stage. The termination stage also gives members and leaders an opportunity to debrief, resolve unfinished business, and process the interpersonal and intrapersonal progress each member made.

Usually, the stages of a group experience unfold in a predictable manner. However, there is one important caution to be aware of when identifying the stage a group may be displaying: It can change at any time! The dynamics of group interaction are fluid and changeable, and members may arrive at sessions with pressing issues that the group is forced to deal with (e.g., life crises, breeches in confidentiality). Skillful group leaders will need to adjust and adapt to harness the power of the group to deal with pressing issues while still suavely segueing back to the primary goals of the group. Thus, while stages give the impression of proceeding progressively from one step to the next, complex group processes frequently lead groups in more of a spiraling path. Part of becoming a skillful group leader is becoming flexible and adept at recognizing these subtle shifts and turns, then skillfully facilitating the process of the group so that the members continue to make progress. With this brief introduction to the stages of group work as context, we are now ready to proceed with a review of the historical foundations of group work.

THE HISTORY OF GROUP WORK

Each era in the history of group counseling has reflected the national, regional, and local climate of that time period. Sociologists and social psychologists began researching collective group behavior in the nineteenth century, although not necessarily in direct relation to therapeutic possibilities. Early research topics focused on exploring the impact of social experiences on behavior, specifically the effects of working in groups on childhood performance in school, group influences on thought processes, and the effect of competition on performance. Today, group work is known to be an effective methodology for meeting various human needs and finding solutions to a multitude of problems. Group leaders are increasingly called upon to address problems that are interpersonally based and have discovered that the social connections provided by counseling groups are often the most effective forms of treatment.

The Late 1800s and Early 1900s

The development of groups in the late 1800s emerged from the fledgling disciplines of psychology, sociology, and philosophy as a result of the need for social reform and education. Those who received treatment in group settings at that time were generally immigrants, poor, or mentally ill. Joseph Pratt, a Boston internist, is credited with establishing the first group experience that was not intended specifically for psychoeducational or

occupational purposes. He used groups to save time in educating and supporting patients, and discovered therapeutic value in the format. Pratt was treating patients with tuberculosis and began seeing them in groups for the sake of efficiency. The patients shared the commonality of having tuberculosis, and over time they became concerned with one another's well-being. This sense of caring had a positive effect, and the patients' spirits seemed to be lifted as they gathered together for weekly meetings (Posthuma, 2002). Startlingly, 75% of Pratt's patients eventually recovered from the disease, despite the fact that they were given no hope of survival upon their initial diagnosis. Pratt provided the first known description of group counseling and the curative effect of group interactions on group members. It is widely believed that his work paved the way for present-day psychotherapy.

Building on Pratt's initial findings, two pioneers of the school-counseling profession began to apply group work within the school context just after the turn of the century. Jesse Davis, a school principal in Grand Rapids, Michigan, introduced group work in a school setting in 1907. Davis's groups were intended to provide students with effective tools for making educational, vocational, and moral decisions (Herr & Erford, 2007). Davis emphasized the use of the group as an effective environment for teaching life skills and values. Frank Parsons, often cited as the founder of the vocational guidance or school-counseling profession, also used groups to facilitate career and vocational development. However, despite their groundbreaking efforts in the field, neither Davis nor Parsons conducted evaluations to empirically test the effectiveness of group work on students.

During World War I (and later in World War II), the importance of group work increased immensely as soldiers were tested and instructed in groups, and teamwork was emphasized. Groups were also used on occasion to treat combat fatigue, known today as Posttraumatic Stress Disorder (PTSD). It is fair to say that throughout the history of counseling, the cost-effectiveness and time-effectiveness of group work has been demonstrated again and again during occurrences of wars and natural disasters; indeed, during any circumstance in which a large number of people required psychoeducational or counseling services.

The 1920s and 1930s

The use of group therapy increased between 1920 and 1930, as did efforts to measure its effectiveness. One of the first outcome studies was noted for individuals with schizophrenia who had previously been considered "untreatable." When Edward Lazell, using a psychoeducational group model, presented lectures on Freudian psychology to groups of these patients with schizophrenia, the medical staff reported that patients consequently exhibited positive behavioral changes and a reduction in the use of sedatives. These findings led other practitioners who had reported success with group work to supplement their anecdotal documentation with observations from additional medical staff, patients' family members, and patients' self-reports. Today, it is still considered an excellent practice to gather multiple sources of information from multiple respondents when measuring the effectiveness of group interventions or counseling outcomes.

During the 1920s and 1930s, several early theorists of group work emerged. Alfred Adler emphasized the innate social nature of human beings to support a group treatment model. He conducted groups in the 1920s that investigated the relationship between children's problems and family experiences (Gazda, Ginter, & Horne, 2008). Adler and his associates developed group family meetings, or family councils, to obtain input from each member about how to best approach disputes and improve family relations. This new, systematic form of group guidance became known as collective counseling. However, Adler did not seek external validation to demonstrate the effectiveness of his techniques because he claimed that effectiveness should be clearly evident to the group leader.

In the late 1920s, Trigant Burrow developed an interest in how individuals were affected by loneliness, and how relationships affected

psychiatric issues. He witnessed individuals interacting in groups and determined that individual relationships in one's community have a tremendous impact on the development of psychopathology.

Another major development of the 1920s was J. L. Moreno's creation of the Theater of Spontaneity, the earliest form of psychodrama. Psychodrama was a technique developed to bring about mental and emotional catharsis for the purpose of tension relief. Techniques that arose from this early group work, including role play, catharsis, and a focus on empathy and the encouragement of group members, are still frequently used today.

Also during the 1920s, some early pioneers began to look at the process variables that underlie group work effectiveness. For example, Lewis Wender articulated the first guidelines for group therapeutic factors (e.g., factors that promote effectiveness of group work with members) after examining the many difficulties associated with making successful psychotherapeutic interventions with inpatient populations (i.e., patients hospitalized with severe mental disorders). Individual transference relations (e.g., individual clients reacting to therapists as they would toward a parent or sibling) were hard to accomplish with inpatients, and the associated time and cost were often prohibitive. After determining that analytic procedures were ineffective, Wender discovered that group therapy produced desired qualities such as intellectualization, patient-to-patient transference, and catharsis in the family, all of which promoted therapeutic progress.

What is known as the Developmental Period in group counseling began in the 1930s and continued into the 1960s. During this time, group work in the school underwent a transformation from predominantly psychoeducational usage to a more balanced use of classroom guidance (psychoeducational) and group counseling, both in elementary and secondary settings. From 1930–1945, substantial laboratory research was conducted to quantify the influence of social interactions on behavior and to determine how different methods of group persuasion and peer pressure changed people's convictions and beliefs. Throughout this time period, research was focused primarily on individual changes in a group setting, rather than on studying the dynamics within the group itself. The work of two leading figures led to considerable expansion of the interest in group work and high-quality group research. Moreno's prominence as a pioneer in the group counseling field continued to grow during the 1930s. He wrote prolifically, organized the first society of group therapists called the American Society for Group Psychotherapy and Psychodrama, and first coined the term *group psychotherapy.* He also introduced the first professional journal on group therapy: *Sociometry, A Journal of Interpersonal Relations.*

S. R. Slavson, an educator and self-taught therapist, founded the American Group Psychotherapy Association (AGPA) in 1942, along with its accompanying publication, the *International Journal for Group Psychotherapy.* AGPA was an interdisciplinary organization for group psychotherapists dedicated to improving the practice, research, and theory of group psychotherapy. Today, AGPA has standards for ethical practice, clinical membership, and a voluntary Clinical Registry of Certified Group Psychotherapists. As part of his research, Slavson offered activity therapy groups for children and reported that group activity sessions were equally as effective as individual counseling for stimulating change. His work was a catalyst for significant increases in the use of group treatment procedures for children and adolescents, and became an impetus for the introduction of group counseling in the schools.

As research provided more evidence of the effectiveness of group therapy, widening patient populations began to seek out this means of treatment for personal growth. Another significant event of the 1930s was the founding of the first major self-help group in the United States, Alcoholics Anonymous. The originators of this group model recognized the power of bringing together individuals in a supportive way to produce change. Listening, empathizing, and teaching were hallmark characteristics.

The 1940s and 1950s

In the 1940s, more and more practitioners began to realize the powerful dynamics created in group therapy settings. The use of this therapeutic medium expanded tremendously during this time due to the needs of military personnel after World War II. Specifically, the war increased interest and innovations in the use of groups due to a shortage of therapists and a need to treat large numbers of veterans through rehabilitation counseling and psychotherapy, as well as psychoeducational approaches for vocational planning and career development. Much of the emphasis in vocational approaches with returning veterans was patterned after psychoeducational group work approaches that had been used with high school students for several decades in schools.

Kurt Lewin, a major figure of this era, is known as the founder of the study of modern group dynamics. In 1940, Lewin began the study of intragroup relations. He viewed groups as agents for change and has been credited with the invention of training groups (or T-groups), which blossomed into the encounter and sensitivity groups of the 1960s and 1970s and which were commonly used in schools at that time. His approach, known as field theory, emphasized the interaction between individuals and their environments, and he was heavily influenced by the ideas of Gestalt psychology, which emphasized the relationship of the part to the whole. Lewin's research on T-groups was conducted at the National Training Laboratories in Bethel, Maine, and resulted in the finding that people's ideas and behaviors were more susceptible to change in group settings than in individual interactions. Lewin also studied the characteristics of group leaders, and he noted the ways in which leaders facilitated growth and change in group members. His research resulted in the identification of predictable stages of group work, and specific change markers for individual clients. In the late 1940s, Wilfred Bion, a member of the Tavistock Institute of Human Relations in Great Britain, studied group cohesiveness and stated that group dynamics often differ greatly from the dynamics of a family unit (Gladding, 2008). The trend toward structured group counseling investigations continued in the 1950s, as additional research was conducted on group structure, climate, leadership, and settings (Gazda et al., 2008). Many therapists recognized that group work was more effective and advantageous than individual counseling, but individual therapists argued that changes made in group therapy were only superficial in nature because proper transference with the therapist could not be achieved. This argument was quelled, however, when evidence was consistently presented to demonstrate that transference was not only achieved, but enhanced in group therapy settings.

While educational institutions continued to implement career guidance, a new emphasis was placed on group and individual counseling to increase academic achievement and enhance the school climate. The 1957 launch of the Soviet satellite, *Sputnik I,* created an urgency in the United States because many U.S. leaders believed the United States had fallen behind in the so-called space race and that public K–12 schools and colleges were not producing students competent enough in math and sciences to compete in the increasingly technological world. In 1958, the National Defense Education Act (NDEA) was signed into law; it targeted money for the training and employment of school counselors in U.S. public high schools. Primarily, these school counselors were given the task of identifying and encouraging students with high math and science aptitudes to pursue college degrees in the sciences. Of course, the role of the professional school counselor over time evolved beyond the emphasis on "test and place" to encompass a developmental approach involving group work and individual counseling (Herr & Erford, 2007). By the end of the 1950s, classroom guidance, a psychoeducational group work approach, while still used quite often to achieve educational and career development goals, was largely replaced by group counseling when the goal was to bring about behaviorally based changes in educational environments.

Later research conducted by Comrey and Stats in the 1950s and Goldman in the 1960s compared individual and group performance in tasks completed by participants of varying ability levels. Results showed that enhanced group performance was linked to the initial ability levels of the individuals working with one another, a finding that demonstrated the importance of individual contributions to group achievements (Posthuma, 2002).

The application of group work to family counseling settings experienced considerable growth during the 1950s. Rudolph Dreikurs used Adler's counseling theory to set up and work with parent groups. Clinician John Bell also conducted work with families, and his therapeutic practice was uniquely characterized by treating the family members like strangers who were new members of a counseling group. He stimulated open discussions and encouraged silent members to share their thoughts and ideas with the other members. Other significant figures of this decade included Nathan Ackerman and Virginia Satir, who modified the psychoanalytic model of group therapy for family work, and Gregory Bateson, who researched group dynamics within families.

The 1960s and 1970s

The popularity of groups flourished during the 1960s and 1970s, largely due to the social climate of that era. The power of groups to create change became evident in light of historical events such as the civil rights movement, the Vietnam War peace protests, and the so-called counterculture movement. Group therapy research decreased from 1960–1980 (Gazda et al., 2008). Although group treatment was used extensively in societal settings, there was a greater emphasis on experiential rather than empirical validation of its effectiveness. Many have speculated that this shift in research practice was fueled by the general disdain for authority that was prevalent during that time period.

Advances in psychoanalytic theory and object relations theory for group therapy were made in the 1960s and 1970s. Several humanistic-existential therapists also aided in the development of group therapy and practice during this time. Fritz Perls developed Gestalt therapy, based upon Gestalt psychology, and demonstrated its use in a group setting through workshops conducted at the Esalen Institute in California. Eric Berne highlighted his transactional analysis approach to therapy in group settings.

During the 1960s and 1970s, Carl Rogers initiated encounter groups, also known as sensitivity training groups, to encourage and assist the pursuit of individual growth and development. These groups emphasized an increased awareness of the group member's emotions and the behaviors of other members, and members were encouraged to explore interpersonal issues within a connected and caring community. Rogers's person-centered approach was very applicable to school settings and helped group counseling to flourish in schools.

Marathon groups also came into prominence during this era. As their title suggests, marathon groups met together for extended periods of time, usually between 24 and 48 hours, throughout which members were expected to become more authentic and engage in true self-disclosure. Fatigue was important in facilitating the breakdown in defense mechanisms and increased openness, which would ultimately lead to deeper levels of personal growth. Proponents of this type of therapy devised techniques to help people learn practical skills for dealing with conflict that could be used in their everyday lives.

An unfortunate side effect of the tremendous popularity of group work was an increase in the incidences of misuse by untrained practitioners seeking to ride the wave of the movement. The exploitation of group therapy was sensationalized by journalists during the 1960s and beyond, especially because many participants with emotional disturbances were harmed by membership in groups which functioned without adequate prescreening. Leaders who abused and distorted the group process set the field back considerably by garnering bad press and ill will among the public. Unfortunately, some of this public backlash also tarnished the use of groups in schools, as well as the reputations of qualified and competent practitioners in clinical settings.

Group work in the 1970s continued to reveal an awareness of the potential hazards of this treatment modality. The term *groupthink* was coined to describe the power that members had over one another to conform. This was seen as a hindrance to individual growth and problem-solving abilities. The classic example of groupthink involved the performance of high-level government officials during the Cuban missile crisis of President Kennedy's administration. In this example, government officials with less close relationships to the president chose not to share concerns or interpretations that varied or did not conform with the concerns or perspectives voiced by more powerful and closely related officials. The power of the group process has both positive and hazardous consequences; skilled leaders know this and address harmful issues when they occur within the group.

Carl Rogers, the leading pioneer of person-centered therapy, bore witness to the powerful changes in attitudes and beliefs that could be achieved in group settings. While many practitioners shared Rogers's enthusiasm for the medium, others came to doubt its validity in the face of overzealous and undertrained therapists, whose practices were controversial and occasionally harmful to clients. For this reason, the need for increasing professionalization of group work was recognized.

In response to this call, the Association for Specialists in Group Work (ASGW) was founded in 1973 for the advancement of professionalism in group work. ASGW, a division of the American Counseling Association (ACA), was founded to "establish standards for professional and ethical practice; to support research and the dissemination of knowledge; and to provide professional leadership in the field of group work" (Association for Specialists in Group Work [ASGW], 2006) and has continued that mission through the present day. In 2000, ASGW revised its *Professional Standards for the Training of Group Workers* (Association for Specialists in Group Work [ASGW], 2000). This important document provides core training standards for all master's and doctoral level counselor education programs, and specialization guidelines for counselor education programs that provide advanced and specific group work training to counselors. An even more important document, and one referenced throughout numerous chapters in this book, is the *ASGW Best Practice Guidelines* (Association for Specialists in Group Work [ASGW], 2007). ASGW (see http//:asgw.org) continues to be an association dedicated to the effective practice of group work by providing consultation, sponsoring continuing education, and contributing to the extant literature through their flagship journal *The Journal for Specialists in Group Work*. Likewise, the American School Counselor Association (ASCA) helped professionalize the practice of group counseling in the schools by publishing its first position statement on group counseling in 1989.

The percentage of research articles on groups in counseling journals rose from 5% in the 1950s to 20% in the 1970s. Particularly important research was conducted by Irvin Yalom, who analyzed group methods and processes, and described therapeutic factors within groups that had positive, curative effects on members. In particular, group leaders' styles and methodologies were found to have a particularly strong impact on group success or failure. Yalom's research was published as the definitive resource on the therapeutic factors in group counseling, and it has retained its prominence into the 21st century. See Table 1.1 for a brief introduction to these therapeutic or curative factors. These factors will be expanded upon in later chapters when contextually relevant.

During the 1970s, group work also received another strong push when soldiers returning from the Vietnam War received rehabilitation counseling, group counseling, and psychotherapy to help readjust to society. Counselors relied on group work as a cost- and time-effective method for addressing the complex issues of numerous soldiers. This trend continued even more recently as soldiers from the first and second wars in Iraq experienced similar war-related trauma and physical or emotional disabilities.

The 1980s and Beyond

In the 1980s, group counseling continued to increase in popularity and professionalism. The AGPA worked to refine group theory and practice through the publication of scholarly articles on group counseling innovations, and in 1980, the ASGW published a professional code of ethics for group workers to address increasing concerns over unprofessional behaviors demonstrated by unqualified or poorly trained individuals. The quest for personal growth and the expansion of counseling theory led to a proliferation in the different types of groups available to clients. Self-help groups, frequently led by group members rather than professionals, but still falling under the group counseling functional model, became particularly prevalent, with between 2,000 and 3,000 self-help groups in existence during the 1980s (Gladding, 2008). Some of these self-help groups were hosted by schools and school-community partnerships. Psychoeducational groups and classroom guidance were also popular, particularly in schools, to address the developmental personal/social, academic, and career needs of children and adolescents. Leaders in the field, such as George Gazda, advocated for the use of developmental group counseling for teaching basic life skills. By the close of the 1980s, group work was widely recognized as a viable option for helping members, and it was readily available to the public.

Division 49 of the American Psychological Association, called the Group Psychology and Group Psychotherapy Division, was founded in 1991 to provide a forum for the practice, research, and teaching of group work in psychology. Division 49 publishes the journal, *Group Dynamics: Theory, Research, and Practice*.

The Council for the Accreditation of Counseling and Related Educational Programs (CACREP) revised its standards in 1994 (and again in 2001 and 2009) to include specific group work specialist preparation guidelines for the graduate-level degrees. The importance of group work was reemphasized by these revisions, which identified specific principles for group dynamics; leadership styles; and group counseling theories, methods, and ethical considerations.

TABLE 1.1 Therapeutic Factors in Group Work

In group work, a therapeutic factor is an element, generally created by the group leader or relationships with other members, that improves a member's overall condition. Building on the work of several researchers (e.g., Corsini & Rosenberg; Hill; Berzon, Pious, & Farson), Irvin Yalom developed what is now considered the landmark classification of curative or therapeutic factors in the 1970s (Yalom & Leszcz, 2005).

1. *Instillation of hope* provides clients with a sense of assurance that the treatment will work.
2. *Universality* is the awareness of the similar concerns of others. As members interact, they come to realize that other members are going through similar situations, and so they feel much less alone and isolated, creating a sense of unity.
3. *Imparting of information* about healthy living is important to the growth of members and their ability to function more effectively. Leaders may provide information about helpful techniques such as those that aid in socialization, while members learn about how to deal with academic, career, personal/social, mental health, mental illness, and other real-life problems.
4. *Altruism* is exemplified by members giving of themselves and working for the common good.
5. *Family reenactment* helps re-create early childhood dynamics so that members are able to relive early family conflicts and effectively resolve them. Psychotherapy (and sometimes counseling) groups can create a caring family environment in which issues of trauma can be safely aired and confronted.
6. *Development of socialization techniques* is necessary for members to function successfully in their everyday lives. Group work allows members to give and receive personal feedback, which facilitates learning about the desirability of one's behaviors.
7. *Imitative behavior* occurs when members have an opportunity to observe the behaviors of other members and witness the positive or negative responses elicited by their actions.
8. *Interpersonal learning* occurs through member interactions with others. Each member affects the other in much the same way that they affect the people they interact with in their everyday lives, and members receive feedback on their conduct and can learn new ways of being while feeling safe and supported.
9. *Group cohesiveness* is similar to a feeling of unity and a sense of being bonded together. Cohesiveness indicates that effective therapy is occurring because it facilitates trust and a willingness to take risks. Groups provide acceptance, belonging, and an outlet to express previously unexplored emotions.
10. *Catharsis* is the expression of strong and often hidden emotions by an individual. Catharsis is characterized primarily by a sense of freeing oneself. Instead of masking one's true feelings, group work provides a forum for releasing tension and venting about whatever a member has kept inside.
11. *Existential factors* are realized when members are encouraged to consider important and sometimes painful truths about life, including an awareness of one's own mortality and the unpredictability of existence.

Group work proliferated in schools during the 1990s as an effective means for improving student academics and social skills. It was also used extensively with special populations outside schools, from those with disabilities to individuals experiencing major life changes. Greater specialization and segmenting in group work occurred during this time period, with practitioners seeking proficiency in areas such as occupational, psychoeducational, and psychotherapy groups (Gladding, 2008). While self-help groups continued to be a dominant force in the field, task groups in schools and other work settings experienced the most remarkable growth in North America. Additional branches such as parenting groups, cooperative learning groups, and focus groups also emerged. During this time, ASGW converged on a preferred language, featuring the term *group work*, and specified four types of group work: task groups, psychoeducational groups, counseling groups, and psychotherapy groups. These four different types of group work will be referred to throughout this book.

ASCA has emerged as a positive force for school counseling and group work in the schools. ASCA's *National Model* (American School

Counselor Association, 2005) featured systemic and data-driven approaches to school counseling delivered through a comprehensive, developmental school counseling program model. Classroom guidance, psychoeducational group work, and group counseling are primary methods for achieving the goals of the school counseling program. ASCA (2007) revised its position statement on group counseling, adding emerging evidence of the effectiveness of group counseling in achieving positive outcomes for students. Also, the 2004 ASCA *Ethical Standards for School Counselors* (see Chapter 2 of this book) included language that addressed issues specific to group work in the schools, including confidentiality, informed consent, and relationships among group members.

Group work has continued to develop and evolve at a rapid pace to meet the needs of the current generation. In the 21st century, group work has become an elemental part of the training and practice of counselors. The effectiveness of group work has encouraged its ongoing refinement and use. Most important, the evolution in the research and practice of group work, from its roots in the early 20th century to its current practice in schools, has produced reliable evidence of its advantages over other approaches to changing thoughts, feelings, and behaviors. Various group work approaches possess particular strengths, depending on the specific therapeutic context and process. Despite the many benefits that can be derived from group work, it is not appropriate for all clients or in all cases. Indeed, there can be both challenges and dangers associated with group work. Some of these strengths and challenges are outlined in Table 1.2.

TABLE 1.2   Strengths and Challenges of Group Work

Strengths of Group Work

1. *Time Efficiency for the Leader.*   Meeting with several members simultaneously for a common purpose (e.g., advising, problem solving, strengthening social support, aiding in personal development) can save substantial time and effort, especially when a counselor's caseload is especially large.
2. *Less Costly per Individual.*   There is generally a lower cost associated with group work compared with individual counseling; all other things being equal, a counselor seeing five to ten members at a time is five to ten times more time- and cost-efficient.
3. *Greater Resources.*   Group members often have access to a greater variety of resources (e.g., concrete information, problem-solving tools, abstract viewpoints and values) from multiple members within a group than does a member in a one-on-one counseling relationship
4. *Feeling of Safety.*   Interpersonal safety can be achieved in groups. Member relationships are developed with a controlled intimacy, which makes it possible for individuals to open up and share their true emotions without the contingent obligations that often arise with this type of self-disclosure in personal relationships.
5. *A Sense of Belonging.*   Most humans have a powerful need to belong. Working with a group of individuals in a therapeutic setting allows members to exchange ideas and feel greater self-confidence as well as a sense of belonging. Members often perceive that their feelings are not shared by others, but in a group setting they come to realize that others are experiencing similar struggles. Members have reported that the acceptance they felt by other members during group counseling was one of the most important aspects of their counseling experience.
6. *Replication of the Everyday World.*   The group is essentially a microcosm of society. Conflicts that arise in group settings are often similar in nature to those that are experienced in the outside world, especially if the group's membership is diverse, and real-life issues are addressed.
7. *Safety in Which to Practice New Skills and Receive Feedback.*   Members can use the group as a sounding board for trying out alternative problem-solving techniques and consequently assess the likelihood that they will be successful when using those techniques in their everyday lives. Groups provide an atmosphere of empathy and trust in which members can build on their existing skills and develop new interaction patterns to facilitate greater interpersonal success in their lives.

(Continued)

TABLE 1.2   Continued

8. *Commitment.*   Group settings often enhance a member's motivation to follow through with commitments that are made during group sessions. The support that members feel from others, as well as the desire to live up to their expectations to avoid letting anyone down, are powerful forces for effecting individual change.
9. *Power of the Peer Group.*   The influence of various groups on an individual's life is almost inevitable and can affect member development in diverse ways, especially in terms of conformity, identity, reward and punishment, and social controls. When all group members are from the same generation, the impact of group dynamics is generally the most significant. This is particularly true during adolescence.
10. *Interpersonal Power.*   In group settings, members have the opportunity to receive help *and* they are empowered to help others. As they witness the positive influence that their interventions have on others, members may become more willing to accept the influence of other members and grow in positive ways.

Challenges of Group Work

1. *Pressure to Conform.*   The power of the group can be problematic if it leads members to actively pursue unrealistic goals, take actions that are detrimental to their well-being, or conform to behaviors that go against their beliefs in order to be accepted by other members.
2. *Reality Distortion.*   Reality distortion (Trotzer, 1999) occurs when the group provides an example of social reality that is not achievable in the outside world. This can be devastating to an individual if the other members or group leader fail to consider reality factors when helping to formulate workable solutions to their problems.
3. *Avoidance.*   Certain group members may not reap adequate benefits from group work if they are less comfortable participating openly or are not given enough attention. Individual members are sometimes able to avoid confronting their problems if they blend in with the group (e.g., camouflage) or if the group setting becomes so safe and accepting that the individual members do not feel compelled to take risks or action toward addressing the issues for which they sought counseling in the first place.
4. *Confidentiality.*   Confidentiality cannot be guaranteed in group settings. Numerous individuals participate in each session, which means a greater risk of information being shared with others outside the group. During prescreening and in the first session, it is critical for group leaders to convey the importance of maintaining confidentiality, as well as the conditions under which content that is disclosed might have to be revealed.
5. *Unhealthy Attachments.*   The counseling group is transitional, not a permanent social outlet. Members who lack a feeling of acceptance from others in their everyday lives can rely too heavily on relationships formed in groups. Experiencing a sense of belonging is only valuable if it facilitates the achievement of a better life outside the group.
6. *Institutional Barriers.*   Some institutions have systemic barriers in place that inhibit effective group work (e.g., parental permission, personnel not realizing the value of group work versus other activities, scheduling challenges, finding space to run groups). Leaders must realize these barriers may exist and persevere. Counselor initiative often determines the prevalence and promise of group work.

Summary

The different types of functional group models highlighted in this chapter included task groups, psychoeducational groups, counseling groups, and psychotherapy groups. Various types of groups provide different ways to meet the needs of members. With regard to leadership, leaders of some groups may take on a more facilitative, less active role (i.e., counseling and psychotherapy groups). With other types of groups, leaders may be more directive and active in the group process (i.e., task and psychoeducational groups). These functional group models will be described in much greater depth in Chapters 11–18.

Throughout recorded history, human beings have gathered in groups for common benefit. Group work is the field of counseling intervention that applies knowledge and skill to assist group members to meet their goals. Numerous influential pioneers have contributed to the development of group work practices commonly used today, including Joseph Pratt, Jesse Davis, Frank Parsons, J. L. Moreno, S. R. Slavson, and Irvin Yalom. Kurt Lewin was particularly influential during the 1940s, inventing T-groups and field theory approaches to group work. During the 1960s and 1970s, leaders of various approaches to individual counseling applied their theoretical approaches to working with group members, including Fritz Perls (Gestalt therapy), Carl Rogers (person-centered counseling), and Eric Berne (transactional analysis). Group work, especially in psychoeducational and counseling groups, is particularly popular in schools.

Several strengths of group work were discussed, including time efficiency, cost efficiency, greater resource contributions by more members, a feeling of safety, experiencing a sense of belonging, replication of the everyday world, providing a safe place to practice new skills and receive feedback, increased member commitment, peer group power, and interpersonal power. Noted challenges of group work include pressure to conform, reality distortion, avoidance, potential lack of confidentiality, and unhealthy attachments.

Finally, Yalom has described a number of curative or therapeutic factors leading to group member progress, including instillation of hope, universality, imparting of information, altruism, family reenactment, development of socialization techniques, imitative behavior, interpersonal learning, group cohesiveness, catharsis, and existential factors.

CHAPTER 2

Ethical and Legal Foundations of Group Work

Lynn E. Linde, Bradley T. Erford, Danica G. Hays, and F. Robert Wilson

PREVIEW

This chapter highlights essential ethical and legal issues in group work, including confidentiality, informed consent, relationships among group members, termination issues, group participation, diversity issues, the Health Information Portability and Accountability Act (HIPAA), and the Family Educational Rights and Privacy Act (FERPA).

ETHICAL ISSUES IN GROUP WORK

One of the attributes of sound group work practice is the continuous assessment and reflection of the way in which a leader interacts with members. This reflective process is necessary to ensure that a leader provides the most appropriate ethical and legal group work services to members and is particularly important given the myriad issues that group leaders face every day. Some issues are clearly governed by either legal or ethical mandates; other issues are not as clear and challenge leaders to determine the appropriate course of action. When challenges arise, it is wise to begin with an examination of the ethical standards and legal issues as the basis for reflection. This process is particularly important when conducting groups because the issues are often more complex than dealing with one client at a time.

Both laws and ethical standards are based on generally accepted societal norms, beliefs, customs, and values. However, laws are more prescriptive than ethical standards, have been codified, and carry penalties for failure to comply. Another difference is that laws "dictate the *minimum* standards of behavior that society will tolerate, whereas ethics represent the *ideal* standards expected by the profession" (Remley & Herlihy, 2005, p. 3). Ethical standards are generally developed by professional associations to guide the practice of members of their profession.

Ethical standards can be further delineated into two categories: mandatory ethics and aspirational ethics. Mandatory ethics describe minimal adherence to the standards. For example, group leaders must act in compliance with the ethical standards of their profession, that is, the imperatives of counseling practice. Aspirational ethics are the ought-to-dos of counseling, wherein group leaders try to aspire to the highest standards and think about the impact of their behavior. According to Herlihy and Corey (2006), to practice aspirational ethics, leaders must go beyond compliance with ethical standards and understand the underlying principles or intent, sometimes referred to as meta-ethical principles.

META-ETHICAL PRINCIPLES

Forester-Miller and Davis (2002) delineated five moral principles that undergird counseling ethical standards and that are important to understand in order to move toward aspirational ethics. These five moral principles are autonomy, beneficence, nonmaleficence, fidelity, and justice. Ethical dilemmas occur when meta-ethical principles conflict with one another. While these principles often overlap and are congruent within group work, group leaders may sometimes be unsure which principle is most beneficial to promote. Dilemmas may also ensue when ethical principles applied to both individual group members and the group as a whole conflict.

Autonomy refers to independence and the right of the member to make one's own decisions. Leaders need to respect the right of members to make sound and rational decisions based on the members' values and beliefs rather than on what the counselor may view as best for members. Leaders do this by addressing and supporting individual group member goals. Goal setting, a task of early group stages, is conducted both by individuals and the group as a whole and is related to autonomy. For example, individual and group goals may not be congruent, at times even appearing to be at cross purposes. It is imperative that group leaders select members who will not impede, or whose well-being will not be harmed by, the group process. Members should be encouraged to set goals that can be addressed in the time allotted for the group.

Beneficence refers to doing what is in the best interests of members and promoting well-being, growth, and an optimal group experience. For example, group leaders promote the greater good for members by providing adequate time for processing group dynamics and content and evaluating the group experience. An optimal group experience for members may begin with informed consent in the planning

phase of the group. Leaders may prepare members from the onset of the group for how and when termination will take place, alternatives to the group experience, follow-up procedures, and potential referrals for continued group work. In addition, group leaders create an optimal group experience by adapting the group content and process as needed and respecting diverse perspectives and cultural identities present within the group.

Nonmaleficence is often referred to as "doing no harm"; that is, leaders avoid doing anything that may harm members. This includes preventing psychological or emotional harm potentially resulting from group member and leader interactions, group leader incompetence, inadequate treatment procedures, member abandonment, or premature termination.

Fidelity refers to honoring commitments and establishing a relationship based on trust. Group leaders promote open communication with members while fostering group relationships. Communication in the form of honest expression of emotions by both group leaders and members can create ethical dilemmas. Along with the challenges of the group process itself, members may experience additional stress if they may feel pressured to conform to member functions (e.g., providing feedback to others, evaluating the group experience).

Justice involves the fair treatment and consideration of each member, that is, doing what is best for each member according to the needs of each member by facilitating equitable and culturally relevant treatment. Equitable treatment may refer to equal access to group resources (e.g., individual time, content relevant to members' needs). Members may feel that their access is compromised by other group members, as in the case of members who monopolize group time, interrupt others, give inappropriate advice, or ask too many questions during group. Unequal access to group resources may cause some members to feel slighted and lead to premature termination.

Group leaders have a fiduciary responsibility to members. This responsibility extends from the time of screening members during the group planning phase to follow-up sessions after termination. It is guided by ethical behavior and consideration of the cultural diversity of all members. Thus, group leaders are entrusted to foster and respect individual development within the context of group learning, facilitate a group in a manner that promotes the group's purpose, avoid and minimize potentially harmful content and process, and be truthful and just with members.

GROUNDING ONESELF IN THE ETHICS OF GROUP WORK

Group leaders are governed by the ethical codes of their professional organizations and certifying bodies. Members of the American Counseling Association (ACA) are bound by the *ACA Code of Ethics* (American Counseling Association, 2005) and are encouraged to adhere to the *ACA Cross-cultural Competencies and Objectives* (American Counseling Association Professional Standards Committee, 1991). Likewise, members of the American School Counselor Association (ASCA) are bound by the *Ethical Standards for School Counselors* (American School Counselor Association, 2004). Counselors certified by the National Board for Certified Counselors (NBCC) are expected to adhere to the NBCC *Code of Ethics* (National Board for Certified Counselors, 2005). Members of the Association for Specialists in Group Work (ASGW) are expected to follow the *ASGW Best Practices Guidelines* (American Specialists in Group Work [ASGW], 2007) and demonstrate mastery of the ASGW diversity competencies (American Specialists in Group Work [ASGW], 1998) (see http://www.asgw.org/PDF/Principles_for_Diversity.pdf). Graduate counselor training programs are encouraged to design their group work training programs to be consistent with the ASGW training standards (American Specialists in Group Work [ASGW], 2000) and national accreditation standards (Council for Accreditation of Counseling and Related Educational Programs [CACREP], 2009).

The American Counseling Association (ACA) is the professional association for all counselors. One of the functions of professional associations is to promulgate ethical standards and thereby provide direction and information to counselors and their clients about appropriate and ethical behavior. The ACA (2005) *Code of Ethics* addresses the responsibilities of leaders toward their clients, colleagues, workplace, and themselves by delineating the ideal standards for conducting one's behavior. All ACA members are required to abide by the *Code of Ethics*, and action will be taken against any member who fails to do so. Because these are the standards of the profession, all group leaders, including those counselors who lead groups in schools, are held to the ACA *Code of Ethics* by the mental health community, regardless of whether they are members of ACA (Linde, 2007).

The ACA *Code of Ethics* is applicable to counseling in all settings and with all populations. More to the purpose of this book, however, are two sections of the code that address issues specific to groups and especially the use of group work in schools. Section A.8 states:

A.8.A. SCREENING

Counselors screen prospective group counseling/therapy participants. To the extent possible, counselors select members whose needs and goals are compatible with the goals of the group, who will not impede group process, and whose well-being will not be jeopardized by the group experience.

A.8.B. PROTECTING CLIENTS

In a group setting, counselors take reasonable precautions to protect clients from physical, emotional, or psychological trauma.

Thus, Section A.8 outlines, in broad terms, the responsibilities of the group leader when creating a group to screen potential members, ensure the appropriateness of members chosen, and to do what is in the best interest of the other members in the group.

Several divisions of the ACA and other counseling organizations have created their own codes of ethics or guidelines for ethical behavior that pertain more specifically to their work setting or specialty area. For professional school counselors, whether or not you are a member of ASCA, the ASCA *Ethical Standards for School Counselors* (2004) are the most relevant guidelines because they provide direction for group counseling in schools. Section A.6, Group Work, states:

The professional school counselor:

> **a.** Screens prospective group members and maintains an awareness of participants' needs and goals in relation to the goals of the group. The counselor takes reasonable precautions to protect members from physical and psychological harm resulting from interaction within the group.
> **b.** Notifies parent/guardians and staff of group participation if the counselor deems it appropriate and if consistent with school board policy or practice.
> **c.** Establishes clear expectations in the group setting and clearly states that confidentiality in group counseling cannot be guaranteed. Given the developmental and chronological ages of minors in schools, the counselor recognizes the tenuous nature of confidentiality for minors renders some topics inappropriate for group work in a school setting.
> **d.** Follows up with group members and documents proceedings as appropriate. (p. 2)

In summary, the ASCA *Ethical Standards* describe the safeguards that a professional school counselor must address in the development and implementation of a school counseling group.

The application of these issues will be addressed in more depth later in this chapter.

The Association for Specialists in Group Work, a division of the ACA, developed the *Best Practice Guidelines* (Association for Specialists in Group Work, 2007) (see http://www.asgw.org/PDF/Best_Practices.pdf at this time and review these guidelines in detail) and ASGW *Professional Standards for the Training of Group Workers* (Association for Specialists in Group Work [ASGW], 2000) (see http://www.asgw.org/PDF/training_standards.pdf at this time and review these training standards in detail). The *ASGW Best Practice Guidelines* identify sound practices when planning a group, selecting members for that group, conducting group sessions, and group processing. These guidelines are consistent with the ACA (American Counseling Association, 2005) *Code of Ethics*, but they contain more detail that is useful when conducting groups.

In 2000, ASGW revised the *Professional Standards for the Training of Group Workers* to use the more inclusive term *group work* to describe what leaders do and to delineate levels of training: core training and four specializations. The standards continue to provide guidance to counselor education programs regarding curriculum and to delineate the coursework and experiential requirements, knowledge and skill objectives, and assessment and planning skills for the core training and each of the specialty areas. Readers are strongly encouraged to review the *ASGW Best Practices Guidelines* and *ASGW Professional Standards for the Training of Group Workers* to become thoroughly familiar with these critical group work documents.

Finally, group work takes place within a community and is subject to that community's culture, norms, and standards of conduct. Whether one is participating in a school, business, or industry task group; providing classroom guidance experiences in a school; conducting a group counseling experience for adolescents with perfectionistic tendencies and concomitant anxiety; or providing group psychotherapy for adults who have been sexually traumatized, the leader and members are influenced by the cultural matrix in which they are embedded. The group work truism, "All group work is multicultural," provides a helpful reminder. To practice successfully in the multicultural context of group work, leaders must be aware of different worldviews and the effect of these worldviews on group work interventions; be aware of personal beliefs and attitudes related to relationships, healing, and health; and learn and provide culturally relevant group work interventions (DeLucia-Waack & Donigian, 2003).

MAJOR ETHICAL ISSUES IN GROUP WORK

Leaders conducting group work will be faced with myriad challenges. Group leaders recognize that conducting groups in any setting is challenging due to the varied and nuanced cultures of different work settings, the age of group members, and policies and procedures that may influence the way in which groups are conducted. This is not to say that planning for and running groups is difficult; ordinarily it is not. But challenges do exist. For example, the nuances of school culture, the demands for increased achievement, and the fact that the vast majority of students are minors and may not hold their own privilege and confidence all make for special challenges to group work in schools that leaders must address. This section provides brief analysis and instructions for dealing with confidentiality, informed consent, relationships among group members, participation and termination issues, counselor competence, and diversity issues.

Confidentiality

Confidentiality is the cornerstone of counseling and helps create the atmosphere in which the member feels able to trust and share with the leader and other group members. Members must feel that whatever they tell the group members will not be shared outside the group, except in instances in which the leader recognizes a duty to warn, or with member consent. Group work presents special challenges for confidentiality because the session is not like individual counseling with just one client and one counselor. If a group is to be productive, members must trust each other. In groups, there is no guaranteed confidentiality among members because there are multiple members in the session. Members can agree to hold information about other members confidential, but there is no law or professional ethic requiring them to do so. However, there is an ethical obligation for confidentiality that leaders must uphold. The *ASGW Best Practice Guidelines* Section A.7.d. (Association for Specialists for Group Work [ASGW], 2007) states:

> Group Workers define confidentiality and its limits (for example, legal and ethical exceptions and expectations; waivers implicit with treatment plans, documentation and insurance usage). Group Workers have the responsibility to inform all group participants of the need for confidentiality, potential consequences of breaching confidentiality and that legal privilege does not apply to group discussions (unless provided by the state statute). (p. 5)

The ASCA (American School Counselor Association, 2004) *Ethical Standards for School Counselors* (A.6.c) indicates that the professional school counselor:

> Establishes clear expectations in the group setting and clearly states that confidentiality in group counseling cannot be guaranteed. Given the developmental and chronological age of minors in schools, the counselor recognizes the tenuous nature of confidentiality for minors renders some topics inappropriate for group work in a school setting.

Conducting groups with minor children, whether in schools or not, places an extra responsibility on leaders to collaborate with parents and guardians, and to provide them with accurate and comprehensive information, while still maintaining ethical responsibilities to the young members.

It is the responsibility of the group leader to emphasize the importance of confidentiality and to establish this as the norm (Cottone & Tarvydas, 2007). A discussion of confidentiality should be part of the group screening interview before the group is established and part of the first group session, and it should be repeated throughout the group experience as appropriate. However, the group leader must also be honest that confidentiality cannot be guaranteed. If confidentiality is broken during the group experience, the group leader must address the issue with the members and reinforce the norm of confidentiality.

There are additional issues involved when counseling minors. Legally, confidentiality rights of minor children belong to the parent or guardian, but the ethical rights belong to the child. Balancing the rights of the parents and guardians against the needs of the child is a continuous process and involves many factors (Linde, 2007). Leaders must try to maintain confidentiality within the group, but they must disclose to parents and guardians when necessary. Leaders should help parents and guardians understand the importance that confidentiality plays in group work and engage their trust as well as the trust of group members. Should a parent or guardian desire to know what is going on in the group, the leader may divulge information only about that parent's or guardian's child as appropriate, and may not share information about other members in the group. Leaders should be aware of state statutes or other institutional policies affecting counseling minor children. Professional school counselors may want to obtain passive consent (commonly called assent), if not informed consent, from parents and guardians to ensure their support of their child's participation in the group and their willingness to respect the confidential nature of counseling. (See the next section on informed consent.)

The ACA (2005) discussed the limitations of confidentiality. The major exception to confidentiality is the duty to warn. Should it become apparent that a group member is being harmed, such as by abuse; harming or threatening someone else; or threatening to harm him- or herself, the leader has a duty to warn the appropriate entity.

Finally, group leaders should encourage members to honor other group members' right to privacy even after termination of the group experience. Group leaders should disseminate information about group members to clinicians to whom the leader refers a group member only with member consent (or the consent of the parent or guardian in the case of a minor child), when it is beneficial to the counseling process, when there is an imminent risk of harm to the group member or others, or there is a court-ordered requirement to disclose information about a group member. In short, confidentiality is for all time, unless legal or ethical circumstances require leaders to divulge confidential information.

Informed Consent and Disclosure Statements

As part of the screening interview process, leaders should obtain informed consent from potential group members or, in the case of minor children, they may want or be required to obtain informed consent from the parents or guardians.

INFORMED CONSENT IN CLINICAL PRACTICE   In clinical practice, it is essential that group members understand their rights as group members; understand the purpose of the group and generally what to expect from the group, including possible outcomes; and that participation is voluntary (or mandatory, if that is the case). Cottone and Taryvdas (2007) emphasized that informed consent also addresses the issue of the match between the member and the group. The screening must be sufficient to ensure that the client is being placed in a group that is consistent with the client's goals and that is compatible with the client.

Professional ethics and licensing statutes often require leaders to create and display a disclosure statement. ASGW standards require that group workers prepare a professional disclosure statement specifically for their group work activities (Best Practice Standard A7.b, ASGW, 2007; Rapin, 2004; Rapin & Conyne, 1999). This disclosure statement should include the following:

- The professional preparation of the group worker (e.g., education; training; licenses held, with the address of the licensing boards; certifications held, with the addresses of the certifying bodies; theoretical orientation).
- The nature of the group services provided (e.g., the nature, purpose[s], and goals of the group).
- The role and responsibility of group leaders and group members, including expectations for member behavior in the group.
- The limits and exceptions to confidentiality with regard to group member health information and disclosures made during the group, especially with regard to individuals coerced into group attendance by third parties.
- Policies regarding psychoactive substance use.
- Policies regarding contact or personal involvement among group members outside the group.
- Policies regarding attendance at group meetings and procedures to be followed in the event of absences.
- Documentation requirements and required disclosure of information to others.
- Procedures for consultation between (among) group leader(s) and group member(s).
- Fees and billing procedures.
- Time parameters of the group.
- Potential effects of group participation.

A fully developed disclosure statement that covers these points can help to ensure that when the prospective group member consents to group participation, it is on the basis of being truly informed (Remley & Herlihy, 2005). A sample disclosure statement is presented in Figure 2.1.

INFORMED CONSENT IN SCHOOLS The ASCA ethical standards (American School Counselor Association, 2004, A.6.b) states that the professional school counselor, "[n]otifies parents/guardians and staff of group participation if the counselor deems it appropriate and if consistent with school board policy or practice." In school settings, professional school counselors must follow the policies and procedures established by the system regarding parental and guardian consent for participation in a group. If the system requires parental or guardian consent, it must be obtained prior to beginning the group. If the system either does not require consent or has no policies regarding consent, the professional school counselor must weigh the merits of the situation. While a professional school counselor may have the legal right to conduct groups without parental or guardian consent, in some systems it may be unwise politically to do so. Having a parent or guardian make a complaint to building administrators or school system officials is rarely a pleasant experience, even if the professional school counselor is in the right. In such cases, the professional school counselor may wish to use either passive consent (assent), which ordinarily involves a written notification, or informally touch base (ordinarily a verbal communication) with the parents and/or guardians to let them know that the child is going to be included in a group.

Regardless of the consent requirement, it is essential that students understand their rights as group members (American School Counselor Association, 2004); the purpose of the group; generally what to expect from the group, including the possible outcomes; limits of confidentiality; and whether participation is voluntary. Cottone and Tarvydas (2007) emphasized that informed consent also addresses the issue of the match between the member and the group. The screening must be sufficient to ensure that the student is being placed in a group that is consistent with the student's goals and that is compatible with the student. Group members must also understand (a) ground rules, the role of the group leader, and expectations for group members; (b) limits and exceptions to confidentiality; (c) logistics of the group, such as the length and number of sessions, expectations for attendance, and follow-up to the group; and (d) potential impact of group participation.

PROFESSIONAL DISCLOSURE STATEMENT

Samuel Smith, M.A., LPCC

CONTACT INFORMATION

City Health Care Center, 123 Anystreet, Anytown, Mystate 43210

Phone: 901.234.5678; **Fax:** 901.234.8765

PROFESSIONAL EDUCATION

Midwestern University, M.A. in Mental Health Counseling (1964–1967)

National Association of Cognitive-Behavioral Therapists, Cognitive-Behavioral Training Institute (1992–1994)

LICENSURE AND CERTIFICATION

Licensed Professional Clinical Counselor and Supervisor (License: 4321S)

Certified Cognitive-Behavioral Therapist (National Association of Cognitive-Behavioral Therapists)

AREAS OF COMPETENCE

Assessment and diagnosis of adult mental and emotional disorders including chemical addiction. Individual and group psychoeducation, counseling, and psychotherapy.

Individual and group training supervision for individuals seeking professional counselor licensure.

GROUP TREATMENT: A TUNE-UP COURSE FOR MARRIAGES

Nature, Purpose, Goals of Group

Type of group: A psychoeducational group for couples with intact, durable marriages.

Purpose and goals for the group: The purpose of the group is marital enrichment. Its goals include: to help married couples assess the quality of their marital life, set goals for marital enrichment, improve communication skills, increase clarity of personal boundaries, increase ability of couples to negotiate for relationship change, and increase the couple's sense of joy in their marriage.

Structure of the group: This group will be limited to six couples who have been married for at least five years. The group will consist of an orientation meeting to take place before the group starts, 10 marital enrichment meetings, and a follow-up meeting one month after the last marital enrichment meeting. Meetings will consist of group warm-up activities, self-assessment activities, didactic inputs, discussion, and small-group skill practice activities. Homework assignments will supplement within-group learning.

Leadership of the Group

Leaders: During this group, I will have the assistance of a co-leader, Ms. Janet Jones, M.A., LISW, with whom I have co-facilitated over 30 marital enrichment groups of various kinds.

Responsibility of the Leaders: The leaders will be responsible for providing meeting space and for conducting the group meetings. The leaders will provide information about marital enhancement skills, attitudes, and values and will lead skill practice sessions to enhance skill development. The leaders will also provide a study guide for recommended reading materials and will assign homework to facilitate transfer of within-group skill acquisition to real-world situations. Members may contact me or my co-leader between

(continued)

FIGURE 2.1 Sample Disclosure Statement.

sessions to discuss problems that may have arisen regarding their membership in the group (e.g., attendance, fee payment, third-party reimbursement) or, on an emergency basis, to discuss matters related to their marriages; however, neither I nor my co-leader will accept a group member for individual or marital therapy during the course of the group.

Membership of the Group

Responsibility of the Members: The members will be responsible for coming to each group session on time, for participating in discussions and skill practice activities, and for completing homework assignments.

- Members join the group as a couple. Couples must attend meetings as couples. If one member cannot attend, the other must also absent him- or herself from the meeting. Couples must attend 80% of the group meetings to maintain membership.
- Members who are taking prescribed psychoactive substances may, of course, continue to take their medication per physician's orders; however, members are expected to come to group sober—not under the influence of a psychoactive substance.
- Members are expected to refrain from discussing their group membership experiences with any group members (other than their spouse) during the course of the group except during group meeting times.

Limits of Confidentiality

- Although it is useful to the development of trust among group members if members promise to maintain confidentiality regarding anything said or done by any member during group meetings, the promise is not enforceable by law in this state. Further, both my co-leader and I are mandated reporters whenever clients threaten suicide or homicide, or are behaving in neglectful or harmful ways toward children, invalids, or the elderly.
- If you wish to use a third-party payer to reimburse you for the cost of this marital enrichment group, you will be requested to sign a release of information so that I may supply your third-party payer with information requested to support your claim for reimbursement.

Fees and Billing Procedures

- The cost of a 10-session ***Tune-up Course for Marriages*** is $250 per couple; however, adjustments in the fee will be made according to City Health Care Center's standard fee-adjustment schedule. There is no charge for attending the orientation meeting or for attending the one-month follow-up meeting.

Potential Impacts of Group Participation

- Marital enhancement groups such as the one I and my co-leader are offering have been shown through research evidence to be helpful to marital couples; however, no guarantees can be made that this particular group will be helpful for any particular couple. In fact, as has also been shown by research, some couples who enter marital enhancement groups find that they have irreconcilable differences that have culminated in the couple seeking divorce. We encourage all couples applying to this program to discuss any concerns they have about joining a group such as our ***Tune-up Course for Marriages*** at the intake interview.

**THIS INFORMATION IS REQUIRED BY THE MYSTATE COUNSELOR LICENSURE
BOARD WHICH REGULATES ALL LICENSED COUNSELORS**

MYSTATE COUNSELOR BOARD
100 East 1st Street, Suite 1234
Capital City, Mystate 43434
Website: www.counsboard.mystate.gov
E-mail: counslicenseinfo@counsboard.state.mystate.us
Phone: 678-123-4567; Fax: 678-123-7654

FIGURE 2.1 *continued.*

SCHOOL LETTERHEAD

SCHOOL COUNSELING DEPARTMENT

Date

Dear Parent/Guardian:

One of the services our school counseling program provides is to work with students in small groups on a variety of topics throughout the school year. Participation in these groups is voluntary. Group sessions are usually scheduled once a week for eight weeks during the school day. The groups are scheduled to minimize the amount of time that students miss from their classes, and students are expected to make up any work they may miss. Confidentiality of what students share will be respected, but it cannot be guaranteed.

Your child, _____, has been invited to participate in a group on _____. The group should begin _____ and should end _____. The purpose of the group is _____ and it is expected that participation in the group will lead to _____. Please sign the form at the bottom of this letter and return it to me by (date) _____ to allow your child to participate.

Please feel free to contact me if you have any questions. I can be reached by telephone at _____ or by email at _____.

Sincerely,

Professional School Counselor

Group Counseling Consent Form

I give permission for my child, _____, to participate in group counseling with the school counselor. I understand this group will focus on _____.

Parent/Guardian Signature   Date _____

FIGURE 2.2   A Sample Informed Consent Letter to Parents and Guardians.

If the professional school counselor sends a consent form home with the student, it should contain sufficient information for the parent and/or guardian to make a determination regarding participation. The form should include information about the topic and/or goal of the group, the number and length of sessions and when sessions will be held, the name and position of the person(s) conducting the group, the expected outcomes, and contact information for the group leader. If informed consent is required, the form should also include a line for the parent's or guardian's signature and date. Passive consent (assent) would not require that the parent or guardian return a signed form to the school. See Figure 2.2 for a sample informed consent letter.

Relationships among Group Members

The issue of personal relationships among group members sometimes is an ethically gray area. In private practice or mental health center groups, it is unlikely that group members will see each other outside the group, although these chance meetings depend on the size of the community, of course. In school settings, students often may interact outside the group. It is very common in schools for students to know each other and perhaps even be in the same class or extracurricular activity. Sometimes leaders plan a group on a specific topic, such as loss and grief or changing families, and must decide whether to include siblings and/or relatives in the same group. Which is ethically more appropriate: to provide the service for all members needing the help and to deal with any relationship issues that arise, or to deny group membership to some members because they have a relative in the group? Leaders sometimes are faced with this and other dilemmas. As long as care is taken to minimize problems and maximize participation, either course of action may be ethically appropriate.

When Should a Group Terminate?

The *ACA Code of Ethics* (2005) states that group leaders should terminate groups when services are no longer effective or required. Services may be considered ineffective when group content and process is not appropriate for members or if leaders lack competence regarding group leadership or content. In addition, group leaders should be cognizant that not all members will be ready to end the group at the same time, creating a dilemma between individual group member and group development. Members develop differently throughout the group as they set goals, overcome resistance, develop and apply new skills, and say goodbye to each other. A number of ethical issues specifically related to a member's readiness for termination can present leaders with ethical dilemmas. Group leaders help members meet individual goals (e.g., applied learning, minimizing unfinished business), but in reality, how responsible are group leaders for ensuring applied learning? How much unfinished business is allowed at the end of a group experience to still have successful termination? What professional and ethical obligation do group leaders have to follow up

with members after termination? These are all questions group leaders face.

In school settings, classroom guidance and counseling groups are generally planned for a finite number of sessions and terminate at the designated date. Professional school counselors must be sensitive to the progress made by individual students during the sessions and provide appropriate follow-up and, if appropriate, referrals for those students in need of continuing assistance.

Group Participation

Group leaders should encourage silent members to participate, acknowledge nonverbal communication, and discourage members from monopolizing the time or content of the group session. Because a key assumption in group work involves verbal expression for group member growth, group leaders should also respect individual differences related to communication patterns. For instance, some members may value nonverbal communication, view group leaders as expert, and thus be less inclined to challenge others. It is good practice to get all members active in the group process early in group sessions to facilitate participation, trust, and cohesion.

The Right to Terminate Prematurely

Premature termination may be beneficial to individual group members, particularly if members perceive that the group is not meeting their needs in some way. In addition, members may choose to terminate prematurely as a result of an improper placement in a group. For closed groups (i.e., groups that will not accept new members once the group sessions have begun), group leaders should encourage members who wish to leave the group early to discuss why they want to leave the group with other group members within a session. Such actions help bring some degree of closure for the members who want to leave and those members who will remain. The discussion also frequently creates interesting content and process related to individual and group goals.

Ethical standards and best practice guidelines (American Counseling Association, 2005;

Association for Specialists in Group Work, 2007) require that leaders not abandon or neglect members. Leaders must monitor their services to ensure that members who are not benefiting from a particular group experience are referred for a more appropriate form of therapy or different type of group.

In the case of mandated clients who involuntarily enter a group, the right to terminate prematurely ordinarily is not an option. However, group leaders still have an ethical and professional responsibility to provide appropriate services to group members while respecting varying levels of group member investment in the group experience. Thus, group leaders should respect the degree that the mandated group member participates in the group. Group leaders should encourage a mandated group member's participation. While attendance may be mandated, individual participation should remain voluntary to avoid harm to the group member.

Counselor Competence

The ACA (2005) *Code of Ethics* cautions professional counselors to practice only within the scope of their education, training, and experience. The ASGW (2007) *Best Practices Guidelines*, Section A, discusses the issues involved in counselor competence when conducting groups, and states that group workers are aware of their strengths and weaknesses when leading groups, practice in those areas for which they meet the training criteria, and assess their knowledge and skill in the type of group they lead. Developing competence in the core areas delineated by the ASGW training standards is the foundation for conducting groups. It is essential that leaders continuously monitor their own competence because different groups and clients require different skills (Remley & Herlihy, 2005).

Leaders must also be aware of how their personality and character influence the way in which the group functions and ultimately affects the success of the group. Group workers must go through the self-reflective process to examine their positions on issues. This is particularly important because value-laden issues often arise in counseling sessions. The group leader's values and beliefs will come out during the group. Gladding (2008) believed that group leaders who try to hide or are unaware of their values may actually do more harm than good and encouraged leaders to model openness by displaying a willingness to explore and accept diverse viewpoints, values, and beliefs.

Competence in group counseling involves group leaders employing interventions that are congruent with group purpose and that are culturally relevant. Group leaders should continually monitor their effectiveness by formal and informal methods to avoid group member harm. In addition, group leaders should seek continuing education in group leadership, including culturally sensitive and culturally relevant group practice (American Counseling Association, 2005; Association for Specialists in Group Work, 2007).

While it is typically viewed as unethical when a group leader prematurely terminates a group, it may be ethically imperative to do so if a group leader does not possess group leadership skills or the specialized knowledge needed to facilitate a group. Ethical standards and best practice guidelines (American Counseling Association, 2005; Association for Specialists in Group Work, 2007) state that counselors in a group setting should discontinue services and provide appropriate referrals to avoid client abandonment.

Figures 2.3 and 2.4 present the Core Group Work Skills Inventory—Importance and Confidence (CGWSI-IC) and Core Group Work Skills Inventory—Quality of Performance (CGWSI-Q), respectively. The CGWSI-IC is an instrument that assesses the extent to which a group leader–in–training believes ASGW's core group work skills are important and feels confident in his or her ability to implement them. Please take a moment now to complete this instrument. Then complete the instrument again during key points in your development as a group leader (e.g., end of your group work course, end of a practicum, end of an internship, end of your first year of clinical practice). The technical manual for the CGWSI-IC can be found at http://asgw.org.

Core Group Work Skills Inventory—Importance and Confidence (CGWSI-IC)

F. Robert Wilson, Mark D. Newmeyer, Lynn S. Rapin, and Robert K. Conyne

Instructions: The CGWSI consists of 27 items. Each item describes a behavior that may or may not be useful to being effective as a group member or group leader. Please rate the importance of each item and your confidence in being able to do what the item describes by circling the number that represents your rating.

	Importance	Confidence
	1: Very unimportant	1: Very unconfident
	2: Unimportant	2: Unconfident
	3: Important	3: Confident
	4: Very important	4: Very confident

	Importance	Confidence
1. Evidences ethical practice in group membership or leadership	1 2 3 4	1 2 3 4
2. Evidences best practices in group membership or leadership	1 2 3 4	1 2 3 4
3. Evidences diversity competent practice in group membership or leadership	1 2 3 4	1 2 3 4
4. Develops a plan for group leadership activities	1 2 3 4	1 2 3 4
5. Seeks good fit between group plans and group member's life context	1 2 3 4	1 2 3 4
6. Gives feedback to group members	1 2 3 4	1 2 3 4
7. Requests feedback from group members	1 2 3 4	1 2 3 4
8. Works cooperatively with a co-leader	1 2 3 4	1 2 3 4
9. Identifies group process	1 2 3 4	1 2 3 4
10. Works collaboratively with group members	1 2 3 4	1 2 3 4
11. Encourages participation of group members	1 2 3 4	1 2 3 4
12. Responds empathically to group member behavior	1 2 3 4	1 2 3 4
13. Responds empathically to group process themes	1 2 3 4	1 2 3 4
14. Keeps a group on task	1 2 3 4	1 2 3 4
15. Requests information from group members	1 2 3 4	1 2 3 4
16. Requests disclosure of opinions and feelings from group members	1 2 3 4	1 2 3 4
17. Provides information to group members	1 2 3 4	1 2 3 4
18. Discloses opinions and feelings to group members	1 2 3 4	1 2 3 4
19. Assesses group functioning	1 2 3 4	1 2 3 4
20. Identifies personal characteristics of individual members of the group	1 2 3 4	1 2 3 4
21. Develops hypotheses about the behavior of group members	1 2 3 4	1 2 3 4
22. Develops overarching purpose and sets goals/objectives for the group, as well as methods for determining outcomes	1 2 3 4	1 2 3 4
23. Employs contextual factors in interpreting individual and group behavior	1 2 3 4	1 2 3 4
24. Conducts evaluation of one's leadership style	1 2 3 4	1 2 3 4
25. Engages in self-evaluation of personally selected performance goals	1 2 3 4	1 2 3 4
26. Contributes to evaluation activities during group processing	1 2 3 4	1 2 3 4
27. Provides appropriate self-disclosure	1 2 3 4	1 2 3 4

FIGURE 2.3   A Reproduction of the Core Group Work Skills Inventory—Importance and Confidence.

Source: CGWSI-IC: Copyright © 2007 by F. Robert Wilson, Mark D. Newmeyer, Lynn S. Rapin, and Robert K. Conyne, University of Cincinnati.

Core Group Work Skills Inventory—Quality of Performance (CGWSI-Q)

F. Robert Wilson, Mark D. Newmeyer, Lynn S. Rapin, and Robert K. Conyne

Instructions: The CGWSI consists of 27 items. Each item describes a behavior that may or may not be useful to being effective as a group member or group leader. Please rate competence (quality of performance) in being able to do what the item describes by circling the number that represents your rating.

<u>Competence</u>

1: Competent
2: Moderately competent
3: Moderately not competent
4: Not competent
N: Not demonstrated

1. Evidences ethical practice in group membership or leadership	1 2 3 4 N
2. Evidences best practices in group membership or leadership	1 2 3 4 N
3. Evidences diversity competent practice in group membership or leadership	1 2 3 4 N
4. Develops a plan for group leadership activities	1 2 3 4 N
5. Seeks good fit between group plans and group member's life context	1 2 3 4 N
6. Gives feedback to group members	1 2 3 4 N
7. Requests feedback from group members	1 2 3 4 N
8. Works cooperatively with a co-leader	1 2 3 4 N
9. Identifies group process	1 2 3 4 N
10. Works collaboratively with group members	1 2 3 4 N
11. Encourages participation of group members	1 2 3 4 N
12. Responds empathically to group member behavior	1 2 3 4 N
13. Responds empathically to group process themes	1 2 3 4 N
14. Keeps a group on task	1 2 3 4 N
15. Requests information from group members	1 2 3 4 N
16. Requests disclosure of opinions and feelings from group members	1 2 3 4 N
17. Provides information to group members	1 2 3 4 N
18. Discloses opinions and feelings to group members	1 2 3 4 N
19. Assesses group functioning	1 2 3 4 N
20. Identifies personal characteristics of individual members of the group	1 2 3 4 N
21. Develops hypotheses about the behavior of group members	1 2 3 4 N
22. Develops overarching purpose and sets goals/objectives for the group, as well as methods for determining outcomes	1 2 3 4 N
23. Employs contextual factors in interpreting individual and group behavior	1 2 3 4 N
24. Conducts evaluation of one's leadership style	1 2 3 4 N
25. Engages in self-evaluation of personally selected performance goals	1 2 3 4 N
26. Contributes to evaluation activities during group processing	1 2 3 4 N
27. Provides appropriate self-disclosure	1 2 3 4 N

FIGURE 2.4 A Reproduction of the Core Group Work Skills Inventory—Quality of Performance.

Source: CGWSI-Q: Copyright © 2007 by F. Robert Wilson, Mark D. Newmeyer, Lynn S. Rapin, and Robert K. Conyne, University of Cincinnati.

Diversity Issues

Chapter 3 will review diversity issues in group work in greater depth. The major point of this section is to reinforce the concept that when group leaders are knowledgeable about diversity issues and skilled in the implementation of approaches to meet diverse member needs, leaders are behaving ethically. The group leader must be culturally competent and sensitive to personal and group member behaviors for the group to be successful (Cottone & Tarvydas, 2007). The ASGW developed *Principles for Diversity-Competent Group Workers* (1998). These principles stress the need for the group leaders to be culturally sensitive and to understand how their cultural and diversity issues affect the group process and dynamics. Group leaders must also be aware of how the backgrounds of the members may influence their acceptance into the group and their behavior once in the group.

As part of their training, leaders should be able to identify, describe, and demonstrate skill in "use of personal contextual factors (e.g., family-of-origin, neighborhood-of-residence, organizational membership, cultural membership) in interpreting the behavior of members in a group" (ASGW, 2000, p. 6). Group workers who gain these skills and self-awareness are able to lead groups that are responsive to issues of diversity.

LEGAL ISSUES IN GROUP WORK

The discussion earlier in this chapter centered on codes of ethics and ethical behavior. Group leaders must also comply with those laws that apply to counseling practice. Laws are generally based on the same, generally accepted norms, beliefs, customs, and values as ethical standards. However, laws are more prescriptive, have been incorporated into code, and carry greater sanctions or penalties for failure to comply. Both laws and ethical standards ensure appropriate behavior for professionals within a particular context, in turn to ensure that the best interests of the members are met. When the two appear to be in conflict, the professional must attempt to resolve the conflict in a responsible manner (Cottone & Tarvydas, 2007). Remley and Herlihy (2005) suggested that there are few conflicts between laws and ethics in professional counseling. If a conflict does occur, group leaders must make their members aware of the conflict and their ethical standards. But because there are greater penalties associated with laws, the leader will often follow the legal course of action if there is no harm to the member. Many ethical standards recognize that other mandates must be followed and suggest that leaders work to change mandates that are not in the best interests of their members (Linde, 2007).

First and foremost, group leaders are governed by law. Before engaging in any form of counseling practice, a leader should become thoroughly grounded in the state statutes that regulate the practice of their profession. These statutes include the specific statute that establishes and regulates the practice of counseling, statutes that regulate a mental health care professional's duty to warn or protect third parties from harm threatened by a client, statutes that limit the conditions under which a client may claim privileged communication rights, and statutes that limit liability should a counselor breach confidentiality by reporting client communications to potential victims or to authorities. Although the Health Information Portability and Accountability Act (HIPAA) set stringent requirements for record keeping, billing, and protecting client health care data, the issue of confidentiality is a special problem for group workers. For counselors who conduct groups in schools, the most important law to be aware of is the Family Educational Rights and Privacy Act (FERPA) of 1974, which governs student records, including records of counseling sessions, but not personal notes.

Federal regulations may require and state statutes may entitle mental health professionals, like group leaders, to refuse to disclose privileged client communications, but client privilege may not extend to disclosures made by a client in a group setting (Rapin, 2004). It is argued that client privilege only binds professionals, such as physicians, psychologists, and counselors, to maintain confidentiality. When a member discloses personal information in the presence of nonprofessional group members, the member has effectively waived privilege. Further, group leaders working with group members who have been mandated into treatment through court order may be required by the court to report attendance records and treatment information to the court as part of the order. Best practice dictates that group workers define confidentiality and its limits (e.g., mandated reporting requirements; waivers implicit when third parties, such as insurance companies, require documentation of treatment before they provide reimbursement) including the fact that legal privilege does not apply to disclosures made during the group, unless specifically provided by state statute (Best Practice Standard A.7.d, ASGW, 2007).

Several laws pertain to counseling records, which are important to review. For counselors who work in schools, the Family Educational Rights and Privacy Act (FERPA) of 1974 governs student records, including records of counseling sessions, but not personal notes. For counselors who practice privately or in other clinical settings, the Health Insurance Portability and Accountability Act (HIPAA) of 1996 governs client information. Both laws are discussed below.

The Family Educational Rights and Privacy Act (FERPA) of 1974

The Family Educational Rights and Privacy Act (FERPA) (20 U.S.C.§1232g; 34 CFR Part 99) of 1974 is the federal law that protects the privacy of all student records in all PreK–12 schools, colleges, and universities that accept funding from programs administered by the U.S. Department of Education (USDE). It is often referred to as the Buckley Amendment. FERPA defines education records as all information collected by a school for attendance, achievement, group and individual testing and assessment, behavior, and school activities. It gives parents, guardians, and nonminor students specific rights regarding this information, including the right to inspect and review their children's records (or their own records if

the record holders are not minors) and the appeals process if they disagree with anything in the record. Second, the law limits who may access records. Under FERPA, only those persons with a "legitimate educational interest" can access a student's record. Some personally identifiable information, usually referred to as directory or public information, may be released without parental or guardian consent and generally includes information such as the student's name, address, telephone number, date and place of birth, honors and awards, and attendance information. The major exemption to the confidentiality of student records relates to law enforcement issues; the school must comply with a judicial order or lawfully executed subpoena. In cases of emergency, information about the student relevant to the emergency can be released without parental or guardian consent (see http://www.ed.gov/print/policy/gen/guid/fpco/ ferpa/index.html for an electronic copy of the law). All states and local jurisdictions have incorporated FERPA's requirements into state statutes and local policies that schools must follow.

The rights of consent transfer to students upon their 18th birthday, although the law does not specifically limit the rights of parents whose children are over the age of 18 years but continue to attend a secondary school, or to a student who attends a postsecondary institution at any age. Noncustodial parents have the same rights as custodial parents and guardians, unless a court order has limited or terminated the rights of one or both parents or guardians. Without court-appointed authority, stepparents and other family members who do not have legal custody of the child have no rights under FERPA.

FERPA requirements affect group work in public schools. Leaders conducting groups in schools must be aware of the limitations that FERPA may impose on any curriculum materials they use in groups, on any assessments used to identify or evaluate students in the group process, and on the types of information that should be kept in counseling notes. While some schools do not require signed, informed consent for participation in groups, professional school counselors may want to consider using informed consent or assent forms to avoid problems, particularly if they are touching on sensitive areas.

Leaders also need to remember that parents and guardians have the right to access their children's records. FERPA delineates personal notes as separate from the educational record and therefore not subject to its provisions. However, counseling notes constructed by the school counselor may be construed as part of the educational record, and therefore subject to review or sharing with others, if a group leader reads from the notes or shares summary findings from the notes with colleagues from the school. Group leaders need to remember this when writing counseling notes. Once the personal notes are shared, the notes are no longer personal notes; they belong to the student's educational record.

The Health Insurance Portability and Accountability Act (HIPAA) of 1996

The Health Insurance Portability and Accountability Act (HIPAA) of 1996 required that the U.S. Department of Health and Human Services (HHS) adopt national standards for the privacy of individually identifiable health information, outlined patients' rights, and established criteria for access to health records. Included in this law was a provision that HHS must adopt national standards for electronic health care transactions. In response to this mandate, regulations named the Privacy Rule were adopted in 2000 and became effective in 2001. This rule set national standards for the protection of health information as it applied to health plans, health clearing houses, and health care providers who conduct transactions electronically. All covered entities had until April 14, 2003, to comply with the Privacy Rule (see http://www.hhs.gov.ocr.hipaa for an electronic copy of the law).

The HIPAA Privacy Rule gives patients the right to obtain and examine a copy of their health records and request corrections, allows individuals some ability to control the uses and disclosures of their health information, allows patients to know how their information might be used and if disclosures have been made, sets limits on the use and release of health records, and provides a complaint process, among other things. It also requires that providers give clients a privacy notice and should obtain a signed acknowledgment of this notice.

States and health entities continue to work on the details of the implementation of HIPAA. Clearly it has implications for group leaders, particularly those who work in health settings, clinics, agencies, and private practice. Leaders must be aware of this law and its requirements, and they must ensure that their practices, including records, are in accordance with its provisions, particularly if they receive payment through insurance companies or health organizations. Group leaders should also ensure that when client information is shared with insurance companies, health professionals, or institutions that they are adhering to HIPAA. It should be noted that the mandates of HIPAA are very consistent with ethical standards and therefore should not be a barrier to sound professional practice. Signed, informed consent; limits to disclosure; and the confidentiality of patient information are all part of the ethical standards and should drive the practice of group leaders (Linde, 2007).

Summary

Ethical and legal issues are of particular import in counseling. Group work, like other forms of counseling, presents a variety of ethical issues, and it is critically important to be aware of codes of ethics, best practice guidelines, laws, and other resources that may help the leader determine the most appropriate course of action when conducting groups. FERPA governs sharing of student information in K–12 schools and universities that accept public funding and is overseen by the USDE.

The ACA (2005) *Code of Ethics*, HIPAA, FERPA, ASGW (2007) *Best Practice Guidelines*, and ASGW (2000) *Professional Standards for the Training of Group Workers* are all critically important documents for counselors conducting group work. All counselors conducting group work should be thoroughly familiar with all of them. Issues that will continue to challenge leaders striving for ethical counseling practice include confidentiality, informed consent, relationships among group members, counselor competence, diversity issues, and record keeping. As a final activity, test your understanding of ethical and legal issues in group work by reading and responding to the brief case dilemmas presented in Case Dilemmas 2.1.

CASE DILEMMAS 2.1

How will you handle the following ethical and legal scenarios?

1. Jonathan comes to group meetings very angry. He accuses Sam of divulging private information about him to other members outside the group—information Sam could only have known because Jonathan shared the information two sessions ago.
2. Sam's wife calls and tells you she is concerned about some information Sam divulged to her about another member in the group named Jonathan.
3. Susan's guardian called and wants an update on Susan's progress in the grief and loss group.
4. The mother of twins, Rowdy and Serenity, in your school called to ask if the twins could be included in the group counseling experience on grief and loss you intended to begin shortly. She indicated that her husband died less than six months ago and the twins are not adjusting as she had hoped.
5. You are beginning a counseling group on substance abuse for current adolescent users and are wondering whether you should obtain parental and guardian consent.
6. You are now in the sixth session of an eight-session group experience for adults who have experienced the loss of a spouse. Leroy has not said a word since introductions during session one. On several occasions he has opted to "take a pass." Several other group members have exchanged looks and seem uncomfortable with his lack of sharing.
7. The day after the sixth session of an eight-session group for adults who have lost spouses, you receive an email from Leroy telling you he is dropping out of group because other group members are giving him and each other looks; he feels uncomfortable sharing anything with them.
8. Juan's mother has asked you to testify in a child custody case on her behalf. Juan has been attending "changing family" group counseling sessions for the past two months. Her lawyer told her that your testimony and personal notes about how Juan feels about his father would help her to gain sole custody.

CHAPTER 3

Multicultural Issues in Group Work

Cheryl Holcomb-McCoy and Cheryl Moore-Thomas

PREVIEW

Group work with diverse members is addressed using oppression and marginalization as the frameworks from which group leaders can conceptualize group members' problems, behaviors, and actions. Because research indicates that people from oppressed backgrounds (e.g., ethnic minorities, disabled persons, the materially poor, gay and lesbian persons) are more likely to avoid counseling experiences, to drop out prematurely from counseling, and to report lower outcomes, it is important that group leaders become more responsive to member experiences of discrimination, prejudice, and inequities. Leaders can act to prevent or address these issues in the group. Also, because oppressed and marginalized persons are accustomed to being silenced, made to feel inferior, and having no voice, leaders must be skilled in working with members who are quiet, suspicious, pessimistic, cynical, and even angry. Second, how issues of oppression and marginalization may influence each stage of the group process will be introduced. Finally, the chapter ends with a discussion of dilemmas that may arise when implementing groups with culturally diverse members.

MULTICULTURAL ISSUES IN GROUP WORK

Whether through varying communication styles, language, sexual orientation, abilities, ethnicity and race, beliefs, behaviors, or perceptions, every group will be influenced by the cultural backgrounds of its members. In essence, a group becomes a social microcosm whereby the group members' values, beliefs, prejudices, cultural biases, and past experiences are played out in the group setting. With the increasing diversity of today's society, the need for more culturally competent work among group leaders is critical and has received much attention in recent literature (Chen & Han, 2001; Conyne, Wilson, & Tang, 2000; DeLucia-Waack, 2000; DeLucia-Waack & Donigian, 2003). This is particularly relevant for today's public schools, where more than one-third of the population is comprised of students of color. In addition to the need for more culturally competent group workers, many scholars have even cited the positive impact of multicultural group work on interethnic group relations (Gloria, 1999; Merta, 1995).

From a multicultural perspective, several goals or frameworks are important to consider when working with multicultural groups. According to DeLucia-Waack (1996a), three common goals of multicultural groups are (1) to understand the situation that brought the person to the group from a cultural perspective, (2) to approach all events and behavior in the group from a functional perspective, and (3) to help members make sense of "new behaviors, beliefs, and skills within a cultural context" (p. 171). Bemak and Chung (2004) believed that group leaders should have two additional goals when working with culturally heterogeneous group members: (1) to foster acceptance and respect for diversity within and between group members, and (2) to promote social justice and social change among members and the communities the leaders represent.

Historically, group work has been based predominately on Eurocentric models of therapy and counseling, with very little attention paid to working across cultures. For instance, it was only recently (1998) that the Association for Specialists in Group Work (ASGW) adopted the *Principles for Diversity-Competent Group Workers*. These principles serve as a guide for multicultural training, practice, and research and marked the beginning of a movement to address multicultural and diversity issues in group work. Gladding (2008) cited three reasons for the delay in addressing culture and diversity in groups. First, he contended that the death of Kurt Lewin in 1947 marked the end of the first movement to include cultural aspects of group work. In the 1940s, Lewin and his associates began a movement to train community leaders to use group work as a means to reduce tensions among interracial groups and to facilitate changes in racially biased attitudes. Gladding believed that the emphasis on reducing racial tension among groups and through group work ended when Lewin died.

Second, Gladding (2008) attributed the delay in addressing cultural issues in group work to the fact that culturally different group members were not considered to be significantly different from dominant group members. In other words, professional counselors believed that it would be best to be color-blind or that issues of race and culture did not have an influence on one's presenting problems. As a result of the multicultural movement in counseling, however, the color-blind approach was deemed inappropriate and unethical (Pack-Brown & Braun, 2003).

Finally, Gladding stated that many counseling professionals did not believe that cultural minority group members' behaviors and attitudes had a significant effect on group dynamics. However, recent thinking has indicated that culture can become the foundation from which a group functions (Baca & Koss-Chioino, 1997; Brinson & Lee, 1997; Johnson, Torres, Coleman, & Smith, 1995). For instance, ethnically or racially diverse members may bring their negative and faulty stereotypical beliefs about one another to a group, creating disharmony and distrust among members.

There are various definitions of multiculturalism found in the counseling literature. The multicultural movement has defined culture in a narrower manner, including only ethnic and racial differences. However, culture can and should be defined broadly to include demographic (e.g., age, gender, sexual orientation) and status (e.g, economic, social, disability) factors. For the sake of clarity, this chapter applies the broadest definition of culture because all of these groups can experience oppression and marginalization. Also, if this broad definition is used, then it is in keeping with the fact that all group work is multicultural. In addition, definitions of the terms *diverse persons*, *minorities*, and *nondominant* will be the same as delineated in the ASGW *Principles for Diversity-Competent Group Workers* (1998). The principles stated that "non-dominant" and "target populations" are

> groups of persons who historically, in the United States, do not have equal access to power, money, certain privileges (such as access to mental health services because of financial constraints, or the legal right to marry, in the case of a gay or lesbian couple) and/or the ability to influence or initiate social policy because of unequal representation in government and politics. (p. 7)

OPPRESSION AND MARGINALIZATION

Oppression manifests differently in varying contexts (Bernardez, 1996). For that reason, it is impossible to identify a single set of criteria that describes oppression. Generally, oppression refers to the unjust use of authority, force, or societal norms and laws to exert control over individuals, a people, or a group. More specifically and contextually important, oppression includes situations of exploitation, marginalization, powerlessness, cultural imperialism, and violence (Zutlevics, 2002). As oppression intensifies and progresses through individualized and systemic manifestations, it may lead to denigration, dehumanization, and scapegoating (i.e., blaming the oppressed for societal problems). Underlying this progression is the faulty belief that the target of oppression is less than or inferior to those of the dominant culture. For instance, a long history of oppression in U.S. schools has led many educators to believe that students of color, particularly African American and Latino and Latina students, are less intelligent or intellectually inferior to White and Asian students. In turn, this faulty belief has led to the achievement gap and lower expectations for many people of color.

Marginalization, one of the specific contexts of oppression, must be seen in reference to the dominant group. Marginalization is the social process of becoming excluded from or existing outside mainstream society or a given group. Given this dominant group reference, marginalization oddly places individuals of the target group on the outside or fringes of the dominant culture while simultaneously placing them inside the dominant culture (Cuadraz, 1996). This outside/inside orientation has social, psychological, political, and economic consequences. Persons from marginalized and oppressed backgrounds often feel as if they will not receive equality, justice, or fair treatment. These beliefs stem from their experiences with discrimination, racism, sexism, injustice, and other types of oppression.

Another important consideration for leaders is the concept of invisible diversity. Even if all of the members have the same skin color or gender, differences in socioeconomic levels, disability, beliefs, and values prevail. The multiculturally competent group leader is aware of potential invisible diversity among members and addresses issues of oppression and marginalization that stem from it.

Stages of Group Development

Oppression and its specific structure of marginalization have implications for group development. Before the group is formed, during the planning phase, leaders are primarily concerned with determining group needs and member characteristics. These issues, although simply stated, are actually quite complex. In particular, determining who may benefit most from a specific group experience requires a series of leader decisions and selections. Each of these leader decisions has implications for culture and for the potential manifestation of the related issues of oppression and marginalization.

Heterogeneous groups, by definition, involve members of diverse cultural identities (e.g., race, ethnicity, sexual orientation, ability, gender). Due to historical, social, and economic factors, there are often power differentials between members of these various groups. Consequently, some members of these cultural groups experience levels of oppression and marginalization that will undoubtedly emerge as the group social microcosm struggles to develop a sense of cohesion. While the emergence and discussion of these issues may lead to some anxiety, they should not be ignored. DeLucia-Waack (1996b) suggested that the discussion of such issues increases group cohesion. Group cohesion is significant for the effective movement through all aspects of group work, including matters of commitment and attendance, goal and norm establishment, and process factors. Although the issues of oppression and marginalization may be more visible in heterogeneous groups (e.g., groups with male and female members, groups with African American and Asian American members), these issues may also emerge in seemingly homogeneous groups. For example, members of a women's group on stress management may need to address marginalization if the subculture dynamics of stay-at-home moms, working moms, and women who do not have children emerge. Ideally, group leaders should explore these issues during the group preselection interviews and the planning phase.

As group work begins in the forming and orienting stage, members struggle to find their place. Trust, safety, and avoidance of rejection are central to this stage of group development. Effective leaders use a variety of skills to assist members in developing a strong sense of security. However, effective leaders must move beyond traditional counseling skills and techniques to address these same issues for group members who may be oppressed or marginalized. In particular, in the forming and orienting stage, group leaders must recognize that the effective development of trust not only occurs between the actual group members but also between the sociopolitical identities that are often played out and stereotyped in society at large. Although this task can be overwhelming, it may be necessary to recognize, in verbal and nonverbal ways, the dehumanizing and weighty baggage that society places on marginalized people. For example, bullying is a form of discrimination, usually against marginalized persons. Until this often unspoken and disregarded reality is acknowledged, trust, safety, and avoidance of rejection may not be possible. If safety, trust, and avoidance of rejection are not established, the greater societal misconceptions that are characteristic at this early stage of group development may be maintained and prohibit deeper, more authentic levels of member growth and exploration.

Different leaders use differing strategies to address these issues, but most leaders bring these issues into the open to allow members to discuss and deal with them in a supportive environment. Growth, understanding, and trust seldom occur when issues of oppression or marginalization are glossed over or treated as taboo topics. As will be discussed in the planning chapter (Chapter 6), recruiting and screening of group members prior to initiating group work is critical. It is essential that leaders become aware of the cultural and ethnic identities of potential members in order to plan for or at least anticipate issues that may arise later in the group.

The transition stage of group development, characterized by struggles for power and control and the building of group cohesiveness, also requires specific group leader functions. The culturally competent group leader recognizes that building awareness, providing support, and modeling must include the potential needs of marginalized members. While recognizing and dealing with potential conflicts and resistance are a leader's primary tasks when facilitating a group's movement through the transition stage, it would be negligent and unethical to fail to address social and political issues that may underlie the emerging group conflicts or resistance. For example, a transition stage conflict that emerges in a male and female adult group on commitment may be fueled not only by the members' anxiety about the group experience, but also by concerns tied to societal power differentials between men and women. To ensure that such a group moves effectively through this stage of development, a skilled group leader must assist the group in effectively managing the surface level conflicts while simultaneously addressing the underlying social and political issues of gender as appropriate. This assistance can include imparting information on the history and politics of gender and issues of gender socialization to the group members in developmentally appropriate ways. Disclosed in appropriate and sensitive ways, this information may inform and inspire creative and effective solutions for members and their individual behavioral situations and needs. The group leader can also continue to explore and develop the leader's own awareness of knowledge and skills related to gender preferences in counseling and the relation of gender and value structure. These topics are discussed elsewhere in this chapter. The extent to which these knowledge and skills sets should be introduced into group work depends on a number of factors, including the developmental level of the group members and the degree to which the particular cultural factor is salient for individual group members and for the group as a unit.

Oppression and marginalization must be vigorously addressed during the working and termination stages of group work. Typically, during these stages, members begin to acquire new insights, behaviors, and skills that are first practiced in the group and then integrated into the members' lives beyond the group. Group leaders should safeguard the group environment so that individualized and systemic applications of oppression do not form barriers for members during this significant time of growth and exploration. While this practice may unfortunately be impossible beyond the group setting, group members can explore the realities of social injustice and come to understand and adapt newly acquired behaviors and skills in ways that are culturally relevant and personally empowering. For example, a leader working with a group of African American students of any age on academic achievement can help the members discover growth-engendering strategies that promote school success. While the strategies may not affect the societal injustices of oppression in any measurable way, acknowledgment and discussion of the dynamic, particularly as it relates to the academic achievement gap, educational opportunities, and learning outcomes, could provide the group members with valuable information and insight that could acknowledge and validate their personal experiences and ultimately fuel their commitment to maximized academic performance. In contrast, denying or ignoring the existence of oppression and its affects on the African American population could prove detrimental. Failing to address, discuss, and act on oppression perpetuates oppression.

Leaders must consider the relevance and developmental levels of members in order to accurately assess the extent and manner in which these should be introduced into group work. For example, the manner in which a leader facilitates group exploration of oppression and achievement with second-grade children or seventh-grade students may differ from the way the leader could appropriately address the same issue with twelfth-grade adolescents.

GROUP LEADERSHIP AND OPPRESSION

To combat oppression and marginalization, group leaders must first engage in a process of self-exploration. By exploring their feelings about their own cultural and political identities, group leaders become more culturally sensitive to others' differences. This process of developing

a sense of cultural awareness also causes group leaders to take into account how they experience their own cultural differences and how their experiences and beliefs may affect their interactions with members from other backgrounds. Leaders should become very familiar with the Association for Multicultural Counseling and Development (AMCD) Multicultural Counseling Competencies (http://www.amcdaca.org/amcd/competencies.pdf) and explore their own attitudes, beliefs, and values regarding diversity and marginalization.

Before implementing groups with diverse members, it is also important for group leaders to explore and understand the complexities of oppression and how members from historically oppressed cultural groups may view the group process and the group leader. When group leaders recognize that group members come to the group with various perspectives based on their experiences with oppression, they are better equipped to help group members process their thoughts and feelings and to overcome any cultural conflict in the group. The reality of ethnic and racial superiority themes in our society, as well as classism, sexism, and the history of depriving certain groups of rights and resources, should all be considered when exploring one's cultural self-awareness.

Group leaders should also be open to the differences exhibited by diverse people. It is important for group leaders to be accepting and nonjudgmental about the values, lifestyles, beliefs, and behaviors of others and to appreciate difference and diversity (Toseland & Rivas, 2001). Because group work tends to be based on Eurocentric values, leaders must be cognizant of the fact that members of culturally diverse backgrounds may have values that conflict with the norms of many group members and leaders. For instance, being on time and taking turns to speak are two societal norms for Eurocentric persons that may not be the expectation of other cultural groups.

It is also important for a group leader to learn about the backgrounds of client groups. Leaders can gain cultural knowledge through researching literature pertaining to particular cultural groups, consulting with members of a particular cultural group, or by visiting a cultural community and becoming a participant observer. Living or spending time in a cultural community (i.e., immersion) can help a group leader better understand the common values, norms of behavior, and worldviews held by members of a particular culture, in all of its contextual richness and without stereotyping.

If immersion is not possible, a group leader might go through the process of social mapping, which consists of observing and analyzing formal and informal relationships among members of a community. For instance, a leader conducting a group for adolescent boys in a community where a majority of its students are African American and Latino could observe classrooms, special school activities, and after-school programs, as well as meet with parents and other community members, to get their perspective on the needs of boys in the community.

Group leaders must also attempt to learn how members identify themselves. It is important for leaders to be aware of the politically correct reference to groups, but most important, to be sensitive to how group members want to be identified. If a leader is in doubt as to a group member's cultural or racial identification, the group leader should ask and spend time discussing the issue openly. For instance, a group leader may ask a group member, "Carlos, I notice that you refer to yourself as a Chicano, rather than Hispanic or Latino. Would you mind telling us more about what that label means to you?" It is important for the group leader to demonstrate respect for the group member as well as interest in knowing more about the group member's cultural background. If the group member appears uncomfortable with the request for more cultural information, the group leader should then accept the member's feelings and decision not to discuss her cultural identification. A member should never feel pressured to self-disclose about cultural issues.

Developing culturally sensitive group strategies is another important task for culturally competent group leaders. Although there is very little research regarding the effectiveness of specific group strategies for diverse populations, there is some promising literature related to culturally sensitive group formats. For instance, Pearson

(1991) suggested that leadership be more structured for Asian and Asian American people. Using a traditional style, with less structure and a reliance on members to take responsibility for group interactions, would cause discomfort and contradict the cultural expectations of some Asian group members. On the other hand, Rittenhouse (1997) suggested that feminist group work use an unstructured format to minimize the power distance between members and the leader. Other culturally sensitive formats suggested in the literature include using empowerment groups for urban African American girls (Bemak, Chung, & Siroskey-Sabdo, 2005), structured task groups for Latino youth (Lopez, 1991), the use of poetry in groups for immigrants (Asner-Self & Feyissa, 2002), using survival skill training groups for African American adolescent males (Bradley, 2001), and using a Native Hawaiian healing method for Native American adolescent groups (Kim, Omizo, & D'Andrea, 1998).

And finally, leaders should have information about group process in "naturally occurring groups" (Lee, 1995). Naturally occurring groups include groups where culturally different persons come together for some type of ritual, ceremony, or entertainment. Typically, these groups include persons with similar or shared cultural experiences. Some examples of naturally occurring groups would include an African American church congregation, Latino youth clubs, gay families, and Native American tribal councils. Group leaders, if given the opportunity to observe naturally occurring groups, should note the nonverbal behaviors of individuals in groups. For instance, eye contact and conversational distance will vary across cultures. However, through the observation of naturally occurring groups, a group leader can acquire knowledge about how members may react in the group.

GENDER AND GROUP WORK

Group experiences provide opportunities for members to explore their personal narratives and challenges within the context of gender and its associated social roles and stereotypes (Lazerson & Zilbach, 1993; Schoenholtz-Read, 1996). Consequently, group leaders work in ways that either support or undermine members as they explore and confront important issues of gender and gender bias. Taking steps to evaluate personal beliefs, feelings, and assumptions regarding gender and gender–based sociopolitical issues (e.g., socioeconomic status, employment opportunities, child rearing, thinking and communication patterns) and consider how those factors may affect the group and group processes is critical to working toward positive group outcomes and experiences for all group members. Group leaders should also familiarize themselves with relevant theory and perspectives. Feminist theory, for example, may provide group leaders with meaningful conceptualizations of the interaction of gender and culture (Lazerson & Zilbach, 1993).

Research and theory regarding the merits of single gender and mixed gender groups is extensive (Bernardez, 1996; Lazerson & Zilbach, 1993; Schoenholtz-Read, 1996). Group leaders must consider the purpose of the group and the needs of members to determine which composition is most appropriate. Homogeneous groups may provide members with a level of security, acceptance, and shared experience while simultaneously limiting the barriers of gender-based oppression, unintentional miscommunication, and other gender-related challenges within the group context. However, mixed gender groups allow members to explore problems and concerns within a cultural context that more closely matches society. Regardless of group composition, group leaders must keep in mind that both women and men are affected by a host of gender-influenced factors, including, but not restricted to, developmental processes, value structures, belief systems, behavioral repertoires, sex-role stereotypes and expectations, power dynamics, and gender-related oppression and marginalization. Racial and ethnic diversity may add dimensions of complexity to all aspects of gender and gender interaction. This may be particularly true for cultures that have extremely differentiated roles and expectations for males and females. Case Study 3.1 explores issues of gender and group work.

CASE STUDY 3.1

Gender

Karla, a European American, is a counselor working in a community counseling center. She is running a group on grief and loss for eight adults who have lost partners or spouses in the last year. Each group member voluntarily sought counseling support, although each had previously received varying levels of encouragement to seek counseling from family and friends. The group is comprised of five women and three men. Two of the women are African American. All other group members are European American.

The group has met for four sessions. Although members report that the group is helpful, Karla is concerned about several issues of early group development, including universality and cohesion. Although all members are beginning to interact in productive ways, Karla cannot help thinking that the group members are not really hearing each other. She realizes that the development of trust and emergence of authentic, meaningful disclosures occur over time, but she wonders what she can do to facilitate the process.

After consulting with her supervisor, Karla realized that her group members' lack of hearing may be related to gender-based factors. In addition to more obvious differences in gender-based communication patterns, Karla and her supervisor considered gender-based roles and expectations regarding responses to grief. Karla challenged herself to consider her own stereotyped views of men's and women's experiences of grief. She wondered, for example, if society expects men who have lost a

Continued

CASE STUDY 3.1 (*Continued*)

loved one to take on different roles than women who have lost a loved one. Karla was also aware of the possible implications of race and ethnicity on the grief and loss process. Careful to avoid inappropriately attributing these issues to the group and its process, Karla decided to encourage the group to explore gender and race in the next session. Karla believed the group could best determine the salience of these issues for itself within and outside the group context.

During the fifth session, Karla posed a series of interpersonal and intrapersonal processing questions to encourage the members to self-determine the salience of gender in their personal and collective experiences of grief and loss. Although the group initially resisted Karla's questions, members slowly began to express a range of emotions regarding their views of society's gender-based expectations. In particular, one of the male group members stated he was angry that people expected him to "get over his wife's death and get back to work." He reported that many of his friends wanted him to "get on with his life, as if grieving had a time limit." A female member shared that she was sure her family and friends saw her as "a weak, helpless widow who could not be left alone." The group agreed that perhaps they had been unintentionally interacting with each other based on gender-based stereotypes and expectations.

Karla and the group members were pleased with the group session. Karla was happy to see the members' willingness to address the here and now of the group by examining the person-to-person interactions. Overall, Karla believed broaching the issues of gender enabled the group members to gain significant insight into their emotions and experiences and to achieve deeper levels of trust.

SEXUAL ORIENTATION AND GROUP WORK

Gays, lesbians, and bisexuals (GLBs) comprise a diverse population with diverse perspectives, needs, and concerns. Due to these varying needs and perspectives, GLBs, like their peers who are not sexual minorities, are well served in a variety of group counseling structures: homogeneous groups, heterogeneous or mixed groups, and special groups (e.g., issue-centered groups that may have particular relevance for GLBs) (Hawkins, 1993). In determining which group setting is most appropriate, the group leader should use, in part, the pre-group selection process during the planning stage to assess the degree to which sexual orientation and the presenting problem overlap, and the current, self-identified reference group of the client. For example, a young woman who is questioning her sexual identity while struggling with her transition to college and life away from home may not be comfortable in a transitions lesbian group run by her college counseling center, while a young woman of a similar demographic who came out in high school and has accepted her sexual identity as lesbian may appreciate and benefit from group counseling support in the described context (see Chojnacki & Gelberg, 1995).

Although many in American society have made some gains in appreciating and accepting the diversity of the GLB population, the GLB community still experiences a good deal of oppression, prejudice, and harassment. Group leaders working with this population must be keenly aware of the extreme levels of oppression experienced by this population and the resulting manifestations, which include substance abuse, family conflicts, academic and career concerns, emotional turmoil, and suicide attempts (Hawkins, 1993; Robinson, 1994; Sears, 1991; Teague, 1992). Furthermore, group leaders must be extraordinarily committed to maintaining confidentiality, establishing trust and an environment that promotes emotional security, examining their personal perspectives and assumptions regarding sexual minorities, and developing awareness of cultural and intrapsychic issues of the GLB population (Hawkins, 1993). Case Study 3.2 further explores many of these issues.

CASE STUDY 3.2
Sexual Orientation

Paul is a counselor at a career center on the campus of a small, private, religious college. He is running a time-limited, career exploration group for four female and two male college students. The work of the group has progressed well during the previous six sessions. With only two more sessions left, the group members are beginning to process significant learning from the group experience that they will be able to transfer to their impending career decisions. Douglas, one of the group members, disclosed that he learned a lot about who he is and the relation of true self and satisfaction in work through the many group experiences. He further shared that, during the group process, he came to accept his identity as a bisexual man and no longer feels the need to hide. Tamara, another group member, is obviously shocked and troubled by Douglas's disclosure and shared that she believes the disclosure had nothing to do with group and was totally "inappropriate and unnecessary." Paul recognized the importance of both disclosures and encouraged the group members to work through the current tension. Using advanced empathy and processing skills, Paul was able to help the group move forward and, in particular, provide Douglas with the supportive and affirming environment that he needed at that particular moment. In coming out, Douglas self-identified as a sexual minority that could unfortunately be subject to oppression, prejudice, and harassment. To safeguard Douglas's well-being and the validity of the process, Paul ended the session with a review of confidentiality and its importance in group work. The members agreed that, out of respect for each other and the work they had done over the past several weeks, confidentiality must be maintained.

DISABILITIES AND GROUP WORK

The interactive nature, high levels of peer support and encouragement, group sense of belonging and cohesion, opportunities for interpersonal and intrapersonal learning, and opportunities to develop and practice new skills may make counseling groups ideal delivery interventions for individuals with physical and mild disabilities, including learning disabilities, emotional disorders, and mild mental retardation (Arman, 2002; Deck, Scarborough, Sferrazza, & Estill, 1999; Livneh, Wilson, & Pullo, 2004). Of course, individuals with disabilities represent a very diverse community and are entitled to appropriate counseling services. This significant population, about 9% of school-age students and perhaps an even higher percentage of adults, may receive the most appropriate counseling service when the counseling is provided in coordination with other required services, which could include educational, medical, and remedial supports (Tarver-Behring & Spagna, 2004). Leaders must also be mindful that members with disabilities who maintain status as a marginalized people due to factors of gender, race, and socioeconomic status may face special counseling concerns. Called double oppression by some researchers and simultaneous oppression by others, minorities with disabilities are often relegated to positions in an invisible and ignored segment of society that is cast well beyond the fringes of the dominant culture (Stuart, 1992).

In serving all populations of individuals with disabilities, counselors must clarify their own feeling and attitudes about counseling members with disabilities, gain knowledge and training to increase competence in this area, and consult and collaborate with other professionals (e.g., supervisors, special educators, physicians, psychiatrists, social workers) and family members to provide the best possible counseling service. Case Study 3.3 illustrates these principles in a school setting.

CASE STUDY 3.3

Disabilities

Ms. Diaz is an elementary school counselor. She is planning to run a third-grade group on resiliency for students referred by classroom teachers and administrators. Through the selection process, Ms. Diaz has decided to include five students. Two of the students, Rochelle and Brian, have been identified as having specific learning disabilities.

Anticipating the needs of the students, Ms. Diaz spent weeks observing all of the group members in their classrooms and in less structured school settings (e.g. hallways, cafeteria), and talking with the students' teachers. Ms. Diaz also met with the school's special education teacher to gain general information about specific learning disabilities and the needs of Rochelle and Brian in particular. The special education teacher consented to give Ms. Diaz feedback on the activities and discussion prompts she planned to use for the group to ensure that the activities would be appropriate for Rochelle and Brian. Finally, in preparation for the group, Ms. Diaz consulted with one of her former college professors so that she could access the most recent literature on resiliency and African American students. Through the pre-group interview with Rochelle, Ms. Diaz began to suspect that Rochelle's issues of double minority status may intersect in ways that it did not for the other students in the group. Overall, Ms. Diaz spent many hours preparing for the third-grade resiliency group. Although the time was hard to find given her busy schedule as an elementary school counselor, Ms. Diaz realized that the time was not only well spent, but also a professional imperative because the new knowledge would come in handy in the future when working with other students with disabilities and multiple oppressions.

SPECIAL ISSUES THAT MIGHT ARISE WHEN LEADING MULTICULTURAL GROUPS

A number of challenging issues may arise when implementing groups with culturally diverse members. These issues are not difficult to overcome, but they require that the group leader understand and acknowledge the influence of culture on the actions and beliefs of the group members. Below are some common issues that may arise and a discussion of how a group leader may overcome them.

When a Group Leader Is Culturally Different from Group Members

As stated previously, it is important for the group leader to recognize that the group members' cultural background can have a significant effect on how members participate in the group. The same is true when the group leader is culturally different from the group members. The culturally different group leader should carefully consider how the leader's cultural background might affect the members' behaviors in the group. The members may stereotype the leader based on preconceived notions of how the members believe persons from a particular culture behave. For instance, White group members may have faulty beliefs about a group leader of Asian descent. They might base their expectations of the group leader on stereotypical notions about "how Asian people act."

While there is a substantial amount of literature on the composition of multicultural groups (Brown & Mistry, 1994; Davis, Galinsky, & Schopler, 1995), particularly the racial composition of groups, there is very little written on the influence of the group leader's background when compared to group members (Marbley, 2004). When a group leader is ethnically or culturally different from the members of the group, the leader should consider how members from different backgrounds might view the leader's cultural and/or ethnic background. It can be helpful for leaders to initiate a discussion of difference and to positively frame the discussion so that members can see the benefits of having diversity in a group. By initiating an open, honest discussion about cultural differences, the group leader is modeling a positive behavior for future group sessions.

When a group leader is culturally different from the members, it is also important for the leader to be aware of personal stereotypes and reactions to the group members. It is possible that the leader's discomfort or biased perceptions can influence the group's dynamics. Marbley (2004) even suggested that leaders of color may want to seek a co-leader who identifies with the culture of the members. She further suggested that leaders seek a co-leader with a high status of racial identity and an acute awareness of and sensitivity to cultural issues both inside and outside group work.

When Group Member Hostility Arises

In culturally diverse groups, members may bring their preferred patterns of behaviors, values, and language to the group (Axelson, 1999). Members may also bring experiences with oppression and negative feelings about themselves, their group identity, and the larger society. When member dissatisfaction or hostility among members occurs, the leader should keep in mind that the problems may be caused by experiences of oppression and marginalization, not by a flaw in the group's process. At the same time, leaders must be aware of the cause for the group member's hostility and label it as such for the members. For instance, consider the example of a group member who is heterosexual and who becomes upset when a group member who is gay complains about being mistreated and discriminated against in

social settings. The member talked about his reaction to what he perceived as the gay member's whining and pouting about "everything." The gay member became frustrated and explained how the other member's reaction is typical of people in general. The group leader then proceeded to reflect the group members' feelings and engaged the remainder of the group in the discussion about gay bias.

When hostility arises, group leaders must not fail to recognize that cultural differences exist or diminish their importance. Facing differences is difficult but it is necessary. Contrary to what many group leaders believe, recognizing and expressing differences does not cause more conflict. Recognizing and accepting differences creates a feeling of safety for members and in turn promotes personal growth among members.

When Advocating for Group Members

Group members from historically oppressed backgrounds or groups may need special assistance in negotiating difficult situations outside the group setting. In working with members from varied cultural backgrounds, the group leader may need to advocate for members. In a support group for sixth-grade Latina girls, for example, the leader may become concerned about the girls' lack of knowledge regarding after-school enrichment activities. The leader not only sends the girls' parents information about the activities, she also encourages her colleagues (fellow professional school counselors and teachers) to distribute after-school information to all of their students. Because of the leader's efforts, the members and their parents were more committed and trustful of the group leader.

Leaders may wish to consider engaging in other advocacy activities on behalf of members. For example, in a parenting group for single mothers, the leader experienced a great deal of absenteeism from members who seemed to enjoy the group. It was discovered that transportation and child care were the reasons for these adults' frequent absences. The leader used this information to advocate for transportation and child care to be provided by a local social service organization. Eventually the YMCA provided a van for transportation and high school students provided child care, thus enabling the single mothers to attend regularly.

BECOMING A MULTICULTURALLY SENSITIVE GROUP LEADER

Although the training and education of group leaders has become more sophisticated, there has still been a lack of attention to culture and diversity issues in group work education (Bemak & Chung, 2004). Future group leaders must be culturally competent and understand how experiences of oppression can affect group process and content, and they must be fully aware of their own cultural values, beliefs, worldviews, biases, prejudices, and tendencies to stereotype.

One approach to integrating cultural information and situations in the group training process is through simulated group counseling models (Brenner, 1999; Romano & Sullivan, 2000). These models consist of group leaders–in–training role-playing different group members in an ongoing group experience of 8 to 12 weeks. From a multicultural perspective, these simulated experiences create an opportunity for students not only to role play a culturally different group member, they also provide students with an opportunity to observe how culture can affect interactions and behaviors among group members.

Another important issue for multicultural sensitivity of group leaders involves the rethinking of traditional group development theories. Most group development theories (e.g., Bion, 1961; Tuckman, 1965) were constructed without the consideration of cultural factors. For this reason, leaders must be prepared to modify traditional group development theories so that they are applicable and sensitive to the differences among cultural groups.

Bemak and Chung (2004), in response to the need for more training of skilled multicultural group leaders, offered the following 17 recommendations:

1. Group work must be considered as an independent therapeutic discipline that stands alone.
2. Understand the concept of culture.
3. Infuse the *Multicultural Counseling Competencies and Standards* into training.
4. Acquire a thorough understanding and self-awareness of your own cultural background.
5. Gain a comprehensive understanding of how your cultural background interrelates with people from other cultural backgrounds.
6. Understand White privilege and its effect on multicultural groups.
7. Acquire a deep and insightful awareness of your cultural biases.
8. Understand the racial identity development of your group members.
9. Understand the importance and relevance of group work in the context of culture.
10. Realize and understand the impact of social justice on multicultural group work.
11. Become comfortable with conflict.
12. Keep in mind differences in perceptions of the group counselor, leader, or person in a position of authority.
13. Emphasize appreciation, respect, acceptance, and tolerance in cultural and racial identity for all cultures.
14. Understand the intersection of personality and culture.
15. Maintain an awareness of how to modify and adapt group theory and technique so that they are compatible with the values, practices, behaviors, and belief systems in a particular culture.
16. Understand how to work with linguistic differences when they are a representation of cultural differences.
17. Model taking risks and discussing tough issues.

Summary

Given the increasing diversity of the U.S. population, the ability to effectively lead groups consisting of culturally diverse members has become a major challenge. In this chapter, oppression and marginalization were used as a framework within which to understand the complex issues that members of diverse cultural groups face. In truth, all groups are multicultural because each member brings a different history with different cultural experiences and expectations, whether visible or invisible. Group leaders can no longer ignore the cultural differences among members and treat everyone the same. To do so is to ignore the richness and benefits of different perspectives in the group membership.

Groups are the ideal setting for members of marginalized and oppressed backgrounds because in groups, feelings can be validated and there is a community support atmosphere (Kottler, 2001). Because many oppressed populations focus on the group rather than the individual as the most significant element of existence, group work is aligned with their cultural practices of cooperation, trust, and relationships. As such, group work provides counseling professionals with an appropriate means of meeting the needs of members from oppressed and marginalized backgrounds.

CHAPTER 4

Distinguishing Group Member Roles

George R. Leddick

PREVIEW

Any discussion of group members should describe what members should both do and not do. This chapter will begin by describing essential tasks for group members (i.e., self-disclosure and feedback) and later identify ways member behavior might prove challenging for leaders. Specific group work techniques include drawing out, giving feedback, I-statements, pairing, paradox, reframing, and self-disclosure.

ESSENTIAL TASKS FOR GROUP MEMBERS

Often, discussions of group member characteristics focus on dealing with problem members. A more pro-developmental perspective involves focusing on what members should be doing in a group. Thus, this chapter will begin with a discussion of two essential member skills, self-disclosure and feedback, and conclude with the more traditional discussion of problematic member roles commonly found within groups.

Self-Disclosure

Among the most important tasks for members is a willingness to take risks to describe themselves (Bednar & Kaul, 1994). Self-disclosure of thoughts, feelings, and behavior are central to participating in the group. In fact, descriptions are valuable substitutes for advice giving. Instead of telling others what to do, members can simply describe how they react to situations. When presented with a variety of reactions, members feel comfortable choosing one that matches their preferences. They have the control of choosing the best match. Understanding how much to disclose and how much to keep private is an early dilemma for most group members. Very young children (grades PreK through 3) frequently display less inhibition and readily share private or personal self or family information. As children get older, ordinarily they become more private, although this is certainly not always the case. Self-disclosure also is often situation-dependent. For example, teenagers often self-disclose more to close friends than close adults.

Describing the Johari Window (Luft, 1984) is one way to help members decide how much they may wish to disclose and how much control they wish to exert to ensure their own privacy.

	Known to Others	**Unknown to Others**
Known to Self	Open, public (e.g., hair color, gender)	Hidden, private (e.g., feelings of inadequacy)
Unknown to Self	Blind (e.g., facial expressions when talking, bad breath)	Unknown, unconscious (e.g., childhood connections to group content)

FIGURE 4.1   The Johari Window.

When one first hears of the Johari Window, it may sound mysterious, but it was simply a device invented by Joe Luft and Harry Ingam to help understand levels of disclosure. The Johari Window (see Figure 4.1) has four "panes," or quadrants. The upper left quadrant symbolizes information you know and others know, too. For example, your name is often public knowledge. The color of the clothes you are wearing is known to anyone who can see you. Such information is not risky to divulge. The lower left quadrant symbolizes information about you known to others but not known to you. Sometimes even your best friend won't mention the bit of lunch still stuck to your teeth or piece of toilet paper stuck to your shoe. The upper right quadrant of the window represents information known to you but not to others. It is private information. Whether you disclose private information sometimes depends on whether it is pertinent to others. If one has an ingrown toenail, this fact might not be shared with other group members. In addition to relevance, another consideration might be whether one trusts the group sufficiently to guard confidentiality. A topic that seems too risky in the beginning of a group might feel easy to disclose later on.

The remaining quadrant of the Johari Window is information that is unknown to you and to others. It represents the unconscious. Group leaders often introduce members to the idea of the Johari Window to provoke a discussion about responsible risk taking and personal boundaries. Discussion of the Johari Window provides structure for consideration of a continuum of degrees of self-disclosure. Leaders often tell members they are allowed to "pass" if they are having difficulty articulating a feeling or they are unwilling to disclose personal, private information. It is hoped members who feel in control of their level of self-disclosure experience less resistance.

Feedback

When members give each other feedback, they are describing the interpersonal interactions they notice and mentioning their reactions. Bednar and Kaul (1994) identified feedback as a characteristic of effective groups. Members must learn to use skill when giving feedback. Otherwise, it is natural for members who receive feedback to be defensive, feel threatened, or tune out. Good feedback is (1) solicited, not imposed; (2) descriptive, not evaluative; (3) specific, not general; and (4) checked for clarity (by restating or reflecting). If feedback is descriptive, it allows the member to have a choice in behavior. If one is labeled a "loudmouth," the member can (1) get defensive and (2) think of this as a character flaw to blame on his ancestors. If instead one tells a member, "You are talking a lot today," the member will notice there is a continuum. Some days the member talks a lot and other days the member says little. Thus, the member can take responsibility for the choice of what to do today.

Feedback should also be timed to happen soon after the event so all members can recall the occurrence and share their observations. When feedback is given by a member on behalf of the entire group, the leader should ask whether this is the impression of just the spokesperson or it is shared by the whole group. Leaders do not allow members to assume they are speaking for the whole group without checking for consensus.

It is typical for members to be tentative about giving and receiving feedback. It is often the case that initial feedback is politely positive and sometimes superficial. In groups with topics and/or membership that make feedback training appropriate, leaders can introduce members to the topic of feedback and allow members to practice developing this skill in a series of dyad activities. For example, in an early session, members might be paired and asked to chat about reasons for joining the group and what they hope will happen (Donigian & Hulse-Killacky, 1999). Each person introduces their partner to the group, and the leader remarks on similarities and common themes. In a subsequent group session, with members paired with different partners, the topic would ordinarily shift to members' fears, concerns, hopes, and expectations for this particular group experience. In a subsequent session, a new pair of members might respond to the question, "When do you feel 'alive' and why is this important to you?" In each exercise, partners introduce each other to the larger group. Topics should be concise, appropriate to the initial stage of group dynamics, and become progressively more involved.

If members feel especially inhibited in groups or find communication in early group stages threatening or frightening, Donigian and Hulse-Killacky (1999) recommended using a simple exercise called Blue Card-Red Card. Each

group member gets several cards of each color (blue and red). Blue represents positive feedback and red represents corrective feedback. At specific points in each session, members are asked to "deal" one card to members soliciting feedback. No verbal explanations are given for the first session, although these might be allowed in later sessions once members feel less threatened. A blue card (i.e., positive feedback) might be given to point out progress toward goals. A red card may signal to a member that she is engaging in a behavior that hinders the group process and/or the task.

If time, ability, or immaturity preclude training in feedback skills, the leader might instead teach members to employ hand signals to indicate approval. When someone makes a statement from the heart or is being genuine, or can identify with the speaker's words, the leader could make a hand signal agreed on by the group. Some groups hold their fingers in the sign language symbol for "I love you." Others make a V and sweep an arm from the heart toward the speaker. If too much verbal feedback is a problem, leaders may wish to use a so-called talking stick, which is traditionally employed by Native Americans in order to take turns speaking. Only the person holding the stick may speak.

One simple way to teach members about feedback is to describe how to make I-statements. I-statements substitute for giving advice. The purpose of an I-statement is to use descriptive feedback to empower members and encourage them to explore their choices. This structure is intended to reduce defensiveness. I-statements describe the speaker's reaction to a situation by completing three sentence stems:

1. When I see/hear _____,
2. I feel _____.
3. I want to _____.

For example, during a classroom guidance lesson on bullying, a second-grade student, Brianna, might say, "Jason, when I see you picking on my friend, Joshua, I feel sad and it makes me not want to play with you anymore." The leader explains the rule that I-statements replace advice giving and cuts off future attempts at giving advice by translating the advice into an I-statement.

In addition to building members' confidence in their disclosure and their feedback through use of progressive dyads and group exercises, the leader can also make process comments about the growth of the whole group in trust levels and cohesion. In this way, leaders encourage individuals' conscious and responsible risk taking when members take risks to confront their issues.

Outstanding leaders manage classrooms and group environments with both discipline and encouragement. To avoid monopolizing attention with problem behavior, leaders know they must "catch them being good." Regardless of the maturity level of a group, leaders should make (age-appropriate) comments when members are "caught" helping, guiding, respecting, being friendly, trusting, cooperating, being forthright, displaying confidence, being realistic, obliging, asking for help, supporting, being sensitive, or explaining what they need.

CONSIDERING MEMBERS' MULTIPLE CULTURES

Group work in a pluralistic country like the United States cannot avoid the dynamics of multiple cultures, and leaders must attend to member differences. DeLucia-Waack (1996a) identified the group work myth of believing group member differences do not affect the process and outcome of groups. Group members are affected by the beliefs, interactions, and experiences that constitute their cultural backgrounds. Cultures influence how and when members interact. DeLucia-Waack and Donigian (2003) gave an example of a time DeLucia-Waack tried to lead a stress management workshop for a group of eight male Italian college students who had recently emigrated to the United States. She discovered these men believed it improper for a woman to be a "teacher" for men. Also, their cultural norms did not permit disclosure of weakness to other males, so there was even less possibility such disclosure would happen in the presence of a woman!

Hulse-Killacky, Killacky, and Donigian (2001) believed that among the first tasks of a group leader is learning as much as possible about each member in the group. The challenge is to look past our own stereotypes and also view each member in the context of the member's own sense of identity development. Doing so contributes to building a group culture in which all members feel more understood.

What if a person identifies with several cultures? Perhaps a group member was the child of a Cuban mother and African American father, and is gay. How do the cultures of this member blend together at this point in time? Salazar (2006) described a systematic way to conceptualize plural identities in a member's life. For each group member, a leader can note the strength of belonging to subcultures and also detect the proportionate stage of identity development. Spending time as a group, appreciating multifaceted identities, and inviting everyone to see beyond polite first impressions are three ways to establish an atmosphere of acceptance and to help members notice both differences and similarities.

CHALLENGES IN WORKING WITH GROUP MEMBERS

All group leaders are anxious at first. What if there is something you can't handle? Are there resistant problem members who wish to make trouble in your next group? Or is the problem actually a nervous and inexperienced leader? Just as Father Flanagan of Boys' Town said, "[T]here is no such thing as a bad boy," and Jay Haley (1987) provocatively reported that client resistance doesn't exist, but counselor misunderstanding does. Members challenging a group leader is a normal and healthy part of the transition stage of group dynamics.

What follows is an attempt to assist leaders in learning what to expect so they can feel grounded and prepared to deal with challenging group members. Problems with members usually fall into two main areas: (1) problems understanding members, and (2) problems with the group process.

Problems Understanding Members

We have all spent time as students and can recognize these student roles: Class Clown, Beauty Queen, Complainer, the Jock, the Critic, Goody-Goody, the Brooding One, the Volunteer-for-everything, the Lover, and the Happy One (McCourt, 2005). Experienced educators juggle such characters while creating a cooperative classroom atmosphere and focusing on the day's topic. Well, group members also adopt roles. These roles occur so frequently they are easily detected by other group members: Monopolizer, Joker, the Silent One, Distracter, Intellectualizer, Attacker, Rescuer, Resister, the Lover, Grouch, Get-the-leader, Crier, and Insensitive. Schein (1969) indicated these roles provide a function for group members. Before members can feel comfortable in the group and attend to others, they may orient themselves by resolving personal emotional issues, which may include:

1. *Identity:* Who am I to be in this group?
2. *Control-power-influence:* Will I be able to control and influence others?
3. *Individual needs and group goals:* Will the group goals include my own needs?
4. *Acceptance and intimacy:* Will I be liked and accepted by the group?

In the process of resolving these issues, group members experience tension, frustration, and anxiety. To cope with these feelings, Schein said three basic coping patterns emerge:

1. *Tough, aggressive responses:* fighting, controlling, and resisting authority.
2. *Tender responses:* helping, supporting, forming alliances, dependency.
3. *Withdrawal or denial responses:* passivity, indifference, overuse of logic and reason.

Group member roles are attempts to become self-oriented and feel in tune as a member of the group. If the roles become distracting, leaders can encourage members to verbally explore the roles they adopted, rather than demanding that members give up their ways of protecting themselves. Leaders can describe the behavior of the member and challenge the member in a caring

and respectful manner to try alternative methods to attain the same goals. Corey and Corey (2006, p. 193) made a number of very helpful suggestions for approaching members in a nondefensive manner:

- Do not dismiss members.
- Express your difficulty with a member without denigrating the character of the person.
- Avoid responding to sarcasm with sarcasm.
- Educate members about how the group works.
- Be honest with members rather than mystifying the process.
- Encourage members to explore their defensiveness rather than demanding that they give up their way of protecting themselves.
- Avoid labeling and instead describe the behavior of the member.
- State observations and hunches in a tentative way, as opposed to being dogmatic.
- Demonstrate sensitivity to a member's culture and avoid stereotyping the individual.
- Avoid using the leadership role to intimidate members.
- Monitor your own countertransference reactions.
- Challenge members in a caring and respectful way to do things that may be painful and difficult.
- Do not retreat from conflict.
- Provide a balance between support and challenge.
- Do not take member reactions in an overly personal way.
- Facilitate a more focused exploration of the problem rather than offering simple solutions.
- Do not meet your own needs at the expense of members' needs.
- Invite members to state how they are personally affected by problematic behaviors of other members while blocking judgments, evaluations, and criticisms.

Typical group member roles are expected and normal, but when textbooks highlight strategies to cope with the most common roles, readers sometimes interpret these roles as deviant behavior. The reason members may select these roles is their frequency and popularity, not out of some desire to express deviancy! Thus, it is most productive for leaders to perceive these transitional roles as a member's attempt to fit in while avoiding the appropriate levels of self-disclosure, feedback, and personal responsibility discussed earlier in this chapter. For example, the monopolizer is a role often spotlighted, perhaps due more to the intimidating effect this member has on a novice leader than to its frequency in groups.

Jacobs, Masson, and Harvill (2006) reported three types of monopolizers. The nervous monopolizer chatters to alleviate anxiety. The rambling monopolizer is self-absorbed and unaware of others' signals. The show-off monopolizer is insecure and craves attention. Jacobs et al. recommended directing two types of responses to a monopolizer, depending on whether it is early or late in the group's evolution. In the beginning of the group, leaders should provide structure and redirect members toward cooperative habits. Once the group begins its transition to the working stage, roles may be gently challenged. Early in the group, the leader wishes to curb nonfacilitative behavior but not be verbally critical. Jacobs et al. suggested three ways to challenge the group's structure when a monopolizer is emerging:

1. The leader uses eye contact and nonverbal body language to convey movement of "air time" to the next member.

2. The leader opens the floor to new speakers by announcing, "I'm going to ask a question and would like to hear from some of you who haven't talked yet."

3. The leader presents the dilemma of the "group hideout excuse." "In order not to hide behind those brave enough to talk first, I'm going to cut everyone off after 15 to 20 minutes. That way we can explore member issues serially, in 3 to 4 segments each week, instead of waiting to move on until the first soul becomes perfect!"

Jacobs et al. (2006) recommended that, during feedback training exercises, the leader pairs with the talker to provide structure for communication and to ensure privacy for the monopolizer's issues. Later in the group (i.e., during the working and termination stages), the monopolizer's defensiveness and anxiety can be gently confronted. Corey and Corey (2006, p. 196) offered these examples:

a. Tanya, you talk often. I notice you typically identify with many of the problems raised. I have difficulty following you. I'm confused about what you are trying to tell us. In one sentence, what do you want me to hear?

b. Tanya, you seem to have a lot to say. I wonder if you are willing to go around the circle and finish this sentence: "What I want you to hear about me is . . ."

(Alternatives) "When people don't listen to me, I feel . . ."

"I want you to listen to me because . . ."

"If I didn't talk . . ."

Alternatively, Gazda, Ginter, and Horne (2008) suggested three responses to a monopolizer: (1) verbally respond to feelings of insecurity, (2) make specific suggestions about appropriate group behavior, and (3) model these first two responses. While more than a dozen group member roles have been identified, several occur more frequently than others. Table 4.1 describes helpful responses to deal with several challenging member types, as suggested by various scholars, including Dye (1968), Gazda et al. (2008), Schein (1969) and Morganett (1990, 1994). The other group member roles not listed in Table 4.1 ordinarily can be addressed by facilitating appropriate member self-disclosure and feedback using the pro-developmental procedures discussed earlier in the chapter. The leader should *never* pathologize the member for adopting one of these challenging group member roles and should always keep in mind that members adopt these roles out of personality needs, avoidance of group goals, or to fit in with the group.

TABLE 4.1   Member Roles and Leader Responses

Problem Roles	Leader Coping Strategies
Aggressor	Avoid negative confrontation. Encourage the member to be specific about his or her personal feelings. Place the member in a role-play situation that involves personal self-disclosure and look for clues to the aggressiveness. Ask for a private conference, share your feelings, and ask for cooperation; point out harmful effects on others; or as a last resort, ask member to leave the group.
Recognition-seeker/ attention-getter	Avoid negative confrontation. Respond to member's feelings of insecurity, if present. Avoid eye contact. Do not respond to off-task comments and/or behavior. Ask for private conference and evaluate member's reasons for the behavior.
Hostile/acting out	Avoid negative confrontation. Respond to possible negative transference phenomena. Keenly observe nonverbal behavior and set limits firmly but not angrily. Ask for private conference and try to resolve member's feelings toward the leader or significant others; refer member if problems cannot be resolved.
Advice-giver	Avoid negative confrontation. Respond to feelings of insecurity. Observe the reaction to the advice on the member who receives it. Encourage self-disclosure on the part of the advice-giver. Place in a role-play situation that limits advice-giver's responses to identifying feelings only. Avoid reinforcing advice-giver's inappropriate advice.

Problems for Group Process

Member behavior is sometimes shared by either a few or most of the group members, not just a single individual. It can be unsettling for the leader who worries the group's process will become nonfacilitative. For example, how should a leader react when the group becomes increasingly silent? It is important to explore the meaning of the silence. Sometimes members are confused about what they are supposed to do next. Other times, they are mulling and pondering what was recently said to gain insight. Sometimes they are embarrassed and withdrawn. Sometimes they are hoping someone else will speak, not knowing how to draw that person out. Gazda et al. (2008) declared that leaders should, in general, respect silence. Leaders verbally recognize when members do contribute, use the skill of drawing out (Jacobs et al., 2006), and emphasize incremental sharing. Leaders can describe the body language they see in the group. They can also use the skill of linking to encourage members to respond to other members.

When two (or more) people in a group whisper and comment only to each other, it is called pairing. Sometimes members try to liven up their experience by making an entertaining running commentary as an aside they believe only they can hear. However, this commentary is distracting to others in the group. Pairing also affects group dynamics by stimulating cliques or subgroups. When members make asides to each other, ask that these be shared with the whole group. If they persist, separate them by changing the whisperers' seating.

New group leaders are sometimes embarrassed when a member in a quiet group announces, "I'm bored!" Instead of becoming flustered or berating yourself for insufficient structure, check to see what the member means by the statement. Leaders need not take personal responsibility for anxiety about transitions between issues. Always poll the group instead of allowing one person to speak for everyone. The leader might also declare the necessity for a new group rule: When bored, members will contribute something new and/or different to the group. Should the group members agree that the new idea has priority, they will pursue it; if they do not, the group will explore other avenues.

Leaders familiar with advanced individual counseling techniques will find these techniques also useful in a group setting. Gladding (1998) mentioned reframing, paradox, and ordeal as potentially useful techniques when working with problematic group member behavior. Reframing is the art of attributing different meaning to a behavior so it will be seen differently. For example, instead of describing an unruly child in a divorce group as incorrigible, the child's behavior could be reframed as sensitive: "Dale is a sensitive group thermostat; each time the tension gets too thick, Dale acts out to direct our attention and protect the group." Alternatively, female African American teens once labeled as rebellious and defiant might be reframed as independent and autonomous: "There's that attitude of independence again—it's important to be able to stand up on your own!" Reframing does not change the situation, but the alternation of meaning invites the possibility of change (Piercy & Sprenkle, 1986).

Paradox is giving permission to group members to do something they are already doing in order to lower their resistance to change. A restraining paradox tells group members, without sarcasm, that they are incapable of doing anything other than what they are now doing. This outcome was inevitable because there was no way to do something differently. A prescribing paradox is reenacting a role play of dysfunctional behavior before the group.

Haley (1987) described an ordeal as helping the members give up behavior that is more troublesome to maintain than it is worth. The ordeal is a constructive or neutral behavior that is prescribed to be performed immediately prior to an undesirable behavior. For example, an ordeal might be to perform aerobic exercise (e.g., 30 minutes on a stationary bike or treadmill) directly prior to the onset of a depression state, if the onset can be predicted. Another example might be a group member who wishes to stop smoking must first donate one dollar per cigarette to a despised organization. The ordeal is never harmful, but it is usually not an activity the member wants to engage in. Will the member give up the behavior to avoid performing the constructive ordeal?

Clarity for Member Behavior

It is not uncommon for new group members to be confused about what they should do during the group. Some leaders favor theoretical counseling orientations (e.g., person-centered, reality therapy) that suggest leader modeling is sufficient to establish member roles in groups. Even when careful explanation is articulated during initial group meetings, members sometimes forget, or they need to have role definitions reinforced. Kottler (2001) provided the following list of member behavior guidelines:

1. Speak only for yourself in the group. Use "I" rather than "we."
2. Blaming, whining, and complaining about people inside or outside the group are discouraged.
3. Racist, sexist, or otherwise disrespectful language will not be tolerated. No name calling.
4. All members take responsibility for making sure they get their own needs met in the group.
5. Nobody will be coerced or pressured into doing something they do not feel ready to do. Each may member "pass."
6. What is said in the group is considered confidential information. Everyone is responsible for maintaining privacy.
7. Time must be distributed equitably among all members.
8. Any member who is late more than three times or misses the group more than three times will be asked to leave.
9. Instead of giving advice, I will tell the story of what I felt and did in a similar situation.
10. My feedback will be descriptive.

Any similar list of guidelines should be brief, parsimonious, and modified so that it is appropriate for the developmental level of the member. The number of items on the list grows shorter when members are younger. One such list for fifth graders during psychoeducational group sessions had three rules:

1. No one is allowed to hurt another's feelings on purpose.

2. No one can interfere with another's right to learn.

3. If the group sees the need for a new rule, we will establish one.

Finally, feedback that members receive on their participation in the group can now be used to draw comparisons to the kind of group member they would like to be. Corey (1981) provided a self-assessment scale that can be used as an in-group activity to provoke independent thought and group feedback about self-perceived and other-perceived group member behaviors. Kottler's guidelines above serve a similar function. If other group members tell a member that his self-perceptions are not accurate, the group can discuss what changes the member can make in order to get where he wants to be. Self-assessment activities can be powerful mechanisms for changing member behaviors.

Summary

Two essential tasks are required of members in a successful group: self-disclosure and feedback. Self-disclosure involves members describing their own reactions and experiences; it emerges as trust and cohesion build from the group process. Exercises such as the Johari Window can help members understand the nature of self-disclosure and determine how much information about themselves they want to disclose. Feedback helps members understand the effects of their behaviors on others, leading to insights and potential behavior changes. Teaching group members to use I-statements can be particularly helpful when giving feedback.

Challenges related to cultural differences and specific group member roles were also addressed. Members frequently use the group experience to resolve personal emotional issues involving identity, control-power-influence, individual needs and group goals, and acceptance and intimacy. Schein proposed that members frequently address these personal issues using tough, aggressive responses; tender responses; or withdrawal and/or denial responses. The literature has identified numerous different difficult member types, including aggressor, monopolizer, attention-getter, hostile/acting out, and advice-giver. Each requires a different leadership approach to deal effectively with the challenging member behaviors. In addition to encouraging member self-disclosure and feedback, commonly used techniques involve drawing out, pairing, reframing, paradox, and ordeals. Members frequently alter challenging behavior patterns when they are helped to gain insight into their behaviors and underlying, often subconscious purposes. This insight is most effectively supplied by other group members engaging in the appropriate use of feedback and self-disclosure.

CHAPTER 5

Leading Groups

Amy Milsom

PREVIEW

The thought of leading a group can feel overwhelming for many counselors-in-training. For students who may just be starting to feel comfortable conducting counseling sessions with one client, thinking about how to attend to and facilitate interaction among many members might seem nearly impossible. Basic knowledge of important group leadership styles, characteristics, and skills for effective group leadership are provided in this chapter. Specific group work techniques include active listening, blocking, clarifying, confrontation, empathy, evaluating skills, initiating skills, instructing skills, linking, modeling, feedback, questioning, and summarizing.

GROUP LEADERS

How do I make sure everyone in the group gets involved? Do I have to lead groups by myself? How can I pay attention to so many people? These questions are common among students in a group work course. As they think about the variety of groups they might eventually lead, counselors-in-training often experience anxiety about meeting the needs of all group members, attending to all members, and in general being effective in group work. By developing an understanding of different leadership styles, characteristics, and skills, counselors-in-training will be better equipped to assess their readiness to lead groups.

Group leaders can use a variety of leadership styles, usually described according to how much structure a leader chooses to impose on a group and how much control a leader exercises over the interactions and communications within a group. Choosing which style is best for a particular group involves assessing the needs of the group members, determining the goals of the group, and identifying personal preferences and tendencies of the leader. Most leaders naturally lean toward one style or another. For example, some leaders have a more difficult time relinquishing control, while others prefer giving a lot of responsibility to group members. At this point, it is essential to understand that various leadership styles can affect the outcomes of the group. By varying the amount of structure and control afforded to the group itself, a group leader can positively or negatively affect group outcomes.

Controlling Group Process

Leadership styles can be understood by visualizing a continuum of low control on the left of a scale to high control on the right. Leaders who provide less control would fall at the left end, while leaders who maintain high levels of control over the group process would fall at the right end of the continuum. The ideal amount of control provided by the group leader depends a lot on the group topic, goals, agenda, or member characteristics (e.g., age, abilities).

HIGH-CONTROL LEADERSHIP Group leaders who provide high levels of control have often been referred to as authoritarian or leader-centered group leaders. High-control leaders might best be described as in control and often take on the role of expert. Their power is evident because they tend to direct conversation, dictate the group's agenda, and provide clear structure. Members are offered little to no opportunity to influence the direction of the group. Group leaders who fall on the high end of the continuum control interaction. Frequently, group members communicate with and through the leader as opposed to other group members. Thus, communication in groups with this type of leader is often limited to interactions between the group leader and individual members. For example, in a task group with a time limit and full agenda, leaders frequently move the group actions and discussions from agenda item to agenda item, gaining quick consensus and decisions, even when some group members believe greater deliberation of the complexities of the decisions is warranted. High-control task group leaders sometimes do not "hear" these concerns in order to stay on schedule and reach closure as quickly as possible. Efficiency is prized. Classroom guidance leaders frequently move into "teacher mode" and impart information that students need to master. Again, because of time constraints in a class schedule, time for discussion may be minimized so that students will receive all of the information needed in the time allotted.

MODERATE-CONTROL LEADERSHIP Group leaders who use moderate amounts of control have been described as democratic, group-centered, or collaborative. These leaders believe that the group process functions best when all members are actively involved and feel their opinions and efforts are valued. This type of group leader communicates to members, either explicitly or implicitly, that responsibility for the group belongs to everyone: leader and members. Leaders who use moderate control provide structure and support, encourage members to share, and maintain flexibility in order to allow group members to provide some direction. For example, leaders of psychoeducational groups often demonstrate moderate control and structure as they impart information necessary to member learning, but they are also quite aware of the need for group members to integrate and process this information via discussion in order to apply it to their everyday lives.

LOW-CONTROL LEADERS Group leaders who provide little to no structure or control might be classified as *laissez-faire,* or leaders in name only. Although leaders displaying low control officially might be considered the leader, these individuals take on almost no responsibilities in the group. This type of leader forces members to assume responsibility if they want to make progress. Leaders of self-help groups or groups in which self-awareness is the primary goal may demonstrate low control. For example, in a counseling group for high school senior honor students worried about transition to college and who are low-assertive students (e.g., shy, inhibited), the leader may take a low-control (nonassertive) approach to "force" students to take more assertive roles and responsibility within the group process. While initially anxiety-producing, the students will realize their own abilities to behave assertively and transfer that ability into social and academic situations when transitioning into the college environment (i.e., demonstrate a success experience).

Member Responsibility

The amount of control provided by the group leader is inversely related to the amount of responsibility placed on members. That is, the more control provided by the group leader, the less members need or are able to take on responsibility for group process and outcomes. Group members must always take responsibility for working on personal goals; they must be willing to spend time and energy during and between group sessions and be open to self-exploration. However, the group leader in essence controls how much opportunity the members have to influence the direction of the group and help each other.

Choosing a Leadership Style

In many ways, group leaders need to be true to themselves and choose a leadership style that fits their personality. Someone who highly values structure and organization might struggle to design and lead a less-structured group. Developing skills and comfort in different leadership styles, however, can help group leaders adapt more easily to the members' needs.

For example, psychoeducational groups would logically require more leader-driven structure and control than would some types of counseling or psychotherapy groups. The instructional or educational component of a psychoeducational group would be challenging to implement effectively if group members were required to take on more responsibility than the leader (Brown, 2004). The assumption could be made that a group leader designs and implements a psychoeducational group because the leader possesses more knowledge of the topic (e.g., anger management skills) than the members. In that sense, the expert role is inherent, and a fairly structured approach is necessary for the leader to ensure that all relevant content is covered. This does not mean that the group could not be run in a fairly democratic manner at certain points in time; group leaders could still engage members by allowing them to guide the discussion (i.e., process) that follows instruction and skill practice (i.e., content). Nevertheless, flexibility to shift back and forth between more and less structure and control both during sessions and throughout the group is important.

Group leaders also must consider the benefits of using different styles during different group stages. Recommendations to provide more structure during the forming/orienting and termination stages of a group suggest that group leaders would benefit from operating from a style more toward the high end of the control continuum during the first few and last few group sessions. As members become more comfortable with each other and enter the working stage, and as they begin to better understand how the group works, they can benefit from less leader structure. As such, knowing when to allow or encourage group members to take on more responsibility can help group leaders facilitate the movement of the group to the termination stage.

Group member characteristics should also be considered when choosing a leadership style. The age and developmental level of group members might indicate a need for more structure. For example, children in the early years of elementary school would benefit from higher levels of leader structure and control because they would not be capable of taking on as much responsibility as adolescents. Additionally, members who have never engaged in group work might need more structure from the leader compared to others who have participated in groups in the past. Knowing what to expect and having previous experience might make a group member more willing or able to take on responsibility earlier in the group.

Finally, a theoretical approach also dictates leadership style to some degree, or perhaps a theoretical approach simply serves as a reflection of group leader preferences. No matter which way you look at it, a direct connection between leadership style and theory appears to exist. Think about which theories lend themselves well to leader structure and control. Theoretical approaches such as cognitive behavioral and solution-focused/brief counseling require group leaders to educate members and lead them through interventions such as skill or thought rehearsal. Naturally greater amounts of structure from the group leader would be required for success with these types of theoretical approaches as opposed to when group leaders use person-centered or existential theoretical approaches.

Group leaders are encouraged to think about their preferences and comfort level in relation to structure and control: How much re-sponsibility do you want group members to have? Which theoretical approaches are you drawn toward and how might they influence the amount of structure and control you afford to members? Group leaders are also encouraged to consider the needs of members: What type of group would best meet the needs of potential members? What special needs might participants possess? All of these questions should be consid-ered when group leaders are in the planning stages so that they can intentionally consider how to incorporate leadership styles that will positively affect the group process.

GROUP LEADER CORE CHARACTERISTICS

Counselor educators often look for evidence of certain personal qualities in potential students during the admissions process, usually focusing on interpersonal skills, insight, or other qualities that would indicate their likelihood for success working with and understanding clients' con-cerns. Qualities that make for an effective coun-selor with individual clients (e.g., genuineness, self-awareness) are also important for group leaders. A few counselor characteristics essential to leading groups include adaptability, belief in the group process, enthusiasm, self-confidence, and a willingness to model positive behavior.

Adaptability

Working with more than one client requires that group leaders be adaptable. Leaders cannot al-ways predict member behavior, and leaders also often have limited control over member behav-ior. Although planning and organization are im-portant, effective group leaders must be able to continuously assess the members' needs. Logically, meeting the needs of multiple mem-bers is challenging and requires the ability to identify and prioritize whose needs are the most important to address in the moment.

Group leaders must keep in mind that some-times not all members are satisfied, and some member concerns might simply reflect normal anxiety or discomfort with the process. Leaders who are adaptable, however, will be flexible enough to change the direction or focus of the group, if necessary, to increase or decrease their control and structure and to solicit member feed-back throughout the process.

Belief in the Group Process

Group leaders should be able to instill hope and explain to members how and why groups might benefit them, and referring to therapeutic factors is one simple way of doing just that. For exam-ple, a group leader might tell members attending a changing families group that they might bene-fit from knowing that other members are also struggling to cope with their new family situa-tions (universality). Similarly, a leader could in-form members attending an anger management group that members who have participated in the group in the past have said that it was help-ful and that it was good to be able to talk about their frustrations.

Enthusiasm

Enthusiasm for group work is closely connected with a leader's belief in the group process. Because the nature of group work prevents all members from being actively engaged at all times (i.e., members cannot all talk at once), the leader must work hard to maintain member involvement and help members realize the importance of en-gaging in the work of other members. This might be particularly challenging when working with children and adolescents who are in a more ego-centric developmental stage. Demonstrating en-thusiasm for the group work that members are doing can help leaders maintain member interest and motivation. However, too much enthusiasm might discourage some group members. The en-thusiasm must be genuine, but leaders should monitor the reactions of group members. Leaders who tend to be very bubbly might frighten or even annoy some group members, so leaders must be prepared to assess what an appropriate level of enthusiasm might be for each group, de-pending on the topic and its members.

Maintaining enthusiasm for group work can be difficult at times, even when a leader truly believes in the work being done. We all have bad days or times when we are distracted or tired. Group leaders must find ways to encourage themselves prior to the group, and planning activities or interventions that members find enjoyable or that engage members will help to keep everyone's energy levels up. Because one negative or withdrawn group member can sometimes influence the whole group process, proactively planning for ways to generate and maintain group member enthusiasm and motivation is critical. To do this, leaders can start with bringing their own enthusiasm to each session. Leader can also play off the energy and enthusiasm that so many members exhibit, and they can proactively try to guarantee high group energy by choosing at least one member who tends to be more extraverted.

Self-Confidence

Group work can be intimidating. Some counselors-in-training who demonstrate confidence and solid basic counseling and attending skills with individual clients may experience difficulty when placed in front of a group. Granted, just because someone can work well with an individual client does not mean she will necessarily work well with a group. Managing many individuals at once can be challenging and does take practice. Nevertheless, basic individual counseling skills serve as a strong foundation for group work. The idea of attending to more than one member can be overwhelming and concerns about giving everyone equal attention might cause anxiety. Just as when working with individual clients, group workers who enter a session believing they can be effective and knowing that they do not have to be perfect will likely experience success.

Bandura (1997) suggested that self-efficacy, a construct closely tied to self-confidence, can be enhanced through mastery experiences (e.g., successful performance of a task), vicarious learning (e.g., modeling), and verbal persuasion (e.g., encouragement). Thus, to increase their self-confidence in relation to leading groups, leaders should consider ways in which they can

experience success, observe others, and receive feedback. For example, setting and achieving realistic, progressive goals for each group session allows leaders to experience success. Those goals might include using any number of the group leadership skills described below. Also, by observing groups and/or participating in a group, counselors-in-training can observe and reflect on effective and ineffective leader behaviors. Finally, by co-leading (discussed at the end of this chapter) with an experienced group leader or providing supervisors with either video- or audiotapes of group sessions, counselors-in-training can receive feedback regarding their skills. Engaging in all or some of these activities can help group leaders improve their confidence.

Willingness to Model

The "do as I say and not as I do" attitude will not work well for group leaders. Counselors who lead groups must maintain awareness of opportunities where they can demonstrate desirable behaviors to group members with the knowledge that group members will, over time, pick up and demonstrate acceptable and desirable behaviors. For example, rather than immediately chastise one member for harshly confronting another member, an effective group leader will acknowledge the concern and model appropriate ways to confront. Leaders who are unwilling or unable to model the behaviors they expect their group members to exhibit will not likely see those behaviors from the members.

Not only must group leaders be willing to model behaviors that members desire to obtain (e.g., social skills), they also should use opportunities to model behaviors that will help members develop trust and cohesion. Modeling in group work can be different from modeling with individuals. By helping members understand how to interact in respectful ways, group leaders can facilitate growth and movement through group stages. Leaders cannot expect members to give honest, caring feedback if the leader cannot do the same with group members. The same also holds true for accepting negative feedback and for exhibiting a number of other interpersonal skills.

SKILLS OF EFFECTIVE GROUP LEADERS

A variety of counseling skills learned when working with individual clients is very applicable to working with groups. The list below is presented in the approximate order each might occur in group work and is not a comprehensive list. However, the list includes skills that may take on new importance in groups. In addition, a few skills that are unique to group work are presented. Some of these skills will be highlighted again as appropriate throughout the remainder of this book because of their applicability to specific stages of various types of group work. Used intentionally and in combination, these skills can help leaders effectively facilitate groups. While it is difficult to trace the origins of many of these skills to specific sources, earlier editions of books by Jacobs, Masson, and Harvill (2006) and Corey (2007) are sometimes noted as the creative originators of some of the skills discussed below.

Initiating

Just as clients who come to individual counseling often need some direction or guidance to feel comfortable or continue making progress, group members can benefit in the same way from leaders' initiating skills. Students, and particularly elementary school students, understandably might need more direction from a group leader or assistance in knowing what is and is not okay to discuss. Counselors who lead groups can provide direction by initiating a topic for discussion in an effort to help members focus their energy in productive ways. Group leaders can also implement activities designed to increase member participation or to move the group to a different level of intensity. Initiating skills will likely be more necessary during the earlier stages of a group, when group members are more anxious and uncertain of what to expect or how to behave. Initiating skills can also be important in later stages either when group members get stuck or during the final stages when members might begin to shut down and resist terminating.

Active Listening

Group leaders use active listening skills (i.e., attending to verbal and nonverbal behavior) to communicate to group members that the leaders are paying attention and to help establish an environment where members feel safe to self-disclose. Effective use of active listening skills might benefit the group in different ways. For example, by giving minimal encouragements (e.g., *uh huh*, head nods), a group leader can encourage a member to continue sharing a new idea for how to solve a problem. Also, by smiling at Miguel, a group member whose nonverbal behavior indicates he might feel anxious, the group leader can help Miguel feel safe and accepted. Groups are most effective when all members are engaged, and through active listening skills, group leaders can help to establish the group as a safe environment.

Clarifying

Group leaders can use clarifying skills to check their own understanding of a member's concern or to help the member identify a main concern. Leaders can also use clarification for the benefit of other group members. For example, after noticing a look of confusion on Dante's face after Jessica described her problem, a leader might use a clarifying statement to make sure Dante understands her problem: "Jessica, I'm getting the sense that a few group members didn't quite understand your concern—did you mean that you didn't initially feel sad about your mom's situation, but now it seems like you can't concentrate?" Also, some members have short attention spans or engage in storytelling; these behaviors can often be developmentally appropriate behaviors. Group leaders must be ready to address these behaviors. For example, Brad tends to give a lot of details and often jumps from one topic to another. To identify his main concerns and help him focus on one thing, the group leader could use a clarifying statement— "So it sounds like the thing you're most concerned about is your problems getting along with your spouse and the trouble you get into at home when you two argue?" Effective use of clarifying skills in a group requires that the leader pay attention to the reactions of other members, noticing when others do not understand what is stated or when they could benefit from clarification. Nonverbal cues can serve as clear indicators of confusion.

Questioning

Group leaders use questioning in the same way they do with individual clients. Questioning can be used to elicit more information from group members. It can also be used to help members focus on an important aspect of their concern or when the leader thinks group members could be more helpful if they knew more background or context about the situation. Note also that leaders can accomplish these objectives using statements as well as questions. For example, after Melissa shares limited information about her miscarriage, the group leader says, "You have talked a lot about your husband's reaction, but please tell us how *you* are feeling about the situation." questioning also can be used to link group members and help them brainstorm ways to cope: "Dean's situation sounds pretty similar to yours, Kim. Did you find any helpful ways to get through it?"

Providing Feedback

Providing feedback is a skill that allows leaders to help members develop greater self-awareness. Members develop insight through feedback provided by the leader and other group members, making it critical that leaders model how to give and receive feedback; encourage members to share feedback with each other; and, most important, facilitate and maintain an environment where feedback can be shared and received respectfully. Feedback might address nonverbal behaviors: "Colby, are you aware that you smile every time you talk about your grandfather?" It could also be used to express honest reactions to behaviors ("I am upset that you are late again, especially since you promised to be on time"), perceptions of group member progress ("It seems like you're really working hard, and you appear a little more comfortable speaking up"), or pointing out patterns ("I noticed that for the past three sessions you have been fairly negative when talking about your mom, and I don't remember hearing that so much from you in the past.")

Empathizing

Empathy is important in any relationship. Leaders can communicate understanding and promote trust through the use of empathic statements. For example, it is not uncommon for members to hesitate sharing information during the early stages of a group. By making a statement such as, "It can be difficult and maybe a bit scary to share things about yourself with people you don't know very well," a leader communicates an understanding of the feelings many members might be experiencing. Through empathic statements, leaders also help members consider how other members might feel, providing them with a greater understanding of others. Trust and cohesion are so critical to the success of a group, and empathy is one group leadership skill that can greatly influence the overall climate and eventual progress of the group members.

Blocking

Blocking is a skill that is unique to group work, and it is used mainly to protect group members. Blocking can be done verbally or nonverbally and can be used to protect a group member from someone else or from him- or herself. For example, members in the early stages of a counseling group might not understand how to confront each other appropriately. When the leader hears Tyler confronting his peer, Tameka, in an attacking manner, the group leader could block Tyler's behavior by verbally stating, "I feel the need to cut you off, Tyler, because while you picked up on the inconsistency in Tameka's story, I'm concerned that you are attacking and criticizing her more than helping her to explore that situation. Tameka, were you aware that you told us something different last week?"

Another example might occur in a psychoeducational group focusing on career development. A group member, Sheri, starts to share information about a loss she experienced as a child. Sensing that the other members are becoming very uncomfortable and determining that the information is not appropriate given the context of the group, the leader would block Sheri from continuing to share that information by refocusing the group members, "Sheri, it sounds like this stirred up some strong memories for you, but let's shift back to how you might narrow down some potential careers." A follow-up meeting with Sheri after the group session would help the leader determine whether or not Sheri could benefit from individual attention to work through the previous loss.

Linking

Linking is a counseling skill that is unique to group work, and its purpose is to help group members connect with one another. Linking involves a leader pointing out similarities among members' experiences, feelings, or concerns. For example, during the forming and orienting stage of a group, members might share basic information about why they are there. As they talk, the leader can make connections among members using statements such as "So it sounds like you and Ben are dealing with some pretty similar stuff."

Linking is a very useful skill in facilitating universality as well as the development of group cohesion. As members become more and more aware of the ways in which they are similar, they develop bonds and support each other. When working with members who often believe that no one else could possibly understand what they are going through, linking becomes a critical skill for leaders. Leaders who can model linking skills often find that group members start to link themselves; one member might say to another, "I had almost the same experience with my brother, but he and I still don't talk about it."

Confronting

Confrontation is used to point out discrepancies in an effort to promote self-awareness. A group leader might confront Gene, pointing out that he just shared a very happy story about his sister, but his face appears to express sadness. A group leader might also note discrepancies in information

shared from session to session. For example, in the past, Terry expressed extreme dissatisfaction with his relationship and even talked about separating from his wife, but this week he said that everything was fine and his problems are resolved. Pointing out this discrepancy might allow a group leader to help Terry honestly explore the situation and his feelings. Has the situation really changed? If so, how did that happen? Are the problems resolved or is Terry just tired of working on it and is now willing to live with the current situation?

Confrontation is important in a group setting because leaders not only want to help members honestly explore their own concerns, they also want to avoid the need to use their blocking skills. For example, if one member, Meena, frequently shares information that is inconsistent, but the leader never confronts her, chances are that other group members will eventually become frustrated and attack her. A leader who confronts Meena's inconsistencies early on can prevent unnecessary attacks and can also model appropriate confrontation skills.

Instructing

Instructing skills can benefit leaders of any type of group. Instructing skills are not restricted to psychoeducational group leaders. For example, a counseling group leader can use instructing skills to explain to members how they can best engage in and benefit from a specific counseling intervention. Or an authoritarian leader working with a task group might use instructing skills to assign various parts of a project to group members, providing specific criteria or guidelines for their work. Not surprisingly, instructing skills are critical for classroom guidance and psychoeducational group leaders (Brown, 2004). These group leaders must be able to present information in an organized manner and tailor the content to match the developmental level of group members. Skills in evaluation, when used in relation to instructing, can help group leaders ensure that members learned or understood the content presented. For counselors who have teaching backgrounds or who possess experience leading classroom guidance, these instructional skills should come easily.

Modeling

As mentioned previously, leaders must be willing to serve as models. Leader modeling may occur naturally because members want to emulate the individual who holds power in the group. Intentional use of modeling, however, can help a group leader establish behavioral norms. In addition to the examples provided above, group leaders can model commitment to the group by arriving on time and being prepared, giving feedback, showing respect for group members, avoiding making judgments, demonstrating professionalism to a co-leader or trainee, or incorporating a variety of other skills and behaviors.

Summarizing

Summarizing is essentially pulling together the important elements of an interaction into a concise statement. Leaders can make summary statements to help ensure that all members take away the same message from another member's work: "So after thinking about it for a long time, you have decided to try speaking up in meetings at work and we can best help you by letting you practice and giving you some feedback." By hearing that type of statement, other group members might have a better idea of how they can be useful. Summarizing is also useful at the end of a session and, in particular, at the end of the group; in these situations, the summary might reflect the overall group process or content rather than focus on one member. This type of summary can be used to help the members reflect on factors such as on how hard they worked, how similar their experiences have been, or how they should prepare for the next session: "So it sounds like everyone is excited to practice their I-messages this week, and all of us should come back next time ready to share how things went."

Evaluating

Evaluating skills are critical to monitoring and affecting group outcomes. In this age of accountability, counselors are often required to demonstrate the effects of their efforts to supervisors, administrators, or others. Evaluating skills can be used to identify issues that might influence group

dynamics and group process, as well as the overall outcomes of the group. Group members who struggle to develop cohesion might not be able to achieve positive outcomes. Leaders can evaluate group dynamics and process throughout the entirety of the group in an effort to identify potential problems and address them early. Evaluating the effectiveness of various interventions and techniques can also help members to determine if or how modifications should be made for future groups. Chapters 10 and 21 contain more information about evaluating groups. Table 5.1 provides a list of leader skills with a self-assessment that leaders can use at the conclusion of a group session.

LEADER FUNCTIONS

Effective leaders must do more than possess desirable leader characteristics and use group counseling skills. They must assume a number of functions to help members get the most out of their experiences. Considering these functions ahead of time enables group leaders to plan activities and interventions that, in turn, will enable them to carry out these functions successfully.

Executive Functioning

Leaders have to engage in a number of administrative tasks to start their groups and to keep them running smoothly. To execute these functions effectively, leaders must possess organizational skills and have access to relevant resources. Leaders need to set aside time to plan the group and attend to logistical issues, including talking with members, teachers, or parents to determine the best time for the group to meet; determining when a group room will be available; and so on. Leaders also need to make photocopies of materials, if relevant, and ensure that group-related materials are available. Groups that are disorganized may not run as smoothly and might result in less positive outcomes for members. Tasks such as advertising the group, recruiting and screening members, and addressing accommodations would fall under this function. Refer to Chapters 6 and 7 for more specifics regarding other types of executive functions.

TABLE 5.1   Self-Assessment of Basic Group Leader Skills

	DND (0)	NI (1)	SK (2)	Comment
Initiating	0	1	2	_____
Active listening	0	1	2	_____
Clarifying	0	1	2	_____
Questioning	0	1	2	_____
Providing feedback . . .	0	1	2	_____
Empathizing	0	1	2	_____
Blocking	0	1	2	_____
Linking	0	1	2	_____
Confronting	0	1	2	_____
Instructing.	0	1	2	_____
Modeling	0	1	2	_____
Summarizing	0	1	2	_____
Evaluating	0	1	2	_____

At the conclusion of a group work session, rate yourself on the following counseling skills; use the following scale: 0 = Did not demonstrate (DND); 1 = Demonstrated, but need improvement (NI); 2 = Demonstrated with skill (SK).

Helping Members Gain Insight and Attribute Meaning

Just as leaders must do more than possess basic skills and characteristics, members must do more than simply engage in activities, self-disclose, or share feelings. They must reflect on or make sense of their experiences if they are to gain the most insight. By using processing skills such as questioning, providing feedback, empathizing, and summarizing, leaders can help members to process their experiences on a deeper level, for example, what it was like to finally say something out loud, how it felt to learn that they are not the only one coping with the loss of their pet, or how they feel about their progress.

While processing skills are associated primarily with counseling and psychotherapy groups, Hulse-Killacky, Kraus, and Schumacher (1999) recommended that task group leaders spend more time processing group dynamics and experiences rather than focusing mainly on content. Task group members who take the time to focus on processing might gain a better understanding of how they contribute to or impede the work of the group. The group as a whole can more clearly assess its effectiveness as well as determine the types of changes that could be implemented in the future to avoid potential problems and identify the components of the group that are working. Furr (2000) also suggested that psychoeducational group sessions include some sort of processing component or activity.

Emotional Stimulation

Group leaders must also consider the ways in which they can help facilitate the safe expression of group members' emotions. Creating a supportive environment and helping members feel safe to share are critical first steps to facilitating emotional stimulation. Group leaders can use skills such as reflecting feelings, empathy, and questioning to elicit emotion. The important point to keep in mind is that the goal here is to provide a safe environment for members to display emotion should they choose, not to convey the expectation that all group members must display intense emotion (e.g., cry) for the group experience to be considered a success.

Johnson and Johnson (2006) identified many benefits associated with group members experiencing emotions, and they emphasized that it does not matter if the emotions are actually expressed. Emotions, whether positive or negative, can lead members to desire change. For example, a group member who feels strongly enough about something will be more motivated to take action (e.g., "I'm really tired of getting into trouble, and I do want my parents to be proud of me, so I want to learn how to stay out of fights at school"). Emotional stimulation can also help members bond and can be cathartic (Yalom & Leszcz, 2005). For example, members who express anxiety during the initial stages of a group may find comfort in knowing they are not alone. Finally, emotional stimulation can provide opportunities for group members to work through a number of issues with support from other members, and it can often lead to insight.

Focus on Here and Now

One of the main benefits of group work is that it allows members to work through concerns and try out new behaviors in a safe and supportive environment, with the hope of carrying over some of the benefits into day-to-day life. By focusing on the here and now (what is happening in the room at that moment), group leaders facilitate open and honest interactions among members and also help to develop increased self-awareness for group members. Leaders can do this by making summary statements that facilitate members' focus on immediate events: "Mary, I've noticed the progress you have made in improving your grades and it seems like you feel really proud of yourself right now."

Promote Interaction

Groups cannot be effective if members don't interact; all of the benefits of the group would be lost. Many therapeutic factors (e.g., cohesion, interpersonal learning) rely on group members interacting with and providing feedback to each other. Group leaders can use many of the skills discussed earlier (e.g., initiating, linking, blocking, modeling) to promote healthy interaction among group members. They can also design and implement activities that require group members to get to know one another. When choosing ice-breakers and other activities to help members interact with and learn more about each other, leaders might consider choosing activities that are related to the focus of the group. For example, for a career exploration group, members could be asked to talk about jobs their relatives hold or careers they would and would not like to have. Similarly, in a counseling group whose purpose is to empower, members could be asked to share information about their heroes or people they admire.

GROUP CO-LEADERS

Counselors might choose to lead groups by themselves, but there are good and not-so-good reasons to consider co-leadership. Just as when determining their leadership style, leaders should consider their personal strengths and weaknesses. When deciding whether to work with a co-leader, leaders must also assess their own ability to work with others as well as the characteristics of the other leader. Nelson-Jones (1992) suggested that effective co-leaders respect each other's skills; work collaboratively; are honest with each other; share in the planning, implementation, and evaluation of the group; and clearly understand and agree upon each other's role in relation to the group. Co-leaders must also determine the most effective style to use.

Group Co-Leadership Styles

Several types of co-leadership have been identified, including alternated, shared, and apprenticed. Each of these types will be reviewed in the sections that follow.

ALTERNATED The alternated style of co-leadership occurs when leaders take turns being in charge of specific sessions or parts of sessions. Some leaders alternate from week to week; others might alternate depending on the topic to be addressed (e.g., the leader with more expertise on the topic might lead) or intervention used (e.g., the leader who has more experience conducting the

---

CASE STUDY 5.1

Jan

Jan works in a community agency serving women and children who are victims of domestic violence. The agency has very little funding to provide services, but they have always conducted counseling groups for the children. A local graduate student, Megan, a potential counseling intern, has approached Jan to inquire if she can help with the groups. She indicated that she has completed a graduate course in group dynamics and has volunteered at community agencies serving minority families and children in the past. Jan currently has more clients than she can fit into a group, and by taking Megan on as a co-leader, she believes she could increase the number of children in the group from 6 to 10 and still meet the needs of the children. The agency has no more funding available to cover the costs of running a second group. What additional issues should Jan consider when weighing the pros and cons of welcoming Megan as a co-leader.

---

intervention might lead). Alternated co-leadership can be useful when two group leaders work together but find they possess very different leadership styles. Rather than struggling to match their styles exactly, alternating leadership can allow the group to benefit from both styles without experiencing awkward co-leader interaction.

SHARED Shared co-leadership occurs when both leaders accept shared responsibility for each group, each session. That is, they do not predetermine who will lead at certain times. Rather, these co-leaders play off each other, interjecting when they can. Sometimes one co-leader assumes more control, but these decisions are made in the moment and occur without discussion between the leaders. Understandably, shared co-leadership is most effective when the two leaders know each other well, respect each other, and have previous experience co-leading together. They must be able to monitor each other to avoid interrupting each other.

APPRENTICED Counselors-in-training frequently participate in an apprenticed style of co-leadership. This style involves an experienced leader working with a less experienced leader. Co-leaders working from an apprenticed style might choose to alternate or share responsibility for the group, but the main emphasis of this style is for the more experienced leader to serve as a model

and to support and provide feedback to the less experienced leader.

Potential Advantages and Possible Problems of Group Co-Leadership

The following is a summary of the potential advantages of and some possible problems in group co-leadership. Co-leadership affords a group the benefits of two individuals who may share different levels of experience, expertise, and skills. A leader might hesitate to implement a particular intervention because he is not very familiar with it. By bringing in a co-leader who has experience with unfamiliar approaches or techniques, the leader allows the group members to benefit from a potentially helpful intervention that they would have missed out on, and the leader benefits by directly observing the implementation of that intervention.

Efforts can be shared when more than one leader is involved. Co-leaders can share in recruitment and screening activities as well as potential follow-up with group members. If one group leader has to miss a session for some reason, the group could still continue in that leader's absence. Having co-leaders also allows for the group size to be increased. Trying to attend to more than eight group members might be challenging for one leader, but with a second leader, the group might realistically be increased to 12 to 14 members. In agencies where funding or space is limited, co-leaders can be used to increase the size of a group and thereby serve more clients.

Group members who are fortunate enough to have co-leaders might benefit from those individuals modeling interactions or other behaviors. Co-leaders can practice skills in advance and come to the group prepared to demonstrate specific interactions or skills (e.g., communication skills) that they are preparing to teach members.

Ongoing evaluation of the group can help to effect positive outcomes. Co-leaders who schedule a regular meeting time after each group session can take that time to reflect on what went well and what did not go well during the session. They can compare perspectives and discuss different factors that each noticed during the group. If one leader is more actively involved, the other could observe and pick up on details possibly not seen by the first leader. When the group does not go smoothly or when the leaders decide to try something new, they can serve as sources of support and feedback for each other.

Finally, using co-leaders allows for a greater likelihood that group members will feel a connection to at least one of the leaders. When possible, co-leaders should consider the type of group and its composition to determine what type of co-leaders might benefit the group. For example, for a heterogeneous group addressing relationship concerns, having male and female co-leaders might help group members feel as if at least one of the co-leaders understand their gender-based perspective. Co-leaders could pair up in many ways to reflect group member diversity in relation to race, age, ability, sexual orientation, religion, and any other characteristic.

Several potential problems might also arise with co-leadership arrangements. Depending on the size of the group, the use of co-leaders might result in the leaders dominating the members. This can also occur when co-leaders both have strong personalities. Participating in a group might be anxiety-provoking for many members, and to enter a group where the leaders clearly dominate might be too overwhelming for some members.

Another possible problem of co-leadership results when the leaders operate from different agendas. As mentioned previously, co-leaders can effectively lead a group even when they possess different leadership styles, if they use an alternated style. Co-leaders who cannot agree on a theoretical approach or who disagree on the direction to take the group will likely create confusion among group members.

Similarly, group co-leaders who fail to share in or agree on an equitable division of responsibilities may struggle to work together effectively. Planning between sessions and follow-up after sessions is important if group leaders want to monitor the effectiveness of the group. Co-leaders who do not take time to prepare together may not co-lead sessions as effectively or as smoothly.

Group co-leaders who do not get along or who feel competitive toward each other might create an environment where group members feel like they have to side with one over the other. Group cohesion cannot easily develop in an environment filled with tension.

Summary

This chapter included a review of various leadership styles, characteristics, and skills that can help leaders successfully implement group work. Leaders must be able to assess their own personal and professional characteristics in order to determine their likelihood of success as group leaders. Understanding which style of leadership they would be most comfortable with helps leaders to determine not only the types of groups they could most likely lead well, but also the ways in which they can become more comfortable leading from various styles. The amount of structure and control offered by the leader affects the amount of responsibility the group members can assume for the group. Theoretical approach, group type, and group member characteristics should also be taken into consideration when determining an appropriate leadership style.

Qualities that make for an effective group leader overlap quite a bit with qualities that help someone become an effective counselor in general. Yet leaders must recognize the unique power that groups have to make a difference in the lives of members. Leaders must consider how their personal characteristics, such as adaptability, willingness to model, and self-confidence, to name a few, can be critical to the overall success of the group. Similarly, general counseling skills can be used by leaders to facilitate group development and member progress toward goals. These skills take on new importance, however, when considering how skills can be used to help group members bond. Without member interaction, the power

of groups is lost. Therefore, leaders are encouraged to use general counseling skills as well as the skills of linking and blocking to facilitate the development of healthy working relationships among members, while at the same time using those skills to facilitate group members' self awareness. Finally, leaders can also use those skills to help members attribute meaning to their experiences.

No one needs to work in isolation, and for counselors-in-training, the use of co-leaders can be a beneficial way to gain confidence and skills in group work. The potential advantages and possible problems associated with co-leadership should be considered in advance of agreeing to co-lead. By observing and working with experienced group leaders, counselors-in-training can obtain feedback about their progress using a variety of leadership styles and skills.

CHAPTER 6

Planning for Group Work

F. Robert Wilson

PREVIEW

Planning is an essential component of successful group work. Key elements of planning, drawn from group work best practices (Best Practices Standard A7.a, Association for Specialists in Group Work [ASGW], 2007) and group work training standards (Association for Specialists in Group Work [ASGW], 2000), are identified and discussed within this chapter. Chapter topics include screening, selecting, and preparing members; selecting methods for deriving meaning and transferring learning; determining needed resources; measuring outcomes; and using closed or open groups.

PLANNING FOR GROUP WORK

An effective group leader carefully plans for the group experience. Contrary to the *laissez-faire*, "go with the flow" leadership style evidenced by some of group work's pioneers, clinical wisdom and research evidence combine to suggest that the key to success is planned flexibility.

Careful planning is required even to launch a program of group-based interventions. Once a group intervention has been launched, a wealth of group process research has revealed that group development follows a relatively orderly developmental progression (Trotzer, 1999). From a starting point of dealing with inclusion and identity issues (which in this book is referred to as the forming and orienting stage), most groups move through a transition stage of dealing with resistance, into a working stage characterized by cohesion and productivity, and finally to a termination stage in which members can be guided to consolidate their gains and conclude their involvement in the group. Prior to the group, successful group leaders immerse themselves in the realities of group process and practice. Leaders must plan groups that not only fit with prospective members' needs but fit comfortably within the culture and climate of the community. In this chapter, the key elements of planning for successful group leadership will be identified and discussed.

The ASGW *Best Practice Guidelines* (2007) has established a list of best practices for planning group work activities that are detailed and specific. Whether a leader is consulting with task or work groups, conducting a psychoeducational or developmental classroom guidance lesson, or providing group counseling or psychotherapy interventions, a solid grounding in these best practices will help him or her achieve greater success in planning group offerings.

A second source of guidance is found in the ASGW *Professional Standards for the Training of Group Workers* (Association for Specialists in Group Work [ASGW], 2000). These training standards outline the knowledge and skills necessary to establish one's scope of practice; assess group members and the social systems in which they live; plan and implement group interventions; become a skillful leader and co-leader of groups; evaluate group outcomes; and observe ethical, diversity-competent best practices while leading groups.

These two ASGW foundational documents identify the key, specific elements of successful planning for group work. These elements include:

- Grounding oneself in the legal and professional regulations governing the practice of group work.
- Clarifying one's own scope of group work competence.
- Establishing the overarching purpose for the group-based intervention.
- Identifying goals and objectives for the intervention.
- Detailing methods to be employed in achieving goals and objectives during the intervention.
- Detailing methods to be used in screening, selecting, and preparing members to be successful in the group.
- Preparing methods for helping students derive meaning from their within-group experiences and transfer within-group learning to real-world circumstances.
- Determining resources needed to launch and sustain the group.
- Determining methods for measuring outcomes during and following the intervention.

The first element was discussed in detail in Chapter 2, but the remaining elements will be discussed in turn throughout the remainder of this chapter.

Clarifying One's Scope of Group Work Competence

It is critical that leaders limit their activities to those permitted under their license or certificate. Leaders must also limit their activities to those for which they have been adequately trained (Best Practices Standard A2, Association for Specialists

in Group Work [ASGW], 2007; Conyne, Wilson, & Ward, 1996; Rapin & Conyne, 1999). Said most simply, "[D]ifferent groups require different leader competencies" (Remley & Herlihy, 2005, p. 203). A counselor who is skillful at working with individual clients or conducting structured psychoeducational interventions in classrooms may be ill-prepared to lead a more loosely structured sexual abuse psychotherapy group or bereavement or anger management counseling groups.

Beyond the basic knowledge and skills described in accreditation standards for counseling programs (Council for the Accreditation of Counseling and Related Educational Programs [CACREP], 2009) and the core group work competencies (Association for Specialists in Group Work [ASGW], 2000), group workers are expected to acquire advanced knowledge and skill in the specific type of groups they intend to lead (i.e., task, psychoeducational, counseling, psychotherapy). Specialized knowledge may be acquired through reading and didactic instruction, but the skills and attitudes necessary for specialized practice are best acquired through training and supervision that features feedback-guided practice while the counselor-in-training is a member and a leader of groups consistent with the specialization being sought (Wilson, 1997).

Counseling theories (e.g., psychodynamic, person-centered, cognitive, behavioral) provide frameworks for organizing the planning for group interventions. These theories have been categorized according to their central goals (gaining insight versus taking action) and core strategies (rational techniques versus affective techniques). Many elementary school students may lack the cognitive development for school counselors to rely on insight-oriented approaches, although more mature adolescents may have the necessary capacity to engage in insight-oriented, meaning-making activities. Instead, counseling with children often focuses more on action-oriented goals and may use role playing or other small-group exercises to generate affective awareness, and use cognitive-behavioral, interpersonal, solution-focused, rational-emotive, or reality-oriented approaches to stimulate knowledge and foster skill acquisition and attitude change. What is critical is the goodness of fit among the leader, members, and broader community environment in which the intervention is to take place.

Self-knowledge and multicultural sensitivity are continuing processes. Best practices in planning (Association for Specialists in Group Work [ASGW], 2007) require that group workers not only "actively assess their knowledge and skills related to the specific group(s) offered," but also "assess their values, beliefs and theoretical orientation and how these impact upon the group, particularly when working with a diverse and multicultural population." Continuing exposure to feedback is necessary for maintaining awareness of one's impact on others. Wilson (1997) suggested that continuing education and participation in professional and peer supervision can facilitate acquisition of new knowledge and skill and increase awareness of the impact the counselor's personal attitudes and values may have on the members served. Continuing education can be obtained through reading professional literature on group work in schools. By attending conferences at which group interventions with children are demonstrated and discussed, counselors may at least have opportunities to learn group facilitation skills via modeling.

Establishing the Overarching Purpose for the Intervention

Skilled group leaders engage in thorough, ecologically grounded needs assessment (Best Practices Standard A3, ASGW, 2007; Rapin & Conyne, 1999). Ecological assessment refers to gathering information about members in their home and community environments, providing the leader with a comprehensive understanding of (1) members' psychological needs, problems, and dynamics; (2) members' primary relationships with family, peers, and others; (3) the economic and sociopolitical environment in which the community is embedded and in which members live; and (4) the broader cultural forces that shape their lives and culture (Addison, 1992). Drawing from suggestions by Rapin and Conyne

(1999), a list of important assessment questions might include the following:

- What needs exist in this school that group counseling might be able to address?
- What resources could be mobilized in order to launch group-based services within this school?
- What group work model or theory fits best with the needs and culture of this school?
- What group-based strategies are culturally appropriate for this school?
- How can we get the school community, administrators, teachers, and students to embrace and use the group interventions designed?

To be successful, leaders must involve the school administrators and teachers in the needs assessment and subsequent design of group-based interventions (Ripley & Goodnough, 2001). Needs assessment will be covered in much more detail in Chapter 21.

Identifying Goals and Objectives for the Intervention

Following a thorough needs assessment, the leader is in a position to develop goals and an intended outcomes framework for the group intervention. Best practices for planning in group work require a leader to set explicit goals that are stated in terms of expected group member benefits (Best Practices Standard A4, ASGW, 2007; Rapin & Conyne, 1999). In addition, the leader may set goals for personal performance or for the climate and process flow the leader intends to establish in the group. For example, the leader of a counseling group may set a goal of using moderate structure and control, and may assess that goal by monitoring the amount of verbal interaction of the leader versus the rest of the group members.

GLOBAL GROUP MEMBER OUTCOME GOALS
Outcome goals are based on member needs and describe what group members are to acquire as a result of participation in the group. What knowledge, skills, or attitudes will group members learn

or develop as a consequence of having participated in the group intervention being planned? For example, the ASCA standards (Campbell & Dahir, 1997) provide clear guidance for goal setting for academic, career, and personal/social development. Under these personal/social standards, for example, professional school counselors are responsible for facilitating student acquisition of self-knowledge, interpersonal skills, decision- and problem-solving skills, and personal safety skills. Goals may be set to increase or improve group members' knowledge (e.g., "learn the goal-setting process,"), skill (e.g., "identify alternative solutions to a problem,"), or attitude (e.g., "develop positive attitudes toward self"). Conversely, goals may be set to decrease or eliminate counterproductive beliefs (e.g., "reduce stereotypic views of cultural differences"), behaviors (e.g., "reduce or eliminate aggressive talk and combative behavior"), and attitudes (e.g., "reduce devaluing of others"). By way of illustration, one could write knowledge, skill, and attitude goals for anger management as follows:

- Group members will identify people and situations that trigger angry feelings and lead to aggressive responses *(knowledge goal)*.
- Group members will demonstrate assertive responses to role-played trigger situations within the group *(skill goal)*.
- Group members will demonstrate increased regard for other people's right to personal safety by choosing to use assertive responses rather than aggressive responses when experiencing conflict with parents, teachers, siblings, and schoolmates *(attitude goal)*.

SPECIFIC INDIVIDUAL OUTCOME GOALS   In addition to goals set prior to the launching of the group, a leader might also design a process for members to identify and commit to personally selected goals. As Trotzer (1999, p. 376) observed, "General group goals are important in organizing a group program, but specific individual goals are necessary to determine outcomes." Individual goal setting should include an explanation about how to set personal goals, what sorts of goals fit within the scope of the planned group, and feedback

about the feasibility of each group member's proposed goals. A common teaching model for goal setting uses the mnemonic "SMART" as a guide for goal setting: effective goals are Specific, Measurable, Attainable, Realistic, and Timely (Nikitina, 2004). A leader might plan to facilitate individual goal setting during a pre-group screening interview, assign goal-setting homework to be completed between a screening interview and the first group session, or conduct structured exercises during one of the early group sessions. An example of an individual member goal might be, "The member will learn two assertive responses to anger-trigger situations."

COUNSELOR PROCESS GOALS   A leader may also set goals for the kind of group process atmosphere necessary for the accomplishment of the member outcome goals set for the group. These leader process goals are typically drawn from the overarching theory of group work to which the leader subscribes, and they typically focus on describing the characteristics of group life necessary to get the group to the working stage. For example, different group member characteristics might require different process goals:

- Group members will contract to refrain from parasuicidal behavior for the duration of the group (e.g., a leader process goal for group members with Borderline Personality Disorder).
- Group members will commit to attend seven out of eight scheduled group sessions (e.g., a leader process goal for students having problems with chronic shyness or absenteeism).
- Group members will take turns speaking and refrain from interrupting others during group discussions (e.g., a leader process goal for a group for students with attention and hyperactivity problems).

Detailing Methods for Achieving Goals and Objectives during the Intervention

With the preparatory self-grounding and goal-setting completed, the leader is ready to plan the specific approach to be used to accomplish goals in the group. Best practices in group planning require that leaders choose the techniques and leadership style that fits with the needs and abilities of the students, the type of group being planned, and the personal abilities and skills of the leader or co-leaders (Best Practices Standard A4, ASGW, 2007; Rapin & Conyne, 1999). Information collected during the comprehensive, ecological needs assessment helps the group leader to select both a group type and group techniques that are a good fit for the members and for their personal environments. Paraphrasing from suggestions made by Cook, Conyne, Savageau, and Tang (2004), ecologically sound interventions could include any or all of the following:

- Explore the inner feelings and conflicts that cause members to have unproductive, unsatisfying interpersonal relationships.
- Use consciousness-raising techniques to heighten member awareness of the neighborhood problems (e.g., bullying, cyberbullying, rumor spreading, cliques and gangs, peer or parental expectations, transition problems), member strengths that could be applied to solving the problems, and commitment to take action.
- Use strategies for meaning making to help bereaved group members regain their ability to function.
- Use rational-emotive exercises to help group members rid themselves of maladaptive habits of perception and thinking.
- Use role-playing and skill-acquisition techniques to practice core interpersonal skills necessary in finding a friend, making a friend, and keeping a friend.
- Use the philosophy and techniques of reality therapy to foster recognition of and respect for other's rights and boundaries.

A leader's choice of group type and intervention techniques rests in part on the prospective members' individual and collective readiness for change. Prochaska and DiClemente's (1982) model for stages of change (i.e., precontemplation, contemplation, determination, and action) and Miller and Rollnick's (2002) motivational

interviewing strategies can be helpful as guides in selecting the type of group approach that fits best for member readiness for change.

People who have not yet realized that they have problems worth addressing (e.g., those at the precontemplation stage) may not be ready for a group where one is expected to commit to making change and to learn new knowledge, develop new skills, or change certain attitudes. To enhance preparedness for change and eventual success, a leader might instead plan a psychoeducational group that focused on consciousness raising, that is, increasing member awareness of the risks or problems associated with their current behavior and lifestyle and helping members evaluate their own mixed feelings about their current approach to life. As members reach the contemplation, determination, and action stages of change, a less structured counseling group may be of more benefit. Members may be ready at this point to focus on articulating reasons for changing and the risks of not changing, developing their sense of change self-efficacy, and increasing their commitment to trying by developing action plans and implementing their planned change. Maintenance of current status and coping with relapse may be supported through both psychoeducational and supportive counseling group interventions; the choice of intervention would be guided by how acute or chronic the member's problems have been and by other events going on in the member's life that may complicate the counselor's attempts to intervene.

Detailing Methods to Be Used in Screening, Selecting, and Preparing Members to Be Successful in the Group

Another important aspect of planning is preparing to admit participants to the group. Candidates for group interventions are typically staff-referred, counselor-identified, or self-referred (Hines & Fields, 2002). Naturally, group leaders seek to include members who need and can profit from the group's activities, but for a group to be successful, leaders must also exclude those who do not need the services provided and those who, because of the acuteness of their problems, cannot participate in the group at a level adequate for success.

SCREENING AND SELECTING   The ACA and ASCA ethical standards (2004) and ASGW best practices (Best Practice Standard A7.a, ASGW, 2007; Rapin & Conyne, 1999) encourage leaders to screen prospective members. Even though dedicating the time required for formal screening may be challenging to accomplish in clinical or school settings, the benefits of screening outweigh the difficulties. Even brief screening activities help initiate the counseling relationship, give prospective group members an opportunity to explore their expectations and concerns about the group, and give the leader a basis for deciding whether the prospective members are appropriate to the type of group being offered (Hines & Fields, 2002). During screening, the leader can find out the following:

- What are the potential member needs? Does the applicant need the sort of intervention or experience offered in the planned group?
- What are the applicant's abilities? Does the applicant have the prerequisite knowledge, skills, and attitudes necessary to succeed at the sort of personal and interpersonal challenges that will be posed during the group?
- What are the applicant's personal and interpersonal limitations? Does the applicant have personal or interpersonal qualities that would make success in the group difficult or impossible or that would seriously interfere with others' success?

A counselor may use a variety of data sources for screening, including individual interviews, group interviews, applicant responses to screening instruments, observations of applicant behavior in formal and informal settings, interviews with or written comments from staff, and historical knowledge gained from personal interaction with the applicants (Hines & Fields, 2002). However, screening is not only about whether the leader deems the applicant to be a good fit with the group; the screening process also helps

the applicant decide if the group is right for him or her.

PREPARING MEMBERS   In addition to screening, ASCA (2004) and ASGW (2007) hold that it is the responsibility of group workers to facilitate a process by which a member (and the member's parents or guardians, if appropriate) can give informed consent to participate in the group (Best Practice Standard A7.b, A7.c). See Chapter 2 in this book for a sample professional informed consent statement. In school-based groups, ASCA ethical standards (2004) indicated professional school counselors should notify parents and guardians when students are involved in group interventions if the counselor deems it appropriate and if such notification is consistent with school board policy or practice. To avoid the frustration of not being able to secure parental or guardian permission for some or even all members chosen to be members of a group, one might seek parental permission for all possible prospective group participants first, with the understanding that not all may be chosen to actually join the planned group (Hines & Fields, 2002). With regard to the members, in addition to verbal descriptions of the purposes of and methods to be used in the group, prospective members should also receive written descriptions that they can keep and review at a later date. Bergin (1993) suggested forming a written contract for prospective group members to sign that lists the purposes of the group and details general guidelines for how the group will be conducted. This makes the group work expectations more concrete for members of all ages and gives members the opportunity to review and recall the group's purpose, goals, and specific operational details (e.g., attendance expectations, confidentiality, responsibility to respect others' opinions and perspectives).

One exceptionally effective, though energy-intensive way to conduct pre-group screening and member preparation is to offer pre-group role-induction training in which members are provided information about the group and its purposes and goals, and training in the sorts of personal and interpersonal process skills that are deemed useful for successful group participation. The first few sessions of the group could be spent in talking about what the group will be about and how to be a constructive group member. Pre-group training has been found useful in a variety of group contexts (DeRoma, Root, & Battle, 2003).

Selecting Methods for Deriving Meaning and Transferring Learning

The main purpose of group work is to experience interactions in the here and now and thus to derive personal meaning from these experiences, then to transfer this learning to life outside the group. The purpose of the following section is to outline this process.

MAKING MEANING FROM THE EXPERIENCE

Group work is much more than a set of techniques. A leader's ability to help members derive meaning from their experience has more impact on promoting growth among group members than does procedural competence (Yalom & Leszcz, 2005). As discussed earlier, a solid theoretical framework for group interventions provides a consistent frame of reference for helping members ascribe meaning to their experience and for planning, assessing, and evaluating the outcomes of a group intervention.

EXPLORING WITHIN-GROUP EXPERIENCE

Skilled leaders engage in within-group processing to help the members make meaning from their experience. In fact, the ASGW standards emphasize the crucial role of processing in helping members integrate their experiential learning and helping leaders obtain the formative feedback needed to guide the unfolding of their group (Best Practice Standard C1, C2, C3; ASGW, 2007). Just as ecological needs assessment focuses on the person, the environment, and their interaction, so within-group processing includes the leader, the members, and the ongoing patterns of group interaction. Certainly, valuable lessons can be learned from spontaneous within-group processing; however, effective group leaders

plan for processing to ensure that it occurs regularly and is conducted skillfully (Rapin & Conyne, 1999). Group leaders may avail themselves of a variety of sources for gathering group process data, including:

- Observations of the members, using carefully crafted processing questions to stimulate within-group disclosure and discussion or brief questionnaires or more formal instruments to collect formative feedback data.
- Systematic observations made by a member who has been designated to serve as a within-group process observer.
- External evaluation of the group activities and interactions made by an outside observer based on live observation or a review of recordings of the group (Trotzer, 1999).

In its most simple form, processing may involve as little as clarifying, "Who said what to whom?" and "What did the receiver hear when the speaker spoke?" Skilled leaders use questions designed to elicit what the members observed (e.g., "What do you see happening in our group? What stands out about other group members' behavior?") and what they experience inside themselves (e.g., "What are you feeling?" "What do you find yourself thinking about?" "What memories or images come to mind?"). Group processing is just as important for task groups, psychoeducational groups, and classroom guidance experiences as it is for counseling and psychotherapy groups.

Modest evaluation tools for helping members examine their experiences in the group include the 3 × 5 card method described by Trotzer (1999), in which the leader simply distributes small index cards and asks members to write down their honest appraisals of the group. Responses may be stimulated by questions such as: "How did you feel during today's group?" "What did you learn that might help you in your day-to-day life?" "What could we do next time to be more helpful to you?" As an alternative, these within-group process evaluation cards may be preprinted with a set of evaluative scales like: boring-interesting; phony-real; honest-dishonest. More sophisticated and standardized group process instruments and evaluation methods will be covered in much greater detail in Chapter 21.

TYING WITHIN-GROUP EXPERIENCE TO LIFE OUTSIDE THE GROUP   Because leaders are responsible for helping members apply their within-group learning to the external world, meaning making may be enhanced by asking members to think through potential real-world applications of within-group experiences. Corey (1995) encouraged members to keep a journal of their experiences during the group and in their daily life outside the group. In his words, "[T]his writing process helps participants focus on relevant trends and on the key things they are discovering about themselves and others through group interaction" (p. 129). Members may also be put in structured role-play situations to practice using skills learned in the group in simulated real-world situations. If the overall group plan includes a follow-up meeting after the group has formally ended, one can plan to ask members to write post-group reaction papers in which they recall significant occurrences during the group and how they have applied their learning to situations that have arisen since the end of the group. They can also be asked to record what they liked and did not like about their group experience to guide future offerings of the group experience.

Determining Resources Needed to Launch and Sustain the Group

In addition to careful planning for the content and process of their groups, leaders must attend to the practical necessities of securing permissions, cooperation, and resources. Group interventions require staffing (e.g., leaders, support personnel), advertising, group meeting space, materials (e.g., audiovisual materials, handouts, evaluation tools), billing services, and record-keeping supplies. Many of these resources require funding.

In any business venture, one must consider both start-up costs and sustainability. Because of a personal commitment to the value of the group, a leader might be willing to personally finance part of the start-up costs of a group (e.g., buying special materials, donating time that could be spent in other activities); however, few counselors can afford to pay for the operational costs of a group out of their personal resources for very long. It is a bitter disappointment to design and launch a group that proves to be successful for its participants and then realize that the group cannot be offered again because no sustaining resources are available. In addition to thinking through the purpose for and methods to be used during a group intervention, group leaders would be well served to develop a business model for each group they intend to offer. In this business model, they should detail both the start-up and sustaining resources needed to implement the group as planned. Leaders should explicitly discuss costs with their administrative leaders, whether the group-in-planning is expected to be a one-shot offering or a continuing group and, in either case, how the group will be resourced.

Getting a specific group offering resourced is one thing, building a culture in which group interventions may thrive is quite another. Ripley and Goodnough (2001) suggest a systematic approach to developing a group-friendly culture in a high school that focused on building collaborative support, institutionalizing group work in the school, and standardizing group rules and procedures to provide a trustworthy product. Ripley and Goodnough launched an ongoing effort to garner and feed faculty support throughout the school year. They institutionalized group work in the school by (1) getting group counseling written into existing policies that regulated excused absences from class,(2) passing a new policy that stipulated that time spent in group counseling would not be counted as an absence from class, (3) passing another new policy barring teachers from denying a student the opportunity to attend group counseling sessions, and (4) getting the start of group sessions incorporated into the policy requiring students to arrive at class on time. Finally, they developed standardized procedures for all groups to ensure that group offerings were consistent, ethically appropriate experiences that had high visibility and credibility among the staff. By creating a group-friendly culture through collaborative engagement with administration and the teaching staff, Ripley and Goodnough were able to provide resources and support for their group work offerings.

Resource issues are multifaceted. To be successful, the planned group must have adequate funding, appropriate staffing, adequate private space, adequate marketing and recruiting, and adequate support from allied or collaborating school units or community organizations and agencies. A special issue in the for-profit sector of group work is the issue of fee setting. For-profit group leaders must observe ethical (American Counseling Association [ACA], 2005) and best practice (Best Practice Standard A5, ASGW, 2007) requirements for setting fees.

Determining Methods for Measuring Outcomes

The final step in implementing program development and evaluation principles as one plans for a group is to create an evaluation plan for assessing the degree to which group member outcome goals and counselor process goals have been met (Best Practice Standard A4; ASGW, 2007). Evaluation of group outcomes must begin during the planning phase.

ASSESSING MEMBER OUTCOMES It is the group leader's responsibility for documenting how members are different as a result of the group interventions. For each group, this evaluation plan should identify how the global group outcome goals and specific individual member outcome goals will be measured. Though group leaders have many evaluation options from which to choose, the evaluation plan should dovetail with the institution's results-reporting system and must also be consistent with policy and practices regarding collecting evaluative data from members and regulatory and reimbursement requirements (Best Practice Standard A4; ASGW, 2007).

ASSESSING LEADER GROUP PROCESS GOALS In addition to evaluating whether students achieved their outcome goals, it is important to evaluate whether the leader's process goals were achieved. To facilitate continual quality improvement, leaders should plan to gather information during and after the group regarding whether the group developed a constructive atmosphere. Many leaders use simple member satisfaction questionnaires at the end of their groups to gather feedback. Typical questions include "What did you like most about this group?" "What didn't you like about this group?" "What did you learn from being in this group?" "What didn't we do that you wished we had?" "Would you recommend a group like this to one of your friends?" "What other kinds of groups should we offer at our school?"

Although member satisfaction surveys can provide useful information for guiding future group offerings, they do not provide the kind of precise information needed to understand the communication patterns within a group. Counselors who want to analyze how their interventions during a group may affect the development of the group atmosphere might use more formal methods. Because the *Interaction Analysis Scale* (Bales, 1950) or the *Hill Interaction Matrix* (Hill, 1966) are observational techniques, these classic procedures work well for studying within-group communication patterns across all developmental levels. With adolescents, the Moos *Group Environment Scale* (Moos, Finney, & Maude-Griffin, 1993) could be used to get more detailed feedback about group climate. These and other scales of their kind, though more time consuming, provide a wealth of data on the personal reactions of, and pattern of interactions among, group members. Group process instruments and evaluation will be covered in much greater detail in Chapter 21.

PLANNING FOR CLOSED GROUPS VERSUS OPEN GROUPS

The standard model for group work ordinarily is the fixed-membership, time-limited and theme-oriented group. Group work literature is filled with examples of such groups: the multiweek anger management or stress management group, the semester-long children of divorcing parents group, the 10-week grief group for individuals with deceased family members, the 20-week smoking cessation group, the 8-week career development group for employees affected by a factory closing. Each of these groups might be designed to be a closed group, a group with fixed membership to be conducted within a predetermined time frame.

However, not all groups fit this model. Sometimes the purpose of the group precludes the establishment of a fixed membership or fixed time boundaries. Open groups, such as groups for supporting bereaved members, members from families with chronic illness, or a 12-step recovery group for chemically addicted individuals may be designed to have no fixed membership. Open groups tend to have no fixed near-term ending date and stay operational across years. Members enter and terminate participation in the group according to their own needs.

Group leaders who are accustomed to fixed-membership groups may find that having members leave and new members join their groups disrupts the cohesion and flow of the group (Capuzzi & Gross, 2002; Corey, 1995). They may also find that the presence of people who are at different developmental levels creates a management problem for them (Corey, 1995; Jacobs, Masson, & Harvill, 2006; Trotzer, 1999). But open groups have a number of advantages as well. With fluctuating membership, new members may infuse the group with new energy and the group is less likely to get stale. The group can repopulate itself when members leave, thus avoiding the risk of not having enough members in the group to remain viable. Old members can acculturate new members, helping them learn the knowledge, skills, and attitudes necessary to be successful in the group.

Groups with no fixed time span also have advantages and disadvantages. With an open-door policy, which allows members to leave at any time, members can "taste" the counseling experience and regulate their "dosage" of counseling according to their need (Hoffman, Gedanken, & Zim, 1993). Members may also feel free to change their goals as they develop more knowledge, skill, and insight into the nature of their problems and

resources. However, a group with no fixed ending point may not sell well. Potential consumers may feel that the personal cost will be too high for them to get involved. Also, feeling unconstrained by time, members may "blue sky" their goals and set wholly unrealistic ones for themselves. Finally, members who experience problems with dependency may develop an attitude that they can stay in the group forever rather than facing the reality that, to be healthy, they must develop a sense of independence and trust themselves to make wise choices about their lives.

A group with fluctuating membership requires a slightly different planning mentality than does a closed group. Even though the best practice guidelines encourage the use of a flexible structure for organizing closed groups, open groups may require even greater structure and even greater flexibility. To manage the shifting membership of the group, the leader may find that a tightly structured format for each session provides stability for the group. At a moment's notice, however, the leader may have to abandon the session's plan in favor of addressing an unanticipated group crisis or need.

Program Development and Evaluation in Open and Closed Groups

Although individual members may have personal goals, it is important for leaders to have a small set of clearly articulated goals for the group as a whole to provide focus for the group and to keep the scope of the group within their personal scope of practice. Leaders can provide structure for the group by developing self-contained units to be used on a rotating basis. Each of these units should be designed as a self-contained unit that does not rely on attendance at previous sessions for a member to be successful. The units should also be designed to accommodate a small, medium, and large group size so the leader can adapt to the number of members who happen to be present on a given day. To accommodate new group members, each session's activities should begin with a reiteration of the purpose of the group and group goals and an acculturation exercise to welcome the new members and help them learn the purpose, rules, and behaviors that promote success in the group. Finally, in order to have data for formative and summative evaluation, leaders of groups with fluctuating membership should prepare or select brief tools for collecting evaluative data after each session of the group.

Although it is good planning to be prepared for slow acceptance of new group members, most students in groups are reasonably accepting of a new member in a group. The first group session with the new member in the group may be a bit more "on the surface" (i.e., returning to an earlier stage of the group process), but often the group will quickly get "back to business." An organized group leader who plans ahead is aware of the shifting level of acceptance of new group members and adjusts expectations of the group accordingly.

Group and Member Preparation in Open and Closed Groups

With open groups, prescreening of members is often quite difficult. Leaders of open groups should plan to conduct screening during the new member's first few group sessions to assess new members for the closeness of fit with the group's ecology and closeness of fit between the group's goals and the member's needs. Critical questions include the following:

- Are the new member's needs and goals compatible with the goals and methods of the group?
- Does the new member have the prerequisite skills necessary to be successful in the group?
- Does the new member have obvious psychological problems that might prove to be an insurmountable impediment to the member's success in the group and that might interfere with the success of other members?

Leaders should be prepared to meet after the group session with new members to conduct a more thorough screening if initial signs suggest a more thorough screening is warranted.

Preparation of members for productive involvement in the group may be facilitated by giving each new member a handout at the beginning of the group that outlines the purpose of the group, its goals, rules, ways the member can gain maximum benefit, and member rights and responsibilities. To increase the stability of membership in an open group, some leaders include a contract for attendance (e.g., for six weeks) with an explicit statement that missing meetings (e.g., two consecutive, unexcused absences) results in dismissal from the group.

VOLUNTARY GROUPS VERSUS MANDATED GROUPS

Most models of counseling assume that group members are present by choice; however, a leader may sometimes be instructed to run a group for members who have been coerced into participating by some authority. Members who have been mandated to attend an anger management group or a sexual perpetrator group may have been offered a choice between punishment (e.g., prison, suspension or expulsion from school) and submitting to treatment (Taxman & Messina, 2002). While leaders prefer members to engage in psychoeducational or counseling groups by choice, some members, though not mandated, may have been pressured by well-meaning spouses, parents, teachers, administrators, employers, or friends to attend. Although these group members may be physically present in a leader's group, psychologically they may be anywhere but present. Prochaska and DiClemente (1982) described these members as being at the "pre-contemplation" or "defensive contemplation" stage of change, not yet considering the possibility that they have a problem or that personal change could reap personal reward. Their most common question is, "Why do I have to be here?"

Counselor ethics (American Counselor Association [ACA], 2005) require that group members give informed consent to treatment. In the case of group members who have been mandated to attend, leaders must inform these members of their rights and responsibilities as group members.

In groups where the members have been referred to the group in lieu of being suspended, expelled, or incarcerated, special care must be taken to inform the member of the consequences for attending but not participating. In all cases, leaders should advise members of limits to confidentiality, for example, required reporting to the officials or, in the case of minor children, parents and guardians, especially in groups where self-disclosure and personal exploration are core elements of the group process.

No one likes to be forced to participate in something they have not chosen for themselves. The coerced group member is likely to be feeling resentful, angry, closed, self-protective, and resistant to engaging in the group process. Members who have been pressured by officials to join an anger management group may feel deep resentment toward anyone they feel is part of the "system." Skilled leaders deal with these issues frankly and openly, with empathy for the feelings that such clients may harbor inside. As Miller and Rollnick (2002) suggested, it is critical to empathize with the member's feelings about being forced to do something he or she does not want to do; recognize the group member's right to self-determination; emphasize that the group member still has choices available and is free to choose not to attend the group and accept the consequences that follow from the choice; state that it is not the leader's job to convince the member to do otherwise; empathize with how awful it feels to have someone try to force the group member to do something he or she does not want to do; invite exploration of alternatives to being in the group; and state a willingness to help the group member with developing options, making choices, or whatever else the group member feels would be most useful.

PROTECTING ONESELF FROM WHAT ONE DOES NOT KNOW

The wisest group leaders are those who know that they do not know all of what will be required for them to be successful. They know that professional growth is a continuous, developmental process that will last throughout their careers. Thus, as part of the planning process, the wisest of group leaders identify sources of professional consultation or supervision to help them see themselves, their group members, and the process of their group as clearly as possible. Leaders strive to maintain professional competence by arranging for continuing education and professional consultation or supervision to:

- Increase group work knowledge and skill competencies (Best Practice Standard A8.a, ASGW, 2007).
- Identify and deal responsibly with ethical concerns that interfere with effective functioning as a group leader (Best Practice Standard A8.b, ASGW, 2007).
- Process personal reactions, problems, or conflicts that threaten to impair their professional judgment or group work performance (Best Practice Standard A8.c, ASGW, 2007).
- Ensure appropriate practice when working with a group that stretches the boundaries of the leader's accustomed scope of practice (Best Practice Standard A8.d, ASGW, 2007).

Summary

Planning is critical to success in group work. Where once group leaders avoided advanced planning for fear it would impede group spontaneity, contemporary leaders know that a well-planned group provides a safe environment in which member goals may be pursued while encouraging and supporting group members' spontaneity and creativity.

Insights into key elements in group planning were provided in this chapter, including examining the importance of grounding oneself in the legal and professional regulations governing the practice of group work and the importance of clarifying one's own scope of group work competence. The chapter addressed the necessity of establishing the overarching purpose for the intervention; identifying goals and objectives for the intervention; detailing methods to be employed in achieving goals and objectives during the intervention; and detailing methods to be used in screening, selecting, and preparing members to be successful in the group. The chapter next described methods for examining group process during group meetings and at the completion of the group intervention, and it underscored the necessity of preparing methods for helping members derive meaning from their within-group experiences and transfer within-group learning to real-world circumstances. It also reviewed methods for measuring outcomes during and following the intervention. Finally, the importance of determining resources needed to launch and sustain the group was emphasized.

To illustrate the importance of planning, the special considerations needed when planning for open groups that may have fluctuating membership or may have no fixed ending date were examined. Finally, this chapter emphasized that the most critical element in planning is recognizing that the wise group leader must constantly engage in ongoing training, collaborative consultation, and personal supervision. Only through systematic participation in activities where one is exposed to new developments in group work theory and practice and in which one exposes oneself to examination and feedback can group leaders learn as much as possible about their work and themselves.

CHAPTER 7

Forming and Orienting Groups

Nathaniel N. Ivers and Debbie W. Newsome

PREVIEW

The purpose of this chapter is to provide an overview of the forming and orienting stage of group work. Provided are descriptions of primary tasks that are accomplished during the forming and orienting stage, discussion of the responsibilities of the group leader during this stage, and a case example that illustrates what might occur during an initial group session. Specific techniques include using enthusiasm, drawing out, holding the focus, shifting focus, cutting off, and journal writing.

GETTING STARTED: FORMING AND ORIENTING

Read case study 7.1. Some questions that Carlos might ask himself include: How safe am I in this group? Can I risk sharing my thoughts and feelings with other group members? Do I belong in this group? Who can I identify with, and from whom do I feel disconnected? Will I be rejected or accepted by other members? Can I really be myself in a roomful of strangers?

The forming and orienting stage of a group can be defined as a time of orientation and exploration. Group members attempt to figure out their place in the group, get acquainted with fellow group members, and explore members' expectations. In this stage, members must endeavor to understand how they are going to achieve their primary goal or reason for joining the group. In addition, during the forming and orienting stage, members attend to ways in which they will

CASE STUDY 7.1

Carlos

Carlos, a 35-year-old male, has decided to attend a counseling group in order to gain greater insight into how he can cope with some of his personal problems. He goes through the screening process of the group, understands the rules and responsibilities of being a group member, and feels prepared for the group. Notwithstanding his excitement and interest in beginning the group, Carlos feels some angst about what to expect from it. He wonders about proper etiquette and holds some skepticism about whether this group experience will truly help him.

relate to each other. Focusing on social relationships within the group helps foster feelings of security, comfort, and satisfaction, thereby creating an environment that will facilitate members' capacity to achieve their primary task.

Consider the case of Allison, a 45-year-old mother of three who is struggling with social anxiety (Case Study 7.2). Her case provides an illustration of the relationship between a group member's primary task and the task of developing social relationships within the group.

Without the security and comfort that came from acquiring acceptance and membership in the group, it would have been very difficult for Allison to work on her social anxiety. In fact, had she not attended to her social relationships in the group, it is likely that she would have succumbed to her anxiety and quit coming to group meetings altogether. Allison's case illustrates the connection between focusing on primary tasks and attending to social relationships within the initial sessions of the group, two key aspects of successful group formation.

Two primary tasks that members attend to during early group formation are identity and inclusion. Finding one's identity in a group involves figuring out who one is in the group in relation to others. It is connected to feeling accepted by and connected to other group members. Inclusion involves a sense of connectedness to the group but also includes determining to what degree one will actively participate in the group and its tasks. Allison took the risk to interact with other group members. She began to identify with the group, increased her comfort in interacting with group members, and thus was able to begin working on her personal goals.

Inherent in the case examples of both Carlos and Allison is the concept of trust. Trust leads to deeper levels of social interaction and self-exploration by giving members confidence to drop superficial interactions. If Allison had not been able to gain trust in her fellow group members as well as the group leaders, she most likely would have hidden her irrational beliefs about group members (e.g., "I make people uncomfortable," "They are judging me and rejecting me"). This, in turn, would have hindered Allison's ability to self-explore and possibly would have thwarted her capacity to overcome her feelings of social anxiety. It is a mistake to suppose that people in the group will openly trust each other at the outset of the first session of a group. Group members must come to

CASE STUDY 7.2

Allison

Allison could feel her anxiety rise as she entered the room for her first group counseling experience. She experienced many feelings, including doubt, anxiety, hope, and fear. As the session began, Allison had a hard time interacting with the group. She was nervous about being rejected and about opening up too much. After a while, through interaction with group members and the group leaders, Allison began to feel more comfortable and accepted, and she no longer felt threatened, rejected, or judged. As a result, she was able to consciously begin working on her primary task (i.e., social anxiety) within the group. She began to feel comfortable enough to test many of her irrational beliefs with the group, beliefs such as: "Everybody's rejecting me and judging me," "I'm annoying everybody," "I make people feel uncomfortable." By expressing these beliefs and allowing the group to process them, Allison was able to begin to recognize the irrationality of her beliefs and therefore begin to change them. Through changing her perceptions of the people in the group, she began to change some of her perceptions of people outside the group (a process known as generalization or transference of learning to the external world), which increased her confidence and security in social situations.

recognize that the group is a safe and accepting environment, a setting that offers more security and approval than the society at large. Group leaders are largely responsible for creating such an environment. One thing a leader can do to foster trust in the group is acknowledge mistrust, thereby encouraging members to discuss factors that impede them from deciding to trust the group. In discussing mistrust ("the elephant in the room"), the leader models openness, risk taking, and congruence. This modeling helps develop the therapeutic atmosphere necessary for members to acquire trust in the group. There are many ways in which a skilled leader can cultivate trust within group members, and these and other responsibilities shall be discussed next.

LEADER RESPONSIBILITIES IN THE FORMING AND ORIENTING STAGE

In the forming and orienting stage, leaders have many functions and responsibilities. Listed below are some of the responsibilities of a group leader in the initial phase of a group; these functions serve as an outline and each will be analyzed individually throughout the remainder of the chapter.

1. Reviewing group goals
2. Helping members establish personal goals
3. Specifying group rules
4. Modeling facilitative group behavior
5. Assisting members in expressing their apprehensions
6. Establishing and maintaining trust
7. Promoting positive interchanges among group members
8. Teaching members basic interpersonal skills such as active listening
9. Instilling hope
10. Resolving possible group problems that manifest in the forming stage

Reviewing Group Goals

During the planning phase and pre-group interviews, group goals are formulated. Goals are outcomes desired by either individual members or by the entire group. Because it is important for members to keep group goals in mind throughout the group process, it is significant that the leaders restate the goals and purpose of the group in the opening session. It is also helpful in the initial session to have group members elaborate on their personal goals for the group.

This process of having group leaders express their goals in the group can be accomplished directly (i.e., asking each member specifically to state her or his goals), as a modified ice-breaker (i.e., an activity that facilitates cohesion among members and the leader), or in another facilitative activity (see Keene & Erford, 2007). An example of an ice-breaker that could be incorporated in the initial session is "Gifts I Bring" (Keene & Erford, 2007). The core of this ice-breaker is to have members make a gift card that lists or describes one positive thing each member brings to this session. The members then pair up and share their gift idea with their partner. Finally, each member of the group takes a turn introducing her or his partner and the gift the partner brings to the group. A group leader can modify this ice-breaker into a goal-setting activity by having each member express one thing each would like to get out of the group that day (i.e., her or his goal for the day), or into a closing activity by positioning it at the end of the group session and having each member announce one gift she or he was given during the group that can be transferred outside the group session (i.e., the goal or need that was met).

Helping Members Establish Personal Goals

Typically during the forming and orienting stage of a group, members have imprecise ideas about what they want to accomplish in their group experience. Therefore, one of the main tasks of a leader during this stage is to facilitate the development of positive, measurable, and specific individual goals. For example, a vague goal clients might have is a desire to get along better with their spouse. The leader may help the member develop the vague goal into one that is more specific through open-ended questions. Some examples of open-ended questions that the leader might use include:

- How would you know when you achieved a good relationship with your spouse?
- What will you do to achieve your goal?
- What keeps you from accomplishing this goal?
- How will you feel when your relationship is better?

By using open-ended questions, the leader helps the member narrow down the member's desires into more succinct, concrete goals.

With respect to making the goal positive, it is important that the group leader help the members avoid negative goals such as, "I will quit fighting with my spouse." Instead, the leader should help members state their goal positively (e.g., "I will improve my relationship with my spouse"). After stating the goal in a positive manner, it is important to help members make the goal measurable (e.g., "I will talk to my spouse at least three times a day about what is going on in my life in order to improve our communication and closeness"). By guiding members in developing positive, specific, and measurable goals, the leader is establishing a group environment that engenders growth and development in individual members and the group as a whole. Phrasing an objective or goal in measureable terms helps everyone involved know when the goal has been reached. Setting measureable goals is essential for any kind of group work, including classroom guidance and task, psychoeducational, counseling, and psychotherapy groups.

Another important aspect of helping members develop individual goals is bringing into the open any hidden agendas that members might have. For instance, members might have goals that run contrary to the purpose of the group. Members might take up as much attention as possible in the group because of an excessive desire to be in control, or they might attempt to be humorous when topics become deep because of their fear of intimacy. It is important that leaders recognize these covert goals and help members work through them in an overt, explicit manner. Covert personal goals often undermine group effectiveness.

Specifying Group Rules

Rules are basic guidelines for how a group operates. During the pre-group planning phase discussed in Chapter 6, leaders formulate the rules by which the group should abide, and during the initial and subsequent sessions, members may make contributions to the rules of the group. Whether in the planning phase or forming and orienting stage, when rules are introduced in the group, a rationale behind the rules should be in place. When rules are made arbitrarily (e.g., group members should wear only dress shoes during group time), the leader creates an atmosphere that may promote rebellion or game playing (Yalom & Leszcz, 2005).

One of the key rules that should be clearly reiterated in the initial session is confidentiality. Confidentiality should have been explained beforehand, during the screening process. Confidentiality is the agreement among all members and leaders that what is said in the group stays in group. Without a guarantee of confidentiality, group members rarely develop trust and cohesion and thus fail to engage in the productive work that leads to accomplishing goals. Therefore, the agreement to keep everything that is said confidential should be addressed in the pre-group process, during the initial session of the group, periodically throughout subsequent sessions as needed, and during the final group session. Just because a group experience has ended does not release members from a promise of confidentiality.

It is imperative that leaders describe confidentiality and insist upon it. Because of the powerful influence confidentiality has in engendering trust, cohesion, and productivity within a group, it may be wise and effective for leaders to take the time to specifically describe problematic situations in which a group member might break confidentiality by accident, or even without knowledge or understanding. A leader may choose to do this anecdotally. For example, the leader may describe a situation in which a group member becomes friends with another group member and they decide that they are going to get together after group. They begin to talk about an issue that they witnessed in group the week before in which a female group member talked about her personal problems with her husband. In talking about someone else's issues outside the group context, even when it is with another member of the group, the two members are breaking confidentiality. In fact, even initiating a conversation with a fellow group member outside the group context about issues brought up in the group would be construed as breaking confidentiality and is potentially harmful to the group process.

Other ways in which group members or leaders may breach confidentiality are by speaking of group members by name to outsiders, even if it is just a first name, and by leaders initiating a conversation with group members in public. In such cases where a leader happens to run into a group member in public, the leader should wait for the group member to initiate any acknowledgment or greeting and avoid talking about the group or any content from the group.

Modeling Facilitative Group Behavior

During the forming and orienting stage, members are often greatly dependent on the leader. Like Carlos (Case Study 7.1), members may wonder to what extent they want to participate, how much the group will even benefit them, and what the appropriate etiquette is for a group. This confusion around group norms can generate feelings of anxiety and apprehension within group members.

On the other hand, leaders who are more experienced with group culture and group norms can play an influential role in soothing members' concerns about how to act. This can be done through modeling appropriate participant behavior. Group leaders can establish and model group norms and set the tone for the group. As the model-setting participant for the group, it is crucial that leaders openly state their own expectations for the group during the initial session, as well as model honesty and spontaneity. It is quite common for leaders, not just the group members, to experience some anxiety surrounding the initial group meeting(s). Thus, in honoring honesty, it may be a relief to members if leaders express their own feelings of nervousness about starting a new group. By expressing one's own feelings of anxiety, the leaders may open up some dialogue among members concerning their own anxiety about beginning a group. This disclosure and dialogue may be very therapeutic and conducive to developing group trust and cohesion. While keeping in mind the importance of honesty and genuineness, it is also important that members understand that leaders truly believe in what they are doing and honestly care about the group process.

Along with honesty and confidence in the group process, it is very important that leaders model respect and positive regard for each member. By expressing cognitive and affective empathy, sensitively attending and responding to what is said, and understanding and replying to subtle messages that are communicated without words to both individual group members and the group as a whole, the leader can model care and positive regard toward members individually and toward the group as a whole.

Assisting Members in Expressing Their Apprehensions

As illustrated in the case study examples of Carlos and Allison, apprehension around membership in a group can inhibit group success. Too much anxiety and too little anxiety can impede group members' performance in the group. On the other hand, a moderate amount of anxiety is appropriate. Case Study 7.3, about Joaquin and Maria, illustrates how too little or too much anxiety can deter member growth.

Because high and low levels of apprehension can impede individual and group progress, it is important that leaders appropriately recognize and address apprehension in the session. For example, in working with Maria and Joaquin, the

CASE STUDY 7.3

Joaquin and Maria

Joaquin and Maria are members of a group. This is the third group that Joaquin has attended in the last two years. He is skeptical about whether it will be helpful because he believes the two previous groups were not. He enters the group with a nonchalant attitude and swagger. He feels very little anxiety and listens halfheartedly as the leader describes confidentiality. When the leader does the rounds, Joaquin describes his thoughts and feelings about the group, but he cannot pinpoint anything poignant about the session or a goal he would like to work toward because he was not paying close attention. Maria, on the other hand, is very nervous. She struggles to pay attention to the group rules and limits. She wonders if she is going to make a mistake. Therefore, when the floor is open for people to talk, she just sits in a silenced panic, counting down the minutes until the group session ends.

leader may use a technique called drawing out, in which the leader purposefully asks more withdrawn or silent members to speak to a particular member of the group or the group as a whole. For example, the leader might say to Maria, "I am interested in knowing your thoughts on this particular topic." This technique could be beneficial in helping Maria get over her anxiety surrounding how to act appropriately in the group.

Another technique used in group sessions is dealing with group member apprehensions at the end of each group session. For example, the leader might interject, "Joaquin, I notice that you seem very withdrawn today. Tell me a little about that." The observation that he is withdrawn and the invitation for him to participate give Joaquin the opportunity to express his skepticism surrounding the group process. Expressing this doubt can be beneficial to Joaquin, but also to the leader and the group as a whole. It is possible that others might also be feeling doubtful about the group's potential effectiveness; therefore, having someone express that concern might allow members to process their skepticism in an open and therapeutic manner, thereby helping the group gain trust and cohesion.

Establishing and Maintaining Trust

The importance of establishing a trusting environment during the forming and orienting stage cannot be overemphasized. There are many ways leaders can facilitate the development of trust in a group. One way is through acknowledging that it is normal to experience mistrust in the beginning stages of a group. This process of acknowledging mistrust, as described earlier in the chapter, is very important in breaking down member defenses and expressing congruence and openness to the group. Other ways in which leaders can establish trust in a group include structuring the group, demonstrating care, and encouraging group members to express their fears.

Groups that are structured are more likely than unstructured groups to engender trust earlier in the group process. The more unstructured the group, the greater the ambiguity and anxiety members feel about how they should behave. Structure is often accomplished during the pregroup preparation and screening of the planning phase, as well as during the initial group session. Leaders who have chosen group members wisely and who have a clear purpose for the group are more likely to nurture trust within the group. Setting ground rules, explaining group procedures, and expressing the importance of confidentiality are also important in creating a group structure where trust can be cultivated among members.

While describing the importance of confidentiality, as well as the rights and responsibilities of group members, it is important that leaders communicate feelings of caring toward each member individually. This can be accomplished by also emphasizing the need for respecting all members of the group. By seriously dedicating time to the issues of confidentiality, members' rights and responsibilities, and the need for respecting others, the leader elicits a serious attitude toward the group.

As members begin to feel invested in the group, they will feel more motivated to "test the waters" of the group through self-disclosure. Generally speaking, during the initial sessions, testing the group waters comes in the form of disclosing safe information (e.g., talking about past situations, conversing about other people). As leaders demonstrate care toward each individual, members will find it easier to explore more important issues and self-disclose personal information, thoughts, and feelings.

Another important technique that helps members feel trust in the group is encouraging group members to express their own fears. For example, if Maria is fearful about speaking up, and she hears Bill, another member of her group, self-disclose his fears and anxieties about participating in the group, she may feel more empowered to describe her own fear and anxiety.

After trust has been established, it is important for the leader to help the group maintain trust. Trust can be lost when members give unwanted advice, often in an attempt to be helpful, or express negative feelings about other members, the leader, or the group process in general. With respect to giving advice, it is important that leaders stop this member's behavior before it stifles open communication and trust.

Leaders may choose many different ways to address advice giving among group members. One such method is both preventive and didactic, and it calls for the leader to present an anecdote that likens a particular problem to a quick and apparently easy solution. For example, a group leader might relate this story:

A parent notices that her child is sitting on the bench during baseball games (the problem). She tells him that he needs to practice at least an hour every day so that he will get better (quick solution). The boy does not heed her advice and continues sitting on the bench.

After relating the anecdote, the leader may ask the group some questions, for example: What other reasons might there be for the boy to sit on the bench? How can the mother better improve her communication with her son? How might advice giving impede open communication and trust?

In this technique, the leaders correlated advice giving in groups to an everyday problem. The leader offered a simple solution (i.e., practice an hour each day), and demonstrated how this solution did not bring results. By having members hear the anecdote and answer questions related to advice giving, group leaders facilitate group members' understanding of some of the potential pitfalls of advice giving. By facilitating understanding, group leaders may be able to lessen the amount of advice giving among members.

Promoting Positive Interchanges among Group Members

Promoting positive interchanges among group members is one of the key responsibilities of a leader during the forming and orienting stage of a group. In fact, if positive interchanges are not appropriately developed, members may discontinue coming to group altogether. Conversely, as already touched upon earlier in the chapter, when group members attend to social relationships and receive positive feedback, they are more able to focus on their reason for joining a group; hence, they become more motivated to continue attending the group. Consequently, it is very important that leaders be active in facilitating the establishment of positive interactions among members. Although promoting a positive interchange among members is discussed in the context of the forming and orienting stage, techniques and interventions described here may also be used during all stages of the group process to facilitate healthy interchange among

TABLE 7.1 Examples of Positive Interchange Techniques

Positive Interchange Techniques	Examples
Using enthusiasm	Leader: "I feel optimistic and excited about what the group has accomplished today, especially in regard to your willingness to open up and express your feelings and insights."
Drawing out	Leader: "Tim, I wonder what your feelings might be concerning this topic."
Holding the focus on interesting topics	Leader: "Now, before we move forward, I would like to return to this feeling of mistrust that a few of you have shared concerning the group process."
Shifting focus	Leader: "I, too, was interested in how the basketball game turned out last night; but rather than focusing on why the team lost, I would like to understand a little bit more about how you felt when your sister turned the TV channel in the middle of the game."
Cutting off hostile interactions	Leader to Marsha (group member): "Instead of stating what Bill (group member) is doing wrong, tell us what you are feeling, and what you think is making you feel that way."
	Marsha: "I feel frustrated and disrespected when I do not have enough time to adequately express myself."

members. A few ways in which group leaders can establish a positive tone and interchanges are included in Table 7.1.

Other ways of producing positive interchange include interactive journal writing and performing ice-breaker activities. Interactive journal writing is a process of having members write journal entries about their thoughts, impressions, feelings, and behaviors in a group, and then having them exchange these entries with other members of the group as well as leaders. Exchanges occur in all directions: member to member, member to leader, and leader to member (Gladding, 2008; Parr, Haberstroh, & Kottler, 2000). Some advantages of effectively engaging the members in interactive journal writing include greater group cohesion, improved trust in individual members and the group as a whole, increased hope, enhanced self-understanding, and stronger social relationships.

Teaching Basic Interpersonal Skills

Several techniques introduced in Chapter 5 are particularly applicable to the forming and orienting stage. Interpersonal skills refer to a broad range of aptitudes that allow a person to interact effectively with others. Some specific skills included in the umbrella of interpersonal skills include active listening, empathy, genuineness, and respect. Of course, it is essential that group leaders possess a high level of interpersonal skills in order for the group to function; nevertheless, it is also very important that group members possess, increase, or acquire interpersonal skills. Even if the group leader possesses exceptional interpersonal skills, the group may have difficulty coming together and ultimately may struggle to grow and progress if members are lacking in these skills. Therefore, it is important that the group leader teach group members basic interpersonal skills. The forming and orienting stage is a good time to do so.

One of the essential interpersonal skills necessary in group counseling is active listening. As discussed in Chapter 5, active listening is the process of actively attending and listening to people's verbal and nonverbal expressions. Engaging in active listening is essential not only for group leaders, it is also very important for group members. One key way in which a leader can facilitate active listening in group members is by appropriately listening and attending to each group member. When members recognize that they are being heard, and their thoughts, feelings, and behaviors are being attended to, they are more likely to sharpen their own active listening skills as they attend to others in the group.

Another important interpersonal skill for members to increase is empathy, which is the ability to "walk in another's shoes," or the capacity to understand and be sensitive to the feelings and situations of others. The development of empathy among group leaders and members is very important to the group process. Empathic understanding motivates leaders and members to open up and share important feelings and thoughts. Thus, it is important for group leaders not only to develop their own ability to empathize, but also to help members increase their capacity to demonstrate empathy. When group leaders are able to model empathy for group members, like they model active listening, members are more likely to gain increased ability to engage in empathic communication with fellow group members.

Some members, and even some group leaders, may feel that they are unable to express empathy because they may not have had the life experiences of other group members. For example, a member who comes from a wealthy family may have a difficult time empathizing with a fellow group member who describes the stress and anxiety she or he feels around the possibility of her or his family being evicted from their apartment for not paying the rent. As group leaders, it is important to model, teach, and convey that it is not always essential that members experience others' situations to truly express empathy. For example, in the above example, although the group member from a wealthy family has not experienced all of the hardships of poverty, she or he has no doubt experienced feelings of stress, fear, and anxiety, even if those feelings have come in different contexts. Therefore, she or he may still be able to demonstrate empathy by being sensitive to and attending to the feelings that her or his fellow group member expresses. The member

from a wealthy family might respond: "I felt an uncomfortable knot in my stomach when you described your fear and anxiety about being evicted. It seems really scary." By expressing her or his feelings, she or he demonstrates an understanding and sensitivity to her or his fellow group member's difficult experience, thereby facilitating further communication. Another response that might be less therapeutic and could even close down communication might be: "That's awful, but I'm sure your family will come up with the money." In this response, the group member from a wealthy family may be attempting to demonstrate empathy, but she or he does not understand her or his fellow group member's position. The group member most assuredly is not at a point where she or he can be reassured. Therefore, hearing something opposite of what she or he is experiencing and feeling may make the member feel unheard and not understood, which could close the door to further group cohesion and self-disclosure. Hence, it is important that empathic communication be taught and developed by both group leaders and members.

Another interpersonal skill that facilitates group cohesion and growth is genuineness, that is, a congruency between what an individual says and does, and what is truly felt inside (Raskin & Rogers, 1989). For example, it is normal for leaders to feel some anxiety before the initial meeting of a group. By self-disclosing their own fears and anxiety about beginning a group, leaders model genuineness, thus making it more likely that group members will learn genuineness and how to display it appropriately within the group and in real-life situations.

Conversely, if members feel some anxiety about beginning a group yet state that there is no reason to feel anxious in a group, they may be setting a precedent that it is not necessarily all right to be genuine in the group. Hence, some trust and honesty may be lost. In order for group members to develop genuineness within the group context, it is important that group leaders model their own congruency among what they feel, think, and do.

Respect is another important interpersonal skill that helps group members grow and progress. When respect is not developed within a group, members may struggle to participate and may feel a sense of insecurity within the group. It is important that leaders help group members develop feelings of respect for each other. Along with modeling respect (e.g., demonstrating positive regard for all group members), it is important that group leaders curtail situations in which disrespect is exhibited between group members. For example, if one member is interrupting another group member or speaking or behaving in a derogatory manner, it may be important for the leader to intervene (Ferencik, 1992; Posthuma, 2002). It might also be important that group leaders intervene to make sure that members are included in group discussion. This may be accomplished by using the technique of drawing out group members.

Instilling and Maintaining Hope

Instilling and maintaining hope are essential to the success of a group. In fact, faith in the group's effectiveness is not only therapeutic in keeping members in the group, it is also therapeutic in itself (Frank & Frank, 1991; Kaul & Bednar, 1994; Yalom & Leszcz, 2005). Yalom & Leszcz (2005) compared the therapeutic power of instilling hope to a placebo effect that patients may experience in scientific experiments. An example of the placebo effect would be members of an experimental control group taking sugar pills rather than an antidepressant medication. Because the control-group participants believe they are receiving the actual antidepressant medication, they feel hopeful that their depression will get better. As a result, the depression subsides. On the same note, if leaders can instill and maintain hope in group members during pregroup sessions, as well as during the initial sessions of a group, they can facilitate growth and progress within individual members and in the group as a whole.

One way hope may be instilled in group members during the first few sessions of a group is through recounting success stories. For example, a leader with some prior experience working with groups might describe instances in

which the leader was able to see the progress that a member made while participating in the group. The leader may describe some of the fear and doubt this particular member had during the forming and orienting stage of the group, the strides that the member made in accomplishing the primary task, and how the group facilitated the member's growth and progress. If the group is open-ended, the leader may be able to rely on veteran group members to describe either their own positive experiences through membership in a group or the success that they have seen in fellow group members. For example, consider Richard's situation in Case Study 7.4.

In essence, Danny's empathy for Richard and his description of the growth that he had experienced in the group helped instill hope in Richard that, in turn, engendered a motivation to actively participate in the group. On a similar note, if a leader is beginning the first group session and the group is a closed group, the leader may be able to relate a positive, growth experience from previous counseling groups.

In addition to relating success stories, it is also vitally important that group leaders believe in themselves and in the efficacy of the group in order to instill hope in group members (Frank & Frank, 1991; Yalom & Leszcz, 2005). When group leaders truly believe that they can help every motivated member of their group to progress and are able to succinctly express this belief to each member, they begin to help members obtain hope and confidence in themselves and in the group.

CASE ILLUSTRATION OF AN INITIAL GROUP SESSION

The following case demonstrates an initial session with a group. Michael and Samantha, two experienced leaders, have decided to form a counseling group. They collaborated on the purpose for the group, advertised the group to receive referrals, interviewed potential group members, selected group members, engaged in pre-group interviews with each member, and set a time for the first group meeting. Now, the day and hour are finally at hand, and it is time for the group to begin.

CASE STUDY 7.4

Richard

Richard has decided to enter a group, but he is very nervous about it. He wonders whether he will feel comfortable enough to participate and even whether the group will benefit from him participating. On his first day, he is really nervous because the majority of the people have already been coming to the open group for a while. Danny, a member who has been attending the group for four months, recognizes Richard's anxiety and recounts how he felt during his first few meetings. Danny describes how he was nervous and scared and that he was not sure he would come back. But once he started participating, Danny started to become more confident. Danny was able to improve upon many of his problems and achieve some of his personal goals. Hearing Danny's experience with the group helps Richard understand that he is not alone in his fear. If Danny can improve upon some of his life struggles and accomplish his goals, then maybe Richard could, too. Consequently, Richard dedicates himself more fully to attending and participating in the group.

Michael and Samantha greeted members as they entered the group room before the first session. In doing so, they feel that they have been able to build rapport more quickly with some members and decrease some of the anxiety inherent in first sessions. After everybody is seated, Michael introduces himself and then turns to Samantha to introduce herself, even though the group members already knew who the counselors were. After introductory remarks about themselves and about the group process and purpose, Samantha and Michael reiterate group rules, specifically focusing on confidentiality.

Samantha describes the importance of respect for each group member, including showing up on time and keeping confidentiality. While illustrating confidentiality, Samantha is careful to specify some simple ways in which confidentiality might be breached by group members. She decides to relate an incident that she encountered in a past group that she led.

"Two male group members, Richard and Ted—I changed their names because of confidentiality—decided to go out to eat one evening after group, and discussed what happened in the group meeting that day. Ted recounted

a problem that Melissa, also a made-up name of a fellow group member, presented. 'I really think that she needs to get out and do something, and then she won't feel depressed or uptight all the time,' said Ted. Richard responded, 'Yeah, I bet she would enjoy hanging out with us. We should invite her next time.' During the next group session, Ted and Richard presented their solution to Melissa. Melissa, rather than thinking that they were being helpful, felt that they had been talking behind her back. Consequently, she lost her trust in the group and wanted to quit. You see, it is important that what is talked about in group, stays in the group. Otherwise, confidentiality may be breached, trust may be lost, and potential group and individual growth may be undermined."

After discussing group rules, Michael and Samantha engage the group in an ice-breaker. Michael explains that, in this ice-breaker, members should describe themselves in the third person, as though they were an outside observer, or how each would like others in the group to see them, while still being factual and accurate. In addition to describing themselves, Michael gives the group instructions to describe their reasons for joining the group. Following are three examples of information shared by group members in the ice-breaker.

> ***Clarence (group member):***   Clarence is a very caring and sensitive person. Also, he is very good with math and science. Clarence is from a big family. He has five brothers and three sisters. All of them are going to college to become or already are doctors, lawyers, or engineers. Clarence, on the other hand, wants to be a high school science teacher. I believe that his reason for joining the group is to learn new ways of relating to others and his family. You see, during family get-togethers Clarence feels like he is the odd guy out, being the youngest and not motivated to be some brainiac.

> ***Mandy (group member):***   Mandy is a, uh, a nice person. She is fun to talk to. She likes reading, and has a really nice boyfriend. Some think that she shouldn't be dating him so seriously, but she seems to be happy. I am not 100% sure why she joined the group, but I do know that she has been struggling in her career, and she has had a falling-out with some of her friends. Maybe she is just curious about the group and wants to learn ways to better cope with everyday stress.

> ***Marshall (group member):***   Marshall is 25 years old. He has an older brother and an older sister. He likes to play basketball. He is in this group because he gets a little upset sometimes on the court, and maybe a little bit at other times as well, and he maybe reacts, you know, without thinking. He wants to control himself before he does something he might regret, if you know what I mean.

After giving each member of the group an opportunity to describe themselves in this manner, Michael begins discussing some of the insecurity and apprehension that he is feeling in this first session. He describes some of the fear and mistrust that he felt before the group session began, and how some of that anxiety persists. After opening the discussion by talking about anxiety, Michael makes it possible for other members to express some of their apprehensions and preoccupations surrounding group membership and etiquette.

ELIZABETH: I am so glad that you said that about feeling nervous. I thought that everybody sounded so together and so comfortable when they described themselves. I thought that I must be the only person in here feeling insecure. I didn't want people to think that I didn't belong in this group, but instead in some group for crazy people. I mean, for a second there, I thought it was a group prerequisite to have yourself completely together.

FELISHA: Oh, I feel nervous as well, and I'm sure I don't have all my stuff together. I don't know about you guys, but this is my first time ever being in one of these group things. I just don't want to start talking about my problems and have people thinking that I'm hogging all the time or something. I just want to make sure that I'm not wasting everybody's time with my own problems.

MARCUS: I can understand that. It would be hard for me to express all my problems knowing that other people might have more important things to get off their chests.

SAMANTHA: So part of what I am hearing is a fear or anxiety about wasting other people's time with your problems.

CLARENCE: Yeah, I think that's accurate. I'm not even sure that my issues are even appropriate for this group.

MICHAEL: Well, Clarence, let's analyze that a little. You mentioned that one of your reasons for joining the group was to relate better with others, especially family members. In fact, as you were describing yourself as the "odd man out" in your family, I noticed you looked away from everybody. Tell me a little about that.

CLARENCE: Well, as I mentioned, my dad is a rocket scientist working for NASA, two of my older brothers are studying to become physicians, two of my sisters are lawyers, my oldest sister is an ophthalmologist, and my two other brothers are chemical engineers. I, on the other hand, just want to be a science teacher at a high school. I feel that I am being looked down upon when I tell them my career goal, like they think that their jobs are more important than being a teacher because they make more money. Or they think that they are more intelligent than teachers because they make more money. Of course, being the youngest in the family doesn't help you, you know?! I don't know. It feels bad!

MANDY: (jumps in) I understand exactly what you mean by not fitting in. I feel like I cannot relate to most of my best friends who I have known since elementary school. They are into the drinking and partying thing, and I'm not really into that.

Now when we're together they just talk about the parties they've been to and how drunk and stoned they get. I just don't feel comfortable with them anymore.

MICHAEL: (responds) Okay, so, Mandy, you feel that you can understand to some degree what Clarence is going through because you don't feel like you fit in with your friends who like to party and drink alcohol. Let's explore this a little further.

The group continues to focus on Clarence and Mandy as they process feelings of being left out. When there is about ten minutes left, Samantha decides that it is time to begin the process of ending the session by checking in with each member of the group. Because it is the first session, she makes sure to focus on group trust and apprehension. The following are some responses from group members as Samantha and Michael were doing the rounds.

ELIZABETH: I am so grateful that we were able to talk about being scared and anxious about being here. At first, as I mentioned, I felt alone in my fear, but hearing from others really helped.

FELISHA: I would like to thank Clarence and Mandy for being so willing to jump out and talk about things. It was really nice to be able to hear their perspectives on things. I think all of us, in some context or another, feel left out or looked down upon. Thank you for sharing. I can't speak for everybody else, but it sure was helpful to me.

CLARENCE: I really appreciate you saying that. I was really beginning to feel nervous about all the focus being on me for such a long time this session. Don't worry, I won't be a time-hog.

MARCUS: No way, you don't have to apologize. I would like to thank you for stepping up to the plate and really talking about this. It was really beneficial to me. I feel a lot less anxiety now than I did at the beginning. I noticed that, even though some sessions might be focused more on one person, all of us can still gain things from it. I think that may help me when I have stuff to talk about in future sessions.

After going around and letting each person express themselves, Michael once again reviewed the group rule on confidentiality, thanked members for coming, and explained that trust and apprehension can be discussed further in subsequent sessions.

CASE ILLUSTRATION OF A SUBSEQUENT FORMING AND ORIENTING STAGE SESSION

It is now the second session of the group that Michael and Samantha have begun. Some of the anxiety and fear that accompanied the first session has decreased, and trust and cohesion are beginning to appear. Along with trust and cohesion, an openness to take some risks in expressing true feelings has emerged.

Also, Michael and Samantha begin to notice hints of some potential group problems, especially with some members who hardly participate. For example, Marshall has displayed a tendency to shy away from discussions and participation. In this session, Samantha and Michael make a point to encourage Marshall to participate before he clams up completely or quits coming to the group altogether.

At one point in the session, Elizabeth begins to talk about some anger problems that she is having. After discussing the situation with Elizabeth for a few minutes, Michael speaks.

MICHAEL: Marshall, I remember in the ice-breaker of our first session, you mentioned a desire to work on your anger. Tell us a little bit more about that.

MARSHALL: Well, I guess I just lose my cool sometimes.

SAMANTHA: What is it like when you lose your cool?

MARSHALL: I don't really know. I just get mad and it's like nothing else matters after that. I just blow up.

MICHAEL: What happens when you blow up?

MARSHALL: I usually either end up in a fight, or I say something that I regret later.

ELIZABETH: That sounds kind of scary. I feel that sometimes, too.

MARSHALL: Yeah, it's not real fun. Like I said, I want to put these angry explosions in check so that I don't have to regret stuff anymore.

SAMANTHA: Okay, so, tell me your goal.

MARSHALL: To not get angry anymore.

MICHAEL: How could you change that goal into something positive?

MARSHALL: Man, I don't know. You're the counselor. How do I make it positive?

SAMANTHA: Well, how do you feel when you are not angry?

MARSHALL: Calm.

SAMANTHA: Okay, then maybe your goal can be to stay calm during basketball games.

MARSHALL: Yeah, but how?

MANDY: I know when I begin to get upset, I sing my favorite hymn. I know if you do that, then you will feel better. One time I was so mad at my little 2-year-old for spilling grape juice on my new carpet that I could hardly stand it. In fact, I didn't know what I was going to do until I remembered to sing a song from the hymnal. I felt much better.

MICHAEL: (attempting to keep the focus on Marshall) Marshall, tell me about a time in your life when you were able to control your anger.

MARSHALL: I guess a few years back when I was in middle school, whenever I began to get upset, Coach Brown took me aside and told me to keep my focus on the fundamentals like staying active, boxing people out, and running the plays. When I stayed focused, I found myself not getting angry as much, and I enjoyed myself more.

SAMANTHA: So keeping your focus on what you need to be doing helps you stay calm.

MARSHALL: Yeah, so I guess I can remind myself of the fundamentals of the game when I recognize that I am getting upset. I'll see how that works.

ELIZABETH: I sure could use some goals for my anger. . . .

The session continues with Elizabeth describing her issues, as well as other group members participating in the session. The group leaders continue to take an active role in the group through modeling, facilitating the establishment of goals, recognizing potential problems, and establishing trust. In effect, the group begins to progress through some of the apprehension and doubt that are pervasive in the forming and orienting stage, and they enter and move through the next step in the development of a group known as the transition stage.

Summary

The forming and orienting stage of a group involves a time of orientation and exploration for group members. During this time, members become more cognizant of their reasons for joining the group. Through interaction with fellow group members, they develop a sense of who they are in the group (identity). They also make decisions about the degree to which they will participate, take risks, and relate to other group members (inclusion). If group members are to interact productively in groups, it is essential that trust be established early. The group leader plays a key role in helping cultivate an environment in which trust develops.

In addition to describing these general tasks that are part of the forming and orienting stage of a group, 10 responsibilities of leaders were discussed. These responsibilities include (1) reviewing group goals, (2) helping members establish personal goals, (3) specifying group rules, (4) modeling facilitative group behavior, (5) assisting members in expressing their apprehensions, (6) establishing and maintaining trust, (7) promoting positive interchanges among group members, (8) teaching members basic interpersonal skills such as active listening, (9) instilling hope, and (10) resolving possible group problems that manifest themselves in the forming stage. At the end of the chapter, a case illustration of two initial group sessions provided examples of group tasks, leadership responsibilities, and membership interactions that are often evident during the forming and orienting stage.

CHAPTER 8

The Transition Stage in Group Work

D. Paige Bentley Greason

PREVIEW

The theory behind the developmental tasks of the transition stage in groups is explored, including the internal and external determinants of transition dynamics, how these dynamics manifest in the group, and what leaders can do to work effectively with the sometimes overwhelming emotions and behaviors of this transition stage.

TRANSITION IN CONTEXT

Leaders work with a variety of types of groups, including task groups, psychoeducational groups, counseling groups, and psychotherapy groups (Akos, Goodnough, & Milsom, 2004; Newsome & Gladding, 2007; Ripley & Goodnough, 2001). No matter the type, all groups pass through what is often called the transition stage. This stage may be quicker and less anxiety producing in some group models (e.g., classroom guidance, small psychoeducational groups, task groups) than others (e.g., counseling groups, psychotherapy groups). For this reason, much of the content and many of the techniques covered in this chapter on the transition stage, while pertinent to all group models, are perhaps most applicable to counseling and psychotherapy group models.

Modern group theorists consider groups to be dynamic and changing systems (Agazarian, 1997; Agazarian & Gantt, 2003; Connors & Caple, 2005; Donigian & Malnati, 1997; McClure, 1998). Like any system, groups are relatively unstable in the early stages of development and progress toward more stability and complexity over time. Early in their development, groups pass through a type of adolescence. Just like a rebellious teenager, the group in transition is testing boundaries and power structures. Depending on the group, this stage manifests as overt or subtle rebellion and conflict, and represents a transition from the superficial niceties and enthusiasm that dominate the beginning of the forming and orienting stage to the more complex and challenging, albeit more cooperative focus that marks the working stage.

If this turbulent transition stage is successfully navigated, the group moves on to a norming period, during which cohesiveness grows, and then to the working stage, in which the productive, goal-focused work of the group can begin. If these forces of the transition stage are not adequately dealt with by the leader and members, these forces have the potential to keep the group stuck in the transition stage and adversely affect the group process and outcomes. Because of the potentially challenging, even destructive nature of transitional forces, it is important for leaders to be aware of the origins of these forces and how to deal with them effectively.

Much of our understanding of the dynamics of the transition stage in groups is based on research of adult groups. That research suggests that the dynamics of the transition stage are driven by anxiety and fear, which manifest as defensiveness, resistance, and interpersonal conflict around power and control (Billow, 2003). Very little research, however, has been conducted on the process dynamics of groups of children and adolescents (DeLucia-Waack, 2000; Shechtman, 2004). In dealing with challenging transitional forces, leaders need to be aware of the potential origins of these forces and the developmental needs and behaviors of members.

TRANSITION AS A CRITICAL GROUP TASK

A number of theorists have postulated about why transitional conflict occurs in the group and the value of conflict for group development. It is instructive to view transition from two important perspectives: group developmental theories and group systems theory, both of which help to explain why conflict is an important developmental task for groups.

Transition from a Developmental Theory Perspective

Despite the different names given to this transition stage, developmental theories are in agreement that, as groups develop, they enter a period characterized by increased tension and testing of the group environment. Members may test each other to see whether the environment is safe and to understand what the various relationships within the group will be like. Members may also test the leader to see if the leader will keep them safe, or they may simply use the leader as a safe target for the expression of their inner anger or hostility. Alternatively, they may become overly dependent

on the leader. They may hold the irrational expectation that the group leader not only understand their innermost problems without their having to say anything, but also make the group itself free of anxiety or tension. Developmental approaches to group work are evident in stage models, such as the one provided in this book and are readily understandable and applicable to task, psychoeducational, counseling, and psychotherapy groups. However, to truly understand the power and promise of group dynamics in counseling and psychotherapy groups, systemic models should also be considered.

Transition from a Systems Theory Perspective

A review of the scholarly literature on groups reveals that systemic approaches to group counseling and psychotherapy groups are becoming more prevalent and influential (Connors & Caple, 2005). Group systems theory provides a framework and language for understanding, defining, and working with the dynamics and processes in the group as a whole, particularly those dynamics that present themselves in the transition stage. Leaders operating from a systemic perspective focus on the big picture of the group while also maintaining awareness of the needs of the individual members. Understanding group dynamics from this perspective helps the leader be more effective in helping the individual group members and the group itself attain goals.

Systems theory posits that behaviors and attitudes that manifest during the transition stage are necessary for the optimal growth and health of the group (Agazarian & Gantt, 2003; Connors & Caple, 2005). The group continues to be useful as long as it is changing and evolving. Once the patterns of behavior become so rigid that the group can no longer adapt to a changing environment, the group ceases to serve its purpose and ultimately ceases to exist. As such, transition is a normal phase of group work and changes in behavior and responsibility are expected and essential elements.

General systems theory was first postulated in the classic work of Ludwig von Bertalanffy

(1968) and was based on the concept of holism—that the whole is greater than the sum of its parts and that the parts are interdependent. Von Bertalanffy proposed that systems are dynamic and ever-changing and that they evolve from disorder, instability, and simple structure into greater complexity through processes such as self-organization and self-stabilization. All the while, systems attempt to maintain homeostasis in the face of an ever-changing environment. Systems theory maintains that all systems include boundary and power structures that guide the development and growth of the system. For the system to survive and grow, boundaries must be flexible to allow input from new information and resources. These boundaries are rarely fixed. They are more open or more closed, depending on the situation.

Likewise, counseling groups can be defined as a system, hence the term *group systems theory*. Groups are self-defining, self-organizing, and self-regulating (Conners & Caple, 2005). From a systemic perspective, the individual members of a group are in a dynamic, interdependent relationship with each other. Each person within the group plays an essential role in the group's development and growth. A change in one person will have an impact on the rest of the group. According to group systems theory, behaviors and attitudes that manifest during the transition stage, however conflict-laden or anxiety producing, are necessary for the optimal growth and health of the group (Agazarian, 1997; Agazarian & Gantt, 2003; Connors & Caple, 2005; McClure, 1998). Conflict, boundary testing, feedback, and adaptation help create a group environment where member issues can be addressed effectively. Each will be addressed in the following chapter subsections.

CONFLICT Stability within the group, or any living system, cannot be maintained forever, no matter how comfortable that stability might feel. Conflict is viewed as necessary for effective growth and functioning. Conflict in a group may arise for a variety of reasons. Consider an example in which members may react to the leader's

failure to provide complete safety and freedom from anxiety. Elementary school students in a counseling group for students facing issues of grief and loss may expect that the leader will run the group like teachers run classes. They may have difficulty accepting that this group will require them to open up to other people and share their feelings. Members may become irritated with each other over how they should behave in the group. Members may have differing views of the group and its potential and how to handle issues in the group. Individuals who have less tolerance for anxiety may advocate for a continued focus on safe topics. Individuals with high needs for affection may want to spend time getting to know each other. In contrast, members with high needs for control may want to get on with the business of the group. These events are important to the evolution of the group because they open up interpersonal boundaries between members and create an opportunity for exploration of defense mechanisms and the establishment of group norms (Rybak & Brown, 1997). Groups that become too rigid in their norms and rules risk stagnation and possible dissolution.

BOUNDARY TESTING Boundaries in group work are defined as "the amount and kind of contact allowable between members" (Becvar & Becvar, 1996, p. 191). Boundaries are part of the overall structure of the group, which includes leader actions, group norms, goals, individual boundaries, and even group activities (Connors & Caple, 2005). For the group to move to higher levels of development and complexity, the boundary structure of the group itself and individual members must be permeable and flexible while preserving enough integrity to maintain safety. For instance, members who are unwilling to share personal information or consider the opinions of others are considered to have impermeable boundaries. If the group as a whole has rigid boundaries and is unwilling to share, the group may become stagnant and uninteresting. Members who are easily influenced by the emotions of others have highly permeable or diffuse boundaries (Nichols & Schwartz, 1995).

Leaders need to help members learn how to effectively open and close their boundaries so that group members can interact in meaningful ways and thus allow change and growth to occur.

FEEDBACK Systems theory suggests that the group receives input from the environment that either encourages change or supports the current status quo, or homeostasis. Connors and Caple (2005) referred to this input as change-provoking and change-resisting feedback. Change-provoking feedback refers to feedback that pushes the system toward growth. In a group, it might be in the form of verbal or nonverbal feedback. For instance, a group member might make an unpleasant facial gesture when a typically self-centered member starts talking about himself again. This gesture sends a message that the usual way of doing things (e.g., listening passively to the group member recount another story) is no longer going to work. The leader could use this opportunity to promote self-disclosure by the first member, perhaps through use of an I-statement about how he feels in response to this self-centered member's storytelling, and feedback that will help both members change the previous status quo. Change-resisting feedback supports the usual way of doing things. For instance, the same self-centered group member may change the subject when confronted about his patterns of behavior in order to avoid facing the issue and making changes, or other group members may simply allow the facial gesture to pass without any further comment.

From a group systems perspective, change-provoking feedback is the source of conflict because of its challenging and disturbing qualities. Coming face to face with something fearful is difficult, and group members experiencing change-provoking feedback are often very uncomfortable. The sense of chaos that can ensue can be disturbing, though it is seen at times as necessary for progress. When faced with these challenges, the group can decide to either retract or expand boundaries or, in rare instances, collapse and terminate the experience.

ADAPTATION Interactions in the group are seen as attempts to maintain homeostasis and regulate behavior in order to alleviate the anxiety of the unknown. These interactions result in the establishment of group norms. When something disrupts the norm (e.g., a heated exchange between group members), the group seeks to reestablish homeostasis. This may mean that the members avoid emotional subjects for some time after the event, or it may develop a new norm around the acceptable level of emotional sharing and intimacy. It takes some time to consolidate the event and accommodate the new information, but once a group survives a conflict event, the group may move more quickly toward greater intimacy and growth (Billow, 2003).

Many members can be resistant to change. Early on, individual group members and the group as a whole will attempt to maintain the status quo in order to alleviate the anxiety of the unknown. It is often easier and more comfortable to stay with what is known than to confront difficult areas of growth. To avoid the challenging work of growth and change, groups often lapse into repetitive patterns that maintain the status quo.

Groups are microcosms of society. Patterns within the group mirror patterns in the individual group members' lives. For example, a male in the group may be loud, dominating, and somewhat ego-centric, even approaching women in the group from a sexually provocative stance. He tends to talk down to females, in particular. This behavior parallels his behavior with significant women in his life, including his sister, mother, and co-workers. This dominating, provocative stance manifests in difficulty establishing strong and stable relationships with women. It may be easier for the male to maintain this behavior than to look at the underlying source of the behavior. Unfortunately, this rigid, patterned approach to life may cut him off from the very intimacy he seeks. Successfully working with these resistances to change will move group members and the group as a whole to a place where change is no longer feared. Instead, change is embraced within the safety of the group (McClure, 1998).

During the transition stage, it is incumbent upon leaders to find a balance between some discomfort in the system and complete chaos, which is usually more destructive than constructive (Nitsun, 1996). Consider an example in which a group member verbally attacked another member who had a pattern of dominating the discussion. Such verbal attacks are reflective of the power struggles typical of the transition stage. Imagine that the dominating member cracked under the attack and began to cry. A sense of tension settles over the group. At this point, the group faces a decision. Should the group rush to the defense of the dominant member, thus maintaining the status quo? Should the group gang up on the dominant member with character attacks? Should the group gang up on the attacking member? How the leader and group members work with these issues will determine whether or not the group survives and grows, maintains the status quo, or devolves.

ANXIETY AS THE SOURCE OF CONFLICT

Anxiety is considered the driving force in the group (Donigian & Malnati, 1997). But it is important to understand that the reasons for the anxiety experienced and expressed during the transition stage are qualitatively different from the forming and orienting stage. The anxiety related to "Will I fit in?" or "Will I get anything out of this group?" is less pronounced. In the transition stage, members are being asked to confront fears about themselves rather than ignore them, and to do so in a very public way. This amplifies core fears such as making a fool of oneself, losing control, or being rejected. For example, if Jane becomes angry about the way Jose treated another group member, she may worry that if she expresses the full force of her rage, she will be ostracized by the group, or worse, she won't be able to control her anger. No wonder group members feel anxious!

Despite the fact that anxiety is normal in group work, too much anxiety can inhibit the group process. Therefore, it is important for leaders to understand the sources of great anxiety in order to create a safe environment for reflection on the myriad ways members deal with their anxiety. This is the premier leader challenge of the transition stage. The group setting itself can trigger these defenses, as can core interpersonal issues among group members. Fortunately, individual psychology and choice theory provide some insight into the sources of transition forces, each of which contributes to sources of anxiety that are qualitatively different from the anxieties apparent in the forming and orienting stage.

The Group Itself as a Source of Anxiety

Groups are inherently anxiety provoking. Individuals are being asked to be vulnerable, to open up to strangers, to come face to face with change and possibly parts of themselves they would rather not see. For many years, the source of anxiety in groups was considered to be within the individual members (Donigian & Malnati, 1997). Literature focused on aggression *in* the group rather than aggression *toward* the group (Nitsun, 1996). This approach does not address the impact of group dynamics or the group setting itself on the elicitation of defensive behaviors. Group work scholars now assume that anxiety and conflict in groups have both an internal and external origin.

In his work on the aggressive forces in groups, Nitsun (1996) stated that the most commonly voiced anxiety about groups is that they can be destructive. He suggested that both constructive and destructive forces exist on a bipolar continuum in the group and that the tension between these forces is necessary for the continued growth and development of the group and its members. He coined the term *anti-group* to describe those forces that threaten the integrity of the group and suggested that the anti-group is an important complement to the creative processes within the group. Nitsun outlined several characteristics of counseling and therapy groups, presented below, that make them challenging and anxiety provoking for members.

GROUPS ARE COMPOSED OF STRANGERS—OR NOT! One of the first "rules" of member composition in counseling and psychotherapy groups is to fill the group with people who don't know each other so that interpersonal dynamics can start fresh. In a school setting, this may not be possible. School groups may be composed of students who interact with each other in many other school settings. Both situations create the possibility for tension in the group. Entering a room full of strangers can be a source of anxiety, as can entering a room full of school acquaintances who know the individual in very different settings. Members often begin group work because of interpersonal issues, and the group format is forcing them to talk about their most private experiences in front of others. Members may feel frustrated and scared that they are being asked to open up to people they aren't even sure they can trust, in the case of strangers, or people who they may have to deal with under different circumstances, in the case of acquaintances.

THE GROUP IS UNSTRUCTURED AND UNPREDICTABLE Task groups and psychoeducational groups aside, counseling and psychotherapy groups typically lack a structured agenda or program. This method invites a here-and-now focus on the dynamics within the group (Yalom & Leszcz, 2005). However, this lack of structure can be frustrating for group members who may be looking to the leader to provide direction. The lack of structure can also arouse anxiety around the unpredictable nature of the group. Members are uncertain what to expect from week to week, and the lack of structure makes it more difficult to feel safe.

THE GROUP IS CREATED BY ITS MEMBERS The paradox of group work is that the very people who are seeking help are the ones who are responsible for the fate of the group itself. Nitsun (1996) likened this to the blind leading the blind. Members may enter the group with hopes of being "fixed" by the leader. These members believe that responsibility for healing and health is external rather than internal. When it becomes clear that this dream of an external cure does not materialize, members may become hostile toward the group or the leader.

THE GROUP IS A PUBLIC ARENA Because the group is outside the typical bounds of members' private lives, it is often experienced as a public space. Because confidentiality cannot be guaranteed in a group, members' anxieties about exposure and humiliation extend beyond the boundaries of the group. In a school setting, this fear is magnified. Students may become anxious, for example, that they will be treated differently by peers after disclosing something deeply personal or embarrassing about themselves. They may also worry that their self-disclosures will be shared with others outside the group. It is important that leaders encourage members not to discuss what happens *in* the group *outside* the group, while also reminding members that confidentiality in a group setting cannot be guaranteed (Corey & Corey, 2006; Newsome & Gladding, 2007).

THE GROUP IS A PLURALISTIC ENTITY A diverse membership creates myriad opportunities for the growth of individual members. However, relating to a group of diverse individuals rather than a single counselor can test even the healthiest of individuals. For members, learning to understand and accept the differences of other people is a key developmental task. Furthermore, members can begin to learn different ways of problem-solving or interpreting events from individuals who are different from them (Newsome & Gladding, 2007).

THE GROUP IS A COMPLEX AND INCOMPLETE EXPERIENCE Communication within the group occurs on many different levels (e.g., explicit and implicit, verbal and nonverbal), and individual members construct meaning of the group experience based on their own phenomenological viewpoint. Due to the inherent limitations on the amount of material that can be covered in the group, individual members may be left with unresolved or unaddressed issues.

This can lead to frustration with the group as well as aggression.

Participation in the group forces members to come face to face with change, which is often very difficult, even if it is change for the better. In a school setting, many students are referred to groups by teachers or parents (Newsome & Gladding, 2007). Although the adult wants the child to change, the child may have very little motivation to change. Students lacking motivation may see the group as an unnecessary waste of time and be resistant to the counseling process.

Core Needs as Sources of Anxiety

In addition to the group setting itself as a source of anxiety, core needs also fuel anxiety and concomitant anxiety-driven behaviors. Anxiety is fostered when a discrepancy exists between needs and present attainment of those needs, as is often the case in groups. The effective leader is cognizant of the underlying needs and fears that generate anxiety and drive defensive behavior. Being mindful and respectful of those reasons helps the leader to decide on an appropriate intervention. A number of theories exist regarding basic human needs. Three of these—psychodynamic, individual psychology, and choice theory—are outlined here because they are particularly relevant to understanding group dynamics.

Psychodynamic theories suggest that a member's previous failed attempts to get basic needs met, as well as the resultant fears and core beliefs about one's ability and adequacy, fuel defensive reactions to perceived threats (McLeod & Kettner-Polley, 2004). In a classic analysis, Schutz (1966) identified three primary needs and suggested that these are satisfied through relationships with others. These primary interpersonal needs include inclusion, control, and affection. "Inclusion is concerned with the problem of in or out, control is concerned with top or bottom, and affection with close or far" (Schutz, 1966, p. 24). Whereas inclusion behaviors are related to forming a relationship, control and affection behaviors relate to how one deals with relationships that

are already established. To be free of anxiety, the member needs to find a balance of these three needs with respect to others. Members differ in the levels to which they are deficient in these areas, reflecting their prior successes or failures in getting these needs met. Schutz suggested that the dynamics within the group reflect these interpersonal needs. For example, a student with strong inclusion needs might try to be "best friend" with everyone in the group or, on the opposite end of the spectrum (i.e., low inclusion needs), might withdraw and avoid contact with others. When the typical defense mechanisms do not fully protect the individual from negative feelings associated with the discrepancy between what is needed and what is attained, anxiety ensues. In the optimal state of equilibrium, defenses are required only minimally.

Individual psychology (i.e., Alfred Adler) provides an insightful theoretical explanation of the needs of children and the related goals of misbehavior (Thompson & Henderson, 2007). According to this theory, children who feel good about themselves attempt to achieve their basic goal of belonging by cooperating and collaborating with others. However, children who are discouraged pursue one of four mistaken goals: attention, power, revenge, and inadequacy or withdrawal. These mistaken-goal behaviors may become more extreme during the transition stage in group work as members try to find their place in the group. For instance, a member who has been mistreated in life may seek to get even by hurting others, or a member who thinks she or he is inferior or incapable may "act stupid" in order to avoid being challenged by the leader.

Finally, choice theory, primarily developed by William Glasser, suggests that humans have five basic needs: survival, freedom, power, fun, and love and that psychological problems are the result of an inability to fulfill these needs. Glasser (1999) suggests that members often try to fulfill their basic needs by infringing upon the basic rights of others through control tactics, resulting in relationship issues. He proposes, therefore, that all psychological problems are relationship problems that stem from attempts to control others. The road to mental health, according to choice theory, is the development of healthy relationships in which each member takes responsibility for one's own behavior as opposed to trying to change the behavior of others.

Regardless of theoretical orientation, these basic needs are associated with a plethora of fears and core beliefs about the self. A number of other common fears observed during the transition stage have been identified by group work authors (Corey, 2007; Corey & Corey, 2006; Ormont, 1984, 1988; Schutz, 1966; Yalom & Leszcz, 2005), including:

- If I show my true self, I will be ignored, or worse, rejected.
- If I speak up or take responsibility, I will make a fool of myself and be seen as incompetent.
- If I look too deep, I'll discover that there is nothing there.
- If I express my anger (fear, sadness, etc.), I will open up Pandora's box and will lose control.
- The group or the leader will expect me to disclose more than I'm comfortable sharing.
- I'm worried about getting close to people who won't be available to me after the group ends. I'm afraid I can't handle that loss. I'm afraid that what I say in the group won't stay in the group.
- I'm afraid that if I tell people about my past behaviors or my deepest fears or fantasies, they will judge me.
- I am afraid that this group will be a waste of my time. I don't see how this can help.
- I am afraid that the group leader won't be able to help me if things get rough.

The group setting creates a rare venue where the member's unique issues with intimacy and contact with others can play out *and* be examined (Yalom & Leszcz, 2005). These theoretical perspectives about how groups develop and the underlying internal and external issues that challenge group members provide a backdrop for understanding the member and leader behaviors that arise during the transition stage. Leaders need to know what specific, concrete behaviors to look for and understand that these behaviors may be driven by anxiety.

THE EXPRESSION OF TRANSITION ISSUES

The interpersonal and intrapersonal dynamics mentioned above manifest in the group during the transition stage in predictable ways. Whereas the forming and orienting stage of group development is characterized by acclimation to the group process and some testing of boundaries to identify "ground rules," the transition stage is marked by more overt hostility and conflict (Yalom & Leszcz, 2005).

Some of the most common behaviors observed during transition are identified and described in this section. All of these behaviors should be viewed in light of their role in the development of the group. For instance, rather than an act of protest, active defiance in the group may actually represent a growing trust in the process and a willingness to express more difficult emotions. Certainly, it could also indicate complete distrust in the process. It is important that the leader explore the origins of various behaviors rather than assuming that he or she understands. Some of these member behaviors can become quite problematic, as was discussed in substantial detail in Chapter 4, and the leader must display skillful, intentional interventions to facilitate member self-disclosure and feedback.

Struggle for Control

During the transition stage, issues around control are present in every group, although they may not always be obvious. To maintain optimal functioning, the group as a whole must find a level of relative equality among members. Conners and Caple (2005) suggested that unequal power dynamics or dominating members must be addressed or else groups will "fall into destructive interpersonal patterns and create negative outcomes" (p. 100).

In this transition stage, members struggle with issues of dependence on the leader's authority and the comfort of the status quo versus independence and freedom of expression (Billow, 2003). As members seek to find their preferred amount of autonomy and power, they must confront all the other group members who, likewise, are struggling with the same issues. They must also deal with the leader, who has been given tacit power simply by virtue of position. The result is conflict and hostility between members and the leader or just among members.

HOSTILITY TOWARD THE LEADER Some hostility toward the leader occurs normally as part of a group's development. In the typically high-dependency state leading up to the transition stage, the group members tend to look to the group leader for guidance and reassurance, as if they are unable to take care of themselves. Kline (2003) stated that members "deskill" themselves and depend on the leader to understand them without members having to say anything (e.g., "The leader should be able to read my mind"). During this period, group members often engage in magical thinking about the group leader's power in the group. Members may expect the leader to be all-knowing and capable of reading their innermost thoughts and concerns. They also may hold the secret wish that the leader will choose them as the "favorite child" (Yalom & Leszcz, 2005). From this perspective, the behaviors of the leader may be misinterpreted as illustrative of a deeper, individual connection between the leader and the member. For instance, when the group leader made eye contact with Sally while another group member was speaking, Sally interpreted the contact to mean: "Ah, he understands exactly what I'm feeling over here. He agrees with me that this person is ridiculous." This illusion of a secret alliance between the leader and member is quickly shattered as the member comes to realize that the leader may have equal interest in the issues of all group members.

When it becomes clear that the group leader will not fulfill these unrealistic expectations, the group members may become angry and lash out at the leader. Hostility toward the leader may take the form of explicit attacks on the leader's character, competence, or methods.

Members may call into question the leader's dedication to members as well as the overall purpose and utility of the group. More passive members may resort to silence in the group or may engage in discussions about the leader with other members outside the group setting (e.g., in the hallways, during other school events).

Aggression toward the leader may come disguised as a challenge or overtly as an attack. An attack typically reflects a judgment about the group leader's character (e.g., "You are insensitive and uncaring") and leaves no room for discussion. A challenge, on the other hand, opens the door for discussion. It reflects a willingness on the part of the challenger to own his feelings. The member who says, "I am nervous about coming to group each week because I am afraid that you will allow other group members to attack me" is questioning the behaviors of the leader rather than attacking the character and opens the door for more dialogue. Young children can also challenge the leader by displaying behaviors such as ignoring the leader's requests that the group get quiet, talking back, and acting out. Challenges reflect members' growing sense of autonomy and independence and a testing of boundaries. Attacks may be indicative of more rebellion to come, particularly if they are not handled skillfully by the leader (Billow, 2003). Recommendations for handling these issues will be discussed later in this chapter.

Certainly, not all group members attack the leader. Some rally to the leader's defense. Yalom and Leszcz (2005) suggested that the "lineup of attackers and defenders" provides good information about the core issues of each member. Challenges or attacks on the leader generally subside as reality sets in and the members begin to recognize the leader's role and limitations.

HOSTILITY TOWARD OTHER GROUP MEMBERS As members come to the realization that they are not the favorite child and that they do not have a special alliance with the leader, feelings of rivalry toward other members may emerge. The very nature of the group setting, as mentioned above, fosters frustration and aggression. As members try to make room for themselves in an environment with limited time, space, and attention, they are likely to hurt the feelings of others (Ormont, 1984). Some of the behaviors that may elicit negative reactions in other group members and that reflect the struggle for control in the group include:

- *Excessive storytelling*. With this behavior, a group member dominates the group by always turning the discussion back on him- or herself. This behavior gives the member control in the group and protects the member from being confronted by other group members, who can't get a word in edgewise.
- *Making comments that are off topic*. This behavior may be an attempt to change the subject or it may simply be an indication of the difficulty the member has in following the thread of the discussion. Either way, it can be irritating for other group members and may be an impetus for conflict.
- *Abdicating responsibility*. Some members of the group may be more submissive in how they handle life events. This tendency will emerge in the way they talk about themselves or handle group events. Other group members may see this as "weak" or "victim-like." They may become frustrated by the lack of personal responsibility for change.
- *Advice giving or rescuing*. These behaviors tend to keep the discussion in a "fix it" mode and may inhibit deeper exploration of feelings. Occasional advice giving is a typical reaction to the pain of others. When this behavior dominates, however, it may indicate a need to be in a "power" position or a tendency to avoid deeper work.
- *Always having to have the last word or assuming a position of moral authority*. This behavior tends to generate negative reactions in group members, even if they agree with the member's position (Trotzer, 1999).
- *Withdrawing from the group and appearing aloof*. This behavior needs to be distinguished from supportive silence that gives

individuals time to think or silence that is related to cultural factors. Obvious indicators of withdrawal are physical distance from the group, rolling eyes or crossing arms, or criticism of the process.
- *Using humor or sarcasm*. This behavior deflects attention from difficult topics. Initially, this behavior is a welcome addition by group members because it takes the pressure off them to do serious work in the group. Over time, however, the jokes may begin to wear on group members who begin to see it for what it is.

Reactions to these behaviors may be flagrant or subtle, and they reflect the interpersonal and intrapersonal issues of the individual group members. Some may lash out verbally at group members or resort to character attacks, such as, "You think you are the most important person on the planet." Others, perhaps frustrated by the member who monopolizes the conversation, for instance, may not have the courage or the skills necessary to express their feelings or aggressive thoughts. Instead, they may use nonverbal behaviors such as crossing their arms, fidgeting, or looking at a watch to indicate their annoyance.

Just as the group members may "gang up" on the leader, members may also unconsciously collude to attack a particular member of the group. This is referred to as scapegoating. The scapegoat may be an innocent victim, but more often it is someone who provokes attack by specific behaviors in the group (Clark, 2002). Yalom and Leszcz (2005) suggested that this phenomenon often occurs when the group leader cannot be openly criticized for some reason. Attacking a peer is less threatening than attacking the leader. Clark (2002) suggested that the phenomenon of scapegoating reflects the displacement of intolerable feelings for another person or the projection of personal characteristics that are perceived to be intolerable or offensive to others. By turning the focus on one target, the group members exert some control over the content of the session and avoid the work of exploring their own feelings.

Resistance to Intimacy

Closely related to the struggle for control is resistance to both interpersonal and intrapersonal intimacy. As group members seek their place in the group, they are also establishing personal boundaries around how much they will divulge about themselves and how willing they are to explore their own feelings. Members may be particularly sensitive about feelings that are ordinarily socially unacceptable (e.g., anger), or indicative of weakness. Therefore, many of the behaviors listed above reflect not only the power drive, but also the mechanisms members use to protect themselves against the anxiety inherent in genuinely connecting with others and delving into painful or difficult feelings.

Resistant behaviors can be indicative of an inability or unwillingness to commit to the group process. Ohlsen (1970) suggested that this lack of commitment in any form should be discouraged. Because they have less investment in the group process, resistant members are more likely to break confidentiality, engage in disruptive behavior within the group, and resist moving beyond superficial topics. However, leaders should be careful not to assume that resistant behaviors are always reflective of intrapersonal issues. Resistant behaviors can also be indicators that something is not working in the group. If group events have been handled ineffectively by the group leader, for instance, group members may rightfully be resistant to opening up and making themselves vulnerable. The group does not feel safe.

It is important to note here that expressions of frustration and anger or avoidance of intimacy in the group are not necessarily problem behaviors. They are natural parts of the process of becoming more genuine and authentic. Labeling group members as resistant or as the Intellectualizer or Advice-giver only reinforces stereotyping and character attacks, even if these labels are never actually spoken in the group.

HANDLING TRANSITION ISSUES: IMPLICATIONS FOR LEADERS

The overarching objective for a leader during the transition stage is to establish a group environment that supports member goals and involves members in this interpersonal learning process. Working through transitional forces, however, can be challenging. Because of the self-perpetuating nature of the interpersonal and intrapersonal phenomena that occur during the transition stage, the group risks being harmed by these forces if they are not dealt with appropriately. For example, underlying resistance to the group can lead to a negative perception of the group experience. A negative perception of the group can reinforce resistance and aversion to participation. Conversely, if these forces are addressed skillfully, the group moves to a place of greater cohesion, intimacy, and growth, and is ready to begin the working stage.

Handling transition dynamics, therefore, is a key task for group leaders. The overt conflict and resistance can be extremely challenging to a leader's sense of accomplishment and sense of self if they are not viewed as a natural part of the process. Trotzer (1999) reminded group leaders that a common factor among group members is a "deep and sincere desire for success" (p. 206) and that this simply gets covered by the defensive reactions members have to the new group environment. Conflict in the group is the very material necessary for personal growth and change and for the cultivation of intimacy.

The work of the leader then is to bring these member defenses into play and work to resolve underlying anxieties. The goal is to increase members' tolerance for anxiety so that they can let go of maladaptive, defensive behaviors and become more accepting of themselves—fears and all (McClure, 1998). Yalom and Leszcz (2005) encouraged group leaders to "plunge the members into the source of the resistance—in other words, not *around* anxiety, but *through* it" (p. 196). Billow (2003) suggested that, after a group has survived the inevitable rebellion and "defenses are sufficiently undone and frustration is contained, the group may move away from authority and dependency preoccupation to phases involved with intimacy and self-affirmation" (p. 334).

Held in this awareness, transition issues become an exciting opportunity rather than an intimidating obstacle for group leaders. This section outlines some common mistakes that leaders make during the transition period and provides an overview of key topics leaders need to keep in mind to work successfully with transition issues.

Common Leader Traps

Working with transition dynamics is challenging even for experienced leaders. Leaders often don't know what to say or where to respond amid a variety of potential issues. Edelwich and Brodsky (1992) outlined four common traps that leaders fall into when trying to handle transition issues, particularly issues around resistance. These traps include doing individual counseling with one group member, justifying the group, inducing guilt in order to gain compliance, and generalizing the feelings of one member to the whole group.

FOCUSING ON ONE MEMBER ONLY A common tendency among leaders is to lapse into individual counseling in a group setting. For instance, when a member states that he doesn't want to participate in the group because he feels uncomfortable, the probing leader might ask the member to explain more about his feelings. Certainly, this is an important step in uncovering emotions and defense mechanisms. However, the goal of group work is to cultivate the capacity of the group to be self-sustaining and autonomous. Complete reliance on the leader to guide the discussion and handle uncomfortable feelings leads to a lack of creativity and to stagnation (Connors & Caple, 2005).

JUSTIFYING THE GROUP Hearing negative comments about the group or the process can easily lead to defensive internal reactions in leaders. Reacting defensively, however, by rushing to explain the benefits of the group does little to increase the motivation of the individual to stay in the group or to participate fully. For instance, explaining all the potential benefits of group participation to a member who has just disclosed that the group doesn't have anything to offer him only sets up a power struggle. Edelwich and Brodsky (1992) argued that it is not the leader's responsibility to keep the group member in the group. A more empowering approach is to put responsibility for making the group useful in the hands of the group member. The leader might say: "We have discussed previously that you are making a choice to come to this group—even those of you who were recommended to the group by someone else. I do care if you stay or go, but that is your choice. Because you are here, you can also make a choice to use this time to your benefit. I'm wondering how you might use the group time today to get something out of it?"

INDUCING GUILT Another defensive reaction that leaders sometimes lapse into is responding judgmentally to a group member's rebellion. A leader might, for instance, accuse a group member of not caring about other group members or suggest that the member's actions reflect lack of concern for the individual's family. "Don't you care about how your family would feel if you dropped out?" Clearly, this type of defensive reaction only perpetuates anxiety, fear, and mistrust of the group process among all group members.

GENERALIZING FEELINGS OF ONE MEMBER TO THE WHOLE GROUP In an attempt to bring the group into the discussion of a topic raised by another group member, leaders sometimes fall into the trap of generalizing the feelings of that one member to the group as a whole. Leaders might say something like, "I sense a lot of people are frustrated with my leadership style." Rather than encouraging true dialogue among members about an issue, this approach is likely to elicit feedback designed to "pump up" what appears to be a demoralized leader. At worse, it may become a self-fulfilling prophecy.

CASE STUDY 8.1

David

David is a 32-year-old, out-of-work plumber who started college but never completed it. He is gregarious and outgoing and has established himself as a "friend of all." He is quick with a joke, but often gets lost in intellectual discourse that is sometimes difficult for the group members to follow. However, the other group members have come to rely on David to break uncomfortable silences in the group. When questioned about his personal life, however, David quickly changes the subject or launches into a theoretical monologue. You sense that there is growing frustration in the group with this member.

What core needs is David having difficulty fulfilling in his life?

How would you conceptualize David's situation?

How will you handle the growing tension?

Read Case Study 8.1. Explore how you would conceptualize David's core anxieties around group participation and what you would do to work with this individual in the group.

Focal Points for Handling Transition

Although some group leaders may fall into the traps listed above from time to time, these traps can also become opportunities for working with conflict in the group. This section outlines specific areas that leaders need to be cognizant of when working with transition issues.

PAY ATTENTION TO DEVELOPMENTAL LEVEL When working in a school setting, it is critical that counselors take into account the developmental level of the student. In the early years of elementary school, young children require very different interventions than do students in middle school. Likewise, middle school students require different approaches than high school students. In fact, approaches that may be helpful with adolescents may be ineffective or even harmful with young children or pre-teens (Newsome & Gladding, 2007; Vernon, 2004a). Although developmental characteristics must be kept in mind when tailoring an intervention for transition issues, some fundamental

practices cut across all developmental levels. These practices are presented in the following chapter subsections.

REINFORCE CONFIDENTIALITY During transition periods in groups, emotions run high, and participants may be tempted to talk to each other or others who aren't in the group about events that take place within the group. Adolescents, in particular, are often acutely concerned with issues of confidentiality (Newsome & Gladding, 2007). It is important that expectations of confidentiality are consistently reinforced beyond the initial group meeting. How confidentiality is discussed varies based on the age of the group participants. With very young students, the leader can use puppets or role plays to help illustrate issues of confidentiality, or the leader might say something like, "In this group, we keep what happens in this group private. That means that if Shawndra says something or does something in the group, we don't talk about it out in the hall or on the playground, or in your classroom. If something that happened here hurts your feelings or makes you uncomfortable, you can let me know." While adolescents and adults may grasp the importance of maintaining confidence more readily than younger members, leaders must still periodically reinforce the necessity of maintaining confidentiality to promote trust and a positive working environment.

COMMUNICATION IS KEY Communication is the key to adequately dealing with conflicts as they arise. The expectation of honest and genuine communication needs to be made explicit repeatedly, starting from the earliest planning stages of the group. Edelwich and Brodsky (1992) suggested that group leaders emphasize the importance of honest communication in the group by saying, "There is no issue so sensitive that we cannot talk about it in this group." With younger students, the leader can set the stage for open communication by saying, "In this group, we will try to be honest about how we are feeling. That means that if you are feeling sad, you can say, 'I'm feeling sad today'." Setting the stage in this way opens the door to allow members to voice their frustrations and irritations. Leaders can also prepare members for the inevitable letdown that can occur as members move from the initial excitement and bonding of early group sessions to the hard work of sharing. By being explicit about what this might look like and emphasizing the importance of discussing this shift when it occurs, leaders lay the groundwork for changes to come (Jacobs, Masson, & Harvill, 2006).

Setting an expectation of communication early sets the stage for productive work, rather than stagnation, in the group. For instance, in their classic work on focal conflict theory, Whitaker and Lieberman (1964) suggested that conflict in groups is dealt with in one of two ways: restrictive solutions and enabling solutions. Restrictive solutions reflect an avoidance of the conflict. Group members' anxiety is lowered because the issue is ignored. This is illustrated by behaviors such as changing the subject or engaging in storytelling. Enabling solutions are associated with confronting underlying fears and may temporarily increase the anxiety of group members. If the solution is successful, however, tolerance for anxiety will increase and the group will become more cohesive.

For members of all ages, it is important that expectations about group participation be discussed prior to the start of the group. In screening interviews, the leader can assess what areas might be difficult for each member. For example, a member may have a passive approach to life and could be expected to be quiet in the group. A one-on-one discussion prior to the start of the group about the expectation of participation and the issues that may be keeping a member from participating can clarify for the leader what may be happening with the member in the group. It also gives the leader some fodder for encouraging the member to participate in the group without pushing the member to participate (Greenberg, 2003). How these expectations are communicated, of course, depends on the developmental level of the member. Leaders can also use the group itself to develop norms about participation.

For example, Sarah is afraid that if she voices her opinion, the group will judge her as stupid or incompetent and reject her. She takes a risk and verbalizes this fear. Rather than being rejected as incompetent, Sarah receives the support of the group. Her willingness to be open about her fears prompts others in the group to share some of their fears as well.

Many times members simply have not learned how to communicate effectively. Research shows that specific instruction in the form of relevant information at critical moments in the group's development is helpful (Morran, Stockton, Cline, & Teed, 1998). It is incumbent upon the leader to model effective communication and perhaps even provide more concrete education about what effective communication looks like. Modeling the use of I-statements, for instance, can set the tone for ownership of feelings and expression of those feelings. For example, during an uncomfortable silence following some act of rebellion, a leader might say, "We've just sat in silence for a full minute. I know I am feeling uncomfortable and at a loss for words. Does anyone else share my feelings?" Edelwich and Brodsky (1992) suggested that the leader can use self-disclosure to address group members' fears. A leader might say: "When I first started working in groups, I was afraid to say anything very close to my heart for fear I would lose control and become emotional in the group. I wasn't sure I could handle that. Who else has had that experience?" Opening the door to discussion about sensitive issues can be followed with: "When I don't speak up about something that concerns me, it's because I'm afraid I won't be accepted or may sound stupid or because I'm afraid of expressing myself about issues. That's why I've found I don't speak up in groups" (Edelwich & Brodsky, 1992, p. 47).

Members may be helped by concrete psychoeducation about effective communication. Topics might include the difference between a character attack and an expression of personal feelings, being assertive versus being passive (or passive-aggressive), or the difference between feeling and thinking. The author has found it effective to provide group members with lists of feeling words so they have a vocabulary with which to work.

In time, group members begin to realize that voicing their fears actually helps them deal with core interpersonal issues. Through this process of conflict, communication, and resolution, the group begins to become more comfortable with the uncomfortable. Yalom and Leszcz (2005) referred to this as "unfreezing" habitual ways of being and relating to others.

PROCESS THE PROCESS A common mistake made by group leaders is to become so involved in the content of a group session that the process is neglected. The Association for Specialists in Group Work *Best Practice Guidelines* (ASGW, 2007) suggested that effective group leaders process the workings of the group by attending to the session dynamics. This could not be truer than in the transition stage, when interpersonal and intrapersonal dynamics are running high. Stockton, Morran, and Nitza (2000, p. 345) defined processing as

> capitalizing on significant happenings
> in the here-and-now interactions of the

group to help members reflect on the meaning of their experience; better understand their own thoughts, feelings, and actions; and generalize what is learned to their life outside the group.

Processing, therefore, includes not only descriptions of the ongoing group experience, but also reflection and extraction of meaning from those experiences (Ward & Litchy, 2004; Yalom & Leszcz, 2005). The leader must help the group members make cognitive sense of what is happening. When used effectively, here-and-now processing serves as a catalyst to deepen interaction among group members and move members toward their personal goals. The object is to shift the discussion from "outside to inside, from the abstract to the specific, from the generic to the personal, from the personal to the interpersonal" (Yalom & Leszcz, 2005, p. 158).

The leader is in a unique position when it comes to here-and-now processing. When group members comment on the process for defensive reasons (e.g., to take themselves out of the client role), they set themselves apart from the other members and may become the target of rage. "Who is he to think he is better than us?" As the observer-participant, the leader has the responsibility of providing objective comments about the cyclical patterns in the group and tying individual goals back into the unfolding of group events. This is not to say that members should never make process comments, particularly as they relate to themselves. In fact, members learning to observe the process can be an important outcome of group work.

Process statements can be either general or more directive. Ormont (1984) suggested that leaders can encourage group members to think in terms of the group and address the holistic nature of the group by asking questions such as, "How is the group operating right now?" and "How is what's happening affecting the feeling of the group?" For younger members, however, this type of abstract thinking may not be possible. Instead, the leader can ask more direct, concrete questions such as, "Emma, you have your arms crossed. I'm wondering if you are angry."

Yalom and Leszcz (2005) suggested that a more directive approach is often well-received by group members. For example, a leader sensing guardedness or withdrawal in the group might say: "We've done a lot of work here today. I sense, however, that something more is going on beneath the surface. I suspect that everyone here has been trying to size up the other group members. Let's take the remainder of the group time to share what we've come up with so far." A less threatening approach—though still directive—is to focus on internal experiences in the group and how those are manifested in the group. "Everyone here is coming to this group with very personal goals and hopes for success that require opening up and being vulnerable. I know that I tend to close up when I feel threatened. I wonder if we could spend some time talking about what each of us is likely to do in this group when we feel threatened or unsafe."

Several models exist for helping leaders process group dynamics. These models include Conyne, Rapin, and Rand's (1997) "grid for processing experiences in group"; Glass and Benshoff's (1999) PARS model (Processing: Activity, Relationship, Self); Stockton et al.'s (2000) "Cognitive Map"; and Yalom's (Yalom & Leszcz, 2005) two-tiered processing model. Although each model has a slightly different approach to organizing and making sense of the ongoing group experience, all of the models have a common focus on bringing attention to the "what" and "how" of critical incidents in the group, illuminating member reactions, and helping members derive meaning that can be applied outside the group.

Read Case Study 8.2. Explore how you would conceptualize Michael's core anxieties around group participation and what you would do to work with this individual in the group.

TIMING COUNTS   Although communication and a process orientation are critical for effective work during transition, this must be balanced with proper timing. Asking groups to do work that they are not yet ready to do may backfire, resulting in increased anxiety, frustration, and aggression (Agazarian & Gantt, 2003). It is important to remember that defenses are in place

---

CASE STUDY 8.2

Michael

On the first day of group, Michael begins to joke with you before group begins about how counselors only repeat back what is said. He states that he doesn't really believe in counseling and cites a quote from a website about the efficacy of computerized counselors versus "live" counselors to make his case. You let the comment drop for the time being and soon see similar behaviors appearing in the group sessions. Michael continues to remain distant from other group members by using jokes to deflect attention. Recently, he has begun to enlist other male members of the group to make fun of the leader and the process as a whole. You realize that there are a number of members in the group who are getting something out of the process, and you fear that if Michael's behavior continues, they will begin to question why they are there.

What core anxiety is Michael displaying?

What aspects of Michael's behavior warrant attention?

How will you enlist the group to work through this resistance?

for a reason and to respect those reasons. Penetrating these defenses too early will not lead to permanent change. Readiness for change involves the ability to discriminate information within the system. If participants are confronted with too much information, the system will be flooded and falter.

Aspects to keep in mind when deciding whether to focus on a critical incident in the group include the impact the focus will have on the group as a whole, the psychological ability and willingness of the group members to handle the topic, and cultural factors that may influence behavior in the group. For instance, ordinarily it is not worth engaging highly defensive individuals who are attacking other members in an exploration of their underlying causes. It may, however, be worth exploring the effect of the attacking behavior on other group members. It may also be beneficial to wait until a defensive method has played out in several members of the group. Pointing out similarities allows members to see their own defenses in others and reduces embarrassment or shame.

Stockton et al. (2000) suggested some types of events that are worth in-depth examination, although they stress that, ultimately, the decision is based on the leader's judgment and empathic understanding of group members. Some of these events include:

- Events that evoke heightened emotional or behavioral reactions.
- Events that reflect a recurring pattern.
- Events that directly relate to goals.
- Explicit hostility or conflict in the group.
- Emotional self-disclosures.
- Body language suggestive of unspoken reactions.

BALANCING CLOSENESS AND DISTANCE As mentioned above, rebellion against the leader is an important factor in group formation and process. As group members band together in this rebellion process, they become more cohesive, and they also take on more responsibility for the group experience itself. As Vella (1999) said, "Independence cannot be granted by Authority,

but must be wrested from it" (p. 17). Therefore, in relating to the group members, the leader must be cognizant of balancing closeness and distance. If the leader is too distant, aggressive feelings dominate the group, and the group may become stuck in rebellion. On the other hand, if the leader is too friendly, no resistance is necessary, and group formation takes longer.

Related to balancing closeness and distance is learning to trust the group process and releasing the reins. This does not mean that the leader is passive. Rather, the leader uses the dynamics of the group to guide from within. For example, this strategy can be used when working with a member who constantly criticizes other group members in the name of honesty but crumbles when group members retaliate. The leader may suspect that this is a pattern that is repeated outside the group when the member is in other social settings. The leader recognizes that the member needs to take responsibility for her or his actions but that, at least initially, she or he would need support in order to withstand the building anger of the group. Taking on the role of the group member's supporter, the leader can provide comfort anytime another member spoke harshly toward her or him. This may free other group members to voice their aggression because they know that the leader will support the offending group participant.

CULTIVATE SELF-AWARENESS Perhaps the most difficult aspect of the transition stage is the effect it can have on the leader's self-esteem if he or she takes the dynamics personally. It is vitally important that leaders are aware of their own defense mechanisms and underlying anxieties because they may be triggered when conflict arises (Ward & Litchy, 2004). The leader needs to be comfortable with personal insecurities and "dark sides" in order to help others do the same. Self-awareness also includes awareness of one's limitations as a group leader. Glass and Benshoff (1999) warned that leaders must have a strong understanding of group dynamics in order to work effectively in here-and-now events within the group.

CASE STUDY 8.3

Kristen

Kristen is a 16-year-old high school sophomore who was referred to counseling for issues of extreme disrespect and impulsive behavior. In the initial interview, you learn that Kristen had a history of self-cutting and had been sexually abused by her mother's boyfriend when she was in elementary school. For the past five years, she has been living with her father and stepmother, and she has very little contact with her mother. At her stepmother's encouragement, Kristen has started working part-time at the local pizza restaurant, where she has met a number of high school males with whom she has engaged in sex.

Kristen has a lot of anger toward her mother as well as her father and stepmother. She believes that her stepmother just wants her to "grow up" and get out of the house and that her father never stands up for her. She states that her stepmother is constantly calling her a "liar" and admits that she often does lie, particularly about her sexual encounters, to keep the peace. Despite this "goal" of keeping the peace, Kristen often ends up in shouting matches with her stepmother and either runs out of the house or to her bedroom. She states that she never knows what kind of mood her stepmother is going to be in and therefore feels on guard all the time. In the past year, she has become increasingly angry and has developed a reputation at school for being sexually "loose" and emotionally volatile.

You decide that, in addition to some individual and family work, Kristen would benefit from a more structured psychoeducation group. During the past three group sessions, Kristen has regaled the group with a never-ending stream of hardships and obstacles. When group members suggest that she try some of the strategies they are learning to help her cope, she shrugs them off as impossible. Her standard line is, "I tried that already, and it doesn't work." Finally, Sam, who has previously remained quiet, bursts forth with a stream of criticisms toward Kristen and you. He charges that you should never have allowed her to go on like this. "It is unproductive and boring."

What are the core anxieties being expressed?

What is your highest priority here?

How can you bring the other group members into the conflict?

Read Case Study 8.3. Explore how you would conceptualize Kristen's core anxieties around group participation and what you would do to work with this individual in the group.

Summary

Change is challenging. For some, the fear of change can make it nearly impossible to move out of a comfort zone. Members in groups come face to face with the need for change and their concomitant anxieties and fears. Developmental and systemic theorists propose that the dynamics of control, conflict, and resistance that appear in the transition stage are important steps in the process of change and growth. Like rebellious teenagers testing their wings, members in the transition stage of a group are testing the group's ability, and their own abilities, to survive the strain of their real selves. It is up to the group leader to help individuals in the group see how they are resistant to change and how their natural defenses against those things that are fearful and anxiety provoking alienate them from connection with others and cheat them out of the fullness of life.

CHAPTER 9

The Working Stage

Kevin A. Fall, H. George McMahon, and Danica G. Hays

PREVIEW

For as long as groups have been studied, researchers have noted the part in the life of the group where members actively and freely work on group and personal goals, honestly share aspects of self, courageously give feedback, and feel a sense of "we-ness" that enable members to truly believe in the process of group like never before. This chapter provides an overview of the working stage of group work, with an emphasis on member and leader functions within this important part of the group process. Components of this stage related to group foundations and design are also discussed to illustrate indicators for optimal working stage process.

OVERVIEW AND ELEMENTS OF THE WORKING STAGE

"So this is the moment I've been waiting for?" This quote, uttered by a counseling intern as she was leading her first "real" group, captures the sense of awe and relief felt by leaders and members as they begin to experience the benefits of the working stage of a group. As a group successfully navigates its way through the conflicts, role confusion, and general tension that characterize the transition stage, it begins to enter into the working stage. The working stage occurs when group members address the purpose of the group and focus their energies on meeting the individual and group goals articulated during the planning phase and the forming and orienting stage. Although group workers have used a variety of terms to describe the stage where the group goals are accomplished, including Performing (Tuckman & Jensen, 1977), Action (George & Dustin, 1988), Commitment (Berg, Landreth, & Fall, 2006), and Middle stages (Jacobs, Masson, & Harvill, 2006), all describe this working stage as the time when the most significant accomplishments are realized by group members. Ideally, the working stage lasts longer than any other group stage. More important than the amount of time spent in the working stage is what is accomplished during that time. The working stage is where members are expected to derive maximum benefit as they strive to meet group goals and work toward increased personal effectiveness (Berg et al., 2006). In many ways, the previous stages are an investment of time and energy to fully prepare members to do the difficult work of the group. Thus, the forming and transition stages are certainly crucial to the success of the group because they help to prepare the group for success. That success, however, is realized in the working stage.

The working stage is distinct from the previous stages in several important ways. First, with the struggles for power and positioning within the group resolved, or at least well in hand, the group members fall into a so-called comfort zone, where each member understands and perhaps even embraces the direction of the group and her or his role in the group. Thus, the time and energy previously spent negotiating internal conflicts are redirected toward fulfilling the purpose of the group, with a more unified and cohesive group ready to get to work. While usually far from a utopian environment, the working stage is typically characterized by certain dynamics expected to be present in the group, such as group cohesion, trust, open communication, teamwork, and a motivation to succeed. To a large degree, those characteristics are a direct result of the resolution of the conflicts of tension during the transition stage. A group that successfully manages the power struggles and role conflicts of the transition stage develops a certain cohesiveness: members identify with one another, understand their roles, and share a collective vision of the group and the direction it is heading. Part of this cohesion is a deep sense of genuine caring that members develop for each other individually and for the group as a collective entity. A sense of trust in each other and in the group process is also present at the working stage, which is often a result of members negotiating conflicts during the control stage with respect and honest communication.

Cohesion is such an important aspect of the working stage that it deserves some special attention before we move on. Cohesion is not something that happens at the working stage but has been developing from the first moment that the group formed. Cohesion is the beneficial outcome of the group members struggling to know one another and find their collective place in the group matrix. It is a fluid element: Cohesion increases when the group participates in activities associated with cohesion (e.g., sharing, trust building, listening, attendance, constructive feedback), and it decreases when member participate in activities that run counter to its formation (e.g., superficial talk, sarcasm, breaking group norms as set by the group members).

Often in the pre–working stage and beginning working stage moments, leaders can perceive evidence of cohesion as group attendance becomes steady, as if a group norm has been set

that "you miss a lot of good stuff when you don't come to group." Group members will also speak directly to each other and rely less on the group leader. As the sense of cohesion solidifies, the group members notice a difference, even if they cannot define it. For example, it is common to hear group members say after a strenuous group session, "This is starting to feel like a nice place to be" or "Things felt different today."

As the group members become more cohesive, with trust and genuine caring present among them, the group is able to take its attention away from preparation and focus more on action. This orientation toward achievement and accomplishment of goals is a very important component of the working stage. Without it, a group may feel very close to each other and enjoy pleasant group sessions, but it may not be growing or experiencing anything therapeutic. Once fully prepared and encouraged, armed with a connection to the group, a sense of purpose, and a feeling of safety that comes from the support of the group, members are motivated to accomplish their goals.

But it is a mistake to characterize the working stage as some perfect environment in which everyone is pulling seamlessly in the same direction and everything is perfectly aligned. Indeed, the working stage still presents leaders and members with plenty of challenges, not to mention that leader and member missteps can lead the group in unanticipated directions or backward into renewed conflict and anxiety. Thus, the leader needs to be vigilant about potential pitfalls, skillful in the implementation of techniques, and mindful of the critical role that group process and dynamics play within successful groups.

The preceding was a brief introduction to and definition of the working stage, and a quick sketch of the characteristics that are typical of a working stage. The next section will more fully explore the working stage, specifically presenting the goals of that stage, the roles that members are expected to play, and the leader's role in the working stage. In addition, the theoretical and conceptual framework often presented in textbooks about groups will be contrasted with a more realistic, practical view of the development of a working stage from the leader's perspective.

GOALS OF THE WORKING STAGE

Leaders are expected to accomplish certain outcomes during the working stage. First and foremost, the primary outcome for the working stage is for group members to meet the individual and group goals identified during the planning phase and the forming and orienting stage of the group. The goals of the working stage should be measurable so that members know when they have met their goals. Although this is certainly ideal and worth striving for, developing measurable goals is more difficult in certain groups and with some members. A smoking cessation group will have an easily identifiable goal: reducing smoking rates. A group for children of divorce, however, may have a more nebulous goal of "coping better with my parents' divorce." In this case, it may be helpful for group leaders to define specific objectives for the group. Objectives for a divorce group may be (1) understanding that children are not to blame, (2) identifying social supports, and (3) developing strategies for staying out of parental conflict. These objectives will be more easily measurable than the overarching goal of "coping with my parents' divorce."

In addition to meeting the individual and group goals, leaders should be aware of several other important aspects of a well-functioning working stage. For instance, during the working stage, group members should develop an appreciation for being part of a well-functioning group. The hope is that group members will develop both an understanding of *what* was accomplished and *how* it was achieved. Several writers (e.g., Klein, 2001) have discussed the importance of teamwork to the ultimate success of the group, with evidence that the act of being committed to and actively participating in a productive team is therapeutic in and of itself (Maples, 1992). This feeling of accomplishment arises not just from meeting goals, but from meeting goals *together*. This can be particularly important for children and adolescents, for whom feeling connected to one's peer group is essential (Berg et al., 2006). Group members can experience satisfaction from knowing they trusted and depended on their peers during their journey, and that the personal and interpersonal risks they took were crucial to their success. Knowing that their peers were able to trust and depend on them can improve students' sense of relational self-efficacy. Whatever the specific goals of the group, the effect of being part of a unified group that has met and overcome challenges on the way to accomplishing goals can have a great impact on the members, particularly for members who may not have had successful experiences working with others.

Another salient group goal of the working stage is the development of group members' social awareness through their interactions with the group. Research has demonstrated that group counseling and psychotherapy provide certain therapeutic factors that are not prominent in individual counseling, including interpersonal learning, altruism, and family reenactment (Fuhriman & Burlingame, 1990), and that the primary vehicle for such therapeutic change in group settings is the relationships formed within the group (Holmes & Kivlighan, 2000). As group members progress through the working stage, they become more self-reflective and better able to take an in-depth inventory of themselves, and they develop an understanding of themselves and their ability to function in a social context. In this way, the group begins to take advantage of the social microcosm provided by the group: members use the group as a "social lab" to practice new behaviors, role-play new identities, and learn more about themselves through feedback in a safe and respectful environment (Yalom & Leszcz, 2005). This is a particularly important aspect of group work with adolescents, when social and interpersonal development plays such a prominent role.

When group members experience genuine feedback about specific behaviors in an environment that is characterized by accurate empathy, trust, and genuine concern, group members may be able to distinguish between their behavior and their sense of self, perhaps for the first time (Yalom & Leszcz, 2005). This can enable members to receive feedback on their social interactions without having that feedback shatter or provide a foundation for their entire self-concept. Given the trust in the group and the ability to separate their behavior from their self-concept, members may no longer feel the need to protect themselves from honest feedback. Instead, they can use that feedback to deepen their awareness and, if desired, alter their social behavior.

MEMBERS' ROLE IN THE WORKING STAGE

In the working stage, the role that the members play in the group can change dramatically. This change is largely a result of the members developing a sense of identity with other members of the group and fully accepting the group's purpose and method. In many ways "*the* group" becomes "*our* group" as the members take on more responsibility for the process of the group within each session and the overall journey the group is making toward its goal. One of the ways members show the responsibility they have taken for the group is by playing a more active role in group discussions. Group members are likely to communicate directly with each other rather than through the group leader. In addition, group members are more willing to start conversations, more able to add insights that take the conversations deeper, and more likely to identify important themes in the group's discussion. One group counselor trainee wrote about these dynamics in her leadership journal:

> The group has begun to "take over" the group. It's like they have incorporated my way of leading the group and have started doing it for themselves. For example, today in group, instead of starting the group by saying, "Let's begin today with a check-in. Who would like to start?" one of the group members said, "Well, let's do check-in. I guess I'll go first." The group then just took off. I don't think I said anything for about 15 minutes. I didn't even have to remind them to speak directly to one another. They were talking about trust and they moved deftly between relating trust issues they have had and are having in group (one member was confronted for being consistently late) and how

it relates to trust issues they have with others outside the group.

Group members are also expected to take more risks in the working stage. Conflict has been experienced and processed in constructive ways in the preceding transition stage, and this sets the groundwork for the risk taking experienced in the working stage. Leaders may notice that members will appear to drop their façades and begin acting in a more authentic, genuine way within the group. This behavior can become contagious; members who may be more reluctant to take risks can find courage in the successes of other members. Members may also practice new behaviors, first in the group itself, then in the "real world," in an attempt to discover a new way of being that is more effective and healthier. Members in the working stage are also willing to ask for genuine feedback from other group members about their new strategies, and they are willing to give genuine and appropriate feedback to other members about their behavior.

Finally, group members engage in appropriate self-disclosure in the working stage. Self-disclosure can be extremely beneficial for a group member as a way to help other members better understand the discloser, as a way to demonstrate empathy for another member, or as simply a cathartic experience. This appropriate self-disclosure is more than just talking about oneself; it is disclosing meaningful and relevant aspects of the individual's self that would previously have remained hidden. For the self-disclosure to be effective, it must be on-topic, productive, and appropriate given the group's stage and level of functioning. During the working stage, self-disclosure is often characterized by immediacy, relating to one's internal reactions to what it currently going on in the group. Here are two examples.

EXAMPLE 1 **Lester**

It's weird, but this whole group thing is uncomfortable. I'm not used to talking about feelings and stuff like that. It's weird because I feel like I don't want to talk, but I usually feel good after I do.

EXAMPLE 2 Anna

When I listen to Alexis struggle with her issues, there is a part of me that understands, but another part is telling me to be quiet, to not share, because my problems seem so small compared to hers.

Both of these self-disclosure examples allow for the group to explore the deeper meanings of the feelings, at a group and individual member level. For many members, Lester's experience of discomfort with emotional vulnerability will be present. Instead of scaring group members with the warning that emotions can uncomfortable, this disclosure at the working stage is an invitation to explore universal vulnerability. Likewise, Anna's disclosure may produce anxiety in earlier stages of the group as members separate into "those with serious issues versus those who are normal" subgroups, but at the working stage, the flow is not interrupted and discussion will probably go deeper into two areas: Anna's need to trivialize her issues and Alexis's genuine response to Anna's categorization of her personal struggles. During the working stage, members are expected to make these types of process disclosures without interrupting the flow; in fact, they are seen as enhancing the process.

As the member's self-disclosures become more real and immediate, group members also take responsibility for the group by supporting other members' growth and development. Group members can help each other grow from the group experience in a variety of ways. First, by being able to demonstrate accurate empathy and a genuine concern for one another, members can encourage others to take the risks inherent in behavioral change or personal growth. By balancing this genuine concern with a willingness to challenge one another, members can help each other find the courage within themselves to take reasonable risks knowing that, if they falter, the group will be there to make sure they don't fall too far. This will likely look very different from

the way group members may have expressed care for one another earlier in the group, when members often attempt to protect or rescue members from difficult situations. Consider this example from a divorce group:

LUCY: It really doesn't matter anyway. It's not like I can do anything about my mom's decision to leave us. I don't even think I care anymore.

CHARLES: I think you do care; otherwise you wouldn't be so mad.

LUCY: I'm not mad!

PATTY: You sound mad to me. I think sometimes it's easier to pretend we don't care than admit we are hurt. I know that's how it is for me. I mean, my dad is gone. What's the use of being mad? He'll never know.

CHARLES: That's what is so crazy! Most of us are confused or hurt by our parents breaking up, and yet we feel like we can't be honest about our feelings or if we are, that it won't matter anyway. That's screwed up.

LUCY: What do you mean, "screwed up"?

CHARLES: I mean that we should do better than what most of our parents are doing. We should learn how to express ourselves openly.

COUNSELOR: It sounds like that is what you are all doing right now.

And then consider this example from a group of male domestic violence offenders:

JIMMY: Look, I don't care what you say! My dad was a good man. I'm sure he had reasons for leaving us and treating us the way he did. I don't really care anyway.

CARL: I think you do care; otherwise, you wouldn't be so mad.

JIMMY: You don't know what you're talking about.

LOUIS: You know, I don't think this is about your dad or what Carl is saying. I think this is about you and your decision to leave your family.

JIMMY: Oh, are you psychoanalyzing me?

LOUIS: No. I'm just trying to hear what you are really talking about. I would understand if you felt bad about leaving your family. Even if you have your reasons, it still feels bad.

JIMMY: I wonder if my dad felt bad.

CARL: Maybe he did. Maybe he didn't, but it looks like you feel pretty sad, angry, or something. Maybe we should stop talking about your dad for awhile and talk about you. I think we would rather hear about you than your dad. I mean, I think we care more about you than your dad.

In these examples, the message that group members send each other changes from "I care about you so I'll protect you from difficult experiences" to "I care about you so I'll support you as you learn from these difficult experiences." In the working stage, members begin to take a much more active role in the process of their group. Capitalizing on the well-developed atmosphere of cohesion, group members more openly share and provide honest feedback to each other in an attempt to solve group and personal goals. As the group becomes more self-sufficient and self-monitoring, the leader is suddenly faced with the question, "Now that the group is running like a well-oiled machine, what am I supposed to do?" The next section outlines how leaders can make the most out of the working stage.

LEADER'S ROLE IN THE WORKING STAGE

Just as the members' roles begin to change as the working stage progresses, the leader's role must also adapt. As the members take on greater responsibility for the group's functioning, the leader may become less directive, serving more as a process monitor and group facilitator. The following story from the *Tao of Pooh* illustrates the possible stance of the group leader during this stage:

> At the Gorge of Lu, a great waterfall plunges for thousands of feet, its spray visible for miles. In the churning waters below, no living creature can be seen. One day K'ung Fu-tse [Confucius] was standing a distance from the pool's edge, when he saw an old man being tossed about in the turbulent water. He called to his disciples, and together they ran to rescue the victim. But by the time they reached the water, the old man had climbed out onto the bank and was walking along, singing to himself. K'ung Fu-tse hurried up to him. "You would have to be a ghost to survive that," he said, "but you seem to be a man instead. What secret power do you have?" "Nothing special," the old man replied. "I began to learn while very young, and grew up practicing it. Now I am certain of success. I go down with the water and come up with the water. I follow it and forget myself. I survive because I don't struggle against the water's superior power. That's all." (Hoff, 1982, pp. 68–69)

In this story, the old man is a good symbol for the leader at the working stage, and the river represents the group. The story illustrates that the leader is not absent from the group but is still part of the process. By the time the group reaches the working stage, the group should have a way of running itself, and leaders often get into trouble when they try to force their will on the group instead of attending to the underlying process. When we hear group leaders talk about problems with their group, it is often because they are blocking the forward momentum of the members. The mental image could be the group leader acting as a dam in the river. Group leaders must learn when to trust the group and when to intervene.

Although the leader should support the members' efforts to take more responsibility for the group functioning, that does not mean that the leaders should give up responsibility for the group. The members may take more of a hands-on approach regarding group discussion and processing, but it is still the counselor's responsibility to lead the group. Ultimately, the leader is still responsible for the group's movement toward its final goal, even if the leader's role is not as obvious. However, the functions that a leader performs in this stage—balancing content and process, modeling behavior, encouraging introspection, and managing difficult situations—are vital to the ultimate success of the group.

Leaders of groups in the working stage must be on the lookout for difficult situations in which they may have to intervene. Even in a highly functioning group, situations can come up that can put the group at risk for stagnation or regression. Personal setbacks, particularly if related to the goal of the group, can discourage members, sapping their motivation to continue taking risks. Likewise, topics that are typically very emotional or sensitive for members, such as issues regarding race, sexual orientation, or members' status in society, can leave members feeling defensive, attacked, or disillusioned. At these times, it is important for leaders to reassert themselves and to be willing to manage the situation through open, genuine, and respectful communication.

Managing the situation does not mean that a leader should become authoritarian and take over the group, even if the members would prefer that at times. For instance, examine the anger management group at a high school discussed in Case Study 9.1.

It is no doubt difficult to decide when to let the group go and when to facilitate. The river metaphor encourages leaders to appreciate the power of the group's process, but it does not give much guidance as to how to interact when a group is regressing to an earlier stage. One metaphor to provide some guidance is an old, very simple childhood game: Take a large tire (the bigger the better) and roll it. That's it. That's the game. Like with group work, much of the work is in the beginning. You have to select a tire, struggle to get it upright and then push it really hard to get it to roll. Also much like group work, once you get it rolling, your job (here comes the fun part) is to run beside the tire and keep it rolling. If the tire starts to wobble or lose speed, that is the time to act. You give it a gentle push, and the tire often corrects itself and continues down the street. Like the tire game, by the time the group reaches the working stage, it is assumed that the leader has done an effective job of co-creating an atmosphere that builds momentum in the group. During the working stage, the leader's job becomes keeping pace with the group and correcting the wobbles, as evidenced by behaviors or attitudes that interrupt the momentum. Often these corrections come in the form of gentle reminders or process observations that the group can incorporate and then use to self-correct.

One of the most important roles that leaders can play during the working stage is negotiating the balance between content and process in the group. In this situation, content is defined as the information related during group discussions, or the what of the group interactions, whereas process is defined as the dynamics that occur within the group during group sessions, or the how of the group interactions (Geroski & Kraus, 2002). Members with reasonable social and communication skills will likely be able to track the content of the conversation, a more basic communication skill (although when leading groups with very young children, even this can be a challenge!) However, it cannot be assumed that children and adolescents will attend to the emotional

CASE STUDY 9.1

The Anger Management Group

The administration asked me if I would start an anger management group, which I was, of course, happy to do. The members of the group were referred from the administration, and originally, the group consisted of three members: one white female, one African American male, and one African American female. The group was open-ended and met once a week for five weeks, without any additional members added. I felt we had developed a solid working relationship with each other, and were really starting to get to work. Slowly, additional members were referred to the group by the school's administration, and each time the new members were welcomed.

However, when the group got to six members, five of which were African American, I began worrying about what the members thought about the makeup of the group not looking like the makeup of the school, which was majority White. I was certainly aware of this. I also worried about how they might view me, a White male, in light of this. More than anything, I was worried that the racial issues may disrupt a group that was functioning so well. I had a choice. To deal with the issue of unbalanced racial representation would take time away from the group's curriculum, and risk damaging the group's working alliance. However, to ignore the issue might save time for the anger management curriculum, but whatever work would be done would likely be very superficial if it is not the issue that the members are focused on.

I decided not only to discuss the racial issue, but to be the one to bring it up. The next session, I said, "I can't help but notice that the makeup of this group is not like the makeup of the school, and I'm wondering what it must be like for you to look around and see that the students identified as having anger problems are almost all African American." This led to an important discussion that took up the majority of the group for the next several sessions. In the end, I know it was productive, and I think many of the members appreciated my asking about it. I think it affected how they saw me, and helped our working alliance. It probably took time away from anger management strategies, but it was definitely time well spent.

Although not part of the curriculum as it was designed, the conversation was vital to the group members getting any further work done, and it set a model for how to deal with difficult and sensitive issues in an honest and forthright manner. In addition, and most important, the discussion helped the group function at a higher level than it had previously.

---

content underlying the discussion or identify the dynamics present in the here and now of the group session. If allowed to focus on content at the expense of the underlying emotions or group dynamics, the group could miss some important opportunities to build self-awareness. On the other hand, a group of adolescents who have learned to make comments on emotions or to process group dynamics can become a little too enamored with process observations, bogging themselves down as they process and process to the point where little

gets accomplished. One can probably imagine this happening with a group of adolescents as they first learn to understand group process and become very proud of their new "depth." Helping the group maintain the balance between attending to content and process remains the leader's responsibility. This balance can be difficult to maintain, but it is an important factor in group learning and growth. Consider this example of group members attending to process from a fifth-grade "Skills for Living" group.

BILLY: I just hate school. It's stupid and nothing we learn is really going to help us at all in life. I mean, who needs quadratic equations anyway? (The content issue here is Billy's dislike of school and his inability to find meaning. The process issue is Billy's search for meaning inside the group. Could it be that he also sees the group as meaningless? The process question is, How does the content comment on the member's perspective of the group? At this point the leader could make that process observation, but in the working stage, group members are becoming skilled at seeing process opportunities.)

STEPHANIE: Billy, maybe you feel group is a waste of time, too. Are you questioning the use of time here? I know I do sometimes, especially when I first started.

BILLY: Well, yeah. It just seems like we don't do much. (Stephanie's process comment brought the discussion into the here and now and avoided the "school is dumb" debate that may have occurred in earlier stages of the group. The comfort level is such that Billy can explore his current feelings.)

STEPHANIE: Yeah, sometimes we don't do much but talk, but talking is good, too. You have good things to say. Maybe you could participate more by giving feedback? You know, to tell you the truth, I don't know that much about you.

ZACH: Yeah, me either. Maybe if you shared a little bit more, you would think this was more worthwhile.

At this point, the group members become engaged to help Billy find meaning in the group by encouraging him to participate in activities that have made the group meaningful to each of the members, namely, through feedback and sharing. In this way, the members reinforce the norms of the groups and attempt to ensure its momentum.

Another important role that a leader can play in the working stage is that of role model. Specifically, leaders model the behaviors that they would like to see from members during the working stage. This modeling may be different from the modeling that the leader has shown in previous stages, when the goal was to help members develop connections among each other and get accustomed to the novelty of being part of a group. Leaders may be among the first in the group to challenge members to take risks and to support members in the efforts to stretch, be authentic within the group setting, and self-disclose appropriately. Take the following example from a group of adults with social anxiety; they are talking about what they've accomplished so far.

SARAH: Well, let's see . . . I know I've made it to every group session; I guess that's an accomplishment for me.

LEIGH: Yeah, I've noticed you've been here for each group, and I do think that is a significant accomplishment. And, at the same time, I feel like I still don't really know you well, even though we've been in group together for eight weeks.

SARAH: (beginning to tear up) That's hard to hear. I want to get to know everyone. I guess I'm just still not sure what to do.

KAKKI: I think I know how you feel, Sarah. Even though Leigh didn't say that to me, I was thinking that she probably doesn't know me very well either. Probably none of you do. I guess I thought I could learn a lot from just showing up, but it's harder than I thought.

LEADER: It *is* hard to let others get to know the real you, isn't it? But I think that's why we are here. It sounds like you would like to get to know each other on a little bit deeper level, and maybe to let others know you a bit better as well. Any ideas how we start doing that?

The members in this example wanted to do more than show up, both in group and in life, but the anxiety they felt prevented them from taking that first step. Once Leigh challenged the group in a supportive way, the members realized that they needed to work on a deeper level if they were to get what they wanted out of the group. This realization fundamentally changed the work to be done in the group, and challenged the group members to strive for more.

It is also important that group leaders continue to deepen and refine their self-reflection, risk-taking, and interpersonal skills throughout the working stage. In reality, the working stage is not a stage but part of a continuum of growth that members will experience throughout the group. Thus, members do not truly reach the working stage; rather, they continually develop through the working stage. As group members begin to demonstrate more self-reflective, authentic, and courageous behavior in group, group leaders can acknowledge the benefits of such risks and motivate members to take further steps. As members feel more comfortable sharing their deep thoughts, group leaders can encourage those members to explore their thoughts even more deeply. As members take small risks, group leaders support their strides and encourage them to take bigger ones. As group members demonstrate trust for one another, group leaders can help develop an even greater sense of intimacy.

THE WORKING STAGE AND CO-LEADERSHIP CONSIDERATIONS

Although the preceding section provided an overview of leadership roles primarily from the perspective of a single leader group, the literature asserts that many groups are facilitated by more than one leader (Roller & Nelson, 1991; Rosenbaum, 1983; Yalom & Leszcz, 2005). Co-leadership is a leadership modality in which the relationship between the co-leaders serves as a therapeutic tool. It is interesting to note that co-leader relationships develop in much the same manner as groups: proceeding through stages of development (Dick, Lessler, & Whiteside, 1980; Fall & Wejnert, 2005; Gallogly & Levine, 1979; Winter, 1976). Ideally, the two develop in tandem, but facilitators should be mindful of the developmental aspects of the co-leader relationship that can affect the growth of the group.

ACTIVITY 9.1

In dyads, brainstorm the benefits and challenges of working with co-leader, particularly during the working stage. Reflecting on a time when you were a member of a group that was facilitated by multiple group leaders (e.g., counseling group, team, course, organization), describe how the experience was more positive as a result of having more than one group leader. If it was a negative experience, how did having multiple group leaders affect your group experience?

Co-leaders who have successfully moved into the working stage specifically use their interpersonal structure as a mechanism to help maintain the momentum of the group and fine-tune the co-leader relationship. Similar to the group's management of resistance and conflict, resistance between the co-leaders can be experienced and managed, and power and expertise issues between the leaders can be processed and resolved. In the working stage, co-leaders use two skills, forecasting and open processing, to maintain a smooth flow of communication. Using forecasting, a co-leader may state, "I am picking up on a theme of honesty in what each of you are saying. Why don't we push below the surface and explore this thread." Instead of abruptly changing the direction of the group, forecasting allows one co-leader to communicate to the other leader and the group as a whole where the line of processing is going. Another key skill is open processing, sometimes called process observation. Open processing is the act of sharing internal dialogue with the entire group. The unique application of open processing for co-leadership includes the discussion or commentary that goes on between co-leaders, in addition to the observations made directly to the group. For example, a co-leader may say, "I noticed a lot of tension in the group as we began to talk about Mark's reaction to last week's discussion." Or the co-leader may say about specific leadership issues, "Leroy (co-leader), can we stop for a minute and talk about what's going on in the group? I think I might be a little lost."

Although both of these techniques may seem basic to quality group leadership and may occur in different ways throughout the life of the group, they are most potent in the working stage. In earlier stages, group leaders are less likely to forecast, and they typically change direction as a way to gain control of the group. They are also probably less likely to use open processing due to inadequacy fears. The hallmark of the working stage is a high-functioning relationship, and both forecasting and open processing allow the leaders to model the behaviors and skills the group strives to attain. In the above examples, note how the forecasting example models the importance of communicating with the group as a method for understanding, an important skill for all group members. Open processing models the importance of not censoring one's inner dialogue, comfort with being vulnerable, and trusting the group as a whole. Two seasoned co-leaders remarked, "Our clients claim the major advantage for them in co-therapy is role modeling . . . part of the process of therapy is teaching people how to be close with each other . . . because we model closeness, we are able to help them achieve it" (Goulding & Goulding, 1991, p. 207).

Much like the experience of the group members, the working stage is a time to reap the benefits of a good working relationship between the co-leaders. Group members move away from the dependence on the leaders and begin to process issues on their own. Co-leaders use the harmony of this stage as a way to deepen the co-leader relationship and its impact on the group. In earlier stages of development, co-leaders are encouraged to receive consultation and/or supervision to minimize and identify unhealthy trends in the co-leader relationship, but in the working stage, co-leaders may become less dependent on supervision because they find they can address issues with one another in an open and honest manner (Fall & Wejnert, 2005). As with group development, co-leaders who maintain awareness of the relationship can continue the productivity of this stage until the group ends or begins the transition to the termination stage.

THE REAL WORKING STAGE

Although the stages of groups are often presented in a linear model with clear boundaries (as they are presented here in this text), in practice, the stages of groups are rarely so clearly defined. In fact, the way group stages are often presented in the literature is primarily an academic concept because the stages are derived from clinical observation rather than evidence provided by research (Berg et al., 2006). In practice, the boundaries between stages of group development are more nebulous than the clearly delineated categories presented in textbooks. In addition, the development of groups often presents with an ebb-and-flow pattern rather than a linear progression. Events that happen between group members outside the group can also affect the group members inside group sessions, and a group that is solidly in the working stage one week can regress to an earlier stage the next. The following example from a fifth- and sixth-grade children-of-divorce group (in a K–8 school) demonstrates how quickly the working stage can be threatened.

> KARA: Ms. Jones, we have a problem we need to deal with right now. I had some fifth-grade girls ask me about what I talked about in here last week, and that means that Jessica told

them what I said in group. I don't think she should be in the group anymore.

JESSICA: That's not true, and I already told her I didn't say anything to anyone. And I don't like being accused of lying or talking behind someone's back, so that's fine. I don't want to be in the same group as Kara anyway.

RITA: Ms. Jones, if they don't want to be together, why don't we just split into two groups? We could have a fifth-grade group and a sixth-grade group. Then Kara and Jessica won't have to be in the same group.

MS. JONES: Well, maybe we can talk about that as an option, but before we jump to that, let me ask you something. Does this situation remind anyone of anything?

RITA: (after a pause) Oh my gosh! We're getting a divorce!

MS. JONES: Wow. Can you explain what you mean?

JESSICA: I get it. We're having a problem, so we just decide to split up, like our parents did.

MS. JONES: Okay. So, now that we know that, I guess you all need to decide if you want to handle this by splitting up, or if you want to try something different.

KARA: I don't want to split up. I'm willing to try to work this out, even if it is difficult.

As the group members identified that they were, in effect, reenacting a divorce scenario, they reconsidered their plan to split up and rededicated themselves to working through the breach of trust. Although this put the group back to an earlier stage where they were once again managing conflict, it was necessary to do that in order to get back to an effective working stage. The process of working out a conflict when it would have been easier to simply split was itself an important therapeutic intervention, especially for this particular population.

Just as a group does not always progress in a linear fashion, the group members may not progress through the stages in unison. Once again, this is particularly true of groups with children and adolescents, where developmental differences within the group can affect how members process the information and the depth of their understanding of the group process. In addition, some group members are sometimes ready to commit to group goals, and others are still holding on to past conflicts or feeling insecure about their place in the group. Consider the Case Study 9.2 about a young men's group.

CASE STUDY 9.2

The Young Men's Group

The group was a place for young adult males to discuss what it meant to them to be a man and to develop strategies to become the type of man they wanted to be. One of the topics that was particularly important to this group was their relationships with their fathers. There were various father-son issues present in the group, with many of the members feeling a strained relationship with their fathers due to frequent conflicts, divorce, and lack of time spent with the fathers. With the exception of one member, all the young adult males were highly motivated to work on these issues and make changes in their current relationships with their father. The exception was a young man, Korey, whose father had left his family and moved away with his new family. While other members bonded over their difficult relationships, Korey shared very little, choosing instead to focus on his relationship with his stepfather because, as he said, his father "didn't matter to him anyway." Yet as the group became more cohesive, encouraged each other to share their experiences, and try new ways of thinking about or interacting with their fathers, Korey grew more distant from the group. They had charged ahead to the working stage, but he was still stuck. What was more, seeing the others begin to work on what he was afraid of most, building a relationship with his dad, led to his feeling even more left out.

Had Korey been part of a group that was more tentative or slower-paced, he might have been more successful in the group. But his vulnerability kept him from taking the risks the others were willing to take, and their excitement to get to work made it difficult for them to know how to encourage him to join them. Although most members of the group were doing the work of a working stage, Korey was not at the same stage.

Presenting the group stages in a linear fashion certainly helps novice group leaders conceptualize the working stage, its goals, and its process. However, there is also benefit in realizing that group development is rarely so neat and streamlined. Knowing that different groups progress at different rates and that members within the same group may progress at different rates can help a novice group leader to be more patient. Like the old man in the river, leaders can allow the group to proceed on its own course and at its own pace rather than struggling against it or giving up. At the same time, understanding that groups ebb and flow can help leaders to identify when a group may be turned around and look for the opportunities to help the group get reoriented so they can get back to work as soon as possible.

Understanding the differences in group development can also help group leaders identify when a group is not working, even when the leader feels that the group has been running long enough and they "should" be in the working stage by now. This is particularly important in more structured groups, psychoeducational groups, or classroom guidance, where leaders plan their groups and organize their topics with a prediction of when a group "should" be in the working stage. But advancing to the working stage is less about time spent in group and more about conflicts resolved. If leaders do not pay attention to where the members are regarding the group stages, they run the risk of forging ahead to the work of the group while leaving the group

members, or many of them, behind. This can lead to frustration on the part of the leaders, who may see the members as "resisting," and can lead to largely ineffective groups.

So how does a group leader know when group members are ready to begin the working stage? The absence of the characteristics mentioned so far (e.g., group cohesion, trust, a willingness to take risks, a commitment to work toward goals) would be one indicator that a group is not functioning as it should. However, there are other indicators as well. For instance, if the group membership appears to consist of several cliques of members rather than a whole group, it is an indication that the group has not come together and developed that sense of "we-ness" that is characteristic of a working group. Until the group members fully form one identity, the members will have difficulty functioning at a high level.

ACTIVITY 9.2

Brainstorm ways in which subgrouping may occur in groups in elementary, middle, and high schools. As a leader, how can you minimize this phenomenon in these settings?

A further complication to recognizing when a group has not yet entered the working stage is that, in many ways, the working stage is a welcome relief from the tension that permeates

CASE STUDY 9.3

The Counseling Group

The members of the group were not unlike many counseling students: highly social, well liked, considerate students who were used to getting along with people. In addition, because they had made it into a master's degree program, they were willing to work hard and they were used to succeeding. As the group began, everyone got along well, and they were anxious to set goals for the group and get to work. I was so excited to have a group that appeared to navigate their way through the transition stage so well. They had open discussions about how they will share honest feedback and handle conflicts with respect and sensitivity. And, to be honest, I wasn't very excited about dealing with conflict anyway. But as they got to what should have been the working stage, I noticed that the conversation seemed superficial. I began to get bored with the group and wondered exactly where the group was heading. I began to realize that perhaps the group, full of individuals used to being liked and seen as highly sociable, sort of faked their way into the working stage. They discussed how they would handle conflict in the group, but they never really allowed a conflict to surface. And I, as the leader, let them get away with it because I was happy not to deal with conflict as well.

the transition stage of the group, for group members and leaders alike. The welcome relief from tension, however, can lead group leaders to believe a group has entered into the working stage when the group may have simply made an implicit group decision to continue without fully resolving conflict. As an example, consider the counseling group presented in Case Study 9.3.

The members of the counseling group in Case Study 9.3 may have said all the right things to indicate they were ready to work and even demonstrated some of the characteristics of a true working stage in the group, such as direct and respectful communication and an increased focus on meeting group goals. However, without having truly worked through conflicts, they entered a fake working stage that was pleasant enough but not productive. A group working around rather than working through internal conflict can certainly make things easier during sessions, but without a deep intimacy, the results of the group will be as superficial as the relationships.

In addition, if the goals of the group and the ways in which group members will reach their goals remain unclear to the members, this may be a sign that not all members are in agreement or that the group as a whole is not in agreement with the group leader. If the group is displaying some resistance in the work expected of them, or if members are missing sessions, being quiet, stalling, or taking the discussion on unproductive tangents, the members may not trust the group enough to take the risk of being authentic, may not trust the process of group work, or may not feel supported in their efforts to grow.

The presence of collusion is also an indication that the group may not be functioning at a high level. Collusion occurs when group members conspire to work against the growth of the group members and often manifests itself in the protection of, or ganging up on, certain members or the leader. It is probably easier to think of examples where group members gang up on a less powerful member—in fact, it is part of the social norms for many later elementary and middle school students! However, it is also common for members to band together against the leader. For instance, when a group member is being challenged to try a different behavioral strategy, other members may come to that member's rescue by making excuses for the member and questioning the rationale behind the group leader forcing them to do work that they do not want to do. Or members may rally around a

CASE STUDY 9.4

The Counselor Supervision Group

We were in week four or five of the supervision group, and I remember feeling like we needed to start getting to work. We had been talking about a lot of conceptual ideas, like ethical considerations in school and what-if scenarios, but the tapes the supervisees were supposed to bring in were slow in coming. Finally, a student, who was seen as a leader among her peers and had good counseling skills, brought in a tape of her meeting with a student. It was not her best work, and she seemed a bit reluctant to share it. After listening to some of the tape, I asked her peers for their thoughts. They were largely supportive, noting that the student seemed comfortable and she seemed to be following the conversation well. I took their feedback as a signal that they did not yet know the rules for feedback, so I told her that I appreciated the risk she took bringing in a tape that she did not appear too happy with. I reported that I was confused about her understanding of the client and wondered aloud where she wanted to go with him. Upon hearing this, the rest of the group quickly came to her defense, stating that she may be having a bad day, and saying how difficult it is to work with a student in the middle of a school day. It felt very much like me against them, and I was taken aback by how protective they were of their peer. It was only later that I saw this collusion as an indicator of their own anxiety. They were not protecting her from my critical feedback as much as they were protecting themselves from future criticism. After all, if I wasn't happy with the work of a student generally acknowledged to have good counseling skills, what would I say about their work? With this new realization, we were able to step back and deal with the anxiety about judgment that was in the room. Once that was (mostly) resolved, we were able to enter a much more productive and comfortable working stage.

particularly powerful group member to begin challenging the leader's strategy as a way to maintain the status quo, thus protecting themselves from being expected to try new things. These types of behaviors, no matter when in the group they are exhibited, are a sign that the group is not yet in a fully functioning working stage; see Case Study 9.4, an example of a supervision group for school counseling students.

Perhaps the most productive way to conceptualize the presence of collusion, like that in Case Study 9.4, is to consider it as evidence of either being stuck or regressing to the transition stage. It is common in the transition stage for group members to practice conflict resolution, with the leader being the target of conflict because the leader is often the one member of the group that members can trust to handle conflict appropriately. As mentioned, if the leader avoids the conflict or mishandles it, the group can fail to proceed or can regress. The following example

illustrates a leader who correctly identifies the transition stage issue, attends to the process, respectfully handles the cultural issues, and facilitates the group through the confrontation.

RICK: (a 35-year-old African American new member in ongoing anger management group) This group is crap. I'm just here 'cause I have to be here. I've been to White counselors and stuff dozens of time, but it never helps. You don't know me, you don't know anything about me, hell, you probably ain't even smart as me. How you gonna teach me anything?

LEADER: You are right, Rick. I don't know you, and because I don't know you, it makes sense that you don't trust me.

RICK: Damn right. I don't trust you or anyone else in this room!

LEADER: That makes sense. I don't blame you for not trusting anyone. I hope that will change, but that's up to you. I don't know who you are as a person, and I don't know if I can teach you anything. For me to assume I know you, having just met you, would be pretty arrogant on my part. I just hope that you will teach me and the others here what we need to know about you and maybe when we get to know you, we will begin to understand. But we'll respect you doing that at your own pace.

RICK: Yeah, well, we'll see.

The leader identified that he was being confronted by Rick, and he was also aware that the group was watching to see how he handled it. He felt attacked, and he wanted to attend to and answer the content issue by proving his competence (e.g., quote his résumé, list his degrees, etc., or try to convince Rick that because the leader is White doesn't matter). Instead he looks for the process issue: "What is he really saying?" By attending to the process message of "You don't understand me," the group leader was able to work with the resistance and demonstrate understanding. The group (an ongoing group in the working stage) was able to get a reinforcement of the skills of conflict management, and Rick received an invitation to participate and an orientation to the ways of the group. This three-minute exchange highlights the complex dynamics and interactions of the working stage.

DIFFERENT WORKING STAGES FOR DIFFERENT GROUPS

Group work textbooks use different names to describe the working stage of a group, but almost all texts describe the stage in fairly general terms. Many of the designations for working stages, as they are presented in texts, appear to be part of

counseling groups based on a humanistic perspective, with a high value on interpersonal learning designed for adult populations. We know from both group work literature and practice, however, that group work varies a great deal and that groups led in schools and with children and adolescents look very different from groups for adults led in agencies or in private practice. With the vast differences in the ways groups are designed and led, it follows that no two working stages would look alike. Depending on the purpose of the group, the group format, and the theoretical perspective of the leaders, group goals may use behavioral changes (e.g., Gazda, Ginter, & Horne, 2008), cognitive restructuring (e.g., Ellis, 1997), corrective emotional experiences (e.g., Yalom & Leszcz, 2005), encouragement and a sense of belonging (e.g., Sonstegard, 1998), or any combination of the above. The following section describes how working stages may look, depending on important group variables, including the group's foundation, the design of the group, and membership variables.

Group Foundations

The group's foundations provide a basis from which many decisions about the group will be made. The foundation is the starting point for designing a group, but it also plays an important role in the working stage. Specifically, the principles that make up the group foundation dictate what is to be accomplished and how goals will be met within the working stage. Factors that are important components of the group's foundation include the general purpose and specific goals of the group, as well as the underlying theoretical perspective.

One of the most important variables affecting the process of a working stage is the goals of the group. Although the decisions about the goals for the group are usually made during the planning phase or forming and orienting stage, those decisions will have important effects on the working stage. In a group with a goal that is easily definable, the focus of the work to be done is often very clear. In a study skills group, for instance, the majority of the group process in the working stage is focused on developing members' organization skills, studying techniques, and perhaps test-taking skills. If the goal of the group is not as clearly defined, such as those for a personal growth group or women's issues group, the work to be done may be a bit more nebulous. *Personal growth* and *women's issues* can mean very different things to different group members, so the content and process during the working stage may vary from group to group, from session to session, and even from member to member.

The working stage is not only affected by the overall goal of the group, but also by how narrow or broad the desired outcomes of the group are. A well-conceived group is developed around a specific goal and sets objectives that are relevant to the overall goal and realistic to achieve given the time allotted for the group and the group format. Unfortunately, goals and objectives are not always well conceived. Furr (2000) notes that a common mistake that group leaders make is trying to having a group goal that is too broad, thus trying to cover too many topics in the course of a group. In these scenarios, the groups can become less like therapeutic experiences and more like survey courses, where a great deal of information is presented but relatively little is absorbed or incorporated into the lives of the members.

Although setting a broad goal is a mistake that is often made in the planning phase, it doesn't become obvious until the working stage. When group leaders have too much information to cover, it may take so long simply to impart the information that not enough time is left for the work to be done. This represents a scenario where there is an imbalance of time spent on content, at the expense of focusing on process. Even if the information is learned, group members may not figure out how to use the information in their lives if they do not have enough time to process it. When leaders in a working stage find themselves in a situation where they feel overwhelmed with pressure to cover a great deal of information, it may be time to reconsider the scope of the group and refine the goals so that members have enough time to integrate what they have learned thus far. It is better to have a group that addresses one issue profoundly than a group that addresses several issues superficially.

The theoretical foundation of a group influences the working stage because it can dictate both the type of change that is desired and the process through which that change should take place. Because each theoretical approach has its own values and favors different processes for effective change to occur (such as insight, interpersonal learning, behavioral change), we can expect the processes favored in the working stages of groups to be very different, too. Even when groups deal with the same population struggling with the same issue, different theoretical perspectives mean different approaches to that issue, thus leading to very different working stages. Consider a counseling group for adults with anxiety. A group coming from a psychodynamic perspective would likely be very insight-oriented, with time spent in the working stage helping members discover how their past experiences are playing out in their current difficulties with anxiety. A group using a cognitive-behavioral perspective would be more content focused and would likely teach new skills for members to practice (Petrocelli, 2002). The working stage in this type of group would likely involve less processing of group dynamics and more practice of new skills that members can use to help manage their anxiety (e.g., calming self-talk) or the use of behavioral techniques (e.g., exposure). A group using a solution-focused approach would be more likely take advantage of skills that members already have by noticing exceptions to the problem and learning from those successes (Murphy, 1997). In this case, the working stage would help students gain insight into behaviors that work for them and generalize their strengths to novel situations. A humanistic group, on the other hand, would be less concerned with directing group members to practice skills and would spend more time processing the emotional experience of the members in the here and now of the group, disclosing immediate emotions and empathizing and supporting other group members (Shechtman & Pastor, 2005). In humanistic groups, the work of the working stage is less about incorporating new information and thinking about how to generalize it to the world outside and more about being different in the moment. Finally, an Adlerian group might use aspects of all the above in the working stage, helping members develop insight into what purpose their anxiety may be serving in their lives, encouraging members to practice new behaviors by "acting as if" in the group, and using homework to encourage members to practice new ways of being when they are not in the group.

Group Design

In addition to the foundations that underlie the group, the specific group design chosen also affects the process of the working stage. Many factors must be considered in the design of the group, including the group type or format, the style of leadership, the duration of the group, and whether the group will be closed or open to new members.

Similar to the effect that the theoretical foundations of the group have on the process of the working stage, the type of group model that is chosen also influences what the working stage will look like. In a psychoeducational format, imparting information would certainly be a central therapeutic factor, and catharsis, existential factors, and altruism may not be emphasized to a great extent. On the other hand, a counseling group would rely more on the interpersonal dynamics within the group for therapeutic growth, utilizing interpersonal learning, catharsis, altruism, and existential factors to a far greater extent. Certainly a counseling group would still utilize the imparting of information and interpersonal learning, but these factors would not be used as intentionally as they would with a psychoeducational group. A psychotherapy group would more likely focus on creating more significant and profound changes in members' lives.

As an example of how the type of group can affect the working stage, imagine two groups for adolescents from divorced homes. One group is an 8-week psychoeducational group, the other group is a 15-week counseling group. The primary goal of the psychoeducational group is for the members to learn about divorce, that it is not the member's fault or responsibility, and to learn strategies for understanding and managing their emotions about the divorce. A great deal of time,

therefore, will be spent imparting the information that is to be learned, while interpersonal factors such as group cohesiveness and interpersonal learning play more of a supportive role in helping members to apply the information to their lives. The counseling group's goals, on the other hand, may include helping members to explore their emotions about the divorce, making meaning of the situation, and finding support and encouragement through the group. In this group, the leader in the working stage would focus less on imparting information to help members learn and more on allowing members to share their experiences and explore their beliefs, fears, and other feelings about the divorce. For this interpersonal learning to be effective, the group cohesiveness would be more crucial than in the psychoeducational group. In addition, interpersonal factors such as catharsis and instillation of hope are more likely to be an important part of a counseling group than they would be in a psychoeducational group.

The group leader's style of leadership also has an effect on the working stage. Whether the leader considers herself to be an educator, a facilitator, or a counselor can have an effect on how she views her role during the working stage. A workshop leader who sees her role as an educator will approach the working stage of the group as the time when the most important information is to be disseminated and processed so that it can be generalized effectively outside the group. A leader who considers himself a facilitator, such as in a support group for partners of the chronically ill, may view the working stage as the time when the members are best able to get the support and empathy they need from other members. Meanwhile, a leader who considers himself a counselor working within a male issues group may see the working stage as the time when he helps members develop insight into the masculine stereotypes that members hold and evaluate those stereotypes honestly, something most members would not feel comfortable discussing anywhere else.

Another aspect of group leadership is the leader's use of exercises or activities within the group. Although not all counseling approaches value the use of exercises in group work, most group leaders seem to agree that exercises can play an important role in group learning when they are implemented thoughtfully. In addition, for developmental reasons, children and adolescents may derive more learning from participating in exercises than through discussion alone. For many leaders, therefore, the question is not about whether to use exercises in groups, but how and when to use them. Leaders who prefer more experiential learning exercises will likely approach the working stage differently than someone who views group process from a purely discussion perspective. For a more hands-on leader who uses exercises, the working stage is when exercises are most effective or when they have the greatest impact on the members. Whereas group leaders may use teamwork-building exercises or exercises to introduce topics early in the group, the exercises used in the working stage should expose members to more complex or higher-risk topics, and they should be used to help members apply principles that were discussed earlier in the group to their own lives in a meaningful way.

Even more important than the exercises themselves is the processing of the exercise; that is when members are able to develop the interpersonal and intrapersonal learning that is the purpose of the group (DeLucia-Waack, 1997). Processing exercises can help members explore their thoughts and feelings at a greater depth, and they can stimulate discussion both about the topic and about the group dynamics that were apparent in the exercise. Processing of exercises in the working stage, therefore, should help members understand the lessons learned from the exercises on a deep level and develop strategies for applying those insights into the world outside the group.

Another important factor that needs to be considered during the working stage is the duration of the group. Preparing for the working stage is an investment and, generally, the more thorough a leader prepares for the working stage, the more effective that work should be. Given the time limits of many groups, however, there may be a point when any more time invested in laying the groundwork is simply time taken away from the working stage. All groups, whether ongoing counseling groups or full-day workshops, have a working stage (Jacobs et al., 2006). To get the most out of a group, group leaders must figure out how to balance preparing a group to function at a high level and ensuring that enough time is saved for the group to actually do the work. If a leader is presenting a 6-hour workshop on cross-cultural understanding, the leader may have to be content with a group cohesion based on the understanding that members share a common goal: to complete the workshop. This may be sufficient enough for the group to work together for a few hours and meet the goals of the workshop. The leader of an 8-session career development group may be able to spend more time helping the group members develop a deeper level of cohesion, but the group is still under considerable time restraints. Certainly the group must resolve obvious conflicts within the group and establish some degree of cohesiveness if the working stage is to be productive but, at some point, the leader may have to sacrifice some of the depth of the group preparation in order to get the group to a working stage. In a longer-term psychotherapy group in a private-practice setting, the leader may have the luxury of being more patient with the group, allowing time to help the group bond on a deeper level so that the group can get maximum benefit from the working stage.

The format for membership can also affect the working group. The stages of a group that is closed to new members will proceed very differently than a group with an open membership format. If the group is closed to new members after the start of the group, the group is more likely to follow what would be considered a typical process for group development, much like the stages presented in this text. If the group is open-ended, however, the process of group development can be altered substantially. A shakeup in membership can have an effect on both certain individuals within the group and the group as a whole. When a member leaves, the role that the member played in the group is no longer filled. Often, another member will step into the departed member's role, creating a ripple effect that can change the dynamics of the group as a whole. This sudden shift of roles can make the members feel less safe about group interactions, leading them to pull back and test the waters for a while. In addition, feelings of loss over the departure of a valued member can dampen the members' willingness to take risks in the group, also leading the group to regress for a time. When a new member comes into an open group, a period of trust building takes place in which the new member learns to trust the group and the group learns to trust the new member. The new member not only shakes up the group dynamics, he or she is operating within the group at a much earlier stage than group members who have been there longer. While those members may provide encouragement to the new member, helping the new member become part of the group faster than they ordinarily would, the group as a whole will not be in a true working stage while it waits for one or more members to catch up.

Group Membership

Understanding the members participating in the group experience is another vital factor in determining what the working stage will look like. The experiences that make up the working stage, whether topics for discussion or experiential activities, certainly need to be directly related to the topic, but they also need to be appropriate for and relevant to the members of the group. Some membership variables that should be considered are age, ability, and cultural characteristics, including the diversity present within the group.

One factor that is vital to managing an effective working stage is the age and developmental level of the members. For a working stage to be effective, the material discussed and the activities presented must be developmentally appropriate for the group members so that they may effectively process the information. Most of the research on group work has been about adult groups (DeLucia-Waack, 2000). Therefore, counselors leading groups in schools may need to adapt the strategies to make the groups more

relevant to and effective for their populations. For instance, we know that children are likely to have shorter attention spans, more concrete thinking, and a less fully developed sense of self-awareness than adults. In addition, younger group members are more likely to project their feelings onto others, and they may be more comfortable having a stronger, more directive group leader than older clients would. Thus, the working stage in a group with children is likely to have more experiential learning than discussion, and to use children's ability to learn through play. These activities should be processed with the group, but on a more concrete level, and should be held to a few minutes.

Group work can be a very effective method of helping adolescents deal with a range of developmental issues, from social skills to values clarification and identity development. However, the working stages of groups serving adolescent populations should also be adapted to ensure that they are appropriate for the developmental stage. Adolescents themselves are in a developmental stage where they can play like children one minute and have a mature discussion about serious issues the next, so groups for adolescents need to be flexible. Providing a variety of activities in the working stage can help ensure that the leader covers a wide range of developmental levels within the group and addresses the many different moods that are likely to appear throughout the group. Many adolescents enjoy hands-on exercises, whether active challenges like team-building exercises or artistic endeavors such as writing stories or creating collages. However, adolescents are able to process these exercises on a much deeper level than children can, and the time spent processing exercises in an adolescent group should be increased accordingly. In fact, a concrete exercise processed in an abstract way is effective for helping adolescents further develop their abstract thinking.

Group leaders working with elderly clients must adapt the working stage to the specific needs of elderly clients, both in terms of the content and process of the working stage. Speaking in general terms, some content areas are more common to groups with the elderly. Older populations may need basic information that is important to them, such as health care and insurance. Working through grief is certainly an important topic for older adults, as is making new social connections at an advanced age. In addition, groups that help older persons feel empowered and capable of contributing may be important topics to cover. But perhaps more important than the specific topics is the process that can occur in the working stage of a group with elderly members. The group members may not be as physically active, but exercises that get them moving and make them think in novel ways can be very effective with older adults. In addition, because many older adults focus on their early lives, groups that help members reminisce about the past are fairly common (Gladding, 2008). This type of storytelling may be seen as parallel to work with young adults, and it can be very productive as well as enjoyable for the elderly. Perhaps most important, however, group leaders should remember that, with most groups, older adults have a variety of needs, and the leader should be aware of the needs of the specific adults in the group.

The degree of heterogeneity in the group membership may also have an effect on the working stage of a group. It is a myth that groups can be truly homogenous because the levels of identities within each person are far too vast (DeLucia-Waack, 1996b), but groups whose members appear to be more homogenous may feel safer trusting each other more quickly due to the comfort group members feel in sharing similarities, superficial though they may be. In spite of this initial bonding that may occur over gender, racial, ethnic, or other similarities, the working stage may not be as rich or fulfilling. A group whose membership is more heterogeneous may have a more difficult time getting to the working stage because cultural or worldview differences can slow the process of group identification and cohesion, and can lead to misunderstandings within group process (Jacobs et al., 2006). DeLucia-Waack (1996b) argues that, although conversations about race and culture are difficult to initiate, having those conversations can help groups become more cohesive. In addition to helping the group form a tighter bond, the

multiple perspectives that can be shared in a more heterogeneous group can provide members with a wider range of feedback than a more homogenous group, making for a potentially richer, deeper experience for the group members.

ACTIVITY 9.3

Cultural issues play an important part in how the working stage plays out in a group. Form dyads to discuss how your personal identities, worldviews, communication pattern preferences, and other sociocultural factors influence your group participation. Consider what potential challenges may occur for you as a group leader. As a large group, discuss how cultural conflicts may be minimized in the working stage.

In addition to the degree of diversity within the group, leaders should also be cognizant of the effects cultural perspectives of group members, as well as the leader's own cultural perspectives, can have on the working stage. Cultural factors can have a strong effect on the way members act and expect others to act within groups. Leaders should be aware of any issues regarding communication that may occur in the group, whether language differences or nonverbal behavior. In addition, leaders should ensure that any activities or exercises in the group take cultural differences into account so that differences in how people perceive personal space, comfort level with touching, and other variables do not make members feel uncomfortable or left out. When members do opt out of exercises because of cultural reasons, it is important for leaders to understand it for what it is and not assume the member is being resistant to the group process. Perhaps most important, leaders need to be aware of when cultural issues may be affecting group dynamics and be willing to have those conversations as part of the group process. Although all leaders want to be sensitive to cultural issues, the truth is that, at some point, something will happen that makes members feel uncomfortable. At those times, leaders must be able to have those discussions that deepen the

CASE STUDY 9.5

The Career Development Group

I felt this group had gotten to the working stage fairly early, but in recent weeks the group seemed a bit stagnant. I decided to spend time doing some team-building exercises to boost the group's cohesion. I found some activities that were active and fun but would require the group members to trust each other and communicate, and would break down some physical boundaries. I was unaware, however, that one of the group members was very devout in his religious beliefs, one of which prohibited him from getting physically close with other members of the group. When he opted out of the exercise without explanation, I admit that my first thought was that he was showing resistance, and perhaps excluding himself from the group was related to the stagnation I had noticed in the group. However, I pulled him aside as the activity was starting and asked him for an explanation, which he answered by telling me briefly about his beliefs. At that point, we began to discuss what he *could* do to participate in the exercise without putting him in an uncomfortable position from a religious standpoint. After a few minutes, he decided he felt comfortable "coaching" the group and participating in the processing between exercises, which the group enthusiastically agreed to.

understanding among members and get back to an effective working stage as soon as possible. As an illustration of how easily this can come up, consider the example in Case Study 9.5 of a group in the 10th week of a 15-week psychoeducational group on career development.

In Case Study 9.5, a cultural misunderstanding could have led to assumptions about resistance on the part of the leader and feelings of isolation on the part of a group member. Though the initial exercise may have put the member in an uncomfortable position, the ability to discuss and be accepting of cultural differences led to greater cultural understanding and a stronger connection among the member, his group, and the leader.

ACTIVITY 9.4

Form dyads or triads in which you discuss and reflect on past group experiences that you have had either as a member or a group leader. How have you experienced the working stage? What methods (e.g., exercises, discussions) were used? What was positive in your experiences? What do you think could have been done differently to make this stage more effective?

EVALUATION AND THE WORKING STAGE

When it comes to the working stage, leaders have two main questions to answer regarding evaluation: "Are we there yet?" and "Are the group members getting what they need?" Regarding the first question, knowledge of the transition stage characteristics and those of the working stage must be assessed to know whether the group has achieved the momentum common in the working stage. Informal means of evaluation, such as group member feedback forms about the members' perceptions of group, can also be helpful to leaders who are interested in the members' perspectives of the process. In addition to informal measures, two more detailed assessments of group interaction, the Johari Window and the Hill Interaction Matrix, are discussed below.

Authors (e.g., Chen & Rybak, 2004) have used the Johari Window model (Luft, 1984) to explain relationship development in groups (see Figure 4.1 in Chapter 4). As described in Chapter 4, the Johari Window can be visualized as a square divided into four quadrants. The top left quadrant, or the open quadrant, contains behaviors and thoughts that are in an individual's awareness and are apparent to others. The top right quadrant, or the blind quadrant, contains behaviors that are out of the individual's awareness but are apparent to others. The lower left quadrant, the hidden quadrant, contains behaviors that the individual is aware of but keeps secret from others. The final quadrant, the unknown quadrant, contains behaviors and thoughts that are out of the awareness of both the individual and others. To increase self-awareness, a group member must increase the size of his or her open quadrant by moving thoughts and behaviors out of the latter three categories into the open quadrant. Material is moved out of the blind quadrant into the open quadrant through the feedback of others, in this case, the group members' feedback. As an example, consider a member who says that her priority is her children and thus consistently puts her children's needs first, at the expense of her social or emotional needs. She may receive feedback from group members that she appears so stretched and stressed that it seems to them that the time she spends with her children might be more rewarding, for both her and the children, if she found time to relax. Likewise, material is moved out of the hidden quadrant by self-disclosure to the group. A member listening to group members talk about how their fathers' views of success skewed their perception of what they needed to accomplish may suddenly realize and share with the group that his pattern of worring so much is an attempt to finally receive his father's approval. Material can be moved out of the unknown quadrant by gaining insight, either on the part of the individual or the group members, then moved into the open quadrant through feedback or self-disclosure.

ACTIVITY 9.5

The Johari Window is an excellent model for understanding the working stage. Using a previous group experience as a guide, describe how the Johari Window is illustrative of your experience at the initial phases of the working stage. Then do the same for the later phases. How might you incorporate the Johari Window in future groups that you lead?

The Hill Interaction Matrix (Hill, 1966) is another tool used to assess the developmental progress of the group (see Figure 9.1). The cells of the matrix are ordered according to therapeutic benefit, as defined by member centeredness, interpersonal risk taking, and interpersonal feedback. The top of the matrix includes elements of content style. This heading refers to what is being discussed in group. The cell headings within content style include:

1. *Topic:* Defined as discussing there and then material, that is, relationships or activities that occur outside the group.
2. *Group:* Discussions that revolve around the group, primarily concerned with the group's rules, procedures, and goals.
3. *Personal:* Exploration of an individual member within the group. It can include personality issues, behaviors, emotions, thought patterns, and current and historical problems or issues.
4. *Relationship:* The most therapeutic of the elements because of its here-and-now emphasis and focus on interactions between and among group members.

The other axis includes the elements of work style, which describes the manner in which members discuss the content elements. Work style elements include:

1. *Responsive:* Basic unit of work characterized by minimal answers to directive questions.
2. *Conventional:* Characterized by social conversation involving general-interest topics. The interaction is appropriate yet superficial.
3. *Assertive:* Interacts in a conflict-based tone and purpose. The outcome of this form of interaction usually shuts down conversation instead of facilitating deeper discussions. The speaker is often rigidly opinionated and argumentative.
4. *Speculative:* Open exploration among group members that includes a cooperative spirit of understanding intrapersonal and interpersonal issues.

WORK STYLE \ CONTENT STYLE	TOPICS I	GROUP II	PERSONAL III	RELATIONSHIP IV
A -- RESPONSIVE	(1)	(2)	(11)	(12)
B -- CONVENTIONAL	(3)	(4)	(13)	(14)
C -- ASSERTIVE	(5)	(6)	(15)	(16)
D -- SPECULATIVE	(7)	(8)	(17)	(18)
E -- CONFRONTIVE	(9)	(10)	(19)	(20)

POWER QUADRANT

FIGURE 9.1   Hill Interaction Matrix.

5. *Confrontive:* Communication that extends below the surface in an attempt to clarify, evaluate, and resolve issues, both in the group and within the members. This is the most potent work style because it acts to engage the members in deeper-level processing.

In assessing whether the group is in the working stage, one would expect that the content and work style would most likely be in the lower right quadrant of the matrix, which would include the combinations of:

1. *Speculative-personal:*

VIRGIL: It seems to me that when you talk about yourself, you feel really scared to open up, like you are afraid to be vulnerable.

2. *Speculative-relationship:*

RILEY: I feel myself getting angry at you because I think you are ignoring me.

GINNY: I'm not ignoring you. I'm just not agreeing with you all the time. Do I have to agree with you for you to feel heard?

3. *Confrontive-personal:*

BUFORD: You say you want to come across as more honest and open and yet you are still the most quiet member of the group.

4. *Confrontive-relationship:*

MIA: I just feel that everyone is blowing me off, like you all don't take my stuff seriously.

JEFF: I find it hard not to be defensive when you accuse me of blowing you off. I want to hear what's behind the insult, but that makes it hard for me. I get the impression that maybe you don't want to connect and you use the insult as way to distract from the real issue between us.

In addition to evaluating the developmental stage of the group, it is important for leaders to determine if the members are getting what they need out of the group. Referring back to the discussion about accountability, it makes sense that counselors want to assess members all through the process, rather than waiting until after all the planning and group leading to find out. Three types of data can be collected for group interventions (see Chapter 21 for detailed discussions): process data (e.g., number of members participating, number of times met), pereption data (e.g., members' reactions to group, evidence of new knowledge and skills learned), and results data (e.g., member success or other results and outcomes of the group). The process data is important to demonstrate the number of members counselors are working with, and the results data is obviously important because it is what most stakeholders ultimately will want to know. The perception data is crucial to examine during the working stage because it can provide information about whether the smaller group objectives are being met. Timeliness of this information is essential so that leaders can make changes to ensure that members learn what they

are supposed to learn before the end of the group. For example, think of a group for high school students designed to improve graduation rates (distal outcomes); one objective may be increasing career adaptability (proximal data). Part of the working stage of the group will be focused on helping students investigate jobs, take interest inventories, and examine personal values as they relate to work. In such a group, it would be helpful for the leader to know if these objectives were being met as early as possible to inform the leader about whether to move the group along or slow down to make sure the skills identified as important were learned. Group members may report that the group is cohesive and a safe environment to explore personal issues, but if the activities are not giving the members what they need, the desired outcomes of the group may not be fulfilled.

Summary

This chapter provided an overview of what one might expect in the working stage of a group. The working stage is characterized by a high level of activity, where group members are readily focused on meeting both interpersonal and intrapersonal goals. Members take more responsibility for the process of the group, and interaction is characterized by much more here-and-now communication as compared to other developmental group stages. The members have experienced and worked through group conflict and have developed a sense of cohesion that propels them into the true work of the group. Group members actively participate at this stage, soliciting genuine feedback from other members and electing to take more risks in the group. One common form of risk taking is self-disclosure. Through self-disclosure, group members demonstrate vulnerability to gain great understanding of self and others to meet individual and group goals set forth at the beginning of the working stage.

During the working stage, leaders often take more of a facilitative role, which is marked by less direct participation and more maintenance and process observation. The leader serves as a

role model for behaviors deemed particularly helpful in this stage, including risk taking, self-disclosure, and demonstrating vulnerability to learn intrapersonally and interpersonally.

Co-leadership can be advantageous during the working stage. Group leaders may rely on each other to implement skills such as forecasting and open processing, which can help to focus group content and manage group resistance to meet individual and group goals. Leaders who choose to colead groups should be mindful of how the developmental process of the co-leader relationship affects the concurrent growth of the group.

Although common characteristics of the working stage portrayed in linear fashion can be helpful to understand this stage, readers are reminded of the uniqueness of each group and its process. Components such as group foundations, group design, and group membership were presented to illustrate specific concerns that may arise depending on the group. In this context, developmental and cultural considerations were presented. Different methods of assessing the working stage were discussed, including the Johari Window and Hill's Interaction Matrix.

CHAPTER 10

Termination

Danica G. Hays, Tammi F. Milliken, and Catherine Y. Chang

PREVIEW

The purpose of this chapter is to provide an overview of the termination stage, including a general description of termination characteristics, goals, and benefits and challenges. Following these general descriptions, three types of terminations will be discussed: premature termination, termination of group sessions, and termination of the group. Group work techniques reviewed in this chapter include rounds, dyads, sentence completion, scaling, values contract, summarization, journaling, reunions, scrapbooks, comfort zone, and personal growth charts.

TERMINATION AND GROUP CLOSURE

Termination may indicate the end of a relationship in its current capacity, the unexpected departure of a group member, the close of a specific group session, or the conclusion of a particular group experience even though the relationship between an individual member and leader may continue in different capacities. Therefore, it is necessary to address the multiple ways in which termination can occur and to develop strategies for successfully negotiating these often overlapping roles. Although termination is also referred to as closure, for the purposes of this chapter we will refer to it as termination.

Termination is typically conceptualized as the final stage of group process. However, it is more than the end of the group. It is an essential part of the entire group process and, if properly executed, serves as a key component to the transfer of learning and change in the behavior of members. Thus, successful termination of each group session and the group experience as a whole has the potential to positively affect member goals.

Facets of termination are embedded within all stages of group work: it occurs when a member leaves, at the end of each session, and after the group experience ends. Although termination occurs throughout all group stages, including as a final stage itself, termination is often minimized in practice. Considering the extent to which counselors engage in group work as a means to address the needs of as many clients as possible, leaders need to be skilled in conducting groups, including effective approaches to termination.

Termination involves reflection and evaluation, which varies according to group size, dynamics, and focus (Vernelle, 1994). It addresses past, present, and future experiences of members. With respect to past experiences, termination deals with actively reflecting on individual and group changes. Present experiences refer to dealing with feelings associated with termination and any unfinished business. Group leaders also assist students with future concerns by co-developing a plan of action, contracting, and assisting members in applying new learning.

Throughout the course of the group, termination as a procedure relates to anecdotal, informal, and formal assessment of individual and group changes. Thus, evaluation of groups is necessary to demonstrate accountability. Evaluation involves an assessment of the group's effects on behaviors and interactions, as well as member self-assessments of change, other report ratings (e.g., teachers, spouses, parents), and counselor observations.

Members cognitively and affectively reflect on personal growth in the context of the group process. As part of this reflection, members consider what they have learned as they have interacted with other group members and prepare to apply new skills to their world outside the group, thus translating insight into action. To maximize the impact of the group experience, members need to identify what they learned, how they learned it, and how to apply it outside group.

GOALS AND BENEFITS OF TERMINATION

The general goals of termination at any stage in the group process are consolidation of learning, skills application, and future recommendations for continued growth and development. Consolidation of learning refers to members within the group actively reflecting upon knowledge and awareness gained about self and others and integrating this information to make changes within their lives. Skills application refers to members applying newly developed skills in their outside relationships. Future recommendations for continued growth and development can range from affirmative statements encouraging members to keep practicing their skills, to formal referrals for services, including occupational support, psychological assessment, additional group counseling,

and individual counseling. Termination is a transition or new beginning for the member rather than an end. As a result, members should view the completion of each session and each group experience as a new beginning for applying new attitudes and behaviors for success.

Effective termination has several benefits for members that focus on reflection, increased knowledge, and evaluation at various levels. It is an opportunity to apply new learning and make meaning of the group experience. Thus, termination may increase members' awareness of self, others, and their relationship with others. Through this reflection, group members may apply learning, evaluate their growth, and plan for future actions. Leaders should consider how to promote reflection among members in all group formats, from small process groups to large psychoeducational groups.

Self-Awareness

Self-awareness in the termination process refers to recognizing personal attributes and behaviors that facilitate skill development and healthy relationships. Developing self-awareness allows members to improve their decision-making ability as well as their interpersonal relationships in and outside the group. While self-awareness is addressed throughout the group experience, it is assessed and processed in the termination stage. The termination process may increase group members' self-awareness as a result of leader-facilitated interactions among group members. For example, the leader might highlight similarities among members, question members' reactions to one another, and encourage members to give feedback to each other.

Awareness of Others

A key component of awareness of others involves establishing universality. Yalom and Leszcz (2005) describe universality as individuals' sense that their issues are normal and experienced by others. While universality is important at all stages of the group process, termination provides leaders with an opportunity to solidify how issues brought up in the group resonated among members. Acknowledging issues that are universal for members may help decrease fears group members have that prevented them from self-disclosing or working on group tasks and goals. This allows members to become aware of how others perceive and respond to their issues. Universality in group process is important to develop because it allows for deeper interpersonal connections. Establishing a connection with others via discovering similarities is a landmark of healthy adult development (Schiller, 1997). For example, a group leader at a substance abuse agency prepares the group for a session's ending. In this particular session, the community counselor has been providing information about common triggers that may lead to drug relapse. The group leader asks the group members to reflect on which triggers were salient for them, including any that may not have been mentioned in the session. Each group member discusses triggers that they personally struggled with in maintaining sobriety. In ending the session, several group members comment on how relieved they were to hear that others had similar difficulties with specific triggers.

Planning for the Future

The termination process allows members a chance to plan for the future. This may involve testing knowledge members have gained in group work, bringing up an issue or subject that was discussed in a particular group session, evaluating destructive patterns from a more constructive perspective, and relating to people within their lives in a more positive manner (Grayson, 1993).

As mentioned earlier, one of the goals of termination is skills application, which includes helping members transfer skills developed in group to the classroom and beyond, as well as discussing strategies and challenges to this task. If the skills application is successful, members will not only be able to apply their skills immediately, they will have developed valuable resources for continuing the process of personal growth and will be able to adapt their learning to new situations.

Having members fantasize about their future can lead to the implementation of new relational, behavioral, or academic skills beyond the group. This can be accomplished through process questions and activities (e.g., "Describe your life one, three, five years from now." "Describe your relationship with [name] one year from now." "How do you see your academic performance affecting your career goals?"), role plays (e.g., have group members role-play different interpersonal scenarios with each other; have group members role-play tasks related to possible professions), and creative arts (e.g., have group members draw a picture of their lives one and five years from the end of the group; have group members write letters to each other reflecting their hopes and wishes for each other). To consolidate your understanding of the goals and benefits of termination, read Case Study 10.1 and respond to the reflection questions.

CHALLENGES OF TERMINATION

Particularly in small, process-oriented groups, as members make changes based on skills they have learned, they become increasingly more independent from the group. Despite the independence gained, many group members experience emotions related to closure, loss, and separation. In dealing with emotions related to termination, some developmental considerations must be addressed for children and adolescents (van Velsor, 2004). Children often formulate their identities within peer and family relationships, and group counseling experiences may facilitate this formulation. Because group work for children is a salient medium by which to define their self-concepts, termination of a group may be particularly difficult if they experience sadness and anxiety. This is developmentally normal and appropriate. Children may quickly form attachments, and leaders should prepare for termination early to minimize possible feelings of abandonment. Leaders should model disclosure of feelings, provide individualized positive feedback for the children,

CASE STUDY 10.1

Noah

At the end of a group addressing career decision making, Noah discusses what he has learned from the group. The leader initiates closure of the last session of the group and asks group members to identify an attribute related to career development that each member possesses that they were not aware of during initial group sessions. Several group members turn their heads down and look away from the leader. Noah reports that he has found the group extremely helpful and that he enjoyed getting to know the other group members, as well as learning the importance of finding a career that matches one's attributes. He states that group discussions and career value assessments have been helpful in showing him the relationship between values and career decision making. Noah further states it was very cool to see his fellow group members connect career values to career decision making. He turns to Sadie and says that, given her interest in and care of others and her desire for creativity in her work, he can see her being a school teacher. When pushed further by the leader to engage more in self-reflection, Noah had a difficult time identifying a specific attribute about himself that he has discovered in the course of the group. The case of Noah displays both benefits and challenges to the termination stage. Process the following questions:

1. Identify the benefits that Noah gained from the group experience.

2. Identify the challenges that Noah is experiencing as the group terminates.

3. As a group leader, how would you encourage Noah to engage in more self-reflection?

and consider appropriate referrals for individual counseling.

Peer groups are an important source of both support and stress for adolescents. Adolescents often strive for closeness yet fear intimacy, making dealing with feelings of termination complex. Thus, adolescents may have difficulty giving and receiving feedback required in termination, particularly in groups with peers who are similar to them.

During termination of a group, members may display emotions such as withdrawal and aggression, which is typically characteristic of earlier phases (Vernelle, 1994). Some members may have conflicted feelings about dissolving relationships formed in the group. Members may express sadness or anxiety, and they may pull back from the group and not introduce new issues. To ease these feelings, they may rely on various defense mechanisms or maladaptive coping mechanisms. For example, members may engage in denial and avoidance

as a way to deal with separation and loss, or they may insist that additional group sessions are needed or that the group experience was not helpful.

Sometimes to avoid closure of a group experience, members will reflect solely on positive changes in other group members, without reflecting on what they have learned, a dynamic known as the farewell party syndrome. A key indicator that members have successfully completed a group experience is movement toward acknowledging and addressing their problems and specific growth experiences. Deflection from personal changes may indicate the farewell party syndrome (see Case Study 10.2).

In addition, members may not be specific about the skills they have learned or specific aspects of self-awareness. They may not be willing to discuss any negative aspects of the group experience. Leaders should model appropriate responses and challenge members who do

CASE STUDY 10.2

The Farewell Party Syndrome

Imagine you are the leader working with a group terminating during its final session. As the group comes to a close, you ask members to describe something they wish they could have addressed during the past group sessions. Several members report that they really enjoyed the group and cannot think of anything that could be different. They discuss how much they enjoyed each other's company and compliment each other's progress. Group members are able to easily identify the progress other group members have made, but they are unable to identify progress in themselves. Members may be engaging in the farewell party syndrome, as well as using defense mechanisms to avoid dealing with closure in an effective manner.

As the leader in this situation, you recognize the farewell party syndrome and that this is a way for the members to deal with the termination of the group. It is also important for you not to let the group end without encouraging the group members to acknowledge their own growth and development as well as acknowledge the difficulty some group members may be having about ending this group experience. To address this issue, you have each group member put his or her name at the top of a blank piece of paper. The group members then pass the paper to their right. Group members are to write one thing that they wished they had shared or elaborated on during the course of the group. Members continue to pass the paper to the right until it comes back to the person whose name is on top. That person also writes what he or she wanted to share but did not. At the end of this activity, each group member reviews his or her list and picks one thing from that list to share with the group. A follow-up to this activity would be to have each group member express one wish he or she has for each of the other members as the group ends.

not discuss personal and specific examples of growth and skill development.

COMMON LEADER FUNCTIONS DURING ALL PHASES OF TERMINATION

Counselors have dual leadership roles related to termination. First, one of the functions of a group leader is to prepare members for the process of termination using various organizational and interpersonal skills. Second, the group leader fosters a sense of closure for the members as they move the members through the termination process.

Preparing Members for Termination

Leaders prepare members for termination by providing logistical and therapeutic structure. With respect to logistical structure, leaders should know when to introduce termination. Within a session, they should leave approximately 10 minutes to close the group, although the time allotment depends on the size and type of the group. The leader provides the members with at least a 10-minute warning and thus acts as the time-keeper for the group. Pertaining to the end of the group experience, leaders should initially make members aware of how many sessions the group will meet and alerts them to the upcoming final session several sessions in advance.

With respect to therapeutic structure, leaders should address termination by reminding group members of the importance of maintaining confidentiality between group sessions and at the end of the group, as well as any additional rules developed by the group members. It is also important for the leader to remind the members of the importance of developing a support system outside the group.

Moving Members through Termination

There are several ways that group leaders in all group formats facilitate movement through termination, including instilling hope, processing feelings with closure, integrating group member experiences, addressing unfinished business, and assessing the group process. As they move groups through termination, leaders modify how each of these variables is addressed based on the type of group conducted as well as on the developmental needs of members.

INSTILLING HOPE   Instilling hope is an important component of group process because members need to feel supported in order to take risks in their lives, practice new behaviors learned in the group (Yalom & Leszcz, 2005), and ultimately see improvements in behavior and performance. While important in every stage of group work, hope must be instilled to prevent premature termination. Leaders encourage members to apply what they are learning during group work to their daily lives both in and out of school. Leaders should reinforce the changes members have made.

To prevent premature termination, leaders instill hope through various methods. One way is through the use of outside role models. Outside role models may be former group members who have successfully completed the group. Highlighting members who have successfully completed the group can encourage current group members to continue to develop skills and take new risks. See Case Study 10.3.

CASE STUDY 10.3
Beth

Beth, an African American female, has been attending a grief and loss group. Beth feels isolated, frustrated, and different from the other group members because she still has not been able to return to work due to the loss of her partner. She perceives that she is not functioning as well as the other group members because they have been able to attend to their daily activities. She shares with the group that she feels like her situation is hopeless and that she should leave the group because she is bringing the others down. The group members tell Beth that she has made progress in the group by sharing her feelings with them and that yes, all their losses are different and they still can support one another. The group members tell Beth that they have noticed positive changes in her, including her ability to increase her support network and attend church—two goals Beth stated that she wanted to address. The group members tell Beth that she would be missed if she left the group now and that she was the group member the others could count on for words of encouragement. The group leader decides to connect Beth with a former member that had a similar loss. After talking to the former group member, Beth reports feeling more hopeful about her situation improving and decides to stay in the group.

What are the primary issues Beth is struggling with?

How did the group members process and respond to Beth's concerns?

As the group leader, what can you do to help members, both inside and outside the group?

How might you use an outside role model with members?

PROCESSING FEELINGS WITH TERMINATION

Because negative feelings and defense mechanisms are a challenge of termination, processing members' feelings with closure may be a difficult yet necessary leadership task. Leaders continue to reiterate the importance of the group experience and termination more specifically to minimize denial and avoidance.

Leaders should remind members that termination may be difficult because members have developed cohesion with a commitment to the well-being of one another and the group itself. Leaders should process how interpersonal connections were formed within the group so that members may emulate these connections in other contexts. They may also promote discussion of how members can continue to foster their relationships in other contexts.

INTEGRATING MEMBER EXPERIENCES

Leaders assist members in integrating experiences acquired in and outside group work. This assistance may occur by helping group members to develop specific contracts and completing homework assignments, or by reflection on key turning points within and outside the group. For example, the leader may highlight a member's marked improvement in following the rules of the group from the beginning to the end of the group experience, as well as the member's improvement in classroom behavior while participating in the group, as noted by the student's teacher.

Leaders can also help members integrate their experiences by focusing on relationship dynamics among group members. Leaders help members to reflect upon reactions to other members in the ending versus beginning phases of the group. If changes were noted by the members, the leader should assess what role members had in changing perceptions or relationships. The termination stage can be used to challenge members to keep these boundaries diffuse and encourage the continuation of friendships beyond the group.

One challenge that leaders may face involves assisting with meaning-making for those who do not perceive the group as a forum for applying learning to the outside world. Some members may consider the group an end in itself and not apply learning to their daily lives. These members may not perceive that skills developed in a group are useful to other situations in their lives. Members may not see how skills learned in group can be applied to positively affect their academic achievement. Case Study 10.4 provides an example of the challenges associated with applying learning outside the group setting.

CASE STUDY 10.4

Kara: Applying Learning after Group Termination

Imagine that you are leading a group on relationships. The purposes of this group are to discuss how to make friends, explore the qualities of being a good friend, understand common friendship problems, learn how to manage conflicts within relationships, and develop a plan to improve relationships. You are beginning to discuss termination with the group with two group sessions remaining. You ask the group members to begin to develop a written plan for what each group member will do to improve their relationships outside the group. Kara, one of the quieter group members, has a difficult time completing this task. She states that she is not sure how it will help her with her friends outside this group. Of course, she can talk about her problems and express her concerns in group, but that is not the same as doing it outside group. As the leader of the group, how could you ask the other group members to discuss Kara's concerns (content issue) and any issues that may underlie Kara's concern (processing)?

ADDRESSING UNFINISHED BUSINESS Another important role of the leader is to facilitate the resolution of unfinished business. Members may have unfinished business related to other group members, the group process, and the goals of the group. Although it is unrealistic to resolve all issues before the termination of a group session or a group, it is the responsibility of the leader to begin the dialogue. In facilitating this dialogue, the leader may motivate members to reexamine their own personal goals for the group and work toward accomplishing those goals before the end of the group.

Group leaders can facilitate this process by asking the following hypothetical questions:

- If the group ended today, what do you wish you could have said to any of the group members?
- If the group ended today, what would you wish you had shared with the group but did not?
- What additional goals do you wish you had accomplished?
- What are your wishes for the other group members?

Leaders may also use this as an opportunity to assess members' needs for additional services. An advantage to school counseling is the opportunity to address students' issues using multiple modalities. Members may be encouraged to continue seeing the counselor on an individual basis, and/or they may be referred for other services, such as emotional assessments, outside counseling, and so on.

ASSESSMENT OF GROUP PROCESS In all groups, leaders assess the progress of the group toward meeting its goals to instill hope and encourage application of learning. Leaders explore with members in various ways how the group is meeting group and individual goals, the degree to which members are satisfied with group content and process, and how successful members are in using their skills in their daily lives. It is ethically imperative that leaders integrate evidence into their practice. Thus, following up

with members at various termination points throughout the group to check on continued progress is essential. Following termination of the group, leaders should assess the group's effect on member behaviors and coping. This evidence should influence future termination techniques and approaches with group members (Pollio, 2002).

In summary, termination is a complex process with many challenges and benefits. It takes a skilled leader to move members successfully through the termination process. Thus far, we have discussed termination in general; however, there are three different types of terminations: premature termination, termination of individual sessions, and group termination. Each of these three types of terminations requires special considerations.

PREMATURE TERMINATION

Premature termination involves a leader or member leaving the group unexpectedly or the group dissolving before its goals have been accomplished. Premature termination is a naturally occurring phenomenon in group work that should be anticipated so that it can be addressed. Leaders realize that premature termination can be minimized or prevented, but it cannot be eliminated altogether. Ethically speaking, group members are free to leave the group at any time. Also, leaders may be unable to continue leading the group, although this case occurs less frequently.

A group can experience premature termination when the leader leaves due to illness, relocation, reassignment, or some other reason and is not replaced with a new group leader. Premature termination due to the leader leaving can result in group members feeling abandoned and anxious. A leader can minimize the group's fears and anxiety by conducting a final session where the leader processes the reason for leaving and provides group members with referrals for other groups with another counselor. For example, the leader may say, "I'm sorry that we have to end this group before the agreed upon time, but my doctor believes it is best that I take maternity leave earlier than expected and so I can no longer continue with this group. How are you feeling about having to end this group? I have talked to Ms. X and Dr. Y about the possibility of joining one of their groups. They will be contacting you to see if you might be interested in meeting with one of them. I will pass out information about their group opportunities as well as information about local groups in the community that you might find helpful." If it is not possible to call together a final group session before the leader leaves, then the leader might consider contacting each group member via telephone to discuss the rationale for ending the group as well as giving the member an opportunity to express fears and concerns related to prematurely ending the group. The leader will want to provide contacts for other counselors at this time.

Premature termination of a group member refers to a member leaving a group without proper closure prior to the group's ending. Thus, members may exit a group prior to the group's last session if they have met their goals, become frustrated over lack of progress, the group is no longer suitable for them, for logistical reasons such as schedule changes that do not allow the member to remain in the group, or if parents or guardians pull them out

of group suddenly. Premature termination is also referred to as dropping out of a group experience.

There are various views on premature termination (Bostwick, 1987). Most of the group literature states that premature termination is detrimental to the group process because progress may be disrupted for those who remain in the group. This disruption may create an increased exodus of others. Dropouts may hinder group process for a significant period of time because a group requires stability. The degree of disruption may vary greatly based on the reason for the member's departure from group. A member who leaves a group due to a job or home relocation is likely to affect the group process far less than a member who chooses to drop out of a group due to boredom or frustration with the process. The latter member may model perceptions and behaviors that are then mimicked by other group members. Antwone in Case Study 10.5 demonstrates some of the group issues related to premature termination.

An alternative perspective asserts that premature termination is a natural process because group members not suitable for a specific group drop out so that other group members' experiences are maximized. However, there is some

CASE STUDY 10.5

Antwone

The purpose of this group is to help individuals gain self-awareness related to their characteristics and uniqueness as well as develop a positive self-image. The group also discusses how to improve peer relationships. This is a voluntary group that meets weekly during the lunch period. After several group sessions, Antwone decides to drop out of the group because he misses having lunch with his friends. After Antwone leaves the group, other group members also state that they miss having lunch with their friends and are thinking about dropping out of the group.

Reflection questions:

As the leader, how would you help the other group members process Antwone's exit from the group?

What are some reason's that may have caused Antwone to terminate prematurely from the group, and how could these issues have been addressed prior to his exit?

caution that this may be true only if such members leave the group early in the group process. While there are mixed effects of premature termination on remaining group members, a group that is cohesive (i.e., with a secure attachment to one another) will experience less disruption when a member leaves a group prematurely (Yalom & Leszcz, 2005).

For members who are appropriate for a particular group experience, premature termination due to the negative experiences for the terminating member may be detrimental for the member as well as the remaining members. If a leader does everything to remove obstacles for a particular member to work effectively in a group and nothing changes, the member may eventually drop out or other members may experience negative consequences by the member remaining in the group. If a member is removed, it is important to emphasize to the member that you as the group leader are looking out for the best interests of that member and those remaining in the group. This will lessen the risk that the member will feel abandoned or rejected. In this case, it may be suitable to offer other services, such as an alternative group, individual sessions, the opportunity to work with a different counselor (if one is available), and/or other outpatient services.

A central paradox of premature termination is that those who would most benefit from group work are more likely to drop out of a group. For instance, those different from the group in some intrapersonal or interpersonal aspect are more likely to drop out (Yalom & Leszcz, 2005). Thus, members with relational problems may be most likely to leave the group prematurely despite group counseling being especially helpful for addressing these very issues.

Why Do Members Terminate Group Prematurely?

Statistics on premature termination (i.e., dropout rates) suggest that 35% of group members (adults and children combined) who join a group drop out of group treatment for various reasons (Yalom & Leszcz, 2005). Because factors for terminating a group prematurely vary, leaders should not automatically assume that members are resistant to group intervention. Some of the reasons for premature termination include psychological characteristics, group dynamics, logistical issues, and leadership factors.

PSYCHOLOGICAL CHARACTERISTICS A key component for members who remain in groups involves their psychological characteristics, which include their level of motivation, general comfort level with intimacy and self-disclosure, mental health status, and appropriate personal boundaries (Gladding, 2008; Yalom & Leszcz, 2005). Members may drop out due to fear of self-disclosure and the subsequent discomfort experienced during group sessions when they are asked to open up. Members may terminate early due to fear of experiencing negative effects from hearing about others' problems. This may be an indication of poor boundaries or maladaptive defense mechanisms. However, level of motivation may compensate for members who have moderate levels of problems with intimacy and self-disclosure. Members lacking motivation are likely to lose interest in the group process and opt for an alternative to the group experience.

Members may leave a group prematurely due to their parents' or guardians' fears (see Case Study 10.6). A parent or guardian may become concerned that others in the group are negatively affecting their child. Minors from families with rigid boundaries may have a parent or guardian who becomes uncomfortable with the level of disclosure in the group and responds by removing the child. Despite a member's level of motivation to participate in a group, the member may not be permitted to take part without parental support. To help prevent premature termination, the leader may directly address parental concerns.

GROUP DYNAMICS Members may terminate prematurely when they perceive unhealthy group dynamics. Healthy group dynamics refer to positive views of a setting, satisfaction with treatment, willingness to self-disclose appropriately (Bostwick,

CASE STUDY 10.6
Nell

Nell is a biracial female attending a changing family group. Her father is Caucasian and her mother is Asian. The purpose of the family group is to support children whose parents are going through a divorce or separation. Nell's parents have recently separated. Her mother is the one who gave parental consent for Nell to attend the group. Although Nell's father did not initially agree with Nell attending the group, he agreed that she could attend. After several weeks of the group, the father becomes increasingly uncomfortable with the level of disclosure as reported by Nell. He tells Nell that she must quit the group immediately. Nell is very upset and tells the leader that she does not want to quit. As the group leader, you invite both Nell's parents for a consultation.

Process questions:

Is it the role of the group leader to "convince" Nell to stay in the group? Explain.

Is it the role of the group leader to "convince" Nell's parents to let her stay in the group? Explain.

What are some issues and concerns that you would want to discuss with Nell's parents?

What are some issues and concerns that you would want to discuss with the group members?

1987), sense of belonging, and comfort level with group intimacy.

A member's perceived acceptance by both the leader and other group members has a significant impact on the member's psychological characteristics. Sometimes members believe that they do not fit in the group or that other members' issues hinder their own success in the group. Subgrouping, both if members are included or excluded, may affect their sense of acceptance and belonging. Thus, members' satisfaction with a group may be in part contingent on the degree to which they have open communication and feel included in the group by others.

Sometimes a member may significantly differ from other group members, a phenomenon termed group deviancy. Group deviancy is different from a general sense of not feeling accepted; a member may be different with respect to personality variables, skills, and degree of insight into problems. Members may be considered deviant if they are not congruent with group goals or impede group process due to unwillingness or incapacity to fulfill group tasks. So-called group

deviants are more likely to experience negative consequences from the group, such as being less generally satisfied with the group, viewing the group as invaluable, or experiencing anxiety (Lieberman, Yalom, & Miles, 1973).

Self-disclosure is another key factor affecting premature termination. Members may self-disclose too much too early in the group process, perhaps because of poor personal boundaries. This premature self-disclosure may not be reciprocated by others in the group, leaving them to feel shame or embarrassment and wanting to drop out of the group (Yalom & Leszcz, 2005).

LOGISTICAL ISSUES Logistical issues may also hinder members from continuing group interventions. These issues may include child care, transportation barriers, financial concerns, changes in work schedules, and concurrent individual therapy. While some of these may arise unexpectedly during the course of the group, leaders should facilitate a discussion in initial group sessions about potential logistical barriers to group work.

LEADERSHIP FACTORS At times leaders may not adequately prepare group members for a group experience, inadvertently prompting premature termination. Leaders should continually assess members' perceptions about their satisfaction with the group. In addition, leaders should monitor member progress through self-evaluation and consultation. With self-evaluation, leaders may attend to their personal reactions to group dynamics as well as members' feedback when terminating individual sessions. For consultation, leaders discuss with other professionals their concerns and successes, interventions, reactions to the group content and process, and perceptions of members' progress. During consultation, leaders should adhere to applicable ethical principles and standards of practice. Case Study 10.7 presents various potential termination scenarios for reflection.

CASE STUDY 10.7
Various Termination Scenarios

The following examples show how the factors discussed in this chapter may cause a member to terminate the group experience prematurely. Reflect on how you could prevent or minimize premature termination in each case.

- Michael, a 49-year-old Caucasian, gay male in a parenting education group, states that he feels that other parents in the group are not accepting of him. He states that he feels judged for his sexual identity and wants to leave the group.
- Nicole, a 23-year-old lesbian in a substance abuse group, constantly interrupts another group member as he talks about his use of marijuana. She gives advice to the member, stating, "You don't really have a problem. You just need to cut back." The group member, Andy, becomes angry with her interruptions.
- Amber, a 32-year-old Native American female, reports at the end of a group session that she will not be able to attend the group anymore. She states that she no longer has child care available to her.
- Owen, a 16-year-old Caucasian male in a managing conflicts group, has a difficult time sitting still and staying focused. He is constantly making inappropriate (and sometimes offensive) jokes, getting up, and disrupting the rest of the group. Other group members are concerned or upset with his jokes and disruptions, and they disclose to the group leader after the session that they want Owen to be removed from the group.
- Maya, an African American female in a child sexual abuse survivors group, becomes anxious as other group members tell their stories of sexual abuse survival. She departs the group unexpectedly in the middle of a group session.
- Tony, a 68-year-old Caucasian male in a depression prevention group, presents with religious delusions and pressured speech. Other group members are concerned with his symptoms and disclose to the group leader after the session that they want Tony to be removed from the group.
- Leigh, a member of a grief and loss group, gets upset as the group members begin sharing the details of their loss. She withdraws and remains silent throughout the session. Then, after the session, she tells the leader that she wants to drop out of the group.
- Jay, an 11-year-old Asian male in an academic success group, has been a leader of the group and appears to be getting a lot from the group. After one of the group sessions, he tells the leader that he can no longer attend the group. His parents have not seen an improvement in his grades and they want him to spend his study period actually studying and not in a group talking about studying.

Preventing Premature Termination

Preventing (or minimizing) premature termination begins with screening during the planning phase and continues as a group develops cohesion. Leaders can minimize the risk of members prematurely leaving a group by adequately preparing them for the group experience during the screening process. This preparation includes reviewing risks, addressing member characteristics, and examining value orientations. Providing structure and consistency are imperative for retaining members and maximizing their satisfaction with the group experience. In most instances, leaders should attempt to have members commit to the designated number of sessions.

REVIEWING RISKS   Regardless of the group format, it is important that leaders thoroughly describe what group content and process will be like in general, including the potential psychological and physical risks involved, to minimize premature termination. Psychological risks include potential group pressure to participate (including self-disclosing), potential scapegoating by other members, being confronted by other members, the fact that confidentiality cannot be guaranteed, and experiencing possible disruptions in members' lives due to psychological and logistical resources needed for group participation.

Particularly for those participating in small process groups, members should be alerted to possible reactions from others outside the group. Others outside a group often desire to join the small group process upon noting the positive experiences of members. However, others may respond in a derogatory manner, potentially causing members to feel ashamed of their circumstances and embarrassed to be part of the group or to need any kind of counseling at all. Members who are prepared to handle negative reactions from peers are less likely to terminate the group prematurely.

ATTENDING TO GROUP MEMBER CHARACTERIS-TICS   Because the success of a group depends significantly on the interactions among members and leaders, leaders should attend to idiosyncratic processes in their groups. Early assessment of each member's group experience is necessary because expectations and satisfaction related to group process may influence group continuation. Leaders should inquire about previous group participation. Throughout the process, leaders should continually encourage members to consider what they are learning and allowing them to be heard. This in turn increases a member's sense of belonging and accomplishment.

Leaders should familiarize themselves with members' vulnerabilities, respect their requests with regard to degree of participation, develop an invitational style, and use objective statements or nonblaming subjective statements when providing feedback or general interaction. Leaders should openly express feelings toward the group process and group members, as appropriate. In addition, leaders should consider the use of concurrent individual and group counseling if they think either or both would be appropriate for their members.

VALUES   Value conflicts play a central role in premature termination for adults and can result in discomfort and possible termination for children participating in groups at school as well. Leaders should inform and discuss with members their value assumptions related to counseling in general and group work more specifically. With respect to group work, leaders should articulate typical group work assumptions and values, including (1) personal risk taking is essential and beneficial for growth; (2) expression of emotions, thoughts, and personal vulnerabilities are key to building authentic and trusting relationships in group work; and (3) assertiveness and autonomy are necessary for getting what you need from others (Corey, Williams, & Moline, 1995). Acknowledging these expectations inherent in group work and soliciting feedback from members may prevent premature termination. This information should be disseminated to parents and guardians as well. If parents' and guardians' misconceptions are addressed in the beginning, it is less likely that they will feel the group process is inappropriate for their children, thus preventing the premature removal of their children from the group.

In addition to discussing group value assumptions, leaders should be clear about their own values to minimize the risk of premature termination, including values related to their cultural worldview or group work itself. Leaders should examine how their cultural values interface with group content and process. For example, leaders who value a collectivistic orientation to skills application (e.g., having members translate newly developed interpersonal skills to family interactions to promote harmonious, collaborative relationships) may need to consider how this value would affect those who do not share this value. Members who may not share similar values may be more inclined to terminate prematurely.

Failure to recognize and attend to cultural values and value conflicts may result in premature termination for members of racial and ethnic minority groups (Leong, 1992). Value conflicts may arise between member and leader cultural values or between member values and the traditional values of group work. For example, self-disclosure may be deemed an important aspect of healthy group development, yet students may terminate prematurely if their cultural norms frown upon self-disclosure.

Leaders should also explore what role group work plays for their members. For instance, leaders may view group counseling as effective if group members self-disclose. However, some members may not feel comfortable self-disclosing in front of their peers because they view it as selfish and thus may terminate early. Addressing these concerns and providing a safe, trusting group environment may result in greater levels of comfort, thus preventing some of these members from prematurely dropping out. If the group format is inappropriate for potential or current members, it is important for leaders to have referral sources and to coordinate services to meet their needs.

Techniques for Preventing Premature Termination

Leaders may use several activities to minimize or prevent premature termination. Three activities are highlighted in this section: values contract, comfort zone, and personal growth charts. Each of these activities is appropriate at different stages of the group process.

VALUES CONTRACT The purpose of a values contract is to discuss values that leaders and members bring to sessions. Developing a values contract is one method for articulating leader and member goals and expectations. This contract should be developed in the initial group session so that individuals are clear about the group purpose, group member roles, and rules. The leader can pose the following questions, which can be modified depending on the developmental level of the members:

- What are your expectations for this group?
- What do you see as your personal role in meeting those expectations?
- What do you see as the leader's role in meeting those expectations?
- What are your personal expectations?
- What are your expectations of the leader?
- What do you view as most important to make this group successful?
- How do you prefer to communicate with others?
- What, if anything, might make you uncomfortable in this group?

After processing these questions and reaching some agreement about group goals and rules from the perspective of the members, the leader should review the group rules, purpose, and goals. The leader should attempt to honor the members' requests as appropriate. This may allow the members to be more invested and committed to the group process, more willing to openly communicate with others, and less likely to terminate prematurely.

COMFORT ZONE The purpose of an experiential comfort zone activity is to identify members' vulnerabilities, fears, and other forms of discomfort in the group. This technique may be used in any session when the leader wants to assess group dynamics. The leader should create a large circle in the middle of the floor using a rope at least 18 feet in length. Have the members stand on the edge of the rope, forming a circle outline around the rope. Instruct the members to move in the middle of the circle to the degree that they agree with the statements below. If the members do not agree with a statement, they should move outside the circle, away from the midpoint. Statements involve exploring members' comfort level with various aspects of daily and group activities, starting with safer statements and ending with riskier ones. Ask members to move in or out of the circle for each statement.

How comfortable are you …:

- Talking to a friend?
- Talking to a stranger?
- Engaging in a conversation with several peers?
- Being in a room with strangers?
- Being silent?
- Being the center of attention?
- Taking risks?
- Communicating with others who may have a different opinion than yours?
- Communicating with others who may have a different cultural background than yours?
- Talking about your strengths?
- Talking about your weaknesses?
- Telling someone when you are dissatisfied with something?
- Giving feedback to others?
- Receiving feedback from a friend?
- Receiving feedback from others?

After the exercise, have the members discuss similarities and differences related to each others' comfort level with communicating, giving and receiving feedback, and working with different people and worldviews. Brainstorm ways in which the group can handle discomfort in the future to avoid premature termination.

PERSONAL GROWTH CHARTS The purpose of a personal growth chart exercise is to have members self-monitor their goals and satisfaction with the group (see Table 10.1). These charts can be shared with the leader to ensure that members are getting their goals addressed, working well with others, and applying their developing skills outside the group experience. Have members complete the chart after each session.

TABLE 10.1 Personal Growth Charts

Please complete the following statements.

Name: _____

My goal in group today was _____.

I made the following progress today to meet my goal:_____.

On a scale from 1 to 10, I would rate my progress as a _____.

I feel that the group was helpful today because _____.

I feel that the group was not helpful today because _____.

My group participation today was _____.

What I liked about today's group session was _____.

What I would like to see change before next session is (are) _____.

At this time, I am concerned about _____.

I may/may not (circle one) return for future group sessions because _____.

I would/would not (circle one) like to discuss these concerns with the group: ____.

TERMINATION OF INDIVIDUAL GROUP SESSIONS

Leaders will want to spend the last few minutes of each group conducting a mini-termination of the group session. This includes pre-termination, termination, and post-termination. Pre-termination involves the planning phase of termination. Post-termination refers to the follow-up procedures that group leaders employ. Throughout these stages, leaders should actively discuss with members what meaning a particular session had for them personally and how the session relates to previous and future learning. Leaders and members should co-construct meanings related to group development, including assessing each other's growth (Birnbaum & Cicchetti, 2000; Birnbaum, Mason, & Cicchetti, 2002). Now process the termination scenarios presented in Case Study 10.8.

The time needed for termination of group sessions depends on several factors, including the type and purpose of the group, member characteristics, and leader characteristics (Gladding, 2008).

Termination of the group session is especially beneficial in short-term groups, open groups, and classroom guidance sessions. Whatever the group type, intensity, and duration, leaders should use an active approach and be intentional about session closures.

Leaders should possess several specific skills for effective session termination. These skills include soliciting feedback from members, establishing norms for session endings, informing members of group process, and dealing with resistance and conflict in the group (Birnbaum et al., 2002). In the early development of a group, leaders discuss how sessions will end and what tasks will be involved. Leaders should allocate a specified amount of time (e.g., 5 to 10 minutes for 30- to 60-minute sessions) to reflect on group content and process of a session.

In terminating a group session, it may be appropriate to integrate feedback from individuals associated with a member in some capacity. Collaborating with parents and guardians, teachers, friends, spouses, and administrators may be

---

CASE STUDY 10.8

Termination Scenarios

Discuss pre-termination, termination, and post-termination techniques that you would employ for ending the following group sessions:

- Psychoeducational group for adults on managing anxiety
- Psychoeducational group for eighth-graders with academic difficulties
- Workshop for adults on maintaining good physical health
- Workshop for college-age females related to dating violence prevention
- Career counseling session for ninth-graders
- Counseling group for recent immigrants
- Support group for people who abuse substances
- Support group for individuals diagnosed with a disability
- Schoolwide psychoeducational group on bullying prevention

Discuss the following in small groups:

- In what ways are your techniques similar across these groups?
- In what ways do developmental and cultural issues affect these techniques?

helpful to gain feedback about the group member. Integrating this outside information is important because it could provide insight into how members are progressing toward their goals as well as how satisfied they are with the group process, which helps assess if members are making meaning from group sessions and avoiding premature termination, respectively.

Benefits

Conducting effective session closures has several benefits. Members may be more satisfied with a group experience and have a greater sense of accomplishment if leaders solicit feedback about the group's effectiveness as well as personal growth for members. Effective session termination may empower members, encourage reflective thinking, and increase genuine interpersonal interactions within and outside the group (Birnbaum et al., 2002).

In general, successful session termination may make transitions between sessions progress more smoothly as both leaders and members reflect on limited and focused instances of group content and process. Members have an opportunity to assess their growth within a particular session from several perspectives: their own, and that of other group members and the leader. Session termination may empower members and leaders to demonstrate that they value members' voices to guide the group's progress. The development of these skills can help members become more confident within the classroom. Members who learn to reflect upon and ask for what they need in the group setting will likely be able to ask for what they need from others outside the group as well.

Whatever the age of the participants, they can be asked to engage in active reflection both during and between sessions. Effective session termination allows members to reflect on the present group experience. What can members take away from today's group session and apply to their daily lives? Members should be encouraged to evaluate and reflect upon their individual and collective work as they make connections between sessions. As part of this reflection, members may identify issues that they would like to explore in future sessions as well as those they feel they have not fully worked through by the session's end. Acknowledging individual growth and unfinished business at the end of a session allows members to have a sense of completion even if all issues were not fully addressed in a particular session. Unfinished business could potentially detract from members' ability to focus when returning to the real world.

Members can also provide suggestions for future groups, such as topics for subsequent sessions. This allows for collaboration among members and between the members and the leader, thus facilitating group cohesion. Members may feel as if they are contributing to future group experiences as they work together in making decisions. Members who bond in the group setting are more likely to maintain positive relations outside the group, which may also reduce interpersonal conflicts.

In addition to member benefits, group leaders receive several benefits when he or she terminates group sessions appropriately. By soliciting feedback at the end of each session, leaders can see how effective the group has been, that is, what is working and not working. Leaders gain a greater understanding of members' needs and acquisitions, and the developmental stage of the group itself. Leaders can learn which interventions were most salient for members and which had the greatest impact.

Challenges

Several challenges or barriers may obstruct effective session termination. A primary challenge is the members' attitudes toward session termination. For example, members may feel that termination is unnecessary or not useful and perceive that termination should occur only at the end of a group. They may be resistant because they feel it is repetitive and takes time away from session content and processes. The leader should address these attitudes, and the value of termination and the consequences of failing to terminate should be discussed.

Leaders should also be cognizant that members may be resistant to ending a group session on time. For instance, a member may bring up a new issue in the last few minutes of a group session. Leaders should validate this member's disclosure and state that the issue may be discussed in a future group session. Or the group member may be seen individually by the leader, allowed to participate in another group, or referred to outside counseling.

Another challenge is presented when members leave a group permanently, such as in the case of open groups. For example, substance abuse treatment groups are often offered in an open format. In open groups such as this, group termination as well as session termination can be conceptualized as occurring in each session because at the end of each session, some members may be returning to the group while others may be exiting permanently. Leaders should be cognizant of any resistance they themselves experience when a particular member leaves. Specifically, if a member has been contributing significantly to a group, the leader could be resistant to the member's termination. Self-awareness can prevent this from interfering with the healthy continuation of the group process. Termination must be more individualized in open groups because members leave at various times. Members should be adequately prepared when someone decides to leave the group, and the impact of an individual leaving a group should be assessed. Communicating to members the nature of open groups at the beginning of the group experience and allowing time during each session to process terminations can prevent disruptions to the group process.

CASE STUDY 10.9

Terminating Group Sessions

The following cases are examples of challenges that may occur when leaders terminate group sessions. Reflect on how you would respond to each scenario.

- Shea, a Caucasian female, has been involved in an Alcoholics Anonymous group for 20 years. Shea has decided that she will no longer attend meetings. Because it is an open group, there are several members who recently started attending group meetings. As the leader reflects on a session, several members discuss how they have learned so much from having Shea in the group and express their wishes that she continue to attend.

- As a leader conducts a round to terminate a session, Chip, a 16-year-old African American male in a study skills group, appears distant and not focused. When it is his turn to participate in the round, Chip discloses to the group that part of the reason he may be having difficulty in his classes is because he is struggling with how to disclose to others that he is bisexual. This is new information for the group.

- Michele, an Asian American female in a stress management group, expresses irritation when the leader conducts a session termination exercise. The leader asks the members to get a partner and talk to each other about what new knowledge they will take with them from today's session. Michele expresses that she doesn't want to waste time doing the exercise and that she would like to spend the last few minutes learning a new stress management technique instead.

- Shawn, a multiracial male in a general psychiatric group, requests that the leader allow the group session to continue for an additional 15 minutes. He states that he needs more time to talk to the group about how to prepare for his upcoming speaking event that is to occur in three days.

Techniques for Terminating Individual Group Sessions

Group leaders may use several techniques to terminate group sessions effectively. These techniques may involve leader or member summarization. In terminating a group session, leader summarization is characterized as commenting or reacting to group process or content in such a way that it helps solidify what was learned within a session, acknowledges specific relationship dynamics among members, and addresses or calls attention to critical events or learning within the session. Member summarization in terminating a group session refers to when a member briefly appraises group content and process.

Techniques for terminating a session may involve rounds, dyads, sentence completion, scaling questions, process questions, journaling, and evaluation of a group session (Corey, 2007). These group work techniques are important because they can be adapted for use during other facets of group work and modified to match the developmental level of the students.

ROUNDS Rounds give each member an equal opportunity to participate in the group because each one is given a chance to comment on a statement or question. Usually, each individual is given about one to two minutes. Rounds are a positive way to end the group as well as to ensure that each member gets an opportunity to participate. See Table 10.2 for stems that a leader can use to begin a round.

DYADS The leader can have members form dyads (i.e., pairs) at the end of the session. As in rounds, the dyads are given stems related to the group session (see Table 10.2), and they are asked to share their answers. By having members form dyads, the leader is ensuring that each member participates in termination, yet less time is taken away from the group work. The leader can either assign dyads based on similar issues or members can form their own dyads.

SENTENCE COMPLETION Having members complete sentences in written or verbal form can be an important part of preparing members for

---

TABLE 10.2 Stems

The following stems may be useful in assisting leaders with session termination. Ask members to respond to the following:

- Today I learned _____.
- I feel _____.
- Based on today's group, I will _____ this week.
- Based on today's group, I will _____ at home this week.
- Three things I will do differently because of this group session are _____.
- What I like about this group is _____.
- Something discussed in group today that I will continue to reflect on is _____.
- If I could sum up my experience in this group so far using one word, it would be _____.
- I will continue to work on _____.
- I will change _____ before next week.
- My experience with others in this group has been _____ because _____.
- One thing I have learned about how I relate to others is _____.
- One way the group has influenced me is _____.
- I would like to address _____ before the group ends.
- I noticed that the group worked well together today because _____.
- One change I would like to make before next session is _____.
- I noticed [member's name] benefited from today's session because _____.

the ending of a group session. Table 10.2 provides a sentence completion activity.

SCALING ACTIVITY   **Scaling** is a valuable tool that allows members to conceptualize incremental changes as they move between sessions. Through this activity, leaders may get a sense of how members internalize certain changes or incorporate these changes into their day-to-day lives. One scaling method involves assessing how satisfied members are with the group in addressing their goals. Table 10.3 provides an example of the use of scaling. Scaling helps to get a sense of members' satisfaction with a counseling group designed to help increase their self-awareness. Case Study 10.10 provides an example of using a scaling procedure in group work.

PROCESS QUESTIONS   Process questions should be congruent with group stage, with more structured questions used during earlier session endings and less structured questions used as the group progresses. For example, questions for summarizing initial sessions may focus on group purpose and goals, member relationships, and member roles. In later sessions, members may start closing sessions on their own (Birnbaum et al., 2002). Some process questions include the following:

- What stood out to you about today's group session?
- How was today's session different from earlier sessions?
- What would you like to see happen in the next group session?
- How will what you learned in group today help you?
- What are your goals for planning for future sessions?
- What did you notice about others' growth in this session?

TABLE 10.3   Evaluation of Group Sessions: A Group Session Rating Form

I am interested in improving future sessions so that you may have a more enjoyable group experience. Using the following scale, please rate the degree to which you feel the statements below describe what occurred in today's group session.

1	2	3	4	5
Strongly Disagree	Disagree	Unsure	Agree	Strongly Agree

Please provide a rating to the left of each item and as much feedback as you would like in the comments section.

Group number: _____

Group topic: _____

_____ The group session was interesting and worthwhile.

_____ My coping will be improved as a result of what I learned in group today.

_____ The group worked toward its goals today.

_____ I worked on my personal goals today in group.

_____ I learned something new about myself today.

_____ I learned something new about others today.

_____ I learned or improved a skill in this group session.

_____ I feel that the group leader was well prepared today.

_____ I feel that the group leader worked toward our goals.

_____ I enjoyed the activities in today's session.

_____ Other group members were supportive and respectful.

Comments:

_____

_____

CASE STUDY 10.10

Scaling Activity for Terminating Group Sessions

During the termination of a group session, a leader wanted the group to process, consolidate, and evaluate gains made in the group by using a scaling activity. The group leader began with the following.

I would like you to rate your satisfaction with the group today in terms of learning something new about yourself. To do this, envision a scale ranging from 1 to 10, with 1 being the least satisfied and 10 being the most satisfied with your personal growth in the group today. What would a 1 look like for you on this scale? What would a 5 look like on this scale? What would a 10 look like on this scale? Where were you on the scale before the group began today? What occurred in the group to change that rating (i.e., what specifically increased or decreased your satisfaction)? Where would you like to be by the end of the next session (i.e., how satisfied with the group do you expect to be in the next session to increase your self-awareness)? What can you do to achieve that rating? What can the group do to assist you in achieving that rating? Imagine that this is the last session. What would be your ideal rating? What would your personal growth look like if you reached this ideal rating?

- In what ways have you begun to meet your goals in this group?
- What has been useful for you in this group experience thus far?
- What are some things that you feel we have not addressed yet?
- What feelings came up for you in group today?
- Which group member did you have the most difficulty relating to and why?
- Which group member did you best relate to and why?
- What things helped the group move toward its goals today?

JOURNALING Journaling can be an important way for members to reflect on a group session in a private manner. Leaders can encourage members to write reactions to the events in a session during the last few minutes of the group. Or members may write in a journal daily between sessions as they continue to reflect and apply new learning.

Evaluation of Group Sessions

Leaders should allow some time to formally or informally assess the group's effectiveness in meeting its purpose. Evaluation related to terminating a group session can occur in many ways, usually by obtaining written or verbal feedback at the end of a session. The effectiveness of a group can be assessed by asking teachers and parents for feedback about changes noted in students since participating in a group. Leaders can also evaluate the group by asking members directly about their experiences. Group leaders can distribute questionnaires or rating scales and ask members to complete them periodically or after each group session. Much more attention is given to group evaluation strategies in Chapter 21.

TERMINATION OF THE GROUP EXPERIENCE

Groups terminate for several reasons. Termination may occur at a preset time, such as in closed groups; when a majority of group members are ready to terminate; or (as discussed earlier) when a leader leaves the group and no other leaders are available.

In open groups, members have consistent models of the beginning, middle, and ending phases of a group because the membership changes with each group session. In this case, a group may not end until each member has met preset goals. Thus, termination in an open group typically will not occur unless there are changes in the group leadership.

A key indicator that a group is ready for termination centers on a task of the working stage: cohesiveness. Group cohesion involves having strong interpersonal bonds with other members yet decreased dependence on them for support. Members from cohesive groups have more genuine interactions and can provide constructive feedback regarding self, the group, and other members. Because the majority of groups conducted in a school setting are closed groups with a set number of sessions, it is imperative that the group leader work to establish group cohesion early to ensure that the members can meet their goals and that the group is ready to terminate when the time arrives.

Evaluation of the Group Experience

Termination of the group experience involves evaluation from both the leader and the members. Group leaders should offer an assessment related to their own effectiveness and the effectiveness of the group process, and they should encourage members to evaluate their own participation, the leader's effectiveness, and the group process.

In preparing for group termination, leaders should engage in some personal reflections. How do they feel about the group? How do they feel about the group getting ready to terminate? How do they feel about the progress the group has made? How do they feel about their own effectiveness in facilitating the group? Leaders should disclose their own feelings about separation, continuing genuine interactions with student members, and normalizing feelings of termination.

The leader should also encourage members to provide feedback about their group experience. This can be done by incorporating rating scales and process questions such as those described in the previous section, but in reference to the entire group experience. The leader may consider the following questions:

- What did you like most about the group experience?
- What did you like least about the group experience?
- What aspects of the group were most helpful? Least helpful?
- What characteristics do you feel make an effective leader?
- What characteristics do you feel make an effective group member?

In evaluating the group, members may provide abstract or vague feedback without concrete examples of what they have learned in the group and how they learned it. The leader should encourage members to provide more concrete, specific responses. In response to the first question (What did you like most about the group experience?), for example, Dee responds, "I liked everything—this has been the most positive experience of my life and I loved every aspect of the group." The leader should follow up and encourage Dee to provide more concrete examples: "I think it's great that you got so much out of this group. Tell us one specific thing that made this group a positive experience for you."

In addition to assessing the group process, following termination, leaders should evaluate the effect of the group on members' performance outside the group. To assess change, leaders can use both formal, existing data, as well as informal sources, such as surveys of or discussions with others (e.g., parents and teachers). This accountability is essential for showing the effectiveness of the group. Group evaluation will be covered in much greater depth in Chapter 21.

Challenges

Group members have a variety of feelings related to termination. As termination of a group nears, some members minimize their improvement because of fears of being abandoned by the group. Thus, they may not appear ready to terminate. Other members may overemphasize their growth and may avoid unfinished business or negative feelings. Leaders can minimize these challenges by preparing the group for termination gradually as well as openly sharing their thoughts and feelings related to termination. Case Study 10.11 provides an example of a group termination challenge.

Techniques for Terminating the Group

The techniques for terminating a group are not all that different from the techniques helpful in terminating group sessions. While all groups, regardless of the model type, should include termination, the procedures may be less formal for task groups, psychoeducational groups, and classroom guidance as opposed to counseling or

CASE STUDY 10.11

A Group Termination Challenge

You have been leading a 10-week group for members who self-harm. The group members have made great progress individually and as a group. With two weeks remaining in the group, you begin introducing the topic of termination. The following week, three of the seven group members come back stating that they had a horrible week and that they are not ready to end the group. One of the members doesn't show up, and when you call her later that day, she tells you that she isn't cutting herself anymore anyway and that she doesn't need to finish the rest of the group sessions. As the leader, reflect on how you would address the members' concerns.

psychotherapy groups. In counseling and psychotherapy groups, members have potentially addressed several personal concerns by the termination stage; therefore, assessment of personal goals and needs are important so that members may see how much they have gained from the group process as well pinpoint specific areas for continued growth. For a few sessions before the last group session, leaders should encourage members to consider what they perceive as accomplishments, what they would have done differently, and what they would like to continue to focus on after the group ends. In particular, the leader should encourage group members to reflect on how what they have learned in the group will continue to affect their lives positively. In addition, members should consider what interpersonal connections they have made and what feelings they have related to termination.

Rounds, dyads, sentence completion, and journaling can help facilitate termination of the group, just as they did for session terminations. Below are sample questions that can be used with these activities:

- What fears did you have coming into this group?
- What fears do you have now as we prepare to end the group experience?
- What is the most important lesson you will take away from this group experience?
- Describe yourself when you first came into the group. Describe yourself now. How are you different? What has made you different?

- How would others close to you describe you before and after the group experience?
- Imagine that you could go back and talk to the person you were before the group began. Based on what you have learned during the group, what advice would you give that person?
- How will you be affected by your experience in this group?

PLANNING FOR THE FUTURE Termination of the group is not only a time for reflection and summarization but also includes looking toward the future and implementing new skills beyond the group. Members can help each other with plans for the future and the implementation of new skills beyond the group through the following activity. Have members put their names on a piece of paper and divide the paper into three sections labeled 1, 5, and 10 years. Have members pass around their paper to other group members. Members are instructed to write down where they believe the group member whose name is on the paper will be in 1, 5 and 10 years from today. After each member has had an opportunity to write on every other group member's paper, the paper is returned to the owner of the paper. Members are given an opportunity to review what other group members have written. The leader facilitates a discussion related to how the members feel about reading what others have written about them. Do they agree with what has been written about them? Did they read about any surprises? What additional details would members add to their lists?

Another activity that facilitates planning for the future is to have members draw a picture of their lives before the group experience, now as they are ending the group experience, and what they would be like in the future. Leaders then facilitate a discussion related to how members' lives are different, how they brought about those differences for themselves, and how they can continue to make positive changes for themselves.

ROLE PLAYS AND BEHAVIORAL REHEARSALS During the last several sessions, members can practice what they have learned in the group through role plays and behavioral rehearsals. Leaders can have members write down scenarios of issues or concerns that they have and encourage them to role-play those scenarios in the group. The leader can either have members participate in their own scenes or watch how others would handle the situation.

GROUP SCRAPBOOK As a group project, the members can put together a group scrapbook. The scrapbook can include pictures, symbols, and statements relevant to the group. The leader should make sure that each person contributes to the scrapbook. In creating the group scrapbook, members are given the opportunity to reflect on their experience as well as see how others experienced the group. The leader can make the group scrapbook available to the group members in his or her office and bring it to follow-up sessions.

A variation of the group scrapbook is to have each member make an individual scrapbook or collage. The leader simply asks members to create a scrapbook that reflects their experiences in the group. As they create their scrapbooks, members should be encouraged to reflect on what they have learned about themselves during the group experience, as well as what they have learned about others. They should also consider their contributions to the group process. After members have worked on their own scrapbooks, they can bring them to a group session. Members are encouraged to walk around; look at other members' scrapbooks; and contribute thoughts, good wishes, and memories to them. Numerous other closure activities can be located in Keene and Erford (2007).

AFFIRMATIONS In addition to reflecting on the experience and planning for the future, the last session of a group in the school setting should include affirmations. This can be accomplished in multiple ways, depending on the nature of the group and the developmental level of the members. For large classroom guidance, the professional school counselor may affirm progress made through a statement to the entire class. For small process groups, affirmations may be expressed through the distribution of certificates and positive statements made to each member. Leaders may opt for a party where refreshments are served and progress is celebrated.

FOLLOW-UP

Following up with group members after a group has ended is imperative because it benefits both the leader and the members. Following up with members after termination helps to assess the group experience and individual progress. One goal of follow-up is to measure member change, which includes examining if (1) members are continuing to work on goals that were contracted in the final session, (2) behavioral and attitudinal changes related to the group process occurred or were sustained for the members, (3) performance was improved as a result of the group experience, and (4) members experienced additional areas of growth. In essence, leaders can gain information regarding how effective the group has been for the group members. The length of time suggested for follow-up ranges from six weeks to several months. Some leaders even conduct 6-month or 1-year follow-ups.

There are several benefits to following up with members, and leaders should determine to what degree they will follow up. Their decisions may depend on the length, type, and purpose of the group as well as the developmental needs of its members. The decision may be guided by members' feedback (leaders should continually assess group dynamics and learning). Leaders have an ethical responsibility to promote member growth and avoid abandonment. If leaders feel that follow-up sessions would fulfill this responsibility, they should use clinical judgment to determine how many follow-up sessions are needed. Follow-ups can range from formal meetings to informal check-ins. Specific methods for following up with members include interviews, group reunions, and survey methods, and leaders may elect to use any or all of these methods for follow-up.

Interviews may be done individually or as a group. In the case of individual interviews, leaders may want to assess individual experiences within the group and the degree to which members have met their goals. Leaders may also want to review referral sources applicable for members who may desire additional group work or individual counseling. In group interviews, leaders can conduct a focus group discussing any changes, new challenges, and issues that members have experienced. If new issues have arisen for some members, leaders can provide referrals for additional counseling or other services. During the interviews, leaders may pose the following questions:

• What effects did the group have on you?
• How has the group influenced you in relation to others?
• How has the group influenced you in relation to your performance?

• What changes have you noticed since leaving the group?
• What recommendations do you have for future groups?

Leaders may consider coordinating a reunion for the members. A reunion may be helpful for both open and closed groups. Group reunions provide a social environment whereby members can reconnect with each other in a less structured setting.

Follow-up provides an opportunity to administer any post-tests. Leaders may want to use a brief questionnaire to assess members' satisfaction with the group as well as for assessing progress toward meeting goals. Surveys may be used at variable time periods to measure both short-term and long-term progress.

During the last group session, leaders explain to group members the purpose of follow-up. They also review how and when follow-up will occur. Similar to preparing members for termination, leaders discuss expectations for follow-up and provide alternatives if members do not wish to follow up formally after termination. One alternative involves providing referrals for other forms of treatment, including individual counseling, community services, or another type of group.

Summary

Termination is an essential part of all phases of group counseling. It occurs when a member leaves prematurely, at the end of each session, and as the group experience ends. If executed properly, termination serves as a critical force in the process of change. Some of the major benefits of termination include self-awareness, awareness of others, and the development of coping skills and interpersonal skills. Despite the benefits of termination, the termination process also involves various challenges, including feelings of separation and loss, difficulty dealing with closure, and conflicted feelings related to ending relationships formed during the group.

There are three types of terminations: premature termination, termination of group sessions, and termination of the group experience.

Premature termination involves either the leader or members leaving the group before the goals of the group have been accomplished or before a predetermined time to end the group. Premature termination brings with it opportunities for group growth and challenges. Termination of group sessions refers to conducting a mini-termination at the end of each group session that provides an opportunity for both the leader and members to summarize their learning and to discuss implementation of skills outside the group. A group can terminate at a preset time or when most of the members are ready to terminate. Rounds, dyads, sentence completion, and journaling are all techniques that can assist with both termination of group sessions and termination of the group.

CHAPTER 11

Leading Task Groups

Janice L. DeLucia-Waack and Amy Nitza

PREVIEW

Task groups are everywhere. Group supervision, planning meetings, clubs, task forces, staff development, community presentations, and classrooms are all examples of task groups. Task groups involve groups of people who come together for a common goal. This chapter contains strategies for using group dynamics, group process, and leadership skills to create successful task groups. Guidelines are included for leading effective task groups aimed at children and adolescents (e.g., classroom guidance lessons, clubs, community service projects, youth organizations) and also adults (e.g., staff or team meetings, professional development). Examples are included to illustrate successful strategies and leadership styles.

LEADING TASK GROUPS

CASE STUDY 11.1

The Book Club

Ms. Dean, a community librarian, wants to invite more adolescents, particularly adolescent girls, to use library services. She hears one girl saying that she wants to be in a book club at school but can't meet early in the morning. Ms. Dean invites the student to create a book club with her friends to meet after school at the library one day a week. Ms. Dean believes this as a good way to teach about women's history, talk about relationship issues with the girls, and cultivate communication and presentation skills. She chooses the book *Seneca Falls Inheritance* (Monfredo, 1992), the first in a series of historical fiction mixed with mystery, as the first book. Her plan is to use the discussion questions on the publisher's website as a place to start. The first meeting goes well, with six girls attending and each talking about what they had read. Some girls had read further than others, so some discussions had to be cut off. Ms. Dean ends the first session by thanking the girls and asking each to read to page 200 by the next meeting (structure). She also emails them two days before the next meeting with two discussion questions to start their next meeting (more structure).

Continued

CASE STUDY 11.1 *(Continued)*

The girls are eager to talk at the next session and quickly get into a discussion of the *Married Women's Property Act* and some of the implications in the book. Ms. Dean then asks how things have changed for women in this century. The girls talk for a while. Ms. Dean then asks about their lives and their plans for the future. One of the girls says, "I didn't know we were going to talk about personal stuff here." Another girl says, "I would rather talk about personal stuff. Let's read something good like *The Sisterhood of the Traveling Pants* (Brashares, 2003) so we can talk about boys." Ms. Dean hasn't read that book so she wants to check with other librarians, and maybe with parents, too, about whether it is appropriate for young teens (appropriate structure with minors). She ends the meeting by saying, "Let's finish this book and then we can select another book to read."

The third meeting begins with Ms. Dean asking each group member to state who is her favorite character (other than the heroine) and why. Amanda goes first and describes her favorite character. Brittany then responds, "How stupid!" Kelsy then says, "Well, I'm not going to answer that question if Brittany is going to be like that." Ms. Dean asks the girls to talk about how they are going to disagree and present different points of view. She reminds them that sometimes it is helpful to ask questions when you don't understand a point of view or see it differently from the person speaking. The girls agree to the following rules: (1) One person speaks at a time; (2) no name calling; (3) no saying, "That's stupid"; (4) everyone can have a different opinion; (5) no one has to answer a discussion question if they don't want to; (6) people can ask you what you are thinking if you are quiet; (7) we are all working on speaking clearly and making our point, so if we don't understand, we will ask for clarification; and (8) we will take turns choosing books and writing discussion questions (with Ms. Dean's approval).

Ms. Dean's intentions with this book club were admirable but not clearly defined. The goals evolved as they begin to work together but not without some disagreement and hurt feelings. It probably would have been helpful for Ms. Dean to communicate what she hoped the girls would learn as a result of the book club as well as to ask the girls to state what they hoped to get out of the book club. With children and adolescents, it is also helpful to inform parents of the goals, purpose, and content. The book suggested by the girls (*The Sisterhood of the Traveling Pants*) might be viewed as too advanced for young teenagers, and parents might not have approved of the choice of books. If the girls choose to talk about personal issues, Ms. Dean might want to ask a community group work specialist to assist or be available to consult, or perhaps use some sort of classroom guidance curriculum on relationship skills appropriate for young adolescents.

Group work and team work are an established part of the community. Group cooperation and learning happen in clubs and organized activities and as teams of counselors work together to establish programs, staff cases, and identify interventions and perhaps curriculum for clients. If one considers all of these events as task groups, then therapeutic factors and leadership principles can be applied to enhance the efficacy of each of them. The Association for Specialists in Group Work (ASGW) published the *Professional Standards for the Training of Group Workers* (2000) with two goals: (1) identification of four types of groups (i.e., task/work, psychoeducational/guidance, counseling, and psychotherapy groups), and (2) to specify the focus and goals of each group and training activities for each type of group. "The focus of task groups . . . is on the application of group dynamics principles and processes to improve the practice and accomplishment of identified work goals" (Conyne, Rapin, & Rand, 1997, p. 117). The *Specialization in Task and Work Group Facilitation* emphasizes:

> The application of principles of normal human development and functioning through group-based educational, developmental, and systemic strategies applied in the context of here-and-now interaction that promote efficient and effective accomplishment of group tasks among people who are gathered to accomplish group task goals (Association for Specialists in Group Work [ASGW], 2000).

Task groups and work groups come together with a specific group goal. The focus of this type of group is on the accomplishment of the group goal rather than on individual member goals. Task forces, planning groups, community organizations, discussion groups, study circles, learning groups, committees, clubs, work groups within organizations, and classrooms are all task and work groups. The use of an activity within a task or work group usually is focused on the accomplishment of the group goal or on creating an atmosphere or procedure that is effective in accomplishing the group goal. The efficacy of task groups may vary depending on the applications of group principles and leadership skills. This chapter will provide strategies for using group dynamics, group process, and leadership skills to create successful task groups. Mental health professionals, educators, and businesspeople may all benefit from these suggestions.

Two types of task groups will be discussed in this chapter: those led by group leaders consisting of staff or professional associates (e.g., team or association meetings, professional development workshops, case supervision) and those led by a group leader consisting of children or adolescents (e.g., clubs, task forces, teams, community service projects, classroom guidance lessons). Successful examples of each are included with the discussion of the suggested principles.

IMPORTANT PRINCIPLES IN LEADING EFFECTIVE TASK GROUPS

It is important to define a successful task group. Hulse-Killacky, Killacky, and Donigian (2001) stated that:

> Successful groups, characterized by accomplishment and personal satisfaction, are those in which people:
>
> - Feel listened to.
> - Are accepted for their individuality.
> - Have a voice.
> - Are part of a climate in which leaders and members acknowledge and appreciate varied perspectives, needs, and concerns.
> - Understand and support the purpose of the group.
> - Have the opportunity to contribute to the accomplishment of particular tasks. (p. 6)

It is also important to think about why task groups are formed. Why work in a group when an individual can accomplish a task? Why not break down the task(s) or goals of a task group and ask five people to work independently rather than trying to coordinate group meetings and collaboration? Everyone has been in a work group that has great difficulty scheduling a time when everyone can meet, where the discussion becomes off-topic, or emotional conflict surfaces. So why work in groups? The primary reason is that task groups often create a synergy of ideas, resources, and plans that does not happen when people work individually on a task. But another reason is that group interdependence, cooperation, and altruism interact so that group goals are created and accomplished more productively than by individuals working alone.

Conyne, Rapin, and Rand (1997) emphasized that certain conditions must be met in order for task groups to be productive: in particular, leadership by a capable professional practitioner, application of theoretical understanding of group process, and recognition of interpersonal interdependence. Thus, it is essential to emphasize both the content and process of groups, just like it is for other types of groups. Task groups, by definition, must have a collective group goal, but group members must also feel connected and part of the group in order to contribute and, if it is a voluntary group, even to attend. Task groups that fail often do not pay attention to the importance of group process and how it influences motivation and efforts to accomplish the group goal. The suggestions that follow are based on the literature regarding effective task groups and teams in schools, business, and industry using group dynamics principles.

Suggestions for Effective Leadership

Leaders of a task group have a significant challenge in creating an atmosphere where the group members embrace the goal(s) of the group and work together cooperatively and effectively. Leadership functions can best be categorized in terms of planning, performing, and processing (Association for Specialists in Group Work [ASGW], 2007). The planning phase involves preparation and planning prior to the beginning of the first group session. Performing focuses on the group leadership skills necessary to lead the task group effectively. Processing asks each group leader to reflect on the group process, dynamics, and effectiveness to plan for future group sessions and interventions. Group leaders should consider guidelines 1-4, discussed below, during the planning phase, then adjust and attend to them as they establish and lead their task groups.

1. ESTABLISH CLEARLY THE GOAL OF THE GROUP FOR THE LEADER(S) AND THE MEMBERS Establishing the goals for a task group requires the leader and members to consider a number of guiding questions, including: What outcome is to be attained? What problem(s) are to be solved? How will the group know it is successful? Why, how, and by whom has this group been established? How does the goal fit with the needs of the organization? Who determines the goal(s)? Has it been predetermined? Does the group set the goal? Are there any perimeters or restrictions?

Goals are the defined outcomes of the task group and are sometimes different than content or the agenda of specific meetings. For instance, the overarching goal of the committee on special education in a school district is to determine whether students need additional services to succeed academically, and if they do, what services are needed. The agenda for such a group would vary depending on the meeting because different students' situations would be placed on the agenda. For a community mental health center planning committee, the overall goal might be to coordinate and plan a group program that offers a series of psychoeducational and counseling groups with different foci in an organized and sequenced way so that clients can participate in one or more groups within a year, or perhaps they begin with a psychoeducational group on a particular topic and then enter a more general counseling group (e.g., begin with a 10-week, structured cognitive behavioral group for eating disorders and then move into an interpersonal counseling group). Early meetings might focus on deciding when groups were most needed, and then subsequent meetings might focus on organizing group intervention materials and creating a schedule. Later meetings might focus on the effective implementation of the groups and case supervision as needed. For an ecology club, the goal might be to make the public aware of ways to recycle through public education, with early meetings focusing on the plans for the year and later sessions focusing on execution of those plans.

If the leader or an outside entity has defined the goals, then how are the goals communicated to the rest of the committee? How will questions and concerns about the goals be discussed? How will the task group members make the goals theirs? How will progress be evaluated and communicated? If the group is to determine their goals, will they be informed ahead of time so they can be prepared for the discussion of goals? For example, a worksite wellness committee might be asked to think about what should be the focus of this committee for the coming year so that goals could be established at the first meeting. How will these goals be articulated? How will they be communicated to other members of the company? How will progress be evaluated?

Conyne, Rapin, and Rand (1997) emphasized that while most teams or task groups are organized around reaching performance goals, individual goals or the means to achieve them may differ from group to group. Goal clarity is essential. For example, all chapters of Mothers Against Drunk Driving (MADD) have the goal of preventing or decreasing the negative effects of drunk driving; each chapter may select different approaches to this problem, from sponsoring an after-prom party to conducting a communitywide public education campaign. For a staff development workshop, the facilitator needs to articulate clearly what new knowledge, attitudes, or skills the counselors will learn as a result of the lesson. If the focus of the staff development is to enhance parent effectiveness, the goals might be to (1) identify appropriate situations in counseling to introduce the topic of effective parenting, (2) identify and practice behavioral strategies for parents to implement, and (3) introduce and brainstorm resources (books, handouts, websites) for use with parents.

In addition, Conyne, Wilson, and Ward (1996) emphasize the mutuality of goals and the importance of group members collaborating to set goals. It is essential for members of any group to establish and agree on goals as part of the forming and orienting stage; the processes of discussion, internationalization of group goals and the collective process, collaboration, compromise, and giving feedback all begin with this discussion. Whether voluntary or assigned, the group members must begin to make the goals theirs. One way to do this is to simply ask members to come to the first meeting prepared to talk about their goals for this group and their ideas about how these goals can be accomplished. Mullen, Johnson, and Salas (1991), in their meta-analyis, noted that more creativity occurs if group members work individually first. In the case of Ms. Dean's book club, identifying and sharing her specific goals for the group, as well as asking each member for her goals and expectations prior to the first meeting or holding a discussion about goals and expectations at the beginning of the first meeting, may have prevented some of the confusion or misunderstanding that occurred during the second meeting.

2. ESTABLISH THE MEMBERSHIP AND GUIDELINES FOR PARTICIPATION   How does this task group establish membership? Is it voluntary? If members are selected, then by whom and based on what criteria? Who informs members of participation in this group? If the administrator of an outside organization appoints group members, it is helpful for the administrator to inform the members and to share with them a vision and goals for this group. Members may not be as committed if the appointment is not communicated directly by the administration. Task groups do not operate in a vacuum. It is essential to understand the context of why the task group was created. Members may also need to know what expertise they are expected to bring to the group. For example, a community is concerned about teenage alcohol and drug use and abuse. Parents, teachers, and counselors come together to create a task force to identify community interventions to deter such use. Membership included parents of children and adolescents of various ages, school personnel, counselors from local schools and agencies, and local businesspeople.

It is also helpful to clarify participation policies. Is attendance mandatory? Will attendance be public information? Will attendance be reported to administration personnel? If the group is voluntary, it is still helpful to have some kind of guidelines about attendance. How many meetings can a member miss before he or she will be considered a dropout? Who should members notify if they will miss a meeting? Who is responsible for informing members of what they missed?

3. ESTABLISH A STRUCTURE FOR GROUP MEETINGS   Meeting structure includes meeting time and duration, group member roles, and guidelines for how members will interact with each other. How often and for how long will the group meet? Will members have assigned roles? Will these roles rotate? How are roles determined (assigned, elected, volunteer)? It is helpful to have a convener or leader, a secretary to record meeting minutes, someone to write down ideas during brainstorming sessions, and someone to act as parliamentarian to keep the discussion on task. Who sets the agenda? When? What is the deadline for putting items on the agenda? For instance, when case supervision occurs every two weeks, it is helpful to decide at the end of a meeting who will present a client or issue at the next meeting. The person who will present then agrees to provide the team with a description of the critical client or issue a week before the next meeting. Other team members are then instructed to bring information to the next meeting related to the issue. Information to be gathered may be specific (e.g., resources for clients with eating disorders, information on other family members), while others may bring more general information based on similar clients or experiences.

Conyne, Wilson, and Ward (1996) also stressed the multidimensionality of goals, particularly as it relates to the structure of task group meetings. "All groups include various combinations of intrapersonal, interpersonal, and task-related goals. A committee, specifically established to accomplish a set of tasks, needs to accommodate intrapersonal and interpersonal goals to be effective" (p. 9). In task groups, those intrapersonal and interpersonal goals relate to how the group

will accomplish its task(s). Two issues, which are related but different, need to be decided. First is a general consensus on how group members will interact with each other. Hulse-Killacky et al. (2001) emphasized the need for group members to develop an ethic of cooperation, collaboration, and mutual respect as well as building a culture that appreciates differences. Conyne, Wilson, and Ward (1996) suggested that the composition "must include sufficient members with enough diversity to fuel group interaction" (p. 7). Guidelines for discussion must emphasize cooperation and allow for differences to occur. The task group leader, through the shaping of the group structure, must motivate members and monitor movement toward goals (Conyne, Rapin, & Rand, 1997).

Typically, the guidelines include statements like: (1) Every person must be treated with respect; (2) personal attacks are not allowed; (3) it is okay to say, "I do not understand _____. Can you tell me more about that?"; (4) allow others to finish before speaking to avoid interruptions; (5) listen carefully as a person speaks—if you are planning what you will say or do, you may not fully understand the person speaking; and (6) outside the group, opinions can be discussed but not people.

Kottler (2001) created a list of guidelines for members of psychoeducational, counseling, and psychotherapy groups, but some of them apply to task groups as well: speak only for yourself in the group; use *I* rather than *we*; blaming, whining, and complaining about people outside the group are discouraged; racist, sexist, or otherwise disrespectful language will not be tolerated; and no name calling.

Now, let's revisit the case of Ms. Dean and analyze her situation from this new perspective. Early in her first book club meeting, Ms. Dean could have engaged the girls in a dialogue to establish ground rules for all discussions, and she could have shared her expectations for the girls' behavior during the group. Having established ground rules may have prevented the hurt feelings that resulted from the disagreements that took place. If members did behave in a manner that was inappropriate, the ground rules would

---

TABLE 11.1   Guidelines for Leading Classroom Discussions with a Goal of Identifying Critical Issues or Points for Discussion and Application of New Information

---

1. What are the goals of this discussion? What do you want the discussants to leave knowing? Doing differently? Thinking differently? Feeling differently? Describe each goal in terms of knowledge, behavior, or cognition. (For a 20- to 30-minute discussion, 2 to 3 goals are reasonable.)
2. From the material to be discussed (either provided beforehand to read or in the form of a minilecture), what are the key points? Bullet these points and then provide an outline of how you will get the members to identify the key points. What questions will you ask? Can you do an activity to help them identify the key points? How can you focus the discussion without giving members the answers?
3. Based on the key points, how can this information be applied and integrated? What questions can be asked? Can scenarios be discussed? Can an activity be implemented to facilitate learning?
4. Summary/wrap-up: How will you end? How will you assess what your members have learned?

---

have provided a structure for correcting the behavior with little disruption to the group. Correction of behavior is often done by the leader or even by another member simply reminding group members of the ground rules. These guidelines, along with clear goals, would have helped the girls see the multiple levels of conversations that can occur: talking about the content of the book, relating the book to their lives, and practicing articulating their opinion and agreeing and/or disagreeing with others.

If the task of some group is to create and deliver a new intervention or plan, then it is helpful to agree on a problem-solving structure. Several are commonly used. Problem-based learning (Duch, Groh, & Allen, 2001) suggests a series of questions that group members answer on their own and then share the answers with the group: (1) Identify the topic or problem to be addressed. (2) What do we know about it? (3) What do we need to know? (4) How can we get what we need? (5) What can we do with all this information? (6) What does it all mean? (7) What are some of the action steps? Conyne (2006, p. 171) suggested a model for agenda setting for a team that includes the following steps: (1) team building; (2) discuss and understand the context, problem, and goals; (3) brainstorm; (4) discuss and clarify terms; (5) include factor analysis in strategy clusters; (6) identify and rank-order the top strategy clusters; and (7) use consensus decision making. Tables 11.1 through 11.4

include variations of these frameworks, as well as guidelines and evaluation checklists for planning a problem-solving session (e.g., planning group, student services team [SST] meeting) and a topical discussion (e.g., professional development workshop, book club, classroom guidance).

If the task of the group is focused on discussion and application of new information, such as in classroom guidance presentations for students

---

TABLE 11.2   Feedback Sheet for Topical Discussions

0	1	2	3	4
Not at all		**OK**		**Very Strong**

____ 1. Use of handouts/outline.
____ 2. Detail of planning outline.
____ 3. Clear opening/introduction to topic.
____ 4. Clear statement of goals of discussion.
____ 5. Help participants to identify key concepts.
____ 6. Redirecting and refocusing when necessary.
____ 7. Shift to application and integration of key concepts.
____ 8. Statements to encourage application and integration.
____ 9. Suggestions of issues and scenarios for application.
____ 10. Clear summary/closure.
____ 11. Facilitation without dominating.
____ 12. Prepared without rote reading.

TABLE 11.3   Guidelines for Leading Problem-solving Discussions to Articulate a Plan of Action

1. What are the goals of this discussion? What problem needs to be solved? Describe each goal or problem in terms of knowledge, behavior, or cognition.
2. Outline how you want to structure the discussion in terms of how much time should be spent on each part of the process such as:
   a. Description of problem (cognitions, affect, behavior)
   b. Relevant background and other interventions already used
      i. Data from multiple sources
   c. Brainstorming possible solutions
      i. First, have each group member write down all possible solutions within a short period of time (2 to 5 minutes) or come prepared to the meeting with this information.
   d. Identification of a plan of action based on group consensus
   e. Identification of key points of the plan
      i. Who, what, when, and where
   f. Timeline for implementation and feedback
      i. Who, what, when, and where.
3. Outline what you will say to introduce and move through your model.
4. Identify how you will gently redirect comments and keep members on task.
5. Summary/wrap-up: How will you end? When will you meet to assess progress?

TABLE 11.4   Feedback Sheet for Problem-solving Discussions

0	1	2	3	4
Not at all		OK		Very Strong

_____ 1. Use of handouts/outline.
_____ 2. Detailed planning outline.
_____ 3. Opening/introduction to topic.
_____ 4. Clear statement of goals of discussion.
_____ 5. Clear communication of process.
_____ 6. Redirecting/refocusing when necessary.
_____ 7. Enough time on each step.
_____ 8. Statements to encourage application and integration.
_____ 9. Statements to clearly identify intervention.
_____ 10. Application and integration for all.
_____ 11. Statements to clarify plan and timeframe.
_____ 12. Facilitation without dominating.
_____ 13. Orepared without rote reading.

or professional development workshops for adults, then an outline that identifies key concepts of the material and suggests applications of the information is useful. For example, a group leader invited to a school to present a classroom guidance lesson on Internet safety might show students a short transcript of conversations in a chat room between a 14-year-old girl and a 50-year-man posing as a 15-year-old-boy. Students are first asked to talk about who they have met in a chat room and how much and what kinds of information they have shared online. Students are then asked to identify what clues the 14-year-old girl gave to her identity and how, by using Internet resources, the other person was able to figure out where she lived and where she would be at a particular time. Then students are asked to collaborate and generate ways to keep themselves and their friends safe and how they can interact online without putting themselves at risk.

Group guidelines or ground rules are needed to clarify what members are expected to do in group and thus encourage positive member participation (Conyne, Rapin, & Rand., 1997). General guidelines are useful for the life of the task group, as is an agenda or organizational structure for each meeting. An estimated timetable for each agenda item is also helpful to keep members on task. It is not useful to plan a meeting for an hour and then spend 50 minutes on the first item. Members are then in an awkward position of leaving if they have another commitment and/or not devoting sufficient time to important topics. One common mistake in problem-focused meetings (e.g., student support team, association meeting, work task force) is spending at least one-half, if not more, of a meeting identifying the problem. If the problem is identified and clearly stated and distributed to all group members prior to the meeting, five minutes ordinarily is sufficient time to clarify the problem. Then the majority of the meeting can be spent on identifying and planning interventions for change and a viable course of action.

An agenda is essential to any task group meeting. Often, it is helpful to distribute the agenda in advance of the meeting so members are prepared to report on and discuss items and progress. The leader makes the agenda based on input from the members. Some questions to consider as part of the guidelines on how the task group will function include: Who actually sets the agenda? How does an item get on the agenda? When, in advance of the meeting, do agenda items have to be submitted? Is the agenda sent out in advance of the meeting? When is it sent? What do members need to do to prepare for the meeting?

When items are brought up in the task group, it is useful to help group members connect their statements to the task group goals. Sometimes, group members are not clear about how items relate to group goals, and they may spend unnecessary time talking about unrelated issues. Hulse-Killacky et al. (2001, p. 88) suggested the following prompts: "What I want to accomplish today is . . .; What I need to do to accomplish my goal is.. . . .; The resources in this group that can help me are . . .; How I will know if I accomplished my goal today. . . ."

4. STRIVE FOR A BALANCE OF PROCESS AND CONTENT ISSUES A task group includes both content and process. Content is the task and/or the goals of the group that need to be clearly outlined and articulated, and much attention each meeting should be focused on the task(s) at hand. Process is what happens to help (or hinder) a task group in achieving its goals. While there is always a propensity in task groups to focus on the task at hand and ignore the relationships that create the group, at some point ignoring relationships probably becomes a problem. In any group, members need to feel a sense of connection to other members and to the group. Cohesiveness and connection (or the lack thereof) ultimately influences the success of the

group. Group process must always be attended to, even in task groups. Group leaders work to shape positive group process and dynamics as well as to intervene and redirect members who interfere with achieving group goals. The earlier three guidelines have discussed how to create a structure within which task group members can clearly identify goals and work together cooperatively.

In initial meetings of task groups, it is important to establish connections and relationships between group members and also connections to the group goal. As mentioned earlier, it is important for group members to articulate in their own words what they see as their goal for the group. For example, the overarching goal of a student support team may be to identify students at-risk, but it would be helpful for each member to talk about what challenges students in their school typically encounter. Following that, it is helpful to ask group members to describe how they have approached such issues on their own to identify multiple perspectives, resources, and strengths within the group (e.g., diversity in experience, perspective, and strengths are valued in task groups). Hulse-Killacky et al. (2001) described the initial session as the warm-up phase of a task group. They suggested three questions that need to be answered: "Who am I? (process), Who am I with you? (process), and What do we have to do? (content)" (p. 31). Some sort of introductory activity that identifies group members' names and their connection to the group is necessary.

In groups with members who do not know each other, it is also helpful to use an activity to help everyone to remember each others' names. It is embarrassing for members in the fourth meeting of a group to have to say, "I agree with what that person in the green sweater said." Hulse-Killacky's (2006) *The Names Activity* helps group members to remember each other's names and begins to establish connections in the group. In a group where members have established relationships (some of which may not be positive), leaders should help group members to think about themselves in terms of the goals of the task group. Helpful activities that focus on characteristics or perspectives that group members may bring to the task at hand will help them to be successful. Gillam's (2006) *What a Character!* and Guth's (2006) *Getting to Know Each Other* highlight characteristics and traits members bring to task groups.

Activities should never be used just for fun. They should also have a goal related to either the content or the process of the group. If the group needs to connect or learn more about each other, then some kind of appropriate self-disclosure activity might be helpful. Conroy's (2006) *Getting to Know You—Now and Then* includes 44 different questions that can stimulate discussion. Warm's (2006) *Map of the World* asks group members to share about themselves and also begin to relate to other group members. DeLucia-Waack, Bridbord, Kleiner, and Nitza's 2006 compilation includes more than 50 activities arranged by group stage, purpose, and type of group. Barlow, Blythe, and Edmonds (1999); Dossick and Shea (1988, 1990, 1995); Foster (1989); and Keene and Erford (2007) all detail group activities that can be used as ice-breakers to promote discussion.

If the goal is to create new interventions with brainstorming and problem solving, then activities that highlight these skills might be useful. Hutchins's (2006) *A What?* and Halbur's (2006) *Ball in Play* encourage levity, humor, and laughter within group work; they also ask group members to think about how groups work effectively in a nonthreatening way. B. Hayes's (2006) *More or Less* is an ice-breaker that may be used to facilitate self-disclosure, cohesiveness, and a discussion of how groups work without being overly intrusive. R. Hayes's (2006) *Why Are We Meeting Like This?* is a good ice-breaker for group members who may have some resistance to meeting or have had trouble in the past working together. In the warm-up stage, it is helpful to accent the positives and strengths of members, and the connections between members. At the same time, it is useful to create a structure that allows for open and honest dialogue and brainstorming, feedback, and respect for all

members. Creating guidelines for discussion and a template for each session's agenda works to create a cooperative atmosphere. Activities and discussions in the warm-up phase should result in cooperation, understanding and appreciation of differences, and active participation of members (Hulse-Killacky et al., 2001). "Intentional and thoughtful coalition building actually contributes to successful outcomes" (p. 33).

Group leaders must pay attention to group process. If the group is working well, then praise should be given: "This was a great meeting." "We did a great job of problem-solving." "We worked hard to get some interventions going. Thanks." It is also helpful to ask group members to reflect on how it worked: "We did a great job of problem solving today. How did we do it so we can make sure it happens again?" "What allowed us to freely generate options and then pick the best one?" "What did each one of you do that contributed to this process?" "Who was helpful to you in being creative (or invested) and how? Thank them." Hulse-Killacky et al. (2001) emphasized the importance of allowing members time to reflect on their work, both at the end of the session and when the task group goal is accomplished.

If the process is not working, then this situation should also be addressed so that group members can identify and evaluate what the problem is and suggest solutions to solve it. When group members may not appear committed to or interested in a discussion, their feedback may be shallow or superficial, or they may suggest solutions that do not appear realistic or helpful, the following questions may be helpful in generating discussion about the group process: "Something seems different in this meeting. What do you think it is?" "We seem to have trouble focusing (or staying on task or getting into details). What do you think is happening?" "No one seems to be very invested in this discussion (or our solutions or options)."

Even if the group leader can identify the obstacle, it is helpful to start by commenting only on what has been observed. It is much more helpful if the group members can identify what the obstacle is and then come up with a solution. Sometimes it is helpful to talk about what it is like to disagree or have different perspectives on an issue. It is one thing to agree that it is okay to suggest different options and another to realize you are the only one in the room voting for a particular option. If the resistance is to the process of problem solving, Trotzer's (2006) activity *Boxed In* helps group members to identify potential obstacles to problem solving and to generate solutions to overcome these obstacles. Smead's (1995) activity, *Responsibility Pie,* is useful in looking at how each group member may contribute to a situation and then what they can do to change it. This activity emphasizes that each person has a responsibility in each situation and also that even a small change can have a big impact. Another type of activity that may be useful in task and work groups is one that asks members to focus on their relationships with others in the group and how it affects productivity. Rapin's (2006) activity *What Is My Relationship to the Group?* asks members to describe their relationship to the group. Brown's (2006) activity *A Group Image* also asks group members to examine their perceptions of how the group works together and to identify potential areas of difficulty.

It is important to remember that different points of view, feedback, conflict, and disagreement are all inherent in the creative process and critical elements in group dynamics. Diversity in resources and approaches is critical to problem solving and task groups. Not all disagreement or differences in opinion are bad. Let's revisit the guideline that Ms. Dean offered to the book club at the beginning of this chapter: "Sometimes it is helpful to ask questions when you don't understand a point of view or see it differently from the person speaking." If a task group can recognize that explaining your point of view to someone else often helps clarify it for you and that others may change their views based on a clear articulation of reasons or point of view, then open discussion of multiple perspectives can lead to fruitful problem solving, planning, and decision making.

EXAMPLES OF TASK GROUPS

This section provides two examples of the use of task groups. The first example involves a task group of adults, while the second involves a professional school counselor working with a task group of high school students. Table 11.5 provides a list of additional resources about task groups in action.

A Interdisciplinary Case Staffing

The director of a community mental health agency attended a conference on interdisciplinary collaboration in mental health treatment. Without giving too much thought to adapting the ideas to her agency's culture, she decided to implement a new interdisciplinary case staffing (ICS) plan into the agency. Following a model presented at the conference, she decided that the ICS was to be held for two hours each week to discuss four clients. The goals of the ICS were to offer a forum for discussion of problematic or

---

TABLE 11.5   Suggested Readings with Task Group Examples

Conyne. (1999). *Failures in group work: How we can learn from our mistakes.* Thousand Oaks, CA: Sage.

Conyne, R. K., Rapin, L. S., & Rand, J. M. (1997). A model for leading task groups. In H. Forester-Miller & J. A. Kottler (Eds.), *Issues and challenges for group practitioners* (pp. 117–132). Denver: Love Publishing.

Conyne, R. K., Wilson, F. R., & Ward, D. E. (1997). *Comprehensive group work: What it means and how to teach it.* Alexandria, VA: American Counseling Association.

DeLucia-Waack, J. L., & Donigian, J. (2003). *The practice of multicultural group work: Visions and perspectives from the field.* Pacific Grove, CA: Wadsworth Press.

Duch, B. J., Groh, S. E., & Allen, D. E. (2001). *The power of problem-based learning.* Sterling, VA: Stylus Publishing.

Hulse-Killacky, D., Killacky, J., & Donigian, J. (2001). *Making task groups work in your world.* Upper Saddle River, NJ: Merrill Prentice Hall.

challenging client cases and to ensure that all staff members were working collaboratively to provide clients with the best services possible. The director hoped that this new approach would improve cooperation and morale among her staff. She decided that the ICS team would consist of the psychiatrist, psychologist, and social worker, as well as the director herself. Rotating members would be the four counselors each week, who were assigned to present cases, as well as the case managers who work with the presented cases.

After selecting a client for presentation and discussion, the counselor fills out a form that provides information on the client's presenting concern, diagnosis and treatment plan, and progress in treatment. Then the psychiatrist, psychologist, social worker, and case manager gather and submit relevant information on the client as well.

It took almost a month to convene the group for the first time because once the counselors were assigned to present cases, information had to be gathered and distributed, and it was very difficult to schedule a 2-hour block of time that was open on the schedules of all 10 people who were to attend. When the meeting finally occurred, it was not very productive. The first 20 minutes were taken up complaining about how difficult it was to get the extra documentation together and to take an additional two hours of nonbillable time from their week. So the discussion quickly turned to "Is there a way to speed up this process so that it does not take away from billable hours?"

The director wisely recognized that she had proceeded too quickly and with an unwieldy process. She realized that if she continued with the ICS plan as it was, staff morale would decrease rather than improve, and she would not accomplish her goals. She then posed the following to her staff: "Our big goal is to improve collaboration across disciplines to improve our services to clients. How can we best do this? We have a protocol in front of us that has worked for other agencies, but it is clear that we need to make adjustments to make it our own." The director

then asked the staff to take a step back and think about what kinds of collaboration, input, and support they would most like to have in order to improve their work. Each person had a different view based on his or her role in the agency and the specific demands of their respective positions. However, they all agreed that the professional collaboration and feedback would be valuable as long as it could be done efficiently. They also agreed that the original plan was comprehensive and looked promising on paper, but in reality it was too cumbersome due to the amount of information being required for every case, some of which seemed redundant. In addition to concerns about the time involved, staff members were concerned that the discussion would become focused on irrelevant issues and not accomplish the goal of helping counselors deal with difficult cases.

Based on this staff feedback, the director suggested that they choose a specific format for discussion with time allotments for each section (e.g., description of the client's presenting problem and current treatment status—5 minutes, discussion of related information—5 minutes, and discussion of clinical issues and potential interventions and treatment plan adjustments—20 minutes). She also decided to allow counselors to sign up for the ICS meetings they wanted to present cases at, rather than assigning the dates herself, and allow the counselor to decide what documentation was necessary to make the discussion meaningful. Everyone in attendance was in agreement that this modified ICS plan was more likely to be successful and beneficial to the agency.

High School Mentoring Program

The following is an example of a counselor-led student task group. A high school counseling department has developed a peer-mentoring program that involves upperclassmen leading small groups of freshmen. The goals are (1) facilitating freshmen adjustment to high school, and (2) promoting a positive school climate through developing connections among students. The program and its goals were generated from feedback received regarding the school's existing freshmen orientation program. The program included a motivational speaker, panel discussions with upperclassmen, and large-group discussions with counselors. After piloting the orientation, feedback from freshmen participants clearly indicated that they found the panel discussions with the upperclassmen volunteers to be the most useful. It was evident that the freshmen highly valued interaction with upperclassmen and that they preferred speaking with the upperclassmen more than hearing adults speak on similar topics.

Based on this information, it seemed beneficial to create a program that would foster this interaction on a year-round basis. It was hoped that ongoing small-group discussions would provide the same quality of interaction and connections between freshmen and their mentors that freshmen experienced in the original panel discussions. It was determined that the program could support the goals of the new ninth-grade academy program that was scheduled to open in the school the following year. The ninth-grade academy was being developed to provide an environment that would improve the process of freshmen transition; thus, a mentoring program that was supportive of incoming freshmen seemed like a natural fit with the academy. In this way, the goals of the program were generated by the guidance staff in response to an identified need and direct feedback from students, and in coordination with broader administrative goals. The success of the program may be considered in part a result of the goals being generated from the combined needs of different stakeholders within the school community.

The structure of the mentoring program involves student co-leaders facilitating weekly small groups of 8 to 10 freshmen, with a focus on a different topic each week, including issues such as cliques, bullying, teacher expectations, time management, etc. Topics are assigned by the program directors, but mentors are allowed some freedom to select activities related to the topic that they feel would best fit the needs of their specific group. In addition to these content topics, an emphasis within the program is on group process. That is, mentors are taught and encouraged not to focus only on the topic at hand, but to use the topic and activities to help the group members process their experiences in a meaningful way, as well as to focus on developing relationships with the freshmen and encouraging them to develop connections among themselves.

Successful implementation of such a program depends heavily on having effective mentors; the program directors have thus developed a comprehensive and thorough program for mentor selection and training. The individuals developing the mentor-training program can be considered a task group that is brought together for the purpose of achieving specific educational goals, and it is an example of a task group in a school that is led by a staff person but made up of students. An examination of the training process highlights how the program addresses each of the task group principles addressed earlier in the chapter.

The goals of the training program are to provide mentors with adequate preparation to deliver the program as intended. The program directors start with the premise that students are an underutilized resource in schools because they have the inherent capability to be a significant positive force in a school when they are empowered. Program directors have identified a specific combination of knowledge, skills, and commitment necessary to enable students to be successful in this new role. Knowledge goals include understanding their role as mentors, procedural guidelines for confidentiality, circumstances that require upward referral, problem solving, and ethics. Skills to be developed include communication skills and group facilitation techniques. Finally, the training is intended to foster a commitment on the part of the students to the mentoring program, the school, and each other.

Selection of mentors is done through a careful application and screening process. Criteria were established based on characteristics of effective peer helpers, including (1) the personality of the mentor, (2) ability to learn new skills and information, (3) the ability of a portion of the student body to relate to the student (i.e., the goal is to select a diverse group of students who represent different types of students in the school), and (4) the student's level of commitment to improving the school climate (Horne, Nitza, Dobias, Jolliff, & Voors, 2008).

Assessment of mentors based on the established criteria is done in a multi-method format that incorporates a written essay component, recommendations from faculty and staff, and a group interview process. Each of these components provides a unique contribution to the overall selection of mentors and helps ensure that the training has the best possible chance of success.

Once mentors are selected, guidelines for participation are developed both formally and informally. Very early in the training, guidelines for being a peer mentor are set out in the form of a peer mentor code of ethics that is reviewed and discussed. Specific attitudes and program philosophies are made explicit and emphasized in the discussion, including a commitment to learning and an "always ask questions" philosophy. These guidelines are supported with a clear rationale so that students understand the reasons behind them and are therefore more likely to embrace and take ownership of them (Horne et al., 2008).

The other approach to establishing guidelines for participation is through the informal shaping of group norms on the part of the trainers. Having little idea of what to expect when they begin the training, students look to the leaders as models of appropriate behavior in this setting. Particularly because students are used to interacting with adults in school in a teacher–student manner, the program directors work hard early in the program to reestablish a different way of interacting. They do this through modeling desired behaviors and attitudes, including energy, enthusiasm, and commitment, and by their emphasis on listening to student voices and establishing a more collaborative atmosphere. Professional school counselors must remember that the tone they set for training frequently will

be the same tone that the mentors develop in their groups, so careful attention to tone is crucial for the overall success of the program.

When training students in this program, careful attention to structure is vital for success. The overall training program is divided into 15 modules: 5 modules from each of 3 major training goals (i.e., foundational knowledge, peer mentoring skills, and team building). Modules are created using a variety of presentation methods, including lecture, large- and small-group discussion, activities, role plays, games, contests, and skill demonstration and practice. Some of the training actually is psychoeducational in function. A theme running through all the modules and formats is ample opportunity for discussion and processing of learning and experiences. The variety of formats in this particular task group is intentional. It is designed to deliver the important content in a way that keeps the students interested and engaged and that allows them to have fun while learning, thereby increasing their motivation.

While a great deal of content must be learned in the mentor training, an equally important emphasis is placed on developing a group identity among the mentors, who are purposefully drawn from different populations within the school and therefore typically do not know each other well. The program directors believe that the program can be successful only if the mentors are highly invested in it and that they must intentionally work to foster cohesion and commitment. In addition to team-building activities throughout the training, follow-up training meetings are used throughout the school year as the mentor program proceeds. While these additional trainings are used to introduce or review content, their primary purpose is to sustain students' enthusiasm and commitment to the program, as well as their connections to each other.

The success of the program in general, and the emphasis on process as well as content, is evident as peer mentors take on leadership roles with the freshmen and in the school in general. They appear to develop a sense of ownership of their school and a commitment to their group members. Finally, when freshmen group members are asked what their group leaders did that was helpful, the clear answer is that, while they found discussions of some of the group topics were helpful, what they valued most was that the peer mentors listened to them and developed relationships with them. This result would likely not occur without careful attention to process throughout the mentor training.

The first session of the training program is planned and organized to accomplish the following goals with the student mentors: (1) Develop an understanding and overview of the peer-mentoring program (content goal); (2) develop foundational knowledge regarding characteristics and ethics of effective peer mentors (content goal); (3) develop a commitment to the peer-mentoring program (process goal); and (4) develop a group identity, cohesion, and commitment to the peer mentors as a team (process goal). To accomplish these goals, a 3-hour training workshop is provided. The agenda for the training workshop is provided in Table 11.6. Note how portions of the agenda look psychoeducational. As mentioned earlier, the psychoeducational portions are needed to teach the task group members what they must know to accomplish the task.

The same format described in Table 11.6 is used in the subsequent training sessions,

---

TABLE 11.6 Agenda for a 3-Hour Mentor-Training Workshop

1. *Introduction and ground rules (10 minutes).*   These brief comments by the facilitators set the tone and provide initial structure by including an overview of the peer-mentoring program, an overview of the training, and basic expectations and ground rules for conduct during the training session.
2. *Creation of small teams (5 minutes).*   The large group is then immediately divided into smaller teams to increase safety by allowing students to break the ice with a smaller number of students initially. The activity *Saying Hello* (Horne et al., 2008) is used to form the teams. This specific activity is used because it necessitates active participation and gets students moving around right away. The teams that are formed using this activity will be used again throughout the training.
3. *Team building (30 minutes).*   In the small teams, two additional ice-breaker activities develop safety and encourage communication and cooperation. The activity *Name Game* (Horne et al., 2008) is followed by a cooperative team activity in which students must work together to create a team name and logo.
4. *Break (15 minutes).*
5. *Initial content module: characteristics of a peer helper (30 minutes).*   Following the team activities, the first content is delivered. The goal of the first module is to help students begin to identify the qualities and characteristics that make a good peer mentor and to define the nature of helping relationships. This is done through the use of *Mona's Story*, followed by small-team discussions to identify the message of the story and the characteristics of peer helpers, and to begin to have students reflect on their own strengths and helping qualities. These discussion topics are then reviewed with the large group.
6. *Content module two: helping skills (40 minutes).*   This module builds on the discussion of the characteristics of peer helpers by introducing the basic helping skills necessary to put those characteristics into action. The skills are introduced, demonstrated, and then practiced in pairs within the small teams.
7. *Break (15 minutes).*
8. *Content module three: peer mentor code of ethics (15 minutes).*   This module builds on the previous two modules; its objectives are to establish guidelines and expectations for mentor behavior and to increase understanding of mentor responsibilities as peer helpers. This takes place through large-group lecture to review the code of ethics, followed by each member signing the code.
9. *Team challenge: pop quiz (10 minutes).*   The closing activity is a team competition to review all the information covered in the workshop. At this point, students have become connected to their teams. The team competitions thus become motivating to the students and promote ownership of the content. This commitment to their small teams also fosters a greater commitment to the overall peer-mentoring program.

including the combination of team-building activities, delivery of content, and team competitions for review. Large-group activities are also incorporated once an initial sense of safety and comfort has been established. Activities that require a greater degree of risk, such as role-playing group leadership skills and crisis situations, are more readily accepted by students after this initial foundation has been established. By the end of the training, task group mentors demonstrate a sense of cohesion and connectedness that promotes a commitment to the program, as well as the knowledge and skills necessary to begin their roles as group leaders.

Summary

Task groups play an important part in community agencies and the workplace. The application of group principles and processes can result in groups that are more effective in meeting their goals, which in turn contributes to the overall functioning of counseling agencies and work settings. Counselors are trained in group leadership and can offer these skills in supporting the functioning of task groups. A consideration of the principles of task group leadership suggested here allows counselors to be successful in facilitating (i.e., leading or consulting with) groups of varying types.

As illustrated by the case examples, these principles can apply to groups made up exclusively of community personnel working together to accomplish particular tasks, as well as to those in which counselors work with parents, children, and adolescents to achieve specific objectives. Careful attention to the planning phase, including establishing clear goals for members and leaders as well as guidelines for membership and participation, increases the likelihood of success by reducing factors that are likely to result in confusion, frustration, or resistance. Establishing a structure for group meetings that takes into consideration the intrapersonal and interpersonal goals and needs of members helps the group maximize opportunities for individual input and collaboration. Finally, the success of any task group is greatly enhanced by working toward a balance between content and process issues in the group. Often, leaders of task groups focus exclusively on content while unintentionally ignoring the process factors that contribute to members' levels of commitment, motivation, and effort, all of which are highly important to a group's ultimate success. At the other extreme, groups with too heavy a focus on process may lack focus or direction, resulting in frustrated members and little progress.

Task group work can be a positive experience. Task groups can accomplish goals that exceed what can be accomplished by individuals working alone. Groups can also increase the ability of counselors to successfully identify and meet the needs of a larger range of clients. As with any other form of group work, the success of task groups lies in the successful application of group processes and principles by knowledgeable and well-trained leaders.

CHAPTER 12

Leading Psychoeducational Groups

Sam Steen, Julia Bryan, and Norma L. Day-Vines

PREVIEW

Psychoeducational groups provide unique learning experiences that support more traditional learning experiences in various settings. This chapter provides information about psychoeducational groups with a focus on both small-group and large-group formats and strategies for enhancing the delivery of classroom or large-group guidance. A group model, Achieving Success Everyday (ASE) and strategies for incorporating bibliotherapy into group work are provided. The chapter begins with an operational definition and rationale for psychoeducational groups; enumerates strategies for the planning, implementation, and evaluation of psychoeducational groups; examines issues of diversity in psychoeducational groups; discusses strategies for classroom guidance and management; and describes two models and their application to psychoeducational groups.

CONDUCTING PSYCHOEDUCATIONAL GROUPS

Psychoeducational groups are structured, time-limited, leader-centered, and usually focused on specific issues and behavioral goals (Aasheim & Niemann, 2006; Association for Specialists in Group Work [ASGW], 2000, 2007; Brown, 2004; DeLucia-Waack, 2006). Whereas counseling groups tend to be less structured and more focused on self-disclosure and extensive processing of feelings, behaviors, and thoughts, psychoeducational groups tend to be more structured, with the group's goals and activities defined primarily by the leader, and with processing focused on helping members understand and make meaning of the information presented. As an example, incoming freshman college students frequently have difficulty transitioning to college life and being away from home, sometimes relocating from one state to another. Ordinarily, a psychoeducational group aimed at addressing the college transition would provide the support and information necessary to help students transition to a new college environment, whereas a counseling group may help students explore their feelings about transition or isolation that come from relocation and then use the group process to help students feel less isolated.

Typically, psychoeducational groups include a teaching component aimed at imparting knowledge and skills to group members, with the goals of prevention and remediation. These groups present group members with the opportunity to learn new information and skills, draw connections to previous knowledge, and make personal meaning of the information. However, the functions of psychoeducational groups are diverse, ranging from merely teaching information and skills to promoting self-understanding and self-empowerment (Brown, 2004). Psychoeducational groups often address developmental concerns related to identity, sexuality, parent and peer relationships, college and career decisions, and educational and spiritual issues. Psychoeducational groups are frequently offered in school settings and often address communication and social skills groups (e.g., friendship groups, anger management groups), academic and career decision-making groups, study skills groups, and self-esteem groups (Gladding, 2008). Psychoeducational groups can help students achieve greater levels of school success and promote student growth and development.

Benefits of Psychoeducational Groups

Psychoeducational groups constitute a critical mode of intervention for professional school counselors who assume responsibility for meeting the academic, career, personal, and social needs of large numbers of students. It is impossible for school counselors to address the needs of large numbers of students using individual counseling as the primary mode of service delivery. Although individual counseling serves important functions within the school context, classroom guidance and psychoeducational groups allow school counselors to maximize the amount of services delivered to students. Maximizing efficiency in service delivery is especially critical when caseloads for school counselors exceed the recommendations of the American School Counselor Association (ASCA). In fact, ASCA recommends student-to-counselor ratios of 250:1;

however, student-to-counselor ratios usually exceed 478:1 across the United States (Hawkins & Lautz, 2005).

Likewise, in private and agency practice, psychoeducational groups play an important role in changing group members' attitudes and behaviors through the acquisition of knowledge. The premise is based on the idea that the information learned within a psychoeducational group can lead to better decision making, enhanced coping mechanisms, and a more positive outlook on life. The emphasis is on education and developing skills. Group members commonly engage in semistructured discussions and activities, role play, and offering and receiving constructive criticism, all while the group leader is acting as a teacher, facilitator, or trainer. The emphasis is on the acquisition of information, learning new skills, and the refinement of existing skills as they pertain to a particular topic.

Psychoeducational groups are also useful for working with culturally and linguistically diverse members whose collective cultural orientations may cause members to be more comfortable in group work settings. Psychoeducational groups provide both the structure and direction that some culturally and linguistically diverse groups value. Some cultural groups may find the lesser orientation toward self-disclosure and greater focus on goal accomplishment more appealing. Nevertheless, counselors who lead psychoeducational groups must be culturally competent and sensitive. It is imperative that they consider the cultural values of culturally diverse members in defining the group's goals. Equally important, leaders must recognize and embrace the strengths of culturally diverse members, rather than view them through a deficit lens. Given the number of racially charged incidents in society, psychoeducational groups offer an appropriate venue and format that leaders can capitalize on to teach members tolerance and acceptance of differences. These groups also provide a forum for helping minority and immigrant members cope with issues of cultural identity, acculturation, and relocation.

Psychoeducational groups provide an effective mode of intervention for working with parents. Leaders sometimes run parent education and support groups to provide parents and guardians with knowledge pertinent to their children's academic and personal success, teach parenting skills, and offer support for parents (Bryan, 2005; Mitchell & Bryan, 2007). Parent education groups increase parents' knowledge of the school system and how to help their children in school; this knowledge in turn increases parents' involvement in their children's education (Chrispeels & González, 2004). It is far more useful for leaders to conceptualize and design parent groups as psychoeducational groups because, in doing so, counselors apply their group leadership skills more intentionally to relating to parents and to facilitating cohesion and understanding among parents in the group. Increased interactions and networks among parents also increase parents' involvement in their children's education. Parent education and support groups facilitate parents' connection with each other and are especially important for parents of culturally and linguistically diverse students, who often feel isolated from schools.

In the next section, strategies for the planning, implementation, and evaluation of psychoeducational groups are discussed. Following that, two group models are presented: the Achieving Success Everyday (ASE) group model, developed to improve motivation and engagement while simultaneously attending to personal-social issues, and a bibliotherapy model that incorporates multiethnic literature to enhance positive identity and literacy among culturally diverse students.

PLANNING PSYCHOEDUCATIONAL GROUPS

Whether in a small-group or large-group format, planning is critical to the success of a group. Leaders should consider several factors when planning for a psychoeducational group, such as assessing member needs, developing the purpose and goals of the group, recruiting members, group size, screening potential members, group composition, determining group procedures and

techniques, and evaluating the group. While some of these facets are similar to those presented in Chapter 6, planning psychoeducational groups requires specific consideration to these facets because of the more structured and directive skill development approach. All of these components are best outlined in a group proposal (Corey & Corey, 2006; Smead, 1995). A group proposal is particularly essential for psychoeducational groups because it provides a roadmap for conducting a group. The proposal should include a rationale for the group, the overall purpose and goals of the group, procedures and techniques to be used, and an outline of each group session. The outline for each session should include the purpose, goals, and objectives of each session; time and materials needed; and a description of teaching and processing activities that will be conducted at the beginning, middle, and end of each session. Smead (1995) suggested dividing each group session into three components: the review, work, and process times, while DeLucia-Waack (2006) recommended breaking each session into four components: the opening, working, processing, and closing times. Dividing each group session into an introduction or review time, a teaching time, a processing time, and a closing time allows leaders to intentionally incorporate processing, which is often overlooked in psychoeducational groups.

Leaders of psychoeducational groups must recognize the importance of staying current with the counseling and group work literature. As leaders develop their group proposal, they will find useful techniques and activities in the literature for use in group work and creative ideas regarding what procedures work best at different stages of the group. Therefore, leaders should include books and resources on groups (e.g., Morganett, 1990, 1994; Search Institute, 2004; Smead, 2000) and professional journals (e.g., *Group Dynamics: Theory, Research, and Practice; Social Work with Groups; Journal for Specialists in Group Work*) in their counseling budget. Other useful resources include professional conferences and workshops offered at the local, state, and national level; see www.schoolcounselor.org,

TABLE 12.1 Suggested Format for Group Session Planning

Group Session Plan

- Session name/topic
- Goal and objectives
- Materials needed
- Developmental activities
  - Review/introduction
  - Teaching
  - Working/processing
  - Closing
- Method(s) of evaluation
- Homework/in-between session activity

www.asgw.org, and www.counseling.org for more information. Note that membership in these organizations may be required to receive some of these benefits.

Prior to implementing group activities, the leader should have completed the group proposal and selected group activities. This detailed pre-group planning assists the leader with planning and organization for each session. Table 12.1 provides a suggested format for planning each group session. Lesson plan formats contain logistical information such as group meeting times, length of the group and length of each session, goals, objectives, materials needed to complete the activities, a detailed discussion of the activities, and questions that leaders can use to facilitate dialogue among members. In the event that a leader needs to be away, another leader could use the group proposal to run the psychoeducational group. In addition, the leaders can continue to improve the group proposal by adding new and more effective activities and strategies to the group each time the group is run.

Special consideration is needed if psychoeducational groups are held in schools. If groups are held during the instructional day, leaders should consider the logistics of getting access to students during class times. Collaboration with teachers, administrators, and parents is critical to the success of groups. Leaders can negotiate with teachers regarding the best strategies for gaining access to students. Some strategies may include staggering the time that the group meets each week so that students do not miss the same class twice, meeting during lunch (although in many cases a single-period lunch does not provide sufficient time), or meeting during nonexamination classes such as physical education and health. To maintain continuity with students and accountability with school personnel, leaders should schedule group meetings so the meetings do not conflict with other responsibilities. Cancellations may sometimes be inevitable, but efforts should be made to minimize scheduling conflicts because they disrupt group continuity. The leader should also make arrangements to meet with students to minimize disturbances to instructional activities. Coordinating the distribution of hall and/or guidance passes in advance helps to inform the student and the teacher of the scheduled meetings. Planning for a psychoeducational group or classroom guidance sessions is essential, as discussed in detail in Chapter 6.

IMPLEMENTING PSYCHOEDUCATIONAL GROUPS

Psychoeducational group development consists of a number of stages. The following chapter subsections describe some important leader tasks of the early (forming and transition), middle (working), and ending (termination) stages, with a specific focus on psychoeducational groups.

Early Stage of Psychoeducational Groups: Forming and Transition

Leader tasks in the beginning sessions of psychoeducational groups include clarifying the purpose and goals of the group, discussing confidentiality and its limits, establishing ground rules, normalizing anxiety, teaching and modeling communication skills, encouraging group norms of participation, creating a safe environment, and facilitating cohesion. Group members may come to the group with preconceived ideas about the upcoming experience.

These expectations may stem from the screening process, from other members discussing their group experiences, or from previous experiences participating in groups. In any case, the initial sessions of the group should include an exploration of members' expectations of the group and group process.

While leaders of psychoeducational groups attend to similar tasks as leaders of counseling groups, psychoeducational group leaders should create the norm of teaching and learning by incorporating didactic activities in the early stage. For example, suppose some of the group members are struggling with incorporating spirituality into their personal identities. Leaders could teach strategies useful for engaging in self-reflection as well as appropriate self-disclosure and outward expression that are important in the group and with the members' peers and family members outside the group. Leaders should also focus on creating a balance between teaching new skills and processing group members' feelings and reactions to group content early in the group. Because information is delivered via teaching, leaders might neglect group process. Leaders should also incorporate interactive group activities during each session.

During the early or initial stage of the group, members tend to function in a honeymoon state. In other words, members have a greater level of focus and willingness to abide by group rules and to work on group goals. During the transition stage, members may be more resistant and reluctant to participate and engage in productive work, especially if members have academic and behavioral challenges. Leaders should help members process why they are responding the way they are in group, make connections between their resistance inside and outside group and the effect of resistance on member success, and support each other in finding strategies to avoid undermining their success in group. Leaders will need to be patient and supportive, focus on encouragement and group management rather than discipline, and highlight members' strengths. Group leaders who facilitate increased self-disclosure will foster greater exploration and learning among group members. See Chapter 7 for an in-depth discussion of the forming and orienting stage, and Chapter 8 for the transition stage of group work.

Middle Stage of Psychoeducational Groups: Working

Although activities (e.g., ice-breakers, energizers) continue to be important during the working or middle stage of the psychoeducational group, this is the stage during which the bulk of the teaching of new information and skills takes place. Psychoeducational groups provide information that helps prevent the onset of difficulties in members' lives or help members cope with current challenges. Group leaders should focus on teaching the skills and behaviors that members need in order to accomplish their objectives. It is important to teach skills and behaviors in small, manageable steps and give members opportunities to experience small successes so that members can generalize their learning to their life outside the group. Therefore, group leaders need to be intentional about incorporating time for skill practice inside the group, homework to help members practice their behavior and skills, and mechanisms to monitor members' success at trying these new behaviors and skills (e.g., keeping a journal, recording the number of times they tried a new behavior or skill). Equally important, homework should involve small, manageable steps so that members can experience some success as they practice new behaviors and skills outside the group.

Group leaders should work to make instruction and accompanying activities interesting and engaging for members, as well as developmentally appropriate. Effective teachers and, by extension, effective psychoeducational group leaders find ways to make the material being taught relevant to members' lives and to elicit and incorporate students' life experiences into teaching. They also help each member feel a sense of belonging to the group. This can be accomplished by using a warm, empathic personal style, which communicates the leader's investment in each group member and that each group member matters. See Chapter 9 for an in-depth discussion of the working stage of group work.

Ending Stage of Psychoeducational Groups: Termination

During the ending stage, group leaders focus on termination, which includes summarizing and wrapping up the themes that emerged in the group; discussing and processing unfinished business; and helping members discuss what they learned in group, describe how they have changed, and determine steps they will take to continue working on their new skills and behaviors on completion of the group. Leaders should help members process their feelings about leaving the group and separating from each other, and help them develop a plan to continue working on their goals. In addition, leaders may need to provide support and follow-up for group members who need further intervention.

Another proactive strategy that counselors can use to support psychoeducational group members is connecting them to support networks (e.g. mentors, reading buddies, and tutoring programs) outside the group. These support networks allow members to participate in meaningful relationships that promote personal, social, and academic development. Finally, as the group comes to a close, leaders must be sure to administer postassessments both for outcome and process data, as appropriate. See Chapter 10 for an in-depth discussion of the termination stage of group work.

DIVERSITY ISSUES IN PSYCHOEDUCATIONAL GROUPS

Leaders must be cognizant of racial and cultural issues and be prepared to initiate and respond to concerns that arise within the context of psychoeducational groups. The leader's inability to respond authentically to member concerns may create ruptures and schisms within the counseling relationship and circumvent members' development. To illustrate, Dr. Davis, a licensed professional counselor, convened a small group around anger management issues for eight male adolescent boys between the ages of 15 and 16 years; most of the group members were African American and Latino. As she reviewed the didactic component of the group that provided the members with new skill sets for improved compliance with requests from authority figures, several of the group members complained that individuals they encounter at school and in the community were racist and provoked many of the conflict situations, which resulted in their referral to receive counseling services. Dr. Davis responded by defensively insisting that teachers and other adults in the community do not see color. Her response effectively silenced the group participants, who felt revictimized by the leader's denial that race may contribute to some of their discipline referrals, and contributed to the boys' perception that she was not trustworthy; did not understand their sociopolitical realities; and, most damaging, was complicit in racial bias.

Day-Vines et al. (2007) developed a model of broaching behavior that leaders will find useful in running psychoeducational groups. The model enumerates behaviors that the leaders exhibit as they both initiate and respond to concerns about racial, ethnic, and cultural issues that may be embedded in members' presenting problems. Leaders along the lower end of the continuum ignore and minimize the effect of race, ethnicity, and culture, while leaders along the higher end of the continuum exhibit a level of social consciousness and comfort examining racial, ethnic, and cultural factors with members. The leader's ability to explore taboo subjects, such as race, is designed to help members explore problem situations, normalize issues related to race and representation, exchange ideas about how group members have negotiated similar concerns, and develop improved decision-making and problem strategies for managing issues such as racial bias. Day-Vines et al. (2007) provided a detailed discussion of how leaders consider racial and ethnic issues within psychoeducational groups.

When working with culturally and linguistically diverse members in psychoeducational groups, leaders must be aware of their own attitudes, biases, and assumptions that may affect members and the group process and thus interfere with the delivery of culturally responsive group work. At the same time, leaders cannot be inhibited by feelings of guilt and fear, which have the potential to immobilize helpful group leadership practices. Day-Vines et al. (2007) encourage leaders to normalize member concerns when issues related to race, ethnicity, and culture arise during the group process. Leaders should monitor their own reactions so that countertransference issues do not interfere with the leader's relationship with members. Leaders should also recognize the sociopolitical issues that govern members' experience. An inability to broach racial and cultural factors may limit the progress that the leader can make with members. For instance, in the scenario above, the leader who rationalized authority figures' behavior may miss an opportunity to help group members gain personal insight and devise strategies for responding appropriately to perceived racism. On the other hand, leaders who openly discuss these issues can help alleviate group members' anxiety and work to improve their potential for decision making.

Again using the case scenario above, the leader could have facilitated a dialogue among the boys that would have helped to increase her understanding of their perceptions of racial bias in their school and community. For instance, the leader might have elicited an example of biased behavior; processed what effect the experience has on their ability to navigate the school and community; explored some of the coping strategies that group members have relied on; and acknowledged that, nationwide, African American and Latino adolescents experience disproportionate rates of suspension and expulsion from school, as well as encounters with law enforcement agencies. Such counseling responses would help participants feel that their concerns were heard, understood, and validated. The leader can also use the adolescents' concerns as a springboard for helping them identify behavioral strategies that will reduce discipline problems. For instance, the leader can assign group members the task of observing how others respond to authority figures and determine what teenager reactions elicit positive or negative reactions from adults within the school and community. This activity helps group members observe a wide repertoire of behaviors that can help them modify their own responses to individuals they encounter. Leaders can also have group members role-play strategies in which they negotiate conflict situations with authority figures.

Leaders must also recognize that some issues are external to members. Although the leader can support the members as they learn more effective behaviors for conducting themselves in public, this may be a necessary but far from sufficient intervention for working with members who are encountering challenges, such as racial bias and other structural barriers in their daily lives. The leader may need to enlist some structural modifications to support the members. That is, the leader may advocate for professional development workshops to be utilized by community members and school personnel on topics such as cultural sensitivity and multicultural knowledge and skill acquisition.

IMPLEMENTING CLASSROOM GUIDANCE

This section highlights considerations for planning, implementing, and evaluating large group guidance, also known as classroom guidance. Because classroom guidance is most frequently implemented in schools, the examples used below will involve school-age youth. However, the principles readily apply to use with adults, such as when adult learning or professional development workshops are constructed. Typically, leaders deliver classroom guidance curriculum comprised of units that contain four to eight lessons. These units can be organized in a number of ways; they often tend to revolve around current initiatives (e.g., bullying prevention, suicide awareness) mandated by administration, critical needs that arise in the school or are unique to the local student body, or a combination of the two.

Planning for Classroom Guidance

In planning classroom or group guidance curriculum and lessons, leaders must attend to similar pre-group tasks, like those involved in planning smaller psychoeducational groups: assessing student needs, developing the purpose and goals of the group, determining group procedures and techniques, and evaluating the group. The needs assessment strategies that are applicable to the small-group format are also appropriate when planning for classroom guidance, including surveying students, parents, building-level administrators, and teachers to identify the most pressing student needs, which can serve as potential topics for classroom guidance. In addition, leaders may use student-related data (e.g., discipline referrals for bullying, reports of bias and prejudice, performance by grade level on state performance tests, numbers of seniors admitted to college in previous years) as a springboard for the development of classroom guidance units. For example, data related to discipline referrals for bullying may indicate the need for a comprehensive bully prevention program to be delivered to all grade levels. Data concerning racially charged incidents may suggest that the counselors need to deliver a school-wide antiracist or antiprejudice curriculum. Data regarding juniors' knowledge of the college admissions process may uncover the need for a guidance unit for all juniors that addresses the college search and college choice processes.

Following the identification of classroom guidance activities, leaders can create specific lessons that incorporate national or state standards or school improvement goals. Leaders should create lessons that are engaging, stimulating, developmentally appropriate, culturally sensitive, and aligned with schoolwide initiatives and instructional objectives. Leaders should seek resources to generate ideas for activities and materials for lessons. The resources can be found in counseling and group counseling texts, at counseling websites (e.g., the ASCA website http://www.schoolcounselor.org), and at professional development venues (e.g., state and national conferences and local workshops). DeLucia-Waack (2006) incorporated numerous resources in her text on leading psychoeducational groups, including a resource guide of books, videos, and games.

Other practical considerations include planning ahead and proactively developing lessons and alternatives in case events do not go as planned. Integrating technology into classroom guidance heightens the need to have a backup plan because malfunctions can and often do happen when teaching with technology. The lesson here is never simply make do. Inadequate preparation creates a potential for disaster, which may include, but is not limited to, the inability of members to profit from the guidance unit, increased disciplinary problems, loss of leader credibility, and decreased confidence levels in the leader. Group leaders should work diligently to portray organization, high levels of energy, passion, and engagement because these characteristics communicate to members that the information being presented is worthwhile; in addition, the leader is more likely to capture members' attention.

Leaders must also explore strategies for effective classroom management in order to decrease issues of discipline in the classroom. In the section that follows, we describe practical strategies of classroom management, with attention to the importance of treating all members with respect.

Classroom Management

Classroom management involves managing classroom dynamics in an effort to prevent potential disciplinary problems and minimize any behavioral problems that arise. Effective classroom management is critical to the success and delivery of classroom guidance. Although, it tends to be easier for counselors to manage the members in the small-group setting, working with an entire classroom can present some unique and interesting challenges. For instance, student-teacher relationships commence the first day of school and evolve thereafter. Counselors are not usually in the classroom on the first day. Consequently, when they conduct classroom guidance, it is important that they adopt the classroom management strategies that the teacher has already implemented, unless those strategies are poorly conceived and ineffective. If adopting the classroom management system in place is difficult, consider building on the work of the teacher. If this is also not feasible, a number of strategies to decrease classroom disruptions can be implemented, as discussed below.

First and foremost, become familiar with each student's name as quickly as possible. Obtain seating charts from teachers in order to learn names quickly. Address students by name in order to enhance familiarity and interpersonal connections between the leader and the students. In middle or high schools, one way to encourage positive counselor-student relationships is to get to the classroom as early as possible and, when appropriate, greet students at the door with a handshake, a pat on the shoulder, or small talk that validates and affirms students. Counselors can also provide students with an assignment such as creating nametags, drawing family portraits, or another developmentally appropriate task as they wait for the lesson to begin.

Establishing classroom rules facilitates the classroom management process. As mentioned previously, the best way to incorporate classroom rules to is to adopt or build on those already established by the teachers. Sometimes this is not possible. In this case, collaborate with the students to generate classroom rules relevant to the context of classroom guidance. For example, do students need to raise their hand before speaking? Are they allowed to be out of their seats? Is music, food, or drink allowed in the classroom? The resulting rules may be appropriate within the context of classroom guidance activities but not within their typical classroom. Nonetheless, working with the students to create appropriate rules and expectations will increase student buy-in to the classroom process and willingness to adhere to the classroom management

system. The classroom rules can also include ideas that hold students responsible for each others' behavior and encourages them to be accountable to one another when the rules are not followed. However, leaders must be sure to include a policy consistent with the school's policy for serious disciplinary infractions. Displaying visuals (e.g., signs, charts) with the classroom guidance rules reduces ambiguity about student conduct, establishes a clear set of behavioral guidelines, and reinforces leader expectations about student conduct.

Positive reinforcement and redirection should be used to remind members of the leader's expectations for appropriate behavior. Leaders can acknowledge and affirm appropriate behavior among members to increase the likelihood that members will continue the behavior. Positive reinforcement builds members' esteem while getting the attention of those who need redirection, incorporates the entire class in focusing on the correct behaviors, and benefits even members who remain on task. A key aspect of positive reinforcement is acknowledging the behaviors of those students who are displaying the correct behavior. For instance, perhaps Cornelius is not interacting appropriately with his peers, but Antwonn is. The leader acknowledges the correct behavior by saying, "I really like the way that Antwonn is treating his classmates." This gets the attention of Cornelius, Antwonn, and others, who immediately react to the prompt in an attempt to win the leader's approval. Of course, this strategy may not work with every child in the classroom, but focusing on the positive reminds members of the expectations for classroom behavior.

Members also need to be treated with respect. Treating members with value and respect helps to decrease the occurrence of discipline issues during classroom guidance. Leaders should use praise to communicate respect to members. This praise should extend to all members, not just the well-behaved members. For instance, Robert has a tendency to blurt out responses rather than waiting to be called on. Rather than becoming annoyed, the leader asks members to review the group rules. The leader also uses a strategy developed by Bireda (2002) known as the stroke-sting-stroke method. Instead of reprimanding Robert in an exasperated tone, the leader addresses Robert's behavior by prefacing her request with a positive comment (e.g., stroke), making a behavioral request (sting), and following up the sting with another positive comment. As an example, the leader says, "Robert, I am excited about your interest in the lesson, active participation, and willingness to share your perspectives with the group (stroke); however, when you talk without raising your hand, you interrupt someone who is following the classroom rules (sting). You are such a confident, competent, and articulate person. I hope you will use your listening and leadership skills to model the classroom rules for the rest of the class (stroke)." Such a response preserves Robert's dignity, highlights his attributes, communicates the counselor's need for his cooperation, and maintains a healthy classroom climate. The leader must use a vocal tone and quality with an air of genuineness, sincerity, respect, and firmness that express these sentiments toward Robert. If stated sarcastically, the leader's tone may undermine the message. If stated earnestly, the leader can command respect not only from Robert, but from other students as well.

A positive climate is critical when delivering classroom guidance. Valuing diverse opinions and viewpoints helps to create a positive climate for all students. When leaders value all members' comments and embrace different opinions, they provide the opportunity for members to be exposed to a variety of perspectives. In turn, hearing a range of viewpoints teaches members about diversity and acknowledges the effect of culture in ways that validate and affirm all members, including those who have experiences and worldviews that are different from the White middle-class culture of most schools. Valuing members' responses fosters a sense of belonging and acceptance among members and improves the likelihood of delivering lessons without major disruptions.

Another illustration of the benefit of creating a safe environment where all members and divergent perspectives are valued in the classroom involves an elementary student named Ghulam, whose family originated from Afghanistan. This student had difficulty on two fronts. First, he appeared to be less willing to engage in any activities that he was not interested in. Second, he would not actively participate in collaborative activities in which females were involved. We could have attributed his behavior to his gender and the fact that his country of origin is a patriarchal society or to his developmental stage as a third grader. Nonetheless, we were willing to work through these differences in light of the reality that this student's worldview was different than ours. We worked to engage Ghulam in group activities while allowing him space to be comfortable. Rather than acknowledging his behavior openly, we addressed this situation by modeling genuine acceptance and consistent messages that all members of the classroom were valued.

Other helpful strategies for valuing members occur through the dialogue between the classroom guidance leader and members. As leaders interact with members, they should do so in a manner that involves all members or, at the very least, does not exclude members on the basis of their class, culture, or religious views. Leaders should strive to achieve balance in their discussions and interactions with members and scan the class regularly to detect the body language of the class members. This will help leaders to gauge how members are responding to the prompts verbally as well as subconsciously.

TWO EXEMPLAR MODELS FOR PSYCHOEDUCATIONAL GROUP WORK

In the following subsections, we describe two exemplar models that may be used in psychoeducational groups to enhance member success: (a) the Achieving Success Everyday (ASE) group model and (b) using bibliotherapy in psychoeducational groups.

Achieving Success Everyday (ASE) Group Model

Given the focus on academic development in schools (American School Counselor Association [ASCA], 2005), leaders can best assist members by implementing group counseling and psychoeducational models that simultaneously address personal/social and academic development (Brigham & Campbell, 2003; Steen & Kaffenberger, 2007). A unique contribution of the Achieving Success Everyday (ASE) group model (Steen, 2009) is the intentional integration of academic and personal/social development using psychoeducational and counseling components. The primary purpose of ASE groups is to enhance members' personal/social development while helping members to improve academic-related behaviors that contribute to success in the classroom (e.g., attending to tasks, completing assignments, asking questions). Using the ASE group model, leaders teach members strategies to address their personal/social concerns and academic difficulties. Leaders also help members identify and build on their internal assets (e.g., achievement motivation, school performance) while drawing on the external assets (e.g., caring, supportive adults; high expectations) available within the school and surrounding community.

Goals may be selected from the ASCA *National Model* (American School Counselor Association [ASCA], 2005). Examples of academic goals include the following for the group members: increase learning behaviors, achieve school success, improve academic self-concept, acquire skills for improving learning, relate school to life experience, and take responsibility for actions. Examples of personal/social goals for students include: learn to communicate feelings, learn strategies to advocate on behalf of oneself, learn to identify internal and external assets, learn to deal with events that provoke negative emotional responses, learn strategies to handle stressful situations, and learn to apply social skills outside the group.

GROUP DEVELOPMENT IN ASE GROUPS The ASE group model is designed to assist members who can benefit from academic as well as personal/social support. ASE groups consist of six phases: assessment, review, acquaintance, challenge, empowerment, and support. These phases develop across the group's lifespan. Each session of the group is composed of an introduction, a personal/social component, an academic component, and a closing.

The *assessment phase* occurs prior to the start of the group and is instrumental in selecting the potential group members. During the assessment phase, the leader gathers information from teachers, parents, and the members for use in assessing the student's academic and personal/social strengths and difficulties. This information may be collected using surveys or at faculty meetings, parent information meetings, or parent-teacher conferences. Leaders may choose to design their own surveys or to use instruments that are available in the literature.

Leaders should use the data to decide who is most in need of services and to help construct the actual group goals, objectives, and lessons. In addition, leaders may use the information gathered in the assessment phase to periodically update teachers and parents about the members' progress. Members should know about these updates and even help decide what information they would like shared with their teachers and parents. Sharing student successes that occur inside and outside the group with teachers and parents can improve teacher-student and parent-student relationships. Overall, collaborating with teachers and parents can help the leader, teachers, and parents keep abreast of member progress, support member efforts at goal accomplishment, empower members, and identify new areas for improvement.

The *review phase* primarily takes place during the first or second sessions of the group. The leader reviews the group's purpose, goals, and ground rules, including confidentiality, and helps members identify individual goals. During this phase, the leader may also review data collected from the assessment phase and share the results with the group members. These data can be used to drive discussions about the purpose of the group's meetings and the benefits that may accrue from member participation. The data from the assessment phase highlight that members may be experiencing similar difficulties. This in turn helps members normalize their concerns (i.e., universality).

In the *acquaintance phase*, the leader facilitates connection among the members to provide a cohesive environment conducive to change. The leader encourages all members to begin actively participating in the group process and helps students to discuss positive self-attributes in meaningful ways. One strategy that leaders can use to increase members' comfort in sharing in the group is exploring uncertainties regarding confidentiality. Facilitating cohesion helps members feel more comfortable in a small-group setting. As the group progresses from the beginning stage to the working stage, leaders should spend a few minutes at the beginning of each session helping members reconnect with each other. Over time, however, it will become less necessary to do so as members become more familiar and willing to engage one another.

During the *acquaintance phase*, the leader should model appropriate interpersonal skills and help members learn how to communicate effectively. Leaders can use engaging activities to encourage members to connect and communicate with each another. Some feasible activities include sentence completion exercises, pair-and-share (i.e., pairing up with another member and then sharing the information with the entire group), or a team drawing activity where students in groups of two or three collectively work on an art project that represents aspects about them. These activities promote safety and self-disclosure among members by highlighting their similarities with one another and examining their differences.

During the *challenge phase*, leaders teach group members productive ways to clarify or confront their own unwanted behaviors and those behaviors they recognize in other members. To facilitate constructive confrontation, leaders need to teach members how to give productive feedback (e.g., stroke-sting-stroke). Leaders also should help members explore their

feelings about feedback received about their behaviors. Equally important, leaders should use their group leadership skills to confront or challenge inconsistencies, negative behaviors and thoughts, and members' misconceptions or misunderstandings regarding issues raised during previous sessions.

During the *empowerment phase*, leaders should focus on providing members with knowledge, strategies, and skills to deal with academic and personal/social obstacles. This typically is where the teaching component in psychoeducational groups occurs. Empowerment is defined as a process of increasing personal, interpersonal, or political power in order for individuals to take appropriate action to improve their lives (Guttierez, 1990). Empowerment is used to help members identify and cultivate personal strengths and take the initiative in overcoming personal challenges. Leaders help members recognize their potential to make changes in their lives that they may not have noticed before. Leaders also help members recognize their strengths by facilitating discussion and exploration of the internal and external assets available to them. The Search Institute's 40 Developmental Assets List may be useful for generating discussion ideas. Assets lists for early, middle, and adolescent years in French, Spanish, and English may be found at http://www.search-institute .org/assets/assetlists.html. Other asset-building resources that leaders may find useful in psychoeducational groups include the following books: *Building Assets Is Elementary: Group Activities for Helping Kids Ages 8–12 Succeed* (Search Institute, 2004), *More Building Assets Together: 130 Group Activities for Helping Youth Succeed* (Grothe, 2002), and *Great Group Games: 175 Boredom-Busting, Zero-Prep Team Builders for All Ages* (Ragsdale & Taylor, 2007). In addition to using asset-building activities, leaders should help students brainstorm unique and creative ideas to overcome their personal or academic challenges.

For leaders to facilitate student empowerment, leaders must recognize the role that environmental and societal pressures (e.g., poverty, institutional racism, stereotypes, negative and unhealthy school climates) play in people's lives. Empowering group members means that leaders must see members from a strength-based rather than a deficit perspective; that is, leaders must identify the strengths in all members regardless of gender, class, race, or religion. Hence, leaders who effectively empower members have a positive view of people and work diligently to confront their own biases and stereotypes.

The *support phase* is used to bring closure to a group. During the support phase, the primary focus is on helping members support each other as the group draws to an end. Leaders should facilitate a discussion about members' initial goals established early in the group, how their goals may have changed, and whether they accomplished their goals. Leaders should also encourage members to give each other feedback about areas of growth observed in one another. Members can encourage each other to improve and to accept each others' unique differences and limitations. Leaders also help members identify supports and resources within and external to the group to help them accomplish their goals. Leaders should help members discover resources available within the group (e.g., acceptance, enhanced self-esteem), within the school (e.g., a supportive adult in the school), and within their families and community (e.g., positive role models, youth or community group). Leaders can brainstorm with members how they may draw on these resources for support as they work toward their goals and as the group terminates. A discussion of external resources during group sessions and at the conclusion of the group can help increase long-term positive results for members (Steen & Bemak, 2007). Finally, as the group comes to a close, leaders should help members explore and celebrate their accomplishments.

Using Bibliotherapy in Psychoeducational Groups

Bibliotherapy refers to the leader's use of literature to help members cope with dilemmas that affect their development. DeLucia-Waack (2006) recommended the use of bibliotherapy in psychoeducational groups to help members process their feelings. Bibliotherapy also supports educational missions by promoting and reinforcing literacy skills. In some counseling contexts, the term *bibliocounseling* may be preferred to avoid the implication that leaders are conducting therapy sessions with members. For the purpose of this chapter, we will rely on the customary term *bibliotherapy*. In any case, the leader selects literature that corresponds with a particular need or challenge that members confront. Selections are usually based on developmental appropriateness, similarities between the protagonist and the members (e.g., age), and relevance of the book's content to the members' problem situation.

The leader has several options for presenting the material to members in psychoeducational groups. For instance, the leader can read the material to members directly; have members read the materially orally or silently; and in some cases, assign reading outside the group session. Following exposure to the literature, the leader facilitates a discussion with members about the book's content. Discussions permit members to (1) recognize that others experience similar dilemmas, (2) identify similarities between their own experience and the protagonist's experience, as well as (3) develop a greater repertoire of more effective problem-solving behaviors and coping strategies.

A fairly extensive body of literature documents the use of bibliotherapy across a range of counseling settings and as a conduit for resolving numerous problem situations. Far less attention, however, has been devoted to the inclusion of multiethnic bibliotherapy selections, despite increasing levels of diversity within schools. Day-Vines, Moore-Thomas, and Hines (2005) developed a model of culturally relevant bibliotherapy (CRB), which refers to the purposeful use of multiethnic books in individual counseling and group work contexts to address the culture-specific concerns of people of color. This model identifies criteria that leaders can use as they select culturally relevant literature. According to the model, protagonists within CRB are from culturally and linguistically diverse groups that reflect the growing diversity in society. Regrettably, less than 2% of literature produced annually for children and adolescents focuses on multicultural concerns (Bishop, 1993).

Day-Vines et al. (2007) recommended that leaders rely on CRB, which was written within the last ten years, because, more recently, authors have made greater efforts to avoid bias in literature. They also note that more exemplary CRB selections are written by people from underrepresented groups because they generally tend to write from a personal lived experience. Within CRB, the plot generally contains at least two themes, a universal theme that applies to all individuals regardless of racial or ethnic group membership, and a culture-specific theme that addresses the unique experiences and developmental concerns of people of color. As an advantage, CRB serves multiple purposes; that is, CRB allows members from the dominant culture to be exposed to literary and cultural perspectives that lie outside a White middle-class imperative. Similarly, CRB permits members of color to have their heritages and cultural perspectives validated and affirmed. CRB literature depicts the integrity of the ethnic minority experience and functions as counternarratives that contest and resist the stereotypes and overgeneralizations that have historically been placed on people from marginalized groups. Most important, CRB can serve as a source of empowerment for culturally and linguistically diverse members. Leaders can integrate CRB seamlessly into their psychoeducational group and classroom guidance activities with members.

Demographers predict that by the year 2050, students of color will comprise more than half of the school-age population in the United States (Sue & Sue, 2003). Leaders can respond to these shifts by incorporating more representative literature in their bibliotherapy efforts, literature that better reflects the student composition. This increasing diversity implies that a larger segment of the U.S. population will speak English as a second language, accented English, or nonstandard forms of English. In any case, members whose discourse styles do not approximate a Standard

English imperative may encounter varying forms of linguistic bias. When confronted with linguistic bias, members may have few resources with which to respond and may internalize their linguistic differences in ways that detract from their sense of well-being, pride, and school success.

Books can assist leaders as they work with members during classroom guidance and psychoeducational groups to address issues pertaining to cultural diversity. For instance, books can be used during small-group guidance to help homogeneous group members explore what it means to be culturally different in settings where differences may not necessarily be appreciated. These books may be infused into self-esteem, study skills, or friendship groups to help members gain greater levels of self-acceptance and self-understanding. Far too many persons of color are viewed from deficit perspectives when certain cultural markers (e.g., their names, discourse communities) are seen as possessing less status. Leaders can help restore social and ethnic pride in members by normalizing their experiences and allowing them opportunities to talk about the effects of culture on their educational experience. Leaders can use their training and expertise to promote multicultural dispositions among members. In fact, leaders can develop classroom guidance activities to help members accept and appreciate cultural differences among peers. Whether leaders incorporate CRB within the context of small psychoeducational groups or classroom guidance, Day-Vines et al. (2005) identified strategies that leaders can use to facilitate discussions.

Following the reading of the CRB selection, leaders can elicit members' general reactions and impressions of the literary content. After ascertaining members' reactions to the book, leaders can inquire whether themes presented in the book parallel issues and concerns of the members or community. Discussions of the broader meaning and implications of the literature facilitate more personalized discussions of the material. Next, the leaders can have members discuss similarities between their own experience and that of the protagonist as well as implications for their own lives. For instance, the leader may sequence questions to inquire about members' perceptions of the book or have members consider how the bibliotherapy selections can inform their thoughts, attitudes, and behaviors. Delucia-Waack (2006) suggests that members can write or make their own books to help other members cope with problems similar to their own.

In addition to the discussions cited above, leaders can facilitate additional creative activities in which members prepare drawings, create collages developed from magazines, write stories or conclusions for their own problems, role-play, and enact new conclusions about the story using dramatic play activities. The creative activities, along with the bibliotherapy, permit members to explore their problems and feelings within the safety of the group context. The members can use these activities to transfer newly acquired skills and understandings to their personal lives outside the group.

Summary

Psychoeducational groups permit leaders to maximize their efficiency by working with members in groups versus individually in their efforts to stimulate and promote improved decision making, coping skills, personal and interpersonal competence, and academic achievement. Ordinarily, psychoeducational groups tend to be more structured than other group formats in order to provide members with useful knowledge, information, and skills.

Personal characteristics of the leader, such as enthusiasm; warmth; friendliness; as well as the ability to create a safe, nurturing group environment, contribute to the well-being of the group. Requisite skills of the leader include the ability to both teach content and attend to group process so that all members have a meaningful and substantive group experience.

Given the rapid demographic shifts in U.S. society, leaders must address universal and culture-specific issues that affect the lived experiences of members. That is, leaders must be aware of their own attitudes, biases, and assumptions to avoid countertransference. An important correlate of multicultural counseling competence involves the leader's willingness to broach the subjects of race, ethnicity, and culture that may arise during the counseling process in a manner that helps members gain a heightened sense of critical consciousness and helps them develop appropriate coping and decision-making strategies so that they can function more optimally in a pluralistic society.

In addition to conducting psychoeducational groups, leaders should develop proficiency in delivering workshop or classroom guidance interventions. The preparatory activities for classroom guidance share many parallels with planning smaller psychoeducational groups: assessing member needs, developing the purpose and goals of the group, determining group procedures and techniques, and evaluating the group.

Steen's (2009) model, Achieving Success Everyday (ASE), holds considerable promise for the delivery of psychoeducational interventions because the model integrates academic and personal/social competencies that are relevant for the healthy developmental functioning of members. Each of the six phases of the model—assessment, review, acquaintance, challenge, empowerment, and support—are designed to help members achieve school success.

Day-Vines et al. (2005) proposed criteria for identifying multiethnic children's literature in an effort to incorporate culturally relevant bibliotherapy (CRB) into the psychoeducational group process. Culturally relevant bibliotherapy serves as a source of empowerment for members from marginalized groups because it validates and affirms their cultural heritage and addresses universal issues that members from all cultures experience, yet at the same time addresses the specific and unique developmental concerns of members from ethnic minority backgrounds. Concomitantly, CRB helps members from th dominant culture recognize the perspectives of ethnic minority group members.

CHAPTER 13

Person-Centered and Existential Approaches to Counseling and Psychotherapy Groups

Laura R. Simpson and Joel F. Diambra

PREVIEW

Humanistic and existential counseling may be viewed as both phenomenological and holistic in their approach to group counseling. The basic tenets suggest that human behaviors are based both in the group members' insight related to their reality and the values and attitudes attached to that perception. It also builds on a foundation of understanding human existence by viewing individuals themselves and in relationship to the contexts in which they live their lives. This chapter examines person-centered and existential group therapy approaches and how each represents these philosophical views.

HUMANISTIC GROUPS

Humanistic approaches to group counseling stress the importance of congruence in human interactions, recognize the effect of personal experiences, and highlight here-and-now phenomena and the formation of personal and interpersonal consciousness. The humanistic theories emphasize personal responsibility for one's life choices rather than considering them a product of heredity or environment. It is assumed that, if given a choice, individuals will choose to be healthy and well adjusted over being unhealthy or self-destructive. The most basic principle is the innate predisposition of the individual to strive toward self-actualization (Gazda et al., 2008; Gilliland, James, & Bowman, 1989; Gladding, 2008).

Among the humanistic theories, the person-centered approach has had great impact. The development of person-centered work is based on the efforts of Carl Rogers. Rogers initially developed his person-centered approach through the introduction of nondirective counseling after realizing that when his clients were in charge of their own therapy and were accepted and understood by him as their therapist, clients improved more rapidly and achieved greater improvement than when he directed their actions (Gladding, 2008).

Types of Humanistic Groups

The T-group was a predecessor of group techniques designed to increase spontaneity, increase personal growth, and maximize members' sensitivity to others (Forsyth, 1999). Ultimately, the name was changed from T-group to encounter group. Expanding his individual work, Carl Rogers sought to bring clients into close and direct contact with one another through encounter groups. Rogers was a leader in the development of encounter groups. He proposed that most people lose sight of their basic goodness because needs for approval and love are rarely satisfied. Rogers felt that encounter groups helped restore trust in one's own feelings, promote self-acceptance, and facilitate openness in interactions with others.

Variations of humanistic groups went by many names. They have been known as personal growth groups, sensory awareness groups, sensitivity groups, and human relationship groups. Ultimately, Rogers became interested in large group-phenomena. He initiated a new group format called the community for learning in which about 100 people lived and worked together for two weeks at a time.

Role and Function of the Leader in Humanistic Groups

The course of humanistic groups is determined by the group members, so leaders are generally less directive than in many other approaches to group work. As a general rule, group leaders do not used planned actions but instead use empathic understanding as a means to perceive the world from the members' perspective. Emphasis is placed on demonstrating genuineness, unconditional positive regard, and empathy in response to all aspects of members' lives, resulting in feelings of self-acceptance.

The leader is genuine in the counseling relationship, and this genuineness is represented by a variety of behaviors. The leader strives to establish a facilitative climate within the group, characterized by congruence, unconditional positive regard, and empathic understanding. According to Egan (1986), the facilitator has freedom from roles and can be professional without hiding behind a professional role. Spontaneity without being impulsive or inhibited is encouraged, thus allowing the leader to respond with tact and without constantly analyzing responses to member concerns. The person-centered leader is also nondefensive and can be open to negative client emotions without feeling attacked. This allows facilitators the opportunity to understand the negative emotion. Facilitators operating from a position of genuineness will also be consistent and not demonstrate great differences among what they think, feel and how they behave. Finally, the humanistic leader uses self-disclosure when appropriate and allows members to know them through open verbal and nonverbal expression of their feelings.

Perhaps the most fundamental condition of person-centered group leader behavior is communication of unconditional positive regard to the group members. This is best represented by the leader giving attention to the members' concerns and feelings while communicating a nonjudgmental attitude and genuineness. The leader must provide an environment in which all members feel safe and there is a climate of mutual trust. The leader consistently responds with empathy and communicates an understanding of the members' point of view. The leader seeks to cultivate the members' resources, which results in insight into their own personal potential and capacity for making change while sharing in the change process. Ultimately, leaders support members' finding their own way in life and accepting the responsibility that goes with self-determination while refraining from giving advice and direction.

Stages in Humanistic Groups

Humanistic group therapy is not presented in terms of stages. Instead, certain conditions potentially facilitate change. Rogers (1961) suggested that if the conditions of psychological contact, incongruence, genuineness, unconditional positive regard, and empathy were present, and the group could facilitate the process in which the member perceives the existence of the conditions, change would emerge naturally. If these conditions were successfully nurtured, members could develop self-acceptance, self-confidence, and self-direction, while becoming less rigid and more flexible, and adopting realistic goals. Ultimately, members would reduce maladjustive behaviors, be more accepting of others, and change central personality characteristics in beneficial ways (Gross & Capuzzi, 2006).

Techniques Commonly Used in Humanistic Groups

In humanistic group work, the therapeutic relationship between the leader and members is the core of the process. It is important that the relationship be one of safety and mutual trust. Once an atmosphere of safety and trust exists, a facilitative relationship can be developed. Because the approach is relationship-oriented, Rogerian strategies for helping are devoid of techniques that involve doing something to or for the members. The strategies are geared to experiential relationships. They occur in the here and now, and they permit members and leader to experience the ongoing process. The leader focuses on the member concerns within the moment. Some major strategies that facilitate empathic understanding are attending, verbal and nonverbal communication of empathic understanding, and using silence (Gilliland et al., 1989). Rogers did occasionally employ role playing to encourage members to experience and express feelings of anger, caring, loneliness, or helplessness. Stripped of defensiveness and façades, Rogers believed that group members would encounter each other authentically."

The group leader achieves authentic therapeutic relationships by attending to the group members and displaying the facilitative conditions from the beginning. Effective leaders focus fully on the concerns of the members. The facial expressions of the leader as well as body posture can relay the message that the leader is listening to the members. Eye contact, smiling, seriousness of expression, and nodding in agreement or encouragement can demonstrate understanding. The physical distance between the leader and members is important and should be considered with sensitivity to the personal and cultural customs of the members.

Verbal communication of empathic understanding is focused on the members' affective and cognitive content. The leader deals with the members' concerns without talking about the members' situation. Nonverbal communication is also transmitted through a variety of ways, including body posture, facial expression, voice quality, and gestures.

Both the leader and the members are sometimes thinking about what has been said and observed. No words are needed. The observant leader senses when the members are meaningfully processing. Ultimately, the members can be encouraged to explore more openly after realizing the leader has no need or desire to direct the topic, tone, or focus.

The person-centered model has been used frequently across all age groups. When the model is applied to young children, it is accompanied with play material and activities appropriate to the age group.

Some Final Comments on Humanistic Groups

Humanistic counseling approaches are based on the assumption that group members can understand the factors in their lives that are causing them to be unhappy. It rests on the belief that individuals have the capacity for self-direction and constructive personal change. The relationship between the group members and leader is emphasized, the leader's attitudes are more crucial than the techniques, and members are encouraged to unleash their growth potential and seek to become more of the person they want to be. The primary responsibility for the direction of the therapeutic process is placed on the group members.

EXISTENTIAL GROUPS

Existentialism examines humanness; the focus is on human existence, including thoughts, feelings, and anxieties. Existential group therapy emphasizes the freedom to choose what to make of our circumstances. It is built on the foundation of freedom and personal responsibility for choices and actions. The basic existential premise is that people are not victims of circumstances but are free to choose who they want to be. The discovery of personal meaning within existence is also a central focal point of this approach. Overall, it is a flexible approach that emphasizes relationships and empowers group members to be who they choose to be.

Types of Existential Groups

Existential groups have become popular since the 1960s because individuals have sought a deeper understanding of who they are and what life means. Yalom, May, and Frankl have all expanded the application of the existential philosophy to apply to everyday life. The existential approach is most often applied to counseling and psychotherapy groups. Psychoeducational and task/work groups are seldom based on this approach because existential groups are not focused on dealing with specific behaviors or concerns. As a general rule, this approach is most useful and beneficial for members who are verbal, can communicate effectively, and are not afraid of dealing with painful issues. It has been suggested that maturity and life experience are prerequisites for an existential approach. At the least, the approach should be limited to members who are developmentally capable of rational thought and are cognitively intact.

Role and Function of the Leader in Existential Groups

In the existential view, the leader is in partnership with the members. The leader is committed to demonstrating a strong presence and nurturing a strong therapeutic alliance. The assumption is that change emerges from the therapeutic relationship itself. The leader also facilitates relationships among and between group members because it is assumed that change is also brought about by relationships with the members.

Existential group leaders assume a basic role of challenging the group members to examine their lives. This involves encouraging members to consider ways that their free will may be constrained, reflect on how they might increase their choices, and assume responsibility for their choices. The leader can be instrumental in helping members see how some of the patterns they have in place hold them back from being who they want to be.

Stages in Existential Groups

An existential therapy group is characterized by an innovative process of examination that can be conceptualized in three general phases (Corey, 2005). In the beginning, group members are invited to consider the ways they process information and cope with the world. They examine their values, beliefs, and assumptions. Group members reconsider the premise that their problems are products of environmental influence. The leader centers on teaching members how to focus on their own existence and to consider their own role in contributing to their problems.

During the middle phase, existential group counseling members are encouraged to examine their value system closely. The process of self-exploration is intended to promote insight into values and attitudes. Members focus on finding meaning through addressing core life issues.

The final phase assists members in putting new insights into action. The group members are encouraged to nurture their strengths and put their abilities into living a meaningful existence. Many members experience the emergence of empowerment when they choose to consciously become the author of their lives.

Techniques Commonly Used in Existential Groups

The interventions that existential group leaders employ are based on philosophical views about the nature of human existence. They are free to draw from techniques that flow from many other orientations. The primary ground rule is that leaders adapt their interventions to their own personality and style while accommodating the needs of group members. Interventions are guided by a philosophical framework about what it means to be human; they include emphasis on self-awareness, anxiety, and the search for meaning and authenticity.

Members are also assisted in coming to terms with the paradoxes of living. One of the leader's tasks is to encourage participants to accept anxiety as growth-producing and to help members find the courage to face and fully experience their anxieties. Similar to the person-centered approach, the therapeutic use of silence, questions, and making interpretations are critical to existential group process.

Some Final Comments on Existential Groups

Existentialists believe people are capable of insight and self-awareness, which empowers them to choose the way they live and become who they want to be. With this responsibility comes anxiety, which is another basic human characteristic. Existential group therapy assists members in creating a life that has meaning and purpose. It embraces the premise that people are not a victim of circumstance but instead have the power to be who they choose to be.

CASE EXAMPLE OF A HUMANISTIC/ EXISTENTIAL GROUP

Existential groups are grounded in several principles: members are free to shape their lives by the choices they make; human beings are aware of the cycle of life and death and that we all eventually die. Healthy members seek meaning or purpose for their lives. Group leaders attempt to help members to become more self-aware, take personal responsibility, and search for meaning in their lives (Yalom & Leszcz, 2005).

The following group dialogue is from a midlife crisis men's group consisting of six members plus the group leader. It is an existentially based counseling group with a closed group format. The men live in or around a fairly large metropolitan area and range in age from 37 to 52 years. Although they are homogeneous in some

respects (e.g., middle-age adult men), they are heterogeneous in other respects (e.g., marital status, ethnic origin, careers, wrestling with different issues). The men meet for 90 minutes weekly, and the group will run 15 weeks in its entirety. The men are in week 11. They have become accustomed to each other, the group session format, and sharing together. This dialogue provides a glimpse into the second half of one group session. The leader is a licensed mental health practitioner, age 48, divorced, Native American, with one child. A brief description of each member follows: Pablo—age 51, married with 3 children, Hispanic American, computer programmer; Randy—age 40, gay with partner, 1 child from previous marriage, European American, real estate broker; Antwane—age 49, divorced and remarried, 2 children from each marriage, African American, architect; Mengjie—age 39, single, Chinese American, restaurant owner; Aldo—age 44, married with 4 children, Italian American, investment broker; and Samuel—age 52, married with 2 children, Jewish American, commercial developer.

LEADER: Let's get restarted, gentlemen. I appreciate you all choosing to take responsibility for returning from our 10-minute break in a timely fashion this week. As I recall, we ended just before break with Mengjie talking about the pressures he experiences related to owning and operating his own business, the enormous time commitment, and the unlikelihood that he would meet a potential marriage partner given his hectic schedule.

MENGJIE: I love work. Not only does it provide a great standard of living for me, but I really know who I am when I'm working. It defines me.

RANDY: I used to feel like that, too. I mean, I still make a decent living selling properties, but this

PABLO: recession has got me rethinking things. I used to think I was something, a big real estate tycoon or something. But I ain't selling jack now. No one is. It makes me realize that I'm not in control of everything.

PABLO: You're right, there.

RANDY: If I let my whole personal identity get wrapped up in my work, then I let my work define me. Well, right now, as a realtor, I'm virtually nonexistent. I can't sell a thing. If my work defines me, I hardly exist. Obviously, this isn't true. So I'm coming to realize that I'm more than just my work.

SAMUEL: Yeah, my business is slowing down dramatically, too. I struggle with the work identity quandary, too. It's like, as men, we're supposed to be the providers. That is one of our major roles. Yet we're much more than that. We're husbands, dads, home repair experts, lawn care maintenance . . . we do a lot. Our identity cannot solely be found in our work. Otherwise, we are simply work droids. I'm not satisfied being a work droid.

ALDO: We're back to the ever present, "What's it all about, Alphie?" question.

LEADER: Yes, many significant conversations tend to lead to the search for meaning in our lives.

PABLO: It's inescapable.

SAMUEL: And not something I think I want to fully escape. The search helps me stay balanced and identify purpose for myself.

RANDY: I have to agree with that. As uncomfortable and as unsettling as these conversations are for me, they seem to help me balance work with relationships, among other things.

ALDO: I still wrestle with the stress of how much time I'm supposed to spend at work, time with my family, and time to myself.

MENGJIE: Yeah, I've been thinking a lot about what you (Aldo) said earlier, in the first half of group, about wanting to be free from your responsibilities as a husband and father. I find it weird that we're about the same age, yet you want to get away from the things I'm trying to attain.

ALDO: I didn't mean I wanted to throw away my family, I just feel a . . . well, a tension between all my family responsibilities and . . . how much time I've got left.

RANDY: Time you've got left? Do you have a disease or illness or something?

ALDO: No, man, I mean I'm 44 and I ain't the guy I used to be, you know? I don't have the same energy, I forget stuff more often, I ache for days after a good workout, and I don't have it in bed like I used to. I'm getting older, man.

RANDY: We're all getting older . . . all the aches and pains . . . those come with the privilege of growing older. That's how I look at it anyway.

MENGJIE: Maybe that's why I'm all worried about hooking up with a lady. I realize I'm not getting any younger and time is short.

I don't have all the time in the world to find a woman, settle down, and have kids. My parents expected me to marry a long time ago, but I got so caught up in building my business it became like my family. I nurtured and raised it like a kid.

LEADER: So the realization of life's brevity makes us reflect, think about ourselves, and reconsider our choices.

ANTWANE: I can relate to that. When my first wife and I divorced, I went through a considerable amount of self-reflective thought and second guessing. I wasn't happy in the marriage and this discomfort forced me to consider other options. I felt stuck for years. I felt like I'd made my bed and needed to lie in it. But when I realized life is too short and I had a choice, I made it. For me, it was a good decision. I truly believe my ex-wife is happier with her new husband and the kids have adjusted pretty well to having two families. Heck, they probably like it (laughing). Now they get two sets of Christmas gifts!

PABLO: Yeah, when I was in my late thirties, I went through a time when I thought about leaving my wife and kids. It lasted a few years, on and off. In the end, though, I knew it wasn't right for me to leave. Commitment is commitment to me. I made vows, for better or worse. Don't get me wrong, I ain't judging you guys who have been divorced; but for me, I made the right decision.

My marriage isn't perfect and my kids don't always agree with me, but we're a family and we get through things as a family.

SAMUEL: You know the Peace Corp slogan? It's the hardest job you'll ever love or something like that. I think they stole it from spouses and parents. (Long, silent pause follows.)

LEADER: Say more Samuel.

SAMUEL: What more do you want to know? I think marriage and rearing kids are two of the hardest, most challenging relationships, or "jobs," that we have as men. I think it is the same for women, too. We made a choice to get married. We made a choice to have kids. We took on the responsibilities that come along with these choices. No matter how much we desire to have a "redo" later on, we must first honor our initial obligations and responsibilities. I made these commitments to God as well as my family. I don't take that lightly. In the end, I believe I've got to answer to God for all my actions here on earth.

PABLO: Yeah, that's a big part of my decision-making process for me, too. Even though Sam and I don't share the same religion, I got married in the Catholic Church. When I got married, I knew it meant forever with the same wife. Whenever I have doubts and start stressing out about it, that original promise pops up in my head. It's weird . . . those marriage vows and being married in the church creates pressure and also provides comfort to me. I wrestle with guilt for even thinking about leaving my wife and kids.

RANDY: You got a case of good old Catholic guilt. You need to refuse to be governed by guilt. You've got to believe you make the best decision you can at the moment and you move forward.

LEADER: Randy, I appreciate what you are saying, but I want to encourage you to say it in first person pronoun by using I-statements. You're giving advice, but I'm not sure you're directing it to the right person.

RANDY: Ahh . . . okay. You got me there, partner. Well, let's see . . . I refuse to be ruled by guilt. I believe you make, er, I made the best decision I could at any given moment and then I forward. Later, I may find myself in different circumstances or I may find out more information about a situation. So I am free to make a different decision at this later point in time.

LEADER: Well done, Randy.

RANDY: It's cool. No problem. Actually, turning the words around like that helped me to realize that what I was saying was more for me to hear than for Pablo to hear. So you got me. I was really giving myself advice. That's cool.

LEADER: Perhaps.

MENGJIE: Regardless of who it was meant for, I can relate to those words. When I chose to run my restaurant to the exclusion of any long-lasting committed

relationships, I made the decision based on the fact that any fledging business needs that type of commitment to succeed. At that time, it was the right decision. Now that my business is doing well, the situation or circumstances have changed. The restaurant doesn't require the same amount of time and commitment from me to succeed. So now I'm able to consider other interests. I like that. I don't feel quite so foolish for pouring myself into my business so much.

ANTWANE: I guess we walk a different path or take a different journey depending on the choices we make.

ALDO: It seems we do, but I find it amazing that we all seem to struggle with some of the same pressures.

ANTWANE: What do you mean?

ALDO: I mean we've all talked about growing older, that life doesn't last forever, and that we struggle with choices we've made— good and bad. It seems like part of the trick is to decide to see the glass as half full and move on.

MENGJIE: I guess I can find satisfaction in the fact that now I have ample resources to care for a wife and family, if I can ever get hooked up.

ANTWANE: So what are you going to do about getting hooked up Meng? Time is short, buddy; you may have to try that speed dating to get hooked up fast! (This provokes laughter from the entire group.)

MENGJIE: I'm not sure about speed dating, but I have thought about joining one of those online dating services. Two couples who frequent my restaurant got hooked up through online dating. One of them actually had their first face-to-face meeting in my restaurant, so they come back for dinner every year to celebrate their anniversary.

SAMUEL: I don't recommend you meeting your online date at your own restaurant, Meng. That would be mixing business with pleasure. (Group laughs again.)

PABLO: He doesn't have to meet her at his restaurant. But, Meng, you better take her to a good restaurant, but not one as good as your place.

RANDY: Good point. He needs to save the best for last.

MENGJIE: Hold on, guys, I don't even have a date yet. I haven't even signed up for an online service yet.

LEADER: Good point, Mengjie. What is the next logical step for you?

MENGJIE: Hmm . . . I guess I can ask my customers which online dating service they used. Or I can get online and Google "dating services."

RANDY: Be *very* careful what you type to do that search. (group laughter)

MENGJIE: Good point.

ALDO: Dude, you mean you can't hook up with all the fine-looking lady customers you've got coming through your doors?

MENGJIE: I really don't like to mix business with pleasure. When I'm

at work, I'm all about work. I don't think I'm as relaxed or approachable that way. Plus, if it doesn't work out, I might lose myself a good paying customer. (chuckles from a few of the guys)

RANDY: I think AOL and Yahoo and those sites have their own Internet dating services, too.

ALDO: How do you know, married man?

RANDY: Don't ask, don't tell. (laughter erupts)

PABLO: Actually, one of my kids told me they've got it broken down into very specific categories now. They've got dating groups categorized by ethnic group, sexual orientation, religion, sexual diseases, marital status . . . all sorts of different subgroups.

ANTWANE: You gotta be kidding? They've got dating sites for married people?

PABLO: Yep.

SAMUEL: I guess there's hope for us married guys, too. (more laughter)

LEADER: I see we're regressing into our typical quips and jokes as the end of our group time approaches. We've talked about a couple of important issues. Let's wrap up tonight's group. What major topics were discussed?

RANDY: Satisfaction or dissatisfaction with work or our jobs.

MENGJIE: Relationships.

LEADER: Okay. How would you summarize the discussion in terms of key points?

ALDO: Some of the points that connect our struggle with work and re-lationships keep coming up.

LEADER: What are these?

ALDO: Time. We're only given a limited amount of time.

SAMUEL: And none of us knows exactly how much we've got.

PABLO: Death. Basically you're both describing death.

ALDO: The other point seems to be about purposefulness. What defines us as men, as human beings.

MENGJIE: Yeah, what's important to us gives us meaning.

ANTWANE: One other threat that seems to tie it all together is the fact that there is a natural tension among living life, limited time, and identifying meaning in or for our lives.

MENGJIE: I'd also say that we go about this journey differently. We make decisions constantly and live with our choices along the way. None of us makes the same exact choices. Even if we make similar choices, we rarely make them at the same time in our lives. This makes each person's journey unique.

LEADER: Succinct and on target. What plans are being made as per our discussion?

MENGJIE: For one, I'm going to ask my customers which online dating service they used.

RANDY: Too scared to go online and search, eh?

MENGJIE: Yep, and too scared to try speed dating. That's not a choice I'm comfortable making, at least not yet.

RANDY: I'm going to be less of a victim. I realized by owning my own advice tonight that I am more in control about how I think, feel, and address situations.

SAMUEL: I'm going to appreciate what I've got in terms of work and family. We're all fortunate to have jobs right now. And I love my family, even during the hard times. I'm going to remind myself about seeing the glass half full, if not three quarters full.

PABLO: Ditto to what Samuel said. I need to add one thing, though. I will replace my guilt with God's forgiveness.

ALDO: Make hay while the sun shines.

LEADER: Tell us what you mean by that.

ALDO: I mean enjoy the time I've got. Realize and remember that each moment is a gift. I'm not promised tomorrow so enjoy today.

LEADER: Can you give us one example of how you will live this out?

ALDO: I've been saving money to buy something for myself, a sports car or something. I've been wrestling with taking my kids to Disney World one last time before they get too old and don't want to do it. I'm going to set up the trip and give up the car.

PABLO: Good for you, man!

ANTWANE: I'm not sure I'm willing to give up my big plans for my dream home, but I am going home to write my "bucket list"—you know, like that movie; things I want to do before I die. So much to do and so little time.

LEADER: Good work, gentlemen. Come next week prepared to give the group a brief update on how you implemented your plans. We've got four more meetings before our group ends. Time is up for tonight, so I'll see you next week, same time, same place.

Summary

Person-centered and existential philosophies have contributed important dynamics to group work. They are focused on the members' subjective life experiences and how these experiences translate to interfering with individuals' abilities to successfully choose who they want to be. Emphasis is placed on the here and now and on the creation of personal insight and interpersonal awareness. Ultimately, these approaches empower group members to examine and evaluate their lives. It encourages members to release destructive life patterns and embrace positive change though a personal quest for meaning.

CHAPTER 14

The Rational-Emotive Behavior Therapy Approaches to Group Counseling and Psychotherapy
Theory, Techniques, and Applications

Ann Vernon

PREVIEW

From its inception, rational-emotive behavior therapy principles have been applied in various group counseling formats to facilitate rational thinking and promote emotional and behavioral well-being. The purpose of this chapter is to describe specific applications of rational-emotive behavior therapy (REBT) to group practice, including an illustration of the process.

RATIONAL-EMOTIVE BEHAVIOR THERAPY (REBT) GROUPS

Group applications have been an integral part of rational-emotive behavior therapy (REBT) since 1959, when Albert Ellis discovered that people by and large improved more from group therapy than from individual therapy (Ellis, 1997). Ellis noted that group therapy has several advantages. First, several group members help dispute the client's irrational beliefs, which usually makes the disputations better and stronger. In addition, group members can collectively suggest better homework assignments that clients are more likely to carry out because they are accountable to several people, not just the leader. Ellis (1997, 2001b) also suggested that, because many people seek counseling for help with significant interpersonal and relationship problems, problems may be more easily assessed and addressed in a group setting because the group itself is a social situation. The fact that group participants can see that others in the group have changed is another advantage of this approach and motivates other group members to help themselves.

REBT groups have been used in many different settings, such as schools, hospitals, and work environments to help people apply rational concepts to problems of everyday living. A variety of problems, such as depression, interpersonal anxiety, self-esteem, bulimia, test anxiety, parenting, assertion, attention deficit hyperactivity disorder, and marital problems, have been addressed effectively in group settings (Dryden, 2002).

According to Ellis (2001a, 2001b), a fundamental premise of REBT is that individuals create their own emotional and behavioral disturbance by thinking in absolute and dogmatic terms, and thus it is not the event itself, but rather how individuals perceive the event that creates problems. Helping people identify and change self-defeating thoughts, feelings, and behaviors by disputing irrational beliefs is a primary goal. Another key concept is that people must learn to accept themselves and others unconditionally and learn how to cope with life's circumstances more effectively.

Rational-emotive behavioral principles are best explained through the A-B-C-D-E-F paradigm. A is the internal or external activating event, which results in feelings and behaviors (C, consequences) that are generated by rational or irrational beliefs (B). In other words, it is not the event itself that creates the emotional or behavioral reactions, but rather the beliefs one holds about the event. If the beliefs are rational, meaning that they are logical, flexible, consistent with reality, and reflect wishes and preferences, the resultant feelings are moderate and appropriate and the behaviors are self-enhancing. In contrast, irrational beliefs result in more extreme negative emotions and self-defeating behaviors. Irrational beliefs consist of "shoulds" and "dogmatic musts" and are rigid, extreme, illogical, inconsistent with reality, and detrimental (Dryden, 2003).

An integral part of the REBT process is helping individuals identify the core irrational beliefs, which are in the form of demands on self (e.g., I must be perfect and infallible); demands on others (e.g., others must treat me exactly as I think I should be treated); and demands on the world, which are characterized by low frustration tolerance (e.g., everything in life should be easy, hassle-free, and comfortable).

If irrational beliefs exist, the next step in the paradigm is to dispute these beliefs (D). The major goal of disputation is to help individuals question the logic, productivity, and reality of the irrational beliefs (Dryden, DiGiuseppe, & Neenan, 2003). Empirical, logical, and pragmatic Socratic disputes, in combination with didactic disputations, are commonly used to help achieve the E (effective new philosophy) and F (effective new feeling). With younger clients, however, disputing should be employed in more creative, developmentally appropriate ways (Vernon, 2002, 2006a, 2006b).

Types of REBT Groups

Vernon (2004a, 2004b, 2007) identified three types of REBT groups. The first is the open-ended problem-solving group, where group members learn the basic REBT concepts and then help each other apply them to current problems that group members take turns presenting. In this type of group, the topics may vary significantly depending on what is troublesome to members at the time, or they may be quite similar if something has happened in the community that affected many people. In conducting this type of group, the leader first invites any member to share a problem (i.e., activating event), identifies how the member felt and behaved (i.e., emotional/behavioral consequence), and then encourages other group members to help identify irrational beliefs and disputes. If the topic is one that most group members identify with, the leader can invite other members to describe their feelings and reactions prior to identifying beliefs and disputes, or reinforce rational beliefs if there were no extreme negative emotions and irrational beliefs. The leader also assigns homework to group members who worked on issues during the session to help them apply rational principles on a regular basis.

To further illustrate, consider an example in which six female college students volunteered to join a problem-solving group at the campus counseling center. After several sessions in which group members had learned the A-B-C-D-E-F paradigm and some cohesiveness had developed, the leader asked if anyone had a problem she would like to discuss. One young woman wanted to talk about problems she was having with her boyfriend. The leader encouraged her to share a specific example of a recent activating event and then asked her to describe how she felt and behaved in relation to that situation. The leader then asked other participants if they had had similar problems and if they felt and behaved in the same manner, which helped him make the point that it wasn't the event itself, but the beliefs about the event that resulted in the degree of emotional upset because all members hadn't reacted in a similar manner. The leader then helped participants identify irrational beliefs, disputes, and coping strategies. In the following session, he asked the young woman who had worked on her problem to share how she was feeling about the issue and whether the coping strategies had worked before inviting others to work on their problems.

A second type of group is the topic-specific group where members all share the same problem, such as anger, anxiety, stress, procrastination, perfectionism, or low-frustration tolerance, or topics such as dealing with divorce or other types of loss, abuse, or transitions such as moving. Group members may volunteer for this group because they identify with the particular topic or they may be referred and requested to join. With this approach, the discussion is limited to the specific topic and the leader helps members apply REBT concepts to deal with current issues relative to the topic. Group participants are encouraged to help each other, but the leader also assumes a more active role, at least initially, and depending on the age and level of participation of the group members. The group setting provides the opportunity for members to learn more about their issues, explore and express feelings, learn how their thoughts affect their feelings and behaviors, and identify more productive and healthier ways of thinking, feeling, and behaving.

In this type of group, it may be appropriate at times for the leader to introduce a more structured activity to help participants learn rational concepts. For example, group members who were dealing with perfectionism benefited from doing a reverse role play, in which one participant assumed the role of the person who had to be perfect at everything and another group member challenged this need to be perfect by asking questions such as, "Is there really any

such thing as a perfect person?" "What does it say about you if you aren't?" or "What's the worst thing that can happen if you aren't perfect?" Through this process, all members developed a better understanding of the irrationality of perfectionism.

A third type of group is the preventive group, which is psychoeducational in nature as opposed to problem-focused. This preventive group is typically more structured and organized around a specific activity or lesson that introduces REBT concepts and encourages group interaction and application of the ideas. Psychoeducational groups are implemented in schools, as well as in other settings, and are developed around a variety of topics that everyone can profit from, such as self-acceptance, problem solving and decision making, emotional and behavioral self-management, and getting along with others. The goal of this type of group is to teach REBT concepts in order to develop more effective life skills. Ideally, these psychoeducational lessons will equip participants with tools that they can use to reframe problems and think more rationally, thus minimizing or eliminating severe negative emotional and behavioral responses.

For example, a self-acceptance activity entitled Don't Soak It Up (Vernon, 2002, p. 77) can be used to help group participants learn how to avoid soaking up negative comments others say about them by using the analogy of a sponge. Participants are asked to pick up a dry sponge and describe it, then pick up a wet sponge and compare the two. They note that the dry sponge is light and airy, but the wet sponge is heavy and soggy. The leader points out the analogy about the sponge that soaks up water and the person who "soaks up" negative comments from others: We feel heavy and weighed down. To avoid that feeling, we need to "wring out" the sponge. In other words, we ask ourselves if what others say about us is true, and if not, we can wring out the sponge and not absorb the negative comments. Or if what they say is true, we can ask ourselves if we are bad people even if we are what they say we are. Teaching the disputing concept in this concrete way is an effective psychoeducational technique that can help minimize self-criticism and increase self-acceptance.

A fourth type of REBT group, the group marathon, may last 12 to 36 hours depending on the leader and the setting (Ellis & Dryden, 1997). This type of group blends encounter group concepts with psychoeducational techniques and problem-focused approaches. It once was an integral part of training at the Albert Ellis Institute, but it is not as widely used now.

Regardless of the type of group, the main goal is for group members to learn to think more rationally, reduce or eliminate unhealthy emotions, engage in fewer self-defeating behaviors, and apply REBT concepts to typical problems (Ellis, 2001a, 2001b). Many different techniques and psychoeducational lessons facilitate acquisition of rational concepts.

Role and Function of the Leader in REBT Groups

In REBT groups, leaders ordinarily display a high activity level and directive approach (Ellis, 1997). Ellis described himself as a teacher who shows group members how they upset themselves and what they can do to change. He believed that, because group members often choose not to modify their behavior, the leader must actively encourage them to change. "As a leader, I try to maximize honest revealing of feelings, cutting through defensiveness, getting to members' core dysfunctional philosophies" (Ellis, 1997, p. 152). He also helped members dispute, accept their discomfort, and engage in in-group and out-of-group experiential and behavioral exercises.

REBT group leaders are not overly close to members for fear of creating dependency, but they are collaborative and supportive and they do understand the importance of developing a sense of community among group members. They use rapport-building exercises as appropriate in the initial session(s), particularly if the group members are children or adolescents. Group leaders may also engage in self-disclosure when appropriate and serve as models to show group members how leaders practice REBT in their own lives. Leaders also monitor the group

process so that one member does not dominate or obstruct the group in any way.

Stages of REBT Groups

In the initial stages of the group, the leader devotes some attention to rapport building and group cohesion, and then introduces participants to the A-B-C-D-E-F theory (i.e., activating event, belief, consequence, dispute, effective philosophy, new feeling). In the working stage of the group, members learn to apply REBT concepts to the problems they introduce in the group setting. For example, in a topic-specific group on dealing with parental divorce, members can learn how to dispute irrational beliefs such as "Nothing could be worse than this" or "I can't stand it" and replace them with rational thoughts. The final stage emphasizes skill acquisition and completion of homework assignments.

Techniques Commonly Used in REBT Groups

Numerous cognitive, emotive, and behavioral techniques have been used effectively in groups with members. Assertiveness training, role playing, behavioral rehearsal, rational-emotive imagery, relaxation training, cognitive restructuring, and information giving are among the most commonly used methods. A few additional techniques will also be described.

COGNITIVE TECHNIQUES A popular cognitive technique, rational coping self-statements, involves asking group members to identify rational beliefs and coping statements to substitute for their irrational beliefs. Members write these on cards and use them repeatedly until they believe them. A rational coping self-statement for a group participant struggling to stay in college might include: "I know I have to study hard, but I've done it successfully before, so I can do it again."

Another effective cognitive technique is to use psychoeducational methods such as REBT books, pamphlets, CDs and DVDs, and other self-help material (Corey, 2007; Ellis, 2001b). For example, adolescents in an anger management group read *How to Control Your Anger Before It Controls You* (Effron-Potter,1993), which explained how to identify the degree to which anger was problematic and what to do about it. The group leader encouraged members to try various techniques and report back to the group on how well these methods worked.

EMOTIVE TECHNIQUES   Shame attack exercises are consistently used to help group members learn that they can stand the anxiety that comes from guilt, embarrassment, and shame and that they can accept themselves even if others think they are behaving foolishly. Shame attack exercises involve some degree of risk taking and can include exercises such as calling out the stops on the elevator or approaching strangers and asking what month it is, explaining that you have just been released from a mental institution, to prove that they can tolerate embarrassment (Nelson-Jones, 2000). Shame attack exercises should not involve anything illegal or highly inappropriate, and they must be used cautiously, especially with younger clients.

Another emotive technique is to use humor to show group members that they take themselves too seriously and to illustrate the ridiculousness of their irrational beliefs. One of Ellis's favorite ways of introducing humor is through humorous songs he has written on a variety of topics. See Ellis (2001a) for examples. Vernon (2002) adapted this concept for children by introducing the concept of "silly songs," and also suggested having young clients write their own humorous songs to help them reframe their issues and not take them too seriously.

BEHAVIORAL TECHNIQUES   REBT group leaders encourage members to reinforce themselves when they do something to change a negative behavior and to penalize themselves when they don't (Ellis, 1997). Penalties may include giving money to a cause they don't support or doing an onerous task, such as scrubbing toilets. Group members can also monitor or suggest rewards and penalties for other members. Homework, typically thought of as a cognitive technique, is also a behavioral strategy when leaders encourage members to do things they are fearful of in order to conquer their fears. Other activity-based assignments can also be used, such as conducting surveys to see if a perfect person truly exists or having adolescents interview parents other than their own to see if these parents allow their children to have all the freedom they want and never make any demands on them that might make their life uncomfortable (Vernon, 2002).

EXAMPLE OF A TOPIC-SPECIFIC REBT GROUP ON ANXIETY

For the sake of illustration, three sessions of a topic-specific group, where all group members are experiencing significant degrees of anxiety, are described. The group members consisted of eight women who volunteered for this group, which was offered at a local mental health center by one of the staff therapists. Some of the participants were also being seen for individual counseling by other therapists at the center. Prior to joining the group, the leader interviewed prospective members to explain the purpose of the group and determine whether a group setting would be beneficial and appropriate for them. Given that this was a closed group that did not allow members to join at any time, the leader also ascertained that the eight who were selected would commit to six group sessions.

In the first session, the leader explained that the purpose of this group was to help participants learn more effective ways of handling their anxiety, She shared some information about her background and group-facilitation experience and then invited participants to generate guidelines they would like to see the group adopt, such as confidentiality, respect for others, openness to sharing, and honesty. Then she asked group members to introduce themselves by stating their name, two things that others couldn't tell by looking at them, and their reason for joining this group. After determining that further rapport building was not necessary because the group members seemed to be connecting, the leader moved directly into the topic of anxiety by distributing index cards and asking each group participant to identify in writing a recent example of when they had been anxious; their degree of anxiety on a scale of 1 to 10; and how the anxiety affected them physically, emotionally, and behaviorally. The leader invited group members to share their experiences. Throughout this sharing, the group leader facilitated interaction among participants, which helped build group cohesion. After everyone had shared, the leader provided some information about anxiety from a cognitive perspective, explaining that the way a person thinks about an event that provokes anxiety contributes to the degree of the emotion. She shared a handout on typical cognitive distortions such as tunnel vision, selective abstraction, personalizing, overgeneralization, catastrophizing, and dichotomous thinking that often contribute to anxiety. After some explanation about these distorted thoughts, she invited group members to identify which thoughts were most problematic for them, encouraging interaction among members. At then end of the two-hour session, the leader explained that short homework assignments would be helpful in reinforcing the learning from the session, and she invited the group members to monitor their thinking and identify specific cognitions that contributed to their anxiety during the week prior to the next session. She ended the session by asking group members to share any learning or reactions. The second and third sessions will be described in a dialogue format.

Session 2

LEADER: Good evening and welcome to our second session. I appreciated the sharing and interaction that occurred in last week's session and I am looking forward to tonight's meeting. First, I would like to ask if anyone has any thoughts about the first session or questions about anything we discussed relative to anxiety.

SYLVIA: I would just like to share that it felt good to be able to talk about my anxiety. Usually I am embarrassed and put myself down because I feel this way, and it was helpful to hear that I am not alone.

LEADER: Thank you for sharing that. I see several others nodding their heads as well, so I am assuming that you also felt some relief in knowing that others experience anxiety. I also think that Sylvia brought up a good point, which is that she often feels ashamed about being anxious and puts herself down. Is that also something that others experience?

LEONIE: Yes, I definitely do that, and I keep thinking that I should be able to live my life without feeling so anxious. And that just makes me more upset and anxious, so I would like to learn what to do about that.

LEADER: What the two of you have brought up is what we call a secondary emotional problem— being ashamed about being anxious. For example, I heard Leonie say that this just makes her anxiety worse. Is that how it is for others? (Heads nod.) Let me ask you this: Does it help you to put yourself down for feeling this way? (Heads shake no.) And what does it say about you if you are anxious? Does it make you a bad person? Are you unworthy because you have some anxiety problems? (Heads shake no.) You are absolutely right. This doesn't make you a bad or worthless person, and it is important for you to remind yourself of that when you catch yourself being ashamed and putting yourself down for being anxious. But the good news is that there are many things that will help you minimize the anxiety, so let's focus on that right now by first reporting on your homework assignment. Would someone like to begin?

LIDIA: I'll share. At first I thought it was hard to identify my distorted thinking, but once I was more aware of it, I found it very helpful.

LEADER: Could you share a specific example?

LIDIA: Sure. I get really anxious when I have to go to the doctor. I have had some health problems and I keep thinking that the next time I go I will have something really serious wrong with me. It's like I can't stop thinking about it. So this week, I had another appointment and I recognized that I catastrophize and have tunnel vision. I see only the bad possibilities and ignore other realities.

LEADER: Thank you for sharing that example. How did your awareness about catastrophizing and tunnel vision affect your level of anxiety?

LIDIA: It really did help. That's not to say that I wasn't anxious, but it wasn't as bad.

LEADER: I'm glad to hear that. Would anyone else like to share?

GRETTA: I learned that I do a lot of overgeneralizing. For example, I had a big project due at work, and I kept thinking that

I would never get it done, that my boss would be furious if I didn't meet the deadline, and that I might even lose my job if I couldn't get this in on time. I was very aware that the more I thought this way, the more anxious I got, to the point where, like always, I am almost paralyzed and have a much harder time focusing on the task. I just don't know what to do about it.

LEADER: You have brought up an important point—that you can recognize how the distorted thinking contributes to your anxiety, but you don't know what to do about it. Would the group like to address that topic now? (Heads nod yes.)

LEADER: Good. First, let me explain that there is a process known as disputing, where you ask yourselves questions or do small experiments to poke holes in your distorted thoughts. Doing this takes practice; you won't necessarily think differently and feel less anxious immediately or all the time, but gradually you can learn how to reduce the intensity of the negative emotion so that you are better able to control your emotions as well as your behavior. It would be easier to illustrate by giving an example. Is there anyone who would like to share her anxious thought about an event so that I could be specific about something meaningful to at least one of you? (Lidia raises her hand to volunteer.)

LEADER: Lidia, you said that you get anxious when you have to go to the doctor and you imagine the worst, is that correct? (Lidia nods.) And despite the fact that you have had only minor health problems, you continue to think the worst? (nods affirmatively) Let me ask you this: How logical is it for you to assume that you will have something very serious wrong with you?

LIDIA: It's not logical. I don't have any family history of serious medical problems and I lead a healthy lifestyle.

LEADER: Good—those are things you can say to remind yourself not to catastrophize. Are there other thoughts that you have when you are going for these checkups?

LIDIA: Well, I just think the doctor will tell me I have a terminal disease and I will die.

LEADER: It is possible that any of us could have a terminal disease and die, but how does it help you to think this way?

LIDIA: It doesn't—but I just can't seem to help it.

LEADER: Let me point out another distorted thought. It seems like you think that you will either get good news or the worst news and that there is no point in between. Does that make sense to you?

LIDIA: Yes, that is exactly what I do.

LEADER: Let me show you something that might be helpful. (The leader places a strip of masking tape on the floor and points out that at one end, there is no health problem at all and that at the other end, Lidia has a

terminal disease and will die soon. Then she hands Lidia several index cards and asks her to write down other possibilities, other things that could happen in between the worst and the best.)

LEADER: (when it appears that Lydia has finished writing) Lidia, would you lay your cards along the continuum according to where they rank on the best-to-worst scale and read them out loud to the group? (Lidia shares possibilities such as learning that she has a serious, but not terminal disease; learning that she has a disease that can be readily cured; learning that she has some elevated blood counts that can be controlled with diet and exercise; and so forth.)

LEADER: So now that you see the many different possibilities, how does that affect your level of anxiety?

LIDIA: It's much less. I can see how I immediately jump to the worst-case scenario instead of looking at this more realistically and seeing all the various possibilities. I think if I can keep that in mind, I won't be nearly as anxious.

LEADER: That would be my prediction,too. So what do you need to tell yourself when you find yourself thinking the worst?

LIDIA: That it is possible that the worst could happen but that, because I am healthy and nothing has been wrong with me yet, it isn't logical to think like that. I only make myself more anxious and that, in itself, could create the health problems I am trying to avoid.

LEADER: Exactly. Can anyone else in the group think of other things Lydia could think or do to reduce her anxiety?

KATIA: I wonder if it would help you to think about this strip of masking tape and your index cards. Then you would remember that there are other possibilities.

LIDIA: That's a great idea.

LEADER: Are there any other suggestions, or does anyone else have an example they would like to share?

SHERRY: I can really relate to what Lidia shared, and I am going to use this continuum to help me deal with my anxieties about something bad happening to my children. I know it isn't good for them to have such an overprotective mother, but when I listen to the news and hear about child abductions, it just makes me want to wrap my kids in a bubble and never let them out.

PAULA: I can relate to that, but when my mother pointed out to me how my behavior was negatively affecting my children, I realized I needed to get a handle on my anxiety.

SHERRY: What did you do?

PAULA: Well, that is partly why I wanted to join this group. But I have made some progress. It had gotten to the point where I wouldn't let my kids play outside in the yard or go next door to the neighbor's house. Finally I just decided that I would let them go for 15 minutes and check on them. If everything was okay,

I would let them stay another 15 minutes, and so forth. All the time they were gone I just did a lot of deep breathing and talking to myself, saying that I just needed to stay calm and that it was better for them to be outside playing like normal kids. After a few times it got a lot easier, but I have to admit I am still struggling with this.

LEADER: Paula, thank you for sharing—and it does sound like you've made progress. Your deep breathing technique is certainly a helpful one, as is setting short time limits. Is there something else you would like to work on relative to this?

PAULA: Well, I still have a lot of anxiety about my kids going to friends' houses, and this has become a real problem. I can tolerate them going next door, but my daughter now has a friend who lives two blocks away and because she is in first grade, she thinks she should be able to ride her bike there instead of having me take her. I don't know what to tell her. Most of the time I just have her invite the friend to our house, but I know this will only get worse as she gets older. I would love some help on this.

MARILEE: I can relate to what you are saying. My children are now 10 and 12, and when they were younger, I was very much like you. But I realized I couldn't keep them close forever, so now I just make sure that they check in with me and that there is adult supervision—and so far so good. One thing my therapist suggested is that I make a plus sign on the calendar every day they come home safe, and that has really helped. In fact, I don't have any minuses. So I keep reminding myself of that every time they ask to go somewhere.

LEADER: I like your suggestion, Marilee, and what I am hearing is that you realized the need to let go, but at the same time you take sensible precautions, which not only helps you deal with your anxiety, but helps keep your kids safe.

PAULA: Thanks, Marilee; I'm going to try that idea.

LEADER: It looks like we are out of time. Would anyone care to share something you learned or an impression you have of today's session?

GRETTA: I really got a lot out of the group and have several ideas that I can use to help me deal with my anxiety. (Several others share similar thoughts.)

LEADER: I appreciated the group interaction and would like to suggest a homework assignment. I would like each of you to make a contract with yourself to do something this week to reduce your anxiety. It might be one of the ideas generated in today's session or something else you think would be helpful. I will look forward to hearing about your progress in our next meeting.

Session 3

Leader: Good evening. I hope you all had a good week. I would like to begin by having you share the results of your homework assignment. Would anyone care to begin?

KATIA: I had a good week, thanks to this group! I have been so embarrassed about my anxiety, and it was so helpful for me to realize that it didn't help to put myself down, that I wasn't a bad person because I got anxious. But nevertheless, I don't like being so anxious, so for my homework assignment, I took Paula's suggestion and forced myself to ride up two floors in the elevator instead of taking the stairs. Some people think I am just a health freak and like taking the steps, but the truth is that I am scared that the elevator will get stuck and I won't be able to get out. It really is something I need to get over because I work in a hospital and it is just a lot faster to take the elevator when I have to run from floor to floor. So this week I started with a small step, and it was okay.

PAULA: Good for you, Katia! (Other members voice their support.)

KATIA: I know I have ways to go until I get to the 10th floor, but I think if I take it a couple of floors at a time, I might be able to do it.

LEADER: I am glad you took the risk, Katia. Did you use any other techniques while you were actually in the elevator?

KATIA: Well, I wasn't alone, so I couldn't talk to myself, which might have helped, but I just kept staring at the door and thinking about my favorite thing to do, which is floating on a lake on a raft.

LEADER: That's another great technique for reducing anxiety—thinking of something pleasant and distracting. Does anyone else use that? (Several heads nod.)

LEADER: Good work, Katia. Would anyone else care to report on her homework assignment?

LEONIE: One of the things I have been quite anxious about is my job performance. I work in a highly competitive advertising agency, and I am always exceptionally nervous when it's time for a performance review. I have one this coming week, so this past week I started to prepare by reviewing my previous evaluations and putting them on the continuum from horrible to wonderful. That really helped! What I realized is that none of my evaluations has been horrible; in fact, not even in the middle. All have been in the "pretty wonderful to wonderful category," so I just told myself to relax about this because I don't have a history of failure. I am so much calmer than I usually am the week before a review!

LEADER: What a great strategy! And I congratulate you on being less anxious. But let's suppose this time was different, and that you got a bad review. If that happened, what would that say about you as a person? Would it mean that you are a failure or that you are totally incompetent now and forever?

LEONIE: Obviously not—but those things have crossed my mind.

LEADER: Of course, but it is important, as you did, to look at your past history and remember that while anything is possible, what is the probability that you will get a bad review given your past performance? And even if you did do poorly this time, you admitted that this doesn't doom you to complete failure at the job or as a person.

LEONIE: Right. I just need to keep working on it.

LEADER: Sounds like you're making good progress and we will look forward to hearing the results of your review.

LEADER: Is there anyone else who would like to report on homework?

SYLVIA: Like I said in the last session, I have always gotten so embarrassed about being anxious. I kept thinking that others would think I was crazy. So for my homework assignment, I decided to tell my sister that I was in this group and that I was learning new ways to deal with my anxiety. I was really afraid that she would be critical, but instead, she shared that she has some anxiety herself, so we ended up having a long conversation about it. I felt so relieved to be able to be honest instead of pretending that everything was great with me.

LEADER: It sounds like that was a good risk for you to take, especially because you anticipated the worst: that she would think you are crazy. Has it happened before, that you think the worst but the worst doesn't happen?

SYLVIA: Yes, a lot.

LEADER: What do you think you could do to stop yourself from imagining the worst?

SYLVIA: I guess I just need to keep reminding myself that the worst doesn't generally happen.

LEADER: And if it did, would you be able to stand it?

SYLVIA: I guess so. . . .

LEADER: As we have discussed before, sometimes the worst does happen, but if you think carefully about the possibility versus the probability of it happening, it helps put the issue in better perspective. However, if the worst were to happen, we often think that we absolutely couldn't stand it. But in fact, how many of you have stood things you never thought you could? (Heads nod.) Exactly. So remembering that may also help alleviate some anxiety. Would anyone else care to share about the homework assignment?

SHERRY: I'll share. Last time I talked a little about being anxious about my children, thinking something bad would happen to them. I got some good suggestions from Paula and Marilee that I tried, and for the most part, I would say they worked. But I still worry about their safety, so I went to the library and found some books about what children should do if a stranger approaches them and we read those together. So now when I let them go out of the yard, I feel a little more comfortable because they have some knowledge about how to protect themselves.

LEADER: I like that idea, and it sounds like the combination of strategies is working for you. Is there anyone who would like to bring up a new issue?

MARILEE: I am still struggling with something that makes me extremely anxious, and that has to do with driving. I was in a bad accident about a year ago, and it was my fault. The other driver was hurt pretty badly and so was I. I felt so guilty, but I think I have worked through that to some extent. I know that accidents happen, and thankfully both of us are okay now. But the problem is that now I am afraid to drive, and this is causing problems because my husband thinks I should just be able to get over it. It's made his life more complicated because he has to drive the kids to school, interrupt his schedule to pick them up and take them to events, and it just isn't a good situation.

LEADER: Has anyone else experienced anything like this? (Nobody has.) What strategies have you tried to help yourself deal with this anxiety?

MARILEE: I really haven't tried anything. I have just avoided the situation, which I think is making it worse because I think I should be able to get in that car and drive like I used to.

LEADER: You actually mentioned two important things: First, that avoidance isn't working, and second, that you are thinking that you "should" be able to do this, which makes you feel bad about yourself, right?

MARILEE: Exactly.

LEADER: How does it help you to put yourself down, thinking that you *should* be able to do this?

MARILEE: It doesn't. . . .

LEADER: What would happen if you changed the *should* to a preference: I would *like* to be able to drive again? Would that take any of the pressure off?

MARILEE: Maybe, but I still don't know if I could do it.

LEADER: Does anyone else have any suggestions that might help Marilee deal with her anxiety about driving again?

PAULA: What about if you just started by taking a drive down the street and then gradually increased your distance?

GRETTA: I think that's a good idea. And maybe at the same time, you could take deep breaths and use self-talk, like "Even though this is hard, it's better if I try."

LEONIE: Marilee, how many bad accidents had you had before this one?

MARILEE: None—not even a fender bender.

LEONIE: So maybe it would help you to think about that each time you got in the car.

LEADER: Does anyone else have any other ideas?

SYLVIA: I think it might be good to write all those ideas on cards, and before you start to drive, you could review them.

LEADER: I think these are all excellent suggestions. I am also wondering about giving yourself a little reward for every successful "journey." Perhaps you could treat yourself to a movie (that you would have to drive to), shopping, or something like that. In other words, pair a reward that is something you could look forward to with what you are trying to overcome.

MARILEE: Thanks, everybody. I am glad I shared this and I hope I will be able to make some progress.

LEADER: Remember, even if your progress is very gradual, it is better to try than not to try— and don't put yourself down if you don't succeed every time.

LEADER: It looks as if our time is up. I appreciate the work you are doing and encourage you to assign another anxiety-attacking task to yourself for this coming session. I will see you next week.

The remainder of the sessions would follow the same format, with an emphasis on skill building, homework completion, and sharing. The final session would culminate with each person making a collage depicting what they had learned and what progress they had made in dealing with their anxiety. Each group member would be encouraged to present hers to the entire group.

SOME FINAL COMMENTS ON REBT GROUPS

A distinct advantage of the REBT approach is that leaders have the flexibility to introduce a variety of developmentally appropriate activities to convey the basic REBT points rather than rely on discussion alone. This is especially important with members who learn best by doing. Another advantage of the REBT group approach is that the basic theoretical assumptions can readily be taught to members who can help each other as well as themselves employ the process to solve typical problems. The fact that both intervention and prevention are incorporated into the group approach is another strength. Another benefit is that homework assignments help members transfer learning from the group to their lives outside the group.

In conducting groups, REBT leaders must be cautious about being too active-directive, which interferes with a collaborative member/leader relationship. If leaders are too didactic and active, members may become passive. Although Ellis prefers a more active and confrontational style, group leaders can be flexible and adopt their own style while still adhering to the basic principles of the approach.

Summary

REBT groups place an emphasis on skill building, which enables group participants to apply skills in everyday circumstances. This psychoeducational focus helps group members learn facts and basic information that can facilitate problem resolution. Like other types of groups, members of REBT groups benefit from the support and empathy they receive from the leader and other group members. In addition, REBT groups comprise an effective option for improving the delivery of mental health services because a number of clients can be reached at one time.

CHAPTER **15**

Reality Therapy and Behavioral Approaches to Counseling and Psychotherapy Groups

Ann Vernon

PREVIEW

Both reality therapy and behavioral groups help individuals lead more productive lives through behavior change. Behavior therapy encompasses more diversity in techniques that are based on learning theory principles, but there is not a single group model that can be labeled a behavioral group, according to Corey (2007). Reality therapy, developed by William Glasser, is based on specific theoretical principles related to how individuals gain control of their lives in an attempt to fulfill their basic needs for survival, love and belonging, fun, freedom, and power. Specific applications of these approaches in group settings will be described in this chapter.

CHOICE THEORY/REALITY THERAPY GROUPS

Reality therapy, which is based on the premise of personal responsibility, has been implemented with individuals, couples, families, and groups. The principles have been successfully employed in a variety of settings, such as mental health agencies, correctional institutions, and schools in particular. Reality therapy is the vehicle for implementing the major constructs of choice theory, formerly called control theory, which asserts that human behavior is purposeful and involves choices.

Glasser contended that most people do not have a clear understanding of why they behave as they do; they choose behaviors they think will help them cope with frustrations caused by dissatisfactory relationships, which constitute many of the problems people have. He also maintained that problems are in the present, and therefore, while people may have been influenced by the past, they do not have to be controlled by it unless they choose to allow the past to dominate their life.

Also central to choice theory is the idea that the choices humans make are based on the physiological need of survival and four psychological needs: love and belonging, power, freedom, and fun (Glasser, 1999). Survival relates to how to maintain good health and live a satisfying life. Love and belonging signify the importance of involvement with people and the need to love and be loved. Power refers to the need to be in charge of one's life and to have a sense of accomplishment and achievement. Freedom is the need to make choices, whereas fun is the need to laugh, experience humor, and enjoy life. While all individuals have these basic needs, the needs differ in degree, and people fulfill these needs differently. People begin at an early age to develop an idea of what feels good and what they want. They store this information in their brain, or in their "quality world." This quality world may include people (the most important component), places, things, or beliefs that give them pleasure; it is the world they would like to live in. Based on their picture of this quality world, people attempt to control their choices in order to satisfy their wants and needs.

Wubbolding (2000) extended the application of reality therapy by formulating the W (wants), D (direction and doing), E (evaluation of self), and P (plans of action) (WDEP), which is a delivery system that the leader uses for helping members remediate deficiencies and make better choices. In a group setting, participants are encouraged to explore their wants, reflect on the direction of their lives and what they are doing, self-evaluate their current behaviors, and develop an attainable action plan.

Reality therapy stresses the present, thereby helping people solve current problems. Instead of emphasizing feelings, the focus is on thinking and acting in order to initiate change (Glasser, 1999). Reality therapy, whether employed in an individual or a group setting, is active, didactic, and directive; reality therapy teaches members to look at whether their actions are getting them what they want, examine their needs and perceptions, and make a plan for change.

Types of Reality Therapy Groups

Corey (2007) noted that in the quality world, people comprise the most important component and therefore, choice theory is naturally well suited to group work because of the emphasis on connection and interpersonal relationships. In the group setting, members can work on how to meet their needs through relationships developed in the group.

Depending on the setting, various types of reality therapy groups can be employed. For instance, in a school setting, reality therapy groups may involve all students in a classroom meeting. Trotzer (1999) described three types of classroom meetings: the social problem-solving meeting, the open-ended meeting, and the educational diagnostic meeting. Classroom meetings increase student responsibility and enhance classroom relationships. For example, during the problem-solving meeting, a problem common to the group is introduced, followed by a brief discussion. Group participants are asked to evaluate whether the behaviors associated with this problem help them achieve their goals, and a plan is developed to address the issue, with periodic follow-up and reevaluation of the plan (Glasser, 1999). In hospital and agency settings, groups are more psychotherapeutic and involve fewer members. The emphasis is on teaching members how to apply reality therapy principles to solve their problems by helping members understand that they choose their behaviors and can empower themselves by making different choices. These principles can also be applied to groups of parents and teachers who interact with each other to identify more effective ways of working with their children or students. Group members look at their present behavior, evaluate what they are doing and what they want to change, and make a plan to accomplish this. Choice-theory based groups are also used with abuse victims and in addiction counseling to help group participants make changes in the present as opposed to focusing on long-term therapy and in-depth exploration of the past.

Role and Function of the Leader in Reality Therapy Groups

One of the basic premises of reality therapy is that connection and interpersonal relationships are very important, which leads to wide applicability of reality therapy to groups. With this in mind, one of the primary roles of a leader is to establish a good relationship with the members by engaging in warm, respectful, and caring interactions, and also to direct any confrontational interactions as appropriate. It is important that leaders not be critical, belittling, or demeaning, but they do need to be determined, conveying to the group members that no matter what their circumstances are, change for the better is possible. Corey (2007) stressed that group leaders must at times be firm and challenge members with questions such as "Is what you are choosing to do getting you what you want? Do you want to change? If you changed, how would you feel better? What do you have to do now to make the changes happen?" (p. 425).

Another role that the reality therapy group leader assumes is that of a skillful questioner, knowing what questions to ask, as well as how and when to ask them. It is important not to misuse questions because members may find this irritating or intrusive. Wubbolding (2000) suggested that the leader combine questioning with reflective thinking and other techniques.

According to Glasser (1999), group leaders must be responsible individuals who can fulfill their own needs in order to help others do the same. They must be mentally and emotionally mature, supportive, involved, accepting, and respectful of all group members. Leaders can serve as role models of responsible behavior and help members evaluate their behavior, stop making excuses, and assume responsibility for their own actions. Group leaders are active, teaching and encouraging members to take control of their lives by thinking and acting differently and helping them understand that these changes indirectly affect the degree of control they have over their feelings. In addition, the leader focuses on the participants' strengths and encourages them not to focus on their failures and limitations because that results in lack of control. Group leaders help members find effective ways to meet their needs, and in conjunction with other group members, the leader helps participants develop specific action plans to help them make

changes to attain goals. The leader also encourages group members to identify ways to maintain the changes they have made once the group has ended.

Of course, leaders need to develop their own style of leadership, consistent with their personality, so that they can employ it with sincerity. This eventually comes with time and experience and as leaders become aware of their own needs and values. It is critical that group leaders demonstrate an openness to their own growth and a willingness to explore their own values with the groups they facilitate. Skillful leaders also learn how to adapt the theory when working with diverse populations. Flexibility is critical.

Stages of a Reality Therapy Group

In the initial stage of a reality therapy group, the leader strives to create a comfortable, supportive atmosphere and establish rapport with group members. Establishing group rules and appropriate boundaries is also part of this initial stage, and it may be appropriate to do some community-building activities, such as inviting group members to share three things from their wallet or backpack that say something about what they value, or engaging in a simple exercise where they share three things that others can't tell about them just by looking at them. According to Wubbolding (2000), leaders need to be empathic, which is demonstrated through skillful questioning and other techniques such as humor and self-disclosure. They must also listen for themes and metaphors, and suspend judgment to help establish a comfortable climate. In this initial stage and throughout the other stages, the leader should be courteous, enthusiastic, and genuine, and may at times do the unexpected because unpredictability can create an environment conducive to successful group interactions.

In the transition stage, the leader addresses typical group issues such as anxiety, control, conflict, and resistance. During the working stage, the leader helps members engage in new, productive behaviors that enable them to achieve present goals. To accomplish this, the leader helps members evaluate their current behavior and teaches them how to take responsibility for these behaviors. Throughout this stage, the leader encourages interaction and feedback among members.

Using the WDEP system developed by Wubbolding (2000), the leader first asks group members what they want, and through skillful questioning, helps them define their needs, what they have, and what they are not getting. Next, members analyze their current behavior to see if what they are doing is consistent with what they want. This assessment helps them determine what specific changes they need to enhance their lives. The leader does not allow discussion of past events unless they relate to present experiences and facilitate group members' future planning. Also, reality therapy leaders do not encourage group members to discuss their feelings; the emphasis is on behavioral change, which is what they can control more directly. The premise is that as actions change, so will feelings (Corey, 2007).

After helping members realize what they are doing and teaching them how to control their behavior in order to make choices that will change their lives, the leader's next task is to engage members in a self-evaluation process, viewed as the core of reality therapy. In confronting group members with the consequences of their behaviors in a nonjudgmental manner, the leader encourages them to evaluate their own actions, which results in greater ownership. It is important to involve all group members in this self-evaluation process.

Once group members have evaluated their own behavior, the leader helps members identify a plan for specific behavioral change. Wubbolding (2000) noted that an effective plan is one that is initiated by the member (but can involve input from the leader); relates to each member's needs; and is realistic, attainable, do-able, and easy to understand. In addition, the plan should include positive actions that can be practiced regularly and carried out

independently of others. Plans should also be flexible, repetitive, precise, and measurable. Wubbolding also suggested that group members give feedback to each other and that the plan be put in writing. The group leader needs to be persistent in helping members work on the plan and revise it as needed in order to be successful. For plans to be effective, however, individuals need to be committed to putting them into action. One of the advantages of group counseling is that members can help each other evaluate and review plans, offer support and encouragement, and hold others accountable for carrying out their plans. Although it is not possible to force members to commit to making changes, the leader and other group members can help those who are resistant to look at what is stopping them make this commitment to change.

Techniques Commonly Used in Reality Therapy Groups

Wubbolding (1991) identified four techniques to employ in a group setting: humor, paradox, skillful questioning, and self-help procedures. According to Wubbolding, humor helps individuals develop an awareness of a situation and should be used only after considering the timing, focus, and degree of trust in the group. If used appropriately, humor can be curative and facilitate bonding in the group. Paradoxical techniques such as reframing, relabeling, redefining, or doing the opposite can also be effective for some group members. Skillful questioning involves using open-ended questions to help clients explore issues. It is also important to focus on behaviors that group members would like to target, with an emphasis on the positive, which constitutes the self-help approach.

Corey (2007) noted that reality therapy is a process, and that there are no absolute questions or techniques. With this in mind, group leaders need to develop their own interventions, tailoring them to the specific group member's needs and keeping in mind that the main focus is on developing satisfying relationships.

AN EXAMPLE OF A REALITY THERAPY GROUP

As previously explained, the initial sessions of a reality therapy group should focus on developing a supportive climate, with an emphasis on developing a warm, caring relationship. There must be genuine involvement, and a friendly and trusting environment should be established. The following transcript illustrates a portion of one session during the working stage of a group for young adults in a college counseling center.

LEADER: It is good to see all of you here tonight, and I hope you all had a good week. I appreciated the opportunity to get to know you all better during the last session, and my impression is that you all have some degree of commitment to making positive changes in your lives. To begin, I would like to ask you to think about your life right now: What do you really want? I invite you to reflect on that and share it with the group if you wish.

ALEX: (after several minutes) The reason I joined this group is because I am about to flunk out of school, and I don't want that to happen.

LEADER: Thanks, Alex. So you want to turn that failure into success. What do you think is stopping you from being successful?

ALEX: I guess that I party too much and don't study enough.

LEADER: So your choice to party and not study isn't getting you where you want to go, is that right?

ALEX: Yeah, I guess so. I just don't know what to do about it.

LEADER: Let me ask you this: What kind of student do you want to be?

ALEX: Well, like I was in high school. I got *A*s and *B*s.

LEADER: So if you know that you have the ability, what stops you from using that ability?

ALEX: Like I said, I guess I just party too much.

LEADER: And you've said that that choice isn't helping you, but it also seems that just being aware of that isn't enough to help you change your behavior. So if you want to study more, what stopped you this week from doing that?

ALEX: I guess I just let my friends talk me into having fun instead of going to the library.

LEADER: And how did that decision help you achieve your goal?

ALEX: It didn't. I ended up cutting three classes because I was too tired to get out of bed.

LEADER: So if it isn't helping you, what do you want to do differently this week?

ALEX: I want to study more and party less.

LEADER: And what is a reasonable, achievable goal you could set for yourself?

ALEX: I could go out every other night and study on the other nights.

LEADER: That sounds like a good short-term goal. I am wondering if there is a way that other group members could help you achieve this goal.

ALEX: I don't know. Maybe someone could call me to remind me that I am going to study every other night.

LEADER: Is there anyone in the group who is willing to help Alex with his plan?

CLAYTON: I could—we live in the same hall, so I could check in with him every day, just to remind him.

LEADER: Alex, how does that sound?

ALEX: That's cool. I know this will be hard, so I could use help.

LEADER: I think you have identified a choice that will help you achieve your goal of studying more and therefore being more successful in school. Who is in charge of determining whether or not you will achieve this goal?

ALEX: I guess I am.

LEADER: You're right. You have the control. It may be that you are giving up some of that control to your friends who want you to party with them, but ultimately, you are the one making the choice to go, right?

ALEX: Right.

LEADER: Well, it sounds like Alex has a plan, and with Clayton's assistance, we will see how well that plan works. Alex, I appreciate the fact that you are clear about what you would like to change and what you want, so my belief is that you will make choices to help achieve your goal.

Subsequent sessions would follow the same pattern, with different members making choices to achieve what they want in life. As much as possible, the leader encourages group interaction so that group members confront and support each other as they engage in self-evaluation, as well as formulate and carry out realistic plans to change behaviors.

Some Final Comments on Reality Therapy Groups

The advantages of reality therapy are that it stresses accountability and includes a structure that helps individuals develop action plans for change. In addition, choice theory is straightforward, flexible, and relatively brief. Large-group applications are very useful because members learn to accept responsibility for their behavior, realize that they can control themselves but not others, and develop their problem-solving abilities. In a small-group setting, members learn how to engage in self-evaluation and deal with present concerns in a supportive environment. Limitations of this approach include the deemphasis on feelings and lack of exploration of the past. Group leaders are cautioned against being too simplistic or acting as moral experts.

BEHAVIORAL GROUPS

Behavioral group approaches, which are becoming more popular because of the emphasis on self-management skills, help members learn life skills and address specific present as well as future problems. Behavioral groups can have an interpersonal and interactive focus that helps members pursue specific goals for self-improvement and self-direction. Because behavior therapy encompasses a variety of techniques and practices from several different learning theories, there is actually no single theory or group model that can be labeled a behavioral group. One common denominator is that the focus is more didactic and educational, stressing teaching and learning.

Several principles underscore behavioral applications in a group setting. First is the notion that problematic behaviors are learned and can therefore be modified and that the problematic behaviors that members express are in fact problems, not just symptoms. Second is the idea that change can occur without insight and that behavioral change will likely lead to greater self-understanding. In addition, behavior therapy is based on scientific procedures, so there is an emphasis on specification and measurement. Finally, a variety of techniques such as positive reinforcement, desensitization, shaping, modeling, contingency contracting, behavioral rehearsal, coaching, and extinction can be systematically employed to help members change maladaptive behaviors. Simplistically stated, behaviorists believe that behaviors that are followed by rewards or positive consequences will occur more frequently than those that are not.

Over the past several decades, traditional behavior therapy groups have been replaced with an approach that is actually more cognitive-behavioral. These groups tend to be short-term, psychoeducational, and action-oriented, so they are very applicable to a variety of settings. According to Corey (2007, p. 360), "cognitive behavioral group therapy is becoming one of the most feasible and efficient forms of treatment for a wide range of specific problems for diverse client populations."

Types of Behavioral Groups

Behavioral groups can be organized around various topics, including learning new social skills; behaving assertively rather than aggressively; and managing weight, stress, pain, or addictions. Learning new ways of thinking and behaving is a focus of cognitive-behavioral groups. The self-management approach of behavioral groups deemphasizes dependence on professional experts. Instead, group members are empowered to become more self-directed. While self-direction is the ultimate goal, this might be somewhat difficult with younger members, so the leader must be more involved at this level.

Role and Function of the Leader in Behavioral Groups

Behavioral groups are structured and problem-oriented, and they employ short-term interventions. Thus, leaders need to be knowledgeable about a variety of strategies that can be developed from diverse therapeutic approaches. Behavioral group leaders are active and directive, often teaching members to learn and

rehearse skills to facilitate problem resolution. At the same time, they are supportive and flexible in their leadership style. As leaders, they also model appropriate behaviors, reinforce members as they learn new behaviors, and collaborate with members on developing homework assignments to practice new skills. Throughout the sessions, leaders assess members' problems, employ strategies to help them achieve their goals, and encourage them to practice new skills in the group setting that they can apply to real-life situations. Leaders model, coach, give feedback, and teach members how to practice skills and monitor their own behavior.

In the behavioral group, the leader assumes the role of an assessor, conducting an initial assessment during the intake interview where prospective members are screened and oriented to how the group operates and how members can benefit from it. Assessment occurs throughout the life of the group, and it occurs concurrently with treatment because the leader not only models appropriate behaviors but also teaches group members how to be more responsible for their own behavior. The leader is also an encourager, reinforcing group members as they make behavioral changes.

Finally, the leader must be flexible and create a climate of trust. Corey (2007) stressed, however, that while a good working relationship between the members and the leader is important, the relationship itself is not sufficient to bring about change. Thus, leaders must develop a relationship style as well as be skilled in a variety of techniques that will help group members make behavioral changes.

Stages of a Behavioral Group

As with most types of groups, the initial stage involves exploring members' expectations and dealing with organizational details. In a behavioral therapy group, the leader also gives relevant information about the group process and how sessions will be structured. Often, a contract that identifies mutual expectations of the leader and participants is developed. Building group cohesiveness in order to establish openness and sharing, and identifying target behaviors to work on also occur during the initial stages.

A variety of rapport-building activities can be implemented to build a sense of community, such as tearing a piece of paper into a shape that identifies something they like to do, or writing their initials on a sheet of paper and drawing something beginning with each letter that represents them. The amount of rapport building depends on the group, of course. Members who already know each other will not need as much emphasis on rapport building as will a group of strangers. During the initial stage, the leader may be quite directive, but this may change as the leader teaches group members how to interact with each other and assume more leadership roles. Ultimately the leader's goal is to train members to assume more therapeutic responsibility.

During the working stage, the leader introduces group members to the behavioral framework. This is most effectively accomplished by teaching members the antecedent-behavior (response)-consequence (A-B-C) model of behaviorism. In essence, this model proposes that all behavior is purposeful but not necessarily productive. The goal is for group members to learn this model and assess and monitor their own actions in light of specific behaviors. As the group progresses, members are asked to identify behaviors they would like to change and to use a variety of behavioral techniques to accomplish this. Assessment occurs throughout the working stages; the leader collects data on the effectiveness of the group sessions, the degree of goal attainment, and what strategies are most effective in helping members make behavioral changes.

In the final stage, the leader focuses on helping members transfer what they learned in the group to their day-to-day environment by engaging them in behavioral rehearsal and practice sessions. Group members give feedback and encouragement. Self-responsibility is emphasized, with members learning how to engage in self-reinforcement and problem solving. In behavioral groups, follow-up sessions are often conducted to help members maintain changes and discuss what they learned. These sessions help keep members accountable.

Techniques Commonly Used in Behavioral Groups

Numerous behavioral techniques can be helpful as group members engage in the process of change. The leader often models and demonstrates many of these techniques during group sessions. Positive reinforcement entails praising or giving positive feedback for contributions members make in the group or when they report on other constructive changes. The ultimate goal is for group members to practice positive reinforcement behaviors within and outside the group setting. Group members are also encouraged to contract with others in the group, calling them throughout the week to report on their progress. Contingency contracts are also employed in behavioral groups. A contingency contract contains a clear description of the behaviors to change; specific identification of the reinforcement that will occur; and a detailed plan about what will occur, and when and how it will be observed and measured. Group members are always encouraged to develop action plans because insight and verbalizing do not produce behavior change. Action plans are especially helpful for school-age participants because they learn to be accountable and see that change is possible.

In behavioral rehearsal, another popular technique, group members are encouraged to practice a behavior they would like to change within the safety of the group setting, and they receive feedback and suggestions from other group members. The goal is to perform this behavior outside the group setting. For example, in a weight management group, one member rehearsed how she could explain to her parents that while she loved to eat desserts, she would appreciate it if they would not serve them while she was visiting because she was on a strict diet to lose weight and improve her health. Group members often assimilate concepts better and transfer skills outside the group if they have opportunities to practice skills.

Shaping is another procedure that helps members learn new behaviors in a gradual process because they practice parts of the targeted behavior in a step-by-step process until they can do it successfully. Another behavioral technique is coaching, where the leader (coach) helps group members rehearse a desired behavior by sitting behind them, intervening, and providing direction as needed. Typically the coach whispers suggestions to the group member who is attempting to change behavior.

Cognitive restructuring is also a technique employed in behavioral groups. This is a process in which members learn how to identify and evaluate their thoughts, assess the negative impact of them, and replace them with more functional beliefs. For example, an individual who wants to be more assertive but fails to do so is taught how to identify erroneous beliefs, such as "If I'm assertive, others will disapprove of me"; assess the negative impact of continuing to be nonassertive; and learn how to challenge the belief that others will disapprove of her by asking her to examine how realistic it is to think this way when she has no evidence to support her belief, or no way of predicting a negative outcome unless she acts assertively to gauge others' responses.

Problem solving is yet another strategy used to teach members how to cope with typical problems, with the goal being to help them find a solution. Group members identify a specific problem and a clear goal. They are taught to brainstorm alternative solutions, thinking of as many ideas as possible without evaluating them. Finally, they select an alternative and agree to try it after examining possible consequences. After they have implemented the alternative they decided upon, members are encouraged to evaluate the effectiveness of what they tried. A helpful strategy is to have one group member identify a specific problem and write it in the center of a circle that is surrounded by other circles and connected to the main one with lines. Then this member and others in the group are encouraged to brainstorm alternatives, writing them in the surrounding circles. After alternatives have been identified, members are encouraged to think of potential consequences, both positive and negative, for each possible solution. This is a graphic way of helping individuals evaluate solutions and select what they think would be the best solution for their problem.

Some Final Comments on Behavioral Groups

The self-help educative approach is a definite strength of behavioral groups, as is the fact that a variety of specific, concrete techniques can be employed to facilitate skill development for a variety of problems. The behavioral approach emphasizes accountability and evaluation of interventions, which increases its efficacy. The self-management aspect of behavioral groups can be very helpful for individuals who want to learn how to control their weight or drinking, manage their stress, or learn organizational skills. The fact that the leader teaches participants how to lead more productive lives can significantly enhance their functioning.

One caution is that members can become too dependent on the leader for direction, and there is some risk that the methods might be employed too mechanically or stringently. Also, the fact that issues from the past or exploration of feelings is not emphasized in behavioral groups may make this approach less appropriate for some types of client problems (e.g., family-of-origin issues, relationship issues).

Summary

Both reality therapy and behavioral groups emphasize behavioral change and self-direction, with an emphasis on helping group members assume responsibility for their own actions. Many of the behavioral techniques described are used in reality therapy groups: evaluating behavior and making a plan for change. In both types of groups, members are encouraged to partner with another to help achieve the desired behavioral change and offer encouragement and reinforcement.

There are some differences between these two theoretical approaches, which obviously affects the applications in groups. Reality therapy is distinct in the identification of basic needs, the quality world, and the emphasis on satisfying relationships as a major source of individuals' problems in life. In behavioral groups, there is more emphasis on specific skill building and teaching problem-solving techniques. And although behavioral group leaders are concerned about establishing a good working relationship with group members, this is not as important as it is in reality therapy, where a basic assumption of this approach is the importance of the relationship and the leader is very deliberate about developing a strong bond. Reality therapy group leaders may

also use the WDEP system, which is unique to that theory.

In behavioral groups, there is more focus on learning theory principles and the scientific method, with an emphasis on assessment and social modeling. The leaders may be more eclectic in the interventions they employ and may incorporate more cognitive-behavioral concepts into their techniques as well, teaching clients how to evaluate and revise cognitions that may impede behavioral change (e.g., cognitive restructuring).

In both types of groups, there is an initial stage, a working stage, and a transition, with an emphasis on helping group members transfer what they have learned to real-life situations. Leaders operating from both perspectives strive to help individuals manage their lives more effectively.

CHAPTER 16

Adlerian and Transactional Analysis Approaches to Counseling and Psychotherapy Groups

Laura R. Simpson, Ann Vernon, and Bradley T. Erford

PREVIEW

Adlerian and transactional analysis principles have been applied in various group counseling formats; they emphasize personal responsibility, insight, communication, and social relationships. The purpose of this chapter is to describe specific applications of both approaches to group practice, including specific techniques and procedures. An illustration of the Adlerian process in group work is also provided.

ADLERIAN GROUPS

Adlerian theory is a socially oriented theory developed by Alfred Adler and used by him and his colleagues in child guidance clinics in Vienna as early as 1922. Other theorists contributed to adapting the concepts for group work; the most notable theorist was Rudolph Dreikurs, who introduced group therapy in the United States in the late 1930s. The basic tenets of Adlerian theory include the purposefulness of behavior, the subjective nature of perception, the holistic nature of people, the importance of a healthy lifestyle, individual self-determination, and the ability to choose from a variety of behaviors after considering consequences. The notion that people are motivated by social interest and have feelings of concern for others is central to the theory.

Adlerian theory emphasizes responsibility, the search for meaning, and striving for superiority. Understanding an individual is accomplished by learning how the individual operates within a social context, which makes it ideally suited for group counseling because relationships are addressed in a group setting (Sonstegard & Bitter, 2004).

Another major aspect of this theory is the emphasis on family constellation and process, which affects personality development during childhood. When children observe family interactions, their values, gender-role expectations, and interpersonal relationships are affected. Analyzing the family constellation forms the basis for interpretations about the client's strengths and weaknesses and the current influence of the family.

Yet another core concept of Adlerian theory is lifestyle, which is influenced by the family constellation and significant experiences within the family, primarily during the first six years of life. Because people are influenced by their perception of the past, particularly childhood experiences, it is important to help members become aware of self-defeating or erroneous ideas so that a more adaptive lifestyle can be created.

Types of Adlerian Groups

Adlerian groups often use components of psychoeducational, counseling, and psychotherapy approaches. Based on the social orientation of this theory, a major premise in all types of groups is that people learn from each other. Because so many problems are interpersonal in nature, a group approach is particularly helpful in promoting change, especially with regard to challenging feelings of inferiority and erroneous concepts that form the basis of many social and emotional problems. Adlerian group approaches are especially applicable for work with school-age children, their teachers, and parents. For example, the Systematic Training for Effective Parenting (STEP) program developed by Don Dinkmeyer and Gary McKay, consists of seven components: collaboration, consultation, clarification, confrontation, concern, confidentiality, and commitment. Other Adlerian parent education groups stress developmental and preventive parenting approaches, with an emphasis on understanding children's behavior, the use of logical and natural consequences, and the use of a family council meeting. Adlerian theory can be integrated into groups with children, focusing on family constellation, encouragement, social interest (e.g., empathy, concern for others, cooperation, listening skills, belonging, relatedness), and mistaken goals of misbehavior.

Role and Function of the Leader in Adlerian Groups

Mosak (2000) emphasized that Adlerian group leaders must be collaborative and open about sharing their feelings and opinions. The personality of the group leader is as critical to the functioning of the group as are the techniques. Leaders need to be accepting of others and open, have a sense of humor and a positive attitude, and be sincere and adaptable. In working with children, in particular, leaders must use encouragement to help children see that behavior change is possible.

Stages in Adlerian Groups

Corey (2007) described four stages in an Adlerian group approach. In the first stage, it is important to develop a democratic atmosphere where cooperation and mutual respect are emphasized. Working together on mutual goals is essential so that group members focus on what is personally significant to them in the change process. In the Adlerian group, an egalitarian relationship is stressed. The second stage involves an analysis and assessment of group members' lifestyles and how lifestyle affects functioning in the present. Recalling early recollections facilitates an understanding of life goals, motivations, beliefs, and values. This lifestyle analysis is interpreted for group members so they can develop a plan for change. Stage three is awareness and insight, which is the basis for change. Interpretation is used liberally in this stage and helps members develop a better understanding of themselves and their problems, as well as what they can do to improve their circumstances. In the final stage, reorientation, members and leaders strive to change mistaken attitudes and beliefs and examine other ways of thinking and behaving. Reeducation is an important part of this stage, along with problem solving and decision making.

Techniques Commonly Used in Adlerian Groups

Several techniques are commonly used by leaders of Adlerian groups to facilitate growth and development within the group setting, including modeling social skills, using visual imagery, observing and interpreting members' nonverbal behaviors, using constructive confrontation, and employing paradoxical intention by asking members to increase negative thoughts and behaviors. With young children in particular, leaders must use caution when using paradoxical techniques because they may be misunderstood. Likewise, confrontation must be used selectively and with care. For example, Shulman (1973) developed the Midas technique, which involved dramatic confrontation involving the leader and a group member acting out roles that create the kind of world and relationships the member would like to have. The technique and its purpose are expected to be freely discussed and understood by the group members, and the purpose must be to help the member, not to discipline or humiliate the member.

Adlerians place a great deal of significance on the social meaning of behavior. The idea is that understanding behavior in its social context is a natural extension of the concept that most problems are social and interpersonal. Adlerian group leaders take an egalitarian approach, encourage members to get to know one another, and take an active role as agents of change. Specifically, Adlerians place emphasis on helping members become aware of their beliefs, values, goals, and lifestyle and on helping them move toward more effective relationships with others by shifting from self-awareness to insight into the motives of others.

In addition to embracing the position that group members are responsible for making changes, the leader may encourage each member to take responsibility for him- or herself. Continued emphasis is placed on a relationship of trust, respect, and cooperation between the leader and members or these techniques may be ineffective. Some examples of Adlerian techniques include task setting, and encouragement techniques that stress concern for the member, instill hope, show the member that there are answers to problems, and emphasize the positive. Helping the member to redefine goals to lessen overambition and decrease fear of failing is another encouragement method.

Other Adlerian interventions that are especially appropriate for children in group settings include play therapy techniques, art, humor, and acting as if they were who they would like to be. Corey (2007) identified other techniques: the pushbutton technique, using stories, and catching oneself. Regardless of the specific technique employed, Adlerians view children's play as an opportunity to view their characteristic way of behaving. It offers information about the child's present status and future direction. Understanding the purpose of children's behavior is the key to effective treatment. Techniques are used to gain insight into mistaken goals, redirecting goals, changing family beliefs, and developing social interest. For example, the enhancement of children's self-concept is addressed through encouragement exercises. Exploration of personal identity might be accomplished by asking a child to draw a picture of his or her family constellation (Dinkmeyer & Nelson, 1986). The child is invited to share who is included and what they are like, often resulting in other members relating to the descriptions. This provides validation of the child's experience and feelings, and encourages further participation.

Special populations also benefit from the use of Adlerian group concepts. For example, groups made up of individuals attempting to address substance abuse recovery issues can benefit from these techniques because they promote "self understanding, encouragement, and a vehicle for developing social interest, a feeling of belonging, and the conviction that one can meet life's responsibilities instead of avoiding or excusing oneself from them through drinking" (Prinz & Arkin, 1994, p. 350).

Some Final Comments on Adlerian Groups

Adlerian group approaches can be used with many different populations and are particularly appropriate with children, adolescents, and parents in a school setting. Drawing from a variety of techniques, Adlerian group members are able to learn concepts relatively quickly. The fact that the group is grounded in a democratic approach and emphasizes belonging enhances participation. One criticism is that groups based on Adlerian theory may be quite narrow in scope. In addition, some problems (e.g., AD/HD, dementia) may not be socially based.

CASE EXAMPLE OF THE ADLERIAN APPROACH IN PRACTICE

The heart of an Adlerian approach involves the discovery and disclosure of the patterns, goals, and purposes that make meaning out of everyday experiences, behaviors, and histories of the group members. Because the leader engages in the interpretive process, it is imperative to be sensitive to the group members. This model places emphasis on forming relationships and the establishment of agreements between and among members based on the work of Sonstegard and Bitter (1998). The five group members are Houston, Kashanta, Jonathan, Nathan, and Donna. They are five teenagers, and the group takes place at a local mental health clinic. The leader, Larry, brings a liberal, tolerant, even appreciating attitude. The leader works to assist every member in contributing to the process. The Adlerian group process promotes members being both recipients of therapy and agents of change within the group. The dialogues in the next sections are representative of the stages of group therapy sessions with an Adlerian approach.

Stage 1: Group Development

LARRY (LEADER): We should probably come to some agreements before we get started. (Avoiding the use of the word *rule* minimizes authoritarian positions or superior relationships. The group is based on the consent and agreement of those who choose to participate in mutually established agreements.)

DONNA: When are we gonna do this? I mean, are we gonna meet every week and are we going to always be in here? (Before Donna speaks, there was silence as group members looked at each other. It is not uncommon for the most uncertain or nervous member or for the person who wants things to go right to speak first. Donna appears compelled to take action and though it seems that she would prefer that others act, she steps in when they don't.)

LARRY: How often do you think we should meet? How often would you like to meet? (The leader turns all questions back to the group for a decision as the foundation for establishing the group process. All group members observe the group process to see if it is going to be group-centered or leader-centered. If the leader offers an opinion here, there is risk of losing the members' input.)

HOUSTON: It seems like how often we meet would depend on what the problems are. I don't care if we met in here. It's okay.

LARRY: (clarifying) Would you like to meet one time per week in this room? (Donna started with a very practical question. The leader responds in a manner that keeps the questions pragmatic.)

HOUSTON: Maybe

LARRY: Well, what do the rest of you think about meeting weekly in this room?

JONATHAN: I think more than once per week is too much. In fact, once per week may be too much!

KASHANTA: I think if somebody has something they want to talk about, they could just call one of the others and we could talk to them. (Kashanta's response is a distraction from group decision making.)

LARRY: (to Kashanta) How often do you think we should meet? (The leader redirects Kashanta back to the decision at hand.)

KASHANTA: As a group?

LARRY: Yes.

KASHANTA: I think once a week is enough.

LARRY: Once a week?

NATHAN: What if there is, like, an emergency? Can we call each other and get together?

LARRY: We could call a special meeting if necessary. (after a pause) Do you think we should start with once a week? (The leader, sensing a decision is at hand, suggests what he believes to be the consensus of the group with a question. While paraphrasing, reflection, and summarizing are staples of the therapeutic process, the leader promotes empowerment through a simple direct question. In this intervention, the leader's question requests an answer from members as final authority.)

NATHAN: Yeah.

LARRY: Are you willing to go along with once per week, Houston?

HOUSTON: Once a week would be okay depending on how long they last. (Houston illuminates a new decision the group will need to consider.)

LARRY: How long do you want them to last? (The leader turns the decision back to the group, starting with the individual who initiates the question.)

HOUSTON: I think it would depend on what you are talking about. If you are really discussing something important, you should go until you are finished.

KASHANTA: Yeah, as long as it takes. If we get through and no one is saying anything, we can quit.

LARRY: (to Nathan) Do you have an opinion on this? (Nathan indicated a tentative willingness to participate in the last decision. The leader encourages him to participate in the second decision at a somewhat earlier stage.)

NATHAN: I don't know how to set a time limit. One day we might need only five minutes and the next we might need 10 hours.

LARRY: Can we leave it to the group each meeting to pick an appropriate time to stop? (Again the leader asks a question that seems to suggest the consensus of the group.)

NATHAN: Yeah.

LARRY: What else should we agree on?

HOUSTON: We can talk about anything that is on our mind.

LARRY: Do you all agree on that? (heads nod) Well, that works for me.

JONATHAN: Can members leave when they want to?

LARRY: (to everyone) What do you think about that? Should people be allowed to come and go as they please?

KASHANTA: Yes.

LARRY: You think so?

HOUSTON: If we make people stay when they don't want to, it would make them feel trapped.

LARRY: Should people be forced to stay?

NATHAN, SUSAN, AND KASHANTA: No!

LARRY: What will they be expected to do?

NATHAN: Quit. Nobody is gonna be forced to do this.

DONNA: I don't think people should have to stay if they don't want to. (All group members nod in agreement.)

LARRY: How do you feel about talking about your personal life?

HOUSTON: It could be good, having people to bounce things off of.

LARRY: What if members talk about it outside the group? (The process of coming to group understanding is far enough along that the leader can raise the issue of confidentiality.)

DONNA: That would suck.

LARRY: What do you propose to keep that from happening?

KASHANTA: We should have to promise not to talk about it outside of here.

LARRY: Do you think we could keep our meetings confidential, meaning that we agree that what we say here stays here?

DONNA: What if people outside the group ask what we talk about?

KASHANTA: We could just name a general topic.

LARRY: If someone asks, then we can say we talked about a subject but not say "Kashanta said this" or "Houston said that" so no one has to worry or have any trouble. (The leader identifies what constitutes harm and what is reasonable communication outside the group.)

Stage 2: Lifestyle Analysis

DONNA: You know, this is my junior year and I feel like it is a complete waste of time. (Donna has continued to present with

the position that she wants to be taken very seriously).

LARRY: Could you be more specific? (Donna is being very basic in her comments and the leader tries to provide clarity by seeking an example. Donna doesn't seem ready to move very deeply.)

DONNA: I am just bored with everything.

LARRY: You mean you don't care about school?

DONNA: Yeah.

LARRY: Houston, what would you say is challenging you? (Donna just made a general statement of discontent, so the leader moves on, using the same topic to involve other members and not get bogged down in an exchange with one member.)

HOUSTON: You mean about school?

LARRY: Anything.

HOUSTON: Nothing.

LARRY: Really? Could you name one thing?

HOUSTON: I am a senior and I am ready for high school to be over and get on to work or college or whatever. (Donna stays safe with a general description and Houston takes a vague position, too.)

LARRY: Kashanta, what about you?

KASHANTA: Not too bad. I have another year and I want to have fun this year. (Kashanta is not interested in taking a position too different from her peers. Her process has been one of discovering the position of others and to fit in by going along. Houston is somewhat the same but not as protective of himself as Kashanta is of herself.)

LARRY: Do you have anything that bothers you right now?

KASHANTA: Not that I can think of.

LARRY: Okay. Nathan?

NATHAN: Well I am sick of people telling me what to do and when to do it. I am sick of everything that is being forced on me. (Nathan is candid. He is direct and specific, and responding to him in a nonjudgmental manner is critical to moving the group process along).

LARRY: Uh huh.

KASHANTA: Why don't you just tell them no.

NATHAN: Because if I tell a teacher no, then I just fail and that doesn't help me get out of Dodge. And if I tell my mom no, she just blows her top and gives me grief.

LARRY: So you just go ahead and do what they tell you?

NATHAN: Yeah, I do it my way, but I do it. (Nathan feels like he is up against a dictatorship.)

LARRY: Jonathan?

JONATHAN: My parents are giving me crap about my bad attitude. (Jonathan continues as Nathan has demonstrated, with frankness.)

LARRY: Anyone else have this problem?

KASHANTA: Yeah.

LARRY: What's up with that?

KASHANTA: You know how it is. (Kashanta has a moment of seeming to connect with Jonathan but returns to her neutral position by avoiding serious personal discussion.)

HOUSTON: Every time I come in the house, my parents interrogate me. They accuse me of all sorts of things.

DONNA: I bet they want to know who you are with, where you have been, and what you were doing.

NATHAN: They don't trust me not to embarrass them.

LARRY: You think this is more about them than you. (This is a reflection that allows the leader to introduce the idea that parents can have a purpose to their actions that can be understood.)

NATHAN: Yeah.

DONNA: Sometimes it seems like my parents just want me to do what they want and don't care what I think. (Donna is beginning to open up. The leader's decision to divert the conversation from Jonathan's specific return seems to have decreased the group's resistance to discussion.)

LARRY: Jonathan, how long have you felt like your parents were riding you about your attitude? (The leader decides to focus on Jonathan's relationship with his parents and give the group an opportunity to help him understand his interactive process. Adlerians have a systemic approach to psychological inquiry. Jonathan is in the relationship with his parents and each contributes to the process.)

JONATHAN: This whole year. I am gone a lot with soccer and football and they give me crap about it. I don't know why,' cause my grades are passing.

LARRY: How many brothers and sisters do you have, Jonathan? (Adlerians might introduce birth order and family constellation at different points in the process. It's useful when considering how an individual has formed coping patterns.)

JONATHAN: I have one sister.

LARRY: Are you the oldest?

JONATHAN: Yes. She is four years younger than me.

LARRY: Do your parents give her grief?

JONATHAN: No, she is the princess. I am the devil. They never like anything I do and they let me know it.

LARRY: (to the group) Does anyone have an idea why Jonathan's parents might be on his case all the time? (The leader encourages discoveries to come from the group itself.)

KASHANTA: Well, since Jonathan is the oldest, maybe they expect him to set an example for his sister.

NATHANIAL: They don't want you to ruin the family name.

LARRY: Do you think people expect more from the oldest children? (This is a natural extension from the previous question and facilitates discussion to proceed into the impact of birth order, which might offer Jonathon insight into his situation.)

HOUSTON: Not in my family. I have an older bother. He used to go out and get loaded and he got away with it every time. But now I can't do anything and they expect me to do everything perfect. (Houston's comment illustrates the importance of family constellation but derails Jonathan's opportunity to gain insight into birth order.)

LARRY: Jonathan, what do you do when your parents get on your case? (The leader is attempting to identify that life happens in everyday activity.)

JONATHAN: I ignore them.

LARRY: You just ignore them or do you leave home?

JONATHAN: I leave or go to my room.

LARRY: You get into an activity? Houston, what about you? (The leader leaves his question for the moment to see if there are others who might contribute to group understanding.)

HOUSTON: If they yell at me and I don't deserve it, I tell them to shut up or just ignore them and watch TV.

LARRY: That helps? (This mild confrontation works because of the relationship the counselor has established.)

HOUSTON: Sometimes it seems to make them realize they don't have a reason to yell at me.

LARRY: Why do you think parents yell? (The leader invites the group into a discussion about purpose and attempts to replace hurt with understanding.)

HOUSTON: Your parents are protecting the family name and they see you as a threat. (Houston is beginning to be more insightful about the parent–child relationship and shows some understanding of the parent's view.)

Stage 3: Awareness and Insight

LARRY: (to the group) What do you think Houston accomplishes when he provokes his parents? (From an Adlerian perspective, the leader would begin seeking a motivation modification and initiate the change by seeking a disclosure and understanding of purpose.)

KASHANTA: I think he is just trying to get his way and try to avoid getting in trouble at the same time. (Kashanta has been an observer throughout the group process and is correctly sensing that Houston doesn't want to get in trouble.)

DONNA: Maybe he is trying to get back at his parents for yelling at him. (Donna is really suggesting the motivation of punishment for his parents, although Houston seems to actually be seeking to avoid surrendering to the control his parents are attempting to exert over him.)

LARRY: I have an idea about it. Would you like to hear it? (This is the beginning of the disclosure process and is intended to be a respectful and nonoffensive confrontation. The leader is letting the members know he has a different opinion and is asking them to consider hearing his position.)

DONNA: Yeah.

LARRY: I think Houston feels a need to be in control of the situation and he tries to back his parents down with an "I'll show you; you can't control me" attitude. (The behavior pattern and goal of the behavior are disclosed.)

JONATHAN: I think you could be right.

HOUSTON: Yeah, that sounds right, especially when I know I haven't done anything wrong. (Goal recognition is occurring on a conscious level.)

LARRY: Does anybody else get irritated with people when they want you to do things you don't want to do?

NATHAN: Yeah, I hardly ever want to do anything my mom wants me to do. She is a nag. I do it a lot of

the time just to keep her off my back. But really, she doesn't know what I need to be doing and I do. (Nathan has a different motivation than Houston because he indicates that he feels like his way is right and his mother's way is wrong.)

LARRY: Because you're smarter than her? (This is a very direct goal disclosure. It works because it follows Nathan's statement and Nathan is direct, so he is not easily offended by directness.)

NATHAN: Yeah, well, it makes me feel good.

LARRY: May I tell you what I think? (Nathan nods.) I think it makes you feel better about yourself when you can make others out to be wrong. (Adlerians assume that behind every declaration of superiority there are feelings of inferiority or inadequacy.)

NATHAN: That could be.

LARRY: It makes you feel important.

NATHAN: Yeah, that's true.

Stage 4: Reorientation

LARRY: (to the group) Now does anybody have any ideas about how Nathan could improve his situation with his mom? (The leader now attempts to move the members' insight into action.)

KASHANTA: Well, it's just gonna make him mad to do everything his mom tells him to.

NATHAN: Well, that ain't gonna happen!

LARRY: Are you willing to do anything different or do you want to just keep fighting with her? (The leader verifies that the member wants to participate in the reorientation process or movement would not be possible because of resistance.)

NATHAN: I don't want to fight with her. She just always thinks she is right and I am always wrong. I just wish she would figure out that I am not stupid.

LARRY: You say that you don't want to fight with her, but you also want to prove her wrong. It's just that the way the two of you have been going at it has accomplished nothing. Do you agree with that? (The leader starts the reorientation process with a restatement of the pattern with Nathan and his mom. Then the leader will engage the other members to initiate the change process.)

DONNA: If he doesn't do something, she is just going to keep telling him what to do.

LARRY: So, you think that he should stick up for himself? (The leader reframes Donna's position to be empowering and positive.)

HOUSTON: You do have to stick up for your rights and you gotta go along with your mom some, too. (Houston is demonstrating awareness that, on some level, even teens must take some responsibility for their relationship with their parents.)

LARRY: You think parents are entitled to some respect.

KASHANTA: Maybe you could do something nice for parents sometimes.

LARRY: Do you think that would help Nathan's situation?

KASHANTA: He could try.

LARRY: Maybe it is worth a try. What else could Nathan do? (The leader validates Kashanta by

illuminating the usefulness of her suggestion.)

HOUSTON: Maybe Nathan needs to figure out how he can feel better about himself so he doesn't have to fight with his mom to feel smart. (Houston is demonstrating an awareness of Nathan's motivation to counteract his feelings of inadequacy, and he enhances it with an interpretation of his own.)

LARRY: Any other thoughts?

NATHAN: There is no reason that I can't be nice to my mom sometimes. It is not gonna hurt anything and maybe she would get off my back a little bit. (Nathan is responding positively to suggestions from the group and demonstrating an initial willingness to consider his own role as an agent of change in his relationship with his mother.)

TRANSACTIONAL ANALYSIS (TA) GROUPS

Transactional analysis (TA) emphasizes interactions between people, so the theory readily lends itself to a group approach. In addition, TA emphasizes intrapersonal understanding, homework assignments, and structured learning. In the group setting, members learn about the three ego states: Parent, Adult, and Child. The Parent ego state is both nurturing and critical, the Adult ego state is logical and realistic, and the Child ego state is spontaneous as well as compliant. Group members achieve autonomy of functioning by understanding how their present behavior is influenced by rules they learned and assimilated as children. As they examine their lives, they can choose a new direction or continue along the same path, if that works well for them.

Transactional analysis was originally developed by Eric Berne, who developed the classic TA as a response to his dissatisfaction with aspects of psychoanalysis. Berne developed the three ego states and maintained that the early years of life are formative because people develop a script that they adhere to throughout their lives. Robert and Marcy Goulding modified the classic approach and developed the redecisional school of TA, which combines Gestalt techniques with psychodrama, family therapy, and behavior therapy.

Role and Function of the Leader in TA Groups

The TA leader fulfills several basic roles. In the protection role, the leader keeps members safe from physical or psychological harm. Next, the leader gives members permission to act against their parents' regulations about roles they should adopt. The potency role involves leaders using appropriate counseling techniques in specific situations. The operations role is when the TA group leader implements techniques such as confrontation, interrogation, confirmation, and interpretation.

The TA group leader assumes the role of teacher, explaining concepts such as the three ego states, life scripts, and games people play. Games involve a "series of transactions that ends with a negative payoff called for by the script that concludes the game and advances some way of feeling badly" (Corey, 2007, p. 342). Not only can the leader teach members about the games, but members can learn about games by observing the naturally occurring behavior of others in the group.

Donigian and Hulse-Killacky (1999) noted that TA groups are leader-centered, and the leader's primary functions are to listen and observe, then diagnose and analyze. Much of the interaction is between the leader and a member; interactions among group members are not as important. The goal is to help members make attitudinal and behavioral changes, and the group leader remains detached in order to analyze and intervene more effectively.

Stages of a TA Group

In the initial stage of the group, the leader develops a relationship with group members. Relationships are essential in TA groups in order to build trust so that members are willing to openly express the issues they would like to work on. During the working stage, the leader helps members analyze their life scripts and take responsibility for their feelings, thoughts, and behaviors, making the decision to change their early life decisions. During the final stage, group members are challenged to apply changes made in the group to the real world.

Techniques Commonly Used in TA Groups

The leader can use a variety of visual and experiential activities to teach TA concepts in the group setting. The development of a contract is essential to TA treatment and places responsibility on group members for identifying the what, how, and when of the problems members want to address. After the development of the contract, groups members begin working on specific issues. Using chairs to describe interactions, drawing the size of different ego states, acting out ego states, and drawing interactions on paper or a writing board are examples of creative techniques to use in TA groups. TA techniques can be modified for use with children, who can readily understand the concept of strokes, injunctions, and ego states. Increasing insight, with the goal of gaining control of thoughts, feelings, and behaviors, is a goal of TA groups with school-age children.

Some Final Comments on TA Groups

Several strengths are associated with the TA group approach. Members make contractual agreements to work on their issues, a procedure that empowers members. TA concepts are easy to teach, can be understood by people of all ages, and can be used in various settings. Also, the structured approach, which is somewhat psychoeducational in nature, lends itself to efficient goal attainment.

Gladding (2008) expressed concern that the simplicity of the concepts may be inadequate to explain what occurs in more complex situations. Yalom and Leszcz (2005) suggested that a limitation in this group approach is that there is not enough emphasis on group process; that is, the leader–member interaction limits interpersonal learning.

Summary

Named for Alfred Adler, Adlerian approaches have also been championed over the years by Rudolph Dreikurs and Don Dinkmeyer. Adlerian approaches emphasize the purposefulness of behavior, the subjective nature of perception, the holistic nature of people, the importance of a healthy lifestyle, individual self-determination, and the ability to choose from a variety of behaviors after considering consequences. Adlerian theory emphasizes responsibility, the search for meaning, and striving for superiority. Stages in an Adlerian group process include group development, lifestyle analysis, awareness and insight, and reorientation. A case example and transcript of the Adlerian group work process were provided in this chapter.

Transactional analysis (TA), developed primarily by Eric Berne, emphasizes human interactions, structured learning, and homework assignments. It is a psychodynamic approach that proposes three ego states: the Child, Adult, and Parent. Stages of a TA group include trust building, working, and application.

CHAPTER 17

Gestalt and Psychodrama Approaches to Counseling and Psychotherapy Groups

Darcie Davis-Gage

PREVIEW

Gestalt and psychodrama groups are used widely across various settings and with a variety of individuals. This chapter will discuss research associated with the effectiveness of Gestalt and psychodrama groups, as well as the role of leaders, stages of group development, and various techniques. Case studies and various examples illustrate how these approaches can be used in group work.

GESTALT GROUPS

Gestalt therapy was developed by Fritz Perls in the 1940s and integrated elements of certain psychoanalytic concepts, along with existential ideas using a humanistic approach (Donigian & Hulse-Killacky, 1999). The emphasis in Gestalt groups is on awareness, which is taught in a variety of ways.

Gestalt group counseling, which emphasizes working in the here and now, operates from four central assumptions. First, full integration, or holism, is achieved through members examining the internal and conflicting messages about their past and getting rid of their unfinished business through various exercises. Through this process, members become more complete. Second is the development of awareness, which leads to personal insight and assists group members in taking responsibility for their own behaviors. Third is a focus on figure-ground, which includes an individual's ability to identify which needs and tasks are central to existence and which are secondary. Healthy individuals are able to differentiate between the two and meet their primary needs first. Congruence, the final concept, is achieved when members are able to identify parts of themselves of which they were unaware. This can be accomplished by using experiments or techniques such as the empty chair (Donigian & Hulse-Killacky, 1999).

Types of Gestalt Groups

Most often, Gestalt groups tend to be classified as counseling or therapy groups, but one could also use the principles in psychoeducational groups. Two general types of Gestalt groups are prominent. In the first type of group, the leader works with individual members one on one, while the other members mostly observe. Particular attention is given to the concepts of self-awareness, centering, and responsibility. The second type of Gestalt group is more interactive, using the here and now and encouraging more direct communication.

Research has found that Gestalt groups can be helpful for individuals presenting with a variety of problems. O'Leary, Sheedy, O'Sullivan, and Thoresen (2001) found older adults respond well to Gestalt therapy groups. In their study, they compared Gestalt group therapy to a control group. Results indicated that participants in the Gestalt groups were less antagonistic and confused and more agreeable than members of the control group. In another study focusing on adults, Gestalt group therapy was particularly helpful for individuals who had unresolved issues in the past such as lingering negative feelings toward another person or unresolved grief issues (Paivio & Greenberg, 1995). The study also found the use of various Gestalt techniques such as the empty chair were more helpful to group members than a psychoeducational group focusing on unresolved past issues. These studies show that Gestalt group therapy can help adults resolve past issues and provide them with new skills to live more productive, peaceful lives.

In addition, Serok and Zemet (1983) found Gestalt group therapy to be helpful for individuals with schizophrenia. Researchers believed that, because Gestalt therapy focused on integrating elements into a whole and focused on the present, patients could develop a clearer perception of reality. The activities for the group were structured and based on exercises initiated by the group member. Serok and Zemet found that group members had significant increases in reality perception when compared to the control group.

Oaklander (1999) advocated using Gestalt play therapy with groups of children to help them learn to express their emotions both verbally and nonverbally. Also, children may become more self-aware by discovering likes and dislikes, which might enable them to make positive choices regarding behavior.

Role and Function of the Leader in Gestalt Groups

In Gestalt groups, the leader coordinates the group by deciding the timing, content, and length of work allotted for each member. Donigian and Hulse-Killacky (1999) noted that one of the main functions of a group leader in a Gestalt group is to make group members responsible for their own behavior. The group leader is an expert in helping and communicating, as well as the one who will frustrate and teach group members. Leaders must emphasize the here-and-now interactions of the group members, facilitate a safe environment where members will be willing to take risks, and set the groundwork for members to experiment or try new behaviors.

Stages of Gestalt Groups

The stages of development in a Gestalt group are very similar to the four general stages of other groups described in this book. During the forming and orienting stage, members become acquainted and are most concerned with finding a place within the group. During the second stage, members often compete for attention and at times will question the leader's ability to facilitate the group. In the next stage, members focus on building relationships and completing goals. The final stage, termination, includes reflections of the group's progress, which some members will resist discussing.

Techniques Commonly Used in Gestalt Groups

Many techniques exist for leaders using a Gestalt approach in a group setting. Spitz and Spitz (1999) described using various role plays and exercises to illicit strong emotional reactions. Once these strong emotions are displayed, members can be assisted to work on congruence and integration. The most commonly used technique to promote awareness and integration is the empty chair, but this technique may not be an appropriate one to implement in some school systems, or with young children. The empty chair technique involves having a member identify a person with whom they have unfinished business. The leader encourages the member to dialogue with the empty chair to help gain insight and awareness and resolve the past issues. For example, a member who is having difficulty communicating with either or both parents or guardians might benefit by practicing a conversation using the empty chair technique. This dialogue may help the member gain awareness of the emotions connected to conversing with parents and/or guardians while practicing effective communication. The empty chair technique can also be used with a person who wants to dialogue with a part of oneself. For example, an adult survivor of abuse may dialogue with herself as a 7 year old girl who was abused. This dialogue may help the person integrate these two aspects of herself. The empty chair technique can also be modified by having members play both roles or by simply rehearsing the role play more than once. By changing the exercise slightly, the group member may gain additional insight and awareness of his or her thoughts and feelings. Other techniques to promote self-awareness are focusing on members' nonverbal communications or helping members bring the past into the present by discussing how the past is influencing their relationships with people in the group.

Group leaders using a Gestalt approach can teach members how to change their questions into statements and help members reveal and discuss their internal dialogue. Leaders may also facilitate this process by simply having members change their use of language, such as by substituting the use of *won't* for *can't*, and *how* or *what* for *why*. These techniques are helpful for all ages, but they can be particularly helpful for children and adolescents (Thompson, Rudolph, & Henderson, 2004). For example, in a friendship group, Madeline often asks, "Why do other kids not like me?" The facilitator helps her to reframe that question to "What do kids like about me?" or

"What do kids dislike about me?" to help her identify what characteristics others might perceive in her. The group members may be able to help Madeline identify the characteristics that others find appealing. Once she is aware of some of these characteristics, then she can decide which ones, if any, she would like to change.

Because the Gestalt approach integrates exercises and experimentation into groups, it can be very appealing and effective for members. According to Gladding (2008), exercises are planned activities in groups, while experiments happen rather spontaneously. Both assist in bringing awareness and insight into the group member's world. For example, in an experiment, a member in a group starts tapping his foot, and the leaders ask him to continue tapping his foot in a given rhythm and to make up a jingle to the beat of the tapping. Other members could then join in by clapping or snapping, creating their own lines until a song is created by the group. The leader could then process the content of the song and how the lines may relate to members' unfinished business.

An example of an experiment is "making the rounds," during which the group leader might develop a sentence stem and then has each member complete the sentence. Some examples of sentence stems are:

In group, I felt most uncomfortable when

_____.

The most important person in my life is

_____.

I feel closest to in the group

_____.

Depending on the goals of the group, the leader can pick the one that is most relevant or that may move the group in a particular direction. A round may be a particularly effective way to improve self-awareness or bring past issues into the here and now.

Addressing unfinished business is an important technique used in Gestalt groups and is often implicit when participating in the empty chair or role plays, but unfinished business may surface in other ways throughout group work.

Unfinished business is usually centered on anger, grief, and past trauma. O'Leary et al. (2001) found processing unresolved anger with older clients was very beneficial and allowed them to live more fully in the here and now.

In addition, unfinished business can also be brought into consciousness by using body awareness activities. Leaders can facilitate deep breathing or grounding activities to promote a heightened sense of awareness. When group members are working through past issues that are stressful or traumatic, grounding techniques may be helpful. For example, members can be given a polished stone to hold on to or rub, and this tactile activity keeps them grounded in the here and now. These grounding techniques may be particularly helpful if the members are experiencing flashbacks or are discussing particularly stressful material. Breathing activities in particular can help group members gain body awareness, and O'Leary et al. (2001) found breathing exercises to be helpful with elderly group members.

One of Perls's (1969) commonly used techniques was labeled Topdog/Underdog. The Topdog tends to operate from the position of "I should" and is best described as authoritarian and righteous. The Underdog works from the "I want" standpoint and can be manipulative, defensive, and apologetic. These two stances often operate in opposition to each other, which can create incongruence. When they agree, such as an individual believing "I want to clean the house" and "I should clean the house," the outcome is usually positive. The Topdog/Underdog can be used in conjunction with the empty chair by having a group member speak while in both roles.

Dream work, another technique used in Gestalt groups, can be integrated into group work by having young children draw pictures of their dreams and share their feelings associated with the dreams. Also, adolescents and adults might benefit from sharing their dreams and discussing the themes that arise in the group.

Some Final Comments on Gestalt Groups

When using a Gestalt approach to group work, the leader must be aware of some limitations.

Although the here-and-now focus can be very beneficial, leaders must be aware that this can produce very strong emotional reactions, so one must be skilled in handling the emotions brought to the surface and prepared to process these feelings in the group. As a result, leaders must use care while assigning experiments for members, and they must consider the amount of support the group members have outside the group.

Strengths of the Gestalt group approach include member feelings of connectedness with others, as well as the sheer number and variety of effective techniques at the leader's disposal. While sparse, the extant literature does appear to support the effectiveness and benefits of the Gestalt group approach (O'Leary et al., 2001; Paivio & Greenberg, 2005).

CASE STUDY EXAMPLE OF GESTALT GROUP THERAPY

The following is a case study transcript of a group of eight male members in a mandated counseling group to address anger. This is the sixth group session, and the group is comfortable now in the working stage of group development. The leader has chosen the Gestalt approach because she believes that, once the men can gain more awareness about their internal emotional states, they will improve their behavior. The leader has created a safe environment where group members are willing to take risks and engage in here-and-now interactions. The leader started the group session with a round asking what each member needs from the group. The transcript opens with Marco sharing a recent incident when he did not handle his feelings the way he had hoped he would.

MARCO: I need some feedback from the group today.

LEADER: What would you like to share?

MARCO: Well, I recently encountered a situation with my neighbor. His dog had been barking at night a lot so I went over to speak with him. My neighbor got extremely angry, quickly saying that I had no right to tell him what to do on his property. I just wanted to ask if he would consider putting the dog in his house at night, but I did not even get a chance to suggest it because he got in my grill almost immediately. Then I just got mad and started yelling and trying to intimidate him. I didn't hit him, but I didn't handle the situation how I would have liked to and did not get the problem solved.

LEADER: You talked about your external response; tell me what was going on inside your body.

(The use of body awareness would be helpful to the group member so that he can better understand his emotional state. Once he can become more aware of his internal changes, he may be able to choose a different behavior earlier in a stressful situation.)

MARCO: My stomach starts to tighten, my heart races, and I know my face gets really red. I can just feel the tension building inside me, and my breathing starts to get faster and then I usually clench my fist.

LEADER: How do others relate to what Marco is describing?

(The leader invites others to relate in order for Marco to hear others' viewpoints. It is hoped that Marco and other group members may gain self-awareness as a result of the sharing.)

ANDRÉ: I understand man, it is so tough when people are in your face, but I have learned that I am the only one that can control me. When I start to get angry, I feel my heart race, too. I find if I am at home, I go to my woodworking shop and try to stay busy until the feelings pass. It usually works well.

MITCH: I work out at the gym when I am really irritated. I lift weights or go for a run.

LEADER: Those are all effective examples of dealing with your anger in more positive ways. I am wondering, what is your internal dialogue?

(It is important for the group members to become aware of their emotions or any incongruence between their current behavior and their desired behavior.)

ANDRÉ: Hmmm. I try not to think about what made me angry and tell myself to take a deep breath and slow down.

MITCH: I just listen to my music and I take all the frustrations out on the machines. I guess I tell myself to just work all the anger out of my system.

MARCO: I had to learn to tell myself that some situations are just not worth getting upset about.

LEADER: It sounds like each of you has learned to tell yourselves something different and that has changed your behaviors.

(With this response, the leader hoped to reinforce the positive behaviors and changes they have made in their lives in and out of the group.)

MARCO: Yes, in the past I told myself I had every right to be angry, and that would just make me angrier. It was like adding fuel to a fire.

TYRELL: Those things just don't work for me. I just feel so angry on the inside and then I have a difficult time calming down.

LEADER: Sometimes the more awareness you have of your internal state, the chances of you controlling your emotions actually increases. I am going to teach you some deep breathing exercises and guided imagery.

(The leader teaches the members deep breathing and encourages them to imagine

a peaceful place. These exercises are helpful because it encourages the men to quiet their minds and pay attention to their internal states. As they begin to learn these skills and incorporate them into their daily living, they may be able to learn to calm themselves quicker in stressful situations.)

LEADER: What did you become aware of during the breathing activity?

STEPHEN: I felt calmer.

ROBERTO: I remembered how relaxing it is to go fishing in my boat.

MITCH: I had a difficult time because I could not get a recent situation with my boss out of my mind. He really made me angry, and I just lost it yelling and screaming at him. I just could not think of what else to do.

ROBERTO: I think situations with bosses are the toughest because they have power over you.

LEADER: Yes, situations with bosses are tough. (Leader gets an empty chair and places it in front of Mitch.) I would like you to think of some things you would like to tell your boss about you and your feelings about this particular situation you are struggling with today.

(With the encouragement of the leader, Mitch shares with his "boss" [the empty chair] how frustrated he feels at work and how unappreciated he feels. Then the leader has Mitch play the role of the boss and respond in a way that is affirming. Then they process how it felt to play both roles. Other group members shared their insights and feedback. Mitch gained insight that his boss may not be intentionally unappreciative but is simply concerned about getting the work on this project done. Mitch also felt that he was able to communicate his needs and wants much better

than normal and plans to try some of these techniques in his daily living.)

ROBERTO: Watching this scenario was really helpful for me. Hey, Craig, was it helpful for you?

CRAIG: Yes.

ROBERTO: Craig, why don't you ever talk in group?

LEADER: It might be more helpful if you phrase that "why" question into a "how" or "what" question.

ROBERTO: Okay. Craig, what makes you not want to share in group?

CRAIG: I do share when I have something to say. Many times others say exactly what I am thinking. I get so much out of listening to others in the group.

LEADER: Craig, did those two questions seem different to you?

CRAIG: Yes, when he asked me why, it made me feel pretty angry and defensive, but when he changed how he asked, I felt like I could share may feelings a bit easier instead of defending myself.

LEADER: That is a simple technique all of you can use in your daily living. Let's end group with a round. I would like everyone to share one thing they became aware of during group.

(Everyone in group shares their thoughts and insights from group, thus demonstrating the building of self-awareness.)

This case study example illustrated the use of various Gestalt techniques, including empty chair, making the rounds, and a variation of turning questions into statements. It also included a psychodrama technique of creative imagery, which will be explained in more detail in the next section. By employing these techniques, the group members were able to build self-awareness and gain congruence.

PSYCHODRAMA

In the 1920s, J. L. Moreno started to use psychodrama as an intervention in group therapy. The basic premise behind psychodrama was for a client to act out feelings toward another person or another part of themselves. The group exercise allows members to gain critical feedback and support in dealing with their issues. The psychodrama provides the member with an opportunity to practice new skills and roles they may apply outside the group.

Types of Psychodrama Groups

Psychodrama can be used in a variety of settings and may be modified to fit the needs of group members. Corey (2007) described how some elements of psychodrama can be used in the schools. For example, a professional school counselor may use role plays and dramatic play within the group setting. Because psychodrama takes a certain amount of creativity and ability to fantasize, children and adolescents are good candidates for this type of work. Using psychodrama techniques with child and adolescent groups helps create group cohesion as well as develop personal insight and self-awareness.

Psychodrama can also be very beneficial to the adult population. After reviewing current literature, Klontz, Wold, and Bivens (2001) also found psychodrama groups have been helpful in treating test anxiety, Posttraumatic Stress Disorder, adjustment issues, antisocial behaviors, and depression. Kipper and Tuller (1996) studied warmth and trust in psychodrama training workshops in Russia and Bulgaria. They found a higher level of warmth and trust in groups when members experience fewer rejections and more positive interaction within group. Psychodrama group leaders can benefit from considering these findings when choosing theoretical approaches.

Role and Function of the Leader in Psychodrama Groups

The leader of psychodrama groups plays the role of producer, facilitator, observer, analyzer, and director. Leaders plan the session, create a therapeutic environment, provide encouragement and guidance for the protagonist, and lead the sharing and discussion after the scene has been acted out. Leaders facilitate warm-up activities as well as ask pointed questions of the protagonist to allow the focus to remain on the process (Kottler, 2001).

Stages of Psychodrama Groups

Ordinarily, psychodrama groups involve three stages, including preparation, working, and application. In contrast, Kottler (2001) described a six-stage model consisting of (1) exploration, (2) assigning roles, (3) role reversal, (4) setting the scene, (5) acting of the scene, and (6) analysis and feedback. Similar elements are present in all of the descriptions of the stages in both approaches; hence an integrated explanation of the stages in both approaches follows.

During the preparation phase, the leader may facilitate warm-up and introductory activities to establish a sense of trust and cohesion in the group. The leader may facilitate dyad work so that members can identify issues or conflicts they may want to work on. The leader and members discuss various issues that group members are willing to explore and then identify the protagonist, who is the subject of the scene being acted out. The leader helps the protagonist explore the issue further and leads a discussion so the group members develop a deeper understanding of the issue. The protagonist, with the leader's guidance, sets the stage by explaining details of the event and then selecting group members to be part of the case. For groups to be adequately prepared for the working stage, trust among the members needs to be established so that risks can be taken. A climate of playfulness and creativity should also be encouraged.

Once the details of the scene are decided, the group moves into the working stage. The protagonist should describe the scene in detail. The leader should help the protagonist by asking questions that focus the protagonist on feelings that the scene provokes as well as messages he or she receives from the other members cast in the scene.

Some group members will be actors in the scene, while others will serve as the audience. With the protagonist's directions and the leader's guidance, the scene is acted out. Protagonists frequently develop greater insights if they engage in role reversal and role switching. Finally, the scene may be repeated as the protagonist tries on new roles and makes behavioral and attitudinal changes.

During the final stage, the group processes the acted-out scene. The group is encouraged to give the protagonist support and feedback focused on the emotional aspects of the scene. Then the leader facilitates a discussion about how to integrate the learning from the psychodrama into the members' lives outside the group. Group cohesion is usually increased as members find commonalities with other members' work. If processing is done correctly, many members can benefit from the work of one member.

Techniques Commonly Used in Psychodrama Groups

Group leaders use a variety of techniques unique to psychodrama as they work through the various stages of the group. Some techniques focus on the roles individuals play in the process of acting out a scene. Members may reverse roles or the leader may assign a double to play a role. In role reversal, the protagonist can view the problem of the story from a different option or role, or someone may act as his double while the protagonist observes. Either approach promotes and improves self-awareness, and the member can learn about himself. Role training may also take place in which the protagonist "teaches" someone else to play his part. This forces the member to discuss and verbalize many of his internal states. Scenes may also be replayed and processed with the group. These replays often cause different endings to emerge, which can promote new learning and awareness. Role playing has been associated with reducing feelings of helplessness and uncertainty, alleviation of the distress that fears may cause, helping to instill hope, healing, enhancing understanding among people, and structuring a consistent and rational sense of identity. Role playing uses people's creativity and spontaneity to achieve a catharsis

and increases one's role repertoire (Kipper & Tuller, 1996).

Other techniques, such as monodrama or soliloquy, develop the psychodrama from a different approach. In the monodrama, the protagonist plays all the roles. A soliloquy allows a group member to act out a scene that is playing in her head. For example, consider a scenario in which a young woman is deciding whether to share her lesbian identity with her parents. Other members may become involved by being assigned to demonstrate approval and/or disapproval to help the group member identify and understand the internal conflicts and explore some of her feelings about parental approval.

Future projections can be used in psychodrama to envision a life without a problem or a change in behavior. For instance, consider an example in which a group member wants to be more successful academically. The member, along with other group members, can discuss how the future might change, such as graduating from high school, attending college, or gaining employment at a prestigious company. Once this is brought into awareness, the group member can focus on changing his/her behavior in the here and now in order to create the future the member identified.

Other creative techniques used in psychodrama are the magic shop, creative imagery, and guided autobiography. The magic shop is a collection of various props such as hats, coins, beads, scarves, costumes, crowns, and some magical animals (unicorns, mermaids). The props can be used in a variety of ways with group members. For instance, the shop can open for business and group members can act out a current situation they are dealing with in their lives. Or a more spontaneous activity might be one in which the leaders open the magic shop and have members pick an object and relate it to their lives. Then these activities can be processed within the group.

Creative imagery is a technique often used at the beginning stage of a psychodrama group. The leader may lead a guided imagery in which members visualize the most relaxing place they have visited. This helps prepare members for the creative process and help them to relax.

The guided autobiography technique within a psychodrama setting is a somewhat structured, topical, group approach to life review, with a written component and a group experience component. The technique gets group members to review situations in the past, while it reinforces enactment and participation in the present. There are nine guiding themes: (1) history of the major branching points in my life; (2) family history; (3) career or major life work; (4) the role of money in my life; (5) health and body image; (6) loves and hates; (7) sexual identity, sex roles, and sexual experience; (8) experiences with and ideas about death and dying and other losses; and (9) influences, beliefs, and values that provide meaning in my life (Brown-Shaw, Westwood, and de Vries, 1999). This process helps a person gain perspective and understanding of herself. This technique also has the potential to increase appreciation (or embarrassment) of life achievements (or lack of). If the member is not happy with the autobiography, she can "restory" her life. By using this in the Gestalt method and the psychodrama process, it helps bring awareness to past events by reliving them in the here and now.

By working on the guided autobiography and sharing parts with the group, the leader can assess whether the member is ready to do a group enactment. Not all situations can be enacted by the group, and some enactment may do more harm than good. Role dynamics are a major influence in both group enactment and guided autobiography because they include intrapersonal, interpersonal, family, organizational, and societal levels of interaction. Combining the guided autobiography and the group enactment helps synthesize two techniques to give a comprehensive foundation for working with members.

Sculpting allows the protagonist to arrange members in symbolic positions to visually illustrate relationships in his life. Creating family snapshots is a form of sculpting. A group member can be asked to envision a family photo taken at a recent gathering. Then, different group members are placed in the pictures in ways that represent relationships within the family. This visual may help the protagonist understand relationships better and learn how to change in order to improve relationships.

Some Final Comments on Psychodrama Groups

Psychodrama groups can be used with different people with many different types of problems. As discussed earlier, elements of psychodrama can be used with young people in the schools as well as with adults with psychological disorders. The elements and techniques of psychodrama can also be integrated easily into other theoretical approaches. Vicarious learning takes place in the group as the protagonist works through the scene and allows actors and members of the audience to relate to and be affected by the work. Gladding (2008) also reminded readers that research proving the effectiveness of psychodrama is limited, and specific training in psychodrama is limited as well. Despite these limitations, psychodrama can be a creative approach to working with groups.

Summary

The Gestalt approach to group work can assist individuals in gaining self-awareness and congruence, and in prioritizing needs and wants. Psychodrama can accomplish some of the same goals, but it uses more creative techniques. The chapter outlined how leaders using these theoretical approaches facilitate groups, how a group develops through various stages, and the many varied techniques used in these types of groups.

CHAPTER 18

Family, Couples, T-Group, and Self-Help Approaches to Counseling and Psychotherapy Groups

Ann Vernon and Darcie Davis-Gage

PREVIEW

Family, couples, T-group, and self-help approaches combine group therapy and other therapy models to facilitate change in group members. Each of these approaches to group work will be discussed, including basic principles, types of groups, the role of leaders, the stages of development, and various techniques.

GROUP WORK WITH FAMILIES AND COUPLES

Family groups and couples groups blend principles of group and family therapy to produce productive group work for families, couples, and individuals. Because family can be considered a person's first group experience, it is logical that group work would be a viable option when treating a family or an individual with family problems (Donigian & Hulse-Killacky, 1999). Indeed, the principles used in small-group work are very applicable to family systems. Special training in group work, family counseling, and couples counseling is needed to apply this approach successfully in clinical practice. Also note that this approach would not be appropriate in school settings. Throughout the remainder of this section, the term *family* will be used to indicate family or couple.

In combining family systems and group work, it is important to understand the similarities and differences between groups and families. Trotzer (1999) identified some similarities of families and groups: (1) families and groups have similar power structures, (2) both often function within a set of rules and norms, and (3) members of both groups and families may play various roles throughout the developmental process. In contrast, some important differences include the fact that groups have an ending point and members usually do not have a lengthy shared history. Families often come to therapy with a lengthy shared history, and when therapy is over, their relationships usually continue.

Types of Family and Couples Groups

Family groups may occur in a variety of settings, such as addiction treatment facilities or outpatient mental health clinics. Donigian and Hulse-Killacky (1999) stated that family group therapy helps members to better understand family-of-origin issues. They also identified birth order, sibling relationships, divorce, and enmeshment and disengagement issues as possible topics for family group therapy.

Groups using principles of family systems can include multiple families (or multiple couples) at the same time. These types of groups bring many families together for group treatment, and research has supported success with various types of problems. For example, Dyck, Hendryx, Short, Voss, and McFarlane (2002) found multifamily psychoeducational groups were successful in reducing the number of hospitalizations for clients with schizophrenia. In addition, Dare and Eisler (2000) found multifamily group treatment to be effective with adolescents being treated for an eating disorder.

Role and Function of the Leader in Family and Couples Groups

Group leaders may sometimes take on the roles of director, facilitator, or participator. At other times, they may be the expert or simply observe the interaction. Leaders in family groups need to be skilled facilitators because these groups can be large, especially when working with multifamily groups. While working in family groups, Donigian and Hulse-Killacky (1999) suggested that leaders take an active role and avoid a laissez-faire approach. Leaders need to balance the role of participator and expert. Some self-disclosure can help members relate to the leader, but too much can interfere with the group process. Similarly, some well-timed giving of leader information can be helpful to group members, but too much may impede the progress of the group.

Stages of Family and Couples Groups

Family and couples groups often progress through similar developmental stages, as in most other types of groups. These stages are also very similar to individual developmental theory as well as family life-cycle stages. Donigian and Hulse-Killacky (1999) identified a five-stage model that includes security, acceptance, responsibility, work, and termination. The stages are interdependent because the identified tasks (e.g., security, acceptance) must be completed before the group progresses to the next stage. If groups can progress through the identified stages, members will usually be able to complete their identified goals.

Techniques Commonly Used in Family and Couples Groups

Many techniques used in traditional family therapy may also be adapted for family group therapy. Trotzer (1999) identified three types of techniques used in family groups: reaction, interaction, and action-based skills. Reaction skills involve the leader intervening on an individual or group level. Skills for this technique involve basic counseling skills such as reflection of meaning, active listening, summarizing, and clarifying. Interaction skills are designed to encourage and facilitate the group process by linking members to one another. These skills include connecting, blocking, and supporting. In addition, the group members are able to process on a deeper and more meaningful level if the leader also uses action skills. Tone setting, modeling, and questioning are all examples of action skills. When a leader can blend all three types of skills in family groups, the group members usually experience positive outcomes.

Some Final Comments on Family and Couples Groups

The combining of group and family systems principles has proven to be helpful for members. Family-centered group work can help members improve relationships and become aware of their patterns of interaction. Although family group therapy can be helpful for members to examine family relationships, Donigian and Hulse-Killacky (1999) cautioned that leaders using family-centered therapy avoid doing family therapy at a distance when family members are not present in treatment. Family group therapy can also be helpful with multiple families and couples in one group. Research has supported success with multifamily groups (Dare & Eisler, 2000; Dyck et al., 2002). Whether using family principles in groups with individuals or with multifamily groups, this approach is a viable option for group leaders.

TRAINING GROUPS (T-GROUPS)

Training groups (T-groups) were developed by Kurt Lewin and became the first popular type of growth group. The T-group is like a training laboratory in which group members learn new things about themselves. When Lewin first developed the T-group, he arranged for his students to observe the group and subsequently discuss the group dynamics (Forsyth, 1999). Although this discussion was intended to be private, several group members asked permission to listen to the students' interpretations. Lewin allowed this, and as a result, learned how beneficial it was for the group to analyze the process and dynamics.

Because this process proved so effective for understanding group dynamics and group development, the role of the process observer emerged. Forester-Miller and Kottler (1997) suggest that all group members be encouraged to assume the role of the process observer. Initially, process observers provided feedback at the end of a group session, but eventually it was determined that at any time during the group meeting, observers could freely share concerns about the group process that they felt were counterproductive to the progress of the group.

According to Forsyth (1999, p. 478), "[t]he T-group was a precursor of group techniques designed to enhance spontaneity, increase personal growth, and maximize members' sensitivity to others." T-groups have a here-and-now orientation, and members are challenged to explore and develop personal goals and better understand themselves.

Types of T-Groups

As the focus shifted from training in group dynamics to an emphasis on developing sensitivity,

the name changed from T-group to sensitivity training group or encounter group (Forsyth, 1999). Regardless of the name used, the emphasis is on learning more about oneself, and members engage in self-exploration and develop goals to better understand themselves and others.

A variation of the T-group is an experiential group in which the leader develops experiential activities that help members learn more about themselves. The Pfeiffer and Jones (1969, 1970, 1971, 1973a, 1973b, 1973c) *Handbook of Structured Experiences for Human Relations Training (Vols. I-VI)* contain numerous examples of activities that increase self-awareness.

Role and Function of the Leader in T-Groups

The traditional T-group is noted for its lack of structure. In fact, during the initial stages of a T-group, members are often anxious about the ambiguous nature of the group and direct their discomfort at the leader (Forsyth, 1999). As Forsyth explained, the ambiguity is intentional because it "shifts responsibility for structuring, understanding, and controlling the group's activities to the participants themselves" (p. 478). Group members determine the organization, agenda, goals, and structure. Through this process, they learn how to express feelings, deal with conflict, and ultimately develop collaborative relationships. In the typical T-group, the leader is nondirective, and the members struggle with the group process, which becomes the laboratory from which to learn.

Stages of T-Groups

Unlike other groups where there is more structure and a more formal warming-up phase, T-groups are unstructured, and participants deal with the ambiguity as they attempt to define the process. During the working stage, more attention is directed at members interacting with each other and giving feedback about perceptions and feelings. In the final stage, closure is reached, and new learning is discussed and reinforced.

A Final Comment on T-Groups

Forsyth (1999) noted that while the long-term effectiveness of T-groups is somewhat questionable, training groups still have a role in organizational development interventions.

SELF-HELP GROUPS

Self-help groups are designed to create a support system for people who share a common problem or dilemma. Self-help groups have increased in popularity since 1980, primarily because of the changing health care system (e.g., health insurance coverage, cuts in government funding), increased stress levels, and the inability to find help within a system (e.g., clinics, private practitioners). Self-help groups can be characterized as psychoeducational, psychotherapeutic, and task-oriented. The most well-known self-help group, Alcoholics Anonymous, has been very influential in changing many lives and has become a model for numerous other types of self-help groups.

Self-help groups allow members to share their experiences and provide support for one another. Participants offer suggestions and direction, and motivate fellow group members to begin changing their lives. Indeed, peer support can be more important and effective than expert assistance.

Self-help groups have no professional leader, but there are often experienced lay leaders or volunteers who assume some leadership or organizational roles. Because these groups are generally self-governing, members rather than mental health professionals structure the activities and agenda. Reciprocal helping, treating all members fairly, and providing time for everyone to express themselves is standard practice (Forsyth, 1999). Because membership is voluntary and participants share a common predicament, bonding occurs quite naturally.

Gladding (2008) identified two forms of self-help groups: (1) groups that originate spontaneously and rely on internal group resources, and (2) groups that are organized by a professional helping organization or by an individual (support groups). Support groups and self-help groups share common characteristics because they are both comprised of individuals who share a similar focus and purpose, and the members use basic counseling skills such as active listening, reflection, and confrontation. In both types of groups there is mutual help, but one is professionally organized and the other is a group of individuals who form a group based on mutual concern.

One of the chief characteristics of self-help groups is that they provide incentive for members to gain more control over their lives so that they can function more effectively. Discussing and sharing member concerns is mutually beneficial, both in terms of giving help to other group members and receiving it themselves.

Types of Self-Help Groups

Forsyth (1999) noted that there are self-help groups for numerous medical, psychological, or stress-related problems: groups to help individuals overcome addictions and weight problems; groups for people suffering from chronic pain, disability, heart or liver disease, AIDS, or cancer; groups to help people manage their time, money or a variety of life problems; groups for people sharing common life experiences such as suffering from grief or being a war veteran; and groups for social advocacy, such as the National Organization for Women or the Gay Activists Alliance, among numerous others.

Stages of Self-Help Groups

Self-help groups often have no clearly defined stages. Typically members introduce themselves, take turns telling their story, and offer support for one another. Depending on the degree of leadership, there may be more clearly defined stages.

Some Final Comments on Self-Help Groups

Self-help groups have become prominent because member needs are not met by educational, social, or health care agencies. The fact that people are reaching out for help is a healthy sign, and professionally led groups are not the only way to help members meet individual goals. Given the fact that life is increasingly challenging, self-help groups obviously meet the needs of many individuals who may not be able to afford professional mental health services. By all indications, the number and types of self-help groups will continue to expand. A downside to self-help groups is the fact that, although participants are brought together because they have a mutual problem and can offer support and understanding, the lack of a trained leader who is guided by a code of ethics and standards of practice may have an adverse effect on group process or individual members.

Summary

This chapter outlined the types of groups, role of leaders, stages of group development, and techniques associated with family and couples groups, T-groups, and self-help groups. In all of these groups, members have the opportunity to learn about relationships and group dynamics and to apply skills learned in the group to their lives outside the group. Access to these groups is usually easier because they can accommodate larger numbers of participants, hence making them somewhat more affordable for clients, and they can increase services to more clients.

CHAPTER 19

Special Issues in Group Work with Children and Adolescents

Susan H. Eaves and Carl J. Sheperis

PREVIEW

This chapter addresses special issues in group work with children and adolescents, including the basic principles of group work with children of alcoholics, children of divorce, sexual abuse victims, and social skills training.

GROUP WORK WITH CHILDREN AND ADOLESCENTS

Having reached this point in the book, you can now see that group work is an effective tool proven useful with a wide range of populations and issues. Like other forms of counseling, however, it must be implemented intentionally and should vary according to the specific population with which it is used. Put another way, for group work to be effective, leaders must not only understand a range of basic group skills, they must also know when and how to apply the various skills acquired. Positive outcomes are more probable when group leaders understand the unique needs of the population with which they are working, match group member capacities with the treatment approach, and modify the approach to accommodate the specific characteristics of the members. If leaders are equipped with appropriate skills and knowledge, adaptations can be made easily so that group members receive the most benefit from their experience within the group.

Because leaders need to know when and how to apply their acquired skills and knowledge in various contexts, no group work textbook would be complete without examining group work with special populations and specific issues, including age (i.e., children, adolescents), aspects of the members' personal development, and preferred characteristics of the group leader.

GROUP WORK WITH CHILDREN

Group work can be an effective and efficient means of serving the needs of children. When children progress through developmental tasks and issues in conjunction with peers, they often develop a greater sense of self-efficacy and resources, leading to fewer problems in the future. Group work can be especially beneficial in this way because children are provided with healthy modeling from both peers and the group leader. Children are referred for group work for a host of issues; however, the most common typically revolve around low self-esteem, grief, abuse, aggressiveness, inability to get along with others, rule violations, depression and anxiety, or crisis.

Group settings are natural environments for children and come with the enormous capability to harm or heal children. Because of this, extreme care must be taken by leaders when working with this population in order to do the least harm and greatest good. Group members often have more influence on one another than the group leader has on any one member. Because peer influence is so valued at this developmental stage, the group leader must be vigilant in facilitating a group that can be reflective of and can validate a child's development (van Velsor, 2004). Counseling small children involves a number of considerations. Leaders must prescreen members prior to inclusion in the group. When meeting with children as potential group members, it is essential to assess the degree to which children can establish relationships and their capacity to want group acceptance enough to give up any inappropriate behaviors they may display. Additional considerations in working with young students (each of which is addressed below) include confidentiality, developing interventions, and group size.

Confidentiality with Children

With children as clients, the concept of confidentiality can be difficult to convey. However, children can be taught how to discuss the group experience in general, without breaking confidentiality, in developmentally appropriate language for their age level. Leaders are encouraged to develop specific examples that can be reviewed in the group as well as guidelines for how to respond when someone outside the group asks children questions about the group. Depending on the ages and developmental levels of participants, written confidentiality agreements can be signed.

Depending on the setting, confidentiality can be difficult to manage for the leader as well. For example, in schools, counselors often remove students from class to participate in group. Teachers or peers may ask questions about the process. Thus, it is important to develop responses to such inquiries ahead of time. In addition, the location of the group in a school may compromise confidentiality to some degree. As a result, leaders should take care in planning the location of the group.

Prior to beginning the first group session, leaders should obtain the written consent or assent of each child's parent or legal guardian to enhance cooperation. In an ideal situation, both parents and leaders have a common goal to promote the well-being of the child. While parental consent is important, parent involvement can also affect the comfort level of the child with regard to confidentiality. While most parents are well meaning, they may ask leaders to break the confidences of the group and give them information about their child's experiences. It is important for you to strike a balance in this area and explain to parents the purposes of the group so that any curiosity or suspicion they may have is resolved, thereby minimizing future inquiries and resistance. At this time, parents can also be encouraged to refrain from asking their child questions about the group. Leaders should also discuss their obligation to confidentiality and how this obligation affects the parent's right to know. Leaders can satisfy this right by sharing general group information, such as weekly session topics, and keeping parents updated in general without divulging a child's personal information. Just as a parent has a legal right to know, a child has an ethical right to confidentiality (van Velsor, 2004).

Developing Interventions

As with any group, it is important for the leader to use appropriate exercises and techniques. An often debated topic pertinent to group work with young children is the use of verbal versus nonverbal techniques. According to Thompson and Rudolph (1996), children respond better to nonverbal techniques because of their limited vocabularies. In fact, for children under the age of 12 years, leaders may rely less on verbal intervention and more on play and action-oriented techniques. In contrast, Ohlsen, Horne, and Lawe (1988) stated that verbal techniques are appropriate to use with even very young children, and those who have difficulty expressing themselves with words can be taught to do so.

In a debate such as this, knowledge regarding child development can be of great use. In general, preschool-age children have limited verbal skills, while children above age 6 years may have the ability to learn verbal expression, although they continue to express themselves primarily in nonverbal ways. It is important for leaders to know the capabilities of the children they serve in the group setting, then combine verbal and nonverbal activities and techniques in a way that is most beneficial to the age group with which they are working (van Velsor, 2004). In addition, the purpose of any technique or exercise should be explained, and children should not be pressured to participate. For example, consider the following scenario where group counseling can be used to work on social skills with preschool children. One of the ways to achieve group goals is by selecting an appropriate story that exemplifies the theme for the group session. Begin the group with a list of rules (e.g., hands and feet to self, use an inside voice), read the story to the participants, ask the children to identify the various social skills (e.g., "How did Tommy the Turtle make a friend?") in the book, and then let the children act out the story. In this process, verbal skills and play are combined to achieve group goals.

Group Size

The size and structure of a children's group are important elements to consider. In general, the leader should be prepared enough for each session to be structured, yet flexible enough to allow the group to take its own direction. Opinions vary regarding the size of the group and length of the sessions. A useful guideline to consider is this: the younger the group members, the shorter the session and the smaller the group. For children, groups larger than nine are considered too large for members to participate, for leaders to prevent subgroups from forming, and for leaders to adequately manage behavior. The leader needs to be a counselor, not a disciplinarian. Likewise, the length of the session should be shorter the younger the children are in age. The attention span of a 6-year-old is typically very different from that of an 11-year-old. Attention spans and general behavior patterns should be taken into consideration when determining length of sessions. As an example, ordinarily preschool groups should last no longer than 30 minutes and contain no more than seven or eight children.

GROUP WORK WITH ADOLESCENTS

As any group leader who works with adolescents will testify, working with adolescents requires patience and a clear understanding of the developmental processes at work. Adolescence is a time of change and uncertainty. During these formative years, adolescents attempt to form a unique and separate identity; solidify a value system; and establish connectedness, yet independence, in relationships with others. This is a time of increased freedoms, but also of increased responsibilities, expectations, pressures, and demands. Teenagers often fluctuate between a need for individuality and independence and a need for connectedness and security. In general, adolescence is a time of polarities, often leading to isolation and loneliness. At the same time, the influence and importance of a peer group increases in importance. For these reasons, group experiences can be of great use for this population and are often even the preferred choice for treatment.

A group counseling format allows adolescents to vocalize emotions, test boundaries safely and appropriately, and feel heard, all while assisting other members in common difficulties. Groups can also be used to help adolescents transition from childhood and to adulthood, providing support and models along the way. Some themes for adolescent groups include self-esteem, managing stress, relating to addicted parents, addictions, social skills, assertiveness, and grief. Several special issues with adolescents deserving further mention include participation and resistance, involuntary participation, leader characteristics, addressing problem behavior, and ethical practice.

Participation and Resistance

Motivation to participate in counseling sometimes can be a problem when working with adolescents. Even with voluntary group members, active and appropriate involvement in the group can sometimes be a challenge. Adolescents typically do better when the group is structured, expectations are given early, and limits and boundaries are made clear. Still, keeping sessions moving in a meaningful direction can prove difficult and may require the leader to actively deal with resistant members, involving as many members as possible, and cutting off inappropriate storytelling. Additional problem behaviors seen in this population include purposeful disruptiveness, withdrawal, subgrouping, and inappropriate disclosure. These behaviors can be ignored, discussed openly as a group, or managed individually. Remember that part of the responsibility of a leader is to facilitate new ways of behaving. Skilled group leaders learn to use resistance and other forms of problematic behavior as learning opportunities within the group. It is important to set limits early with adolescents and to be consistent. As a leader of groups with adolescents, it will be important to hold members accountable for their behavior and to maintain control over the process.

Involuntary Participation

In addition to dealing with difficult behavior from voluntary group members, group leaders also need to be prepared to handle the issues inherent with involuntary group membership. Children and adolescents are occasionally made to attend group counseling (e.g., court-required), resulting in resistance to participation and general feelings of hostility and resentment toward the group leader. Initially, the leader's main focus should be to listen to what members might have to say about being in the group, including their complaints. However, it is advisable to set a time limit for this type of process (e.g., 10 minutes) or the group session could quickly become a complaint session. In addition, it is important to have clear rules about respect and to enforce these rules as members share. Because many of the participants in these groups will have an external locus of control and may blame others for their problems, it will be important to get them to own their behavior rather than to complain about others.

Once members see that it is acceptable to be honest, leaders can work with members toward having a new perspective, helping them to view the group as something other than punishment. It might be helpful to point out that there are still choices within their control. Being in a group, although it may feel involuntary, is still a choice. While the alternative is usually some type of negative consequence, the choice remains theirs. Thus, leaders are encouraged to emphasize the choices members do have and help them move toward an attitude of "as long as I'm here, I might as well benefit from it." Once they begin to view participation in this way, discussion of goals can take place. Additional guidelines, as offered by Gladding (2008), include the following: (1) meet with involuntary members on an individual basis outside the group prior to beginning; (2) work with the resistance rather than against it; and (3) remain nondefensive, caring, and firm. To remain respectful of such members, allow them to vent their frustrations without taking it personally. Leaders working with adolescents in groups should establish clear rules, develop a gentle but firm style of confrontation, and begin holding members accountable in the very first session.

To decrease the risk of burnout when working with this population, it is important to understand the members' worldviews. Understanding their life experiences often puts their behavior in perspective. Group leaders working with this population should learn to celebrate even subtle improvements in behavior. Finally, remember that you can support the group members' feelings without approving of their actions.

Leader Characteristics

Perhaps more than with any other population, the personality and behavior of the group leader are of great importance when working with adolescents. Not only do adolescents respond best to leaders who are caring, enthusiastic, open, and direct, they also respond to leaders who are obviously congruent, genuine, and have come to terms with their own adolescent milestones and issues. An appropriate amount of self-disclosure is not only preferred, it is often expected from these group members. Respect for these individuals and their questions about your own experiences will typically result in reciprocity of both respect and openness. Above all, the effective leader with adolescents will be a good role model, promoting the very behaviors he or she hopes to see from the adolescents.

Addressing Problem Behavior

While many leader behaviors and characteristics are conducive to productive group counseling with adolescents, several behaviors, characteristics, and responses are not. Group leaders are strongly encouraged to take an active rather than a passive role in the process. Leaders should be fair and firm, and they should address behavior that is not appropriate according to the limits set early in the group. For instance, if confidentiality is breached, it must be addressed in the group setting. If behavior toward the leader crosses the boundaries of what is appropriate, the leader must be assertive enough to say so. Remember that you are the leader, not a peer. While it is important not to be judgmental of a member's slang language, you also do not have to incorporate it into your own style of speaking in an effort to be accepted by the group. Finally, avoid advice giving and siding with adolescents in their complaints against parents, teachers, or administrators.

Group work with adolescents can be especially helpful because groups are designed to provide a supportive and healthy environment of peers. Because peer relations are so crucial during adolescence, a group format can be even more beneficial than other modes of therapy.

Adolescents can vent feelings openly, try out new behaviors, learn through modeling, and receive feedback. Adolescents can gain a sense of connectedness with others and a sense of well-being through helping other members. Despite the many positive aspects of group work with adolescents, there can be a number of disadvantages as well, most of which involve inappropriate member behavior. Because peer group pressure is so strong during this time in life, the group leader must be vigilant in screening out members with inappropriate or destructive behaviors, and in keeping behavior productive and supportive after group begins.

Ethical Practice

One final caution to exercise when working with adolescents involves ethical obligations. When working with this population, be thoroughly familiar with the pertinent ethical guidelines and consult with a colleague or supervisor, as appropriate, if problems arise. Depending on the age of the adolescent and the issue the group addresses, it may be necessary to obtain parental consent or assent. Parents may be determined to know the personal details of their teen's involvement in the group. The adolescent may be especially sensitive to any communication between the leader and parent. Remember that the adolescent in this case is the one with whom you have entered into a counseling relationship. Be very clear with all group members regarding your communication with their parents or legal guardians. If the group member is being made to participate, you may have to communicate information to a judge or probation officer. Thus, it is important to be clear with all parties, especially the adolescent, about the amount and nature of the information to be shared. In addition to obtaining consent and/or assent from the parent(s), it is also appropriate to gain consent and/or assent from the group members to ensure that they understand the process of this type of treatment and the potential risks involved. Also emphasize their choice and freedom in the matter. Thoroughly explain your duty regarding threats of danger to self or others. Adolescents are often more prone to statements involving harm, and they must understand your obligation to protect and report.

GROUP WORK WITH MINOR CHILDREN OF ALCOHOLICS (COAs)

An estimated 10 million alcoholics live in the United States. For every alcoholic, it is estimated that four or five family members and friends, 35 to 45 million persons, are directly and negatively affected by the drinking (Wilson & Blocher, 1990). Alcoholism has the greatest negative effect on the spouse and children. Approximately eight million minor children and 18 million adult children of alcoholics (COAs) currently reside in the United States (Riddle & Bergin, 1997).

Children growing up in homes with alcoholism contend with inconsistency and tension on a daily basis, making it the most common reason for severe stress in children. COAs report household arguing and uncertainty about the family staying intact as primary concerns in childhood. COAs are also more likely to experience physical abuse, sexual abuse, and neglect. Their emotional needs are neglected and their feelings are ignored. These children often behave more like miniature adults and become the caretakers of both siblings and parents. Unpredictability in the home, especially concerning rules, norms, and discipline, also contribute to the tension and stress this population feels. Distortion, denial, and isolation are used within these families in order to maintain the family secret. In light of such chaos and turmoil, it is little wonder that these children develop problematic behaviors. Group counseling or therapy emulates the family dynamics, so it is important for the group leader to keep these family norms in mind in order to better understand within-group behaviors (Wilson & Blocher, 1990).

Presenting Problems

Before discussing the symptoms associated with children of alcoholics, it is first important to understand that COAs are not sick. Instead, it would be more accurate and fair to say that they are simply reacting in a normal and self-preserving manner to abnormal and threatening events (Wilson & Blocher, 1990). In general, children of alcoholics have higher frequencies of temper outbursts, truancy, fighting with peers, eating disorders, low grades, low frustration tolerance, substance use, depression, low self-esteem, suicide completions and attempts, and psychosomatic complaints. Regarding substance use, sons of alcoholics are five times more likely to become alcoholic themselves, while daughters of alcoholic mothers are three times more likely. Alcohol is used to compensate for the poor social skills common to this population, as well as an anxiety-reducing agent (Chandy, Harris, Blum, & Resnick, 1994; Harman & Armsworth, 1995; Thompson, 1990; Tomori, 1994; Wilson & Blocher, 1990).

Children raised in such families continue to use the same coping responses that have proven necessary and useful in their home environment. As these children continue to develop and mature, their social skills and coping responses may become maladaptive and detrimental to their well-being, thus preventing optimal functioning. These children will continue to struggle with trust, dependency, control, depression, identification, and emotional expression because previously learned behavior becomes dysfunctional when applied to relationships outside the home (Glover, 1994). Characteristic personality traits of COAs include difficulty with project follow-through, taking themselves too seriously, overreacting to change, constantly seeking approval, feelings of oddity or differentness, denial of needs, high needs for control, an inappropriate sense of personal responsibility, and impulsivity (Seefeldt & Lyon, 1992). These characteristics often result in impoverished interpersonal relationships, chemical dependency, co-dependency, and stress-related illness (Downing & Walker, 1987). Knowledge regarding the problematic results of growing up in an alcoholic home is of great importance in the development and implementation of group work approaches aimed at helping COAs.

Goals and Objectives

Goals listed in the literature for group work with children of alcoholics include appropriate and healthy emotional expression, social skills, identification and expression of needs, self-esteem building, assertiveness training, relaxation to reduce psychosomatic complaints, decision making, resource identification, and increasing support systems (Riddle & Bergin, 1997; Wilson & Blocher, 1990). According to Downing and Walker (1987), in their classic study of COA group approaches, there should be four specific group goals. First, because secrecy is a typical alcoholic family characteristic, the group should provide a safe place to talk honestly about events in the home. Second, the group should confront denial and guilt, traits often seen in children of alcoholics. Third, the group should have an educational aspect, focusing on the disease of alcoholism. Finally, the group assists members in identifying and recovering feelings that have been distorted or lost. The format suggested for the accomplishment of these goals includes: Week 1-building commonality and confronting denial, Weeks 2 and 3-confronting denial and educating about alcoholism and codependency, and Weeks 4 through 8-recognizing and recovering emotions. Structure decreases throughout the life of the group, and member needs increasingly become the focus.

Assessment

While many of the logistics of group work (e.g., number of members, duration, frequency) depend heavily on the age group being served, screening of group members warrants specific attention for each specialty group. An individual interview with each potential group member should be conducted prior to including the member in the group. With COAs, it is important to assess for the following: (1) current functioning, (2) need for intervention, (3) impact of parental alcoholism, (4) current substance use, (5) expectations for treatment, and (6) the match between potential member expectations and what the group can provide (Downing & Walker, 1987). When assessing for current functioning, need for intervention, and impact of parental alcoholism, keep in mind that many COAs display the problematic behaviors discussed above, but some fit into a role termed the superhero.

Within the home of an alcoholic parent, each child develops a survival mode, leading to the adoption of behavior perceived to cause the least amount of upheaval in the home and to cause the greatest amount of chaos reduction. The five typical adaptive roles are as follows: (1) the enabler, whom the alcoholic depends on the most; (2) the scapegoat, who draws attention away from the chemically dependent person with troublemaking behavior; (3) the lost child, who hides and disappears into the chaos; (4) the mascot, who charms and humors the family to deflect negative circumstances; and (5) the superhero, who strives for perfection, bringing pride to a family that will now be perceived as healthy and happy. The potential hazard for excluding the superhero from groups is that they often appear highly successful with model behavior. They seem normal, even extraordinary by society's standards, but they have been neglected by their alcoholic family and risk being overlooked by leaders. However, they are in need of intervention as much as other children of alcoholics (Downing & Walker, 1987; Glover, 1994).

A final note regarding screening of group members is necessary because some potential members can prove inappropriate to the group process. Persons currently experiencing an intense crisis may not be ready for group work. Also, persons who abuse substances should be referred and successfully treated for alcohol or drug abuse first before being included in this type of group therapy. Those believed by the group leader(s) to have the potential for disrupting the group's functioning (e.g., certain personality disorders) should be excluded from this type of group as well (Downing & Walker, 1987).

Benefits of Participation

Group counseling and psychotherapy were shown to be an especially beneficial treatment modality for children of alcoholics. According to Riddle and Bergin (1997), the primary purpose of group counseling for this population is to increase effective coping with the parental alcoholism, thereby minimizing the harmful consequences. Whether or not the parents stop drinking, it is important for the child of the alcoholic parent to learn to attend to one's own needs and cope in spite of the parent's behavior. If the children remain living in the home environment, this purpose can be thought of as parent-proofing the child to survive, and perhaps even thrive, despite their home environment.

A second major purpose of group counseling with COAs is for group members to differentiate between themselves and their parents. Group members are educated about the family dynamics and the disease of alcoholism. They are taught they cannot cause, cannot control, and cannot cure parental alcoholism. Through a kind of demystification process, the disease loses its mystery and therefore much of its power. Family secrets are explored, and perspectives become increasingly objective. Through this work, children learn to detach from the behavior of the alcoholic as they realize that detachment is neither abandonment nor rejection (Glover, 1994; Riddle & Bergin, 1997).

In comparison to individual counseling, group counseling provides a different type of atmosphere for growth and change. The importance of the group environment mimicking the family dynamics cannot be stressed enough. Group members begin to take on characteristics of family members, as perceived by each COA. Children also bring to the group their different family roles. Members see themselves not only mirrored in other group members, they also see their siblings and other family members mirrored by other group members. In this way, they gain valuable insight into their own behavior, feelings, and reactions, thereby increasing their chances for understanding and changing (Glover, 1994).

Format

When working with students in COA groups, Riddle and Bergin (1997) offered suggestions for

the format of the group. Opening activities are suggested for the purpose of providing fun and relaxation. Secret handshakes can be used to close each session and help increase cohesion and camaraderie. Riddle and Bergin also suggested repetition of the group motto: "I can't cause alcoholism. I can't cure alcoholism. I can't control alcoholism. But I can learn to cope with it" (p. 199). In addition, children's books that involve characters who learn to express their feelings are frequently used. Drawing family pictures, making collages of feeling words, and acting out family roles from the pictures and story books are also used. Unspoken rules from home of "don't talk, don't trust, don't feel" (p. 200) are discussed. Additional activities can be found in Riddle and Bergin (1997). The point is that, while the specific activities of groups may differ according to the developmental age of the participants, the group goals are much the same.

The tasks of the group leader are also universal with children of alcoholics. The group leader plays a fundamental role in building cohesion within the group by drawing out and linking members' stories. The leader assists each member in creating an accurate picture of his or her family, free of guilt, distortion, and denial. The members are helped to identify the effects that the alcoholic family has had on them personally, as well as their emotional reactions to these effects. The leader should validate and normalize member reactions, while teaching them that they can control and choose how to respond (Arman, 2000).

GROUP WORK WITH CHILDREN OF DIVORCE

The divorce rate in the United States has become a source of concern. Because divorce has become so common, however, the toll it takes on the children involved is often overlooked. Not only does divorce have short-term effects, but the data also indicates that children of divorce often continue to experience adjustment problems for as many as ten years after the divorce occurs. The process of a divorce can involve family conflict, upheaval, uncertainty, and loss, but during all of this change, parents are also under such personal stress that they are often unable to be attentive to and provide support for their children. It is no wonder that children experience negative repercussions. In fact, it is well established that parental conflict and divorce are precursors to adverse emotional and behavioral consequences in children (Yauman, 1991).

Presenting Problems

Children of divorce often experience loneliness, chaos, feelings of responsibility for the divorce, divided loyalties, and loss of stability. Because of these experiences, they often show increased impulsivity, distractibility, aggressiveness, acting out, lowered academic achievement, depression, anger, insecurity, fear, and withdrawal. Often, even after the divorce, children have to contend with inconsistent visitation, continued interparental hostility, and parental remarriage (Schreier & Kalter, 1990).

"Group counseling is perceived as the most practical, efficient, and effective treatment mode for children of divorce" (Yauman, 1991, p. 131). Group work is beneficial in a number of ways because it provides an avenue for reducing feelings of isolation and shame. Simply talking aloud about feelings and experiences takes away some of the negative power of divorce. According to Schreier and Kalter (1990), the group setting provides safety in numbers and facilitates verbal and emotional expression earlier than would be the case in individual or family counseling. While providing peer support, validation, and modeling, group counseling for children of divorce can assist members to gain new ways of thinking, feeling, and behaving. These changes first occur within the group context, then later are applied in the members' personal lives (Yauman, 1991).

Because divorce leaves parents emotionally and physically drained, they are often unable to provide their child objective support. When parents learn of the possibility of their child being in a group, they typically respond favorably because they are often relieved to have the extra source of support and stability for their child (Yauman, 1991). Once consent is given for the child to participate in the group, and the child is willing as well, an interview with the parent is suggested. Basic information should be obtained in an effort to assess all the changes that have occurred in the child's life. This is beneficial for the group leader to better understand the dynamics operating within the group, and it builds rapport with the parents. Most important, however, it assists the leader in separating fantasy from reality as the child reports it. Children often speak in terms of what they wish would happen rather than what is actually happening. If leaders are aware of the facts, they can recognize this as a defense and help the group member explore her or his needs and fears.

It is also suggested, under optimal circumstances, that parents receive treatment separately but at the same time as the child. Because parents are instrumental in their child's ability to adapt to the changing circumstances, parents should, at a minimum, be educated regarding the effects that divorce can have on their child as well as ways in which they can better meet their child's needs during this time. Parent education and support groups can be of great value to both parent and child (Yauman, 1991).

Goals and Objectives

Because children of divorce have and continue to experience excess amounts of upheaval and uncertainty, a structured environment with clear and fair rules is suggested (Yauman, 1991). Within this structured environment, group leaders should make it a priority to offer support, teach coping skills, validate feelings, reinforce appropriate expression, offer resources, and facilitate communication among members. Leaders should make sure they enforce the message that it is not the child's divorce, and no one is divorcing the child. The child neither caused this nor can he or she fix the situation between the parents.

Schreier and Kalter (1990) also offered five specific goals for children of divorce groups: (1) normalize the divorce experience, (2) clarify divorce-related concerns, (3) reexperience painful emotions, (4) improve coping, and (5) communicate each child's reactions and questions to the parents to facilitate increased parental support. These goals are met through a structured group that meets for eight sessions. These sessions initially focus on the need for fairy-tale endings and the reality and sadness of the lost family unit. The group shifts its focus to feelings about parental hostility, loss, fear, divided loyalties, and confusion regarding custody. In later sessions, the group discusses feelings about the noncustodial parent, parental dating, and remarriage. A number of techniques and activities are used throughout the life of the group to discuss these themes.

Techniques Used in Groups for Children of Divorce

When used appropriately, selectively, and in a flexible manner, specific techniques can assist in stimulating group interaction and clarifying feelings, especially when working with children and adolescents. The group techniques used most often for this population include bibliotherapy, movies, board games, drawings, brainstorming, role playing, and puppets. One of the most commonly used methods, bibliotherapy, is recommended because it is often helpful to approach the issues surrounding divorce in an indirect manner early in the group. This technique is most productive when used with other techniques and in only one or two sessions. Similar to storybooks, short movies can also be used to open the group members to discussion and expression of feelings through their reactions to what they've read or viewed. Movies are especially useful for reassuring children that their feelings and reactions are normal. Children also benefit because they can typically identify with the characters they see depicted. Depending on the one chosen, games can generate enthusiasm and maximize group interaction. Many specific games have been created for specific subpopulations; they foster cognitive restructuring, behavioral rehearsal, feedback, and positive social behaviors (Yauman, 1991).

According to Sonnenshein-Schneider and Baird (1980), one of the most successful combinations of techniques is brainstorming, role playing, and rehearsal. When a group member expresses a divorce-related concern, the group first brainstorms possible courses of action. The children then role-play and rehearse the solution agreed upon as most likely and beneficial. Teaching children how to clarify and act on their feelings is greatly enhanced by this process because it desensitizes the group to the problems, clarifies the issues, generates active problem solving, and fosters communication.

Remember that techniques should be well thought out; reviewed prior to the group session; and used appropriately, selectively, and intentionally. The purpose of using specific techniques is to facilitate discussion and processing of information in a way that it becomes personally relevant for each child (Yauman, 1991).

Strengths and Resources

One additional suggestion for working with children of divorce involves the importance of attending to the positive aspects of the child's situation. Members must not only be encouraged to mourn their loss, but also to consider the positive aspects of their new family structure. Reframing the divorce and considering the positive events and conditions that have resulted from it is invaluable in changing the child's perception (Yauman, 1991).

Group leaders must set realistic expectations for themselves, the group, and the members. A group counseling experience for children of divorce serves many purposes, including offering support and normalizing feelings. It can result in many positive changes, including improved concentration, mood, social skills, resolution of feelings, and behavior, and overall well-being and adjustment. However, the group will not radically change anyone's situation, nor save any particular child. The loss involved in a divorce is similar in some ways to losing a loved one to death. However, with divorce, there is sometimes no closure and the child often continues to wish for a reunion between the parents. It is important for the leader to recognize this as normal and not as therapeutic failure.

GROUP WORK FOR SOCIAL SKILLS DEFICITS

Group work for children and adolescents capitalizes on the aspect of social interaction, which is pertinent to the developmental process of this age group. According to Bandura (1997), most social learning takes place through observation of the actions and consequences of others. By its very nature then, group counseling provides ample opportunity for this to occur and allows for observation, comparison, interaction, and practice.

Presenting Problems

Positive interactions with others serve as an important protective factor for children and adolescents. Positive peer relationships serve as a safeguard against anxiety, depression, and loneliness and assist in the development of healthy self-worth and social problem solving. However, when social interactions are negative and entail rejection or aggressiveness, children's self-esteem, academic performance, and feelings of belongingness can all be affected (Sim, Whiteside, Dittner, & Mellon, 2006). According to Kupersmidt and Coie (1990), peer rejection is associated with school truancy, suspension, delinquency, and dropout.

A social skills deficit implies that a child does not have the necessary repertoire of social abilities useful in navigating various social situations, avoiding problematic situations, and also building connections and relationships. Though not always, most children with social skills deficits typically have a number of other risk factors. When the lack of appropriate social skills then leads to rejection, isolation, and conflict, the original problems are compounded. In addition, social skills are considered a necessary component for success in life well beyond childhood and adolescence. Among other things, parents and teachers can ask themselves if a child has (1) trouble approaching new groups, (2) difficulty waiting his or her turn in a conversation, (3) trouble discerning appropriate distances from other children, or (4) difficulty managing emotional reactivity (Sim et al., 2006).

The use of social skills training within a group is a popular idea in most school settings. Such training has been supported by extensive reviews of the research showing three skills to be most important to student success. These skills include cognitive skills (e.g., memory, goal setting), social skills (e.g., problem solving, listening), and self-management skills (e.g., motivation, controlling anger). Research findings have been used to support the connection among social, emotional, and academic functioning, with improvements in one area affecting improvements in other areas (Brigman, Webb, & Campbell, 2007).

Specific Leader Qualities

In general, it is both helpful and necessary that the leader can personally demonstrate the social skills in which the group members are to be trained. In other words, potential group leaders need to be socially competent. For instance, if a leader is passive and unable to assert himself, it is going to be difficult for him to then teach and model that behavior to a group member. Similarly, the counselor should be able to distinguish among aggressive, assertive, and passive behavior. At a minimum, the school counselor should be able to establish eye contact, share her emotions assertively, use I-statements, and make direct requests (Rotheram-Borus, Bickford, & Milburn, 2001).

Goals and Objectives

While social skills are extremely important, many members do not have ample opportunity to develop these skills, are lacking the appropriate models or guidance needed to develop them accurately, or are impaired due to emotional or behavioral disorders. The goals of group work for the purpose of social skills training encompass several interrelated objectives. In general, it is important to focus on training a member in nonverbal and verbal skills that will assist him in using more prosocial and appropriate behaviors and also to recognize the impact of his behavior on others. More specifically, children and adolescents should have both the opportunity and guidance to develop skills such as managing emotions, cooperation, compromise, empathy, and listening. Specific goals of social skills training often involve tasks that most adults find commonplace. Meeting friends, making good first impressions, joining groups, praising others, being a good host, coping with teasing, conversation skills, reading social cues, and problem solving to reduce conflict are all examples of such goals. To address these goals, groups typically use education, group activities, exercises, behavior rehearsal techniques, peer feedback, and homework to improve social skills. Practice assignments are heavily relied upon to encourage generalization of skills to other settings and environments outside the group (Sim et al., 2006).

Techniques or Format

The format of a social skills group can vary, but most are either structured discussion groups involving a specific topical agenda or activity groups that go beyond discussion and incorporate guided and purposeful tasks for skill acquisition. An example of a typical activity group might involve a three-step phase for skill acquisition. The first few sessions of the group might provide information about social skills deficits and the benefit of counseling. Sessions falling in the middle portion of the program might incorporate skill-building exercises focused on social cues, social problem solving, assertiveness, and cognitive restructuring. The latter sessions then could provide opportunities to incorporate these skills into actual demonstrations through within-session exposure and homework assignments. During this skill generalization process, parental involvement has been advocated (Schindler, 1999). Researchers suggest that parental involvement can improve treatment outcomes regarding skill acquisition and use outside-the-group environments (Kolko, Loar, & Sturnick, 1990). Specifically, research findings have been used to support parental involvement because it has been found to result in improved social skills ratings and decreased aggression (Frankel, Myatt, Cantwell, & Feinberg, 1997).

Several social skills training programs have been designed specifically for the counselor and have been shown through research to be effective (Rotheram-Borus, Bickford, & Milburn, 2001). Typically these programs are theory driven and enjoyable, and they require repeated practice of new skills. Most social skills training programs have a manual that specifies exactly what is needed to conduct the group. Activities, exercises, and often an exact example for carrying out intended objectives are provided. It is also typical to find role-play scenes, self-assessments, and homework exercises included.

One such skills program, the Assertive Communication Training (ACT) Game, was designed specifically for children in grades 3 through 6, some of whom are lacking in social skills and some who are socially skilled. The idea is to have skilled members serve as learning models for those who are not skilled. Also, social skills training is considered to improve the adjustment of all children regardless of skill deficit or attainment, and so was implemented at the classroom level for all children through the use of the ACT Game. Typically, a problematic social situation is presented by the leader, and members are chosen to role-play the situation, with the roles of facilitative coaches, dilemma-presenting challenger, and problem-solving actor being filled by the members. The leader usually plays the role of director and guides the role play in an appropriate and meaningful direction (Rotheram-Borus et al., 2001).

Student Success Skills (SSS), another social skills training program, is designed to teach academic, social, and self-management skills. This program focuses directly on improving student behavior and academic achievement and aligns itself with the American School Counselor Association (ASCA) *National Model* (Brigman et al., 2007). Under the SSS, the group meets for eight weekly and four monthly sessions, each lasting approximately 45 minutes. Each session focuses on skills necessary for improved social, self-management, and academic skills. Specific strategies of this group include music, movement, storytelling, role playing, and peer coaching.

Specifically, the SSS group follows a specific format for each group meeting, meaning that each session is conducted in a three-part series. In the beginning of any particular session, the group focuses on setting goals and monitoring progress. During the middle portion of the group, members work toward solving a social problem specific to each identified issue using dramatization and feedback. The end of each group session is used to report progress in each area specific to the group through a formal instrument, and members are encouraged to report any useful tools they learned (Brigman et al., 2007).

Children suitable for social skills training groups typically have poor listening skills, low frustration tolerance, inability to perceive social cues, inappropriate social boundaries, difficulty expressing themselves, passivity, or aggressiveness. The very characteristics that are in need of remediation also contribute to difficult group processes. Because group work is a social environment and because the members of a social skills group are likely to have poor social skills, smaller groups, typically around six members, are suggested for optimal results. More than six members can become counterproductive because members will learn from one another as intended, but inappropriate behaviors may be learned instead of newer and more socially appropriate ones (Schindler, 1999).

Summary

Group work is effective with both children and adolescents for a variety of reasons. Important considerations are involved when conducting group work for individuals in various developmental stages, and with specific issues. When group leaders are prepared and intentional, and when they understand the needs of the group, positive outcomes are most likely.

Recall that group settings are natural social environments and therefore are highly influential. The group leader facilitates a positive group environment because peer influences and feedback actively shape each group member. Confidentiality is a concern with this particular population, and the group leader must take extra care to make certain that children understand the limits of confidentiality. Parents of these children can also press the group leader for information about their child, and a balance has to be achieved between a parent's right to know and a child's right to confidentiality. The size and structure of the group are especially important considerations. Typically, the younger the members, the shorter the sessions and the smaller the group should be. In general, knowledge of child development can be of great use when planning and implementing group counseling for children.

Group counseling is often the preferred treatment approach for adolescents; however, it is not without special concerns. Disruptiveness, withdrawal, cliques, inappropriate disclosure, and poor boundaries are all special issues related to group work with adolescents. A lack of motivation can be especially problematic. Thus, it is important for group leaders to help members reframe their thoughts about participating in group. Leaders should also remind themselves to use resistance in a therapeutic manner, avoid becoming defensive, resist personalizing adolescent behavior, model appropriate behavior, and remain both firm and fair. Finally, because peers are so influential at this stage, it is even more important for group members to be vigilant in screening and keeping behavior productive during the group. If group interactions are not appropriate, according to the rules and limits set early within the group, leaders must attend to this immediately, keeping in mind that they are the group leader and not a peer.

This chapter offered overviews of three specific groups commonly used with children and adolescents. First, groups used for children of alcoholics can become distorted if the family of origin is emulated within the group setting, with similar dynamics and norms. The group leader must keep this in mind to better understand within-group processes and use them to facilitate healing and changed behaviors. This environment can be especially helpful in assisting members to try new coping responses in a setting that feels similar to their home environment. Additional treatment goals include providing a safe place to talk honestly in an effort to combat secrecy, confronting common characteristics of denial and guilt, education regarding the disease of alcoholism, and the identification and recovery of feelings that have been distorted or lost.

Second, group work is the most effective treatment modality for children of divorce. Not only does the group setting provide safety in numbers, it can also be validating, supportive, and encouraging of emotional expression. A group that is structured and has clear and fair rules is especially important for these members because they often continue to experience uncertainty and a changing environment. The group techniques used most often for this population include bibliotherapy, movies, board games, drawings, brainstorming, role playing, and puppets. Techniques should always be well thought out; reviewed prior to the group session; and used appropriately, selectively, and intentionally. Also, when working with this population, the positive aspects of the child's situation must be stressed. In other words, children must be encouraged to mourn their loss and also to consider the positive aspects of their new family structure.

Finally, social skills groups for children and adolescents were reviewed. The very nature of group work is such that social learning takes place. Such groups are widely used within the school setting because the relationships between social functioning and behavior, as well as social functioning and academics, have both been established in research. Social competence is viewed as a buffer against trauma, crisis, anxiety, and depression. Likewise, the lack of social skills, which will ultimately lead to conflict and rejection among peers, compounds the effects of risk factors already existing within the child. The most often cited school-related issues affected by a social skills deficit include school truancy, delinquency, dropout, and lower grades. Many social skills programs provide for learning that is structured to improve the chances for positive social learning and skill acquisition. Due to the nature of the socially deficient child, smaller groups of around six children are recommended. Within these groups, which must be led by socially competent counselors, skills such as nonverbal behaviors, compromise, listening skills, and emotion regulation are taught through a variety of techniques, including role play, education, peer feedback, and homework.

Regardless of the developmental stage of the group or the specific issue to be addressed, the effective and competent group leader must be intentional and purposeful in every stage of the development and implementation of the group: the initial planning of the group; screening of the members; deciding on specific mechanics of location and the number, frequency, and duration of sessions; setting of rules and guidelines; choosing activities and interventions; and facilitating the group process itself. Knowledge specific to each group and awareness of member characteristics and needs assists this process.

CHAPTER 20

Group Work with Adult Populations

Susan H. Eaves and Carl J. Sheperis

PREVIEW

This chapter addresses aspects of group work with adults, including the basic principles of group work with elderly clients, survivors and perpetrators of sexual abuse, and substance abuse.

GROUP WORK WITH MEMBERS IN YOUNG AND MIDDLE ADULTHOOD

While adulthood covers more than twice the number of years as childhood and adolescence combined, most people, including adults themselves, tend to simplify the process of adulthood, assuming it to be a time of smoother development. However, adulthood can be a complex period of development. For this reason, it is especially important to look at the issues inherent in adulthood as they may apply to group work processes. What is known about adulthood is that it spans much of one's life (from approximately age 20 to 65 years) and it encompasses a number of developmental, social, emotional, and psychological issues. Early in adulthood, issues of intimacy and identity continue to be of primary importance. In middle adulthood, issues related to generativity and the aging process are the focus. Men; women; parents; nonparents; and single, married, divorced, and widowed adults experience the process of adulthood differently. Each group leader must seek information to better understand the specific life stage and issues of importance when working with adult groups.

Relevant Developmental Issues

Counselors employ both psychoeducational and therapeutic groups to explore issues of adulthood. The transitions inherent in this part of the life cycle are eased in the group setting because members can talk to and identify with others in similar situations. The scope of this chapter does not allow for an extended discussion on developmental issues related to adulthood. However, we provide some examples, grounded in Erikson's stages, that may be relevant for group counseling. For instance, young adults typically feel pressure to establish a career, become emotionally and financially independent from their family of origin, and perhaps settle into their own primary relationship and begin a family. Behaviors and activities that were accepted in the recent past are suddenly no longer appropriate (e.g., college student-type social activities). Young adults face the decision to move forward with their cohort or get left behind, the latter leading possibly to loneliness and isolation. Although age expectations for this behavior are changing, young adults who delay making adult commitments are still sometimes criticized by mainstream society. Many floundering and unproductive young adults fail to mature and transition. Still others rush through this process and prematurely take on responsibilities of marriage and family life, potentially leading to overwhelming feelings plagued by doubt and resentment. Group work can play a role in addressing the anxiety, depression, loneliness, frustration, and confusion felt by many young adults.

Somewhere between the late 30s and early 40s, early adulthood ends and middle adulthood begins, typically lasting until around age 65 years. Middle adulthood is a time for evaluating the life that has been lived thus far and making decisions and adjustments to be enacted in the remaining years. For some, this midlife transition can be difficult because the realization of mortality becomes obvious. When adults remain in denial of their own mortality, they are more prone to behaviors designed to escape, overcompensate, or decompensate. When they can incorporate the reality of death into their lives, they typically focus on generativity, or working to benefit others, and self-actualization, or fulfilling their potential. These same adults are often also coping with their aging parents and launching their children. Groups for the midlife adult are varied and primarily focus on learning, wellness, and change. Other groups, however, focus on specific issues related to children, abuse, stress, career, and grief, among numerous other potential topics.

Gender Differences

Men and women share many commonalities in adulthood, but they may differ dramatically in their approach to their concerns. Within a group setting, men and women may participate very differently as well. For women, primary issues of focus in group work may center on being seen, being heard, reduced guilt for expressing oneself, and being real rather than simply being nice. In other words, prescribed roles dictated by society often affect women negatively. Women may feel an inconsistency between what they feel and what is socially acceptable to express. Historically, women have been expected to support others, with little support for themselves. Men, too, have been heavily influenced by socialization and societal expectations. Men are socialized to hide any traits they may possess that are considered feminine, such as sensitivity and emotional expression, and to display competitive and powerful behaviors. Because of this, they often struggle with conflicting drives, too. In general, men are often considered even more restricted in their behavioral repertoire than women; that is, men are often viewed as "set in their ways."

Within groups, women tend to differ from men in a number of ways. Women are often more verbal than men, yet they feel shame for their verbalizations afterward and attempt to withdraw. Women identify other group members' nonverbal cues more readily and accurately. Women also tend to be caregivers, which can lead to more supportive behaviors in groups but can also turn into rescuing. Men often have difficulty participating in a group because of strict sex-role traditions involving verbalization and emotional expression. With skillful leadership in a group, men can benefit from group participation by learning to clarify gender roles and receiving support for the struggles associated with being providers and protectors. Both men and women can learn to manage and combine the often opposing sides of themselves that society attempts to keep separate according to prescribed gender roles.

GROUP WORK WITH ELDERLY PERSONS

America is graying as a population. Individuals over age 65 years are the fastest growing segment of the U.S. population. As a result, the need for social services among this population is also growing. Although the population of older Americans has increased 30-fold since 1870, availability of counseling services for the elderly have generally not kept pace. The reasons for this are varied, but they include stereotypical thinking, such as ageism, or the acceptance of negative myths associated with the elderly. Elderly persons are in fact creative, capable of change, and full of knowledge, and they continue to lead meaningful lives. While some are certainly more active than others, elderly persons in general continue to participate in life, especially as it revolves around family.

Stage of Life Issues

Given the fact that many older individuals live happy and productive lives, those who might participate in group counseling tend to have specific problems related to this phase of life (e.g., adjustment to retirement, chronic health problems, widowhood). In this section, we address issues specific to older individuals who are experiencing some level of psychological distress and who might participate in group counseling. For older individuals who struggle with phase-of-life changes, there is often an accompanying breakdown in social support systems. Those belonging to a minority culture or who are considered financially poor have an even more difficult time with such adjustments. Issues related to financial costs of aging, medical care, loss, loneliness, social isolation, purposelessness, despair, fear, and regret are prevalent when working with the elderly (Moody, 2002).

The above-mentioned concerns specific to the elderly population can be attended to in a group format. In fact, group work is especially helpful to elderly who feel loneliness and isolation because it provides a source of socialization and support. Due to retirement and the loss of friends and family members to death, an elderly person's social group may be lost, making her or him more vulnerable to depression and physical ailments. Through participation in a group, a sense of belongingness and purpose is enhanced. If their life experiences

and wisdom can be of use to another group member, elderly people feel a sense of contribution and empowerment. Groups offer a unique advantage over other therapeutic tools when used with this population (Thomas & Martin, 1992).

Benefits of Participation

Group work serves to promote the renewal of social interaction at a time when support systems are their weakest. Group members join together to work through common problems and thus can develop a more realistic and positive self-image through the reflection of others. They are able to develop increased self-respect and self-worth, leading to greater involvement in the experience of living. The elderly often need to be heard and understood. The group provides an ideal atmosphere of support, enabling members to share and relate concerns related to aging as well as to connect central meanings and disconnected parts of life (Thomas & Martin, 1992).

Groups can also provide an atmosphere for learning of new knowledge and a place to try new behaviors. Like groups for other ages, groups for the elderly focus either on issues specific to counseling or education. The most common groups for elderly persons involve reality testing, investment in life, life review, and adjustment. Reality orientation assists those who are disoriented as to time and place and can also help prevent further cognitive deterioration. Participants in this group are typically hospitalized (inpatient) and seriously mentally impaired. Investment in life groups, or remotivation, help less severely impaired members, both inpatient and outpatient, gain renewed interest and involvement in their surroundings. In this way, mental processes are stimulated and active involvement in life is encouraged (Thomas & Martin, 1992).

Reminiscing, or life review, groups include more functional and independent members and work with such members in an effort to enhance their sense of belonging and continuity. Reconstructing a positive past is also important, as is identifying themes to create meaning.

Adjustment groups, also called psychotherapy groups, help members work through adjustments inherent with aging in order to lessen feelings of fear and loneliness (Thomas & Martin, 1992). Other groups for this population focus on specific topics of concern to the particular group, such as widowhood, grief, health, or sexuality. Additional groups of value for the elderly may focus on physical fitness, occupational therapy, music and art therapy, dance and movement, family therapy, or assertion training, among many other topics.

Leader Characteristics and Skills

When working with groups comprised of elderly persons, leadership skills are similar to those necessary when working with other groups. There are some distinct differences, however, requiring more than a kind disposition and a fondness for this age group. The effective group leader perceives aging as a transition stage in the process of self-actualization and also recognizes the importance of linking the present to a meaningful past. Awareness and sensitivity to the specific issues common to this population are also important. Leaders must often come to terms with their own eventual death and issues surrounding aging in order to best serve elderly persons. In fact, Hawkins (1983) suggested imagining your own life at this stage of development, and asking yourself what concerns and issues might be important to you. As a leader, the most important characteristics you can display with this group are that of a listener and a supporter/encourager. That is not to say that you should never use more active skills with members of this age group; it is a reminder to you that the typical elderly person will benefit most from a supportive, encouraging environment and group where she or her can engage in conversation (Thomas & Martin, 1992).

Potential Pitfalls

Most unsuccessful groups for older persons fail due to inappropriate member selection. Screening is important and requires some specialized skills.

The leader must be able to assess cognitive functioning, sensory deficits, memory loss, mobility, attention span, ability to communicate, and mental disorders. These aspects must be explored in order to determine member appropriateness for group treatment, and for which type of group. Also important to consider when working with this population is the physical setting of the group meetings. Typically, warmer temperatures are needed for comfort, and larger rooms may be necessary for wheelchair mobility. Leaders should also consider level of impairment when deciding on frequency and length of sessions. In general, the greater the impairment, the greater the frequency and the shorter the length of group meetings (Thomas & Martin, 1992).

Also important to keep in mind is that the overall pace of these groups will need to be slower. Be aware that medication, physical or psychological difficulties, and onset of senility may interfere with members being fully present in the group. Regular attendance at sessions may also be difficult due to appointments, illness, and transportation problems. As a group leader, make certain not to stereotype your group members, even if they have already been labeled and categorized by the mental health system. Do not assume that all older persons are kind and subtle. The same difficult member types that you see in younger groups may show up in these groups as well. Attempt to understand the broader meaning of such negative behaviors. Also, do not treat this older group of adults as you would children. While the group should not be about meaningless busywork, neither should it be about confrontation and strong emotional catharses. In general, group leaders working with an elderly population should have caring and respect for older people, a desire to learn from them, sensitivity to their burdens, and a healthy attitude regarding their own eventual aging and death (Corey & Corey, 2006).

As with other age groups, special knowledge is required when working with the elderly because it is important to understand the unique issues that face adults in this phase of life. However, it cannot be overstated that, in addition to this knowledge, it is imperative that leaders remain aware of their own feelings in relation to this age group, how they feel about their own mortality, and what stereotypical thinking patterns they hold. Issues of age bias and countertransference can interfere with successful therapeutic outcomes and may have negative consequences for the elderly adult. When the group setting is supportive, it can assist the older adult in working through concerns, regain control of life, and reactivate social interaction so that the final years will be ones of fulfillment and dignity.

GROUP WORK WITH SURVIVORS AND PERPETRATORS OF SEXUAL ABUSE

Depending on how abuse is defined, it can be estimated that between one-third and one-half of all women in the United States experience some form of sexual abuse during their lifetimes. Regarding the effects of sexual abuse, several factors contribute to the level of trauma experienced by the victim. First, the family atmosphere in which the abuse occurred seems to play the most significant role in terms of outcome. Individuals whose families are viewed as unsupportive, blaming the victim, neglectful, or dealing with substance abuse seemed to have the most difficulty coping with the sexual abuse. Second, the younger the age at which the abuse occurs, the more devastating the effects on the survivor. Third, the more violent the abuse, the more traumatic the effects. Of all the forms of sexual abuse, father-daughter incest is considered the most difficult to recover from, primarily due to the beliefs society holds regarding fathers as protectors. The child who is abused by a father has to accept that the father did not protect her *and* caused direct and purposeful harm (Newbauer & Hess, 1994; Turner, 1993).

A host of psychological effects can occur as a result of sexual abuse, and they will differ from person to person, with no two survivors reacting the same. A person's crisis history, support network, emotional stability, coping skills, and unique experience of abuse, including the type of abuse, the perpetrator, and the reaction of

others, will all affect the range, duration, and severity of symptoms that the survivor experiences. In general, survivors of sexual abuse typically report depression, shame, guilt, anxiety, worthlessness, lowered self-esteem, stigmatization, isolation, anger, difficulty trusting, problems with sexuality, obsessive-compulsive tendencies, self-destructive behaviors, and perhaps dissociation (Darongkamas, Madden, Swarbrick, & Evans, 1995; Turner, 1993).

Benefits of Group Membership

Despite the high number of sexual abuse survivors and knowledge about the resulting trauma, society continues to send the message that sexual abuse is not to be talked about. Because victims are so often silenced, feelings of isolation and alienation are increased. Belonging to a group designed specifically for survivors of sexual abuse not only allows the communication and open discussion prohibited by society, it also provides a safe environment in order to encourage such openness. It is believed that each time a survivor speaks about her experiences, she distances herself from the pain. The more she talks, the less power the abuse has and therefore the less victimized she feels. Such a group is believed to foster a sense of empowerment and a connection to others, and to facilitate the ability to trust, a trait that is nearly always shattered after abuse occurs (Turner, 1993).

Group counseling and psychotherapy are thought to be the most effective and timely treatment modality for survivors of sexual abuse because it allows for the ventilation of feelings necessary for the construction of a new cognitive framework, or simply a new perception of the abuse (Darongkamas et al., 1995; Herder & Redner, 1991). These goals can also be accomplished in individual therapy. The difference between group and individual therapy lies in the all-in-the-same-boat idea, described by Shulman (1992). Essentially, a group setting enables survivors to share among others who feel similarly, thus lessening isolation and providing a sense of relief. Within a group therapy format, the members are as healing to one another as the leader is to each member (Darongkamas et al., 1995; Turner, 1993).

Not only is the group setting conducive to treating the symptoms associated with abuse, the therapeutic social interactions can also greatly reduce feelings of isolation, aloneness, and shame. Another benefit that a group experience provides is that it replicates family dynamics. Because of this group trait, each member has the opportunity to explore behaviors learned in the family of origin that might be influencing behavior (Marotta & Asner, 1999). Ideally, the group has a skilled leader and restorative and nurturing members, and functions as a healthy surrogate family. In this way, members are further supported, learn that boundaries are respected, begin to trust again, and practice new and healthier behaviors (deYoung & Corbin, 1994).

A final note regarding group counseling and psychotherapy as preferred treatment options for sexually abused individuals revolves around one of the dangers of individual treatment with this population. Individual therapy can have characteristics that may in some ways feel similar to the abusive relationship because both an abusive relationship and individual therapy are emotionally intense dyadic relationships based on trust, but with an unbalanced power relationship. Group therapy, on the other hand, emphasizes equal and open relationships and reduces secrecy (deYoung & Corbin, 1994).

Assessment in Sexual Abuse Groups

As with any group experience, decisions have to be made regarding screening and selection of group members. While screening criteria are well documented for group inclusion in general, some specific guidelines are needed when screening members for a sexual abuse group; deYoung and Corbin (1994) stressed the importance of this phase in group preparedness and emphasized that each member selected must be ready for the group experience. Readiness is assumed if the member is no longer being abused, is not in contact with the perpetrator,

has a support system, has a willingness to share with others in the group, and is ready to realize the impact the abuse has had on current functioning and decision making.

For the group experience to be therapeutic rather than damaging, it is important for each member selected to have ego strength and be able to cope with what occurs within the group. Potential members should have a positive opinion about their potential inclusion into the group (Darongkamas et al., 1995). Herman and Schatzow (1984) even weighted this factor as more important than other factors in predicting successful group outcomes. Prior therapy and disclosure of the abuse is preferred, too. For instance, if a potential member had just become aware of past abuse or had just recently disclosed it to a helping professional, group participation would need to be postponed until individual work had been done. Someone new to treatment for this issue tends to be in a crisis mode and requires much more individual attention than a group format can provide (Darongkamas et al., 1995).

When screening potential members, it is preferred that the potential member's personal life is relatively stable from day to day. *Stability* is a relative term for each individual. However, it might prove beneficial to exclude members who have had recent hospitalizations or suicide attempts. Though it is expected for some mental health symptoms to be present, those with active psychotic symptoms should also be excluded. Not only would these members be too fragile for the group setting, they might also overwhelm other group members and become a counterproductive force in the group experience. A potential group member should perceive and accept the sexual abuse as a primary problem or main impetus for the problematic issues currently being experienced.

Conjoint Group and Individual Counseling with Survivors of Sexual Abuse

One final issue debated in the professional literature involves concomitant group and individual counseling with survivors of sexual abuse.

Herman and Schatzow (1984) considered an on-going relationship with an individual counselor a necessary criterion for inclusion in a sexual abuse group. Likewise, deYoung and Corbin (1994) also stated the importance of ongoing individual therapy during the course of group work in order for each member to continue gaining insights initiated in the group as well as to work on issues unrelated to the sexual abuse. However, it was the reasonable opinion of Darongkamas et al. (1995) that concurrent individual work may take away from the group experience and that any difficulties that arise from participation in the group should be discussed as part of the group process. In this way, insights generated from the group process are fed back into the group process rather than being topics for isolated discussions with individual counselors.

Format

Less than four members or more than ten members make establishing a healthy group dynamic difficult, especially with this population. For sexual abuse groups specifically, five to six members seems to be the most frequently cited number (Marotta & Asner, 1999). The length of the group, duration, frequency of meetings, and whether it is open or closed will often be determined by treatment goals, clinical setting, and the age range of the members (i.e., children, adolescents, young adults, middle-age adults, or elderly adults). However, it is generally agreed that, if possible, groups should be closed and time-limited. The closed group format promotes trust, cohesion, safety, and some degree of predictability, all of which are paramount to survivors of sexual abuse. When groups are time-limited, it encourages members to focus and work toward their goals more efficiently, and also provides a sense of closure and completion (Darongkamas et al., 1995; deYoung & Corbin, 1994; Marotta & Asner, 1999).

Group rules, including those related to attendance, timeliness, and being respectful to other members, are essential for the development of trust and the protection of members.

However, rules without reasons can lead to rebellion for some group members, while others may become overly compliant. When setting rules, keep in mind their purpose, limitations, and exceptions because these group members have experienced the abuse of power and authority. In addition to rules, structure is also important. Each group meeting should have a structured format, yet enough flexibility to be responsive to the needs of the group at that moment. The goal is to provide enough structure to promote safety and predictability, yet allow enough flexibility that the members feel they have autonomy and choices because these are especially important issues for sexual abuse survivors (Darongkamas et al., 1995; deYoung & Corbin, 1994).

In addition to reducing feelings of isolation, shame, oddity, and alienation, sexual abuse groups also serve the function of resocialization within a surrogate family. Such groups assist in transforming secretiveness into openness, confusion into certainty, and numbness into expression. Group members work toward creating meaning from the chaos following the abuse. Hearing others' stories serves as a mirroring process. Giving and receiving feedback is empowering. Seeing rules set, explained, and followed builds a sense of safety and trust in the group, which then transfers to the members' larger environments outside the group. Insight can be gained into the effects the abuse has on current functioning. As the group leader normalizes the thoughts and feelings of each member, survivors are able to reorganize perceptions and reinterpret events so that they no longer assume responsibility. Overall, traumatic memories are perceived in a new way so that they may be more easily incorporated, thereby giving them less power (deYoung & Corbin, 1994).

Models of Sexual Abuse Group Treatment

Group counseling and psychotherapy for victims of sexual abuse have been so widely advocated that many formats have been created solely for that purpose. One such model is trauma-focused sexual abuse treatment groups that focus on adolescents. Probably the main element of this group is the member's disclosure about the experience of sexual abuse. The leader goes to great lengths to facilitate storytelling and even uses a guided exercise. If a member has already had the experience of family members, law enforcement officers, or child welfare professionals disbelieving the details of her story, she may be very reluctant about having that same experience with the group leader. The guided exercise acts as a prompt for sharing details. It begins with an affirmation that reinforces each member's control over the disclosure, and relieves each girl of responsibility for the sexual abuse. The guided exercise then suggests the details of the sexual abuse that are important to the story, such as who the perpetrator was, how many times the abuse occurred, the pressures for secrecy, the impact it had, and the nonabusive parent's response to it. The exercise then ends with an affirmation of each member's right to respect and safety (deYoung & Corbin, 1994).

Although telling the story has great value, it is not enough. The task of the leader, therefore, is to normalize these thoughts and feelings, reorganize perceptions, and provide a new interpretation that relieves the survivors of responsibility. As a result, traumatic memories are transformed so that they may be incorporated more easily into the member's life (deYoung & Corbin, 1994).

The "new family" model is a therapeutic group for adult survivors of sexual abuse. The focus of the group is on altering behavior within a family and developmental context. Behaviors that were initially adaptive responses, or conditioned reactions to abuse during childhood but were elaborated upon and generalized over time, are seen as inappropriate in the victim's adult personality. Because revictimization by self and others continues into adulthood, it is necessary to identify and confront family structure and family-of-origin roles and rules of the past. Each group member is encouraged to move away from the view of the victimized child and develop a healthier view of self and family. The process of

changing behavior is accomplished through the group as members become the survivor's surrogate family. Each member is given half an hour to describe the family of origin, the abuse, and maladaptive coping mechanisms affecting present thoughts and behaviors. After each presentation, other group members are asked to give immediate verbal support (Kreidler & Fluharty, 1994).

Male Victims of Sexual Abuse

Men molested as children are often overlooked because male sexual abuse is underreported, and male victims are much less likely to seek help than female victims. Studies show that as many as 16% of men are sexually abused as children or adolescents. Some symptoms more common in male than female victims include normalization of the abuse, homophobic concerns, sexual identity confusion, sexual compulsiveness, difficulty dealing with anger, aggression, and wariness of other men (Thomas & Nelson, 1994).

A process group for males who were abused as children and adolescents has been formatted to address the specific problems associated with being a male victim (Thomas & Nelson, 1994). This process group recommends an ongoing experience with no set time to end. It is believed that healing from sexual abuse is a process, and each member has to resolve a different combination of issues. A structured group with set expectations and time limits may cause more harm than good. It is emphasized that recovery is a process that involves several stages and steps, and no one follows the same pattern. Long-term group counseling is necessary to treat the total problem rather than simply treating the symptoms.

Treating Sex Offenders Using Group Counseling and Psychotherapy

Not only have group approaches been used for treating survivors of sexual abuse, group counseling and psychotherapy have also been highly recommended for treatment of sex offenders. Treatment of survivors and offenders in the same group is very controversial, has been tried, and is not recommended.

Group therapy for sex offenders is often at a disadvantage before it even begins. First, many agencies and helping professionals are reluctant to work with this type of offender. Second, most treatment groups for this population are involuntary and mandated by the court system. Perpetrators of sexual abuse are usually required to attend, and therefore they are reluctant to engage in this type of group work. These two dynamics paired together create barriers to the therapeutic process. Therapy viewed as punishment is seldom effective. While group counseling and psychotherapy with this population is challenging, the manipulative tendencies of the typical offender are often addressed effectively by other group members, making group work much more effective than individual therapy with this population.

As early as the 1970s, groups for sex offenders were being used for the prevention of abuse reoccurrence. In one early group program, Mickow (1973) required attendance, with one of the only exceptions for leaving the group being exclusion by the group's unanimous vote. In other words, group members were allowed to remove a group member if this person's participation was felt to be harmful to the group. Mandatory attendance for the members was possible because they were parolees and still under court order. Mandatory attendance was viewed as necessary because past experience showed that members lost motivation for participating somewhere after the third or fourth session.

Mickow (1973) further discussed techniques used with this population and found that insight-oriented approaches "created more problems for the clients than they solved" (p. 99). Offenders often manipulated their environment to purposely place themselves in unsupervised situations with children, often the same age as the victims of their offenses. Mickow stated that, in these instances, direct confrontation typically did not work, but a present-oriented approach seemed to work best. The group did not respond well to an unstructured, democratic setting because as discussion dissipated, subgrouping

occurred, or one member would dominate the discussions.

Some of the goals of a member in a group for perpetrators of sexual abuse include the following: to protect the community, to prevent additional offenses, to develop empathy, to manage emotions, to increase responsibility, to improve decision making, to develop boundaries, to enhance relationship skills, and to develop a reoffending prevention plan (Corey & Corey, 2006). Leaders should use a combination of humanistic, cognitive-behavioral, and experiential techniques, along with confrontation as required. Feedback, role plays, and homework can be used to work on issues such as intimacy, conflict, pressures, and past offenses.

Working with sexual offenders in any capacity is not an easy task for a host of reasons. To improve the likelihood of successful group outcomes, some important steps can be taken. First, screening members is especially important with this population. Corey and Corey (2006) insisted that, in order to be accepted into a treatment group for sexual offenses, the potential member must be at low to moderate risk for reoffense, have an adequate support system, be supervised, and must admit to some of the offenses that he has been accused of. Second, contracts containing very specific rules and guidelines for acceptable behavior during the group is especially necessary. Such contracts may need to be more thorough and strict than with other populations. When members act in a manner inconsistent with guidelines, group leaders must hold them accountable. Third, member resistance should be explored rather than ignored or diverted, with leaders making sure to acknowledge whatever issues and emotions may be contributing to the resistance. Finally, leaders must remind themselves often that by helping sexual offenders, they are helping to prevent further sexual assaults.

GROUP WORK AND ADDICTIONS

Addictive behaviors encompass a variety of issues, including food, gambling, sexual activity, and substances. Many characteristics pertinent to these types of groups span across addictive issues; however, some are specific to a particular addiction and do not necessarily apply to others. For the purposes of this chapter, group work with addictions in general will be discussed; when information pertains only to a particular addiction, such an acknowledgment will be made.

Group counseling and psychotherapy are the most common treatment modalities for persons suffering from addictions, and they are also commonly considered an essential and core aspect of treatment (Line & Cooper, 2002; Weiss, Jaffee, de Menil, & Cogley, 2004). In addition to the obvious cost-effectiveness of the group format, the dominant use of group work with members with addictions is related to the strong influence of peer groups. The influence of others who have experienced similar problems is especially relevant in reducing the denial, rationalization, and minimization that is so common among individuals with addictions. Not only does the feeling of sameness reduce these common defenses, so, too, does the fact that group members are able to support and confront one another. As group members challenge one another's distorted interpretations of behavior, defenses lessen more quickly than might be expected in individual therapy. Group members who share the commonality of addiction tend to trust other members more readily than the group leader, who may be viewed as an authority figure (Line & Cooper, 2002).

Group work essential in confronting the typical defenses of members with addictions, and it is also an integral part of healing the shame that is commonly present and that typically contributes to additional addictive behaviors. Individuals with addictions often engage in secretive behavior and internalize negative societal perceptions. As members get to know one another, empathy and understanding for other members develop. This in turn leads to self-empathy and self-understanding as members realize that others also have misguided rationales for their addictive behavior and are not inherently "bad." In addition, group leaders should provide a safe and nonjudgmental atmosphere to facilitate shame reduction (Line & Cooper, 2002).

Although various treatment approaches have proven effective with addictive behaviors, group work is especially promising because it uses various strategies to increase social support, social skills, coping responses, and role changes. The group itself becomes a microcosm of each member's personal society so that members may reflect on their lives and the dynamics of their addictions in order to recognize and overcome issues that interfere with their recovery. In addition, group work should ideally contribute to members' recognition of the void created by addiction, and help them to reflect on ignored emotions, understand their motivations for addictive behavior, and decide how to behave without their addiction (Washington & Moxley, 2003). A final goal of group work with addiction is to assist members to develop more appropriate coping responses for negative emotions, situations, and issues. Members should learn healthier strategies (e.g., using others for support, honest communication, self-care) to replace old habits (e.g., sexual acting out, eating, substance use) (Line & Cooper, 2002).

Certain member characteristics appear with chemically addicted populations that bear mentioning here because they will no doubt affect group processes. Persons who are chemically dependent often exhibit behaviors that can interfere with both the ability to develop effective communication and interpersonal relationships, characteristics necessary for successful group outcomes. During times of substance use, social, personal, and work activities are negatively affected because time is diverted away from these life areas and instead used for the addictive behavior. Because of this neglect and preoccupation, dysfunctional and maladaptive behaviors emerge. Among such behaviors are compulsiveness, impulsiveness, overspending, overeating, hypersexuality, depression, low self-worth, societal estrangement, social isolation, impaired judgment, aggressiveness, rebelliousness, and anger (Campbell & Page, 1993).

Not all persons with addictions are equally well suited for group work. Those who have particular personality features may be unable to attach emotionally, which is a necessary component of successful group work. Many members are openly defiant, rebellious, or conning, all of which can undermine the potential work of other group members. It is preferable to have like-minded individuals in a group, thereby increasing the chances of effectiveness. This is not always possible, so it is important for the group leader to keep in mind that most persons with addictions have a commonality regardless of their addiction or their personality traits. Typically, most members with addictions are looking outside themselves for an escape that keeps them from facing their inward emptiness (Flores, 1997).

Other factors that call for special consideration with this population are lack of motivation to change, lack of engagement, retention issues, and co-occurring disorders. When working specifically with chemical addiction, symptoms of physiological withdrawal may also interfere with group work. Also, for those who are chemically addicted, if substance abuse began in adolescence, research has showed completion of crucial developmental tasks was likely delayed. For instance, development of prosocial behavior, interpersonal skills, and the assumption of family and work responsibilities are often delayed because the necessary opportunities and coping skills are not realized when an adolescent engages in heavy substance use (Waldron & Kaminer, 2004). All of these factors can impede group work and, at a minimum, should be a consideration of group leaders.

In a review of the existing literature on group work for addiction, Weiss et al. (2004) identified five common models of group work for persons with addictions: (1) the education model, where the leader acts as a teacher, educating members about addiction; (2) the recovery skills training model, where the leader teaches specific skills to decrease relapse; (3) the group process model, where outcomes are a result of group process and interaction; (4) the check-in model, which entails brief individual assessments within the group; and (5) the specific issue group model, where the focus is on an issue related to the addiction. While these same authors found few differences among group therapy models or focus in terms of treatment effectiveness, Washington and Moxley (2003) urged group leaders to be intentional and diligent in selecting group interventions so that the group experience is tailored to the individual needs of the members. While group work in general was shown to be effective with individuals with addictions, it is uncertain which group characteristics and interventions truly contribute to recovery. The different phases of recovery, various needs of group members, and diverse social issues should be taken into account when developing an addiction group.

Others (Flores, 1997; Line & Cooper, 2002) also point out that group work with addicted persons should look different in the beginning stages of the group as compared to the latter, as well as for those new to the recovery system compared to those who have done work in the past. Specifically, Flores (1997) stated that the group leader should provide high levels of support and structure in the beginning sessions of the group. As members increase their recovery time, however, confrontation is necessary to encourage the members to look at themselves and their lives honestly and to deal with the very feelings they have been avoiding. Forcing this view of oneself too early, however, can lead to anxiety or depression and possibly trigger relapse. Similarly, Line and Cooper (2002) suggested a high level of structure, psychoeducation, and a cognitive-behavioral approach in the beginning of group because this often feels *safer* to new members.

Dayton (2005) also agreed that leaders developing treatment approaches should be concerned with whether the issues of grief will undermine a group member's sobriety. Many persons with addictions have self-medicated (e.g., with drugs, alcohol, food, sex, gambling) as a way to manage their emotional pain. This pain may reemerge during the recovery process when these self-medicating tools are no longer an available option. Members may need to grieve for lost time, often years that were spent in addiction, and for the pain they have caused others. In general, in early recovery, members with addictions may not benefit from revisiting painful matter from the past because it can trigger relapse. However, the very opposite can be true in later recovery. Avoiding such painful material after the group member has developed ego strength and support can undermine recovery (Dayton, 2005).

GROUP WORK WITH CLIENTS WITH CHRONIC ILLNESS

In recent years, counselors have expanded their treatment to include persons coping with health issues, chronic illness, and disease. Clients respond to medical diagnoses and treatments in psychological ways that directly affect their quality of life and, potentially, even their life expectancy (Greer, 2002; Wenzel & Robinson, 1995). Faced with a new diagnosis such as cancer, human immunodeficiency virus (HIV), or fibromyalgia, most initially react with shock and disbelief followed by anxiety, anger, and depression. Typically the reaction is very similar to the stages of grief that one would experience with a loss. Though this stress reaction subsides after several weeks with the majority of cases, a large number of clients continue to develop psychological symptoms due to the emotional strain caused by the initial diagnosis, side effects of treatment, or advancing disease (Greer, 2002).

Members that may be involved in group work for assistance in coping with a medical diagnosis can present with a wide range of psychological symptoms. Typical reactions to chronic illness or disease include anxiety, depression, emotional distress, impaired self-worth, negativity toward self, helplessness, dependency, guilt, alienation, suicidal ideation, anger, vulnerability, a loss of purpose, fear, impaired social relationships, reduced sexual functioning, impaired work productivity, and excessive health concerns (Greer, 2002; Kelley & Clifford, 1997; Molassiotis et al., 2002; Spiegel et al., 1999; Wenzel & Robinson, 1995). It is important to remember that these symptoms are merely the reactions of psychologically normal individuals subjected to severe stress (Greer, 2002).

Some seem to be at a higher risk for poor coping and therefore greater psychological impairment. Those who are socially isolated, have recently experienced a loss, have multiple roles and obligations, or who have rigid coping patterns tend to cope less well than others when faced with a chronic illness or disease. Research has shown that the use of avoidance and denial as a coping response places a client at higher risk for psychological impairment as well. Feelings of helplessness and hopelessness also show a relationship to poor quality of life. On the other hand, those who believe they have some control over the course of the disease and the remainder of their lives have better psychological responses (Greer, 2002; Spiegel et al., 1999; Wenzel & Robinson, 1995).

Group work is an effective way of helping people cope with crisis. Psychological intervention can improve the quality of life for persons coping with chronic illness by at least increasing feelings of control and reducing avoidance and denial. Intervention has been shown to improve not only psychological adjustment, but also functional adjustment (e.g., returning to work) and anticipatory symptoms related to treatment (Greer, 2002). According to Spiegel et al. (1999, p. 483), the literature "provides uniform evidence for a positive systematic improvement in mood, coping and adjustment as a result of group therapy." Specifically, group counseling and psychotherapy offer three unique advantages as a treatment choice for clients with chronic illness: (1) the social support can counter the isolation often experienced with this population, (2) members can develop feelings of usefulness because they are helpful to other members, and (3) costs are reduced because group therapy may be up to four times more affordable for patients when compared to individual treatment. Finally, medically ill patients who are participating in group counseling or psychotherapy have been shown to recover more quickly after a surgery, have shorter hospital stays, and have less distressing outpatient doctor visits (Spiegel et al., 1999).

Several different models appear in the literature as effective group treatments with medically ill persons. Some of these models incorporate existentialism, which focuses on anxiety about death and uncertainty about one's life purpose. Such existential themes can easily be woven into various models of treatment. One such model is proposed by Kissane et al. (1997); it is a cognitive-existential approach commonly used with cancer patients. Six goals were identified and aimed at improving patients' quality of life: (1) promoting a supportive environment, (2) facilitating grief work, (3) changing unhealthy cognitions, (4) increasing problem solving and coping, (5) fostering a sense of mastery, and (6) prioritizing one's future.

During the initial phase of the cognitive-existential approach, leaders actively promote the therapeutic factors of self-disclosure, cohesion, and commonalities of experience in an attempt to decrease isolating behaviors. Leaders listen as each member shares his or her experience with illness. Leaders resist assuming the role of medical expert by inviting the group to be the reference point regarding accuracy of medical aspects of the experience (Kissane et al., 1997).

During the middle phase, anxiety about death arises and losses are grieved as members come to terms with their own mortality. The eventual goal of this type of work is for each member to adopt a new perspective of control over the remainder of one's life, regardless of its length. Victor Frankl (1963) stated that it was not the length of one's life that gave it meaning, but the quality of it. As more adaptive coping through healthier cognitions begins to replace helplessness, a sense of hope and mastery is instilled. Leaders are cautioned to help members distinguish between realistic and healthier ways of thinking and false reassurance. Guilt, anger, and the doctor-patient relationship are central themes of this phase of group work as well (Kissane et al., 1997).

In the final phase of the cognitive-existential group, loss and grief are revisited as the group's end is mourned. This mourning is balanced by a reappraisal of future commitments and priorities. In general, incorporation of existential themes into a cognitive framework emphasizes the finitude of life and accepting responsibility for one's life, while at the same time facilitating more appropriate and rational thinking and coping.

A second model seen in the literature is the supportive-psychoeducational model, which has been associated with reduced distress and increased coping for HIV-infected patients. The goals of this model are to (1) offer patients accurate information about their illness, (2) provide a supportive atmosphere, (3) address fears and concerns, (4) improve coping with negatively affected relationships, (5) renew hope, (6) improve anxious and depressive cognitions, and (7) facilitate grieving. The initial session was left open-ended and focused on introductions, guidelines, confidentiality, and exploring anxiety related to the group. The next several sessions concentrated on trust and cohesion. Remaining sessions centered on themes of abandonment, stress related to medical diagnosis, social stigma, education regarding the illness, and identifying available social support systems. The final sessions concentrated on termination of the group and the loss experienced by group members (Levine, Bystritsky, Baron, & Jones, 1991).

Focusing more on the emotional response than the supportive-psychoeducational group, the supportive-expressive model proposed by Spiegel et al. (1999) encouraged open emotional expression and catharsis within a supportive environment as a way to reduce mood disturbance and improve feelings of control. A central theme of this model is to assist patients in confronting their worst fears and experiencing related emotions rather than simply hoping for the best and ignoring withheld anxiety. Through open exploration, the leader's role was to guide discussion toward personal and emotionally expressive content. Topics were allowed to emerge naturally without planned agendas for the group session. Common topics that seem to appear across groups include social isolation, helplessness, fear of dying, reordering priorities, enhancing relationships, and pain and anxiety management. Unlike many group interventions, this model encouraged members to see one another outside the group sessions. Similar to other models with this population, leaders were advised against providing medical advice or information. Leaders were also cautioned against personality analysis, historical causes of the present problems, or direct confrontation (Spiegel et al., 1999).

The narrative model and the reconstructive model are also used with clients with chronic illness. Both of these models include the telling of personal stories and experiences, while exploring alternative realities or interpretations (Kelley & Clifford, 1997; Viney & Allwood, 1991).

An additional note of importance when choosing which framework or model to use with the chronically ill population is that some authors (Greer, 2002; Kissane et al., 1997) proposed that cognitive models may be more appropriate for patients in the initial stages of disease diagnosis to assist with coping and adjustment. Alternatively, supportive-expressive types of therapy, which encouraged discussion about existential concerns, may be more suitable for patients with more advanced illness (Greer, 2002).

Finally, leaders should keep in mind two potential downfalls of group therapy with this population. First, it has been reported by members who have dropped out of treatment that the group therapy was simply too anxiety-provoking (Kissane et al., 1997). Also, within the group therapy setting, patients seek interactions with other clients who have either overcome their illness or are adjusting well (Spiegel et al., 1999). When members of the group experience advances in their diseases, not only does this cause enormous distress for the other group members, but the member who needs support the most may be ostracized.

Summary

Adulthood is a complex time of development, and it is a time that should not be oversimplified. Adulthood entails a number of social, emotional, and psychological issues that may either be important for a group to address or that can affect the group process. Young adults in particular begin to realize that rules and norms are changing and that behaviors acceptable up until recently in their lives are no longer appropriate in their young adult lives. They feel pressure to move forward or get left behind. Those in middle adulthood may begin to reevaluate their lives and the decisions made thus far. The realization of mortality becomes obvious and the middle adult may either remain in denial or grow because of it. While older adults are often happy and productive, those who present for group treatment may be having difficulty with this time of life. Loss and grief are issues pertinent to this developmental stage, and groups can be especially important for providing social support and a sense of contribution.

When working with older adult populations, group leaders must be mindful of their own perceptions of aging and death. Aging should be viewed as part of the self-actualization process. The group leader should also take care in screening members because lack of screening is the reason for most unsuccessful groups.. Also, when working with elderly group members, the leader should keep in mind that elderly members are not children, but rather are full of wisdom, experience, and knowledge that should be capitalized upon within the group.

Several specific group formats were discussed, including group work with survivors of sexual abuse, perpetrators of sexual abuse, individuals with addictions, and persons with chronic illness and disease. When working with survivors of sexual abuse, it is important to accept only those members who have already recalled, acknowledged, and worked on issues stemming from the abuse within an individual therapy setting. Survivors of abuse who have only recently opened up about the abuse are considered to be in crisis and are therefore not appropriate for group work because they need more individual attention than the group setting can provide. Also, the group leader should bear in mind that not all group members are affected in the same way by sexual abuse. Several factors that may determine the level of trauma experienced by the survivor include family atmosphere, age at the time of the abuse, the violence of the abuse, and the relationship of the perpetrator to the abuser.

Similar to groups for children of alcoholics, groups for sexual abuse survivors can also begin to take on characteristics of the family of origin. Ideally, the new therapeutic group family is a healthy surrogate in which the members can talk openly about the abuse that the family of origin may have insisted on keeping secret. Finally, specific guidelines must be considered when screening for and setting up groups, including frequency, duration, and number of group members.

When working with sexual abuse perpetrators, rules may need to be more detailed and less flexible, perhaps in the form of a contract. Also, perhaps even more so than with other groups, member resistance should be addressed openly rather than ignored or diverted. Some group leaders have an especially difficult time working with this population due to personal beliefs, but they can remind themselves that in working with this population, they are helping protect the community and reduce repeat offenses.

An additional specialty group offered in the chapter is group work with addictions. Group therapy is not only the most common approach with this population, it is considered essential to recovery. Members within the group can often accomplish honest confrontations and offer support that the group leader is not capable of in the eyes of the members. Specific goals pertinent to an addictions group include recognition of the repercussions of addiction, owning previously ignored emotions, gaining insight into motivations for the addiction, and learning new ways of behaving without the addiction.

Persons with addictions typically exhibit difficulty in communication and in relationships. Both of these elements are essential for successful groups and can therefore pose an additional challenge within the group setting. Group leaders must remain intentional at all times in an effort to tailor the group to the individual needs of the members. Also, it is necessary for group leaders to recall that confrontation is a necessary component to group work with addicted individuals, though not necessarily in the beginning of their recovery.

The chapter provided information for group work with individuals diagnosed with chronic illness and disease. More and more, counselors are called upon to assist with the adjustment and coping of persons diagnosed with a chronic illness. Group leaders should remember that the psychological symptoms often displayed by these individuals are normal reactions to severe stress. As with other traumatic events, however, some seem to have more difficulty coping and are therefore more adversely affected. Group therapy has been shown to not only improve the quality of life for such people, but to also increase feelings of control and reduce denial. Group leaders are warned, however, to distinguish between more positive but realistic ways of thinking, and false reassurance and hope.

Regardless of the developmental stage of the group or the specific issue to be addressed, the effective and competent group leader will be intentional and purposeful in every stage of the development and implementation of the group: the initial planning of the group; screening of the members; deciding on specific mechanics such as location, number, frequency, and duration; setting of rules and guidelines; choosing activities and interventions; and facilitating the group process itself. Knowledge specific to each group and awareness of member characteristics and needs will assist in this process.

CHAPTER 21

Accountability in Group Work

Bradley T. Erford

PREVIEW

The following facets of accountability are addressed in this chapter: needs assessment, program evaluation, process evaluation, and outcome studies. Each facet contributes to a cycle of quality improvement for group work practice.

ACCOUNTABILITY IN GROUP WORK

Research has established that group work is an effective treatment delivery system (see Chapter 22). However, this knowledge alone does not satisfy the public's justified need for continued **accountability** in counseling services, particular on a case-by-case or group-by-group basis. Whiston (1996) stated, "Clients, third-party payers, and school administrators are only a few examples of those who may want data based information concerning a professional counselor's effectiveness" (p. 616). For group counseling to remain valued by the public and covered by third-party payers, group leaders must provide evidence demonstrating that their work is worthwhile and produces results. Lack of accountability can cause the elimination of counseling positions, specific counseling practices, and delivery systems.

Accountability in group work answers the following question: How are group members different as a result of the services provided by group leaders? By using assessment techniques to measure outcomes, leaders can provide a means for accountability to members, funding sources, administrators, and other stakeholders and demonstrate how their program is affecting member outcomes, development, and even achievement.

According to various scholars (Erford, 2007a; Issacs, 2003; Loesch & Ritchie, 2004; Myrick, 2003), accountability ordinarily involves the following:

- Identifying and collaborating with stakeholder groups (e.g., advisory committees, administrators, parents, teachers, students).
- Collecting data and assessing the needs of clients, students, staff, and community.
- Setting goals and establishing objectives based on data and determined need.
- Implementing effective interventions to address the goals and objectives.
- Measuring the outcomes or results of these interventions.
- Using these results for program improvement.

TABLE 21.1 Advantages and Challenges of Accountability Studies

Advantages

1. Data is almost always as good or better than perception when it comes to guiding decision making about programs, practices, and interventions.
2. Accountability studies help demonstrate necessity, efficiency, and effectiveness of counseling services.
3. Accountability studies can help identify professional development and staff development needs.
4. Leaders can network to share program results, thereby spreading the word about effective practices.
5. Conducting accountability studies is a professional responsibility and demonstrates one's commitment to personal and professional improvement.
6. Accountability results can serve a public relations function by informing stakeholders and the public of a counseling program's accomplishments.

Challenges

1. Outcome measures and surveys take some training and skill to develop.
2. It takes time and resources to do quality outcomes research and evaluation; these time and resources could be dedicated instead to additional service delivery.
3. Many do not understand the nature and purpose of accountability because of misperceptions or previous bad experiences.
4. Data is sometimes "overinterpreted" or given undue meaning (e.g., the facts may not support the conclusion). All studies have limitations that must be considered when arriving at conclusions.
5. Comprehensive evaluations are seldom conducted. More often, bits and pieces of evaluative information are collected, and the big picture is often incomplete.

- Sharing results with major stakeholder groups (e.g., administration, teachers and staff, parents and guardians, students, school boards, community and business leaders, school counselors and supervisors).

There are advantages and disadvantages to conducting accountability studies. Both are outlined in Table 21.1. It is important to note that many of the challenges can be remedied if practitioners work with colleagues with research expertise to evaluate group work effectiveness.

It is the professional and ethical responsibility of leaders to ensure that the services offered to stakeholder groups are truly effective. The focus of this chapter is on the wide-ranging accountability functions of the professional counselor, including needs assessment, program evaluation, and outcome research. The content of this chapter is among the most important in terms of (1) understanding the needs of a clientele and community (needs assessment); (2) determining the extent to which a program is implemented (program evaluation); (3) evaluation of leader, member, and group processes (process evaluation); and (4) group work effectiveness (outcome or results studies). This information will also allow leaders to speak the language of decision makers, thus allowing social and academic advocacy for clients with diverse needs when encountering systemic barriers to academic, career, or personal/social success. Finally, every professional counselor should be constantly asking and gathering information to answer the following question: Is what I'm doing working with this group member?

CONDUCTING A NEEDS ASSESSMENT

At least two primary purposes underlie the use of a needs assessment in counseling programs. First, needs assessment helps leaders understand the needs of various subpopulations of a community. These subpopulations may include clients, congregations, neighborhoods, teachers, parents, students, administrators, community organizations, local businesses, and the general citizenry. Each of these groups holds a stake in the success of the total program; thus, they are called stakeholder groups. Second, needs assessment helps establish the priorities that guide the construction of a counseling program or group work intervention, as well as continuous quality improvement of the program. A needs assessment emphasizes what currently exists in comparison with identified goals and objectives (Erford, 2008). Assessing the needs of a community or community population provides a trajectory for addressing what the community values and desires to pursue. Needs assessments can be classified as data-driven needs assessments and perceptions-based needs assessments.

Data-Driven Needs Assessment

Data-driven decision making deals with real needs and impact, not perceived needs. Data-driven needs assessment is most frequently used in school systems but can be applied just as easily to group work in other settings. In an example from clinical practice, Table 21.2 provides treatment change data from the Beck Anxiety Inventory (BAI) (Beck, 1993) for 50 clients seen for a group counseling treatment regimen with no concurrent medication treatment. Analyzing the aggregated data, one would conclude that the 50 clients began with an average BAI raw

score of 30 (moderate to severe levels of anxiety symptoms) and finished the group counseling treatment regimen with an average BAI raw score of 20 (mild to moderate levels of anxiety)—an average raw score change of 10 points. On the surface, and on average, this data shows that the group treatment was successful in reducing average symptoms of anxiety for the group. However, conscientious group leaders are interested in determining whether the treatment differentially affected members with various characteristics (e.g., sex, race, socioeconomic status).

By disaggregating the total sample data in Table 21.2, you will notice that some differences do appear to exist regarding the effectiveness of the treatment on certain subgroups. For example, lower socioeconomic status (SES) group participants experienced only a 3 raw-score-point improvement after treatment, while nonlow SES group participants experienced nearly five times that level of symptom relief (i.e., a change of 14.6 raw score points for nonlow SES participants versus a change of 3 points for low SES participants). Likewise, African American clients reported average BAI raw-score-point declines of only 3.5, while White participants reported a 12.5 raw-score-point decline. On the surface at least, one may reach a tentative conclusion that the group counseling treatment was more effective for White and nonlow SES participants. Thus, disaggregated data can help leaders make decisions about treatment efficacy for prospective clients,

TABLE 21.2 Aggregated and Disaggregated Data of 50 Clients Treated for Anxiety with a 24-week Group Counseling Regimen on the BAI (Raw Score)

	n	BAI Baseline (A)	BAI (24 sessions) (B)	BAI Change (A − B)
Total sample	50	30.0	20.0	10.0
Males	20	26.0	17.2	8.8
Females	30	32.7	21.9	10.8
White	36	33.3	20.8	12.5
Black	14	21.5	18.0	3.5
Low SES	20	25.5	22.4	3.1
Nonlow SES	30	33.0	18.4	14.6

as well as make program improvements to help future clients benefit equitably from an otherwise effective approach or program. In summary, data-driven approaches to needs assessment use existing data, or easy-to-collect data, to determine client population needs and treatment equity.

These differences can be determined through more advanced statistical procedures or by eyeballing the data to note gaps in performance. Identified gaps provide objective (not perception-based) evidence of differential results, thus identifying needs to be addressed. When such needs are identified, leaders can begin the process of addressing these needs through well-written objectives, interventions, and programmatic initiatives (see Converting Needs to Program Goals and Objectives below).

Perceptions-Based Needs Assessments

In contrast to a data-driven needs assessment, a traditional needs assessment process is more content and perception driven. Group leaders are often interested in what members, community leaders, citizens, teachers, and parents perceive as primary needs to be addressed. Prior to undertaking a perceptions-based needs assessment, group leaders would be wise to consider issues such as how often to conduct a needs assessment, which stakeholder group(s) to assess, and how to design an efficient needs assessment.

FREQUENCY OF CONDUCTING A NEEDS ASSESSMENT While it may seem tempting to design and conduct a global needs assessment on an annual basis, such an endeavor would be a massive administrative and costly undertaking that would likely result in findings being outdated by the time changes are made to the total program. It is probably best to follow a continuous cycle of assessing program needs. This will allow ample time for program development and improvements over the course of the cycle. The timing of needs assessments will vary for community and school venues. For example, in schools, the

American School Counselor Association (ASCA) *National Standards* (Campbell & Dahir, 1997) and *National Model* (American School Counselor Association, 2005) designate the areas of academic, career, and personal-social development as cornerstones of a comprehensive developmental guidance program; therefore, it makes sense that school community needs can be assessed according to these components on a rotating basis. Community-based mental health counseling programs may require a comprehensive needs assessment only every three to five years, or when societal or political changes deem it essential to maintaining quality service levels within the community. The main point here is that assessing needs is part of a much bigger endeavor: that of implementing program changes to continuously improve the counseling program. Implementing changes can be quite time intensive and simply a waste of time if they are not guided by accurate needs assessments and program outcome research. An effective program uses this information to fine-tune its efforts in data-driven decision making.

POPULATIONS TO BE ASSESSED In the broadest sense, any stakeholder group can provide helpful information about the needs of a population or community. However, it is most practical and efficient to seek those who are most informed and likely to respond. Community leaders, teachers, administrators, potential or current members, and parents are the most likely to be informed about community and school issues and needs, and under most circumstances they will be the primary stakeholder groups surveyed during a needs assessment. Valuable information can be garnered from community organizations, local businesses, and the general citizenry as well. It is just more difficult to obtain a large response sampling from these groups. Information from these stakeholders is probably best obtained through personal contacts and interviews.

Return rate is an important consideration in the needs assessment process. Return rate is the percentage of returned surveys out of those sent. As in any research sampling procedure, the higher the return rate, the lower the sampling error; this leads to greater confidence in the accuracy of the results. Return rate is generally maximized when the participants are a captured audience. For example, if a social skills needs assessment of fourth-grade students is conducted in the classroom, the response rate should be nearly 100%. On the other hand, if a needs assessment for parents is sent home, the counselor may be lucky to receive 25 to 50% of the surveys back. Whenever possible, surveys should be distributed and collected immediately during community gatherings, faculty meetings, class meetings, and parent gatherings.

Triangulation of needs across populations should be attempted when possible; that is, the highest priority needs should be those agreed to by all or most populations assessed. This ensures that the community's needs, not an individual's agenda, drive programs and services. For instance, if an administrator has decided to place a high priority on social skills, but community leaders, parents, and clients indicate this is a low priority and far below other issues such as depression, anxiety, and substance abuse, the triangulated responses of the teachers, parents, and students can provide compelling, data-driven evidence to guide the program's focus.

DESIGN ISSUES IN AN EFFICIENT NEEDS ASSESSMENT

Designing an efficient needs assessment is essential to meaningful results. While some advocate for a comprehensive needs assessment that simultaneously assesses all goals and topics associated with a comprehensive counseling program, others have found it more helpful to focus the assessment on specifically defined topics or issues that are being updated or altered (Erford, 2007b, 2008). This chapter will focus on the latter method.

Stone and Bradley (1994) recommended seven methods for determining needs: (1) questionnaires and inventories, (2) analysis of records, (3) personal interviews, (4) counseling statistics, (5) classroom visits, (6) use of outside consultants, and (7) systematic evaluation of the guidance program. Perhaps what is most important is that the needs assessment uses objective methods for data gathering and analysis. It is essential to understand that some questions are addressed by different methodologies. Although all of these methods are important and useful, questionnaires (formal or informal surveys) are most commonly used and will be the focus here. While open-ended questionnaires are generally easier to design and yield rich and diverse information, such questionnaires are usually more difficult to interpret and translate into goals and objectives.

From a return-rate perspective, it is good practice to design a needs assessment that is only one to two pages in length and can be completed in about 3 to 5 minutes. The content of the needs assessment should be topical (e.g., social skills, changing families, substance abuse, college application procedures) rather than service-related (e.g., individual counseling, group counseling, consultation, etc.). Group leaders should keep in mind that services are simply methods for meeting needs, not needs in themselves. Of course, the topics should be related to the program goals or organizational mission so that priority status can be placed on addressing the most pressing needs in comparison to the mission and/or goals. A good needs assessment directly translates into program development.

In general, the following steps form the basis of an efficient needs assessment:

1. Decide what you need to know.
2. Decide on the best approach to derive what you need to know.
3. Develop the needs assessment instrument or method.
4. Enlist the support of colleagues and a few individuals from the target groups to review and try out items for clarity of understanding.
5. Implement the final version on the target groups.
6. Tabulate, analyze, and interpret the results.
7. Translate the results into program goals and objectives.

Name: _____

Place a checkmark (✓) in the appropriate space below to indicate how well you handle each issue.

	Almost Never	Sometimes	Often	Almost Always	I need Help with this	
					Yes	No
1. I am able to focus my thoughts when I need to.						
2. I have a good workout schedule.						
3. I have good time management skills.						
4. I can control my breathing when I am upset.						
5. I can control my level of stress.						
6. I have good organizational skills.						
7. My muscles are relaxed.						
8. I have good nutritional habits.						
9. I think positive thoughts about myself.						
10. I can readily identify stressors in my life.						

FIGURE 21.1 **A Focused Stress Management Needs Assessment.**

Questions or response stems should be short, to the point, and easily understood. The reading level of the items should also be appropriate for the target audience. Figure 21.1 provides an example of a topic-focused needs assessment. Substantial consideration should also be given to the response format. If the purpose of the survey is to determine the importance or frequency of a potential problem, it is generally best to use a multipoint scale with four to seven choices. For example, Figure 21.1 asks about the frequency of the display of stressors, so the response choices "Almost Never," "Sometimes," "Often," and "Almost Always" are appropriate. Note that the response choices "Never" and "Always" do not

appear. It is rare that behaviors never or always occur; to include these descriptors may force responses to the center of the distribution and truncate the range of possible results. Also notice how each category has a descriptor. Gone are the days when a survey lists the response categories of 0 ("Almost Never") and 4 ("Almost Always"), and then provide the center points of 1, 2, and 3 with no accompanying descriptor. The reliability problems of such a scale are obvious: Will all respondents agree on what an unlabeled 1, 2, or 3 represents? All choice categories must be accompanied by a verbal descriptor.

Another important response component of a needs assessment is a frequency count. Suppose a group leader wants not only to assess the importance of an issue, but also to determine how many potential members were likely in need of services to address the problems stemming from the issue. When possible, the needs assessment should be designed to include an indication of whether the respondent should be targeted for intervention. In Figure 21.1, notice how the far right-hand column asks for a yes or no answer to the statement, "I need help with this." An affirmative response targets the potential member for intervention to address a self-perceived weakness.

Tallying or computing the information from a needs assessment is relatively simple. Tallying involves counting the number of potential members who may benefit from intervention. Computing the results of a needs assessment is probably best accomplished by assigning a number value to each response category and averaging all responses for a given item. In Figure 21.1, assume that the response categories are assigned the following values: "Almost Never" = 0, "Sometimes" = 1, "Often" = 2, and "Almost Always" = 3. For item 1, "I am able to focus my thoughts when I need to," simply add all student response values and divide by the number of responses. Refer to the data in Table 21.3. If 50 members completed the needs assessment, and for item 1, 10 members marked "Almost Never" ($10 \times 0 = 0$), 12 members marked "Sometimes" ($12 \times 1 = 12$), 21 members marked "Often" ($21 \times 2 = 42$), and 7 members marked "Almost Always" ($7 \times 3 = 21$), simply sum the points ($0 + 12 + 42 + 21 + 75$) and divide by the number of member responses (75 divided by 50 students = 1.50) to compute the average frequency rating (1.50). Although this assumes a ratio scale and is somewhat nebulous from a statistical interpretation perspective (that is, what does a 1.50 really mean?), it does offer a reasonable estimate of the average frequency of a behavior, or the importance of one issue in comparison to the other issues under study. For example, when viewing the mean computations of the 10 items in Table 21.3, the leader gets a good idea about how important item 1 is in comparison to the other nine items in the needs assessment.

HELPFUL TIPS FOR DEVELOPING A NEEDS ASSESSMENT The program evaluation and assessment cycle for counseling programs may require up to 5 to 6 years (Rye & Sparks, 1999, p. 34), with the first year focusing on the needs assessment component:

1. Preparing and organizing the advisory team into a working group.
2. Reviewing and refining the beliefs, vision, and mission of the counseling program.
3. Conducting a needs assessment among students, parents, and school personnel.
4. Identifying high priority needs.
5. Writing objectives.
6. Helping the counseling staff develop activities to address identified needs.

Program implementation, monitoring, evaluation, and revision compose the next four years of this cycle. In the sixth or final year, another needs assessment should be undertaken to determine whether any needs or priorities have shifted. Of course, at this point, the cycle repeats itself, leading to a continuous process of modification, refinement, and improvement.

A helpful set of commonsense guidelines for questionnaire or survey development was provided by Worthen, Sanders, and Fitzpatrick (1997, pp. 355–356):

1. Sequencing questions
   a. Are later responses biased by early questions?
   b. Does the questionnaire begin with easy, nonthreatening, but pertinent questions?
   c. Are leading questions (ones that lead to a certain response) avoided?
   d. Is there a logical, efficient sequencing of questions (e.g., from general to specific questions; use of filter questions when appropriate)?
   e. Are closed- or open-ended questions appropriate? If closed, are the categories exhaustive and mutually exclusive? Do responses result in the desired scale of data for analysis (i.e., nominal, ordinal, interval)?

TABLE 21.3 Data from the Stress Management Needs Assessment ($n = 50$)

	Almost Never (0)	Sometimes (1)	Often (2)	Almost Always (3)	Yes	No	Ave (Rank)
1. I am able to focus my thoughts when I need to.	10 (0)	12 (12)	21 (42)	7 (21)	21	29	1.50 (9)
2. I have a good workout schedule.	22 (0)	17 (17)	7 (14)	4 (12)	33	17	0.86 (3)
3. I have good time management skills.	15 (0)	12 (12)	14 (28)	9 (27)	22	28	1.34 (6)
4. I can control my breathing when I am upset.	29 (0)	12 (12)	7 (14)	2 (6)	42	8	0.64 (1)
5. I can control my level of stress.	24 (0)	9 (9)	10 (20)	7 (21)	33	17	1.00 (4)
6. I have good organizational skills.	14 (0)	9 (9)	17 (34)	10 (30)	19	31	1.46 (8)
7. My muscles are relaxed.	28 (0)	8 (8)	8 (16)	6 (18)	35	15	0.84 (2)
8. I have good nutritional habits.	19 (0)	15 (15)	7 (14)	9 (27)	35	15	1.12 (5)
9. I think positive thoughts about myself.	17 (0)	12 (12)	7 (14)	14 (42)	23	27	1.36 (7)
10. I can readily identify stressors in my life.	6 (0)	9 (9)	10 (20)	25 (75)	4	36	2.08 (10)

Note: The tally (number of clients responding) is entered in each column first, followed by the product of the tally and response value. For example, item 1 under the Almost Always (3) column reads 7 (21), meaning that 7 clients responded Almost Always and this tally was multiplied by 3, resulting in a product of 21. The rank indicates the order of greatest need, with the lower average scores indicating greater degrees of need.

f. Are the major issues covered thoroughly, while minor issues are passed over quickly?

g. Are questions with similar content grouped logically?

2. Wording questions

a. Are questions stated precisely? (Who, what, when, where, why, how?)

b. Does the questionnaire avoid assuming too much knowledge on the part of the respondent?

c. Does each item ask only one question?

d. Is the respondent in a position to answer the question, or must she make guesses? If so, are you interested in her guesses?

e. Are definitions clear?

f. Are emotionally tinged words avoided?

g. Is the vocabulary at the reading level of the audience? If any technical terms, jargon, or slang is used, are the terms the most appropriate way to communicate with this audience?

h. Are the methods for responding appropriate? Clear? Consistent?

i. Are the questions appropriately brief and uncomplicated?

3. Establishing and keeping rapport and eliciting cooperation

a. Is the questionnaire easy to answer? (Questions are not overly long or cumbersome.)

b. Is the time required to respond reasonable?

c. Does the instrument look attractive (i.e., layout, quality of paper, etc.)?

d. Is there a respondent orientation?

e. Does the cover letter provide an explanation of purpose, sponsorship, method of respondent selection, anonymity?

f. Is appropriate incentive provided for the respondent's cooperation?

4. Giving instructions

a. Is the respondent told clearly how to record her responses?

b. Are instructions for return clear? Is a stamped return envelope provided?

Group leaders conducting needs assessments must choose an appropriate response format, ordinarily yes or no (or sometimes), multi-scale formats (e.g., almost never, sometimes, frequently, almost always), Likert-type scales (e.g., very dissatisfied, dissatisfied, satisfied, very satisfied), or true/false or multiple-choice formats. Note the wording of the item, scaling method, and single-page format of the needs assessment presented in Figure 21.1.

CONVERTING NEEDS TO PROGRAM GOALS AND OBJECTIVES If the needs assessment was designed correctly, translating the results into goals and learning objectives is relatively easy. The first step is to prioritize the needs in order of importance and their relationship to existing components of the program. Prioritization can be accomplished most easily by using the tallying, computing, and triangulation strategies mentioned above. Next, the needs must be matched with or translated into goals aligned with the program mission and standards. Finally, the goals are operationalized through development of learning objectives. See Erford (2007a; 2009) for an excellent nuts-and-bolts discussion of how to write learning objectives using the **ABCD model**: (A) audience, (B) behavior, (C) conditions, and (D) description of the expected performance criterion.

A reasonable goal stemming from the needs assessment shown in Figure 21.1 would be "to increase members' abilities to manage stress and anxiety." Notice how the wording of a goal is nebulous and not amenable to measurement as stated. In developing learning objectives related to goals, particular emphasis is given to specific actions that are measurable. For example, a possible objective stemming from this goal could be "After participating in a group counseling program and learning thought stopping procedures, 80% of the members will experience a 50% reduction in obsessive thinking over a one-week period." Another possible objective might be "After participating in a 6-week program on the importance of exercise with follow-up goal-setting monitoring, 80% of members will engage in at least 20 minutes of aerobic exercise at least three times per week." Notice how the objectives designate the audience, the stated behavior, how the behavior will be measured, and the level of expected performance. Several excellent resources exist for additional information on constructing needs assessments (e.g., Erford, 2007a, 2008).

ACCOUNTABILITY: EVALUATING PROGRAMS AND ASSESSING OUTCOMES

In this age of accountability, program evaluation is more important than ever. Traditionally, however, professional counselors for many reasons have failed to hold their programs and services accountable or to provide evidence that the activities undertaken were achieving intended results. Some complained that the nature of what group leaders do is so abstract and complicated as to render the services and results unmeasurable. Others were so busy attempting to meet the needs of members that they shifted time that should have been spent in evaluation to responsive interventions. Some lacked an understanding of how to implement the methods and procedures of accountability studies. Still others were unsure of the effectiveness of the services provided and shied away from accountability unless forced to do so by supervisors.

Whatever the reason, the end result is a glaring lack of accountability that poses dangers for the future of the profession. Lack of accountability contributes to a shirking of professional and ethical responsibility for ensuring that the services provided to group members are of high quality and are effective in meeting intended needs. Think about it from a business perspective. How long would a business last if it continued to engage in indiscernible or ineffective activities, the value of which was unknown to the business's consumers, managers, or employees? Such businesses are selected out for extinction! Now extend that thought to group work. Without accountability data to back them up, counseling services are often among the first services to go during budget cutbacks.

In the context of group work, leaders must be concerned with two areas of accountability: (1) process evaluation and (2) results or outcome evaluation. Both are important facets of program evaluation. Evaluation is the measurement of worth and indicates that a judgment will be made regarding the effectiveness of a program (Erford, 2008). In an evaluation process, it is essential to be very specific about what you are measuring and how you are measuring it. This is made clear in the writing of specific learning objectives (see Erford, 2009). Too often, leaders are not specific about what they are trying to accomplish and become frustrated when they fail to measure what they may or may not have achieved. If a person doesn't know where she is heading, she must either get specific directions (write a specific, measurable objective) or be satisfied with wherever she ends up (perhaps being unable to demonstrate an ineffective group program)!

PROCESS EVALUATION

Process evaluation refers to assessment of the group dynamics and interaction processes occurring within the group sessions, usually related to the leader, members, and the interactions between the leader and members. Understanding the group dynamics helps to improve the efficiency and effectiveness of the interactions. Several resources provide ideas for conducting process evaluations. The *Handbook of Group Psychotherapy: An Empirical and Clinical Synthesis*, edited by Fuhriman and Burlingame

(1994b) identifies numerous measures and methods for evaluating group process and outcomes, as has DeLucia-Waack (1997, 1999) and Delucia-Waack, Gerrity, Kalodner, and Riva (2004).

Some interaction and process evaluation instruments used in the past include the Hill Interaction Matrix (Hill, 1966), Bales's (1950) Interaction Analysis Scale, and Simon and Agazarian's (1974) Sequential Analysis of Verbal Interaction (SAVI). Trotzer (1999) also developed structured leadership and member process instruments and, most recently, the Association for Specialists in Group Work (ASGW) has undertaken a project to develop a standardized and psychometrically robust process evaluation instrument.

In addition to standardized measures, process evaluation can be conducted through a variety of other methods, including peer/supervisor observation, informal member evaluation, and evaluation of video. Colleagues with expertise in group work can observe sessions and provide feedback in an informal or formal supervisory relationship. This is sometimes requested by the group leader when a group is at an impasse or not moving in an appropriate direction, but observation by a colleague may provide helpful feedback at any point in a group counseling process.

Informal member evaluations should be conducted during each session to help the leader understand how group members are progressing and perceiving the group process. Members frequently give helpful feedback and make suggestions for improvement when presented with basic questions, such as the following:

- What did you like most (or least) about this session?
- What did and didn't work well or go well in this session?
- How could the session have been improved?
- What could the leader or members have done differently to make the session more successful?
- What was the most important gain or insight you realized in today's session?

Alternatively, members can journal about their session experiences and insights to communicate similar thoughts, feelings, and behaviors to clients. Leaders should always keep in mind that some members may give inaccurate negative feedback, give inaccurate positive feedback, or say what they believe the leader wants to hear (i.e., social desirability).

Video has the advantage of being an actual record of real-life events that can be reviewed at the leisure of the group leader, colleague, or supervisor. It is difficult to dispute the advantages of actually seeing and hearing oneself, repeatedly if need be, engaging in the actual group process. Comments, sequences, and interchanges can be broken down and analyzed so that strengths can be identified and areas in need of improvement targeted. Videotaping is used extensively in training programs, but unfortunately it is used infrequently in clinical practice. Videotaped sessions are among the most effective process evaluation tools available.

RESULTS OR OUTCOMES EVALUATION

Outcome evaluation (often called results evaluation) answers the question, How are members different because of the group work? Many leaders view outcome evaluation as a discrete component, but it is actually an integral part of a continuous process for program improvement. All accountability procedures must have the institution's mission in mind because the institutional values and needs will determine the focus of study. Questions of worth and effectiveness are derived from a confluence of values, needs, goals, and mission, and these questions lead to the determination of what evidence must be collected. Evidence may exist in many places, but typically it is derived using preplanned measures or from the performances or products clients produce during program activities. Once information has been gathered, it must then be interpreted, and conclusions must be drawn from it regarding the program's or activity's worth, strengths, and weaknesses. Finally, the interpretations and conclusions must be used to

change the program or parts of the program to improve it.

Assessment information is used to prompt program changes, and goal setting and the posing of new questions about the revised program produce additional revisions. Many professional counselors gather evidence and then stop, believing that the program has been evaluated and the job finished. Why spend valuable time collecting evidence and not use it to improve what you are doing?

Sources of Evidence

Both people and products merit discussion as potential sources of accountability evidence. Almost anyone can serve as a helpful source of evidence: clients, members, students, teachers, staff, administration, parents, employers, graduates, community resource people, and so on. Numerous products from data collection methods can also be used. A short list includes portfolios, performances, use of ratings from external judges or examiners, observations, local tests, purchased tests, self-assessments, surveys, interviews, focus groups, and client/student work. Each of these sources or products can produce helpful evaluative data, but what is collected will result from the specific question to be answered.

Selecting Outcome and Process Measures

Perhaps the simplest of the individual (or ideographic) outcome assessment techniques is the behavioral contract. Behavioral contracts with criteria for success are negotiated during a group session, signed by the member making the contract, witnessed by the other group members, and distributed among the group members so all of them know what goals each member has made a contract to meet (Trotzer, 1999). Groups oriented toward treatment of mental health concerns might use the Target Symptom Rating Form (Battle, Imber, Hoen-Saric, Nash, & Frank, 1965), which identifies symptom targets and provides a scale for rating severity. Target symptom rating can be adapted easily for use in other applications.

A more complex method for assessing individual outcomes is Kiresuk and Sherman's (1968) Goal Attainment Scaling methodology, a criterion-referenced approach to describing changes in group members (Roach & Elliott, 2005). After stating a SMART (specific, measurable, achievable, realistic/relevant and timed) goal, the member determines descriptive criteria for five scale levels, which range from $+2 =$ "best possible outcome" through $0 =$ "no change in behavior or performance" to $-2 =$ "worst possible outcome." Ratings for multiple goals can be combined through application of Kiresuk's pseudo T score formula, yielding overall client growth values, which can be averaged across group members to produce an overall evaluation of the group (Kiresuk, Smith, & Cardillo, 1994). Though originally developed for mental health applications, goal attainment scaling has been used successfully in schools to monitor academic growth or behavioral change with children and adolescents (Roach & Elliott, 2005).

A criticism frequently made of these ideographic methods is that goals or complaints are judged on a relative rather than an absolute basis and may ignore standard criteria for adjustment. When clients set multiple goals, they are often not independent of one another and may even be stepped goals, with one goal dependent on another for success.

The Progress Evaluation Scales (Ihilevich & Glesser, 1979), a set of seven empirically supported goals for individual and group counseling and psychotherapy, tracks progress toward goal attainment based on a continuum of objectively scaled outcomes using standardized definitions. The Progress Evaluation Scales map to the Kiresuk Goal Attainment Scaling format and may be summarized by using Kiresuk's summary formula.

Beyond ideographic or individual outcome assessment measures, a group worker has a wealth of symptom, behavior, and attitude measures from which to choose. For example, a group leader planning a group to alleviate test anxiety among high school students might choose a standardized measure of test anxiety, such as the State-Trait Anxiety Inventory to assess group outcomes. Normed outcome assessment tools provide a way of putting individual group member scores into a broader context.

Descriptions of a multitude of outcome measures for individual and group applications have been provided in many published works (see, for example, Antony & Barlow, 2002; Lyons, Howard, O'Mahoney, & Lish, 1997; Ogles, Lambert, & Fields, 2002; Ogles, Lambert, & Masters, 1996), and DeLucia-Waack (1997) has provided a description and discussion of outcome and process evaluation instruments most popular among group workers. Table 21.4 provides a list of group work measures related to screening and selection, leader behaviors/skills, climate, therapeutic factors, and member behavior.

Practical Program Evaluation Considerations

To be of practical value, assessment must be connected to real program concerns as well as the core values of the program. Avoid overwhelming the data collectors, focus on only one or several important questions at a time, and always select measures that will yield reliable and valid scores for the purposes under study. Ineffective program outcomes often stem from poor or inappropriate measurement rather than faulty programming. Be sure to involve the relevant stakeholders and use a variety of approaches. Perhaps most important, do not reinvent the wheel. Use what you are already doing to generate useful data about program effectiveness. Also, don't be afraid to call on outside experts to consult on the development and evaluation of a program (Vacc, Rhyne-Winkler, & Poidevant, 1993).

It is good advice to start small and build on what has been found to work; the methods and goals of individual programs are celebrated, and successes can be shared across programs. This often leads to a cross-pollination effect that yields both diversity of approach and homogeneity of results. In other words, over time, leaders will learn from each other what works and will implement these strategies with their own populations after necessary refinements based on the needs

---

TABLE 21.4   Process and Outcome Measures Used in Group Work

Screening/Selection Measures
Elements (Schutz, 1992)
Group Psychotherapy Evaluation Scale (Van Dyck, 1980)
Group Therapy Survey (Slocum, 1987)
Hill Interaction Matrix (Hill, 1965, 1973)

Leader Behaviors/Skills Measures
Corrective Feedback Self-efficacy Instrument (Page & Hulse-Killacky, 1999)
Group Counselor Behavior Rating Form (Corey & Corey, 1987)
Group Leadership Self-Efficacy Instrument (Page, Pietrzak, & Lewis, 2001)
Leadership Characteristics Inventory (Makuch, 1997)
Skilled Group Counseling Scale (Smaby, Maddux, Torres-Rivera, & Zimmick, 1999)
Trainer Behavior Scale (Bolman, 1971)

Group Climate Measures
Group Climate Questionnaire—Short (MacKenzie, 1983, 1990)
Group Environment Scale (Moos, 1986)

Therapeutic Factors Measures
Curative Factors Scale—Revised (Stone, Lewis, & Beck, 1994)
Critical Incidents Questionnaire (Kivlighan & Goldfine, 1991)
Therapeutic Factors Inventory (Lese & McNair-Semands, 2000)
Therapeutic Factors Scale (Yalom, Tinklenberg, & Gilula, 1968)

Member Behavior Measures
Group Cohesiveness Scale (Budman & Gurman, 1988)
Group Observer Form (Romano & Sullivan, 2000)
Group Sessions Rating Scale (Cooney, Kadden, Litt, & Gettler, 1991)
Hill Interaction Matrix (Hill, 1965, 1973)
Individual Group Member Interpersonal Process Scale (Soldz, Budman, Davis, & Demby, 1993)
Interaction Process Analysis (Bales, 1950)
Systems for Multiple Level Observation of Groups (SYMLOG) (Bales, Cohen & Williams, 1979)

---

of a differing client population. Different can still be effective!

Aggregated Outcomes

The use of an aggregated hierarchical evaluation system is common in psychoeducational approaches in which there is a defined curriculum, goals, outcomes, and measurable objectives. Aggregation is the combining of results to provide a more global or generalized picture of group performance. While such a practice may deemphasize subgroup or individual performance, aggregation can also be a valuable tool when it comes to evaluating how well counseling programs meet higher-level standards or goals. Due to their more abstract or generalized wording, goals (sometimes called standards) are difficult, if not impossible, to measure directly. This is why curriculum development begins with a statement of goals (standards) that are then described further through a series of outcomes (sometimes called competencies). While more specific and well-defined, these outcomes are still ordinarily not amenable to direct measurement in the classic sense. Instead, we rely on specific objectives, such as those discussed in the section above, Converting Needs to Program Goals and Objectives. Objectives are written in such specific, measurable terms that everyone (e.g., members, leaders, teachers, parents, administrators, significant others) can tell when an objective has been met. The use of objectives, outcomes, and goals composes an aggregated hierarchical model and is an important way that leaders can demonstrate the effectiveness of a counseling program. Figure 21.2 provides an example of this aggregated hierarchical model.

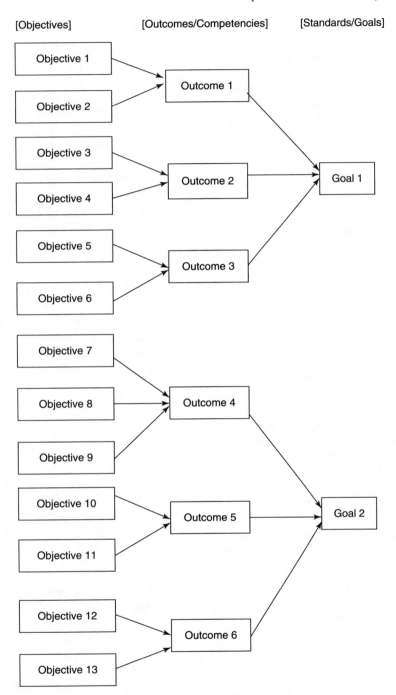

FIGURE 21.2   Aggregated Hierarchical Model for Evaluating the Effectiveness of a School Counseling Program.

In Figure 21.2, note the alignment of objectives to outcomes to goals. Objective 1 measures outcome 1, which is aligned with goal 1. Likewise, objective 13 measures outcome 6, which is aligned with goal 2. Such a hierarchical structure allows the leader to conclude that meeting the lower-order objectives provides evidence that higher-order outcomes and goals have been met successfully. For example, assume the leader of a psychoeducational group provides evidence that objectives 1–6 have been met. By extension, if objectives 1 and 2 were met, then outcome 1 was met. If objectives 3 and 4 were met, then outcome 2 was met. If objectives 5 and 6 were met, then outcome 3 was met. Because outcomes 1–3 were met, the leader has provided evidence that goal 1 was met. Success! In addition, areas of program strength have been identified.

Refer again to Figure 21.2 and consider a second example in which the leader of a psychoeducational group provides evidence that objectives 7–10 were met, but objectives 11–13 were not. By extension, if objectives 7–9 were met, then outcome 4 was met. If objective 10 was met but objective 11 was not, then outcome 5 was either not met or, more accurately, was met only partially. If objectives 12 and 13 were not met, then outcome 6 was not met. Now, because of some inconsistent results, interpretation is a bit cloudier. It is most appropriate to conclude that goal 2 was met only partially because outcome 4 was met, outcome 5 was partially met, and outcome 6 was not met. Given the inconsistency in meeting the outcomes, it would be inappropriate to conclude that goal 2 had been met; it would be equally inappropriate to conclude that goal 2 had not been met. A conclusion of "partially met" identifies the hierarchical set of goals, outcomes, and objectives as a program area in need of improvement and/or in need of additional attention, or the criteria must be revised for successful performance. From these examples, one can see that an aggregated hierarchical model can be a valuable curriculum evaluation method. It also underscores the importance of a measurable objective as the building block of an effective developmental curriculum.

Designing Outcome Studies

While any data collected on counselor effectiveness can be helpful, in most instances, counselors should measure outcomes or results by designing a research-type study: not necessarily one using a true experimental design with participant randomization, but one that yields verifiable, meaningful results through systematic data collection and analysis. The systematic collection of outcome data can yield some evidence that a leader's interventions have had some effect on members. A bit of forethought and planning can lead to much more meaningful conclusions. Research studies are typically empirical in nature and involve providing some control over how members are assigned to counseling interventions and the timing and circumstances under which data is collected. Erford (2008) discussed helpful, easy-to-implement designs, and several of these designs that may be particularly useful to group leaders have been included in Table 21.5.

While a comprehensive treatise of this topic is beyond the scope of this book, what follows are some of the relevant points leaders should consider when designing outcome studies. Leaders generally receive an entire course in research that can be useful in this context. The interested reader should consult Erford (2008) for a helpful source on research methodology and statistical analysis written specifically for counselors.

Answering several questions can help the counselor determine which research design to use:

1. *Has the treatment already been implemented?* So much for planning ahead! If the intervention has not already occurred, the leader has many possible options. If the intervention has already occurred, one is relegated to a nonexperimental design, probably a case study or static-group comparison design. It is critical to think about outcomes assessment in the early stages of planning for a group and certainly before the group has begun!

TABLE 21.5 Common Designs Used for Outcomes Research

Nonexperimental Designs

1. Pretest–posttest single-group design		O I O
2. Case study		I O
3. Static-group comparison	Group 1	O
	Group 2	I O

Quasi-Experimental Designs

4. Two-sample pretest–posttest design	R O
	R I O
5. Nonequivalent control group design	O I O
	O O
6. Time series design	O O O I O O O

True Experimental Designs

7. Randomized pretest–posttest control group design	R O I O
	R O O
8. Randomized post-test-only control group design	R I O
	R O

Note: R = participants are randomly assigned to groups; I = intervention (implemented treatment or program); O = observation or other data collection method.

2. *Can I randomly assign members to treatment conditions?* If the answer is yes, outstanding! Control over the random assignment of members is critical to implementing true experimental designs. If one does not have control over assignment of members, the leader must choose a quasi-experimental or nonexperimental design.

3. *Can I conduct (one or several) pretests, post-tests, or both?* Usually, measuring the dependent variable both before (pretest) and after (post-test) is desirable, although not always essential.

The answers to each of these questions will help the leader choose the most useful and powerful design. For example, if the answers to the three questions are no, yes, and yes, respectively, the leader may opt for an experimental design (i.e., designs 7 or 8 in Table 21.5). If the answers are yes, no, and posttest only, the leader can opt for a nonexperiment design (designs 2 or 3 in Table 21.5). As one can no doubt surmise, outcome studies require some level of planning early in program development.

Most true experimental designs involve randomization of participants, which also randomizes various sources of error, thus allowing for the control of numerous threats to validity. True experimental designs allow causative conclusions to be reached. This is a big advantage when the leader wants to know conclusively if his or her interventions caused significant improvements in group members. For example, if a leader wants to know if a group intervention designed to improve symptoms of depression in members was effective, she could use the randomized pretest–posttest control group design (design 7 in Table 21.5). She would begin by randomly assigning her members into two groups of optimal size, one designated control and the other treatment, and determining a data collection method (e.g., test, survey, observation) to measure an outcome of interest (e.g., anger management skills, social skills). She would begin by administering the "test" (called the pretest) to all participants in both the control and treatment conditions. Next, she would implement the intervention (e.g., group counseling experience) to the treatment group but not to the control group. (*Note:* The control group would either experience nothing [i.e., wait list control] or may undergo a placebo group counseling experience for some issue other than anger management skills or social skills.) Upon conclusion of the treatment program or intervention, the group leader would again administer the test (this time called the post-test) to members in both groups. It would be expected that no change in the control group members' scores would be observed (i.e., no statistically significant difference between pretest and post-test scores would be observed). However, if the group counseling experience was successful, it would be expected that a significant change would be observed in the treatment group (e.g., post-test scores are higher than pretest scores). Of course, the other designs in Table 21.5 also could be used with this or other examples. However, quasi-experimental and nonexperimental designs do not allow the group leader to conclude that the treatment was the "cause" of the changes noted in the participants. Thus, in many ways, results or outcomes from studies with experimental designs are more valuable and powerful. Note in this example, if randomization of participants was not possible, the same research design could be used, but it would be considered quasi-experimental (see design 5 from Table 21.5).

A lot of thought must be given to the design of the outcome measure used. Often, nonsignificant results are not due to the group work intervention, but to the selection of an outcome measure not sensitive enough to demonstrate the effect of the treatment. Some outcome measures can be obtained easily because they are a matter of record (e.g., grade point average, number of homework assignments completed), or they already exist in published form (e.g., Conners-3, Achenbach System of Empirically Based

Assessment [ASEBA], Beck Depression Inventory [BDI-II], Children's Depression Inventory [CDI]). The number of available outcome measures may be limitless. Sometimes group leaders still need to design an outcome measure with sufficient sensitivity and direct applicability to the issue being studied (e.g., adjustment to a divorce, body image, social skills, peer self-efficacy). When leaders need to develop an outcome measure from scratch, the basics of scale development covered above in the discussion of needs assessments can be helpful. In addition, Weiss (1998, pp. 140–142) provided a dozen principles the assessor should consider:

1. Use simple language.
2. Ask only about things that the respondent can be expected to know.
3. Make the question specific.
4. Define terms that are unclear.
5. Avoid yes-no questions.
6. Avoid double negatives.
7. Don't ask double-barreled questions (e.g., two questions in one).
8. Use wording that has been adopted in the field.
9. Include enough information to jog people's memories or to make them aware of features of a phenomenon they might otherwise overlook.
10. Look for secondhand opinions or ratings only when firsthand information is unavailable.
11. Be sensitive to cultural differences.
12. Learn how to deal with difficult respondent groups.

These principles apply to most types of data collection procedures. Leaders can use a wide range of procedures, each with advantages and disadvantages. Table 21.6 presents descriptions of several of the most common methods of data collection used by leaders.

Single-Subject Research Design (SSRD)

Leaders do not always have access to members who can be randomly assigned to various experimental conditions. In fact, the majority of leaders

TABLE 21.6 Common Data Collection Methods

1. *Interviews* of the counselors, key personnel, or members of stakeholder groups can provide valuable data. Interviews can be structured, semistructured, or unstructured. Structured interviews present a formal sequence of questions to interviewees with no variation in administration, thus generating clear evidence of strengths and weaknesses. Unstructured formats allow for follow-up and deeper exploration, and are commonly used in qualitative studies. Usually, multiple respondents are required for patterns and conclusions to emerge. Face-to-face interviews are generally better than phone interviews, although they are usually more costly and inconvenient. Careful consideration must be given to question development, and interviewers must guard against introducing bias.

2. *Observations* can also be classified as informal or formal. Informal observations tend to yield anecdotal data through a look-and-see approach. Formal or structured observations usually involve a protocol and predetermined procedures for collecting specific types of data during a specified time period. Structured procedures tend to minimize bias. As an example of observation, counselors can be observed implementing a group counseling session by a supervisor or peer.

3. *Written questionnaires, surveys, and rating scales* are usually paper-and-pencil instruments asking a broad range of open- or close-ended questions. Questionnaires and rating scales typically ask for factual responses, while surveys generally solicit participant perceptions. By far, the greatest weakness of this data collection method is that many participants do not complete or return the instrument (i.e., low return rate). It also requires a certain level of literacy. Few respondents take the time to write lengthy responses, so usually it is best to keep the questions simple and close-ended, with the opportunity for participants to expand upon a response if needed. Multiscaled response formats (e.g., Likert scales) often provide more helpful results than yes-no questions. Emailed or online versions of these instruments are becoming more common.

4. *Program records and schedules* are a naturally occurring and helpful source of evaluation data. If stored on a computer in a database format, this kind of data is particularly accessible, and a counselor is well advised to consider this format ahead of time, when determining how best to maintain electronic records and schedules. Archives should also be kept in good order to facilitate record searches. In particular, counselors should keep previous program improvement documents and outcome study reports.

5. *Standardized and educator-made tests* provide objective sources of measurable student performance and progress in the academic, career, and personal-social domains. Individual, classroom, and schoolwide tests can be extremely helpful and powerful measures. Tests are available to measure academic achievement, depression, anxiety, substance use, distractibility, career indecision, and myriad other student behaviors. Likewise, professional counselors can design and develop tests to measure behaviors and characteristics, much like teachers design tests to measure academic achievement.

6. *Academic performance indicators* may include a student's grade point average (GPA) or classroom grade, but they also include daily work behaviors and habits (e.g., attendance, homework completion, disruptions) and attitudes (e.g., academic self-efficacy, attitude toward school).

7. *Products and portfolios* are real-life examples of performance. A product is anything created by a group member (or the counselor) that stemmed from a program standard (e.g., artwork, composition, poster). A portfolio is a collection of exemplar products that can be evaluated to determine the quality of an individual's performance.

need to document effectiveness of services one group at a time and for widely varying presenting problems. An interesting form of experimental research design used by practicing group leaders is the single-subject research design (SSRD) (orsingle-case research design). SSRD involves intensive study of a single individual or a single group. This type of study examines member changes over a period of time both before and after exposure to some treatment or intervention. The pressure for accountability and managed care within all fields of the counseling profession make SSRDs particularly helpful to leaders as they strive to document outcomes.

SSRDs start by measuring the state of the members before the intervention begins. This is called a baseline (no treatment) and is designated by A. The intervention is designated B. Ordinarily, the condition of each member is observed or measured several times during the baseline phase (A) and several times during the intervention phase (B). A line graph is usually used to display the member's behavioral changes over time. Line graphs are interpreted visually rather than statistically, so they are popular among mental health professionals and health maintenance organization workers. The behavior being observed or tracked (i.e., the dependent variable) is displayed on the vertical axis. Scores on a behavior rating scale, number of times a member gets out of his seat without permission, scores on a depression scale, or number of negative self-talk statements are some examples of observed or tracked behaviors that members may be trying to change. The horizontal axis usually indicates the observation session (i.e., passage of time). Member observations may occur each hour, day, or session, as determined by the leader. Data points indicate the member's score at each time of collection throughout the study, and the slope of the condition line indicates whether the member's condition has changed over time. Figure 21.3 provides a diagram of a commonly used SSRD, the AB design.

There are numerous types of SSRDs, including the A-B design, A-B-A design, A-B-A-B design, B-A-B design, A-B-C-B design, and the multiple-baseline design. The two most commonly used designs by leaders (A-B and A-B-A-B) will be discussed below, but the interested reader should

see Erford (2008) for an expanded discussion of SSRDs. The most common, the A-B design, introduces an intervention to the members after a baseline period during which the members act as their own control. In the AB design, the member is observed or measured for several sessions (i.e., the pretreatment baseline phase, A), the intervention is implemented, and the member is observed or measured for several more sessions (the treatment phase, B). The general rule of thumb regarding the number of sessions to measure is to keep measuring until a stable pattern emerges, whether the pattern shows the treatment to be effective or ineffective. A disadvantage of using the A-B design is that it does not control for extraneous or confounding variables. The A-B-A-B design may minimize this problem because it includes two baseline periods interspersed with two intervention periods. Initially, the baseline (A) is established and then treatment (B) is introduced. Once the treatment is shown to have the desired effect, the intervention is withdrawn to collect a second baseline (A). If the member's scores on the dependent variable return to a level of diminished effectiveness, the leader has provided evidence that the intervention was indeed responsible for the changes that the members exhibited during the B phase. At that point, the treatment is reintroduced (B) and more observations are taken, the expectation being that a reintroduction of the previously effective treatment will return the members to a more effective condition. The A-B-A-B response pattern provides strong evidence that the intervention, not some extraneous

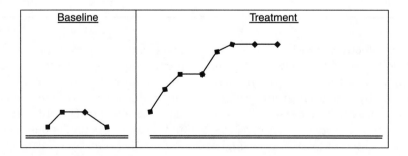

FIGURE 21.3   A-B Design.

or confounding variable, was responsible for changes in the condition of the members.

Putting It All Together: Working for the Future

The current accountability movements in both schools and clinics point to the need for leaders to focus on process and outcome evaluation. It is more essential than ever before that leaders, leaders-in-training, and researchers work together to establish effective group work practices. In the past, leaders have often viewed research as artificial, or a necessary evil. Such a view is counterproductive. Instead, members, practitioners, and researchers must work together—quite literally—to become collaborators in research and evaluation as well as consumers of research. Such collaboration will significantly improve our understanding of efficient and effective group practices and thus improve personal practice and member outcomes.

Summary

Accountability involves the demonstration of responsibility for professional actions. Group leaders demonstrate accountability by providing evidence that answers several primary questions. First, what are the needs of the member and stakeholder population? A needs assessment can be implemented using one of two primary methods. A data-driven needs assessment evaluates real needs demonstrated through derived information. Aggregated results are broken down (disaggregated) so they can be examined on the subgroup level. Such analysis is critical to demonstrate whether all members are benefiting from the counseling program and services. A perceptions-based needs assessment assesses what primary stakeholder groups (e.g., teachers, parents, members) perceive as needs. These perceptions can be gathered through a variety of methods, but some form of quantifiable result is preferred so that various perceived needs can be compared and prioritized.

Second, what was the result of the implemented services? Some argue that process evaluation or outcomes studies are the most valuable facet of group work accountability. Data is collected to evaluate actions and interventions so that judgments can be made on the worth or value of services and programs. Often, traditional research designs can yield helpful and authoritative information about program or event quality. Because of the broad ranging nature of goals and outcomes, leaders attempting to demonstrate the effectiveness of psychoeducational group work interventions may want to use an aggregated hierarchical model in which evidence is collected at the objectives level in order to demonstrate whether higher-order outcomes and goals have been met.

Accountability applies to every facet of a counseling program. Leaders must be prepared to engage in accountability activities, collect evidence continuously, and report on program performance. Being responsible for one's actions and the quality of services provided is an important ethical and professional responsibility.

CHAPTER 22

Outcome Research in Group Work

Bradley T. Erford

PREVIEW

Leaders have an ethical responsibility to "use techniques/procedures/modalities that are grounded in theory and/or have an empirical or scientific foundation" (Herlihy & Corey, 2006, p. 39). Research has concluded that group work can affect members in powerful ways. This chapter reviews research on the effectiveness of group work with children, adolescents, and adults across a variety of settings.

OUTCOME RESEARCH IN GROUP WORK

Leaders have an ethical responsibility to use effective techniques and processes when working with members (American Counseling Association, 2005; Herlihy & Corey, 2006; Lambert, 1991; Lambert, Masters, & Ogles, 1991). Thus, group leaders must become familiar with current extant literature on group work effectiveness, commonly known as outcome research.

Ordinarily, outcome research in group work has involved three types of methodology: clinical trials, qualitative reviews, and meta-analytic reviews. Clinical trial studies are very common in the extant literature, typically consisting of a single study of a specific type of treatment or approach. Clinical trials are important and helpful because they use comparison groups (e.g., placebo, wait-list control, alternative treatment), outcome measures, and standardized treatment protocols (Sexton, Whiston, Bleuer, & Walz, 1997). Use of such instruments and procedures enhances the replicability of results. However, clinical trials offer only a single result from a single study, and different studies using different methodologies frequently yield inconsistent or even contradictory results. One sees the problems with clinical trials frequently on television news programs. Nearly every day a new study is reported that contradicts previous studies on health, diet, or parenting. Inconsistency in the results of clinical trials can lead to great confusion among professionals and the public. Thus, leaders are normally better off relying on accumulations and summarizations of numerous research results to inform practice, rather than on a couple of potentially unreliable studies. These accumulations of research can be conducted using either qualitative or quantitative research methodologies, each approach having strengths and weaknesses.

Perhaps qualitative analyses of accumulated research studies are more commonly employed than quantitative summarization approaches. Ordinarily, a qualitative approach finds researchers examining and summarizing consistent and meaningful trends and findings across contexts, clients, and studies. Qualitative analyses conducted by content experts can yield reliable and meaningful results, but due to their subjective nature, biased conclusions sometimes can result from qualitative reviews. Thus, procedural safeguards and criteria must be developed to insure robustness and replicability of results (Ellis, 1991).

Meta-analysis is a specific quantitative technique that aggregates the results of numerous clinical trials using a meaningful quantitative index, commonly known as an effect size (ES). For experimental studies (e.g., clinical trials), an effect size ordinarily is computed using the formula $(M_e - M_c)/SD_c$ (or some variation of this formula). Basically, this means that an effect size is obtained by subtracting the mean of the control group from the mean of the experimental group, then dividing that difference score by the standard deviation of the control group. Thus, an ES is an index score reported in standard deviation units of the control group sample. By extension, the effect sizes from various comparable studies can then be combined and averaged to yield a result across several, even hundreds of, studies. This index is usually weighted according to the sample size so that larger, more stable sample results are given greater weight than smaller, less stable sample results. To determine the strength of a given effect size, it is compared to some criterion-referenced effect size range, such as the popular ES range developed by Cohen (1988). Cohen proposed that an ES of 0 indicates no effect of treatment, an ES equal to .20 indicates a small effect of treatment, an ES equal to .50 indicates a medium effect of treatment, and ES = .80+ indicates a large effect of treatment. Thus an ES = .60 indicates a medium effect, while an ES of .15 indicates little to no effect.

Another way to interpret effect sizes is in terms of the number of standard deviations above or below the control group mean a given treatment score lies; basically this involves z-score transformations. For example, ES = 0 means that the treatment and control group means were the same. Assuming that the variances of the treatment and control group samples are similar, one can conclude that the average client in the treatment group performed no better or no worse than the average participant in the control group. In other words, the treatment had no effect. On the other hand, if ES = .50, this means that the treatment mean was one-half standard deviation (SD) above the mean of the control group. The medium effect associated with an ES = .50 can also be expressed in terms of a percentile outcome; that is, an ES = .50 means that the average client in the treatment group attained a better outcome than 69% of the control group participants (.50 standard deviations above the mean [z = +0.50] is a percentile rank of about 69). Likewise, an ES = 2.00, is not only a large effect (i.e., >.80), it also indicates that the average treatment group participant performed better than 98% of control group participants (i.e., 2.0 standard deviations above the mean [z = +2.00] is the 98th percentile rank).

When an empirical study is correlational (usually involving computation of a Pearson family r), Cohen (1988) suggested interpreting effect sizes according to the following criterion-referenced interpretive range: $r = .10$, (small), $r = .30$ (medium), $r = .50$ (large). There are many additional formulas for estimating effect size estimates, but the reader of group outcome research will encounter these two indexes most frequently in the extant research.

At this point, it should be clear to the reader how meta-analysis can help compensate for methodological problems in some clinical studies by summarizing results across numerous similar studies. This helps to minimize study-specific error and generalize trends and significant results. While meta-analysis has been common in counseling and psychological research, it is by no means free of critics (Ioniddis, Cappelleri, & Lau, 1998; Shadish, 1996; Sharpe, 1997; Sohn, 1997), some of whom conclude that combining numerous studies into a single result simply spreads errors stemming from poorly designed studies into well-designed studies. At the very least, readers should view meta-analysis as a potentially helpful procedure for analyzing robust trends across studies, but they should view results with some caution, as is the case with any research study. With all of this information on clinical trials, qualitative reviews, and meta-analysis as context, we are now ready to explore the research outcomes literature in group work. Enjoy!

HOW EFFECTIVE IS GROUP WORK? AN INTRODUCTION TO GROUP WORK OUTCOME RESEARCH

Hundreds of studies over the past half century have explored the effectiveness of group work, and the short answer to the question, "How effective is group work?" is: very effective. This conclusion is consistently reached for both children and adults, and regardless whether the reviews of extant literature are qualitative or narrative (Abramowitz, 1976; Bednar & Kaul, 1994; Dagley, Gazda, Eppinger, & Stewart, 1994; Fuhriman & Burlingame, 1994a; Gazda, 1989; Kanas, 1986; Kaul & Bednar, 1986; MacKenzie, 1994, 1995; Orlinsky & Howard, 1986; Sternbarger & Budman, 1996; Toseland & Siporin, 1986; Zimpfer, 1990a), or empirical meta-analyses (Bednar & Kaul, 1994; Burlingame, Fuhriman, & Mosier, 2003; Fuhriman & Burlingame, 1994a, 1994b; Hoag, 1997; Hoag & Burlingame, 1997; Lambert & Bergin, 1994; McDermit, Miller, & Brown, 2001; McRoberts, Burlingame, & Hoag, 1998; Miller & Berman, 1983; Mitte, 2005; Robinson, Berman, & Neimeyer, 1990; Shapiro & Shapiro, 1982; Smith, Glass, & Miller, 1980; Tillitski, 1990; Whiston, Eder, Rahardja, & Tai, 2005).

Bachar (1998) (see Table 22.1) reported that results of meta-analytic reviews of group counseling outcome studies ordinarily yield effect sizes of about 0.70 or higher in comparison with control groups, and about 0.40 or higher in comparison with placebo. As explained above, an effect size of .70 means that the average member receiving counseling displayed a better outcome than 76%

of control group participants (i.e., +.70 standard deviations above the mean is the 76th percentile rank). In addition, most studies indicate little or no difference between individual and group counseling treatment effectiveness, although this generalization does not account for the fact that some specific conditions may be better addressed through individual counseling approaches (Hoag & Burlingame, 1997; McRobert et al., 1998).

Group work has also been demonstrated to be effective with specific client groups experiencing internalizing disorders, such as clients with depression (Scott & Stradling, 1991; Vandervoort & Furhiman, 1991), eating disorders (Zimpfer, 1990b), obsessive-compulsive disorder (Krone, Himle, & Nesse, 1991), grief (Zimpfer, 1991), and sexual abuse trauma (Alexander, Neimeyer, Follette, Moore, & Harter, 1989; Cahill, Llewelyn, & Pearson, 1991; Winick & Levene, 1992), and there is general agreement that group treatment is both outcome effective and cost-efficient (Scheidlinger, 1993, Yalom & Leszcz, 2005). In addition, groups have also been shown effective in addressing externalizing disorders, particularly treatment of spousal abuse (Dutton, 1986; Tolman & Bennett, 1990), as well as a vast assortment of developmental and clinical issues. For example, Zimpfer offered meaningful reviews of important clinical topics of importance to group leaders, including midlife career change (1989), divorce and separation (1990a), bulimia (1990b), and bereavement (1991).

A frequently debated question over the years has been whether group or individual counseling is the more effective approach. In short, group treatment is as effective as individual treatment for most conditions as long as the group treatment is specific to the condition (Fuhriman & Burlingame, 1994a). And sometimes, a simultaneous combination of individual and group approaches is most effective, such as is likely the case with Borderline Personality Disorder (Slavinsky-Holey, 1983), and eating disorders (Bohanske & Lemberg, 1987; Franko, 1987). It is also essential to realize that some individuals benefit much more from group treatment than do others (Piper, 1994). McRoberts et al. (1998) indicated no significant effects

TABLE 22.1 Selected Meta-Analytic Studies from the Extant Literature of the Effectiveness of Group Work with Adults or Heterogeneous (i.e., Child, Adolescent, and Adult) Samples

Source	Outcome Explored	Population	ES
Burlingame, Fuhriman, & Mosier (2003)	Group counseling effectiveness	Heterogeneous	0.58
Dush, Hirt, & Schroeder (1983)	Group counseling effectiveness	Heterogeneous	0.58
Faith, Wong & Carpenter (1995)	Group sensitivity training	Heterogeneous	0.62
	Behavioral measures	Heterogeneous	1.03
	Self-report measures	Heterogeneous	0.44
Hoag (1997)	Group counseling effectiveness	Children	0.50
Hoag & Burlingame (1997)	Group treatment	School-aged	0.61
McDermit, Miller & Brown (2001)	Group therapy for depression	Heterogeneous	1.03
Miller & Berman (1983)	Group counseling effectiveness	Heterogeneous	0.79
Robinson et al. (1990)	Group counseling effectiveness	Clients with depression	0.84
Shapiro & Shapiro (1982)	Group counseling effectiveness	Heterogeneous	0.89
Smith et al. (1980)	Group counseling effectiveness	Heterogeneous	0.83
Tillitski (1990)	Group counseling effectiveness	Heterogeneous	1.35
Whiston et al. (2005)	Group interventions	School-aged	0.36

between individual and group counseling interventions when therapist characteristics such as gender, training, experience, or use of a coleader/cotherapist were studied.

Table 22.1 provides a summary of some available meta-analyses that will be referred to at times throughout the remainder of this section. The remainder of this review of outcome research on group work effectiveness will focus on three primary areas: (1) process issues, (2) group research with adults, and (3) group research with children and adolescents.

PROCESS ISSUES IN GROUP OUTCOME RESEARCH

The process variables in group work can be complex and difficult to isolate and analyze because of the holistic nature of human interaction. Ordinarily, group process variables include facets such as (1) group planning characteristics, (2) group

structure, (3) pre-group training, (4) therapeutic factors, and (5) leader characteristics.

Group Effectiveness Related to Group Planning Characteristics

In a fascinating, complex, and comprehensive meta-analysis, McRoberts et al. (1998) found no significant differences based upon group size (less than nine versus more than nine participants), group type (psychoeducational versus process), or group membership (open versus closed). In addition, McRoberts et al. (1998) reported that group work was more effective than individual counseling when 10 or fewer sessions were conducted, confirming the use of group work as a short-term treatment alternative (Budman, Simeone, Reilly, & Demby, 1994; Burlingame & Fuhriman, 1990). Faith, Wong, and Carpenter (1995) reported larger effect sizes for larger group sizes and groups that met for a greater number of sessions in their meta-analytic study of sensitivity training groups.

Group Structure and Effectiveness

Gazda (1989) identified a trend favoring use of more structured approaches to group work. Structured groups are more leader-directed than are process-oriented groups, leading to greater standardization, efficiency, and replicability of the group experience. Rhode and Stockton (1994) reported that a lack of structure led to client difficulties with interpersonal fears, cognitive distortion, subjective distress, and premature termination, leading to the suggestion that structure introduced early in the group process helps to define boundaries and build trust.

The use of structured activities to build trust and cohesion has been well documented. Stockton, Rhode, and Haughey (1992) used structured group exercises to build group cohesion at the start of a group experience, while Caple and Cox (1989) found that early structured exercises helped enhance group cohesion at critical points later in the group's life. On the other hand, Lee and Bednar (1977) found that increased structure can lead to lower group cohesion probably mediated by certain member personality characteristics. Therefore, structured group approaches should be used strategically and always matched with member personalities to enhance effectiveness. This is especially the case when counseling low risk takers because Evensen and Bednar (1978) found that low risk takers evaluated group experiences more negatively as group structure increased. Summing up this complexity quite nicely, Gazda et al. (2001, p. 85) concluded, "The interaction between structure, group composition, leader characteristics, and group stage is always complex" and deserves great attention in future research efforts.

The Effectiveness of Pre-Group Training

Pre-group training involves personal, written, audio-, or videotaped procedures meant to prepare group members for entry into the group (Yalom & Leszcz, 2005). Pre-group training has been shown to boost treatment outcome (Hilkey, Wilhelm, & Horne, 1982), interpersonal interactions (Yalom, Houts, Zimberg, & Rand, 1967), and attendance (France & Dugo, 1985).

The Effectiveness of Therapeutic Factors

Therapeutic factors (e.g., cohesion, instillation of hope, altruism, universality) appear to affect different populations and member disorders differentially (Kaul & Bednar, 1986) and even at different stages of group development. For example, Kivlighan and Mullison (1988) indicated universality was very important early in the group process but less so in later stages, while interpersonal learning was less important early on and gained importance in the later group stages. A study by Butler and Furhriman (1983) indicated that group members perceived catharsis, interpersonal interaction, and self-understanding to be the most important therapeutic factors, providing evidence of the need for particular attention to these factors by group leaders. In contrast, Shaughnessy and Kivlighan (1995) criticized studies such as these for being too simplistic and, through a cluster analysis, showed that "self-reflective responders" valued the triad of therapeutic factors mentioned above, but "broad spectrum responders" (the majority of group member participants) actually endorsed and benefited from all of Yalom's proposed curative factors.

Effective Leader Characteristics

When it comes to therapeutic factors, a great deal of the group work literature explores group leadership characteristics and their effect on client outcome. Effective leaders have been shown to nurture a sense of hope in group members (Couch & Childers, 1987; Dykeman & Appleton, 1998), and display positive personal characteristics (e.g., positive attitudes, emotionally supportive behaviors) (Combs, Avila, & Purky, 1978; Stockton, Morran, & Velboff, 1987).

GROUP OUTCOME RESEARCH WITH ADULTS

The outcome research on adults is much more robust than that available for children and adolescents. This brief section will review the effectiveness of group work relative to (1) structured treatment regimens, (2) differential effects of various outcome reporting sources, (3) group composition, and (4) effectiveness of group work with members with various clinical diagnoses.

The Effectiveness of Structured Group Treatment Regimens

The 1990s produced a significant increase in group treatment protocols targeting specific diagnoses with standardized treatment regimens replicable across clients, practitioners, and settings (Fettes & Peters, 1992; Hoag & Burlingame, 1997). For some, this represented a significant advance over the previous process-oriented and generic use of groups for heterogeneous clients and presenting problems. In general, there seems to be an outcome advantage to groups using structured treatment, manual-based approaches to group work. This has occurred concomitantly with the increased demand for group treatment by health maintenance organizations (HMOs) as a more time- and cost-effective delivery system for mental health services. Burlingame et al. (2003) indicated that these two factors, the maturation of the group counseling literature to provide diagnosis and client-specific group treatments and the efficiency orientation of the current health care movement, have coalesced to create the current demand for effective and efficient group work leaders.

Outcomes Based on Different Response Sources

Burlingame et al. (2003), in a very interesting meta-analysis of adult outcomes across 111 experimental and quasi-experimental studies, concluded that the source of the outcome made a difference in the overall effect size. For example, objective sources of member progress yielded an effect size of .31; therapist report, .35; self-report, .56; independent rater, .73; and significant other report, .81. It can be surmised that the more objective the outcome source, the less effective the group treatment. Another way of framing this

result could be that group members and those they associate with most frequently (i.e., significant others) may be expressing an element of satisfaction with the group treatment that empowers them to perceive the members as making more progress than do the more objective sources of outcome information.

Differential Effects of Group Composition in Adults

Members of heterogeneous groups attained an overall effect size of only .25, while members of homogeneous groups attained a significantly higher level of improvement (ES = .56) (Burlingame et al., 2003). Thus, group interventions aimed more directly at underlying, common difficulties that are the focus of the group appear more effective.

Outpatient groups (ES = .55) outperformed inpatient groups (ES = .20), although this is likely explained by the severity of members' conditions and the current level of crisis prevalent (Bulingame et al., 2003). Mixed-gender adult groups were more efficacious (ES = .66), overall, than all male (ES = .41) or all female groups (ES = .39). Perhaps the diverse perspectives and interpersonal learning opportunities available in mixed-gender groups accounted for this difference.

Effectiveness of Group Work with Members with Various Clinical Diagnoses

Group treatment of depression in adults (Robinson et al., 1990; Vandervoort & Fuhriman, 1991) and Bipolar Disorder is quite effective. Group interventions for members with these mood disorders appear helpful in providing interpersonal support, learning effective coping skills, and understanding the nature and course of the conditions. In the treatment of adults with eating disorders, group interventions appear to be very effective, and even more so when coupled with individual counseling. In his review of more than 30 studies of eating disorders, Zimpfer (1990b) concluded that every study resulted in treatment gains such as reduced binging and purging, improved body image, and lower levels of depression.

Group therapy was highly effective (ES > .80) in the treatment of adults with depression, eating disorders, personality disorders, substance abuse, and anxiety disorders, and moderately effective (.50 < ES < .80) for adults with thought disorders, criminal behavior, stress, neuroticism, or who were sexually abused. No significant relationships were found related to degree of patient diagnosis, group size, pregroup training, membership (open versus closed), therapist experience, or client gender or age (Burlingame et al., 2003).

GROUP OUTCOME RESEARCH WITH CHILDREN AND ADOLESCENTS

Numerous narrative reviews have been conducted on the effectiveness of group work with children and adolescent populations (e.g., Dagley et al., 1994; Dies & Riester, 1986; Sugar, 1993). Unfortunately, a general conclusion is that the sophistication of the research methodology was inferior when compared to the extant literature available for adults. However, a number of meta-analytic studies have been conducted and, collectively, indicate that group work with children and adolescents is effective and as effective as individual counseling (Baer & Nietzel, 1991; Casey & Berman, 1985; Grossman & Hughes, 1992; Prout & DeMartino, 1986; Roberts & Camasso, 1991; Russell, Greenwald, & Shirk, 1991; Shirk & Russell, 1992; Weisz, Weiss, Alicke, & Klotz, 1987). Of course, some studies have pointed to interesting differential effects. For example, Tillitsky (1990) indicated that adolescents reported better outcomes when they were treated with group counseling rather than with individual counseling, but children reported the opposite effect (i.e., individual treatment was more effective than group work).

In general, group outcome research with the child and adolescent populations falls broadly into the following areas: (1) large group psychoeducational approaches, and (2) small-group approaches addressing developmental and clinical concerns.

The Effectiveness of Large-Group Psychoeducational Approaches with Children and Adolescents

Borders and Drury (1992), in a qualitative review of the literature, found support for classroom guidance activities, a staple of the comprehensive developmental guidance movement so commonplace in school counseling programs today, but Whiston and Sexton (1998) and Wiggins and Wiggins (1992) found little empirical support in the experimental literature. In fairness, few high-quality experimental studies existed at the time, and of those that did, more heartening evidence was available to support guidance activities at the elementary level (Hadley, 1988; Lee, 1993). Still, and to the contrary, several of the more rigorous studies have either found no improvement because of large-group intervention (Laconte, Shaw, & Dunn, 1993) or less progress than that found when using individual interventions (Wiggins & Wiggins, 1992). In a somewhat dated review, Strein (1988) concluded that 103 of the 344 studies of large-group classroom guidance studies reviewed reached statistical significance, and the vast majority of the most rigorously controlled studies did not. And, finally, Gosette and O'Brien (1993) found only 70 of 278 treatment comparisons supported the use of large-group classroom guidance. These results are troubling given the emphasis on providing large-group guidance activities in schools today, a practice stemming from the comprehensive developmental guidance movement championed by professional associations such as the American School Counseling Association. Certainly, more and better studies are needed to resolve this controversy.

Small-Group Approaches Addressing Developmental and Clinical Concerns with Children and Adolescents

Most of the counseling research studies involving school students explored the effectiveness of group counseling approaches (Prout & Prout,

1998), although the quality and sophistication of these studies was inferior compared to those of adult group outcome studies overall (Hoag & Burlingame, 1997). Still, Whiston and Sexton (1998) concluded that group approaches with school-age children were very effective in addressing social skills, discipline, and family adjustment problems. Hoag and Burlingame (1997) reported effect sizes of .72 for depression, .56 for behavioral disorders, .55 for learning disorders, .53 for children of divorce, and .32 for social problems.

Regarding depression in adolescents, Beeferman and Orvaschel (1994) reported that group counseling is a very effective treatment, with the best results coming from a combination of supportive group processes, cognitive-behavioral interventions, and some behavioral skills training and homework. Reynolds and Coats (1986) showed that relaxation training was just as effective as cognitive-behavioral interventions with adolescent group members. Among high school students, groups focusing on cognitive-behavioral approaches and relaxation appear particularly effective (Bauer, Sapp, & Johnson, 2000; Kiselica, Baker, Thomas, & Reddy, 1994).

Group approaches were shown to produce positive outcomes for children of divorce in both the short-term (Omizo & Omizo, 1988; Pedro-Carroll & Alpert-Gillis, 1997) and long-term (Pedro-Carroll, Sutton, & Wyman, 1999). Group counseling has also been used for many years to treat disruptive behavior disorders in children and adolescents. Braswell (1993) reported cognitive interventions to be especially effective, particularly her structured "think first—act later" procedure.

In general, Whiston (2007) suggested that group approaches with children have ample support in the outcome research literature, while further study of group work effectiveness with high school students is needed, primarily because of methodological issues. This is interesting given the general perception that adolescents learn and process best in peer group interactions. Given the context that group work is effective with children and adults, it is reasonable to conclude that it is also likely to be effective with adolescents, but that group

leaders and researchers must collaborate to promote research with this population of students.

PREVENTING HARM IN GROUP WORK

The ethical imperative of nonmaleficence (i.e., do no harm) is a paramount consideration when engaging in group work. Unfortunately, as with any approach to helping, group leaders do acknowledge the possibility that some clients may experience treatments that are not just ineffective, but potentially harmful. Kaplan (1982) reported that casualty rates for group interventions varied widely by approach, but acknowledged that these rates were no higher than for other types of counseling. Group leaders can prevent harm to members primarily through efficient member screening and effective counselor behaviors.

Efficient Member Screening

Dykeman and Appleton (1998) listed a number of client contraindications for participating in group work: acute self-disclosure fears, Borderline Personality Disorder, extreme interpersonal sensitivity, low anxiety tolerance, low frustration tolerance, low motivation for change, marked emotional lability, paranoia, psychopathy, psychotic thinking, schizophrenia, severe depression, severe impulse control problems, and unstable medical condition. Clients with any of these conditions will probably not benefit from group counseling and may lead to ineffective treatment for other group members. That said, a number of research studies have shown group work to be an acceptable and effective treatment for a number of these conditions, such as Borderline Personality Disorder or low motivation. Obviously more research is needed before potential members can be summarily excluded from group counseling or psychotherapy experiences.

Effective Counselor Behaviors

Not surprisingly, Hadley and Strupp (1976) warned that poorly trained or skill-deficient group leaders can be harmful to group members. Obviously, leaders who permit clients with the contraindicated conditions listed above to participate in group work risk client harm—and not just to the clients with the contraindicated condition.

Hadley and Strupp (1976) also concluded that group leaders with certain personality traits could be harmful to clients. These traits include absence of genuineness, coldness, excessive need to make people change, excessive unconscious hostility, greed, lack of interest or warmth, lack of self-awareness, narcissism, pessimism, obsessiveness, sadism, and seductiveness. Lieberman et al. (1973) reported that nearly 50% of all group work casualties are produced by the "aggressive stimulator" leadership style, which involves the leadership characteristics of high stimulus input, intrusiveness, confrontation, challenging but demonstrating, and high positive caring. Obviously, group leaders who seek advanced group coursework and quality supervision are better able to increase skills and identify ineffective and harmful personal behavior.

IMPLICATIONS OF THE CURRENT STATE OF THE OUTCOME LITERATURE FOR GROUP WORKERS

While much helpful outcome research has accumulated over the years, much is still needed to help leaders skillfully implement group work. And this is where you, as a member of the next generation of group leaders, can build a better profession. There are three primary ways that group leaders can help: (1) collaborate with researchers, (2) advocate for outcome research funding, and (3) read the outcome literature and practice accordingly.

Collaborate with Researchers

Students and practitioners must collaborate with researchers whenever possible. Students interested in becoming group leaders should volunteer to help professors and other researchers. Research can be a long and intense process; it often takes several years to complete a study and publish the results. However, students can provide valuable aid in conducting portions of studies, thus contributing to the final product. During this process, students will learn valuable practice, research, and evaluation skills. Likewise, practitioners can collaborate with researchers to conduct site-based action research and program evaluation with members.

One practitioner's results with a handful of members when combined with the handfuls of member results from other group leaders can lead to meaningful results. Researchers frequently attempt to coordinate these field trials, but struggle for lack of contacts in the field. Consider making your worksite available to researchers so that results can be aggregated across a number of sites. The large populations served by group leaders in schools and community agencies can be particularly useful for outcomes research. Students who become active in research studies begin to understand the research process and are more likely to stay active in research after entering the field. Providing access to participants and helping to collect data are the two components of outcome research with which practitioners can be of greatest aid.

Advocate for Outcome Research Funding

All group leaders must advocate for increased funding for outcome research. Ordinarily, funding for research comes from government agencies, private foundations, universities, and professional organizations (Erford, 2008). Advocating for research funding by these sources is a professional responsibility that will generate new practice-improving findings: findings that will help group leaders understand how to better help group members meet their goals, help researchers communicate this information to group leaders, and help researchers conduct basic research meant to inform counseling practice. But this all starts with your advocacy efforts.

Read the Outcome Literature

Group leaders improve the effectiveness of their practice by reading and using the outcome research. In particular, group leaders should peruse the *Journal for Specialists in Group Work* (published by the Association for Specialists in Group Work [ASGW]), *Group Dynamics: Theory, Research, and Practice* (published by the American Psychological Association [APA]), and the *International Journal of Group* *Psychotherapy* (published by the American Group Psychotherapy Association [AGPA]). Group leaders can serve an incredibly helpful service to colleagues by passing along helpful resources sifted from the literature.

Summary

Hundreds of studies have explored the effectiveness of various facets of group work; however, much still remains to be learned. This chapter briefly reviewed the extant literature on group counseling outcomes research as it relates to process issues and our work with adults, adolescents, and children. While much is already known about group work effectiveness, counselors should collaborate with researchers and conduct their own action research and evaluation studies to create new evidence of group counseling outcomes. Counselors should advocate for increased funding for group work research, and read and disseminate outcome research on effective group counseling practice to other practitioners.

Accountability applies to every facet of a counseling program. Leaders must be prepared to engage in accountability activities, collect evidence continuously, and report on program performance. Being responsible for one's actions and the quality of services provided is an important ethical and professional responsibility.

REFERENCES

Aasheim, L. L., & Niemann, S. H. (2006). Guidance/psychoeducational groups. In D. Capuzzi & D. Gross (Eds.), *Introduction to group work* (4th ed.) (pp. 269–294). Denver, CO: Love Publishing.

Abramowitz, C. V. (1976). The effectiveness of group psychotherapy with children. *Archives of General Psychiatry, 33,* 320–326.

Addison, J. T. (1992). Urie Bronfenbrenner. *Human Ecology, 20*(2), 16–20.

Agazarian, Y. M. (1997). *Systems-centered therapy for groups.* New York: Guilford.

Agazarian, Y. M., & Gantt, S. (2003). Phases of group development: Systems-centered hypotheses and their implications for research and practice. *Group Dynamics: Theory, Research, and Practice, 7,* 238–252.

Akos, P., Goodnough, G. E., & Milsom, A. S. (2004). Preparing school counselors for group work. *The Journal for Specialists in Group Work, 29,* 127–136.

Alexander, P. C., Neimeyer, R. A., Follette, V. M., Moore, M. K., & Harter, S. (1989). A comparison of group treatments of women sexually abused as children. *Journal of Consulting and Clinical Psychology, 57,* 479–483.

American Counseling Association. (2005). *ACA code of ethics* (3rd ed.). Alexandria, VA: Author.

American Counseling Association Professional Standards Committee. (1991). Cross cultural competencies and objectives. Retrieved December 19, 2005, from http://www.counseling.org/Content/NavigationMenu/RESOURCES/MULTICULTURALANDDIVERSITYISSUES/Competencies/Competencies.htm

American School Counselor Association (ASCA). (2004). *Ethical standards for school counselors.* Alexandria, VA: Author.

American School Counselor Association. (2005). *The ASCA national model: A framework for school counseling programs* (2nd ed.). Alexandria, VA: Author.

American School Counselor Association. (2007). *ASCA position statement on group counseling.* Retrieved December 24, 2008 from http://www.schoolcounselor.org

Antony, M. M., & Barlow, D. H. (Eds.). (2002). *Handbook of assessment and treatment planning for psychological disorders.* New York: The Guilford Press.

Arman, J. F. (2000). A small group model for working with elementary school children of alcoholics. *Professional School Counseling, 3,* 290–294.

Arman, J. F. (2002). A brief counseling model to increase resiliency of students with mild disabilities. *Journal of Humanistic Counseling, Education and Development, 41,* 120–128.

Asner-Self, K. K., & Feyissa, A. (2002). The use of poetry in psychoeducational groups with multicultural-multilingual clients. *Journal for Specialists in Group Work, 27,* 136–160.

Association for Specialists in Group Work (ASGW). (1998). Principles for diversity competent group workers. Retrieved November 8, 2008, from http://www.asgw.org

Association for Specialists in Group Work (ASGW). (2000). Professional standards for the training of group workers. Retrieved February 23, 2006, from http://www.asgw.org

Association for Specialists in Group Work (ASGW). (2006). Retrieved December 21, 2006 from www.asgw.org/purpose.asp

Association for Specialists in Group Work (ASGW). (2007). Best practice guidelines. Retrieved December 24, 2008 from http://www.asgw.org

Axelson, J. A. (1999). *Counseling and development in a multicultural society* (3rd ed.). Pacific Grove, CA: Brooks/Cole.

Baca, L. M., & Koss-Chioino, J. D. (1997). Development of a cultural responsive group counseling model for Mexican American adolescents. *Journal of Multicultural Counseling and Development, 25,* 130–141.

Bachar, E. (1998). Psychotherapy—an active agent: Assessing the effectiveness of psychotherapy and its curative factors. *Israel Journal of Psychiatry and Related Sciences, 35,* 128–135.

Baer, R. A., & Nietzel, M. T. (1991). Cognitive and behavioral treatment of impulsivity in children: A meta-analytic review of the outcome literature. *Journal of Clinical Child Psychology, 20,* 400–412.

Bales, R. F. (1950). *Interaction process analysis: A method for the study of small groups.* Cambridge, MA: Addison-Wesley.

Bales, R. F., Cohen, S. P., & Williams, S. A. (1979). *SYMLOG: A system for the multiple level observation of groups.* New York: Free Press.

Bandura, A. (1997). *Self-efficacy: The exercise of control.* New York: Freeman.

Barlow, C. A., Blythe, J. A., & Edmonds, M. (1999). *A handbook of interactive exercises for groups.* Needham Heights, MA: Allyn & Bacon.

Battle, C. C., Imber, S. D., Hoen-Saric, R., Nash, C., & Frank, J. D. (1965). Target complaints as criteria of improvement. *American Journal of Psychotherapy, 20,* 184–192.

Bauer, S. R., Sapp, M., & Johnson, D. (2000). Group counseling strategies for rural at-risk high school students. *The High School Journal, 83,* 41–50.

Beck, A. (1993). *Manual for the Beck Anxiety Inventory.* San Antonio, TX: The Psychological Corporation.

Becvar, D. S., & Becvar, R. J. (1996). *Family therapy: A systemic integration* (3rd ed.). Needham Heights, MA: Allyn & Bacon.

Bednar, R. L., & Kaul, T. J. (1994). Experiential group research: Can the canon fire? In A. E. Bergin & S. L. Garfield (Eds.), *Handbook of psychotherapy and behavior change: An empirical analysis* (4th ed.) (pp. 631–663). New York: John Wiley & Sons.

Beeferman, D., & Orvaschel, H. (1994). Group psychotherapy for depressed adolescents: A critical review. *International Journal of Group Psychotherapy, 44,* 463–475.

Bemak, F., & Chung, R. (2004). Teaching multicultural group counseling: Perspectives for a new era. *Journal for Specialists in Group Work, 29,* 31–41.

Bemak, F., Chung, R., & Siroskey-Sabdo, L. A. (2005). Empowerment groups for academic success: An innovative approach to prevent high school failure for at-risk, urban African American girls. *Professional School Counseling, 8,* 377–390.

Berg, R. C., Landreth, G. L., & Fall, K. A. (2006). *Group counseling: Concepts and procedures* (4th ed.). New York: Routledge.

Bergin, J. J. (1993). Small-group counseling. In A. Vernon (Ed.), *Counseling children and adolescents* (pp. 299–332). Denver: Love.

Bernardez, T. (1996). Women's therapy groups as the treatment of choice. In B. DeChant (Ed.), *Women and group psychotherapy: Theory and practice* (pp. 242–262). New York: Guilford.

Berzon, B., Pious, C., & Farson, R. (1963). The therapeutic event in group psychotherapy: A study of subjective reports by group members. *Journal of Individual Psychology, 19,* 204–212.

Billow, R. M. (2003). Rebellion in group. *International Journal of Group Psychotherapy, 53,* 331–351.

Bion, W. R. (1961). *Experiences in groups.* New York: Basic Books.

Bireda, M. R. (2002). *Cultures in conflict: Eliminating racial profiling in school discipline.* Lanham, MD: Scarecrow Press.

Birnbaum, M., & Cicchetti, A. (2000). The power of purposeful sessional endings in each group encounter. *Social Work with Groups, 23,* 37–52.

Birnbaum, M. L., Mason, S. E., & Cicchetti, A. (2002). Impact of purposeful sessional endings on both the group and practitioner. *Social Work with Groups, 25,* 3–19.

Bishop, R. (1993). Multicultural literature children: Making informed choices. In V. Harris (Ed.), *Teaching multicultural literature in grades K-8* (pp. 39–53). Norwood, MA: Chistopher-Gordon.

Bohanske, J., & Lemberg, R. (1987). An intensive group process-retreat model for the treatment of bulimia. *Group, 11,* 228–237.

Bolman, L. (1971). Some effects of trainers on their T-groups. *Journal of Applied Behavioral Science, 7,* 309–325.

Borders, L. D., & Drury, S. M. (1992). Comprehensive school counseling programs: A review for policy-makers and practitioners. *Journal of Counseling and Development, 70,* 487–498.

Bostwick, G. J., Jr. (1987). "Where's Mary?" A review of the group treatment dropout literature. *Social Work with Groups, 10,* 117–132.

Bradley, C. (2001). A counseling group for African American adolescent males. *Professional School Counseling, 4,* 370–373.

Brashares, A. (2003). *The sisterhood of the traveling pants.* New York: Delacorte Press.

Braswell, L. (1993). Cognitive-behavior groups for children manifesting ADHD and other disruptive behavior disorders. *Special Services in the Schools, 8,* 91–117.

Brenner, V. (1999). Process-play: A simulation procedure for group work training. *Journal for Specialists in Group Work, 24,* 145–151.

Brigman, G., & Campbell, C. (2003). Helping students improve academic achievement and school success behavior. *Professional School Counseling, 7,* 91–98.

Brigman, G. A., Webb, L. D., & Campbell, C. (2007). Building skills for school success: Improving the academic and social competence of students. *Professional School Counseling, 10,* 279–288.

Brinson, J., & Lee, C. (1997). Culturally responsive group leadership. In H. Forster-Miller & J. A. Kottler (Eds.), *Issues and challenges for group practitioners* (pp. 43–56). Denver: Love.

Brown, A., & Mistry, T. (1994). Group work with mixed membership groups: Issues of race and gender. *Social Work with Groups, 17,* 5–21.

Brown, D., & Trusty, J. (2005). School counselors, comprehensive school counseling programs, and academic achievement: Are school counselors promising more than they can deliver? *Professional School Counseling, 9,* 1–8.

Brown, N. W. (2004). *Psychoeducational groups: Process and practice* (2nd ed.). New York: Brunner Routledge.

Brown, N. (2006). A group image. In J. L. DeLucia-Waack, K. H. Bridbord, J. S. Kleiner, & A. Nitza (Eds.), *Group work experts share their favorite activities: A guide to choosing, planning, conducting, and processing* (revised) (pp. 65–66). Alexandria, VA: Association for Specialists in Group Work.

Brown-Shaw, M., Westwood, M., & de Vries, B. (1999). Integrating personal reflection and group-based enactments. *Journal of Aging Studies, 13,* 109–119.

Bryan, J. (2005). Fostering educational resilience and academic achievement in urban schools through school-family-community partnerships. *Professional School Counseling, 8,* 219–227.

Budman, S. H., & Gurman, A. S. (1988). *The theory and practice of brief therapy.* New York: Guilford Press.

Budman, S. H., Simeone, P. G., Reilly, R., & Demby, A. (1994). Progress in short-term and time-limited group psychotherapy: Evidence and implications. In A. Fuhriman & G. M. Burlingame (Eds.), *Handbook of group psychotherapy* (pp. 370–415). New York: Wiley.

Burlingame, G. M., & Fuhriman, A. (1990). Time-limited group therapy. *Counseling Psychologist, 18,* 93–118.

Burlingame, G. M., Fuhriman, A., & Mosier, J. (2003). The differential effectiveness of group psychotherapy: A meta-analytic perspective. *Group Dynamics: Theory, Research, and Practice, 7,* 3–12.

Butler, T., & Fuhriman, A. (1983). Curative factors in group therapy: A review of recent literature. *Small Group Behavior, 14,* 131–142.

Cahill, C., Llewelyn, S. P., & Pearson, C. (1991). Treatment of sexual abuse which occurred in childhood: A review. *British Journal of Clinical Psychology, 30,* 1–12.

Campbell, C., & Dahir, C. A. (1997). *The national standards for school counseling programs.* Alexandria, VA: American School Counselor Association.

Campbell, L., & Page, R. (1993). The therapeutic effects of group process on the behavioral patterns of a drug-addicted group. *Journal of Addictions & Offender Counseling, 13*(2), 34–46.

Caple, R. B., & Cox, P. L. (1989). Relationships among group structure, member expectations, attraction to group and satisfaction with the group experience. *Journal for Specialists in Group Work, 14,* 16–24.

Capuzzi, D., & Gross, D. R. (2002). *Introduction to group counseling* (3rd ed.). Denver: Love Publishing.

Carey, J., Dimmitt, C., Kosine, N., & Poynton, T. (2005). An evidence-based practice approach to school counselor education. Retrieved February 1, 2008, from http://www.umass.edu/schoolcounseling/CSCORPowerPoints.htm

Carrier, J. W., & Haley, M. (2006). Psychotherapy groups. In D. Capuzzi & D. Gross (Eds.), *Introduction to group work* (4th ed.). Denver, CO: Love Publishing.

Casey, R. J., & Berman, J. S. (1985). The outcome of psychotherapy with children. *Psychological Bulletin, 98,* 388–400.

Chandy, J. M., Harris, L., Blum, R. W., & Resnick, M. D. (1994). Female adolescents of alcohol misusers: Sexual behaviors. *Journal of Youth and Adolescence, 23,* 695–707.

Chen, M., & Han, Y. S. (2001). Cross-cultural group counseling with Asians: A stage specific interactive approach. *Journal for Specialists in Group Work, 26,* 111–128.

Chen, M., & Rybak, C. J. (2004). *Group leadership skills: Interpersonal process in group counseling and therapy.* Belmont, CA: Brooks/Cole.

Chojnacki, J. T., & Gelberg, S. (1995). The facilitation of a gay/lesbian/bisexual support-therapy group by heterosexual counselors. *Journal of Counseling & Development, 73,* 352–354.

Chrispeels, J., & González, M. (2004). *Do educational programs increase parents' practices at home? Factors influencing Latino parent involvement.* Cambridge, MA: Harvard Family Research Project.

Clark, A. J. (2002). Scapegoating: Dynamics and interventions in group counseling. *Journal of Counseling & Development, 80,* 271–276.

Cohen, J. (1988). *Statistical power analysis for the behavioral sciences* (2nd ed.). Hillsdale, NJ: Erlbaum.

Combs, A. W., Avila, D. L., & Purky, W. W. (1978). *Helping relationships: Basic concepts for the helping process.* Boston: Allyn & Bacon.

Connors, J. V., & Caple, R. B. (2005). A review of group systems theory. *Journal for Specialists in Group Work, 30,* 93–110.

Conroy, K. (2006). Getting to know you—Now and then. In J. L. DeLucia-Waack, K. H. Bridbord, J. S. Kleiner, & A. Nitza (Eds.), *Group work experts share their favorite activities: A guide to choosing, planning, conducting, and processing* (revised) (pp. 33–36). Alexandria, VA: Association for Specialists in Group Work.

Conyne, R. K. (2006). *Critical incidents in counseling children.* Alexandria, VA: American Counseling Association.

Conyne, R. K., Rapin, L. S., & Rand, J. M. (1997). A model for leading task groups. In H. Forester-Miller & J. A. Kottler (Eds.), *Issues and challenges for group practitioners* (pp. 117–132). Denver: Love Publishing.

Conyne, R. K., Wilson, F. R., & Tang, M. (2000). Evolving lessons from group work for involvement in China. *Journal for Specialists in Group Work, 25,* 252–268.

Conyne, R. K., Wilson, F. R., & Ward, D. (1996). *Comprehensive group work: What it means and how to teach it.* Alexandria, VA: American Counseling Association.

Cook, E. P., Conyne, R. K., Savageau, C., & Tang, M. (2004). The process of ecological counseling. In R. K. Conyne & E. P. Cook (Eds.), *Ecological counseling: An innovative approach to conceptualizing person-environment interaction* (pp. 1–21). Alexandria, VA: American Counseling Association.

Cooney, N. L., Kadden, R. M., Litt, M. D., & Getter, H. (1991). Matching alcoholics to coping skills or interactional therapies: Two-year follow-up results. *Journal of Consulting & Clinical Psychology, 59,* 598–601.

Corey, G. (1981). *Manual for theory and practice of group counseling.* Monterey, CA: Brooks/Cole.

Corey, G. (1995). *Group counseling.* Pacific Grove, CA: Brooks/Cole.

Corey, G. (2005). *Theory and practice of counseling and psychotherapy* (7th ed.). Belmont, CA: Brooks/Cole.

Corey, G. (2007). *Theory and practice of group counseling* (7th ed.). Belmont, CA: Thomson Brooks/Cole.

Corey, G., Corey, M. S., Callahan, P., & Russell, J. M. (2004). *Group techniques* (3rd ed.). Belmont, CA: Thompson Brooks/Cole.

Corey, G., Williams, G. T., & Moline, M. E. (1995). Ethical and legal issues in group counseling. *Ethics & Behavior, 5,* 161–183.

Corey, M. S., & Corey, G. (1987) *Group counseling: Process and practice* (3rd ed.) Monterey, CA: Brooks/Cole.

Corey, M. S., & Corey, G. (2006). *Groups: Process and practice* (7th ed.). Belmont, CA: Thomson Brooks/Cole.

Corsini, R. J., & Rosenberg, B. (1955). Mechanisms of group psychotherapy: Processes and dynamics. *Journal of Abnormal & Social Psychology, 15,* 406–411.

Cottone, R. R., & Tarvydas, V. M. (2007). *Ethical and professional issues in counseling* (3rd ed.). Upper Saddle River, NJ: Pearson Merrill/Prentice Hall.

Couch, R. D., & Childers, J. H. (1987). Leadership strategies for instilling and maintaining hope in group counseling. *Journal for Specialists in Group Work, 12,* 138–143.

Council for Accreditation of Counseling and Related Educational Programs. (CACREP). (2009). 2009 standards. Retrieved February 23, 2009, from http://www.cacrep.org/2008Standards.html

Cuadraz, G. (1996). Experiences of multiple marginality: A case study of Chicana scholarship women. In C. Turner, M. Garcia, A. Nora, & L. Rendon (Eds.), *Racial and ethnic diversity in higher education* (pp. 210–222). Needham Heights, MA: Simon & Schuster.

Dagley, J .C., Gazda, G. M., Eppinger, S. J., & Stewart, E. A. (1994). Group psychotherapy research with children, preadolescents, and adolescents. In A. Fuhriman & G. M. Burlingame (Eds.), *Handbook of group psychotherapy* (pp. 340–369). New York: Wiley.

Dare, D., & Eisler, I. (2000). A multifamily group day treatment programme for adolescent eating disorders. *European Eating Disorder Review, 8,* 4–18.

Darongkamas, J., Madden, S., Swarbrick, P., & Evans, B. (1995). The touchstone therapy group for women survivors of child sexual abuse. *Journal of Mental Health, 4*(1), 17–30.

Davis, L., Galinsky, M., & Schopler, J. (1995). RAP: A framework for leadership of multiracial groups. *Social Work, 40,* 155–165.

Dayton, T. (2005). The use of psychodrama in dealing with grief and addiction-related loss and trauma. *Journal of Group Psychotherapy, Psychodrama, & Sociometry, 39,* 15–34.

Day-Vines, N., Moore-Thomas, C., & Hines, E. (2005). Processing culturally relevant bibliotherapeutic selections with African American adolescents. *Counseling Interviewer, 38*(1), 13–18.

Day-Vines, N., Wood, S., Grothaus, T, Craigen, L., Holman, A., Dotson-Blake, K., & Douglass, M. (2007). Broaching the subjects of race, ethnicity, and culture during the counseling process. *Journal of Counseling and Development, 85,* 401–409.

Deck, M., Scarborough. J., Sferrazza, M., & Estill, D. (1999). Serving students with disabilities: Perspectives of three school counselors. *Intervention in School and Clinic, 34,* 150–155.

DeLucia-Waack, J. L. (1996a). Multiculturalism is inherent in all group work. *Journal for Specialists in Group Work, 21,* 218–223.

DeLucia-Waack, J. L. (1996b). Multicultural group counseling: Addressing diversity to facilitate universality and self-understanding. In J. L. DeLucia-Waack (Ed.), *Multicultural counseling competencies: Implications for training and practice* (pp. 157–195). Alexandria, VA: American Counseling Association.

DeLucia-Waack, J. L. (1997). What do we need to know about group work: A call for future research and theory. *Journal for Specialists and Group Work, 22,* 146–148.

DeLucia-Waack, J. L. (1999). *Group psychotherapy and outcome measures.* Paper presented at the annual convention of the American Psychological Association, Boston.

DeLucia-Waack, J. L. (2000). Effective group work in the schools. *Journal for Specialists in Group Work, 25,* 131–132.

Delucia-Waack, J. L., Gerrity, D. A., Kalodner, C. R., Riva, M. T. (Eds.). (2004). Handbook of group counseling and psychotherapy. Thousand Oaks, CA: Sage.

DeLucia-Waack, J. L. (2006). *Leading psychoeducational groups for children and adolescents.* Thousand Oaks, CA: Sage.

DeLucia-Waack, J. L., Bridbord, K. H., Kleiner, J. S., & Nitza, A. (Eds.). (2006). *Group work experts share their favorite activities: A guide to choosing, planning, conducting, and processing* (revised). Alexandria, VA: Association for Specialists in Group Work.

DeLucia-Waack, J. L., & Donigian, J. (2003). *Practice of multicultural group work: Visions and perspectives from the field.* Belmont, CA: Brooks/Cole.

DeRoma, V. M., Root, L. P., & Battle, J. V. (2003). Pretraining in group process skills: Impact on anger and anxiety in combat veterans. *Journal for Specialists in Group Work, 28,* 339–354.

deYoung, M., & Corbin, B. A. (1994). Helping early adolescents tell: A guided exercise for trauma-focused sexual abuse treatment groups. *Child Welfare, 73,* 144–154.

Dick, B., Lessler, K., & Whiteside, J. (1980). A developmental framework for co-therapy. *International Journal of Group Psychotherapy, 30,* 273–285.

Dies, R. R., & Riester, A. E. (1986). Research on child group psychotherapy. Present status and future directions. In A. E. Riester & I. A. Kraft (Eds.), *Child group psychotherapy: Future tense* (pp. 173–220). Madison, WI: International University Press.

Dinkmeyer, D. C., Sr., McKay, G. D., & Dinkmeyer, D. C., Jr. (2007). The Parent handbook: Systematic training for effective parenting. Minneapolis, MN: Step Publishers.

Dinkmeyer, D., & Nelson, A. (1986). The use of early recollection drawings in children's group therapy. *Individual Psychology: The Journal of Adlerian Theory, Research and Practice, 42,* 288–292.

Donigian, J., & Hulse-Killacky, D. (1999). *Critical incidents in group therapy* (2nd ed.).Boston: Brooks/Cole Wadsworth.

Donigian, J., & Malnati, R. (1997). *Systemic group therapy: A triadic model.* Pacific Grove, CA: Brooks/Cole.

Dossick, J., & Shea, E. (1988). *Creative therapy: 52 exercises for groups.* Sarasota, FL: Professional Resources Press.

Dossick, J., & Shea, E. (1990). *Creative therapy II: 52 more exercises for groups.* Sarasota, FL: Professional Resources Press.

Dossick, J., & Shea, E. (1995). *Creative therapy III: 52 exercises for groups.* Sarasota, FL: Professional Resources Press.

Downing, N. E. & Walker, M. E. (1987). A psychoeducational group for adult children of alcoholics. *Journal of Counseling and Development, 65,* 440–442.

Dryden, W. (2002). *Fundamentals of rational emotive behaviour therapy: A training handbook.* London: Whurr.

Dryden, W. (Ed.). (2003). *Rational emotive behaviour therapy: Theoretical developments.* New York: Brunner-Routledge.

Dryden, W., DiGiuseppe, R., & Neenan, M. (2003). *A primer on rational emotive therapy* (2nd ed.). Champaign, IL: Research Press.

Duch, B. J., Groh, S. E., & Allen, D. E. (Eds.). (2001). *The power of problem-based learning.* Sterling, VA: Stylus Publishing.

Dush, D. M., Hirt, M. L., & Schroeder, H. (1983). Self-statement modification with adults: A meta-analysis. *Psychological Bulletin, 94,* 408–422.

Dutton, D. G. (1986). The outcome of court-mandated treatment for wife assault: A quasi-experimental evaluation. *Violence and Victims, 1,* 163–175.

Dyck, D. G., Hendryx, M. S., Short, R. A., Voss, W. D., & McFarlane, W. R. (2002). Service use among patients with schizophrenia in psycho educational multiple family group treatment. *Psychiatric Services, 53,* 749–754.

Dye, H. A. (1968). *Fundamental group procedures for school counselors.*Boston: Houghton Mifflin.

Dykeman, C., & Appleton, V. E. (1998). Group counseling: The efficacy of group work. In D. Capuzzi & D. R. Gross (Eds.), *Introduction to group counseling* (2nd ed.) (pp. 101–129). Denver: Love Publishing Company.

Edelwich, J., & Brodsky, A. (1992). *Group counseling for the resistant client.* New York: Lexington Books.

Effron-Potter, R. (1993). *How to control your anger before it controls you.* Minneapolis: Johnson Institute.

Egan, G. (1986). *The skilled helper: A systemic approach to effective helping* (3rd ed.). Pacific Grove: CA: Brooks/Cole.

Ellis, A. E. (1997). REBT and its application to group therapy. In J. Yankura & W. Dryden (Eds.). *Special applications of REBT: A therapist's casebook* (pp. 131–161).New York: Springer.

Ellis, A. E. (2001a). *Feeling better, getting better, and staying better.*Atascadero, CA: Impact.

Ellis, A. E. (2001b). *Overcoming destructive beliefs, feelings, and behaviors.*Amherst, NY: Prometheus Books.

Ellis, A. E., & Dryden, W. (1997). *The practice of rational emotive behavior therapy* (2nd ed.). New York: Springer.

Ellis, M. V. (1991). Conducting and reporting integrative research reviews: Accumulating scientific knowledge. *Counselor Education and Supervision, 30,* 225–237.

Erford, B. T. (2007a). Accountability. In B. T. Erford (Ed.), *Transforming the school counseling profession* (2nd ed.) (pp. 236–278). Columbus, OH: Pearson Merrill/Prentice Hall.

Erford, B. T. (Ed.) (2007b). *Assessment for counselors.* Boston: Houghton Mifflin/Lahaska Press.

Erford, B. T. (Ed.). (2008). *Research and evaluation in counseling.* Boston: Houghton Mifflin/Lahaska Press.

Erford, B. T. (Ed.). (2009). *Professional school counseling: A handbook of theories, programs, and practices* (2nd ed.). Austin, TX: Pro-ed.

Evensen, E. P., & Bednar, R. L. (1978). Effects of specific cognitive and behavioral structure on early group behavior and atmosphere. *Journal of Counseling Psychology, 25,* 66–75.

Faith, M. S., Wong, F. Y., & Carpenter, K. M. (1995). Group sensitivity training: Update, meta-analysis, and recommendations. *Journal of Counseling Psychology, 42,* 390–399.

Fall, K. A., & Wejnert, T. J. (2005). Co-leader stages of development: An application of Tuckman and Jensen (1977). *Journal for Specialists in Group Work,* 30, 309–327.

Ferencik, B. M. (1992). The helping process in group therapy: A review and discussion. *Group, 16,* 113–124.

Fettes, P. A., & Peters, J. M. (1992). A meta-analysis of group treatments for bulimia nervosa. *International Journal of Eating Disorders, 11*(2), 97–110.

Flores, P. J. (1997). *Group psychotherapy with addicted populations: An integration of twelve-step and psychodynamic therapy* (2nd ed.). Binghamton, NY: The Haworth Press.

Forester-Miller, H., & Davis, T. (2002). *A practitioner's guide to ethical decision-making* (2nd ed.). Alexandria, VA: American Counseling Association.

Forester-Miller, H., & Kottler, J. A. (1997). *Issues and challenges for group practitioners.* Denver: Love Publishing.

Forsyth, D. R. (1999). *Group dynamics* (3rd ed.). Belmont, CA: Wadsworth.

Foster, E. S. (1989). *Energizers and icebreakers for all ages and stages.* Minneapolis: Educational Media Corporation.

France, D. L., & Dugo, J. M. (1985). Pretherapy orientation as preparation for psychotherapy groups. *Psychotherapy, 22,* 256–261.

Frank, J. D., & Frank, J. P. (1991). *Persuasion and healing: A comparative study of psychotherapy* (3rd ed.). Baltimore: Johns Hopkins University Press.

Frankel, F., Myatt, R., Cantwell, D. P., & Feinberg, D. T. (1997). Parent-assisted transfer of children's social skills training: Effects on children with and without Attention-deficit Hyperactivity Disorder. *Journal of the Academy of Child and Adolescent Psychiatry, 36,* 1056–1064.

Frankl, V. (1963). *Man's search for meaning.* New York: Washington Square Press.

Franko, D. L. (1987). Anorexia nervosa and bulimia: A self-help group. *Small Group Behavior, 18,* 398–407.

Fuhriman, A., & Burlingame, G. M. (1990). Consistency of matter: A comparative analysis of individual and group process variables. *Counseling Psychologist, 18,* 6–63.

Fuhriman, A., & Burlingame, G. M. (1994a). Group psychotherapy: Research and practice. In A. Fuhriman & G. M. Burlingame (Eds.), *Handbook of group psychotherapy* (pp. 3–40). New York: Wiley.

Fuhriman, A., & Burlingame, G. M. (Eds.) (1994b). *Handbook of group psychotherapy.* New York: Wiley.

Furr, S. R. (2000). Structuring the group experience: A format for designing psychoeducational groups. *Journal for Specialists in Group Work, 25,* 29–49.

Gallogly, V., & Levine, B. (1979). Co-therapy. In B. Levine (Ed), *Group psychotherapy: Practice and development* (pp. 296–305). Prospect Heights, IL: Waveland.

Gazda, G. M. (1989). *Group counseling. A developmental approach* (4th ed.). Boston: Allyn & Bacon.

Gazda, G. M., Ginter, E. J., & Horne, A. M. (2008). *Group counseling and group psychotherapy: Theory and application* (2nd ed.). Boston: Allyn & Bacon.

George, R., & Dustin, D. (1988). *Group counseling: Theory and practice*. Englewood Cliffs, NJ: Prentice Hall.

Geroski, A. M., & Kraus, K. L. (2002). Process and content in school psychoeducational groups: Either, both, or none? *Journal for Specialists in Group Work, 27,* 233–245.

Gillam, L. (2006). What a character! In J. L. DeLucia-Waack, K. H. Bridbord, J. S. Kleiner, & A. Nitza (Eds.), *Group work experts share their favorite activities: A guide to choosing, planning, conducting, and processing* (revised) (pp. 41–43). Alexandria, VA: Association for Specialists in Group Work.

Gilliland, B., James, R., & Bowman, J. (1989). *Theories and strategies in counseling and psychotherapy* (2nd ed.). Englewood Cliffs, NJ: Prentice-Hall.

Gladding, S. T. (1998). *Family therapy: History, theory, and practice* (2nd ed.). Upper Saddle River, NJ: Prentice-Hall.

Gladding (2008). *Groups: A counseling specialty* (5th ed). Upper Saddle River, NJ: Merrill/Prentice Hall.

Glass, J. S., & Benshoff, J. M. (1999). PARS: A processing model for beginning group leaders. *Journal for Specialists in Group Work, 24,* 15–26.

Glasser, W. (1999). *Choice theory: A new psychology of personal freedom*. New York: Harper Collins.

Gloria, A. M. (1999). Apoyando estudiantes Chicana: Therapeutic factors in Chicana college student support groups. *Journal for Specialists in Group Work, 24,* 246–259.

Glover, G. J. (1994). The hero child in the alcoholic home: Recommendations for counselors. *School Counselor, 41,* 185–190.

Gosette, R. L., & O'Brien, R. M. (1993). Efficacy of rational-emotive therapy (RET) with children:

A critical re-appraisal. *Journal of Behavioral Therapy and ExperimentalPsychiatry, 24,* 15–25.

Goulding, R. L., & Goulding, M. M. (1991). An intimate model for co-therapy. In B. Roller & V. Nelson, (Eds.), *The art of co-therapy* (pp. 189–209). New York: Guilford.

Grayson, E. S. (1993). *Short-term group counseling*. Arlington, VA: American Correctional Association.

Greenberg, K. R. (2003). *Group counseling in K-12 schools*. Boston: Allyn & Bacon.

Greer, S. (2002). Psychological intervention: The gap between research and practice. *Acta Oncologica, 41,* 228–243.

Gross, D., & Capuzzi, D. (2006). Group work: Theories and applications. In D. Capuzzi, D. Gross, & M. Stauffer (Eds.), *Introduction to group work* (4th ed.). Denver: Love Publishing.

Grossman, P. B., & Hughes, J. N. (1992). Self-control interventions with internalizing disorders: A review and analysis. *School Psychology Review, 21,* 229–245.

Grothe, R. (2002). *More building assets together: 130 group activities for helping youth succeed*. Minneapolis: Search Institute.

Guth, L. (2006). In J. L. DeLucia-Waack, K. H. Bridbord, J. S. Kleiner, & A. Nitza (Eds.), *Group work experts share their favorite activities: A guide to choosing, planning, conducting, and processing* (revised) (pp. 44–46). Alexandria, VA: Association for Specialists in Group Work.

Gutierrez. L. M. (1990). Working with women of color: An empowerment perspective. *SocialWork, 3,* 150–153.

Hadley, H. R. (1988). Improving reading scores through a self-esteem intervention program. *Elementary School Guidance and Counseling, 22,* 248–252.

Hadley, S. W., & Strupp, H. H. (1976). Contemporary views of negative effects in psychotherapy. *Archives of General Psychiatry, 33,* 1291–1302.

Halbur, D. (2006). Ball in play. In J. L. DeLucia-Waack, K. H. Bridbord, J. S. Kleiner, & A. Nitza (Eds.), *Group work experts share their favorite activities: A guide to choosing, planning, conducting, and processing* (revised) (pp. 47–48). Alexandria, VA: Association for Specialists in Group Work.

Haley, J. (1987). *Problem-solving therapy* (2nd ed.). San Francisco: Jossey-Bass.

Harman, M., & Armsworth, M. (1995). Personality adjustment in college students with a parent perceived as alcoholic or nonalcoholic. *Journal of Counseling & Development, 73,* 459–462.

Hawkins, B. L. (1983). Group counseling as a treatment modality for the elderly: A group snapshot. *Journal for Specialists in Group Work, 8,* 186–193.

Hawkins, D. (1993). Group psychotherapy with gay men and lesbians. In H. I. Kaplan & B. J. Sadock (Eds.), *Comprehensive group psychotherapy* (3rd ed.) (pp. 506–515). Baltimore: Williams & Wilkins.

Hawkins, D. A., & Lautz, J. (2005). *State of college admission.* Retrieved on December 12, 2007, from http://www.nacacnet.org/NR/rdonlyres/AF40D947-D5B0-4199-A032-5C7A3C5D0F49/0/SoCA_Web.pdf

Hayes, B. (2006). More or less. In J. L. DeLucia-Waack, K. H. Bridbord, J. S. Kleiner, & A. Nitza (Eds.), *Group work experts share their favorite activities: A guide to choosing, planning, conducting, and processing* (revised) (pp. 49–50). Alexandria, VA: Association for Specialists in Group Work.

Hayes, R. (2006). Why are we meeting like this? In J. L. DeLucia-Waack, K. H. Bridbord, J. S. Kleiner, & A. Nitza (Eds.), *Group work experts share their favorite activities: A guide to choosing, planning, conducting, and processing* (revised) (pp. 51–53). Alexandria, VA: Association for Specialists in Group Work.

Herder, D., & Redner, L. (1991). The treatment of childhood sexual trauma in chronically mentally ill adults. *Health & Social Work, 16,* 50–58.

Herlihy, B., & Corey, G. (2006). *Ethical standards casebook* (6th ed.). Alexandria, VA: American Counseling Association.

Herman, J. L., & Schatzow, E. (1984). Time-limited group therapy for women with a history of incest. *International Journal of Group Psychotherapy, 34,* 605–621.

Herr, E. L., & Erford, B. T. (2007). Historical roots and future issues. In B. T. Erford (Ed.), *Transforming the school counseling profession* (2nd ed.) (pp. 13–37). Columbus, OH: Pearson Merrill/Prentice Hall.

Hilkey, J., Wilhelm, C., & Horne, A. (1982). Comparative effectiveness of videotape pretraining versus no pretraining on selected process and outcome variables in group therapy. *Psychological Reports, 50,* 1151–1159.

Hill, W. F. (1966). *Hill Interaction Matrix (HIM) monograph.* Los Angeles: University of Southern California, Youth Studies Center.

Hill, W. F. (1973). *Hill Interaction Matrix* (HIM) conceptual framework for understanding groups. In J. W. Pfeiffer, & J. E. Jones (Eds.), *The 1973 annual handbook for group facilitators* (pp. 159–176). San Diego, CA: University Associates.

Hines, P. L., & Fields, T. H. (2002). Pregroup screening issues for school counselors. *Journal for Specialists in Group Work, 27,* 358–376.

Hoag, M. J. (1997). Evaluating the effectiveness of child and adolescent group psychotherapy: A meta-analytic review. *Dissertation Abstracts International: Section B: The Sciences and Engineering, 57* (7-B), 4709.

Hoag, M. J., & Burlingame, G. M. (1997). Evaluating the effectiveness of child and adolescent group treatment: A meta-analytic review. *Journal of Clinical Child Psychology, 26,* 234–246.

Hoff, B. (1982). *The Tao of Pooh.* London: Mandarin.

Hoffman, S., Gedanken, S., & Zim, S. (1993). Open group therapy at a university counseling service. *International Journal of Group Psychotherapy, 43,* 485–490.

Holmes, S. E., & Kivlighan, D. E. (2000). Comparison of therapeutic factors in group and individual treatment processes. *Journal of Counseling Psychology, 47,* 478–484.

Horne, A., Nitza, A., Dobias, B., Jolliff, D., & Voors, W. (2008). *Connectedness is key: Using group process and peer influence to reduce relational aggression in high schools.* Manuscript in progress.

Hulse-Killacky, D. (2006). The names activity. In J. L. DeLucia-Waack, K. H. Bridbord, J. S. Kleiner, & A. Nitza (Eds.), *Group work experts share their favorite activities: A guide to choosing, planning, conducting, and processing* (revised) (pp. 54–55). Alexandria, VA: Association for Specialists in Group Work.

Hulse-Killacky, D., Killacky, J., & Donigian, J. (2001). *Making task groups work in your world.* Upper Saddle River, NJ: Prentice Hall.

Hulse-Killacky, D., Kraus, K. L., & Schumacher, R. A. (1999). Visual conceptualizations of meetings: A group work design. *Journal for Specialists in Group Work, 24,* 113–124.

Hutchins, M. (2006). A what? In J. L. DeLucia-Waack, K. H. Bridbord, J. S. Kleiner, & A. Nitza (Eds.), *Group work experts share their favorite activities: A guide to choosing, planning, conducting, and processing* (revised) (pp. 79–84). Alexandria, VA: Association for Specialists in Group Work.

Ihilevich, D., & Glesser, G. C. (1979). *A manual for the Progress Evaluation Scales.* Shiawasse, MI: Community Mental Health Services Board.

Ioniddis, J. P. A., Cappelleri, J. C., & Lau, J. (1998). Issues in comparisons between meta-analysis and large trials. *JAMA, 279,* 1089–1093.

Issacs, M. L. (2003). Data-driven decision making: The engine of accountability. *Professional School Counseling, 6,* 288–295.

Ivey, A. E., Pedersen, P. B., & Ivey, M. B. (2001). *Intentional group counseling: A microskills approach.* Belmont, CA: Wadsworth.

Jacobs, E. E., Masson, R. L., & Harvill, R. L. (2006). *Group counseling: Strategies and skills* (5th ed.). Belmont, CA: Thompson/Brooks Cole.

Johnson, D. W., & Johnson, F. P. (2006). *Joining together: Group theory and group skills* (9th ed.). Boston: Allyn & Bacon.

Johnson, I. H., Torres, J. S., Coleman, V. D., & Smith, M. C. (1995). Issues and strategies in leading culturally diverse counseling groups. *Journal for Specialists in Group Work, 20,* 143–150.

Kanas, N. (1986). Group psychotherapy with schizophrenics: A review of controlled studies. *International Journal of Group Psychotherapy, 36,* 339–351.

Kaplan, R. E. (1982). The dynamics of injury in encounter groups: Power, splitting, and the mismanagement of resistance. *International Journal of Group Psychotherapy, 32,* 163–187.

Kaul, T. J., & Bednar, R. L. (1986). Experiential group research: Results, questions, and suggestions. In S. L. Garfield & A. E. Bergin (Eds.), *Handbook of psychotherapy and behavior change* (2nd ed., pp. 671–714). New York: Wiley.

Kaul, T. J., & Bednar, R. L. (1994). Experiential group research: Can the cannon fire? In S. Garfield & A. Bergin (Eds.), *Handbook for psychotherapy and behavioral change: An empirical analysis* (4th ed.) (pp. 201–203). New York: Wiley.

Keene, M., & Erford, B. T. (2007). *Group activities: Firing up for performance.* Columbus, OH: Pearson Merrill/Prentice Hall.

Kelley, P., & Clifford, P. (1997). Coping with chronic pain: Assessing narrative approaches. *Social Work, 42,* 266–277.

Kim, B., Omizo, M., & D'Andrea, M. (1998). The effects of cultural consonant group counseling on the self-esteem and internal locus of control orientation among Native American adolescents. *Journal for Specialists in Group Work, 23,* 143–163.

Kipper, D., & Tuller, M. (1996). The emergence of role playing as a form of psychotherapy. *Journal of Group Psychotherapy, 49*(3), 99–120.

Kiresuk, T. S., Smith, A., & Cardillo, J. (1994). *Goal attainment scaling: Applications, theory and measurement.* Hillsdale, NJ: Lawrence Erlbaum.

Kiresuk, T. J., & Sherman, R. E. (1968). Goal attainment scaling: A general method for evaluating comprehensive mental health programs. *Community Mental Health Journal, 4,* 443–453.

Kiselica, M. S., Baker, S. B., Thomas, R. N., & Reddy, S. (1994). Effects of stress inoculation training on anxiety, stress, and academic performance among adolescents. *Journal of Counseling Psychology, 41,* 335–342.

Kissane, D. W., Bloch, S., Miach, P., Smith, G. C., Seddon, A., & Keks, N. (1997). Cognitive-existential group therapy for patients with primary breast cancer-techniques and themes. *Psycho-Oncology, 6,* 25–33.

Kivlighan, D. M., Jr., & Goldfine, D. C. (1991). Endorsement of therapeutic factors as afunction of stage of group development and participant interpersonal attitudes. *Journal of Counseling Psychology, 38,* 150–158.

Kivlighan, D. M., & Mullison, D. (1988). Participants' perceptions of therapeutic factors in group counseling: The role of interpersonal style and stage of group development. *Small Group Behavior, 19,* 452–468.

Klein, T. J. B. (2001). Predicting team performance: Testing a model in a field setting. *Journal for Specialists in Group Work, 26,* 185–197.

Kline, W. B. (2003). *Interactive group counseling and therapy.*Upper Saddle River, NJ: Merrill/ Prentice Hall.

Klontz, B. T., Wold, E. M., & Bivens, A. (2001). The effectiveness of a multimodel brief group experiential psychotherapy approach. *Action Methods, 4,* 119–135.

Kolko, D. J., Loar, L. L., & Sturnick, D. (1990). Inpatient social cognitive skills training groups with conduct disordered and attention deficit disordered children. *Journal of Child Psychology and Psychiatry and Allied Disciplines, 31,* 737–748.

Kottler, J. A. (2001). *Learning group leadership: An experiential approach.* Boston: Allyn & Bacon.

Kreidler, M. & Fluharty, L. B. (1994). The 'new family' model: The evolution of group treatment for adult survivors of childhood sexual abuse. *Journal for Specialists in Group Work, 19,* 175–182.

Krone, K. R., Himle, J. A., & Neese, R. M. (1991). A standardized behavioral group treatment program for obsessive-compulsive disorder: Preliminary outcomes. *Behavior Research and Therapy, 29,* 627–631.

Kupersmidt, J. B., & Coie, J. D. (1990). Preadolescent peer status, aggression, and school adjustment as predictors of externalizing problems in adolescence. *Child Development, 61,* 1350–1362.

Laconte, M. A., Shaw, D., & Dunn, I. (1993). The effects of a rational-emotive affective education program for high-risk middle school students. *Psychology in the Schools, 30,* 274–281.

Lambert, M. J. (1991). Introduction to psychotherapy research. In L. E. Beutler & M. Crago (Eds.), *Psychotherapy research: An international review of programmatic studies* (pp. 1–23). Washington, DC: American Psychological Association.

Lambert, M. J., & Bergin, A. E. (1994). The effectiveness of psychotherapy. In A. E. Bergin & S. L. Garfield (Eds.), *Handbook of psychotherapy and behavior change* (3rd ed.) (pp. 143–189). New York: Wiley.

Lambert, M. J., Masters, K. S., & Ogles, B. M. (1991). Outcome research in counseling. In C. E. Watkins &

L. J. Schneider (Eds.), *Research in counseling* (pp. 51–83). Hillsdale, NJ: Erlbaum.

Lazerson, J. S., & Zilbach, J. J. (1993). Gender issues in group psychotherapy. In H. I. Kaplan & B. J. Sadock (Eds.), *Comprehensive group psychotherapy* (3rd ed.) (pp. 682–693). Baltimore: Williams & Wilkins.

Lee, C. C. (1995). Group work for a new millennium. *Together, 24,* 4.

Lee, F., & Bednar, R. L. (1977). Effects of group structure and risk taking disposition on group behavior, attitudes, and atmosphere. *Journal of Counseling Psychology, 24,* 191–199.

Lee, R. S. (1993). Effects of classroom guidance on student achievement. *Elementary School Guidance and Counseling, 27,* 163–171.

Leong, F. T. L. (1992). Guidelines for minimizing premature termination among Asian American clients in group counseling. *Journal for Specialists in Group Work, 17,* 218–228.

Lese, K. L., & McNair-Semands, R. R. (2000). The *Therapeutic Factors Inventory:* Development of the scale. *Group, 24,* 303–317.

Levine, S. H., Bystritsky, A., Baron, D., & Jones, L. D. (1991). Group psychotherapy for HIV-seropositive patients with major depression. *American Journal of Psychotherapy, 45,* 413–424.

Lieberman, M., Yalom, I., & Miles, M. (1973). *Encounter groups: First facts.* New York: Basic Books.

Linde, L. E. (2007). Ethical, legal, and professional issues in school counseling. In B. T. Erford (Ed.), *Transforming the school counseling profession* (2nd ed.) (pp. 51–73). Columbus, OH: Pearson Merrill/Prentice Hall.

Line, B. Y., & Cooper, A. (2002). Group therapy: Essential component for success with sexually acting out problems among men. *Sexual Addiction & Compulsivity, 9,* 15–32.

Livneh, H., Wilson, L., & Pullo, R. (2004). Group counseling for people with physical disabilities. *Focus on Exceptional Children, 36* (6), 1–18.

Loesch, L. C., & Ritchie, M. H. (2004). *The accountable school counselor.* Austin, TX: Pro-ed.

Lopez, J. (1991). Group work as a protective factor for immigrant youth. *Social Work with Groups, 14,* 29–42.

Luft, J. (1984). *Group processes: An introduction to group dynamics*(3rd ed.).Palo Alto, CA: Mayfield.

Lyons, J. S., Howard, K. I., O'Mahoney, M. T., & Lish, J. D. (1997). *The measurement and management of clinical outcomes in mental health*. New York: John Wiley.

MacKenzie, K. R. (1983). The clinical application of a group climate measure. In R. R. Dies, & K. R. MacKenzie (Eds.), *Advances in group psychotherapy: Integrating research and practice* (pp. 159–170). New York: International Universities Press.

MacKenzie, K. R. (1990). *Introduction to time limited group psychotherapy*.Washington, DC: American Psychiatric Press.

MacKenzie, K. R. (1994). Where is here and when is now? The adaptational challenge of mental health reform for group psychotherapy. *International Journal of Group Psychotherapy, 44,* 407–428.

MacKenzie, K. R. (1995). Rationale for group psychotherapy in managed care. In K. R. MacKenzie (Ed.), *Effective use of group psychotherapy in managed care* (pp. 1–26). Washington, DC: American Psychiatric Press.

Makuch, L. (1997). *Measuring dimensions of counseling and therapeutic group leadership style: Development of a leadership characteristics inventory*. Unpublished doctoral dissertation, Indiana University.

Maples, M. F. (1992). STEAMWORK: An effective approach to team-building. *Journal for Specialists in Group Work, 17,* 144–150.

Marbley, A. F. (2004). His eye is on the sparrow: A counselor of color's perception of facilitating groups with predominately White members. *Journal for Specialists in Group Work, 29,* 247–258.

Marotta, S. A., & Asner, K. K. (1999). Group psychotherapy for women with a history of incest: The research base. *Journal of Counseling & Development, 77,* 315–323.

McClure, B. (1998). *Putting a new spin on groups: The science of chaos*. Mahwah, NJ: Lawrence Erlbaum.

McCourt, F. (2005). *Teacher man*. New York: Scribner.

McDermit, W., Miller, I. W., & Brown, R. A. (2001). The efficacy of group psychotherapy for depression: A meta-analysis and review of the empirical research. *Clinical Psychology: Science and Practice, 8,* 98–116.

McLeod, P. L., & Kettner-Polley, R. B. (2004). Contributions of psychodynamic theories to understanding small groups. *Small Group Research, 35,* 333–361.

McRoberts, C., Burlingame, G. M., & Hoag, M. J. (1998). Comparative efficacy of individual and group psychotherapy: A meta-analytic perspective. *Group Dynamics: Theory, Research, and Practice, 2,* 101–117.

Merta, R. J. (1995). Group work: Multicultural perspectives. In J. G. Ponterotto, J. M. Casas, L. Suzuki, & C. M. Alexander (Eds.), *Handbook of multicultural counseling* (pp. 567–585). Thousand Oaks, CA: Sage.

Mickow, G. (1973, July). Group therapy for sex offenders. *Social Work, 18,* 98–100.

Miller, R. C., & Berman, J. S. (1983). The efficacy of cognitive behavior therapies: A quantitative review of the research evidence. *Psychological Bulletin, 94,* 39–53.

Miller, W. R., & Rollnick, S. (2002). *Motivational interviewing: Preparing people for change* (2nd ed.). New York: The Guilford Press.

Mitchell, N. A., & Bryan, J. (2007). School-family-community partnerships: Strategies for school counselors working with Caribbean immigrant families. *Professional School Counseling, 10,* 399–409.

Mitte, K. (2005). Meta-analysis of cognitive-behavioral treatments for Generalized Anxiety Disorder: A comparison with pharmacotherapy. *Psychological Bulletin, 131,* 785–795.

Molassiotis, A., Callaghan, P., Twinn, S. F., Lam, S. W., Chung, W. Y., & Li, C. K. (2002). A pilot study of the effects of cognitive-behavioral group therapy and peer support/counseling in decreasing psychologic distress and improving quality of life in Chinese patients with symptomatic HIV disease. *AIDS Patient Care and STDs, 16,* 83–96.

Moody, H. R. (Ed.) (2002). *Aging: Concepts and controversies* (4th ed.). Thousand Oaks, CA: Sage.

Moos, R. H. (1986). *Group Environment Scale manual*. Palo Alto, CA: Consulting Psychologists Press.

Moos, R., Finney, J. W., & Maude-Griffin, P. (1993). The social climate of self-help and mutual support groups: Assessing group implementation, process, and outcome. In B. S. McCrady & W. R. Miller (Eds.), *Research on alcoholics anonymous: Opportunities and alternatives* (pp. 251–274). Piscataway, NJ: Rutgers University, Center of Studies on Alcohol.

Monfredo, M. G. (1992). *Seneca Falls inheritance.* New York: Penguin Group.

Morganett, R. (1990). *Skills for living: Group counseling activities for young*adolescents. Champaign, IL: Research Press.

Morganett, R. S. (1994). *Skills for living: Group counseling activities for children.* Champaign, IL: Research Press.

Morran, D. K., Stockton, R., Cline, R. J., & Teed, C. (1998). Facilitating feedback exchange in groups: Leader interventions. *Journal for Specialists in Group Work, 23,* 257–268.

Mosak, H. H. (2000). Adlerian psychotherapy. In R. J. Corsini & D. Wedding (Eds.), *Current psychotherapies* (6th ed.) (pp. 54–98). Itasca, IL: Peacock.

Mullen, B., Johnson, C., & Salas, E. (1991). Productivity loss in brainstorming groups: A meta-analytic review. *Basic and Applied Social Psychology, 12,* 3–23.

Murphy, J. J. (1997). *Solution-focused counseling in middle and high schools.*Alexandria, VA: American Counseling Association.

Myrick, R. D. (2003). Accountability: Counselors count. *Professional School Counseling, 6,* 174–179.

National Board for Certified Counselors. (2005). *Code of ethics.* Retrieved December 19, 2007, from http://www.counselingexam.com/nce/resource/code.html

Nelson-Jones, R. (1992). *Group leadership: A training approach.* Pacific Grove, CA: Brooks/Cole.

Nelson-Jones, R. (2000). *Theory and practice of counseling and therapy* (4th ed.). London: Sage.

Newbauer, J. F., & Hess, S. W. (1994). Treating sex offenders and survivors conjointly: Gender issues with adolescent boys. *Journal for Specialists in Group Work, 19,* 129–136.

Newsome, D., & Gladding, S. (2007). Counseling individuals and groups in schools. In B. T. Erford (Ed.), *Transforming the school counseling profession* (2nd ed.) (pp. 209–230). Upper Saddle River, NJ: Merrill/Prentice Hall.

Nichols, M. P., & Schwartz, R. C. (1995). *Family therapy: Concepts and methods* (3rd ed.).Needham Heights, MA: Allyn & Bacon.

Nikitina, A. (2004). Goal setting guide. Retrieved January 16, 2006, from http://www.goal-setting-guide.com/smart-goals.html

Nitsun, M. (1996). *The anti-group: Destructive forces in the group and their creative potential.* New York: Routledge.

Oaklander, V. (1999). Group play therapy from a Gestalt perspective. In D. S. Sweeney & L. E. Homeyer (Eds.), *The handbook of group play therapy: How to do it, how it works, whom it's best for.* New York: Jossey-Bass.

Ogles, B. M., Lambert, M. J., & Fields, S. A. (2002). *Essentials of outcome assessment.* New York: John Wiley & Sons.

Ogles, B. M., Lambert, M. J., & Masters, K. S. (1996). *Assessing outcome in clinical practice.* Boston: Allyn & Bacon.

Ohlsen, M. M. (1970). *Group counseling.*New York: Holt, Rinehart & Winston.

Ohlsen, M. M., Horne, A. M., & Lawe, C. F. (1988). *Group counseling* (3rd ed.). New York: Holt, Rinehart & Winston.

O'Leary, E. O., Sheedy, G., O'Sullivan, K., & Thoresen, C. (2001). Cork older adult intervention project: Outcomes of a Gestalt therapy group with older adults. *Counseling Psychology Quarterly, 16,* 131–143.

Omizo, M. M., & Omizo, S. A. (1988). The effects of participation in group counseling on self-esteem and locus of control among adolescents from divorced families. *The School Counselor, 16,* 54–60.

Orlinsky, D. E., & Howard, K. I. (1986). Process and outcome in psychotherapy. In S. L. Garfield & A. E. Bergin (Eds.), *Handbook of psychotherapy and behavior change* (2nd ed.) (pp. 361–381). New York: Wiley.

Ormont, L. R. (1984). The leader's role in dealing with aggression in groups. *International Journal of Group Psychotherapy, 34,* 553–572.

Ormont, L. R. (1988). The leader's role in resolving resistances to intimacy in the group setting. *International Journal of Group Psychotherapy, 38,* 29–45.

Pack-Brown, S. P., & Braun, C. (2003). *Ethics in a multicultural context.* Thousand Oaks, CA: Sage.

Page, B. J., & Hulse-Killacky, D. (1999). Development and validation of the Corrective Feedback Self-Efficacy Instrument. *Journal for Specialists in Group Work, 24,* 37–54.

Page, B. J., Pietrzak, D. R., & Lewis, T. F. (2001). Development of the group leader self-efficacy instrument. *Journal for Specialists in Group Work, 26,* 168–184.

Paivio, S. C., & Greenberg, L. S. (1995). Resolving "unfinished business": Efficacy of experiential therapy using empty-chair dialogue. *Journal of Consulting and Clinical Psychology, 63,* 419–425.

Parr, G., Haberstroh, S., & Kottler, J. (2000). Interactive journal writing as an adjunct in group work. *Journal for Specialists in Group Work, 25,* 229–241.

Pearson, V. (1991). Western theory, eastern practice: Social group work in Hong Kong. *Social Work with Groups, 14,* 45–58.

Pedro-Carroll, J. L., & Alpert-Gillis, L. J. (1997). Preventive interventions for children of divorce: A developmental model for 5 and 6 year old children. *Journal of Primary Prevention, 18,* 5–23.

Pedro-Carroll, J. L., Sutton, S. E., & Wyman, P. A. (1999). A two-year follow-up of a preventive intervention for young children of divorce. *School Psychology Review, 28,* 467–476.

Perls, F. S. (1969). *Gestalt therapy verbatim.* Lafayette, CA: Real People Press.

Petrocelli, J. V. (2002). Effectiveness of group cognitive-behavioral therapy for general symptomology: A meta-analysis. *Journal for Specialists in Group Work, 27,* 95–115.

Pfeiffer, J. W., & Jones, J. E. (1969). *A handbook of structured experiences for human relations training* (Vol. 1). Iowa City, IA: University Associates Press.

Pfeiffer, J. W., & Jones, J. E. (1970). *A handbook of structured experiences for human relations training* (Vol. 2). Iowa City, IA: University Associates Press.

Pfeiffer, J. W., & Jones, J. E. (1971). *A handbook of structured experiences for human relations training* (Vol. 3). Iowa City, IA: University Associates Press.

Pfeiffer, J. W., & Jones, J. E. (1973a). *A handbook of structured experiences for human relations training* (Vol. 4). Iowa City, IA: University Associates Press.

Pfeiffer, J. W., & Jones, J. E. (1973b). *A handbook of structured experiences for human relations training* (Vol. 5). LaJolla, CA: University Associates Press.

Pfeiffer, J. W., & Jones, J. E. (1973c). *A handbook of structured experiences for human relations training* (Vol. 6). LaJolla, CA: University Associates Press.

Piercy, F. P., & Sprenkle, D. H. (1986). Family therapy theory building: An integrative training approach. In F. P. Piercy (Ed.), *Family therapy education and supervision* (pp. 5–14). New York: Haworth.

Piper, W. E. (1994). Client variables. In A. Fuhriman & G. Burlingame (Eds.), *Handbook of group psychotherapy* (pp. 83–113). New York: Wiley.

Pollio, D. (2002). The evidenced based group worker. *Social Work with Groups, 25*(4), 57–70.

Posthuma, B. W. (2002). *Small groups in counseling and therapy: Process and leadership* (4th ed.). Boston: Allyn & Bacon.

Prinz, J., & Arkin, S. (1994). Adlerian group therapy with substance abusers. *Individual Psychology: The Journal of Adlerian Theory, Research and Practice, 50,* 349–359.

Prochaska, J. O., & DiClemente, C. C. (1982). Transtheoretical therapy: Toward a more integrative model of change. *Psychotherapy: Theory, Research, and Practice, 19,* 276–288.

Prout, H. T., & DeMartino, R. A. (1986). A meta-analysis of school-based studies of psychotherapy. *Journal of School Psychology, 24,* 285–292.

Prout, S. M., & Prout, H. T. (1998). A meta-analysis of school-based studies of counseling and psychotherapy: An update. *Journal of School Psychology, 36,* 121–136.

Ragsdale, S., & Taylor, A. (2007). *Great group games: 175 boredom-busting, zero-prep team builders for all ages.* Minneapolis: Search Institute.

Rapin, L. S. (2004). Guidelines for ethical and legal practice in counseling and psychotherapy groups. In J. L. DeLucia-Waack, D. Gerrity, C. R. Kalodner, & M. T. Riva (Eds.), *Handbook of group counseling and psychotherapy* (pp. 151–165). Thousand Oaks, CA: Sage.

Rapin, L. (2006). Your place in the group. In J. L. DeLucia-Waack, K. H. Bridbord, J. S. Kleiner, & A. Nitza (Eds.), *Group work experts share their favorite activities: A guide to choosing, planning, conducting, and processing* (revised) (pp. 88–89). Alexandria, VA: Association for Specialists in Group Work.

Rapin, L. S., & Conyne, R. K. (1999). Best practices in group counseling. In J. P. Trotzer (Ed.), *The counselor and the group: Integrating theory, training, and practice* (pp. 253–276). Philadelphia, PA: Accelerated Development.

Raskin, N. J., & Rogers, C. R. (1989). Person-centered therapy. In R. J. Corsini & D. Wedding (Eds.), *Current psychotherapies* (4th ed.) (pp. 155–194). Itasca, IL: F. E. Peacock.

Remley, T. P., & Herlihy, B. (2005). *Ethical, legal, and professional issues in counseling* (2nd ed.). Upper Saddle River, NJ: Prentice Hall.

Reynolds, W. M., & Coats, K. I. (1986). A comparison of cognitive-behavioral therapy and relaxation training for the treatment of depression in adolescents. *Journal of Counseling and Clinical Psychology, 54,* 653–660.

Rhode, R. I., & Stockton, R. (1994). Group structure: A review. *Journal of Group Psychotherapy, Psychodrama, and Sociometry, 46,* 151–158.

Riddle, J., & Bergin, J. J. (1997). Effects of group counseling on the self-concept of children of alcoholics. *Elementary School Guidance & Counseling, 31,* 192–201.

Ripley, V. V., & Goodnough, G. E. (2001). Planning and implementing group counseling in a high school. *Professional School Counseling, 5,* 62–65.

Rittenhouse, J. (1997). Feminist principles in survivor's groups: Out of group contact. *Journal for Specialists in Group Work, 22,* 111–119.

Roach, A. T., & Elliott, S. N. (2005). Goal attainment scaling: An efficient and effective approach to monitoring student progress. *Teaching Exceptional Children, 37* (4), 8–17.

Roberts, A. R., & Camasso, M. J. (1991). The effects of juvenile offender treatment programs on recidivism: A meta-analysis of 46 studies. *Notre Dame Journal of Law, Ethics, & Public Policy, 5,* 421–441.

Robinson, K. E. (1994). Addressing the needs of gay and lesbian students: The school counselor's role. *The School Counselor, 41,* 326–332.

Robinson, L. A., Berman, J. S., & Neimeyer, R. A. (1990). Psychotherapy for the treatment of depression: A comprehensive review of controlled outcome research. *Psychological Bulletin, 108,* 30–49.

Rogers, C. R. (1961). *On becoming a person.* Boston: Houghton Mifflin.

Roller, B., & Nelson, V. (1991). *The art of co-therapy: How therapists work together.* New York: Guilford Press.

Romano, J. L., & Sullivan, B. A. (2000). Simulated group counseling for group work training: A four-year research study of group development. *Journal for Specialists in Group Work, 25,* 366–375.

Rosenbaum, M. (1983). Co-therapy. In H. I. Kaplan & B. J. Sadock (Eds.), *Comprehensive group psychotherapy* (2nd ed.) (pp. 167–173). Baltimore: Williams & Wilkins.

Rotheram-Borus, M. J., Bickford, B., & Milburn, N. G. (2001). Implementing a classroom-based social skills training program in middle childhood. *Journal of Educational & Psychological Consultation, 12*(2), 91–111.

Russell, R. L., Greenwald, S., & Shirk, S. R. (1991). Language change in child psychotherapy: A meta-analytic review. *Journal of Consulting and Clinical Psychology, 59,* 916–919.

Rybak, C. J., & Brown, B. M. (1997). Group conflict: Communication patterns and group development. *Journal for Specialists in Group Work, 22,* 31–42.

Rye, D. R., & Sparks, R. (1999). *Strengthening K-12 counseling programs: A support systems approach.* Philadelphia: Accelerated Development.

Salazar, C. F. (2006). Conceptualizing multiple identities and multiple oppressions in clients' lives. *Counseling and Human Development, 39,* 1–18.

Scheidlinger, S. (1993). The small healing group-A historical overview. *Psychotherapy, 32,* 657–668.

Schein, E. H. (1969). *Process consultation: Its role in organization development.* Reading, MA: Addison-Wesley Publishing Company.

Schiller, L. Y. (1997). Rethinking stages of development in women's groups: Implications for practice. *Social Work with Groups, 20,* 3–19.

Schindler, V. P. (1999). Group effectiveness in improving social interaction skills. *Psychiatric Rehabilitation Journal, 22,* 349–354.

Schoenholtz-Read, J. (1996). Sex-role issues: Mixed gender therapy groups as the treatment of choice. In B. DeChant (Ed.), *Women and group psychotherapy: Theory and practice* (pp. 223–241). New York: The Guilford Press.

Schreier, S., & Kalter, N. (1990). School-based developmental facilitation groups for children of divorce. *Social Work in Education, 90*(13), 58–67.

Schultz, W. C. (1966). *The interpersonal underworld.* Palo Alto, CA: Science & Behavior Books.

Schutz, W. (1992). Beyond FIRO-B-three new theory derived measures-element b: Behavior, element f: Feelings, element s: Self. *Psychological Reports, 70,* 915–937.

Scott, M. J., & Stradling, S. G. (1991). The cognitive-behavioral approach with depressed clients. *British Journal of Social Work, 21,* 533–544.

Search Institute. (2004). *Building assets is elementary: Group activities for helping kids ages 8–12 succeed.* Minneapolis: Author.

Sears, J. T. (1991). Helping students understand and accept sexual diversity. *Educational Leadership, 49,* 54–56.

Seefeldt, R. W., & Lyon, M. A. (1992). Personality characteristics of adult children of alcoholics. *Journal of Counseling & Development, 70,* 588–594.

Serok, S., & Zemet, R.M. (1983). An experiment of Gestalt group therapy with hospitalized schizophrenics. *Psychotherapy: Theory, Research, and Practice, 20,* 41–424.

Sexton, T. L., Whiston, S. C., Bleuer, J. C., & Walz, G. R. (1997). *Integrating outcome research into counseling practice and training.* Alexandria, VA: American Counseling Association.

Shadish, W. R. (1996). Meta-analysis and the exploration of causal mediating processes: A primer of examples, methods, and issues. *Psychological Methods, 1,* 47–65.

Shapiro, D. A., & Shapiro, D. (1982). Meta-analysis of comparative therapy outcome studies: A replication and refinement. *Psychological Bulletin, 92,* 581–604.

Sharpe, D. (1997). Of apples and oranges, file drawers and garbage. Why validity issues in meta-analysis will not go away. *Clinical Psychology Review, 17,* 881–901.

Shaughnessy, P., & Kivlighan, D. M. (1995). Using group participants' perceptions of therapeutic factors to form client typologies. *Small Group Research, 26,* 250–268.

Shechtman, Z. (2004). Group counseling and psychotherapy with children and adolescents: Current practice and research. In J. L. DeLucia-Waack, D. A. Gerrity, C. R. Kalodner, & M. T. Riva (Eds.), *Handbook of group counseling and psychotherapy* (pp. 429–444). Thousand Oaks, CA: Sage.

Shechtman, Z., & Pastor, R. (2005). Cognitive-behavioral and humanistic group treatment for children with learning disabilities: A comparison of outcomes and process. *Journal of Counseling Psychology, 52,* 322–336.

Shirk, S. R., & Russell, R. L. (1992). A reevaluation of child therapy effectiveness. *Journal of American Academy of Child and Adolescent Psychiatry, 31,* 703–709.

Shulman, B. H. (1973). A psychodramatically oriented action technique in group psychotherapy. In B. H. Shulman (Ed.). *Contributions to individual psychology* (pp. 206–228). Chicago: Alfred Adler Institute.

Shulman, L. (1992). *The skills of helping individuals, families and groups.* Itasca, IL: Peacock.

Sim, L., Whiteside, S. P., Dittner, C. A., & Mellon, M. (2006). Effectiveness of a social skills training program with school age children: Transition to the clinical setting. *Journal of Child & Family Studies, 15,* 408–417.

Simon, A., & Agazarian, Y. (1974). Sequential Analysis of Verbal Interaction (SAVI). In A. E. Simon & G. Boyer (Eds.), *Mirrors for behavior III: An anthology of observation instruments.* Philadelphia: Humanizing Learning Program, Research for Better Schools.

Slavinsky-Holey, N. (1983). Combining homogeneous group psychotherapies for borderline conditions. *International Journal of Group Psychotherapy, 33,* 297–312.

Slocum, Y. S. (1987). A survey of expectations about group therapy among clinical and non-clinical populations. *International Journal of Group Psychotherapy, 37,* 39–54.

Smaby, M. H., Maddux, C. D., Torres-Rivera, E., & Zimmick, R. (1999). A study of the effects of a skills-based versus a conventional group counseling training program. *Journal for Specialists in Group Work, 24,* 152–163.

Smead, R. (1995). *Skills and techniques for group work with children and adolescents.*Champaign, IL: Research Press.

Smead, R. (2000). *Skills and techniques for group work with young adolescents* (Vol. 2).Champaign, IL: Research Press.

Smith, M. L., Glass, G. V., & Miller, T. I. (1980). *The benefits of psychotherapy.* Baltimore: Johns Hopkins University Press.

Sohn, D. (1997). Questions for meta-analysis. *Psychological Reports, 81,* 3–15.

Soldz, S., Budman, S., Davis, M., & Demby, A. (1993). Beyond the interpersonal circumplex in group psychotherapy: The structure and relationship to outcome of the individual group member interpersonal process scale. *Journal of Clinical Psychology, 49,* 551–563.

Sonnenshein-Schneider, M., & Baird, K. L. (1980, October). Group counseling children of divorce in the elementary schools: Understanding process and technique. *The Personnel and Guidance Journal, 59,* 88–91.

Sonstegard, M. A. (1998). The theory and practice of Adlerian group counseling and psychotherapy. *The Journal of Individual Psychology, 54,* 217–250.

Sonstegard, M., & Bitter, J. (1998). Adlerian group counseling: Step by step. *Journal of Individual Psychology, 54,* 176–217.

Sonstegard, M. A., & Bitter, J. R. (2004). *Adlerian group counseling and therapy.* New York: Brunner-Routledge.

Spiegel, D., Morrow, G. R., Classen, C., Raubertas, R., Stott, P. B., Mudaliar, N., Pierce, H. I., Flynn, P. J.,

Heard, L., & Riggs, G. (1999). Group psychotherapy for recently diagnosed breast cancer patients: A multi-center feasibility study. *Psycho-Oncology, 8,* 482–493.

Spitz, H. I., & Spitz, S. T. (1999). *A pragmatic approach to group psychotherapy.* Philadelphia, PA: Brunner/Mazel.

Steen, S. (2009). *Linking social skills, learning behaviors, and social skills through group work: An exploratory study.* Unpublished manuscript.

Steen, S., & Bemak, F. (2008). *Group work with high school students at-risk of school failure: A pilot study. Journal for Specialists in Groups Work, 33,* 335–350.

Steen, S., & Kaffenberger, C. J. (2007). Integrating academic interventions into group counseling with elementary students. *Professional School Counseling, 10,* 516–519.

Sternbarger, B. N., & Budman, S. H. (1996). Group psychotherapy and managed behavioral care: Current trends and future challenges. *International Journal of Group Psychotherapy, 46,* 297–309.

Stockton, R., Morran, D. K., & Nitza, A. G. (2000). Processing group events: A conceptual map for leaders. *Journal for Specialists in Group Work, 25,* 343–355.

Stockton, R., Morran, D. K., & Velboff, P. (1987). Leadership of therapeutic small groups. *Journal of Group Psychotherapy, Psychodrama, & Sociometry, 39,* 157–165.

Stockton, R., Rhode, R. I., & Haughey, J. (1992). The effects of structured group exercises on cohesion, engagement, avoidance, and conflict. *Small Group Research, 23,* 155–168.

Stone, L. A., & Bradley, F. O. (1994). *Foundations of elementary and middle school counseling.* White Plains, NY: Longman.

Stone, M. H., Lewis, C. M., & Beck, A. P. (1994). The structure of Yalom's *Curative Factors Scale. International Journal of Group Psychotherapy, 44,* 239–245.

Strein, W. (1988). Classroom-based elementary school affective education programs: A critical review. *Psychology in the Schools, 25,* 288–296.

Stuart, O. (1992). Race and disability: Just a double oppression? *Disability, Handicap & Society, 7,* 177–188.

Sue, D. W., & Sue, D. (2003). *Counseling the culturally diverse: Theory and practice* (4th ed.). New York: John Wiley & Sons.

Sugar, M. (1993). Research in child and adolescent group psychotherapy. *Journal of Child and Adolescent Psychotherapy, 3,* 207–226.

Tarver-Behring, S., & Spagna, M. (2004). Counseling with exceptional children. *Focus on Exceptional Children, 36*(8), 1–12.

Taxman, F. S., & Messina, N. P. (2002). Civil commitment: One of many coerced treatment models. In C. G. Leukefeld, F. Tims, & D. Farabee (Eds.), *Clinical and policy responses to drug offenders.*Retrieved February 25, 2006, from www.bgr.umd.edu/pdf/coerced_treatment.pdf

Teague, J. B. (1992). Issues relating to the treatment of adolescent lesbians and homosexuals. *Journal of Mental Health Counseling, 14,* 422–239.

Thomas, C., & Nelson, C. (1994). From victims to victors: Group process as the path to recovery for males molested as children. *Journal for Specialists in Group Work, 19,* 102–112.

Thomas, M. C., & Martin, V. (1992). Training counselors to facilitate the transitions of aging through group work. *Counselor Education and Supervision, 32*(1), 51–60.

Thompson, C. L., & Henderson, D. A. (2007). *Counseling children* (7th ed.). Belmont, CA: Thomson.

Thompson, C. L., & Rudolph, L. B. (1996). *Counseling children* (4th ed.). Pacific Grove, CA: Brooks/Cole.

Thompson, C. L., Rudolph, L., & Henderson, D. (2004). *Counseling children* (6th ed.). Belmont, CA: Brooks Cole.

Thompson, L. (1990). Working with alcoholic families in a child welfare agency: The problem of under diagnosis. *Child Welfare, 69,* 464–471.

Tillitski, L. (1990). A meta-analysis of estimated effect sizes for group versus individual versus control treatments. *International Journal of Group Psychotherapy, 40,* 215–224.

Tolman, R. A., & Bennett, L. W. (1990). A review of quantitative research on men who batter. *Journal of Interpersonal Violence, 5,* 87–118.

Tomori, M. (1994). Personality characteristics of adolescents with alcoholic parents. *Adolescence, 29,* 949–960.

Toseland, R. W., & Rivas, R. F. (2001). *An introduction to group work practice.* Needham Heights, MA: Allyn & Bacon.

Toseland, R., & Siporin, M. (1986). When to recommend group treatment. *International Journal of Group Psychotherapy, 36,* 171–201.

Trotzer, J. P. (1999). *The counselor and the group* (4th ed.). Philadelphia: Accelerated Development.

Trotzer, J. P. (2006). Boxed in: An activity for overcoming resistance and obstacles to problem-solving in groups. In J. L. DeLucia-Waack, K. H. Bridbord, J. S. Kleiner, & A. Nitza (Eds.), *Group work experts share their favorite activities: A guide to choosing, planning, conducting, and processing* (revised) (pp. 96–100). Alexandria, VA: Association for Specialists in Group Work.

Tuckman, B. W. (1965). Developmental sequence in small groups. *Psychological Bulletin, 63,* 384–399.

Tuckman, B., & Jensen, M. (1977). Stages of small group development revisited. *Group and Organizational Studies, 2,* 419–427.

Turner, S. (1993). Talking about sexual abuse: The value of short-term groups for women survivors. *Journal of Group Psychotherapy, Psychodrama & Sociometry, 46*(3), 110–122.

Vacc, N. A., Rhyne-Winkler, M. C., & Poidevant, J. M. (1993). Evaluation and accountability of counseling services: Possible implications for a midsize district. *The School Counselor, 40,* 260–266.

Van Dyck, B. J. (1980). An analysis of selection criteria for short-term group counseling clients. *The Personnel & Guidance Journal, 59,* 226–230.

van Velsor, P. (2004). Training for successful group work with children: What and how to teach. *The Journal for Specialists in Group Work, 29,* 137–146.

Vandervoort, D. J., & Fuhriman, A. (1991). The efficacy of group therapy for depression. *Small Group Research, 22,* 320–338.

Vella, N. (1999). Freud on groups. In C. Oakley (Ed.), *What is a group? A new look at theory in practice* (pp. 8–38). London: Rebus.

Vernelle, B. (1994). *Using and understanding groups.* London: Whiting & Birch.

Vernon, A. (2002). *What works when with children and adolescents: A handbook of individual counseling techniques.*Champaign, IL: Research Press.

Vernon, A. (2004a) *Counseling children and adolescents* (3rd ed.). Denver, CO: Love Publishing.

Vernon, A. (2004b). Applications of rational emotive behavior therapy. In A. Vernon (Ed.), *Counseling children and adolescents* (3rd ed.) (pp. 163–187). Denver, CO: Love Publishing.

Vernon, A. (2006a). *Thinking, feeling, behaving: An emotional education curriculum for children* (rev. ed.). Champaign, IL: Research Press.

Vernon, A. (2006b). *Thinking, feeling, behaving: An emotional education curriculum for adolescents* (rev. ed.). Champaign, IL: Research Press.

Vernon, A. (2007). Application of rational-emotive behavior therapy to groups within classrooms and educational settings. In R. W. Christner, J. L Stewart, & A. Freeman (Eds.), *Handbook of cognitive-behavior group therapy with children and adolescents: Specific settings and presenting problems* (pp. 107–128). New York: Routledge.

Viney, L. L., & Allwood, K. (1991). Reconstructive group therapy with HIV-affected people. *Counseling Psychology Quarterly, 4,* 247–259.

von Bertalanffy, L. (1968). *General system theory: Foundations, development, applications.* New York: George Braziller.

Waldron, H. B., & Kaminer, Y. (2004). On the learning curve: The emerging evidence supporting cognitive-behavioral therapies for adolescent substance abuse. *Addiction, 99,* 93–105.

Ward, D. E., & Litchy, M. (2004). The effective use of processing in groups. In J. L. DeLucia-Waack, D. A. Gerrity, C. R. Kalodner, & M. T. Riva (Eds.), *Handbook of group counseling and psychotherapy* (pp. 104–119). Thousand Oaks, CA: Sage.

Warm, S. (2006). Map of the world. In J. L. DeLucia-Waack, K. H. Bridbord, J. S. Kleiner, & A. Nitza (Eds.), *Group work experts share their favorite activities: A guide to choosing, planning, conducting,* *and processing* (revised) (pp. 58–59). Alexandria, VA: Association for Specialists in Group Work.

Washington, O. G., & Moxley, D. P. (2003). Group interventions with low-income African American women recovering from chemical dependency. *Health & Social Work, 28,* 146–156.

Weiss, C. (1998). *Evaluation* (2nd ed.). Upper Saddle River, NJ: Prentice Hall.

Weiss, R. D., Jaffee, W., B., de Menil, V. P., & Cogley, C. B. (2004). Group therapy for substance use disorders: What do we know? *Harvard Review of Psychiatry, 12,* 339–350.

Weisz, J. R., Weiss, B., Alicke, M. D., & Klotz, M. L. (1987). Effectiveness of psychotherapy with children and adolescents: A meta-analysis for clinicians. *Journal of Consulting and Clinical Psychology, 55,* 542–549.

Wenzel, L. B., & Robinson, S. E. (1995). The effects of problem-focused group counseling for early-stage gynecologic cancer patients. *Journal of Mental Health Counseling, 17,* 81–94.

Whiston, S. C. (2007). Outcomes research on school counseling interventions and programs. In B. T. Erford (Ed.), *Transforming the school counseling profession* (2nd ed.). Columbus, OH: Pearson Merrill/Prentice Hall.

Whiston, S. C., Eder, K., Rahardja, D., & Tai, W. L. (2005, June). Research supporting school counseling: Comprehensive findings. Paper presented at the annual meeting of the American School Counselor Association, Orlando, FL.

Whiston, S. C., & Sexton, T. L. (1998). A review of school counseling outcome research: Implications for practice. *Journal of Counseling and Development, 76,* 412–426.

Whitaker, D. S., & Lieberman, M. A. (1964). *Psychotherapy through the group process.* New York: Atherton Press.

Whiston, S. C. (1996). Accountability through action research: Research methods for practitioners. *Journal of Counseling and Development, 74,* 616–623.

Wiggins, J. D., & Wiggins, A. H. (1992). Elementary students' self-esteem and behavioral ratings related to counselor time-task emphases. *The School Counselor, 39,* 377–381.

Wilson, F. R. (1997). Group psychotherapy. In R. K. Conyne, F. R. Wilson, & D. Ward (Eds.), *Comprehensive group work: What it means and how to teach it* (pp. 169–197). Alexandria, VA: American Counseling Association.

Wilson, J., & Blocher, L. (1990). The counselor's role in assisting children of alcoholics. *Elementary School Guidance & Counseling, 25,* 98–107.

Winick, C., & Levene, A. (1992). Marathon therapy: Treating rape survivors in a therapeutic community. *Journal of Psychoactive Drugs, 24,* 49–56.

Winter, S. K. (1976). Developmental stages in the roles and concerns of group co-leaders. *Small Group Behavior, 7,* 349–362.

Worthen, B. R., Sanders, J. R., & Fitzpatrick, J. L. (1997). *Program evaluation: Alternative approaches and practical guidelines.* New York: Longman.

Wubbolding, R. E. (1991). *Understanding reality therapy.* New York: Harper & Row.

Wubbolding, R. E. (2000). *Reality therapy for the 21st century.* Philadelphia, PA: Brunner-Routledge.

Yalom, I., Houts, P., Zimberg, S., & Rand, K. (1967). Predictions of improvement in group therapy. *Archives of General Psychiatry, 17,* 159–168.

Yalom, I. D., & Leszcz, M. (2005). *The theory and practice of group psychotherapy* (5th ed.). New York: Basic Books.

Yalom, I. D., Tinklenberg, J., & Gilula, M. (1968). *Curative factors in group psychotherapy.* Unpublished manuscript.

Yauman, B. E. (1991). School-based group counseling for children of divorce: A review of the literature. *Elementary School Guidance & Counseling, 26,* 130–139.

Zimpfer, D. G. (1989). Groups for persons who have cancer. *Journal for Specialists in Group Work, 14,* 98–104.

Zimpfer, D. G. (1990a). Groups for divorce/separation: A review. *Journal for Specialists in Group Work, 15,* 51–60.

Zimpfer, D. G. (1990b). Group work for bulimia: A review of outcomes. *Journal for Specialists in Group Work, 15,* 239–251.

Zimpfer, D. G. (1991). Groups for grief and survivorship after bereavement: A review. *Journal for Specialists in Group Work, 14,* 98–104.

Zutlevics, T. L. (2002). Towards a theory of oppression. *Ratio, 15,* 80–102.

INDEX